T0406166

Forschungen zum Alten Testament

Edited by

Corinna Körting (Hamburg) · Konrad Schmid (Zürich)
Mark S. Smith (Princeton) · Andrew Teeter (Harvard)

164

Jürg Hutzli

The Origins of P

Literary Profiles and Strata of the Priestly Texts
in Genesis 1 – Exodus 40

Mohr Siebeck

Jürg Hutzli, born 1963; 2005 PhD University of Bern; since 2012 Lecturer for Hebrew and Aramaic language and literature at the Universities of Geneva and Lausanne; 2019 habilitation, University of Zurich; 2020-2022 working on the project "Primus: Textuality in the Second Temple Judaism: Composition, Function, and Transmission of Texts", Charles University Prague.

The prepress production of this book and the eBook were published with the support of the Swiss National Science Foundation.

ISBN 978-3-16-161545-0 / eISBN 978-3-16-161641-9
DOI 10.1628/978-3-16-161641-9

ISSN 0940-4155 / eISSN 2568-8359 (Forschungen zum Alten Testament)

The Deutsche Nationalbibliothek lists this publication in the Deutsche Nationalbibliographie; detailed bibliographic data are available at *http://dnb.dnb.de*.

The book was typeset in Minion 3 and SBL Hebrew by Samuel Arnet, Bern, printed on non-aging paper by Gulde Druck in Tübingen, and bound by Buchbinderei Spinner in Ottersweier. Published by Mohr Siebeck Tübingen, Germany. www.mohrsiebeck.com.

Printed in Germany.

Table of Contents

III. Synthesis

1. Stratigraphy of P: Sources and Redactions in the Priestly Texts of Genesis 1–Exodus 40

2. The Literary Profile of the Priestly Texts in Genesis 1–Exodus 40

3. The Literary-Historical Relationship between the Priestly and Non-Priestly Strata in Genesis 1–Exodus 40

Tables and Figures

Preface

This book is the revised version of my habilitation, submitted in 2019 to the University of Zurich. It is the result of a long-term study that began with analyses of Priestly texts in the book of Genesis. In its final form, the work includes analyses of all Priestly texts in Genesis–Exodus. Crucial questions concerning P, namely inner stratification, literary profile, historical setting, and relationship to the non-P "environment," are analyzed separately for each Priestly unit or section. Each analysis begins with a discussion of the unit's most important textual problems. This is followed by the larger analysis of the unit. At the end, a synthesis summarizes the results of the comprehensive analytical part with regard to the ensemble of the Priestly texts, the Priestly composition (P^c), and its later supplements.

The delimitation of the Priestly texts that form the basis of analysis for this study, i.e. the P texts in Genesis 1–Exodus 40, is the result of preliminary observations concerning the differences in profile between Priestly texts in Genesis on the one hand and those in Exodus on the other. These differences can only be demonstrated by a thorough analysis of all the relevant texts in both books. Since the study must address the important question of the relationship between the tabernacle account in Exod 25–29*, 39–40* and the Sinaitic sacrificial legislation, a preliminary survey of Lev 1–16 is included as well. Priestly(-like) texts in Leviticus, Numbers, and beyond would have stretched the scope of the work too far, and so the difficult question concerning the extent of the Priestly composition is addressed only briefly and provisionally.

An important result of this study is the conclusion that the Priestly texts form a stratum that is more composite and less homogeneous than was previously thought. Existing studies of P emphasize the presence of corresponding elements at the end of the opening text (Gen 2:1–3) and the end of the tabernacle account (Exod 39–40). The choice of shared vocabulary creates a parallel between the achievement of creation and that of the tabernacle's construction. However, thematic imbalances and theological tensions between different sections and units often go unobserved in studies on P. In addition to the construction and inauguration of the tabernacle, P^c has a second focus: the covenants with Noah and with Abraham. Single units like Gen 1, the Priestly flood story, and the Priestly Abraham narrative have their own distinct theologies that do not fit that of the comprehensive Priestly composition in every respect. Furthermore, as recent studies by E. Blum, J. C. Gertz, and J. Wöhrle point out, the literary profile of P is not the same in every section. Some units have characteristics of autonomous composition, whereas others depend conceptually or even syntactically on non-P narratives and should therefore be considered redactional. This observation suggests a rejection of the controversial and overly simplistic binary of "source or redaction." Yet, in contrast to the three aforementioned scholars, who attribute both the source texts and the redactional texts within the P stratum to the same literary layer (Priestly *Grundschrift* [P^G] / Priestly Composition [P^C]), the present study assigns the two dissimilar literary profiles to distinct literary strata: the source texts, which are present in the primeval history and the Abraham narrative, predate the redactional texts, which are predominantly found in the other sections. While the former should be assigned to a proto-Priestly level, the latter bear typical characteristics of the comprehensive Priestly composition.

Since the study provides a detailed survey of the multifaceted textual and literary problems of the Priestly texts in Genesis–Exodus, it can be read as a comprehensive critical commentary on P in this larger section. In this capacity, the study should be useful for many readers who are interested in the Priestly texts and their discussion in traditional and recent research.

I am grateful to many people who assisted me in various ways during my study. I thank in particular Prof. Thomas Römer and Prof. Konrad Schmid for their support; they have been committed discussion partners during various phases of this work. I benefitted from the constructive and encouraging habilitation reports by Prof. Konrad Schmid and Prof. Thomas Krüger. I would like to thank Dr. Jan Rückl, Axel Bühler, Dr. Jordan Davis, and Prof. Nathan MacDonald (in chronological order) for reading parts of the manuscript and for subsequent fruitful discussions. I have also presented certain sections of the study at symposia and project meetings and received valuable comments; particularly worthy of note is the Sinergia project "The History of the Pentateuch. Combining Literary and Archaeological Approaches" (hosted by the Universities of Lausanne, Tel Aviv, and Zurich). The discussions in this framework widened my focus to include additional observations from archaeology, historical geography, and material culture in the investigation. I also benefited from participating in the stimulating project "Primus: Textuality in Second Temple Judaism: Composition, Function and Transmission of Texts," Charles University, Prague. Exchanges on the book's topics and texts with my colleagues at the Institute of Biblical Studies at the University of Lausanne, in particular Dr. Jaeyoung Jeon, Prof. Jean-Daniel Macchi, and Alain Bühlmann, have also been helpful and pleasant.

I also thank Dr. Sarah Shectman for her insightful editing of the manuscript and for her valuable comments, Dr. Samuel Arnet for his attentive help in preparing the final print file and Nina Jaillet and my wife Carmelia Pinheiro Hutzli for their efficient support in verifying the biblical references and creating the indexes.

La Sarraz, February 2023   Jürg Hutzli

I. Introduction

1. State of Research and Preliminary Considerations concerning Profiles and Strata of the Priestly Literature

1.1 The Theory of P: Evidence and Open Questions

The Priestly literature is easily identifiable through its style (repetition, concentric structure), certain particular linguistic features (distinct vocabulary, designation for God), and coherent theological convictions (theonym theology, monotheism). It is striking that most scholars, for several decades, have agreed in ascribing the same texts of the books of Genesis, Exodus, Leviticus, and Numbers to P (P^G/P^C, P^S, H).[1] When it comes to the general attribution of texts to P or to non-P, only a few verses are disputed.[2]

There are nonetheless several important open questions concerning this theory: (1) the demarcation of the document, that is, the identification of its "endpoint" (Exod 40; Lev 9; 16; Deut 34:7–9; Josh 18:1; 19:51); (2) the literary profile (is P composed as a source or as a redaction layer?); (3) the inner stratification of the Priestly writings (for some texts, which traditionally are, as an ensemble, assigned to P^G/P^C, a diachronic differentiation between two or more layers seems necessary; i.e., a differentiation between proto-P and the Priestly composition [P^C], or between P^C and P^S, or between P^C and H); and (4) the historical locations of the identified Priestly layers.

(1) The difficulty of demarcating P lies in the identification of its endpoint: strong arguments for each position have been put forward, yet no theory is completely convincing or without problems.

The classical theory that the report of Moses's death (Deut 34) is P^G's end encounters difficulty in the lack of a coherent and self-contained P thread in the book of Numbers.[3] Notably, the language of Deut 34:7–9, traditionally ascribed to P, is not typ-

---

[1] For an explanation of the sigla, see below I.2.7.

[2] See the compilations in K. ELLIGER, "Sinn und Ursprung der priesterlichen Geschichtserzählung," *ZTK* 49 (1952): 121–22, and N. LOHFINK, "Die Priesterschrift und die Geschichte," in *Congress Volume: Göttingen, 1977*, ed. J. A. Emerton, VTSup 29 (Leiden: Brill, 1978), 198, n. 29, which are basically in agreement with Nöldeke's detailed reconstruction from 1869 (T. NÖLDEKE, *Untersuchungen zur Kritik des Alten Testaments* [Kiel: Schwers, 1869]). According to the isolated view of G. Fischer, however, the Priestly texts cannot be divorced from their context; see G. FISCHER, "Keine Priesterschrift in Ex 1–15?," *ZTK* 117 (1995): 203–11.

[3] Scholars who have put forward this theory include M. NOTH, *Überlieferungsgeschichte des Pentateuchs*, 2nd ed. (Darmstadt: Wissenschaftliche Buchgesellschaft, 1960), 181–208; ELLIGER, "Sinn"; C. FREVEL, *Mit Blick auf das Land die Schöpfung erinnern: Zum Ende der Priestergrundschrift*, HBS 23 (Freiburg im Breisgau: Herder, 2000); J. BADEN, *The Composition of the Pentateuch: Renewing the Documentary Hypothesis*, AYBRL (New Haven: Yale University Press, 2012).

ical of P.[4] Similar problems apply to the idea that P would end with the achievement of control over the land by Joshua (Josh 18:1 or Josh 19:51).[5] With regard to these problems and to linguistic differences between the Priestly texts in Genesis–Exodus on the one hand and those in Numbers on the other, T. Pola has postulated Exod 40 as the endpoint of P.[6] Pola was followed by E. Otto,[7] who argues that P ends in Exod 29. But this proposal raises the question whether the account of the construction of the sanctuary (or perhaps only the construction order) makes sense without the description of the sacrificial cult. In this vein, E. Zenger and C. Nihan regard the cult regulations in Lev 1–9 or Lev 1–16, respectively, as part of P[G].[8] More generally, one might also ask whether the idea of a report beginning in a universal manner with the world's creation but ending abruptly in the desert is plausible.[9]

(2) One of the most contentious points in the actual debate on P is the question whether P was written as an independent or autonomous document, that is, as a source, or whether it was, from its very beginning, composed as a redaction layer.

P's distinct ideological tendency, which deviates strikingly from the non-P texts, is used as an argument to support the source theory.[10] Aspects of P's ideological out-

---

[4] Cf. L. PERLITT, "Priesterschrift im Deuteronomium?," in *Lebendige Forschung im Alten Testament*, ed. O. Kaiser, BZAW 100 (Berlin: de Gruyter, 1988), 65–87.

[5] LOHFINK, "Die Priesterschrift," 198, n. 29; E. A. KNAUF, "Die Priesterschrift und die Geschichten der Deuteronomisten," in *The Future of Deuteronomistic History*, ed. T. Römer, BETL 147 (Leuven: Peeters, 2000), 101–18; IDEM, *Josua*, ZBK 6 (Zurich: TVZ, 2008), 19–20; P. GUILLAUME, *Land and Calendar: The Priestly Document from Genesis 1 to Joshua 18* (New York: T&T Clark, 2009).

[6] T. POLA, *Die ursprüngliche Priesterschrift: Beobachtungen zur Literarkritik und Traditionsgeschichte von P[G]*, WMANT 70 (Neukirchen-Vluyn: Neukirchener Verlag, 1995) (P ends in Exod 40:33b). Pola was followed by M. BAUKS, "Genesis 1 als Programmschrift der Priesterschrift (P[G])," in *Studies in the Book of Genesis: Literature, Redaction and History*, ed. A. Wénin, BETL 155 (Leuven: Peeters, 2001), 333–45, who sees the end of P in Exod 40:34b (345), and R. G. KRATZ, *The Composition of the Narrative Books of the Old Testament*, trans. J. Bowden (London: T&T Clark, 2005), 243, who puts the end of P in Exod 40:34.

[7] E. OTTO, "Forschungen zur Priesterschrift," *TRu* 62 (1997): 35.

[8] E. ZENGER, "Priesterschrift," *TRE* 27:435–46; C. NIHAN, *From Priestly Torah to Pentateuch: A Study in the Composition of the Book of Leviticus*, FAT II/25 (Tübingen: Mohr Siebeck, 2007).

[9] Cf. E. BLUM, "Issues and Problems in the Contemporary Debate Regarding the Priestly Writings," in *The Strata of the Priestly Writings: Contemporary Debate and Future Directions*, ed. S. Shectman and J. Baden, ATANT 95 (Zurich: TVZ, 2009), 41.

[10] Scholars who consider P a source include (among others) LOHFINK, "Die Priesterschrift," 183–225 = IDEM, *Studien zum Pentateuch*, SBAB 4 (Stuttgart: Katholisches Bibelwerk,1988), 213–53; K. KOCH, "P – kein Redaktor! Erinnerung an zwei Eckdaten der Quellenscheidung," *VT* 37 (1987): 446–67; P. WEIMAR, "Gen 17 und die priesterliche Abrahamsgeschichte," *ZAW* 100 (1988): 52–60; D. CARR, *Reading the Fractures of Genesis: Historical and Literary Approaches* (Louisville: Westminster John Knox, 1996), 43–140; A. DE PURY, "Abraham: The Priestly Writer's 'Ecumenical' Ancestor," in *Rethinking the Foundations: Historiography in the Ancient World and in the Bible; Essays in Honor of John Van Seters*, ed. S. L. McKenzie, T. Römer, and H. H. Schmid, BZAW 294 (Berlin: de Gruyter, 2000), 163–81 = IDEM, *Die Patriarchen und die Priesterschrift / Les Patriarches et le document sacerdotal: Gesammelte Studien zu seinem 70. Geburtstag / Recueil*

line pointed out or asserted by scholars are strict monotheism, "theonym theology" (YHWH reveals his name only at Sinai), and strict cult centralization (cult and sacrifice begin only in the Sinai, after the consecration of the tabernacle). Because of P's marked (albeit not always consistent) theological tendency, many scholars reject the idea that P was written as a redaction layer built on already existing non-P compositions that do not share its ideological maxims. Another argument put forward in favor of the source theory is the fact that in certain sections P and non-P share the same content, creating doublets. This particular textual-profile element is explained as resulting from the combination of the P source with the non-P source by a redactor. Yet, other scholars reply that in such cases one of the two textual strands is interpreting and correcting the other.

Scholars advocating the redaction model point to certain sections of P that show significant dependence on non-P texts. Major gaps are visible in the Priestly narrative thread, rendering P incomprehensible without the neighboring non-P texts.[11] In response, scholars defending the source model claim that P is a separate, autonomous document that was written "in constant relation to non-P material."[12] What remains, however, is the problem of the gaps in the narrative of P. Some argue that passages were lost during the process of joining together the non-P and P texts, but this explanation does not take into account that there are entire sections in P where no gaps are visible, as for instance in the Priestly texts of the primeval history and in the Terah-Abraham narrative. Most of these latter texts do not seem to be dependent on or related to non-P texts, for example, Gen 1* (base layer), the Priestly flood story, the Priestly version of the Table of Nations, and the bulk of P's Abraham narrative. The question of dependence is of course also disputed for these texts and must be examined for each unit, but this disparity, if confirmed by further investigation, favors E. Blum's idea that some P texts were composed as autonomous narratives, whereas others were written as revisions of non-Priestly texts.[13]

---

d'articles, à l'occasion de son 70e anniversaire, ed. J.-D. Macchi, T. Römer, and K. Schmid, ATANT 99 (Zurich: TVZ, 2010), 73–89 (74); T. Römer, "The Exodus Narrative according to the Priestly Document," in The Strata of the Priestly Writings: Contemporary Debate and Future Directions, ed. S. Shectman and J. Baden, ATANT 95 (Zurich: TVZ, 2009), 158–59.

[11] Cf. F. M. Cross, Canaanite Myth and Hebrew Epic: Essays in the History of Religion in Israel (Cambridge: Harvard University Press, 1973), 301–22; J. Van Seters, Abraham in History and Tradition (New Haven: Yale University Press, 1975), 279–85; R. Rendtorff, The Problem of the Process of Transmission in the Pentateuch, trans. J. J. Scullion, JSOTSup 89 (Sheffield: JSOT Press, 1990), 136–70; C. Berner, Die Exoduserzählung: Das literarische Werden einer Ursprungslegende Israels, FAT 73 (Tübingen: Mohr Siebeck, 2010); R. Albertz, Exodus 1–18, ZBK 2.1 (Zurich: TVZ, 2012); idem, Exodus 19–40, ZBK 2.2 (Zurich: TVZ, 2015); H. Utzschneider and W. Oswald, Exodus 1–15, IEKAT (Stuttgart: Kohlhammer, 2013).

[12] Cf. Carr, Reading, 47.

[13] E. Blum, Studien zur Komposition des Pentateuch, BZAW 189 (Berlin: de Gruyter, 1990), 229–85; idem, "Noch einmal: Das literargeschichtliche Profil der P-Überlieferung," in Abschied von der Priesterschrift? Zum Stand der Pentateuchdebatte, ed. F. Hartenstein and K. Schmid, VWGT 40 (Leipzig: Evangelische Verlagsanstalt, 2015), 32–64. See also R. H. Pfeiffer, "A

(3) The question of the inner differentiation of P is necessarily linked with that of its extent. If P^G/P^C is limited to texts found in Genesis–Exodus (or Gen–Lev 9/16), then the P texts of Numbers must be attributed to P^s (that is, they must be secondary P texts). Most scholars ascribe Lev 17–26 to a separate document, the so-called Holiness Code (H), and recently several scholars have assigned additional P texts to authors close to H.[14] With the exception of these latter, studies and commentaries on P often give the impression that in terms of their style and theology P^G/P^C and H are both coherent and uniform entities. Redaction-critical differentiations within P (in its entirety or in large part) – see, for instance, the studies of von Rad or P. Weimar – have not had a great impact in the interpretation of the Priestly writings.[15] Nevertheless, we should address the question whether we can, from a literary and conceptual perspective, interpret P^C, P^s, and H as monolithic blocks and whether the attribution of all P texts to one of these three strata is evident in every case.[16] Several observations contradict this assumption. First, there are indications favoring the idea that several P texts are based on sources with distinct stylistic and ideological features. This is especially the case with the creation narrative of Gen 1, certain genealogical lists (Genesis),

Non-Israelite Source of the Book of Genesis," *ZAW* 48 (1930): 67; J. C. GERTZ, *Tradition und Redaktion in der Exoduserzählung: Untersuchungen zur Endredaktion des Pentateuch*, FRLANT 186 (Göttingen: Vandenhoeck & Ruprecht, 2000), 391; IDEM, "Genesis 5: Priesterliche Redaktion, Komposition oder Quellenschrift?," in *Abschied von der Priesterschrift? Zum Stand der Pentateuchdebatte*, ed. F. Hartenstein and K. Schmid, VWGT 40 (Leipzig: Evangelische Verlagsanstalt, 2015), 91; J. WÖHRLE, *Fremdlinge im eigenen Land: Zur Entstehung und Intention der priesterlichen Passagen der Vätergeschichte*, FRLANT 246 (Göttingen: Vandenhoeck & Ruprecht, 2012), 147–60.

[14] I. KNOHL, *The Sancuary of Silence: The Priestly Torah and the Holiness School* (Minneapolis: Augsburg Fortress, 1995); J. MILGROM, *Leviticus 17–22: A New Translation with Introduction and Commentary*, AB 3A (New York: Doubleday, 2000), 1344; IDEM, "H_R in Leviticus and Elsewhere in the Torah," in *The Book of Leviticus: Composition and Reception*, ed. R. Rendtorff, R. A. Kugler, with the Assistance of Sarah Smith Bartlet, VTSup 93 (Leiden: Brill, 2003), 24–40; J. WÖHRLE, "The Integrative Function of the Law of Circumcision," in *The Foreigner and the Law: Perspectives from the Hebrew Bible and the Ancient Near East*, ed. R. Achenbach, R. Albertz, and J. Wöhrle, BZABR 16 (Leipzig: Harrassowitz, 2011), 71–87.

[15] G. VON RAD, *Die Priesterschrift im Hexateuch literarisch untersucht und theologisch gewertet*, BWANT 65 (Stuttgart: Kohlhammer, 1934). Cf. the influential refutation of von Rad's thesis by P. HUMBERT, "Die literarische Zweiheit des Priester-Codex in der Genesis (Kritische Untersuchung der These von von Rad)," *ZAW* 58 (1940–41): 30–57. For Weimar's redaction-critical studies, see P. WEIMAR, "Chaos und Kosmos: Gen 1,2 als Schlüssel einer älteren Fassung der priesterschriftlichen Schöpfungserzählung," in *Mythos im Alten Testament und seiner Umwelt: Festschrift für Hans-Peter Müller zu seinem 65. Geburtstag*, ed. A. Lange, H. Lichtenberger, and D. Römheld, BZAW 278 (Berlin: de Gruyter, 1999), 196–211; IDEM, "Die Toledot-Formel in der priesterschriftlichen Geschichtsdarstellung," *BZ* 18 (1974): 84–87; IDEM, "Gen 17," 22–60; IDEM, *Die Meerwundererzählung: Eine redaktionskritische Analyse von Ex 13,17–14,31*, ÄAT 9 (Wiesbaden: Harrassowitz, 1985), 175–99.

[16] This question is one of the starting points of the collected essays in F. HARTENSTEIN and K. SCHMID, eds., *Abschied von der Priesterschrift? Zum Stand der Pentateuchdebatte*, VWGTh 40 (Leipzig: Evangelische Verlagsanstalt, 2015).

and also the specific stipulations for sacrifice (Leviticus). Many scholars assume that an originally independent and ancient "book of *tôlĕdōt*" existed. Second, certain texts like those belonging to the *tôlĕdōt* framework and to the network of statements concerning the ancestors' ages (which are traditionally attributed to P) depend on non-P texts, which raises the question whether these texts really are part of the Priestly composition (as commonly supposed) or belong to later redaction layers. In general, the observation (see 2, above) that P constitutes an uninterrupted thread in some sections and in others consists of only a few short, punctual statements and passages bears directly on the question of inner differentiation. This variation in P's literary profile might indicate different literary strata: Where P constitutes an independent, continuous, and self-contained strand, it *may* constitute an autonomous *proto*-Priestly composition. Where P builds on the non-P strand and reinterprets it, one should consider it a redaction layer that aims to combine a (proto-)P and a non-P section in order to create a more comprehensive composition.

(4) Most European and North American scholars agree in dating the Priestly composition in the late Neo-Babylonian (second third of the sixth century BCE) or the early Persian period (last third of the sixth and beginning of the fifth century BCE).[17] They follow the arguments of nineteenth-century scholars such as E. Reuss, A. Kuenen, and J. Wellhausen in part. The "revolutionary" historical location of P (youngest source, from the exilic/postexilic period) by those scholars was and is still a cornerstone of biblical research. The point of departure for this theory was the observation by Reuss, taken up by K. H. Graf and Kuenen, that the Priestly cultic laws are not known either in the historical books of Judges, Samuel, and Kings or in the writings of the preexilic prophets and therefore postdate them.[18] In Wellhausen's theory, the main argument for the postexilic date of P was that Deuteronomistic cult centralization was presupposed or even taken for granted by this source.[19] Nowadays, not all of these arguments carry the same weight. Several scholars consider the possibility that some of the stipulations in Lev 1–5 stem from preexilic times,[20] and the

---

[17] Cf. T. RÖMER, "Der Pentateuch," in *Die Entstehung des Alten Testaments: Neuausgabe*, ed. W. Dietrich et al., Theologische Wissenschaft 1 (Stuttgart: Kohlhammer, 2014), 93.

[18] J. CONRAD, *Karl Heinrich Grafs Arbeit am Alten Testament: Studien zu einer wissenschaftlichen Biographie*, ed. U. Becker, BZAW 425 (Berlin: de Gruyter, 2011), 73–178; A. KUENEN, *Historisch-critisch onderzoek naar het ontstaan en de verzameling van de boeken des Ouden Verbonds I* (Leiden: Engels, 1861) = IDEM, *A Historical-Critical Inquiry into the Origin and Composition of the Hexateuch*, trans. H. P. Wicksteed (London: Macmillan, 1886), 140.

[19] J. WELLHAUSEN, *Prolegomena zur Geschichte Israels* (Berlin: Reimer, 1895), 412 = IDEM, *Prolegomena to the History of Ancient Israel* (New York: Meridian Books, 1957), 404–5; repr. of *Prolegomena to the History of Israel*, trans. J. Sutherland Black and A. Menzies, with preface by W. Robertson Smith (Edinburgh: Black, 1885). Wellhausen is followed by BLUM, "Issues and Problems," 32.

[20] For different views on the origins of these texts, cf. M. NOTH, *Das dritte Buch Mose: Leviticus*, ATD 6 (Göttingen: Vandenhoeck & Ruprecht, 1962), 11–12; R. RENDTORFF, *Leviticus*, BK 3.1 (Neukirchen-Vluyn: Neukirchener Verlag, 1985), 5–7, 20–21; NIHAN, *From Priestly Torah*, 198–231.

extent of the Josianic reform is also debated. Furthermore, Wellhausen's claim that cult centralization is presupposed by P has been questioned by Y. Kaufmann and continues to be challenged by scholars.[21] T. Römer, for example, argues that the localization of the sanctuary in the wilderness (Sinai) might express the authors' neutrality toward competition or conflict between different ʏʜᴡʜ sanctuaries in the Persian era.[22]

Other scholars, following Kaufmann, argue for a preexilic date on the grounds of linguistic dating of P. A. Hurvitz inferred from amassed biblical lexicographical data that P was written in "Classical Biblical Hebrew" and therefore would date from the preexilic period. He is guided by two criteria: the listed vocabulary consists (1) of Priestly terms that are absent from Ezekiel and that establish the chronological priority of P vis-a-vis Ezekiel (e.g., אִשֶּׁה, "sacrifice") and (2) of Priestly terms that are replaced by a synonym in Late Biblical Hebrew (e.g., שֵׁשׁ, "linen," replaced by בּוּץ, "linen").[23] More nuanced is the study by R. Polzin who differentiates between Pᴳ and Pˢ and assigns the two strata to a transitional stage.[24] Scholars defending a setting in exilic or postexilic eras question the conclusion drawn from linguistic data assuming that later authors would have been able to adapt to the conventions of Classical Biblical Hebrew.[25] They furthermore point out terms and themes in P that are typical of postexilic writings.[26]

In current scholarship additional arguments favoring a setting at the end of the Babylonian or the beginning of the Persian era have been put forward and are gaining influence. Scholars point to the proximity of P to texts in Ezekiel and Second Isaiah, with which it shares vocabulary and ideological motifs.[27]

---

[21] Y. Kᴀᴜꜰᴍᴀɴɴ, *The Religion of Israel from Its Beginnings to the Babylonian Exile*, trans. M. Greenberg (Chicago: University of Chicago Press, 1960). Kaufmann maintained that the P prescriptions were meant to regulate cultic practice at local sanctuaries. See also J. Mɪʟɢʀᴏᴍ, "Priestly ('P') Source," *ABD* 5:460.

[22] Cf. Röᴍᴇʀ, "Der Pentateuch," 92. See also Aʟʙᴇʀᴛᴢ, *Exodus 19–40*, 193–94, and Kɴᴀᴜꜰ, *Josua*, 19.

[23] A. Hᴜʀᴡɪᴛᴢ, *A Linguistic Study of the Relationship between the Priestly Source and the Book of Ezekiel: A New Approach to an Old Problem*, Cahiers de la Revue biblique 20 (Paris: Gabalda, 1982). See also ɪᴅᴇᴍ, "Dating the Priestly Source in Light of the Historical Study of Biblical Hebrew a Century after Wellhausen," *ZAW* 100 (1988): 88–100. G. Rᴇɴᴅsʙᴜʀɢ, "Late Biblical Hebrew and the Date of 'P,'" *JANESQU* 12 (1980): 65–80 and J. Mɪʟɢʀᴏᴍ, *Leviticus 1–16: A New Translation with Introduction and Commentary*, AB 3 (New York: Doubleday, 1991), 3–5, basically agree with Hurwitz.

[24] Polzin establishes the chronological sequence "JE – Court History – Dtr – Pᴳ – Pˢ – Chronicles"; see R. Pᴏʟᴢɪɴ, *Late Biblical Hebrew: Toward an Historical Typology of Biblical Hebrew Prose*, HSM 12 (Missoula, MT: Scholars Press, 1976), 85–122.

[25] See the detailed discussion below I.2.6.2 (lit.).

[26] See B. Lᴇᴠɪɴᴇ, "Late Language in the Priestly Source: Some Literary and Historical Observations," *WJCS* 8 (1983), 69–82.

[27] Cf. T. Pᴏʟᴀ, "Back to the Future: The Twofold Priestly Concept of History," in *Torah and the Book of Numbers*, ed. C. Frevel, T. Pola, and A. Schart, FAT II/62 (Tübingen: Mohr Siebeck, 2013), 39–65; J. Jᴇᴏɴ, "A Source of P? The Priestly Exodus Account and the Book of Ezekiel," *Semitica* 58 (2016): 77–92.

Because P is assumed to presuppose the centralization of the cult in Jerusalem and because of several commonalities between the Priestly tabernacle account and the report of the First Temple's construction, the Priestly composition is generally located in Jerusalem or in a milieu in Mesopotamia attached to Jerusalem. More recently, another geographical setting has been proposed by A. Rofé and P. Guillaume, who point to the important role that Bethel plays in texts that precede the Sinai pericope (see Gen 35:6, 9–14). They conclude that it is therefore more likely that P[G] was composed in Bethel than in Jerusalem.[28]

However, with regard to the above-mentioned indications favoring the diachronic stratification of P, one should address the question of chronological setting and geographical location not only for the supposed comprehensive Priestly composition but also for single, i.e., proto-Priestly or "secondary" Priestly (P[s]) units. The evidence from different texts indeed points to different periods. As I will show below, the trousers (מכנסים) worn by priests, mentioned in Exod 28:42; 39:28; Lev 6:3; 16:4; and Ezek 44:18, hint at a Persian setting for these texts, as pants were a Persian innovation in the ancient Near East.[29] As for the Table of Nations, in contrast, the fact that Persia is not mentioned speaks against a setting for this text in the Persian era.

The counterargument, that the author would have passed over the Persians because he considered the emergence of the Persian Empire too recent a development, is not cogent.[30] First, one should note the presence of a similarly "young" nation, Javan (Greece), in the Priestly text of Gen 10 (Javan is mentioned in the Hebrew Bible mostly in postexilic texts).[31] Second, certain nations figuring in the Table of Nations (Cimmerians [Gomer in Gen 10:2]; Medes [Madai in 10:2]; and Lydia[32] [Lud in 10:22]) became important regional powers (eighth–early sixth century BCE), relatively shortly before the emergence of Persia. Taken together, these observations make a setting before the Persian era probable.[33]

The same holds true for the question of geographical location, which should be examined individually too, in particular for the self-contained pre- or proto-Priestly units.

---

[28] A. Rofé, *Introduction to the Literature of the Hebrew Bible*, Biblical Studies 9 (Jerusalem: Simor, 2009), 228–29; Guillaume, *Land*, 183–87.

[29] Cf. S. D. Sperling, "Pants, Persians and the Priestly Source," in *Ki Baruch Hu: Ancient Near Eastern, Biblical, and Judaic Studies in Honor of Baruch A. Levine*, ed. R. Chazan, W. W. Hallo, and L. H. Schiffman (Winona Lake, IN: Eisenbrauns, 2003), 373–85; cf. P. Calmeyer, "Hose," *RlA* 4:472.

[30] Against C. Nihan, "L'écrit sacerdotal entre mythe et histoire," in *Ancient and Modern Scriptural Historiography / L'historiographie biblique, ancienne et moderne*, ed. G. Brooke and T. Römer (Leuven: Peeters, 2007), 185, n. 116.

[31] 1 Chr 1:5, 7; Isa 66:19; Ezek 27:13; Joel 4:6; Zech 9:13; Dan 8:21; 10:20; 11:2. For an overview of these occurrences, cf. H. Gonzalez, "Jawan, 1: Hebrew Bible/Old Testament," *EBR* 13:1–2.

[32] Lud is identified with the Lydian kingdom in Asia Minor (playing an important role during the seventh–sixth century BCE). Cf., for instance, J. Simons, *Geographical and Topographical Texts of the Old Testament* (Leiden: Brill, 1959), §§150–51.

[33] Cf. the more detailed argument, below, II.4.8.

1.2 Double Focus within the Priestly Texts in
Genesis 1–Exodus 40/Leviticus 16

Among the Priestly texts, the section Gen 1–Exod 40 stands out because it forms, over long sections, an uninterrupted narrative thread that runs toward a climax (Exod 40). As for the suggested comprehensive Priestly narrative of Gen 1–Deut 34, coherence and narrative aim are less evident. Deuteronomy 34, which reports Moses's view of the land and his death, contains only a few P elements. The statement of Moses's death and burial (34:5–6) is clearly non-P. For these reasons, a recent tendency among scholars is to search for the supposed base layer of the Priestly strand within Gen 1–Exod 40 (or within Gen 1–Lev 9/16).

However, the following observations cast doubt on the idea of a coherent and unified P document within Gen 1–Exod 40. First, P^c has not one but two thematic focuses in this section. On the one hand, the construction and inauguration of the tabernacle (and eventually the cultic procedures) at Sinai are considered the goal of the narrative. On the other hand, the promises to the patriarchs and the covenants concluded with Noah and with Abraham provide another major theme.

The first focus is set in view by the opening chapter, Gen 1, which is often considered a key text in the inner organization of the Priestly composition;[34] many scholars have observed that the end of this opening text (Gen 2:1–3) and the end of the tabernacle account (Exod 39–40) form an inclusion. The choice of a shared vocabulary creates a parallel between the achievement of the creation and that of the tabernacle's construction.[35]

In contrast, the focus on the promises in the patriarchal stories in P^c is manifest in the extent of textual material dedicated to the patriarchs. Partly related to it is the important motif of the covenant, which is developed in the flood story and the patriarchal story.[36] Interestingly, the covenant motif does not occur in the Sinai pericope.[37] Among the promises to the ancestors in P, the one addressed to Abraham is clearly the most fully elaborated (Gen 17). Here one finds the distinct promise that Abraham will be a "father of multiple nations." The Priestly Abraham narrative leads to the

---

[34] M. Bauks labels it a "Programmtext." Cf. BAUKS, "Genesis 1," 333.

[35] Cf., among others, POLA, *Die ursprüngliche Priesterschrift*, 227–29, 361; B. JANOWSKI, "Tempel und Schöpfung: Schöpfungstheologische Aspekte der priesterschriftlichen Heiligtumskonzeption," *JBT* 5 (1990): 46; BLUM, *Studien*, 301–12.

[36] C. STREIBERT, *Schöpfung bei Deuterojesaja und in der Priesterschrift: Eine vergleichende Untersuchung zu Inhalt und Funktion schöpfungstheologischer Aussagen in exilisch-nachexilischer Zeit* (Frankfurt: Lang, 1993); T. J. KING, *The Realignment of the Priestly Literature: The Priestly Narrative in Genesis and Its Relation to Priestly Legislation and the Holiness School*, Princeton Theological Monograph Series (Eugene, OR: Pickwick, 2009), 85–87; K. SCHMID, *Genesis and the Moses Story: Israel's Dual Origin in the Hebrew Bible*, Siphrut 3 (Winona Lake, IN: Eisenbrauns, 2010), 246–48.

[37] In accord with most European scholarship, Exod 31:12–17, which declares the observation of Sabbath a "covenant" (ברית, cf. 31:16), should be assigned to H or an H-like stratum. See below, II.10.4.1 (a).

genealogical lists of the Ishmaelites, Edomites, and Israelites. It is striking that in the Priestly strand after Genesis, these texts and the Abraham motif find no resonance at all. In fact, in the Priestly texts after Genesis, Abraham is never referred to again on his own, but rather only together with Isaac and Jacob (Exod 2:24; 6:3, 8). Moreover, references to the promise to the ancestral triad are rare in P and stop after Exod 6.

Furthermore, the ties between the two sections of the two focuses – patriarchal narratives on the one hand and the tabernacle account on the other – are weak: a commonality of the two sections consists of God's promise "to be Abraham's/Israel's God," which is found once in the patriarchal narrative (Gen 17:7, 8), once in the exodus narrative (Exod 6:7), and once in the tabernacle account (Exod 29:45). Interestingly, this phrase is used several times in H.[38] For this reason, I. Knohl assigns the three texts to H rather than to his PT (Priestly Torah),[39] whereas Blum, who emphasizes Knohl's observation, considers it an important reason to include H in his KP (Priestly composition).[40]

Scholars working on P underline the correspondence between Gen 1 and Exod 40 (inclusion) above all. But the emphasis put on the promises to Abraham and the other patriarchs of Genesis has also been observed by several scholars.[41] Nevertheless, the fact that the presupposed Priestly composition has two focuses that stand in isolation from one another has not attracted attention in scholarship.

1.3 Concentration of Priestly Key Motifs and Central Thematic and Stylistic Features in Genesis 1–50

In addition to the aforementioned double focus of the Priestly document, there is a striking concentration of key motifs and stylistic and linguistic features in the Priestly texts of Genesis.

(1) It is commonly recognized that the genealogical and narrative texts introduced by the characteristic formula ואלה תולדת ("these are the descendants of"/"this is the history of") structure the P account. Interestingly, with the exception of Num 3:1–4, all are found in the book of Genesis. With regard to certain anomalies (mention of Moses and Aaron at the head of the genealogy, the circumstantial phrase in 3:1b, and remoteness from the *tôlĕdōt* in Genesis), Num 3:1–4 is rightly considered by most scholars to be a late, post-Priestly addition. The fact that the other genealogies are only found in the book of Genesis has attracted little attention in current scholarship.[42]

(2) As for the pivotal motif of the covenant, in the aftermath of W. Zimmerli's

---

[38] Lev 22:33; 25:38; 26:12, 45. Cf. also Lev 11:45 and Num 15:41.
[39] Cf. KNOHL, *Sanctuary*, 102, 104.
[40] See BLUM, "Issues and Problems," 33–34.
[41] Cf. n. 34.
[42] Cf., however, RÖMER, "Der Pentateuch," 94–95.

important study on the subject[43] scholars have emphasized the fact that the Priestly composition does not provide a covenant with Moses.[44] According to P's conception, God concluded a covenant only with the two non-Israelites Noah and Abraham (see above). It is true that the covenant with Abraham is directed to Israel and Moses.[45] However, in light of the central promise of Gen 17:1–6 concerning Abraham's future "multinational" offspring, the transfer of the covenant to Isaac and then to Jacob is surprising and seems somewhat forced. Furthermore, it is striking that the Priestly Sinai pericope never refers to the key event from the Priestly patriarchal narrative, God's covenant with Abraham. Wellhausen's inaccurate characterization of P as a "book of four covenants" (abbreviated Q, for *quatuor*) certainly must be taken in relation to this imbalance within P (according to Wellhausen, in addition to Noah and Abraham, Adam and Moses were also each given a covenant).[46] Likewise, von Rad, who suspected that in P the Sinai event was originally described as a covenant, but that the motif would have been lost as a result of the merging of the sources, obviously sensed a certain disparity[47]

(3) Even if they are not depicted as nuanced characters, Noah and Abraham are introduced in their respective Priestly narratives and are endowed with certain honorable qualities (Gen 6:9; 17:1). Similar depiction of pivotal figures is lacking in the Priestly texts of Exodus: for Moses and Aaron, even a short introduction is lacking.

Given the commonly accepted theory of a Priestly *Grundschrift* (P[G]) or Priestly composition (P[C]) covering at least the books of Genesis and Exodus, this striking concentration of key motifs and important stylistic and linguistic features of the Priestly texts in Genesis deserves further explanation.

1.4 Conclusion: Different Redactions, Origin of P in Genesis?

How can the double focus of P[C] and the striking concentration of key motifs and linguistic features in Gen 1–50 be explained? The double focus alone could be explained as the Priestly author's (authors') intent to combine two originally independent

---

[43] W. ZIMMERLI, "Abrahambund und Sinaibund: Ein Beitrag zum Verständnis der Priesterschrift," *TZ* 16 (1960): 268–80.

[44] Cf. the summary of scholarly views in C. NIHAN, "The Priestly Covenant: Its Reinterpretation, and the Composition of 'P,'" in *The Strata of the Priestly Writings: Contemporary Debate and Future Directions*, ed. S. Shectman and J. Baden, ATANT 95 (Zurich: TVZ, 2009), 91–103.

[45] Cf. Gen 17:17–22; 28:1–5; Exod 6:2–9.

[46] Cf. WELLHAUSEN, Prolegomena zur Geschichte, 342–45 = IDEM, Prolegomena to the History, 338–40.

[47] See G. von Rad, Theologie des Alten Testaments, Band I: Die Theologie der geschichtlichen Überlieferung Israels, 10th ed. (Munich: Kaiser, 1992), 247, n. 6: "(...) Andererseits aber muss man sich fragen, ob P das Sinaigeschehen wirklich nicht als einen Bundesschluß Jahwes mit Israel angesehen hat, denn eine solche Abweichung von der älteren Sinaitradition wäre doch sehr auffallend."

traditions, the patriarchal narrative on the one hand and the exodus story on the other.[48] But the fact that important linguistic, stylistic, and thematic features of P are limited to Gen 1–50 alone suggests the following diachronic explanation: the original kernel(s) of P lie(s) in Genesis; the combination of P's Genesis with P's Sinai (tabernacle) account should be considered a secondary development.[49]

Certain aspects of the literary profile of the Priestly strand in the two books support this conclusion. Several Priestly texts found in the book of Genesis seem to have been composed independently of parallel non-P texts. They form self-contained units, such as the creation account in Gen 1;[50] the Priestly flood story (Gen 6–9);[51] the Priestly Table of Nations (Gen 10);[52] and the Priestly Abraham narrative (Gen 11:27–25:9).[53] A characteristic of these compositions is that they are well- marked units having a beginning and an end. The situation is different in Exodus, for which several recent analyses have argued that the P texts are related to the non-P strata.[54] Considered on the whole, the Priestly narrative strand in Exod 1–40 contains several lacunae.[55] Furthermore,

---

[48] Cf. Schmid, *Genesis and the Moses Story*, 238–48.

[49] Cf. Rolf Rendtorff's considerations pointing in this direction: he argues that the "cohesive group of priestly texts" is found only in Gen 1–Exod 6 (see Rendtorff, *Problem*, 191–94 [quote on 191]). King, *Realignment*, sees a separate origin for the Priestly texts in Genesis as well, attributing them to a distinct document, a single written source stemming from the northern tribes.

[50] Several commonalities of language and motif between Gen 1 and Gen 2–3 favor the idea that one text depends on the other. Arguing for the dependence of Gen 2–3 on Gen 1 are E. Otto, "Die Paradieserzählung Genesis 2–3: Eine nachpriesterschriftliche Lehrerzählung in ihrem religionsgeschichtlichen Kontext," in *"Jedes Ding hat seine Zeit ...": Studien zur israelitischen und altorientalischen Weisheit; Diethelm Michel zum 65. Geburtstag*, ed. A. A. Diesel et al., BZAW 241 (Berlin: de Gruyter, 1996), 167–92; J. J. Blenkinsopp, "A Post-Exilic Lay Source in Genesis 1–11," in *Abschied vom Jahwisten: Die Komposition des Hexateuch in der jüngsten Diskussion*, ed. J. C. Gertz, K. Schmid, and M. Witte, BZAW 315 (Berlin: de Gruyter, 2002), 54–55. See further below, II.1.6.

[51] Cf., among others, T. Krüger, "Das menschliche Herz und die Weisung Gottes," in *Rezeption und Auslegung im Alten Testament und in seinem Umfeld (Festschrift O. H. Steck)*, ed. R. G. Kratz and T. Krüger, OBO 153 (Fribourg: Presses Universitaires; Göttingen: Vandenhoeck & Ruprecht, 1997), 73–76; E. Bosshard-Nepustil, *Vor uns die Sintflut: Studien zu Text, Kontexten und Rezeption der Fluterzählung Genesis 6–9*, BWANT 165 (Stuttgart: Kohlhammer, 2005), and M. Arneth, *Durch Adams Fall ist gänzlich verderbt ...: Studien zur Entstehung der alttestamentlichen Urgeschichte*, FRLANT 217 (Göttingen: Vandenhoeck & Ruprecht, 2007). See below, II.3.6.

[52] Cf., among others, J. Blenkinsopp, *The Pentateuch: An Introduction to the First Five Books of the Bible*, ABRL (New York: Doubleday, 1992), 87–88; M. Witte, *Die biblische Urgeschichte: Redaktions- und theologiegeschichtliche Beobachtungen zu Genesis 1,1–11,26*, BZAW 265 (Berlin: de Gruyter, 1998), 100–116; Arneth, *Durch Adams Fall*, 92–96. See below, II.4.

[53] Cf. de Pury, "P[G] as the Absolute Beginning," 13–42.

[54] J. Van Seters, *The Pentateuch: A Social-Science Commentary*, Trajectories 1 (Sheffield: Sheffield Academic Press, 1999), 160–89; C. Berner, *Die Exoduserzählung: Das literarische Werden einer Ursprungslegende Israels*, FAT 73 (Tübingen: Mohr Siebeck, 2010); Albertz, *Exodus 1–18*; H. Utzschneider and W. Oswald, *Exodus 1–15*, IEKAT (Stuttgart: Kohlhammer, 2013).

[55] Cf. Blum, *Studien*, 260, with n. 116. The lacunae are well-known: Moses is not introduced; for the last and decisive plague, P does not provide a fulfillment report; the detailed itinerary

the Priestly strand of Exodus lacks units with clear demarcations, containing both a beginning and an end. It is possible that certain Priestly texts in Exodus and Leviticus – i.e., the Priestly plagues account and the story about the miracle at the sea, the tabernacle account, and certain cultic laws – were initially composed as autonomous compositions.[56] Nevertheless, their literary character is different from the mentioned Priestly texts in Genesis: none of them have a marked literary introduction comparable to that in Genesis ("these are the *tôlĕdōt* of NN"). Certain indications reveal that the authors of the Priestly plagues account, the story of the miracle at the sea and also the tabernacle account knew and had in mind the non-P texts.

This observation concerning P's distinct literary profiles in Genesis (or in some parts of it) on the one hand and in Exodus on the other may further support the idea that, diachronically speaking, the beginnings of P's narrative tradition lie in the book of Genesis.

These preliminary observations have a direct impact on the delimitation of the texts forming the basis of analysis for this study. The differences in profile between Priestly texts in Genesis on the one hand and those in Exodus on the other can only be demonstrated by a thorough analysis of all texts of both books.

---

notice in Exod 14:2 does not fit the end of the Priestly Passover account (Exod 12:42, 51), which mentions Israel's exodus without noting any toponym. See below, II.8.5.

[56] Some scholars consider the (primary) Priestly plagues account and the story about the miracle at the sea autonomous compositions (cf. BLUM, *Studien*, 250–52; GERTZ, *Tradition*; T. RÖMER, "From the Call of Moses to the Parting of the Sea: Reflections on the Priestly Version of the Exodus Narrative," in *The Book of Exodus: Composition, Interpretation, and Reception*, ed. T. B. Dozeman, C. A. Evans, and J. N. Lohr, VTSup 64 [Leiden: Brill, 2014], 121–50). Yet the regular structure of these compositions and their elaborate character may be explained by assuming that the units were first composed as independent texts and then were integrated into the non-P narrative strand (cf. ALBERTZ, *Exodus 1–18*, 122, 141–42). See further below, II.7.4 (a). The cultic laws in Leviticus (Lev 1–3) probably once constituted a law collection belonging to a sanctuary, which P took up. See NOTH, *Das dritte Buch Mose*, 11, 16, 26; NIHAN, *From Priestly Torah*, 198–215, and, more generally, R. RENDTORFF, "Two Kinds of P? Some Reflections on the Occasion of the Publishing of Jacob Milgrom's Commentary on Leviticus 1–16," *JSOT* 60 (1993): 80, who shares the estimation of Israeli scholars that the Priestly cultic laws stem from the pre-exilic period. See also above, I.1.1 (4), with n. 20, and below, II.10.6.

2. Methodological Considerations

2.1 Identification of the Priestly Texts

The solid points of departure for identifying Priestly texts are the commonly shared observations concerning their language (distinct vocabulary), style (repetition, concentric structure), and theological convictions (theonym theology). Current scholarship agrees on the general attribution of texts to P or to non-P; only a few verses are disputed. That means that in general a text's classification as Priestly (P^C) will be adopted without additional explanation.[1] Dubious or contested classifications are nevertheless discussed.[2] In a few cases, new "positive" (a text commonly identified as non-P is classified as P) and "negative" (a text generally considered Priestly is identified as non-P) identifications are taken into consideration.[3] A surprising result is the classification of the dating (first part) in 1 Kgs 6:1aα. This chronological notice, which has the same particular shape as the frequent chronological statements and age indications scattered throughout the Priestly stratum in Genesis–Exodus, is consequently classified as Priestly (P^C).

2.2 Evaluating Significant Textual Differences

Text-critical assessment of the various Priestly passages and units is the means for ascertaining the most original text of each unit. For some among the numerous textual differences, careful evaluation is particularly important, because the latter bear directly on the comprehension of the unit in question (see, for instance, the textual variants in Gen 1; 5; Exod 1:1–5; and in the tabernacle account). It may appear that a redaction-critical analysis depends on an uncertain text-critical decision. To give an example, the main textual witnesses to Gen 5 contain a number of differences with regard to the ages of the ancestors. According to the Masoretic Text (MT), the number of years of Lamech's lifetime is 777 (Gen 5:31). The Samaritan Pentateuch (SP) and Septuagint (LXX) have distinct numbers (653 and 753, respectively). In all probability, the number in MT alludes to the motif of the seventy-seven-fold vengeance in Gen

---

[1] The present study bases itself on the "standard" compilations by Elliger and Lohfink (see above, n. 1 in section I.1).

[2] Disputed are (among others): Gen 8:6–7 (see II.3.3 [b]); 11:28–30 (see II.6.3 [a]); 16:15; 21:2 (see II.6.3 [c]); Exod 1:1–5 (see II.7.3 [a]); Exod 6:6–8 (see II.7.3 [b]).

[3] Exod 6:12bγ; 7:2–8 (see II.7.3 [d]). Outside of Genesis–Exodus: 1 Kgs 6:1aα (first part of the chronological indication, see III.1.2.2 [b] [3]).

4:24.[4] This connection with Gen 4 is one reason (among others) why certain scholars argue that the Sethite genealogy in Gen 5 (P) depends on the Cainite genealogy in Gen 4 (non-P/J).[5] Textual differences cannot be explained conclusively in every case. In the aforementioned example of Gen 5:31, the reading of MT may be explained as a secondary attempt to allude to Gen 4:24; in contrast, the readings of SP and LXX may be due to an intention to dissolve such a connection (the Lamech of the Sethite genealogy, the father of the "positive" Noah figure, should be detached from the "negative" Lamech figure of the Cainite list).[6] It is similarly difficult to give priority to one of the variant readings in other cases.[7] Such impasses may complicate redaction-historical reconstruction. However, considered on the whole, only a few textual uncertainties affect redaction-critical analysis.

The text-critical investigation must restrict itself to the most important differences relevant to the content and the literary-historical interpretation of an unit. Because of this limitation an important step in the text-critical investigation is the brief preliminary, global assessment of the main textual witnesses for each of the two large sections of Genesis and Exodus. The aim is to present important characteristics of the textual witnesses according to recent relevant studies. These comments precede the text-critical commentary on each of the two large sections, namely Genesis and Exodus (see the analyses of Gen 1 and of Exod 1–14).

2.3 Specific Criteria for Diachronic Differentiation between Literary Strata

(a) Spelling, Vocabulary, Style

Distinct spelling, expressions, and stylistic characteristics that occur only in certain texts and plots in the Priestly strand but not in others may suggest differentiation between literary Priestly strata. In the creation account in Gen 1:1–2:4a, different spellings in the so-called word account section on the one hand and in the so-called deed account section on the other give (additional) support to the idea that the unit is

---

[4] Cf., among others, WELLHAUSEN, Prolegomena zur Geschichte, 309; E. A. SPEISER, *Genesis: A New Translation with Introduction and Commentary*, AB 1 (New York: Doubleday, 1964), 43; M. BARNOUIN, "Recherches numériques sur la généalogie de Gen. V," *RB* 77 (1970): 351–52; B. ZIEMER, "Erklärung der Zahlen von Gen 5 aus ihrem kompositionellen Zusammenhang," *ZAW* 121 (2009): 15.

[5] See, among others, WELLHAUSEN, *Prolegomena zur Geschichte*, 309, and ZIEMER, "Erklärung," 15.

[6] In this concrete case, consideration of the global system of numbers in the main textual witnesses of Gen 5 and of the meanings of the names of the patriarchs will nevertheless help to overcome the impasse: they hint at the originality of the numbers in SP in general; see below, II.2.2 (a).

[7] Although in certain cases two or more readings appear equally appropriate in the context, it is probable that one of them is more original than the other; cf. E. Tov, *Textual Criticism of the Hebrew Bible*, 3rd ed. (Minneapolis: Augsburg Fortress, 2012), 164–65.

composed from two different literary strata. While the word account uses the noun מִין, "kind," with the contracted suffix ו for the third-person singular (לְמִינוֹ, cf. 1:11, all main textual witnesses[8]), the deed account consistently prefers the longer form לְמִינֵהוּ (cf. 1:12 [2×], 21, 25, all main textual witnesses[9]). The former, furthermore, contains the archaic paragogic suffix ו in the construct state (cf. חַיְתוֹ אֶרֶץ, "wild animals of the earth," in 1:24 MT[10]), whereas the latter prefers the ordinary spelling חַיַּת הָאָרֶץ, "wild animals of the earth" (cf. 1:25, all main textual witnesses[11]).

Linguistic discrepancies in a literary unit may point to two different authors. In the Priestly flood story, for instance, the distributive idea is expressed in two different ways. In two statements found in the passage of YHWH's instruction to Noah the distributive notion has to be deduced from the context (see Gen 6:19, 20: שְׁנַיִם, "two [of every kind]"). In two statements within the section of the fulfillment of the order, however, the idea is expressed by repetition (7:9 and 7:15: שְׁנַיִם שְׁנַיִם, "two of every kind") which is frequent in Priestly texts (tabernacle account, H and Priestly texts in Numbers) and in Late Biblical Hebrew in general.[12] This intriguing difference points to two different literary strata within the Priestly strand in Gen 6–9. Another example: the story in Gen 23, assigned to P^G/P^C by a majority of scholars, contains expressions such as גֵּר וְתוֹשָׁב, "stranger and sojourner" (23:4), and עַם הָאָרֶץ, "the people of the land" (23:7, 12, 13), which do not appear in the Priestly texts of Genesis and Exodus. These terms, however, are found in the so-called Holiness Code.[13] Noticeably, the topic of the preservation of Israelite ownership of the land, present in Gen 23, is of great importance in the Holiness Code. These commonalities with H favor the idea that Gen 23 (and the related passages in Gen 25:9–10; 49:29–32; 50:13) stems from the same author or from the same milieu. Moreover, the peculiar construction יֵשׁ with infinitive in 23:8 appears frequently in late biblical texts such as Chronicles but never in P^C.[14] In these and other cases, the mentioned observations concerning language use are a sure indicator for the inner differentiation between literary strata and thus for their relative dating. In other cases, however, the observed linguistic particularities may be due to the topic or to the genre of the section in which they are found.

---

[8] MT, SP, 4QGenb. – Unfortunately, in the word account מִין with the third-person singular suffix is attested only once.

[9] 1:12: MT, SP, 4QGen^b; 1:21: MT, SP, 4QGen^b; 1:25: MT, SP.

[10] SP: חית הארץ.

[11] MT, SP, 4QGen^d.

[12] Repetition is used in these texts to express either the notion of totality or the distributive idea. See POLZIN, *Late Biblical Hebrew*, 47–51; GKC §123c, d, with n. 2, 134q. See furthermore in II.3.2 (a).

[13] גר ותושב: Lev 25:23, 35, 47 (2×), outside of H only in Gen 23:4 and Num 35:15; עם הארץ: Lev 20:2, 4; cf. furthermore Lev 4:27; Num 14:9. See below II.6.4 (f).

[14] On this construction, the basic meaning of which is "it is possible to (…)," see S. R. DRIVER, *Notes on the Hebrew Text of the Books of Samuel* (Oxford: Clarendon, 1890), 286, and IDEM, *A Treatise on the Use of the Tenses in Hebrew and Some Other Syntactical Questions* (Grand Rapids: Eerdmans, 1998), §202.1.

For instance, the tabernacle account contains a number of technical terms, expressions relating to the inventory of the tabernacle, that are not used elsewhere in Priestly texts. Another difficulty in applying language criteria for the inner differentiation is as follows: certain Priestly texts with a redactional literary profile refer to preceding (or subsequent) non-Priestly texts by taking up certain motifs and specific expressions not found elsewhere in P. Thus the presence of "alien" terms in a Priestly passage does not necessarily indicate that the text in question was revised and that the expression or sentence in question derives from a post-Priestly redactor. The following example may illustrate the problem: in Exod 1:7 (generally ascribed to P), the use of the lexeme עצם, "to become mighty," which does not occur in other Priestly texts, may be considered an allusion by the Priestly author to the non-Priestly context in which the expression is used (Exod 1:9, 20)[15] rather than a harmonizing post-P addition.[16]

Variations in use of certain expressions within P may suggest a differentiation between literary strata too: in Gen 2:1, the expression כל צבאם, "all their host," denotes all living creatures that populate the habitats of the created world. In several Priestly texts of Exodus and Numbers, the same term designates Israel as an organized army (Exod 6:26; 7:4; 12:17, 41, 51 and the frequent use of the noun in Num 1–10 and 31[17]). This may point to distinct literary strata. There are indeed other indications favoring the idea that Gen 2:1 belongs to the *Vorlage* of the Priestly creation account.

(b) Ideological (Theological) Coherence

There is a general consensus among scholars concerning the existence and importance of certain ideological features of P. For instance, it is generally acknowledged that P expresses an inclusive monotheism. However, as already noted above, a close reading of the texts reveals that certain passages contain contradictory statements. The motifs concerning the bringing forth of animals by the sea and by the earth in Gen 1:20, 24 and the conception of the royal household of God in 1:26 (see the plural נעשה, "let us make") are unique in P and stand in tension with the Priestly source's inclusive but strict monotheism. Another example: a key Priestly text, Gen 17, states that the covenant is destined only for Abraham as "a father of multiple nations," yet according to other verses in the same chapter the gift of the covenant is offered to Isaac and his descendants as well. Such ideologically conflicting positions in one and the same passage or unit may point to the presence of two literary strata. However, in certain cases, one should also envisage the possibility that the Priestly author relied on one or even several oral traditions that he was keen to combine with his own theological standpoint or to combine with one another. In this respect, what may clarify the question of unity in a certain passage is the application of more than one of the aforementioned

---

[15] Cf. Albertz, *Exodus 1–18*, 42.

[16] Thus T. Römer, *Moïse en version originale* (Paris: Bayard; Geneva: Labor et Fides, 2015), 44–45.

[17] In Num 1–10: 61×; in Num 31: 13×; cf. other occurrences in Numbers (P): 26:2; 32:27; 33:1.

criteria. For instance, what favors a differentiation between the word account in Gen 1:24 and the deed account in 1:25 is not only the ideological discrepancy but also the difference in spelling (see above).

(c) Literary Profile: Relationship to Non-P Texts

As noted above, different literary profiles are discernible in the Priestly strand: some units have characteristics of autonomous compositions, whereas others clearly depend on non-P narratives. Sometimes, the two profiles are apparent in one and the same greater Priestly unit.

Observations concerning differences in the literary profiles of the P strand[18] might serve, when supported by other arguments, as criteria for diachronic differentiation between Priestly texts.

What are the characteristics of P's different literary profiles (independent thread on the one hand, dependent thread on the other)? A sign of a unit's "independence" is a self-contained and coherent plot. An example is the Priestly Abraham narrative, which is self-contained and flows continuously. In contrast, Priestly units with an interrupted narrative thread and obvious gaps that have to be "complemented" with contents from the non-P context presumably were written in relation to the non-P context. Often they take up non-Priestly expressions and motifs that otherwise do not occur in Priestly texts (see above, [a]). A good example of this second case is the Priestly Jacob-Esau story, with its well-known gaps and lexical "borrowings" from the neighboring non-P texts.[19] Other examples are the recurrent statements mentioning the age of the patriarchs and giving chronological information. In the Abraham narrative they are numerous and related one to the other. Some of them obviously depend on the non-P strand, in contrast to the overall profile of the self-contained and independent (proto-)Priestly Terah-Abraham narrative.

Interestingly, those scholars who point to differences in the literary profile of P do not take into consideration the possibility that their observations might be evaluated diachronically for an inner differentiation of the Priestly strand.[20] In Blum's analysis, for instance, the observed differences in the literary profile, as far I can see, never serve as indicators of distinct Priestly layers. According to Blum, both Priestly "source" texts (i.e., texts from the primeval history, the continuous Priestly Abraham narrative) and the complementary Priestly passages in the Esau-Jacob narrative were composed as "preliminary works" (*Vorarbeiten*), which were then combined with the pre-Priestly texts (non-P primary story; late exilic patriarchal narrative).[21] R. H. Pfeiffer,

---

[18] Cf. above, I.1.1 (2).

[19] See the analysis in II.6.5.1 (a).

[20] E. Blum, J. Gertz, and J. Wöhrle; see above, n. 13 in section I.1.

[21] See Blum, "Noch einmal," 51–54 (quotation on 52). Blum also reckons with a long, multistage formation of the Priestly *Kompositionsschicht*. However, the supposed long duration of the formation of the Priestly layer is due to manifold later additions (Pˢ) (see Blum, "Noch einmal," 51–54).

J. C. Gertz, and J. Wöhrle likewise attribute source and redactional texts in P to the same literary layer (P^G/P^C).[22]

2.4 Focus on Individual Priestly Units

An important methodological principle of this study of the Priestly texts in Gen 1–Exod 40 is its focus on the *individual* Priestly section or unit, that is, its own literary profile, its plot (if applicable), its specific language, and its relationship to the non-P "environment." This principle is based on the observation that certain Priestly texts, found in particular in Genesis, appear as well-marked units having a clear beginning and end. For other Priestly texts, the demarcation is not self-evident. In the ancestral narrative and in Exodus it is more difficult to delimit single Priestly units; therefore, the Priestly strand has to be dealt with within larger, thematically determined sections. The present investigation deals with each delimited part of the Priestly strand individually, following the canonical order of the Priestly texts. Only a few studies share this format (consecutive treatment of single units or sections in canonical order).[23] Most analyses of Priestly texts in Genesis and Exodus rest on the tacit assumption that the individual unit fits well in the extensive Priestly composition (document) and was composed by the Priestly author; therefore, a focus on the individual profile, plot, and specific language of single units is far less pronounced or even nonexistent in those studies. This assumption of a (nearly) monolithic Priestly document is not shared by the present study, which reckons from the outset with the possibility that not one but multiple different authors contributed to the Priestly composition (P^C) and that some of the Priestly texts are based on older written *Vorlagen*. Another difference from recent studies on P is the minute focus on Priestly texts *in both* Genesis and Exodus. Recent detailed studies concentrate on Priestly texts in certain sections of either Genesis or Exodus.[24]

---

[22] R. H. Pfeiffer, "Non-Israelite Source," 67; Gertz, *Tradition*, 390–91; idem, "Genesis 5," 90–91; Wöhrle, *Fremdlinge*, 147–60.

[23] See, in particular, Wöhrle, *Fremdlinge*; C. Berner, "Der literarische Charakter der Priesterschrift in der Exoduserzählung: Dargestellt an Exodus 1 bis 14," in *Abschied von der Priesterschrift? Zum Stand der Pentateuchdebatte*, ed. F. Hartenstein and K. Schmid, VWGT 40 (Leipzig: Evangelische Verlagsanstalt, 2015), 94–133; P. Weimar, *Studien zur Priesterschrift*, FAT 56 (Tübingen: Mohr Siebeck, 2008), 246–49 (collected essays on Priestly texts, discussed in canonical order).

[24] See E. Zenger, *Gottes Bogen in den Wolken: Untersuchungen zu Komposition und Theologie der priesterschriftlichen Urgeschichte*, SBS 12 (Stuttgart: Verlag Katholisches Bibelwerk, 1983); Wöhrle, *Fremdlinge*; Berner, *Die Exoduserzählung*, 38–41; idem, "Der literarische Charakter."

2.5 Focus on the Comprehensive Structure(s) and Framework(s)

This study will give special attention to recurrent and mutually corresponding elements that structure the Priestly texts in Genesis and Exodus and beyond, such as the *tôlĕdōt* formulae, chronological information (which often is related to indications of age), and intertextual correspondences between the creation narrative in Gen 1:1–2:4a and the end of the tabernacle account (Exod 39–40), among others. A thorough analysis of these elements may provide insights about the conceptual structure(s) of the Priestly composition.

Whereas most of these elements are easy to survey and can be adequately discussed in the analytic sections, the different chronological notes appear more frequently and seem more disparate in form. They contain considerable chronological information, which is part of a comprehensive framework. Both the significance and the complexity of this latter theme, including methodological considerations, should be briefly outlined here.

Despite the fact that the chronological statements and age indications predominantly appear in the book of Genesis, it is noteworthy that some of them are related to assertions of identical shape outside this book (Exod 12:40–41 and 1 Kgs 6:1). A difficulty consists in the differences in the main textual witnesses (MT, SP, and LXX): above all, the main textual witnesses for the two genealogies in Gen 5 and 11 differ from each other significantly. By contrast, almost all statements about the ages of the ancestors found in the Priestly patriarchal narrative (Gen 11:27–47:28) are shared by all main witnesses of the biblical text (only exception: Gen 11:32). Combined with the 430 years of Israel's stay in the land of Egypt (Exod 12:40 MT, 41 MT), these shared data point to the round periods from Abraham's birth to the exodus (720 years) and to the dedication of the First Temple (1,200 years; see 1 Kgs 6:1), respectively.

According to some scholars, the different chronological indications are all connected to each other; they see the beginning of this overall chronological system in the genealogies in Gen 5 and 11. In an influential study, A. Jepsen considered the dedication of the First Temple in the year 2800 *anno mundi* to be the goal of the Priestly chronological system.[25] In cases of disagreement between the main witnesses, his calculation follows SP in part (for Gen 5) and MT in part (for Gen 11:10–26). Other scholars considered the date of the exodus in 2666 *anno mundi*, calculated according to MT, to be significant. This number would have been considered two-thirds of a world era (4,000 years). Furthermore, the chronological system in MT would make the year 4000 coincide with the Maccabean temple dedication in 164 BCE.[26] According to B. Ziemer's calculation using the data in MT, which adds a year for each entry in the genealogies in Gen 5 and 11:10–26 in order to account for the time between procreation and birth, Abraham was born exactly 300 years after the flood.[27]

---

[25] A. Jepsen, "Zur Chronologie des Priesterkodex," *ZAW* 47 (1929): 251–55.
[26] See Schmid, *Genesis and the Moses Story*, 17–19.
[27] Ziemer, "Erklärung," 9, n. 41.

The problem with these calculations is that they all depend on external interpretations of the text.[28] Theories according to which a certain calculation was aimed toward a specific date in the Persian or Hellenistic period are based on questionable premises concerning the existence of accurate historical records in the postexilic Judean community.[29]

Independent of these problems, from a methodological point of view, it seems more sound to analyze the numbers first within the context of their own units, taking into account the possibility that the various numbers in Gen 5 – perhaps together with those in Gen 11:10–26 – formed a system in their own right. Similarly, the chronological indications in the patriarchal narrative and the exodus story may have constituted an independent and closed system as well. The latter idea is supported by the fact that the statements in these sections point to round periods of 720 or 1200 years (for the periods from Abraham's birth to the exodus and to the dedication of the First Temple).[30] It is noticeable that in Gen 5 the sum of years indicating the beginning of the flood does not seem important (in none of the three main textual witnesses is this number round or meaningful). The focus is rather laid on such individual figures as Enoch (365 years) and the patriarchs who die in the year of the flood (according to the SP).[31]

The calculation resulting in round periods from Abraham's birth to the exodus and to the consecration of the First Temple is based on the following indications: Abraham's age at Isaac's birth (100 years; Gen 21:5), Isaac's age at Jacob's birth (60 years; Gen 25:26), Jacob's age at his departure for Egypt (130 years; Gen 47:28 [and 47:9]), the duration of Israel's stay in Egypt (430 years; Exod 12:40–41 MT[32]), and the time from the exodus to the construction of the First Temple (480 years; 1 Kgs 6:1 MT, LXX[33]). Almost all these dates are shared by the main textual witnesses. In the two instances where the main textual witnesses diverge, MT is preferable.

As for Exod 12:40–41, the alternative reading (SP, LXX) is clearly harmonistic. In SP and LXX, the 430 years are related to Israel's stay in Canaan and Egypt. This reading harmonizes with

---

[28] See, for instance, the question raised by ZIEMER, "Erklärung," of how to treat the time between procreation and birth. Another question is how to deal with the indication in 11:10 that Shem fathered Arpachshad two years after the flood. This information is ignored by the (putative) calculation of MT directed toward the year 4000 (see R. S. HENDEL, "A Hasmonean Edition of MT Genesis? The Implications of the Editions of the Chronology in Genesis 5," *HBAI* 1 [2012]: 11).

[29] See HENDEL, "Hasmonean Edition," 4–5.

[30] Pointing to the importance of the data found in the patriarchal narrative are K. KOENEN, "1200 Jahre von Abrahams Geburt bis zum Tempelbau," *ZAW* 126 (2014): 494–505, and B. ZIEMER, *Abram–Abraham: Kompositionsgeschichtliche Untersuchungen zu Genesis 14, 15 und 17*, BZAW 350 (Berlin: de Gruyter, 2005), 347.

[31] See below, II.2.2 (a).

[32] See the argument in the following passage in small font.

[33] LXX[BA]: 440 years.

the information given in Exod 6:16–25.[34] The deviation of LXX in 1 Kgs 6:1 = 3 Kgdms 6:1 (440 years) may be explained as follows: the translator or a scribe of the *Vorlage* preferred to assign a round number of years to the reign of the good king Asa rather than to that of the dubious king Solomon. According to 3 Kgdms 6:1; 11:42; 15:9, Asa became king in Judah exactly 500 years after the exodus. Asa was evaluated as "good" because of his merits in the domain of the cult: in contrast to Solomon, he removed heterodox cults.[35]

Since the 430 years of Exod 12:40–41 are not derived from the plot of Gen–Exod, they were probably inspired by the length of time between Solomon's building of the temple and the capture of Jerusalem and end of the Judean monarchy (430 years, according to the data in the books of Kings [MT]).[36] The duration of the patriarchs' stay in the land of Canaan (215 years) is half the length of Israel's stay in Egypt.

Accordingly, all the indications of time and statements of age in the Priestly strand after Gen 11:27 show or imply the following periodic structure:[37]

0:     Abraham's birth (Gen 11:27)
       period of 75 years: Abraham lives 75 years in Mesopotamia
75:    Abraham moves to Canaan (Gen 12:4)
       period of 215 years: time of patriarchs' life in the land of Canaan
290:   Jacob enters Egypt (Gen 47:28 [and 47:9])
       period of 430 years: period of Israel's stay in Egypt
720:   Exodus (Exod 12:40–41)
       period of 480 years: time between the exodus and Solomon's construction of
       the temple
1200: Construction of the temple (1 Kgs 6:1)

This broad network of chronological references and its goal, Solomon's construction of the temple in Jerusalem, raise the question of literary classification for the statements about the patriarchs' ages. Generally, they are all ascribed to P^G/P^C, except the notice in 1 Kgs 6:1aα, which generally is considered Deuteronomistic although it shares the characteristic form of the other Priestly chronological indications which is not found elsewhere in Deuteronomistic chronological notices in the Former Prophets.[38]

---

[34] Cf. KOENEN, "1200 Jahre," 498–99, and also SCHMID, *Genesis and the Moses Story*, 90, n. 245; and see the discussion in II.7.2.2 (f).

[35] What may indeed advocate that this was an intentional device by the translator or scribe of the *Vorlage* of LXX is the reading in 3 Kgdms 15:18: LXX deviates from MT in that Asa took only the silver and the gold that was found in the treasures of the the palace and not the silver and the gold that was stocked in the temple of YHWH. It is most likely that the plus of MT is the more original reading and that the LXX has left out the statement in order to "optimize" the image of Asa. (There is no visible motive for a deliberate modification in MT; for what reason would a scribe of MT have intended to charge Asa with such a problematic act?)

[36] Cf. KOENEN, "1200 Jahre," 498–99. Koenen also notes that the period from the exodus to the temple's construction (480 years) is framed by two 430-year periods (501).

[37] Cf. KOENEN, "1200 Jahre," 496.

[38] See M. NOTH, *Überlieferungsgeschichtliche Studien* (Halle: Niemeyer, 1943), 18–27; IDEM,

2.6 Elucidating the Historical Contexts

2.6.1 Significance of the Task

Elucidation of the historical contexts and dating constitute an essential task for exegesis of biblical texts for the reason that there can be no comprehensive understanding of the latter without some knowledge of the world of the addressees of these texts.[39] This aspect was an important element of the historical critical investigation of the Hebrew Bible since its beginnings and is going on to be although its pertinence has been put in question by the adherents of the so-called New-Documentary Hypothesis.[40] The "New-documentarians" consider the composition of the Pentateuch a "strictly literary problem."[41] According to one of their exponents, J. Baden, the New-Documentarian Hypothesis "is a proposed literary solution to the literary problems of the Pentateuch, no more, no less. It does not purport to date the texts or to be the key to the history of Israelite religion."[42] The disregard of the history in the analytic approach of the New-Documentarians marks a fundamental shift with classical documentary theory as it was proposed by Kuehnen and Wellhausen. In the latter's analysis of P, the reconstruction of the historical context played a crucial role. According to Wellhausen, P presupposes Josiah's cult centralization, the exile and the "restauration" of the temple and aims to provide a legitimation for the Jerusalem temple and its priesthood. P can only be understood in the context of this concrete historical situation.[43] Accordingly Wellhausen criticized a "mechanical separation between sources" purely based on literary observations.[44] This historical approach is shared by most critics. Redactional criticism cannot do without the (tentative) reconstruction of the historical context.

Könige, BKAT 11 (Neukirchen-Vluyn: Neukirchener Verlag, 1968), 110; E. WÜRTHWEIN, *Die Bücher der Könige. 1.Kön. 1–16*, ATD 11,1 (Göttingen 1977), 62; V. FRITZ, *Das erste Buch der Könige*, ZBK 10.1 (Zurich: TVZ, 1996), 68–69; KOENEN, "1200 Jahre," 504. See further below III.1.2.2 (b) (3).

[39] See E. BLUM, "The Linguistic Dating of Biblical Texts: An Approach with Methodological Limitations," in *The Formation of the Pentateuch: Bridging the Academic Cultures of Europe, Israel, and North America*, ed. Jan Christian Gertz et al., FAT 111 (Tübingen: Mohr Siebeck, 2016), 303.

[40] See for instance J. S. BADEN and J. STACKERT, "Convergences and Divergences in Contemporary Pentateuchal Research," in *The Oxford Handbook of the Pentateuch*, ed. J. S. Baden and J. Stackert (Oxford: Oxford University Press, 2021), 17–37; B. J. SCHWARTZ, "The Documentary Hypothesis," in *The Oxford Handbook of the Pentateuch*, ed. J. S. Baden and J. Stackert (Oxford: Oxford University Press, 2021), 165–87.

[41] K. SCHMID, "The Neo-Documentarian Manifesto: A Critical Reading," *JBL* 140 (2021): 468–70, here 468.

[42] BADEN, *Composition*, 32.

[43] See WELLHAUSEN, *Prolegomena zur Geschichte*, 342–45 = IDEM, *Prolegomena to the History*, 404–5.

[44] See WELLHAUSEN, *Prolegomena zur Geschichte*, 8, n. 2; 299 = IDEM, *Prolegomena to the History*, 8, n. 2; (quotation is from here), 295.

In pursuing this goal scholars look out for textual features and contents pointing to a specific setting and at the same time rendering others improbable. The relevant information contained in the texts belong to different domains such as language, geography, material culture and ideology. This study strives to incorporate data from all of these different areas; as a result, it will contribute more and new observations related to geography and material culture in particular. Methodologically important in this respect is furthermore, that it attempts to answer this question not only for the Priestly composition in general, but for each unit individually (in accordance with the principle set out above).

2.6.2 Linguistic Evidence

In the discussion on P's setting and dating of the last decades the linguistic criterion plays an important role. Since the seventies of the twentieth century scholars have argued for a preexilic date of P on the grounds of linguistic dating (see above).[45] An engaged debate has developed on the differentiation between different stages of Biblical Hebrew (i.e. Archaic Biblical Hebrew [ABH], Classical Biblical Hebrew [CBH], Transitional Biblical Hebrew [TBH], Late Biblical Hebrew [LBH]), their chronology and their implications for scholarly dating of biblical literature in general.[46]

Linguistic analyses are an indispensable task for serious biblical exegesis, not only for dating a text unit but also for its inner differentiation (see above) and its interpretation. However, dating texts on the basis of language and style meets a number of problems. A fundamental difficulty consists in the interpretation and classification of linguistic singularities of a textual unit; do they point to a distinct historical period (and should therefore interpreted diachronically) or to a distinct geographical or socio-historical setting (which both would not necessarily have diachronic implications)? Notwithstanding this question, in many cases the relative dating of a textual unit through assignment to CBH or LBH seems reasonable. Correlation with precise absolute dates, however, is more difficult for several reasons.[47] First one should take into account the absence of sufficient non-biblical epigraphic data for Hebrew in pre-Hellenistic periods. Sources are in particular rare in Persian times. Establishing absolute dates seem possible only through other data available to historical exegesis such as content related features, references to social-political constellations, close connections to a specific

---

[45] See above, I.1.1 (4).

[46] Recent publication include I. YOUNG, R. REZETKO, with the Assistance of M. EHRENSVÄRD, *Linguistic Dating of Biblical Texts. An Introduction to Approaches and Problems*, 2 vols. (London-Oakville: Equinox, 2009); A. HURVITZ, in Collaboration with L. GOTTLIEB, A. HORNKOHL, E. MASTÉY, *A Concise Lexicon of Late Biblical Hebrew. Linguistic Innovations in the Writings of the Second Temple Period*, VTSup 160 (Leiden: Brill, 2014); BLUM, "Linguistic Dating," 303–25; R. S. HENDEL and J. JOOSTEN, *How Old Is the Hebrew Bible? A Linguistic, Textual, and Historical Study*, ABRL (New Haven: Yale University Press, 2018); K. SCHMID, "How Old Is the Hebrew Bible? A Response to Ronald Hendel and Jan Joosten," *ZAW* 132 (2020), 622–31.

[47] See BLUM, "Linguistic Dating," 306.

text or literary stratum (that can reliably be dated).[48] A problem consists furthermore in the inner stratification of biblical books and textual units. Existing linguistic studies tend to assign globally entire books and even more comprehensive units (Pentateuch, Former Prophets) to a certain stage (CBH, TBH or LBH) and the (presumably) corresponding historical period. Such generalization stands in conflict with the insights of historical-critical research in the composite nature of the biblical books and the ongoing editorial activity that has affected most of them. For instance, it is problematic to choose the book of Ezekiel *en block* as reference for the dating of the Priestly texts which themselves are treated *in toto* as A. Hurwitz does (even so he recognizes the methodological problem).[49] The complex literary history of most books renders relative dating on the basis of comparisons a complicated task.[50] Inner stratigraphy apparently cannot be detected by means of linguistic dating alone. This is due to the archaizing style used by learned redactors and authors in exilic and postexilic periods; they were able to write classical Hebrew. Some scholars such as A. Hurwitz and more recently R. Hendel and J. Joosten, however, resolutely deny this possibility.[51] Pointing to some "pseudo-classicisms" in late texts, they argue that later scribes who applied CBH's conventions inevitably made a mistake here and there. In their opinion, "the argument that Persian or Hellenist-Roman period scribes could write in perfect CBH lacks evidential warrant. It is a thought experiment, a logical possibility ... It lacks consilience with the historical and linguistic data."[52] However, the results of several decades of historical-critical exegesis on the contrary confirm the argument in question and, in fact, provide some "evidential warrant."[53] Several studies, based mainly on non-linguistic aspects such as intertextual connections, dependence on Greek literature, and socio-historical considerations, date large portions of the CBH books such as Leviticus, Numbers, Joshua, and Judges (Appendix) to the Persian period.[54] Studies on the book of Numbers, for example, have shown that this book (or its bulk) should be considered a "close relative" of the book of Chronicles in terms of its main themes, theology, and social-historical background.[55] Most of its texts, despite the fact that

---

[48] See BLUM, "Linguistic Dating," 304–5.

[49] HURWITZ, *Linguistic Study*, 20–21. Hurwitz refuses to consider results of literary-historical studies because of their conjectural nature. His study "examines the biblical texts as they crystallized in their last historical phase and does not seek to trace their growth and development during previous 'pre-historical' stages" (see p. 20).

[50] See BLUM, "Linguistic Dating," 307.

[51] HURWITZ, *A Linguistic Study*, 163–64; HENDEL and JOOSTEN, *How Old Is the Hebrew Bible?*, 125.

[52] HENDEL and JOOSTEN, *How Old Is the Hebrew Bible?*, 124–25.

[53] See P. R. DAVIES, "Biblical Hebrew and the History of Ancient Judah: Typology, Chronology and Common Sense," in *Biblical Hebrew: Studies in Chronology and Typology*, ed. I. Young, JSOTSup 369 (London: T&T Clark, 2003), 150–63; SCHMID, "How Old Is the Hebrew Bible?," 626–27.

[54] See SCHMID, "How Old Is the Hebrew Bible?," 626–27.

[55] In two recent contributions H. P. Mathys documents a number of shared themes and motifs in the two books such as the relationship between priests and Levites; increased significance of

they are written in CBH, should therefore be dated to the Persian period. Moreover, the inference from the documented pseudo classicisms to the de facto impossibility for postexilic authors and scribes to imitate CBH-style without committing errors is not evident at all. The phenomenon of consequent and competent recourse to the conventions of a previous "classical" literary language stage is well attested for Sumerian, Standard Babylonian, Attic Greek, Latin and Quranic Arabic.[56] For these reasons, one should rather assume that there were scribes in the Persian period who wrote in Classical Biblical Hebrew. This does not mean that they adapted to the conventions of CBH without making small adaptations to the rules of the later language stage with whom they were more familiar. Closer examination reveals indeed that the CBH texts of the Pentateuch linguistically are non a monolithic block; this is confirmed also by analyses of scholars correlating language typology with chronological setting.[57] As example of linguistic inconsistency in a CBH text, one may adduce the repetition of the numeral "two" to express the distributive idea in the secondary P-stratum in the flood narrative (see above).

When considering this question, it should be kept in mind that in certain genres, as for instance repetitive genealogies, it was probably easier for redactors to reproduce CBH correctly than in others. Ron Hendel draws attention to the use of ילד‎ *qal* with a masculine subject with the meaning "to beget" in J/non-P genealogies in the book

---

Pesach; tithe and Temple financing; registration of the people; stylized holy war descriptions. See H.-P. Mathys, "Numeri und Chronik: Nahe Verwandte," in *The Books of Leviticus and Numbers*, ed. T. Römer, BETL 215 (Leuven: Peeters, 2008), 555–78; idem, "Numbers and Chronicles: Close Relatives 2," in *Chronicles and the Priestly Literature of the Hebrew Bible*, ed. J. Jeon and L. Jonker, BZAW 528 (Berlin: de Gruyter, 2021), 79–107. See furthermore R. Achenbach, "Theocratic Reworking in the Pentateuch," in *Chronicles and the Priestly Literature of the Hebrew Bible*, ed. J. Jeon and L. Jonker, BZAW 528 (Berlin: de Gruyter, 2021), 53–78.

[56] See Davies, "Biblical Hebrew and the History of Ancient Judah," 158–59; Sh. Gesundheit, "Introduction: The Strengths and Weaknesses of Linguistic Dating," in *The Formation of the Pentateuch: Bridging the Academic Cultures of Europe, Israel, and North America*, ed. J. C. Gertz, B. M. Levinson, D. Rom-Shiloni, and K, Schmid, FAT 111 (Tübingen: Mohr Siebeck, 2016), 298–99, with n. 12.

[57] In a study on the differences between the syntax of CBH and that of LBH J. Joosten focuses on instances of second person prefix conjugation forms preceded by ו‎ in the Hebrew Bible which are a marker of LBH (see J. Joosten, "The Distinction between Classical and Late Biblical Hebrew as Reflected in Syntax," *HS* 46 [2005]: 330–34). While Joosten enumerates nine cases of we + second person prefix form in LBH books he nevertheless identifies three occurrences in CBH texts (Exod 15:17; 21:3, Num 17:25), from which he excludes the first one because of its distinct genre (poetry). Joosten's motivation to refer to these two or three occurrences seems only to illustrate the ratio 2:9 in the use of this construction for the two corpora; an interesting question he does not ask, however, is how it comes that a CBH author follows a convention from a later time. One obvious possibility to answer the question is that that the CBH-text in question was composed by a later author who though being willing to write constantly flawless CBH for once slipped and "fall back" into the later convention with whom he was more familiar. Interestingly enough all three occurrences are found in texts that are all considered late insertions in recent research.

of Genesis which contrasts with the use of ילד *hiphil* in Priestly lineages. Since ילד *qal* possibly represents the older form, Hendel cautiously deduces the diachronic priority of the J/non-P stratum.[58] In this case, however, it would not seem to have been so difficult for a learned author in the Persian period to adapt to the conventions of CBH and create the sober and repetitive genealogical phrases in question including ילד *qal*, "to beget" with a masculine subject (and similarly ילד *qal passive*, "to be born"), as archaizing element(s). There are indeed some clues for a post-Priestly (or post-proto-Priestly) origin of the mentioned J/non-P genealogies or genealogical notices.[59]

2.6.3 Significance of Realia

For the question of the historical location of the Priestly texts, certain cultural and political realities reflected in P will also be taken into account. These data should be productive not only for the analysis of the extensive Priestly composition as a whole but also for individual units and passages.[60]

The tabernacle account, with its detailed description of the tent, its inventory and in particular the high priest's vestments, yields important information about the material culture of the time of its author(s).

Of great importance in general are toponyms, which are found in several Priestly texts but which are used, when considered on the whole, in a rather sporadic and unsteady manner. How significant is the use of these toponyms for the understanding of P? As for this question, an important criterion is whether the toponym is introduced for the first time by the Priestly author or is already found in a pre-priestly stratum, which is presupposed by the Priestly text. A toponym is all the more significant if it is the Priestly (or proto-Priestly) author who has introduced it.

An accumulation of geographical names appears in the Priestly Table of Nations (Gen 10*) that probably predates the non-Priestly stratum. Both the presence of certain names, and the absence of others (Persia and Arabia) in this text seem significative for the question of historical location, they point to a setting before the Persian era. A certain importance seems to be given to Mamre (Abraham's burial place), Bethel (where El Shaddai reveals himself to Jacob; Gen 35:9–15), Baal Zaphon (Mount Cassius, where the miracle at the sea happens; Exod 14:2, 9), and in particular Mount Sinai (where the tabernacle is erected). Whereas Mamre and Baal Zephon were introduced by the proto-Priestly or Priestly author respectively, Bethel and Mount Sinai played already an important role in the pre-Priestly stratum. The case of Bethel shows

---

[58] See R. S. HENDEL, "'Begetting' and 'Being Born' in the Pentateuch: Notes on Historical Linguistics and Source Criticism," *VT* 50 (2000).

[59] In the case of the Table of Nations (Gen 10), for instance, an increasing number of scholars consider the self-contained Priestly stratum the older stratum and the punctual J passages – using several times ילד *qal*, "to beget" with a masculine subject – later additions (see II.4.5). For the phrases including ילד *qal* in Gen 4:18, see II.2.4.2.

[60] For examples, see above, I.1.1 (4).

that mention or even (seemingly) prominence of a toponym does not necessarily indicate its importance for the author nor that it can be considered a sure clue to the geographical location of the pericope. In fact, as will be shown below, the passage Gen 35:9–15 focusing on Bethel is reacting to the Bethel etiology in Gen 28 and, in reality, diminishes Bethel's status as a place of revelation. Bethel is not the place where God dwells (as Gen 28:10–22 claims) but just a place of temporary encounter with God, just like Mamre in the Priestly Abraham narrative (cf. Gen 17:22).[61]

In other cases, the mention of a toponym or specific geographical information might indicate that the author was well informed about a particular region and not necessarily that he (had) lived there (cf. the miracle story in Exodus 14 and the tabernacle account), although the latter possibility should also be taken into consideration.[62]

2.7 Terminology and Sigla

Since the terminology for the presumed literary strata partly deviates from common usage in scholarship, the designations used shall be briefly explained. The comprehensive literary stratum spanning the books of Genesis and Exodus and including non-priestly texts is called "Priestly Composition" (P^C); this term is chosen with regard to the composite nature of the layer. When referring to studies that follow the source model, I use the traditional designation "Priestly source" ("Priestly *Grundschrift*," P^G). Self-contained individual units within the Priestly stratum that predate P^C are called "proto-Priestly" ("proto-P"). Later additions to the comprehensive Priestly composition (P^C) having strong affinities with so-called Holiness Code (Lev 17–26) are labeled H ("Holiness texts"). They could stem from the same circles as the texts of the texts of the Holiness Law. Secondary insertions that have nothing in common with H-texts, are assigned to P^s ("secondary Priestly stratum"), although the latter should not be considered a unified stratum. Rather this designation is used as provisional designation of different sorts of later additions written in the style of P^C.[63]

A note on the terminology of the non-Priestly texts is also necessary here. Since in the primeval narrative the non-P units share several linguistic and ideological characteristics and are mutually interconnected, I prefer the conventional siglum J ("Yahwist") to the general and vague designation "non-P" as designation for these texts in the section Gen 1–11.[64] Given that the Tetragram appears in all of the texts and that YHWH as unique deity intervenes in primeval history – which for the primarily

---

[61] Cf. E. BLUM, *Die Komposition der Vätergeschichte*, WMANT 57 (Neukirchen-Vluyn: Neukirchener Verlag, 1982), 265–70; IDEM, "Noch einmal," 47–50.

[62] Certain *aegyptiaca* in Priestly texts in Exodus (P-version of the plagues-narrative, miracle story in Exod 14 the tabernacle account) *prima facie* support the latter possibility.

[63] See NIHAN, "Priestly Covenant," 88–89.

[64] Concerning the linguistic and ideological commonalities between the J and J^s units in Gen 1–11, see, for instance, BLENKINSOPP, "Post-Exilic Lay Source"; HUTZLI, "Transgression," 113–26; IDEM, "J's Problem with the East," 107–117.

national deity ʏʜᴡʜ is not evident, the Yahwist (J) designation seems appropriate for this section. A dominant motif appearing in most of the J texts in Gen 1–11 is that of humans' transgression and God's harsh punishment.[65]

This does not mean that I consider the J texts of the primeval narrative to be unified and to belong to one and the same strand. On the contrary, there are certain indications favoring the idea that the earliest J stratum in the primeval narrative once ran directly from Gen 2–4 to Gen 11.[66] For later non-P texts in this section, which often, as in the flood story, constitute redactional additions to Priestly texts, I use the siglum Jˢ (S stands for "secondary").

Non-P texts of following sections, which are traditionally assigned to J, are less interconnected among themselves and the theme of humans' transgression and God's punishment is much less present here.[67] These texts are therefore designated "non-P."

Sigla used in this study for presumed literary strata:

Dtr	Deuteronomistic texts
J	Yahwistic primeval story
Jˢ	Yahwistic primeval story, secondary additions
non-P	non-Priestly texts
Pᶜ	Priestly composition (used in the framework of the "redaction model")
Pᴳ	Priestly source ("*Grundschrift*"; in the framework of the "source model")
proto-P	proto-Priestly unit
H	Holiness texts

---

[65] See below, II.3.6 (b).

[66] See Sᴄʜᴍɪᴅ, *Literaturgeschichte*, 153–56, and below, II.2.5.

[67] See however Gen 19: The inhabitants of Sodom are wicked and perverse (Gen 13,13; 19), so that the city is destroyed by ʏʜᴡʜ.

II. Analyses of the Priestly Texts in Genesis 1–Exodus 40

1. The Creation Account in Genesis 1:1–2:4a

1.1 Introduction: Important Issues in Scholarly Discussion

This section will deal extensively with all the questions that are generally considered important for a literary-historical analysis of Gen 1.[1] Several textual differences between MT, SP, and LXX in the composition's arrangement necessitate an initial investigation of the most important differences between the main textual witnesses (see II.1.2). A central and complex question concerns the literary unity of Gen 1:1–2:4a, which has been a matter of controversy among scholars for more than a hundred years. Until the 1970s, scholars generally agreed on the differentiation between two different layers in Gen 1: one containing an account of divine acts of creation and the other consisting of an account of divine words of creation. In 1975, in a detailed study, O. H. Steck defended the literary unity of the story, marking an important turning point in the history of scholarship. Steck's interpretation has found much support in scholarship. Recently, however, his understanding has received some criticism (see II.1.3).

Also relevant to the question of literary history is the larger context of ancient Near Eastern traditions. Both earlier and more recent interpretations of Gen 1 have paid considerable attention to the possible influence of the latter, in particular those stemming from Mesopotamia or Egypt (see II.1.4). Furthermore, Gen 1 shares important linguistic commonalities and motifs with other biblical texts, and comparison with those texts, too, is important for the historical location of the primary composition (II.1.5). Of particular importance is comparison with the creation account in Gen 2:4b–3:24. In the last two decades, with the decline of the classical Documentary Hypothesis and its fixed relationship between J and P (the former predating the latter), the question of the relationship between the two creation texts has become increasingly controversial (II.1.6).

1.2 Significant Textual Variants

1.2.1 Introduction

As noted above, there are several significant differences between the main textual witnesses in Gen 1:1–2:4a. In particular, the text of the LXX deviates from MT in many

---

[1] This discussion of Gen 1:1–2:4a is a reworked version of J. Hutzli, "Tradition and Interpretation in Gen 1:1–2:4a," *JHS* 10, art. 12 (2010), doi:10.5508/jhs.2010v10.a12.

instances, and some of the deviations are relevant to the investigation of the composition's literary history. Interestingly, the structure of the word account is more intact
in the LXX than in MT and SP. The discrepancies between the textual witnesses are
controversial and raise several questions: What is the nature of the LXX translation?
Is it faithful or free? And, closely related to that question: Do the variant readings
reflect a distinct Hebrew *Vorlage* or should they be considered harmonizations on the
part of the translator? Are there instances where the reconstructed Hebrew *Vorlage* of
the LXX preserves the more primary reading in comparison to MT (and SP)? There
are clear indications that the LXX of Gen 1:1–2:4a is mainly a faithful translation of a
Hebrew *Vorlage* that differed in several small instances from MT. Certain variant readings of LXX that deviate from MT are shared by the fragmentary scrolls from Qumran
or SP (see below, [d], [e], and [g]).[2] A further clue is the literal translation of יום אחד,
"a first day," as ἡμέρα μία in Gen 1:5, which does not conform to the usual Greek use
of ordinal numbers for the enumeration of days.[3] A sign of another extremely literal
translation is the lack of agreement between the noun ὕδωρ (sing.) and the pronoun
αὐτῶν (plur.) in the expression τὰς συναγωγὰς αὐτῶν in Gen 1:9 LXX, which is due
to the plural form of the equivalents (המים, "waters," and מקויהם, "their gatherings")
in the idiomatic Hebrew formulation of LXX *Vorlage*.[4] Given these "confirmations,"
the assignment by a few scholars of almost all LXX readings that deviate from MT
to the translator is not convincing.[5] It seem more appropriate to conclude that the
Greek translator deviated from his *Vorlage* only occasionally, for instance in cases
where he did not understand his *Vorlage*.[6] An example is the rendering ἀόρατος καὶ

---

[2] See J. R. DAVILA, "New Qumran Readings for Genesis One," in *Of Scribes and Scrolls:
Studies on the Hebrew Bible, Intertestamental Judaism and Christian Origins presented to John
Strugnell on the Occasion of His Sixtieth Birthday*, ed. H. W. Attridge, J. J. Collins, and T. H. Tobin
(Lanham, MD: University Press of America, 1990), 3–11 (with n. 22); the thorough and well-bal-
anced investigation by R. S. HENDEL, *The Text of Genesis 1–11: Textual Studies and Critical Edi-
tion* (New York: Oxford University Press, 1998), 16–39; and several studies by E. Tov, "The
Nature and Background of Harmonizations in Biblical Manuscripts," *JSOT* 31 (1985): 21–22;
IDEM, "Textual Harmonization in the Stories of the Patriarchs," in *Rewriting and Interpreting
the Hebrew Bible: The Biblical Patriarchs in the Light of the Dead Sea Scrolls*, ed. D. Dimant
and R. G. Kratz, BZAW 439 (Berlin: de Gruyter, 2013), 19–50 = IDEM, *Textual Criticism of the
Hebrew Bible, Qumran, Septuagint: Collected Essays, Volume 3*, VTSup 167 (Leiden: Brill, 2015),
166–88, esp. 169–72; IDEM, "The Harmonizing Character of the Septuagint of Genesis 1–11," in
*Die Septuaginta: Text, Wirkung, Rezeption, 4; Internationale Fachtagung veranstaltet von Septua-
ginta Deutsch (LXX.D), Wuppertal 19.–22. Juli 2012*, ed. W. Kraus and S. Kreuzer, WUNT 325
(Tübingen: Mohr Siebeck, 2014), 322–23 = IDEM, *Textual Criticism: Collected Writings*, 470–89;
P. PRESTEL and S. SCHORCH, "Genesis/Das erste Buch Mose," in *Septuaginta Deutsch, Erläuterungen und Kommentare (I)*, ed. M. Karrer and W. Kraus (Stuttgart: Deutsche Bibelgesellschaft,
2011), 145–51.
[3] See PRESTEL and SCHORCH, "Genesis," 158, and *BDR* 198, §247.1.
[4] See below, II.1.2.2 (e).
[5] See M. RÖSEL, *Übersetzung als Vollendung der Auslegung: Studien zur Genesis-Septuaginta*,
BZAW 223 (Berlin: de Gruyter, 1994); BÜHRER, *Am Anfang*, 25–37.
[6] See HENDEL, *Text of Genesis 1–11*, 18–19.

ἀκατασκεύαστος ("unseen and unorganized") for the obscure expression תהו ובהו in Gen 1:2, which seems inspired by Platonic cosmology (the term ἀόρατος is used by Plato to designate the preexisting world of ideas).[7] Another example is the rendering of the toponym Ur of the Chaldeans (אור כשדים) by "the region of the Chaldeans" (Χαλδαίων) in the Abraham narrative (Gen 11:28, 31; 15:7; cf. Neh 9:7). Probably the translator, located in Alexandria, far away from Babylonia, was not acquainted with the place name Ur of the Chaldeans. There are indications that Ur (Tall al-Muqay-yaren) became unimportant after the Persian period.[8] Apparently, there is also an entire section (the Joseph story) where the LXX translation in general is freer than in the others.[9]

Given the corroboration concerning the distinctiveness of LXX's *Vorlage* from MT and SP, one needs to ask more generally about the characteristics of the main textual witnesses, namely MT, SP, and LXX (Hebrew *Vorlage*) in the book of Genesis. Are general tendencies recognizable? What is the relationship between them? Investigations into the textual history of the book of Genesis show a tendency in LXX's *Vorlage* and SP to harmonize the text with its immediate context.[10] At the same time, a number of retroverted Hebrew readings of LXX indicate originality; in some of these cases, proto-MT seems to be deficient due to scribal errors,[11] and in others it appears to be deliberately modified.[12] There is one literary unit where LXX reflects a more

---

[7] See *Sophist* 246a–c; *Theaetetus* 155e; *Timaeus* 51a. Supposing Platonic influence, see R. Hanhart, "The Translation of the Septuagint in Light of Earlier Tradition and Subsequent Influences," in *Septuagint, Scrolls and Cognate Writings*, ed. G. J. Brooke and B. Lindars, SCS 33 (Atlanta: Scholars Press, 1992), 367; M. Harl, *La Bible d'Alexandrie, I: La Genèse; Traduction du texte grec de la Septante, Introduction et Notes* (Paris: Cerf, 1986), 87; Rösel, *Übersetzung als Vollendung*, 31; Hendel, *Text of Genesis 1–11*, 19.

[8] Archaeological and epigraphic records for Ur (Tall al-Muqayyaren) ceased in the Seleucid period; see below, II.6.2 (a). As for the unfamiliarity of the LXX translator with Mesopotamia, see M. Kepper, "Genesis, Das erste Buch Mose," in *Einleitung in die Septuaginta: Handbuch zur Septuaginta/Handbook of the Septuagint*, ed. M. Karrer, W. Kraus, and S. Kreuzer, JSCS 49 (Gütersloh: Gütersloher Verlagshaus, 2016), 114.

[9] See Prestel and Schorch, "Genesis," 148–49; Kepper, "Genesis," 114.

[10] Examples are Gen 2:4b (LXX and SP harmonize the order of the nouns in the accusative with Gen 1 [שמים וארץ] instead of ארץ ושמים).

[11] See the discussion of the plus of LXX in Gen 1:9 below (II.1.2.2 [e]); and see: 1:14 (see Hendel, *Text of Genesis 1–11*, 41–42); 2:20 (see Hendel, *Text of Genesis 1–11*, 44); 4:8 (see Tov, *Textual Criticism*, 221); 21:9 (see Speiser, *Genesis*, 155); 22:12 (see Tov, *Textual Criticism*, 229); 49:19–20 (see Tov, *Textual Criticism*, 234–35).

[12] Gen 14:22 (identification of "God Most High" [El Elyon] as yhwh; cf. Tov, *Textual Criticism*, 261); 13:18; 14:13; 18:1 (dissimilation of the holy oak at Mamre; see J. Hutzli, "Interventions présumées des scribes concernant le motif de l'arbre sacré dans le Pentateuque," *Sem* 56 [2014]: 313–31; the minus of MT, SP in 21:9 might also be theologically motivated (ancient rabbinic exegesis was bothered by the verb צחק *piel* because of its possible sexual connotation [see Gen 39:17 and A. Tal, *Biblia Hebraica Quinta: Genesis* (Stuttgart: Deutsche Bibelgesellschaft, 2016), 964; Speiser, *Genesis*, 155]; similar concerns might have induced a scribe to omit the verb's complement, the reference to Isaac).

developed redactional stage: in the genealogy in Gen 11, LXX provides an additional entry about Kenan (Gen 11:12–13: καιναν), to which further plusses in 10:22 LXX and 10:24 LXX are related.[13] In contrast, there is one passage where LXX *Vorlage* seems to preserve a more ancient redactional stage compared to MT and SP (Gen 31:46–48).[14] It is certainly true that in the majority of cases of divergence between the main textual witnesses, MT and its congeners preserve the more original reading.[15] Nevertheless, the number of cases where MT seems to be corrupt or theologically modified should prevent us from prejudging the differences between MT, SP and LXX's *Vorlage*. Furthermore, even though it seems reasonable to preliminarily assess the main textual witnesses for each book – following the assumption that some revisors limited their activity to one single book – one should be conscious of the fact that revising scribes often restricted themselves to smaller textual units or sections instead of an entire book.[16] For this reason, the text-critical investigation must be undertaken separately in each case. Sometimes the evaluation proves to be complicated and a firm decision is not possible.

The most significant textual variants in Gen 1:1–2:4a are discussed in the following paragraphs.

1.2.2 Textual Differences

(a) Genesis 1:6–7, 20

Differences Concerning the ויהי כן Formula

The section detailing the creation of the sea animals and birds lack the ויהי כן ("and it was so") formula in MT, SP, and 4QGen[b,d]. This formula occurs consistently in every other section. In LXX it is also present in this passage (see Gen 1:20). In the creation of heaven, the ויהי כן formula in MT, SP, 4QGen[b,d] seems shifted and remote from the corresponding announcement (see 1:7), which it normally follows immediately. The LXX, however, has the sentence in the "appropriate" place (1:6). One may suppose that the LXX – the translator or its *Vorlage* – inserted the formula (and put it in the "right" place [1:6, 7]) in order to harmonize it with the other sections. However, concerning LXX's plus in 1:20, a modification of the text in proto-MT tradition is not to be excluded either. One occurrence of the ויהי אור/ויהי כן-formula could have been left out of MT so that there would be a biblically significant *seven* total occurrences of

---

[13] See below, II.5.2 (b) and II.4.2 (e).

[14] E. Tov, "Der Charakter der hebräischen Quellen der Septuaginta und ihr textkritisch-textgeschichtlicher Wert," In *Septuaginta Deutsch, Erläuterungen und Kommentare (I)*, ed. M. Karrer and W. Kraus (Stuttgart: Deutsche Bibelgesellschaft, 2011), 81.

[15] See the judgment in Tov, "Harmonizing Character," 332.

[16] For examples in 1–2 Samuel, see J. Hutzli, *Die Erzählung von Hanna und Samuel: Textkritische und literarische Analyse von 1. Samuel 1–2 unter Berücksichtigung des Kontextes*, ATANT 89 (Zurich: TVZ, 2007), 31–34; 145–51.

the phrase. One might explain the curious lack of the approbation formula in the MT of Gen 1:6–8 similarly: it could have been omitted to meet the "requirement" of seven occurrences of the approbation formula.[17]

(b) Genesis 1:7

MT, SP, 4QGen[b,g]:   ויבדל
LXX: καὶ διεχώρισεν ὁ θεὸς
       = ויבדל אלהים

There is an ambiguity in the deed account of Gen 1:7 MT: in light of the fact that God functions as subject in the foregoing sentence (ויעש אלהים את הרקיע), one is inclined to see the deity as the subject of the separation act. But theoretically, the firmament could also function as the grammatical subject of ויבדל. In contrast to MT, LXX mentions God as subject in both sentences explicitly (ὕδατος). Possibly a scribe of the LXX's *Vorlage* was attempting to resolve the ambiguity.[18] Alternately, a scribe in the proto-MT tradition might have omitted אלהים in order to avoid contradicting the word account (v. 6), in which the firmament clearly functions as subject of the water's separation ("and let it divide").

(c) Genesis 1:8

MT, SP, 4QGen[b,g]:   שמים
LXX: οὐρανόν καὶ εἶδεν ὁ θεὸς ὅτι καλόν
       = שמים וירא אלהים כי טוב

The text of MT, SP, contains a total of seven occurrences of the approbation formula (six standard phrases ["it was good"] and one variation [1:31: "and behold, it was very good"]); only in the present section about the construction of heaven do MT, SP lack the formula. They share this minus with 4QGen[b,d]. LXX provides the formula here as well and has eight occurrences in total (seven standard phrases and the variation at the end). Again, one may be inclined to ascribe this plus in the LXX to the harmonizing tendency of a scribe of the proto-LXX text. The initially strange lack of the formula in MT, SP, and 4QGen[b,d] might be explained as follows: after the creation of heaven, the formation of the living spaces was not yet finished but continued with the creation of sea and earth (Gen 1:9–10); therefore the approbation formulation might have been seen as appropriate only after the creation of the sea and the land had been achieved. However, one should also consider the possibility that a scribe of proto-P intended

---

[17] See below, (c). The quantitative argument concerning the number of textual witnesses is not decisive in evaluating the differences in Gen 1:6–7, 20 (*contra* BÜHRER, *Am Anfang*, 26–27). The text of the two very fragmentary Qumran scrolls 4QGen[h1,k], which in other places deviate from MT but agree with LXX (see 1:9), are unfortunately nonexistent in the relevant sections, and it cannot be ruled out that these two Qumran texts might have agreed with LXX in Gen 1:6–7, 20.

[18] See, for instance, HENDEL, *Text of Genesis 1–11*, 23, who considers the reading of LXX an explicating plus, and PRESTEL and SCHORCH, "Genesis," 158.

to limit the number of the formula's occurrences to seven (in accordance with the seven-day chronology). As noted above, an astonishing "lack" is observable in MT among the occurrences of the ויהי אור/ ויהי כן-formula as well (after the announcement sentence in 1:20). That formula, too, appears precisely seven times.[19] It could therefore be that a tendency to reduce the number of repetitive formulas (ויהי כן / ויהי אור-formula, approbation formula) to seven was at work in proto-MT.

(d) Genesis 1:9

MT, SP, 4QGen[b]:	מקום
4QGen[h1]:	[מקוה
LXX:	συναγωγὴν
	מקוה =

Even before the discovery of the Dead Sea Scrolls, scholars claimed that LXX followed a *Vorlage* distinct from MT, suggesting that Hebrew מקוה, "gathering," lay behind LXX's συναγωγὴν in Gen 1:9. This view is supported by the fact that LXX consistently renders מקום, "place," with τόπος in the book of Genesis (in all 47 occurrences of מקום in the book of Genesis, excluding Gen 1:9).[20] In addition, the relatively rare noun מקוה is translated by συναγωγή in Lev 11:36. The reading of 4QGenh1 now confirms the Hebrew origin of the LXX's variant. More difficult is to answer the question of which reading – מקום or מקוה – is more ancient. Both readings fit the context. Given the graphic similarity, simple confusion of the final letter may have caused this variation.

(e) Genesis 1:9

MT, SP, 4QGen[b,g]:	—
4QGen[k]:	[ותרא היב[ש]ה]]
LXX:	καὶ συνήχθη τὸ ὕδωρ τὸ ὑποκάτω τοῦ οὐρανοῦ εἰς
	τὰς συναγωγὰς αὐτῶν, καὶ ὤφθη ἡ ξηρά
	ויקוו המים מתחת השמים אל מקויהם ותרא היבשה =

The MT omits a fulfillment report about the gathering together of the waters and the emergence of the dry land (Gen 1:9–10). LXX's *Vorlage* and – most probably – 4QGen[k] did contain such a fulfillment report.[21] Again, a Qumran reading points to the reliability of the Greek translation. Before the discovery of the Dead Sea Scrolls, Wellhausen had already offered an argument for the view that LXX here preserves a plus of its Hebrew *Vorlage*: the lack of agreement between ὕδωρ and αὐτῶν is only

---

[19] See above, II.1.2.2 (a).

[20] See HENDEL, *Text of Genesis 1–11*, 24.

[21] As HENDEL, *Text of Genesis 1–11*, 26, convincingly argues, ותרא, the form attested in 4QGen[k], should not be considered a short *yiqtol*: since the short *yiqtol* form is virtually non-existent in late biblical Hebrew (see E. QIMRON, *The Hebrew of the Dead Sea Scrolls*, HSS 29 [Atlanta: Scholars Press, 1986], 81; A. SÁENZ-BADILLOS, *A History of the Hebrew Language*, trans. J. Elwolde [Cambridge: Cambridge University Press, 1993], 129), it is improbable that the harmonizing scribe of 4QGen[k] would have written the jussive in short spelling (ותרא); MT, SP, and 4QGen[b] all have the long form (ותראה) for the jussive in v. 9.

explicable as an effect of the literal translation of the idiomatic Hebrew formulation of its *Vorlage* (plural noun המים, "waters" – מקויהם, "their gatherings").[22] E. Tov adds further arguments:[23] First, he points to the literal, word-for-word translation of the preceding sentence (v. 9a, word account) in LXX. Second, by noting a difference between the phrasing of the word account and that of the corresponding deed account (συναγωγὴν – συναγωγὰς), he shows that v. 9b (the deed account statement) was not composed by the translator as a harmonization (with regard to the other sections, based on the existing v. 9a). In the case of a harmonizing addition by the translator, one would expect that the latter would have strictly conformed to the phrasing of the word account. This last point also argues for the originality of the retroverted Hebrew reading, compared with the shorter reading of MT, SP, and 4QGen[b,g]. A late scribe in the proto-LXX tradition aiming to fill in the "gap" in order to harmonize with the other sections would probably have respected the phrasing of the corresponding word account's statement.[24]

As will be shown below, in most other sections the deed account differs from the corresponding word account in significant details.[25] These discrepancies point to the existence of two different literary layers. The reading of LXX's *Vorlage* (4QGen[k]) in 1:9 fits nicely with this characteristic of the deed account statements. The author of the deed account probably considered the plural (מקויהם, "their gatherings") more realistic (corresponding to multiple seas) than the singular (מקוה, "gathering," v. 9a and 10) that he found in his source text.

What was the reason for this textual difference? Why was the plus lost in MT, SP, and 4QGen[b,g]? As J. R. Davila argues, the phrase may have been lost in proto-MT by parablepsis due to homoioarkton. The eye of a scribe would have skipped from ויקוו, "and they were gathered," (first [retroverted] word from the "plus") to ויקרא (first word of v. 10).[26]

(f) Genesis 1:10

MT, SP, 4QGen[b]:	מקוה
LXX:	τὰ συστήματα
	מקוי? מקוה? =

This difference is relevant for understanding the naming clause. MT, SP juxtapose a singular (מקוה, "gathering") and a formally plural noun (ימים). However, the entry in

---

[22] J. WELLHAUSEN, *Die Composition des Hexateuchs und der historischen Bücher des Alten Testaments* (Berlin: Reimer, 1899), 184.

[23] Cf. Tov, "Nature and Background," 3–29.

[24] Cf. HENDEL, *Text of Genesis 1–11*, 27.

[25] Cf. the multiple discrepancies between commandments by Elohim (word account) and the following report of fulfillment (deed account) in 1:6–7, 21–22, 24–25 and 1:26–27. See below, II.1.3.3.

[26] DAVILA, "New Qumran Readings," 3–11.

HALOT shows that יָמִים predominantly has a singular meaning ("sea");[27] this under-standing also seems to be required for the present context because of the preceding singular, מִקְוֶה. Moreover, one should take into account the singular יָם in Gen 1:26.

LXX has two plural nouns: συστήματα and θαλάσσας. συστήματα, the Greek translation of מִקְוֶה, is surprising given the twofold rendering συναγωγή in 1:9 (see above). The plural contrasts with the singular in MT but fits well with the context of LXX's *Vorlage* (see the plural αὐτῶν/מקויהם in the preceding execution sentence and the plural θαλάσσας/יָמִים, "seas," in the subsequent naming clause).

Which reading is more original? P. Prestel and S. Schorch consider the plural συστήματα a harmonization by the translator with the formal plural יָמִים (θαλάσσας) in the subsequent naming clause.[28] The translator would not have understood יָמִים as singular. However, such a harmonization is also imaginable on the level of the Hebrew *Vorlage* of the LXX and with regard to the plural מקויהם (συναγωγὰς) in the preced-ing execution sentence in LXX's *Vorlage*. A (deliberate) modification in MT, SP (from the plural מקוי to the singular מִקְוֶה) is more difficult to imagine; the interpolator probably would also have changed יָמִים to יָם.

(g) Genesis 2:2

MT: הַשְּׁבִיעִי

SP, LXX (τῇ ἕκτῃ), Syr. (ܫܬܝܬܝܐ), Jub.:   הַשִּׁשִּׁי

The statement of MT that God *completed* (וַיְכַל) his work on the seventh day con-tradicts the preceding verse (2:1), which states that "the heavens and the earth *were completed* (וַיְכֻלּוּ), and all their hosts." The interpretation of the sequential *wayyiqtol* וַיְכַל as pluperfect ("had completed") by some scholars is not convincing;[29] anterior-ity of action would be indicated by *w-x-qatal*.[30] How can MT's difficult reading be explained? It should probably be understood in the sense that the creation finds its achievement only through the creator's rest. The statement places great value on the Sabbath.

In contrast to MT, the reading of LXX, SP, and Jub. for 2:2 is in line with the pre-ceding context. With R. Hendel, we should assume that the shared variant "on the sixth day" in SP, LXX, Syr., Jub. is derived from a common ancient Hebrew reading rather than being an independent development from a common exegetical tendency in all these texts.[31]

---

[27] Judg 5:17; Ezek 26:17; 27:4, 25, 26, 27, 33, 34; 28:2, 8; 32:2; Jonah 2:4; Ps 46:3; Dan 11:45 (among others). The meaning "sea" (singular) for יָמִים is the only meaning *HALOT* 414 gives.

[28] PRESTEL and SCHORCH, "Genesis," 158.

[29] U. CASSUTO, *A Commentary on the Book of Genesis, Part I* (Jerusalem: Magnes, 1972), 612–62; G. J. WENHAM, *Genesis 1–15*, WBC (Waco, TX: Word, 1987), 35.

[30] Similarly HENDEL, *Text of Genesis 1–11*, 32. For the notion of anteriority expressed by *w-x-qatal*, see Joüon §112c, 118d; W. R. OSBORNE, "Anteriority and Justification," *OTE* 25/2 (2012): 376.

[31] HENDEL, *Text of Genesis 1–11*, 33, in discussion with E. Tov, *The Text-Critical Use of the*

How should this difference be evaluated? A majority of scholars prefer the more difficult reading of MT and assume that LXX/SP have corrected the text to "on the sixth day" in order to harmonize it with the preceding context (2:1) or to avoid the idea that God would have worked on the seventh day.[32] Other scholars, however, hesitate to give preference to the reading of MT; the contradiction with the preceding verse, 2:1, is considered too blatant to allow it to stem from the same author.[33] The question is whether MT's contextually difficult and theologically subtle assertion (God completed his work by resting) should be assigned to the author of 2:2–3 or to a later scribe. Speaking in favor of the second option is the fact that biblical Sabbath legislation consistently contrasts the six workdays on which the Israelites should do their labor (מלאכה) with the seventh day as a rest day on which the Israelites should abstain from work (מלאכה). The notion that a work (מלאכה) was completed on the seventh day in Gen 2:2 does not fit this logic. Additionally, the two parallel statements about the completion of the sanctuary in the tabernacle account (Exod 39:32 and 40:33) associate completion *with activity* and not with rest; notably, this also applies to the second assertion in Exod 40:33, which parallels Gen 2:2. For these reasons, I tentatively assign the reading "on the seventh day" to a later scribe of proto-MT rather than to the author of the seven-day/Sabbath framework. His interest would have been to underline the significance of the Sabbath.[34] Perhaps this change on the level of proto-MT can be associated with the tendency in the same textual witness to reduce the number of repetitive formulas (ויהי אור/ויהי כן formula, approbation formula) to seven (see above, [a], [c]).

(h) Genesis 2:4a

MT, SP: אלה תולדת
LXX: αὕτη ἡ βίβλος γενέσεως
    = זה ספר תולדת

The reading of LXX parallels the statement of Gen 5:1 (all main witnesses: זה ספר תולדת אדם). Generally, the reading is considered a harmonization with the latter text.

Septuagint in Biblical Research, Jerusalem Biblical Studies (Jerusalem: Simor, 1981), 28; cf. 3rd ed. (Winona Lake: Eisenbrauns, 2015), 88.

[32] Thus, for instance, also Tov, *Textual Criticism*, 244; Bührer, *Am Anfang*, 36, with n. 68; J. C. Gertz, *Das erste Buch Mose (Genesis): Die Urgeschichte Gen 1–11*, ATD 1 (Göttingen: Vandenhoeck & Ruprecht, 2018), 28, with n. 21.

[33] Speiser, *Genesis*, 40; Hendel, *Text of Genesis 1–11*, 32–34; T. Krüger, "Schöpfung und Sabbat in Genesis 2,1–3," in *Sprachen – Bilder – Klänge: Dimensionen der Theologie im Alten Testament und in seinem Umfeld, FS R. Bartelmus*, ed. C. Karrer-Grube and J. Krispenz, AOAT 359 (Münster: Ugarit-Verlag, 2009), 155–69.

[34] Not to be excluded but less probable is the proposal of R. S. Hendel, who explains the variant השביעי (MT) as an unintentional anticipation with regard to the occurrence of this expression in 2:2b, 3. Cf. Hendel, *Text of Genesis 1–11*. Krüger, "Schöpfung und Sabbat in Genesis 2,1–3," 166, similarly considers it a scribal error.

1.3 Literary Stratigraphy of Genesis 1:1–2:4a

1.3.1 Introduction

In the early part of the twentieth century, several scholars – among them F. Schwally, J. Morgenstern, and M. Lambert – argued that Gen 1:1–2:4a consists of two different layers, one containing a *Tatbericht* (account of the creative divine act) and the other consisting of a *Wortbericht* (account of the creative divine word).[35] This view came to dominate scholarship.[36] The main reason for this literary-critical differentiation was the recognition of two dissimilar theological conceptions behind the text of Gen 1:1–2:4a: creation by word on the one hand and creation by act on the other. J. Morgenstern stated:

> the present form of the narrative is the result of the literary fusion of two originally independent and even contradictory versions of the creation story. The one told that God created the universe and all its contents by his word alone, while the other told that God actually worked and made the various creatures, heavenly bodies, monsters, fish, fowl, animals, and man, by his very hands, as it were.[37]

These two conceptions are found throughout the entire story. In addition to the repeated expression ויהי כן, "and it was so," (and ויהי אור) which in each case corresponds to the preceding divine commandment, several statements relating to creative acts of God occur (expressed by ויברא אלהים and ויעש אלהים). In LXX, this arrangement with two distinct accounts in each section is worked out regularly; in MT and SP it is less consistent but nevertheless clearly visible.

Until the 1970s, scholars generally agreed on the differentiation between these two accounts in Gen 1. A lively debate emerged around the question of which layer – the

---

[35] F. SCHWALLY, "Die biblischen Schöpfungsberichte," *AR* 9 (1906): 159–75; J. SKINNER, *Genesis*, ICC (Edinburgh: T&T Clark, 1910), 8; J. MORGENSTERN, "The Sources of the Creation Story: Gen 1:1–2:4," *AJSL* 36 (1919–20): 169–212; M. LAMBERT, "A Study of the First Chapter of Genesis," *HUCA* 1 (1924): 3–12; O. PROCKSCH, *Die Genesis*, 2nd ed., KAT 1 (Leipzig: Deichert, 1924), 444, 453. The basic idea was already expressed by B. STADE, *Biblische Theologie des Alten Testaments I* (Tübingen: J. C. B. Mohr, 1905), 349.

[36] Cf. R. KITTEL, *Geschichte des Volkes Israel, erster Band: Palästina in der Urzeit, das Werden des Volkes, Geschichte der Zeit bis zum Tode Josuas*, 7th ed. (Stuttgart: Kohlhammer, 1932), 246, n. 7; VON RAD, *Die Priesterschrift*, 11–18, 167–71, 190–92; NOTH, *Überlieferungsgeschichte*, 10, n. 21; 255; H. LUBSCZYK, "Wortschöpfung und Tatschöpfung: Zur Entwicklung der priesterlichen Schöpfungslehre in Gen 1,1–2,4a," *BibLeb* 6 (1965): 191–208; W. H. SCHMIDT, *Die Schöpfungsgeschichte der Priesterschrift: Zur Überlieferungsgeschichte von Genesis 1,1–2,4a und 2,4b–3,24*, 3rd ed., WMANT 17 (Neukirchen-Vluyn: Neukirchener Verlag, 1973); C. LEVIN, "Tatbericht in der priesterschriftlichen Schöpfungserzählung," *ZTK* 91 (1994): 121–25; J. VERMEYLEN, "Tradition et rédaction en Genèse 1," *Transeu* 16 (1998): 127–47; T. KRÜGER, "Genesis 1:1–2:3 and the Development of the Pentateuch," in *The Pentateuch: International Perspectives on Current Research*, ed. T. B. Dozeman, K. Schmid, and B. J. Schwartz, FAT 78 (Tübingen: Mohr Siebeck, 2011), 125–38.

[37] MORGENSTERN, "Sources," 170.

deed account or the word account – was older. The majority of scholars came down on the side of the layer reporting God's deeds.[38] In 1975, Odil Hannes Steck presented a detailed argument for the literary unity of the story.[39] Steck's main argument for the literary unity of Gen 1:1–2:4a was that the term ויהי כן in the Hebrew Bible never refers to the fulfillment of a command in itself but is always accompanied by an additional report of execution. Steck believed that the ויהי כן formula expressed the adequate correspondence between an order and its fulfillment.[40] As for Gen 1, Steck concluded that the three elements – divine order/ויהי כן formula/report of fulfillment – form a coherent unity. Steck also argued against both the idea of an independent word account and the claim of an independent deed account because the two reconstructed accounts would lack at least one important work. The impact of Steck's investigation continues to be felt strongly today; his interpretation of the ויהי כן formula in particular has found much support in scholarship;[41] only recently has it earned some critical reaction.[42] For this reason, in the present chapter I will take up and refine the critical examination of Steck's arguments that I published in a previous study (II.1.3.2).[43] This examination will be followed by a discussion of the important thematic and linguistic differences between the divine word statements and divine act statements (II.1.3.3). On the basis of this evidence, I will reexamine the literary-historical relationship between the two layers (II.1.3.4–5), and will tentatively determine the content of the two accounts (II.1.3.6–10).

1.3.2 Steck's Arguments for the Literary Unity of Genesis 1

(a) Steck's Definition of the ויהי כן Formula

Steck first considers the ויהי כן formula in the Hebrew Bible outside of Gen 1, in Judg 6:38; 2 Kgs 7:20; 15:12:[44]

---

[38] Cf., among others, SKINNER, *Genesis*, 8; PROCKSCH, *Die Genesis*, 444, 453; M. LAMBERT, "Study," 3–12; VON RAD, *Die Priesterschrift*, 17; W. H. SCHMIDT, *Die Schöpfungsgeschichte*, 16, 160–93; LEVIN, "Tatbericht," 121–25, KRÜGER, "Genesis 1:1–2:3."

[39] O. H. STECK, *Der Schöpfungsbericht der Priesterschrift: Studien zur literarkritischen und überlieferungsgeschichtlichen Problematik von Genesis 1,1–2,4a*, FRLANT 115 (Göttingen: Vandenhoeck & Ruprecht, 1975).

[40] The term would express "the assertion of a consistent equivalence" ("Feststellung folgerichtiger Entsprechung"); STECK, *Der Schöpfungsbericht*, 36.

[41] Cf. WENHAM, *Genesis 1–15*, 7–8; ZENGER, *Gottes Bogen*, 52–53; LEVIN, "Tatbericht," 123–24; R. G. KRATZ and H. SPIECKERMANN, "Schöpfer/Schöpfung II," *TRE* 30:270; O. KEEL and S. SCHROER, *Schöpfung: Biblische Theologien im Kontext altorientalischer Religiosität* (Göttingen: Vandenhoeck & Ruprecht, 2002), 176.

[42] Cf. HUTZLI, "Tradition and Interpretation," 4–6; W. BÜHRER, *Am Anfang…: Untersuchungen zur Textgenese und zur relativ-chronologischen Einordnung von Gen 1–3* (Göttingen: Vandenhoeck & Ruprecht, 2014), 40–75.

[43] As presented in HUTZLI, "Tradition and Interpretation." See above n. 1.

[44] Cf. STECK, *Der Schöpfungsbericht*, 32–39.

Judges 6:36–38

[36] Then Gideon said to God: "... [37] I am going to lay a fleece of wool on the threshing floor; if there is dew on the fleece alone, and it is dry on all the ground, then I shall know that you will deliver Israel by my hand. ..." / [38] And it was so [ויהי כן]. / When he rose early next morning and squeezed the fleece, he wrung enough dew from the fleece to fill a bowl with water.

2 Kings 7:19–20

[19] The captain had answered the man of God, "Even if YHWH were to make windows in the sky, could such a thing happen?" And he had answered, "You shall see it with your own eyes, but you shall not eat from it." / [20] It did indeed happen to him [ויהי לו כן]; / the people trampled him to death in the gate.

In these two instances, the notice of fulfillment, the ויהי כן formula, is followed by a short report of fulfillment. In the third instance, 2 Kgs 15:12, a notice of fulfillment is lacking:

2 Kings 15:12

[12] This was the promise of YHWH that he gave to Jehu, "Your sons shall sit on the throne of Israel to the fourth generation." / And so it happened [ויהי כן].

However, the historical events to which the equivalence formula refers are reported in the *preceding* narrative context (2 Kgs 10:35–15:11). After Jehu, four descendants (Jehoahaz, Jehoash, Jeroboam II, and Zechariah) rule.

Finally, Steck provides a fourth instance (Judg 6:39–40), in which the fulfillment notice uses עשה instead of היה. Like the initial two instances above, the correspondence formula is followed by "the assertion of a consistent equivalence":

Judges 6:39–40

[39] Then Gideon said to God, "Do not let your anger burn against me, let me speak one more time; let me, please, make trial with the fleece just once more; let it be dry only on the fleece, and on all the ground let there be dew." / [40] And God did so [ויעש אלהים כן] that night. / It was dry on the fleece only, and on all the ground there was dew.

These four instances form the basis for Steck's interpretation of the ויהי כן formula. In his eyes, the formula itself cannot express the notion of fulfillment but instead must be accompanied by an assertion of fulfillment.

I see two problems with Steck's argument. First, since in the third example (2 Kgs 15:12) the context for fulfillment is quite large, it is questionable whether the ויהי כן formula functions only as an expression of the equivalence of the predicted events, as Steck claims. Second, and more important, Steck provides only one example (Judg 6:39–40) of the formula with the elements עשה and כן. This is problematic since the formula with עשה appears frequently, and there are several cases in which the ויעש כן ("and he did so") formula occurs *without* the accompaniment of a fulfillment report (cf. Gen 42:25; Exod 14:2–4; 17:5–6; Judg 6:20; 2 Sam 5:23–25; Jer 38:12; Esth 2:2–4). In these instances, the formula with כן + עשׂה must *express the fulfillment itself.* See for instance Exod 17:5–6:

Exodus 17:5–6
[5] YHWH said to Moses, "Go on ahead of the people ..., take in your hand the staff ...
[6] ... Strike the rock, and water will come out of it, so that the people may drink." / Moses did so [ויעשׂ כן], in the sight of the elders of Israel.

The continuation of the narrative omits any (additional) report of fulfillment (v. 7):

Exodus 17:7
[7] He called the place Massah and Meribah, because the Israelites quarreled and tested YHWH, saying, "Is YHWH among us or not?"

Likewise in Judg 6:20–21 a report of accomplishment is lacking:

Judges 6:20–21
[20] And the angel of God said to him [Gideon], "Take the meat and the unleavened cakes, and put them on this rock, and pour the broth over them." / And he did so [ויעשׂ כן]. / [21] Then the angel of YHWH reached out the tip of the staff that was in his hand, and touched the meat and the unleavened cakes; and fire sprang up from the rock and consumed the meat and the unleavened cakes; and the angel of YHWH vanished from his sight.

Neither does the evidence in Gen 1 support Steck's understanding of the ויהי כן formula.[45] Only four (Gen 1:9 [4QGen[k], LXX], 11, 15, 24) out of the eight passages (corresponding to the eight works of creation) place the formula between the divine order and the notice of fulfillment.[46] In fact, in Gen 1:7, 30 the ויהי כן formula obviously stands alone, without an accompanying fulfillment statement.

From this reevaluation of the texts used by Steck we may conclude that there is little evidence supporting his strict definition of the ויהי כן formula as a statement only of "consistent correspondence" between an order (prediction) and its fulfillment, not as statement of the fulfillment itself. It is possible to interpret the two instances in Judg 6:36–38 and 2 Kgs 7:19–20 as Steck does, but at the same time nothing hinders us from understanding the ויהי כן formula in these contexts as a "proleptic summary" of the fulfillment, with the following sentences as additional concretizations.[47] It is of considerable importance that counterexamples occur both in Gen 1 (Gen 1:7, 30) and outside this chapter (several instances with the similar ויעשׂ כן formula) without a report of

---

[45] Cf. STECK, *Der Schöpfungsbericht*, 39–61 (and also 144–49).

[46] In 1:9, the reading of LXX and 4QGen[k], including a fulfillment report, should be preferred; see above, II.1.2.2 (e).

[47] Cf. J.-L. SKA, "Sommaires proleptiques en Gn 27 et dans l'histoire de Joseph," *Bib* 73 (1992): 518–27; IDEM, "Quelques exemples de sommaires proleptiques dans les récits bibliques," in *Congress Volume, Paris: 1992*, ed. J. A. Emerton, VTSup 61 (Leiden: Brill, 1995), 315–26.

accomplishment. In these cases, the ויעש כן formula and the ויהי כן formula enunciate the fulfillment. On the basis of this evidence, we can conclude that the ויהי כן formula in Gen 1 *can* express the notion of fulfillment.

(b) Incompleteness or Completeness of the Presupposed Sources?

Steck's second argument against both the idea of an independent word account and the claim of an independent deed account is that the two reconstructed accounts would each lack at least one important work, rendering both incomplete. First, on methodological grounds one may object that the lack of one work in the supposed sources is not a cogent argument against the existence of the latter. The absence might have resulted from the loss of text passages during the procedure of matching together the two accounts. Second, in this case, too, we must examine the validity of Steck's observations.

Steck is right to argue that the deed account is missing one or even two works. Since the phrase ויהי אור, "and it was light," it is to be attributed to the word account (see the similarity with the ויהי כן formula),[48] and a fulfillment sentence such as ויעש אלהים את האור, "and God made the light," does not occur, the deed account is lacking the creation of light. Attempts by W. H. Schmidt and by C. Levin to reconstruct an independent deed account, which lacks the creation of light, are not convincing:

> "And the earth was waste and void; and darkness was upon the face of the deep: and the wind of God moved upon the face of the waters. And God separated the light from the darkness" (Schmidt).[49]
>
> "But the earth was waste and void. And God separated the light from the darkness" (Levin).[50]

In both reconstructed texts, the sudden, unprepared emergence of the light is awkward.

The MT also omits a fulfillment report about the gathering together of the waters and the emergence of the dry land (Gen 1:9–10). However, we should probably follow the LXX and 4QGen[k] and argue that the missing passage has dropped out of MT's v. 9.[51] There is, however, no such explanation on offer for v. 4 (creation of light). Here, Steck's claim of incompleteness seems sound with regard to the deed account.

As for the assumed word account, Steck maintains that a report of man's creation

---

[48] Cf. also W. H. Schmidt, *Die Schöpfungsgeschichte*, 57; C. Westermann, *Genesis 1–11*, BK 1.1 (Neukirchen-Vluyn: Neukirchener Verlag, 1974), 153, 155.

[49] Cf. W. H. Schmidt, *Die Schöpfungsgeschichte*, 161: "Und die Erde war wüst und leer, und Finsternis (lag) auf der Urflut, und der Wind Gottes bewegte sich über dem Wasser. Und Gott trennte zwischen dem Licht und der Finsternis."

[50] Cf. Levin, "Tatbericht," 116: "Die Erde aber war wüst und öde. Da schied Gott das Licht von der Finsternis."

[51] See above, II.1.2.2 (e).

is missing.[52] But in the relevant section we actually find a sentence that has the same form as the preceding word accounts:

Genesis 1:26a

ויאמר אלהים נעשה אדם בצלמנו כדמותנו [26a]

[26a] Then God said, "Let us make man in our image, after our likeness."

The fact that in v. 26 God's word relates to an act to be done by God himself has led scholars to believe that this verse belongs to the deed account. However, the feature actually makes good sense in the context of the word account. It is true that this statement is unique when compared with the other divine-word statements because it reports the *act of God himself*, whereas in every other passage the word account contains a divine order addressed to *other entities* (light, firmament, the waters under the heaven, earth, luminaries, sea waters again, and earth again). Yet the statement nevertheless matches the word account insofar as in the context of the latter the last act of creation is indeed peculiar and forms a climax.[53] Of all beings, only humanity is created "in God's image and likeness": he has the closest relationship to God. Thus it is fitting and an intentional feature that in the word account only humankind is made by Elohim himself, without the participation of other entities.[54]

Another difficulty for the reconstruction of a complete word account lies in the creation of the sea animals and birds, for which most of the main textual witnesses (MT, SP, 4QGen[b,d]) lack the ויהי כן formula; it appears only in LXX (see Gen 1:20). In all other sections, the ויהי כן formula appears in all the textual witnesses (see the detailed discussion above[55]).

In conclusion, we can agree with Steck's contention that in the present text of Gen 1 (as attested in MT and SP), none of the two supposed source texts is complete. However, we should not put too much significance on the absence of one or two elements from the two supposed accounts. This lack might result from the combination of word account and deed account by a redactor who was not interested in conserving his source text(s) completely. In particular, the inconsistencies in the word account are minimal (and in the LXX are nonexistent), and the structure and shape of the supposed source text(s) are nevertheless clearly visible.

---

[52] STECK, *Der Schöpfungsbericht*, 246–47.

[53] In the word account, the passage on the seventh day of rest, which forms a climax in the present form of the text, does not exist (see below, II.1.3.6 [c]).

[54] At first sight, a difficulty arises, however, from the fact that the ויהי כן formula follows only four verses later, in v. 30. Yet one might explain this by the insertion of statements belonging to the deed account redaction.

[55] II.1.2.2 (a).

1.3.3 Discrepancies between the Word Account and the Deed Account

Having rebutted arguments against the existence of an older source behind Gen 1:1–2:4a, we will now discuss evidence that suggests a literary-critical differentiation between the various strata in the present text. A close reading reveals remarkable tensions between the content of certain commandments by Elohim (word account) and the following report of fulfillment (deed account). Further, we note some discrepancies of vocabulary and spelling.

(a) Theological Tensions and Contradictions

The reports of the creation of the sea animals (1:21) and the land animals (1:25) by Elohim do not match the preceding commandments (1:20, 24), which are addressed to the sea waters and the earth:

> Genesis 1:20–21
>
> [20] And God said, "Let the waters bring forth [ישרצו המים] swarms of living creatures, and let birds fly above the earth across the dome of the sky." (And it was so.)[56]
> [21] So God created [ויברא אלהים] the great sea monsters and every living creature that moves, of every kind, with which the waters swarm, and every winged bird of every kind. And God saw that it was good.

> Genesis 1:24–25
>
> [24] And God said, "Let the earth bring forth [תוצא הארץ] living creatures of every kind: cattle and creeping things and wild animals of the earth [וחיתו ארץ] of every kind." And it was so. [25] God made [ויעש אלהים] the wild animals of the earth [חית הארץ] of every kind, and the cattle of every kind, and everything that creeps upon the ground of every kind. And God saw that it was good.

In the word account, the respective living spaces of the sea animals and of the land animals are also the places of their origin.[57] In the deed account, Elohim is the lone creator. There is also a linguistic difference between 1:24 and 1:25 (cf. חיתו ארץ and חית הארץ) which will be discussed below.

Different subjects can also be observed in the creation of the firmament. In Elohim's command, the action of separating the waters above from the waters beneath is attributed to the firmament, whereas in the deed account the deity itself is responsible for the separation:

> Genesis 1:6–7
>
> [6] And God said, "Let there be a firmament [יהי רקיע] in the midst of the waters, and let it separate [ויהי מבדיל] the waters from the waters." [7] So God made the

---

[56] The correspondence formula occurs only in the LXX. See above, II.1.2.2 (a).
[57] Cf. also W. H. Schmidt, *Die Schöpfungsgeschichte*, 121, n. 3.

firmament and separated[58] [ויעש אלהים את הרקיע ויבדל בין] the waters that were under the firmament from the waters that were above the firmament. And it was so.[59]

According to the word account, the heavenly bodies have the task of separating day and night (1:14). In the deed report in v. 4, however, the division between light and darkness (identified later as day and night) is attributed to God.

Genesis 1:14
[14] And God said, "Let there be lights in the firmament of the heaven to separate [להבדיל] the day from the night; and let them be for signs and for seasons and for days and years."

Genesis 1:4b
[4b] and God separated [ויבדל אלהים] the light from the darkness.

Finally, we note a tension in the creation of humanity as well. The idea of the "plurality" of God found in the announcement sentence in Gen 1:26 (the first-person plural is used three times) does not occur in the following verse (deed account).

Genesis 1:26–27
[26] And God said, "*Let us* make [נעשה] humankind in *our* image [בצלמנו], according to *our* likeness [בצלמנו] ..." [27] And God created humankind in his own image [בצלמו], in the image of God he created [ברא] him; male and female he created [ברא] them.

We must stop briefly to ask whether Gen 1:26 really expresses a "polytheistic" conception (which would then create tension with 1:27). Scholars have suggested at least four interpretations of the use of the first-person plural in v. 26: the formulation stands in relation (a) to the conception of the "royal household of God"[60] or (b) to the idea of a divine couple,[61] or it expresses (c) a "self-consultation" (*pluralis deliberationis*)[62] or (d) sovereign rule and majesty (*pluralis majestatis*).[63] As for understandings a and c, there are several instances in the Hebrew Bible where

---

[58] There is an ambiguity in the deed account of MT: the firmament could also function as the grammatical subject of ויבדל. LXX explicitly mentions God as the verb's subject (see the detailed discussion above, II.1.2.2 [b]).

[59] In LXX, the ויהי כן-formula is placed before the deed account statement (concerning this textual difference, see the detailed discussion above, II.1.2.2 [a]).

[60] Cf. H. GUNKEL, Genesis, 3rd ed., HKAT I/1 (Göttingen: Vandenhoeck & Ruprecht, 1922), 111; J. C. GERTZ, "Antibabylonische Polemik im priesterlichen Schöpfungsbericht?," ZTK 106 (2009): 142–43.

[61] This new interpretation is advanced by T. RÖMER, "The Creation of Humans and Their Multiplication: A Comparative Reading of Athra-Hasis, Gilgamesh XI and Genesis 1; 6–9," ITS 50 (2013): 126. This interpretation sees Gen 1:26 in relation to the subsequent statement (in 1:27) that humans who are created in the image of God are male and female.

[62] Cf. WESTERMANN, Genesis 1–11, 199–201.

[63] Cf. H. SEEBASS, Genesis I: Urgeschichte (Neukirchen-Vluyn: Neukirchener Verlag, 1996), 79.

such a use may be intended by the authors. A difficulty with interpretation b is that the Hebrew Bible never positively refers to the divine couple. Interpretation (d) also seems less probable, since there is only one late instance (Ezra 4:18) of the *pluralis majestatis* in the Hebrew Bible (in a statement of the Persian king).

Deciding between a and c is difficult, since possible parallels (Gen 11:7; Isa 6:8; 2 Sam 24:14) are open to both interpretations. Nevertheless, there is an argument to be made for explanation a. Given that the royal household of God is well attested in the Hebrew Bible (see 1 Kgs 22:19–23; Job 1:6–12; 2:1–6; 38:7), and an Assyrian text uses the same plural formulation for the creation of humanity (a number of deities consult among themselves and announce the decision by using the first-person plural),[64] it is in principle *possible* to understand 1:26 in relation to the conception of the royal household. The author of the text must have been aware that if he used this formulation, the statement would be open to or even suggestive of a polytheistic interpretation. *He would not have chosen the formulation if he judged the idea of the royal household incompatible with his own theological perception.*

In addition to the fact that the peculiar plural forms of v. 26 do not appear again in v. 27, we can point to other linguistic differences between the word account and the deed account in this final work of the deity (see below).

A further difference between word account and deed account sentences is observable in the section on the creation of the earth and the sea (Gen 1:9–10; the deed account sentence is preserved in LXX and most probably in 4QGen[k] and can easily be reconstructed; see above, II.1.2.2 [e]).[65] The word account (Gen 1:9) contains the peculiar statement that the waters "below the sky should be gathered into *one* place" (LXX: "one gathering"). In contrast, the deed account uses the plural: "And the water which was under the heaven was gathered into its gatherings." The deed account clearly contradicts the announcement sentence, which emphasizes the uniqueness of the place, expressed by the number אחד. The author of the deed account seems to have corrected his *Vorlage* in order to adjust this creation work and render it more realistic (Judeans and Israelites knew several seas: the Mediterranean Sea, the Dead Sea, the Sea of Reeds, and the Sea of Galilee).[66]

Steck generally explains the divergence in formulation and conception between the commandment and the fulfillment sentences by arguing that the announcement sentence relates to the enduring permanent living form ("andauernde Daseinsgestalt"),[67] whereas the execution sentence focuses on the respective creation act as an initial act ("Erstausführung im Rahmen der Schöpfung").[68] This explanation fits the second day (creation of the firmament), but it does not match the land animals' creation. In this case, the image used in the commandment sentence expresses the punctual event of

---

[64] Cf. *AOTAT* 135 [B 13–17, 22–23].

[65] For the text-critical value of the LXX reading and the reconstruction of its Hebrew *Vorlage*, see above, II.1.2.2 (e).

[66] Attested in the Hebrew Bible under the names ים הגדול, ים המלח, ים סוף, and ים כנרת (see *HALOT* 414).

[67] STECK, *Der Schöpfungsbericht*, 65.

[68] STECK, *Der Schöpfungsbericht*, 65.

creation (earth "gives birth" to the land animals) but not the process of furnishing the animals with "life energy," as Steck and now Bührer claim.[69] Nothing in the wording of 1:24 suggests the latter interpretation, for which one would rather expect the order of the two statements to be reversed (the sentence about God's "initial act" should precede the announcement concerning the earth's "permanent producing of life energy"). The motif of the earth's giving birth is attested elsewhere in the Hebrew Bible (see Job 1:21[70]; Ps 139:15) and is widespread in the ANE.[71] Also for this reason, it seems evident to understand the assertion in 1:24 (and also that in 1:20) in its proper sense.[72]

(b) Differences in Vocabulary and Spelling

In addition to the theological divergences between the announcement and the execution sentences, one should note some striking linguistic discrepancies between them.

In the section on the creation of humans, in addition to the difference in the number of the subject (singular/plural), there are important differences in the choice of verb (עשׂה in v. 26 vs. ברא [3×] in v. 27), the use of the expression אדם (without article in v. 26 vs. with article in v. 27), and the fact that the statement about humanity's two sexes is found only in v. 27.

> Genesis 1:26–27
> [26]And God said, "Let us make [נעשׂה] humankind [אדם] in our image, according to our likeness ..." [27]And God created [ויברא] (the) humankind [האדם] in his own image, in the image of God he created [ברא] him; male and female he created [ברא] them.

As will be shown below, the use of ברא is restricted to deed-account sections; its distribution, which is in accord with the blessing motif, is theologically meaningful.

There are other differences of vocabulary as well. In the account concerning the emergence of vegetation on the earth, the verbs of the announcement and execution sentences are different (דשׁא *hiphil*, v. 11/יצא *hiphil*, v. 12).

In the section about the creation of the sea animals and birds, the deed account (v. 21) is extended by one species and is also differently formulated in comparison to the word account (v. 20): "greats sea monsters" (התנינם הגדלים) are added and the birds are called עוף כנף instead of simply עוף as in the announcement sentence.

---

[69] According to STECK, the earth provides "die für den Fortbestand der Landtiere entscheidende Kraft"; STECK, *Der Schöpfungsbericht*, 121. BÜHRER, *Am Anfang*, 64–65, notes: "ist die Anordnung nun dahin zu verstehen, dass die Erde all das hervorbringen soll, wessen die von Gott erstmalig erschaffenen Tiere für ihren Fortbestand bedürfen (die Tiere wachsen ja nicht wie die Pflanzen aus der Erde heraus)."

[70] In Job 1:21, biological mother and earth seem to be identified; see KEEL and SCHROER, *Schöpfung*, 56–58.

[71] See KEEL and SCHROER, *Schöpfung*, 52–58.

[72] For this understanding, see also GUNKEL, *Genesis*, 447–48 (for 1:24); W. H. SCHMIDT, *Die Schöpfungsgeschichte*, 121, n. 3.

Finally, there are striking differences of spelling. As mentioned above, Gen 1:24 contains an "archaic" paragogic *wāw* in the construct state (חיתו ארץ), while 1:25 shows the usual spelling of the compound noun (חית הארץ).[73] Another divergence in spelling between the word account and the deed account can be observed in the section reporting the genesis of vegetation: whereas in the word account למינו is used (cf. 1:11), the deed account prefers למינהו (cf. 1:12 [2×]; cf. also 1:21, 25).

To sum up: these theological tensions and linguistic discrepancies between the word accounts and deed accounts lead us not to share the opinion of the majority of modern scholars who view Gen 1:1–2:4a as a literary unity; taken together, they are clear evidence for the presence of two different strata.

1.3.4 The Literary Relationship between the Word Account and the Deed Account

Scholars who advocate a deed account as the original layer of the creation story must reckon with the problem that the creation of light is not reported. Attempts to reconstruct a meaningful original deed account that lacks the creation of light are not convincing (see above). The fact that this work is lacking in the deed account is elegantly solved by viewing this account as *a later redaction layer*. A redactor appears to have reworked the word account by adding a deed account; however, he did not find it necessary to insert a deed report for every act of creation. For instance, it would be inappropriate to supplement the statement ויהי אור with a deed report (ויעש אלהים את האור, "and God made the light").[74]

The genetic relationship between the two accounts proposed here (the word account as the original report and the deed account forming the redaction layer) is supported by a further important argument. The four differences between the two accounts in 1:20/21; 1:24/25; 1:6/7; and 1:14/4 (see above) suggest the following theological explanation: the idea expressed in the word account – that heaven, earth, sea, and stars are addressed by the divine command to carry the act out – seems to have been problematic for the author of the deed account. This author (or better: redactor) aimed to correct the word account *by limiting creation activity to Elohim alone.*

There is, however, one case that seems to contradict this theological explanation. In the deed account concerning the emergence of vegetation on the earth, it is not God but rather the earth that is the actor (1:12: ותוצא הארץ דשא, "And the earth brought forth vegetation"). Remarkably, this is the only example among all the deed account sentences where Elohim is *not* the grammatical subject.[75] How are we to explain this? In contrast to the more mythical conceptions of other

---

[73] B. Wysshaar, of the University of Zurich, pointed to this difference in a term paper. For a discussion of the differences in spelling, see above, I.2.3 (a).

[74] The assumption, conversely, that God's creation of light was originally reported (deed account) and was later removed by the author of the word account seems more complicated but is also possible.

[75] In the text of LXX's *Vorlage* and 4QGen[k] we note another exception. In the fulfillment report about the gathering of the waters and the emergence of the dry land (1:9), Elohim is not

sections (preserved only in the word account; see 1:20, where the water brings forth sea animals; 1:24, where the earth brings forth land animals), the idea that the earth brings forth *vegetation* is realistic and corresponds to human experience. For this reason, it is imaginable that in this case the deed account redactor agreed with the word account and conceded the earth's active role.

1.3.5 The Deed Account Layer as the Priestly Redactor's Contribution

Since there are – as shown above – certain reasons to conclude that the deed account is a later supplement, we may ask if the deed account should be ascribed to the author of the Priestly composition (P[C]). There is in fact some evidence for this assumption. First, the lexeme ברא occurs several times in statements relating to Elohim's deeds but is missing from the word account statements.[76] This verb appears elsewhere in the Priestly strand (four times in Gen 5) and occurs mainly in exilic or postexilic texts.[77] Second, the blessing motif (ברך *piel*) also plays an important role within P[C].[78] It is significant that the distribution of ברא in the deed account sections accords with the blessing motif: ברא is used for the creation of the sea animals and birds (1:21) and humanity (1:27, three times). These are exactly those beings that receive a blessing from God. In contrast, for all other products of God's creation, the verb עשה (and once יצא *hiphil*) is used, and all are bereft of God's blessing. This is ideologically significant. Since mankind and land animals have to share the same living space, they cannot both be blessed. According to the conception of the deed account, the humans find themselves in a privileged position.

Creation of the Firmament (Genesis 1:7a)

‏7a‏ ויעש אלהים את הרקיע ויבדל בין המים אשר מתחת לרקיע ובין המים אשר מעל לרקיע

Creation of the Vegetation (Genesis 1:12a)

‏12a‏ ותוצא הארץ דשא עשב מזריע זרע למינהו ועץ עשה פרי אשר זרעו בו למינהו

Creation of the Luminaries (Genesis 1:16–18a)

‏16‏ ויעש אלהים את שני המארת הגדלים את המאור הגדל לממשלת היום ואת המאור הקטן לממשלת הלילה ואת הכוכבים ‏17‏ ויתן אתם אלהים ברקיע השמים להאיר על הארץ ‏18a‏ ולמשל ביום ובלילה ולהבדיל בין האור ובין החשך

---

the subject either. However, with regard to the previous context (1:2, 9), formulating a statement that the deity would have made sea and earth is of course impossible.

[76] In the sections dealing with the eight single acts of creation, ברא is used in Gen 1:21 and 1:27 (3×). The lexeme also occurs in 1:1; 2:3, 4a. Verses 1:1; 2:4a should probably be attributed to the "deed account"; for 2:2–3 an attribution to a second redactional layer seems possible; see below, II.1.3.6.

[77] Cf. K. H. BERNHARDT, "ברא II 2," *TDOT* 2:245. The verb ברא occurs predominantly in Second Isaiah (17×) and the P stratum of Gen (in Gen 1:1–2:4a and 5 [11×]). It is found less often in Ps (6×), Ezek (3×), and Third Isaiah (3×).

[78] Sixteen times in P in Gen and Exod (Gen 1:22, 28; 2:3; 5:2; 9:1; 17:16 [2×], 20; 25:11; 28:1, 3, 6 [2×]; 35:9; 48:3; Exod 39:43). Cf. BAUKS, "Genesis 1," 342–43; KING, *Realignment*, 85–87.

Creation of the Sea Animals and the Birds (Genesis 1:21abα.22)

ויברא ^{21abα} אלהים את התנינם הגדלים ואת כל נפש החיה הרמשת אשר שרצו המים
למינהם ואת כל עוף כנף למינהו ²² ויברך אתם אלהים לאמר פרו ורבו ומלאו את המים
בימים והעוף ירב בארץ

Creation of the Land Animals (Genesis 1:25)

²⁵ ויעש אלהים את חית הארץ למינה ואת הבהמה למינה ואת כל רמש האדמה למינהו

Creation of Humanity (Genesis 1:27–28)

²⁷ ויברא אלהים את האדם בצלמו בצלם אלהים ברא אתו זכר ונקבה ברא אתם ²⁸ ויברך
אתם אלהים ויאמר להם אלהים פרו ורבו ומלאו את הארץ וכבשה ורדו בדגת הים ובעוף
השמים ובכל חיה הרמשת על הארץ

In this respect it is important to see that this well-planned alignment, that is, the parallel use of the verb ברא and the blessing motif, is observable only in the deed account. The verbs used in the preceding announcement sentences differ from those that occur in the deed account sections. It is especially remarkable that the word account of the creation of humanity uses the verb עשה (1:26, נעשה אדם בצלמנו), which does not concur with the threefold use of ברא in 1:27 (deed account). Scholars have always been troubled by the fact that two verbs of similar meaning – ברא and עשה – are used within the same passage. No satisfying explanation has been found yet for the distribution of the two verbs in the final form of the text.[79] Yet the problem should be explained diachronically. According to the redaction-critical differentiation proposed here, the lexeme ברא together with the blessing motif is restricted to the later deed account layer. Since the two motifs play an important role within P[c],[80] the deliberate parallel use of the verb ברא and the blessing sentences is a strong argument for the attribution of the deed account layer to the Priestly author.

The attribution of the deed account to the Priestly redaction seems clear for a second reason as well. Whereas the word account contains certain motifs that are difficult to combine with the theology of P (e.g., the "birth" of certain beings by the earth and the sea), the deed account fits well with P's monotheistic theology because it stresses God's role as the lone creator. Furthermore, there is a notable "plus" in the deed account when compared to the word account, which can be explained in the context of the comprehensive Priestly composition. As shown above, the "great sea monsters" (התנינם הגדלים) in 1:21 have no counterpart in the corresponding

---

[79] Cf. W. H. Schmidt, *Die Schöpfungsgeschichte*, 164; Westermann, *Genesis 1–11*, 120–21. M. S. Smith, *The Priestly Vision of Genesis 1* (Minneapolis: Augsburg Fortress, 2010), 48, is right in pointing out that the verb ברא "frames the account, and in this way it stresses God's unique role as the Creator." As for the use in between, however, he lists the occurrences of the two verbs ברא and עשה without giving an explanation for their distribution: "In between, this verb [ברא] applies to the creation of sea creatures and humanity on days 5 and 6 of creation (1:21 and 27). In contrast, a more generic verb, 'to make' (עשה), occurs on days 2 and 4 and in combination with the verb, 'to create' (ברא) on day 6 (see also 2:3)."

[80] See above, n. 77, 78.

word account section (1:20). In the Priestly miracle narrative about the competition between Hebrew and Egyptian magicians the motif of the תנין plays an important role in the first miracle (see Exod 7:9, 10, 12).[81] The author of the deed account might have added the "great sea monsters" under the influence of that passage.

1.3.6 Further Elements of the Redaction Layer(s) (Deed Account)

(a) Food Provision (Gen 1:29–30)

Certain linguistic particularities suggest that God's provisioning of food in Gen 1:29–30 probably constitutes a later addition. The designation and enumeration of the plants and animals deviate partly from the preceding parts of the composition. In contrast to the twofold occurrence of the expression דשא עשׂב מזריע זרע found in 1:11–12, the statement in 1:29 has את כל עשׂב זרע זרע (זרע) *qal* replaces זרע *hiphil*; דשא is omitted). The specification אשר בו נפש חיה, "[every moving thing] in which there is the breath of life," is also striking; the phrase is unique in Gen 1:1–2:4a but resembles the expression אשר הוא חי, "[every moving thing] that is alive," in Gen 9:3.[82] Genesis 1:29–30 and 9:1–7 perhaps stem from the same Priestly redactor.[83]

(b) Title (1:1) and Postscript (2:4a)

The key term ברא also occurs in the frame sentences of Gen 1:1 and 2:4a. In these two sentences, the verb is used in a summarizing way for the entire creation. Are these clauses to be attributed to the redaction layer?

The two sentences frame Gen 1:1–2:4a. That they relate to one another is made obvious by the use of three identical expressions (הארץ, השמים, ברא):

Genesis 1:1

¹בראשית ברא אלהים את השמים ואת הארץ

Genesis 2:4a

⁴ᵃאלה תולדות השמים והארץ בהבראם

The occurrence of ברא, which is found only in deed account sections, suggests that these verses should be ascribed to the Priestly redaction as well. The redactor probably

---

[81] In Exod 7:9, 10, 12 תנין is understood as "serpent" (see, e.g., Propp, *Exodus 1–18*, 322), "sea dragon" (see, e.g., Dozeman, *Commentary on Exodus*, 210), or "crocodile" (see, e.g., Jeon, "A Source of P?," 85–6, with n. 21).

[82] See K. Budde, "Wortlaut und Werden der ersten Schöpfungsgeschichte," *ZAW* 35 (1915): 86.

[83] Also according to Steck, *Der Schöpfungsbericht*, 100, and U. Neumann-Gorsolke, *Herrschen in den Grenzen der Schöpfung: Ein Beitrag zur alttestamentlichen Anthropologie am Beispiel von Psalm 8, Genesis 1 und verwandten Texten* (Neukirchen-Vluyn: Neukirchener Verlag, 2004), 153, Gen 1:30 is formulated in view of Gen 9:3.

considered this verb, which expresses a special qualification, necessary for these framing statements, which refer to the totality of Elohim's creation deeds.

According to several scholars, Gen 2:4a belongs to a post-Priestly redaction; it
was meant to serve as an introduction to the following non-P unit, Gen 2:4b–4:26.[84]
However, with regard to its vocabulary and contents,[85] 2:4a matches the preceding
account, Gen 1, much better; it seems obvious that it was composed in view of the
latter composition.[86]

Are there other arguments for the attribution of these sentences to the deed account
redactional layer? The opening verse, Gen 1:1, stands in tension to v. 2:

Genesis 1:1–2

¹ בראשית ברא אלהים את השמים ואת הארץ ² והארץ היתה תהו ובהו וחשך על פני
תהום ורוח אלהים מרחפת על פני המים

According to Gen 1:1, heaven and earth are created by Elohim, whereas v. 2 reveals
that the earth has existed *ab initio*.[87] Like Gen 1:2, several creation accounts from the
ancient Near East begin with a description of the primordial world.[88] Furthermore,
some scholars have argued that the syntax at the beginning of v. 2 (*w-x-qatal*) is often
used at the commencement of a story.[89] These could be indications that "1:2 originally
was an opening verse."[90] The preceding verse, Gen 1:1, would be a later supplement.
It fits well with the theological profile of the Priestly redaction layer outlined above.
Immediately at the beginning of the unit, Elohim appears as lone creator. It is possible
that the redactor, in order to further stress a theocentric theology, wanted to introduce
the notion of *creatio ex nihilo* by God.

---

[84] B. D. EERDMANS, *Alttestamentliche Studien I: Die Komposition der Genesis* (Giessen: Töpelmann, 1908), 3, 78; CROSS, *Canaanite Myth*, 302; BLUM, *Studien*, 280; A. SCHÜLE, *Der Prolog der
hebräischen Bibel: Der literar- und theologiegeschichtliche Diskurs der Urgeschichte (Gen 1–11)*,
ATANT 86 (Zurich: TVZ, 2006), 45, 48–50. Others consider 2:4a a redactional "bridge" between the two creation accounts: CARR, *Reading*, 74–75; BÜHRER, *Am Anfang*, 142–52.

[85] Cf. the sequence השמים והארץ, the use of the lexeme ברא, and the idea that the earth
brings forth living beings, which is corrected by the addition בהבראם (the living beings were
created).

[86] For the traditional assignment of Gen 2:4a to the Priestly creation account, see, among
others, WESTERMANN, *Genesis 1–11*, 21–22; WEIMAR, *Studien*, 27–28, 93–99; C. LEVIN, *Der Jahwist*, FRLANT 157 (Göttingen: Vandenhoeck & Ruprecht, 1993), 89; SEEBASS, *Genesis I*, 90;
WITTE, *Die biblische Urgeschichte*, 55.

[87] This tension between the two first verses is observed by WEIMAR, "Chaos," 198–99 = IDEM,
Studien, 137–38; M. WEIPPERT, "Schöpfung am Anfang oder Anfang der Schöpfung: Noch
einmal zu Syntax und Semantik von Gen 1,1–3," *TZ* 60 (2004): 12, 20–21.

[88] See, for instance, Cosmogony from Nibru (cf. *TUAT* 3:353–54); Enuma Elish I 1–9 (cf. I 1–9
in *TUAT* 3:569); "Eine zweisprachige Beschwörung mit Schöpfungsmythos" (cf. *TUAT* 3:608–9).
See also Gen 2:4b–3:24.

[89] See Gen 3:1; Exod 3:1; Judg 11:1; 2 Sam 3:17; 2 Kgs 6:8.

[90] Cf. M. BAUKS, *Die Welt am Anfang: Zum Verhältnis von Vorwelt und Weltentstehung in Gen
1 und in der altorientalischen Literatur*, WMANT 74 (Neukirchen-Vluyn: Neukirchener Verlag,
1997), 84, n. 123: "ein ursprünglicher Erzählbeginn gewesen ist."

As for 2:4a, here too the idea that heaven and earth have been *created* is under-lined by the final expression בהבראם. The two sentences – 1:1 and 2:4a – form an *inclusio*.

Since the expression תולדות השמים והארץ ("descendants/posterity of heaven and earth") does not match the theocentric theology of the Priestly redaction, it is possi-ble that the sentence אלה תולדות השמים והארץ was formulated by the author of the word account and later, with the addition of בהבראם, was reinterpreted by the Priestly redactor ("these are the descendants of the heaven and of the earth *when they were created*"). Let us note further that the first part of the phrase would fit as a superscrip-tion or title of the primary account.[91]

(c) The Section Relating to the Seventh Day (2:2–3) and the Six/Seven-Day Schema

Two characteristic elements of the deed account – ברא and the blessing motif – also appear in the section on the seventh day (Gen 2:2–3). For this reason it is tempting to ascribe the entire passage to the Priestly redaction as well. However, the use of both elements is somewhat different: In 2:2–3, the blessing is not connected with the order of reproduction as it is in 1:22, 27. Likewise, this section uses the verb ברא, but the verb עשׂה occurs three times, too. The two verbs are utilized here in the same way: both refer to God's work of creation as a whole (cf. the identical formulations, מכל מלאכתו אשר עשה [v. 2] / מכל מלאכתו אשר ברא [v. 3]). The variation in the use of the lexeme ברא (parallel to עשׂה) in this section favors the idea that a secondary Priestly redactor, rather than the first Priestly redactor, is responsible for this addition. The differentiation between two Priestly redactions is further supported by the distinct vocabulary of Gen 2:2–3: the term מלאכה occurs three times there but never appears in the preceding section, Gen 1:1–2:1. Additionally, Y. Amit and J. Milgrom point to קדש *piel* and שבת that appear in this passage but are lacking in Gen 1:1–2:1. They consider these typical "Holiness school terms." Amit ascribes the entire account of 1:1–2:4a to "H"; for Milgrom only 2:2–3 form an "H" insertion.[92] Since the institution of the Sabbath plays a major role in H – but not in P^C – it is tempting to assume that the author responsible for this passage stems from the milieu that produced H or was close to it.[93]

The section on the seventh day is related to the six-/seven-day schema that shapes Gen 1:1–2:4a. This probably means that the arrangement with six working days and a rest day was devised by the second Priestly (perhaps H) redactor. The striking absence of the seven-day scheme in the numerous allusions to Gen 1 in other biblical texts (in particular in Psalms; see below) hints at a second redactional stage. Since the Sabbath

---

[91] See below, II.1.3.7.

[92] See AMIT, "הבריאה ולוח הקדושה," 13*–29*, and MILGROM, *Leviticus 17–22*, 1344.

[93] In my article of 2010, I was, despite of the mentioned observations, still indecisive whether the section 2:2–3 and all related statements referring to the 6/7 day scheme should be ascribed to P^C or to second a Priestly layer (H), cf. HUTZLI, "Tradition and Interpretation," 17.

and the seven-day scheme constitute distinctive features of the present composition, we would expect some reference to them in those texts if their authors knew these elements.

1.3.7 Further Elements of the Word Account as Original Report

Is it possible to attribute further elements, apart from the announcement sentences and the subsequent ויהי כן formula, to the word account layer, too? In Gen 1:2, one may see the old beginning of the creation story of Gen 1 (word account, see above). It is probable that the main part of 2:4a – אלה תולדות השמים והארץ – belonged to the stipulated source text, perhaps as its "title," as some scholars have suggested.[94] The sentence fits much better with the theology of the word account than with that of the Priestly redaction layer (see the idea that the earth brings forth living beings).[95]

We may now consider how this report ended. One possibility is the concise concluding sentence of Gen 2:1: ויכלו השמים והארץ וכל צבאם, "Thus the heavens and the earth were completed, and all their host." At first sight, we might be inclined to attribute the lexeme כלה *pual* to the Priestly redaction layer; כלה *piel* often occurs in P texts.[96] A number of recent treatments see Gen 2:1 in close relationship to Exod 39:32a (use of כלה *qal*[97]) in the tabernacle account.[98] This observation is certainly correct. However, it is probable that this verse already belonged to the word account as the source text of the Priestly redactor. Indeed, there are two arguments against the idea that this verse stems from the Priestly redactor. Its passive voice contrasts with the style of the redaction layer in Gen 1:1–2:4a: the Priestly redactor generally chose the active voice and mentioned Elohim as subject explicitly.[99] Concerning the use of the lexeme צבא, "host (of beings)," (וכל צבאם, "and all their host") it is noteworthy that in Gen 1 the expression refers both to the heavenly bodies (as is often the case in the Hebrew

---

[94] Cf., among others, A. KUENEN, *Historisch-kritische Einleitung in die Bücher des alten Testaments hinsichtlich ihrer Entstehung und Sammlung*, 3 vols. (Leipzig: Schulze, 1885–94), 1.1:309; GUNKEL, *Genesis*, 101; WITTE, *Die biblische Urgeschichte*, 55; BLENKINSOPP, *Pentateuch*, 60, 71. In contrast to my contention, the aforementioned authors consider the element בהבראם an original part of the supposed title.

[95] However, the idea that the heavens have "posterity" is not explicitly expressed in Gen 1; nevertheless, the word account of 1:14 may be interpreted in this sense.

[96] Cf. Gen 2:2; 6:16; 17:22; 49:33; Exod 40:33; Lev 16:20; Num 4:15; 7:1.

[97] According to the MT vocalization (וַתֵּכֶל). A vocalization as *pual* would perhaps also be fitting.

[98] Cf., among others, BLUM, *Studien*, 306–7; SCHÜLE, *Der Prolog*, 82, n. 227; K. SCHMID, *Literaturgeschichte des Alten Testaments: Eine Einführung* (Darmstadt: Wissenschaftliche Buchgesellschaft, 2008), 147; IDEM, "Der Sinai und die Priesterschrift," in *"Gerechtigkeit und Recht zu üben" (Gen 18,19): Studien zur altorientalischen und biblischen Rechtsgeschichte, zur Religionsgeschichte Israels und zur Religionssoziologie; Festschrift für Eckart Otto zum 65. Geburtstag*, ed. R. Achenbach and M. Arneth, BZABR 13 (Wiesbaden: Harrassowitz, 2010), 121.

[99] See above, II.1.3.3 (a) and II.1.3.4.

Bible, as for instance in Isa 40:26) and to the creatures of the sea and the earth. In P, however, צבא occurs only in the plural and relates only to Israel in connection to its "regiments" (צבאות, cf. Exod 6:26; 7:4; 12:17, 41, 51). Both observations favor ascribing Gen 2:1 to the ancient word account as its conclusion rather than the Priestly redaction layer. The word account layer is thus found in Gen 1:1–2:1*.

The *naming* of the creation works ("and God called") in Gen 1:1–2:4a is probably also to be ascribed to the supposed ground layer. Naming clauses occur after the formation of light (1:5a), the creation of the firmament (1:8a), and the gathering of water and appearance of dry land (1:10a). The designations שמים, "heaven," (1:9, 14, 20, 26), ארץ, "earth" (1:11, 20, 24, 26), ים, "sea" (1:26), יום, "day" (1:14), and לילה, "night" (1:14), which all occur in word account statements, presuppose the preceding naming, and so the attribution of this redundant element to the word account seems probable.

Finally, the *approbation formula* ("and God saw that it was [very] good") might have been part of the word account as well. Because it appears seven times (according to MT, SP, 4QGen[b,g]), this formula might at first glance seem to belong to the Priestly redaction, which implemented the six/seven-day scheme in the text.[100] However, LXX, which has eight occurrences in total of this formula (seven standard phrases and the variation at the end), might reflect the original pattern.[101] Furthermore, the climax of the formula in the creation of humanity (see the alteration of formulation: "behold, it was *very* good" in 1:31) matches the word account, which – as the analysis above has shown – culminates in the same section and lacks the motif of rest. For these reasons, I attribute the approbation formula to the word account.

EXCURSUS I: The Relationship between the Creation of Light and the Formation of the Heavenly Bodies in the Word Account

Two of the eight works from the word account reconstructed above, the creation of light and the formation of the heavenly bodies, are considered to be in tension with each other by certain scholars (D. Hermant, J. Vermeylen, P. Weimar). These interpreters, operating with various redaction-historical models, attribute one of the two sections (in its full extent, including the word account statement) to a redactional layer. Whereas Herman,[102] followed by Vermeylen,[103] views the creation of the astrological bodies as a later addition, Weimar[104] claims that the first work, the genesis of light, has been supplemented by the Priestly redactor.

Herman and Vermeylen argue that the section on the fifth section disturbs "la

---

[100] The first Priestly redaction (P[C]) or another, subsequent Priestly redaction (see above, II.1.3.6 [c]).

[101] In the second section MT, SP, and 4QGen[b,g] lack an approbation sentence, while the LXX provides it in 1:8. A detailed discussion of the difference is offered above, II.1.2.2 (c).

[102] D. HERMANT, "Analyse littéraire du premier récit de la création," *VT* 15 (1965): 437–51.

[103] VERMEYLEN, "Tradition," 127–47.

[104] WEIMAR, "Chaos," 196–211 = IDEM, *Studien*, 135–50.

progression logique"[105] of the account: having located its point of departure in the installation of the "cosmic framework," the account then descends to earth (cf. the fourth section: the coming-forth of the vegetation). The subsequent return to the firmament (fifth section) seems to disturb the movement, since the following continues again on earth (sixth, seventh, and eighth sections).[106] However, the direction of movement is ambiguous in other sections as well: in the word account of the sixth section, the firmament is mentioned again (v. 20: "and let birds fly above the earth in the open firmament of the heavens [על פני רקיע השמים]"). The main argument against the reconstruction of the traditional account without the fifth section is that it seems natural that a creation account like Gen 1, which aims systematically to describe every domain of the cosmos, would also include the heavenly bodies, which are of great importance in ancient societies. One argument for the inclusion of the fifth section in the assumed source text is the occurrence of the expression "all their host" (ויכלו השמים והארץ וכל צבאם) in 2:1, which certainly refers to luminaries of heaven as well.

Weimar, in discussing the significance of the formation of light and the separation of light and darkness for the seven-day framework, takes for granted that the section belongs to the Priestly redaction; for the fifth section, in contrast, he ascribes certain parts to the traditional account.[107] This idea also seems problematic: if one assumes that the formation of light (first section) was lacking from the original account, it is hardly imaginable that its author would place the formation of the luminaries after the creation of beings that are dependent on light sources (e.g., the coming-forth of the vegetation). It is not credible that the author – an accurate observer of nature[108] – would ignore this causality. In addition, with regard to the possible attribution of the approbation formula to the word account (see above), the creation of light is an essential work and indispensable to all subsequent creation acts; the idea that Elohim approves a work when still being girded by darkness seems awkward.

Taking into account the assignment of Elohim's separation of light and darkness in 1:4b to the redactional layer (see II.1.3.3 [a], above),[109] the word account statements of the two sections do not share the same elements and thus there is no discernible tension or contradiction between them.

---

[105] VERMEYLEN, "Tradition," 133.

[106] HERMANT, "Analyse," 445; VERMEYLEN, "Tradition," 133.

[107] Cf. WEIMAR, "Chaos," 199: "Angesichts der grundlegenden Bedeutung der Erschaffung des Lichts sowie der damit einhergehenden Scheidung von Licht und Finsternis für die als Strukturierungsmerkmal der priesterschriftlichen Erzählfassung dienende Tageszählung erscheint für Gen 1,3–5 eine Herkunft aus der Hand des priesterschriftlichen Erzählers unabweisbar, wohingegen für Gen 1,14–19 manches dafür spricht, dass die Erschaffung der Leuchten im Gegensatz zum Werden des Lichts schon ein Element der Tradition darstellt."

[108] This is evident especially from his differentiated, "scientific" enumeration in the fourth section, on vegetation (cf. 1:11).

[109] The statement of 1:15a in the fifth section might also be considered a later addition (see below, II.1.3.8).

1.3.8 Conclusion: Redactional-Critical Differentiation in Genesis 1

Assigning additional elements of Gen 1:1–2:4a to specific layers is more difficult. As shown above, Gen 2:2–3, together with the related statements that introduce the six-/seven-day schema in Gen 1, may belong to a second, H-like Priestly redaction. Besides these verses, questions remain concerning single sentences: for instance, in the creation of the heavenly bodies, the word account is quite long, and 1:15a, with the repetitive expression והיו למאורת ברקיע השמים, could plausibly be a later addition. In this case and others, we might consider the possibility of insertions by a second redactor or a later scribe.

However, the main question addressed here is *whether it is possible to identify the full extent of the text of the redactional layer(s) of Gen 1:1–2:4a (Priestly deed account and additions) on the one hand and that of the base layer (word account) on the other.* The difficulty of accurately identifying the texts of the different layers may be a result of the fact that not one but two redactors are at work. Furthermore, we must take into account the possibility that the redactor decided to include only some parts of his source text. Nevertheless, the forgoing analysis has shown that every act of creation includes a word account, which means that the redactor preserved his source text to some extent, at least in the eight creative works.[110] Even if 1:20 MT – which lacks the ויהי כן formula – preserved a more ancient reading, the global framework of the word account and its rigid structure (with the correspondence between announcement sentence and execution formula) is sufficiently discernible.

Scholars who consider Gen 1 to be a unified composition often admit the presence of two conflicting conceptions, but at the same time they think that the Priestly author relied on different oral traditions that he was keen to combine. Yet the fact that the word account and the deed account contradict one another in several sections speaks against this contention. Why would the author have taken up two conflicting traditions instead of favoring only one of them or simply developing his own? Why, for instance, would the Priestly author have preserved the idea that the earth brings forth living beings, which has no point of contact with the theology of P? It is much more likely that the author (or rather, the redactor) of the present text reworked and corrected a written source that was too important to be disregarded and replaced with a new and independent account. Particularly speaking against the theory of a unified text relying on two conflicting oral traditions are the different spellings in the word account on one hand and the deed account on the other.[111]

As will be shown below, there are further indications that the Priestly author reused a form of the word account as his written source text: in addition to the fact that the extant word account forms a well-structured and self-contained unit, it has some characteristic themes that do not find resonance in the extensive Priestly composition (whatever its extent may be).

---

[110] See above, II.1.3.2 (b).

[111] See above, I.2.3 (a) and II.1.3.3 (b).

The stratigraphy of the text is outlined below, with the original account without underline, the first Priestly redaction (P^c) with single underline, and the second Priestly redaction (H) with double underline. Unless otherwise noted, the text follows MT. The text is divided according to the inherent structure of the presumed primary story (word account, see below 1.3.9).

Genesis 1:1–2:4a

[1] בראשית ברא אלהים את השמים ואת הארץ [2] והארץ היתה תהו ובהו וחשך על פני תהום ורוח אלהים מרחפת על פני המים [3] ויאמר אלהים יהי אור ויהי אור [4] וירא אלהים את האור כי טוב ויבדל אלהים בין האור ובין החשך [5] ויקרא אלהים לאור יום ולחשך קרא לילה ויהי ערב ויהי בקר יום אחד [6] ויאמר אלהים יהי רקיע בתוך המים ויהי מבדיל בין מים למים [7] ויעש אלהים את הרקיע ויבדל בין המים אשר מתחת לרקיע ובין המים אשר מעל לרקיע ויהי כן [8] ויקרא אלהים לרקיע שמים ויהי ערב ויהי בקר יום שני [9] ויאמר אלהים יקוו המים מתחת השמים אל מקום אחד ותראה היבשה ויהי כן ויקוו המים מתחת השמים אל מקויהם ותרא היבשה[112] [10] ויקרא אלהים ליבשה ארץ ולמקוה המים קרא ימים וירא אלהים כי טוב [11] ויאמר אלהים תדשא הארץ דשא עשב מזריע זרע ועץ[113] פרי עשה פרי למינו אשר זרעו בו על הארץ ויהי כן [12] ותוצא הארץ דשא עשב מזריע זרע למינהו ועץ עשה פרי אשר זרעו בו למינהו וירא אלהים כי טוב [13] ויהי ערב ויהי בקר יום שלישי [14] ויאמר אלהים יהי מארת ברקיע השמים להבדיל בין היום ובין הלילה והיו לאתת ולמועדים ולימים ולשנים[114] [15] והיו למאורת ברקיע השמים להאיר על הארץ ויהי כן [16] ויעש אלהים את שני המארת הגדלים את המאור הגדל לממשלת היום ואת המאור הקטן לממשלת הלילה ואת הכוכבים [17] ויתן אתם אלהים ברקיע השמים להאיר על הארץ [18] ולמשל ביום ובלילה ולהבדיל בין האור ובין החשך וירא אלהים כי טוב [19] ויהי ערב ויהי בקר יום רביעי [20] ויאמר אלהים ישרצו המים שרץ נפש חיה ועוף יעופף על הארץ על פני רקיע השמים [21] ויברא אלהים את התנינם הגדלים ואת כל נפש החיה הרמשת אשר שרצו המים למיניהם ואת כל עוף כנף למינהו וירא אלהים כי טוב [22] ויברך אתם אלהים לאמר פרו ורבו ומלאו את המים בימים והעוף ירב בארץ [23] ויהי ערב ויהי בקר יום חמישי [24] ויאמר אלהים תוצא הארץ נפש חיה למינה בהמה ורמש וחיתו ארץ למינה ויהי כן [25] ויעש אלהים את חית הארץ למינה ואת הבהמה למינה ואת כל רמש האדמה למינהו וירא אלהים כי טוב [26] ויאמר אלהים נעשה אדם בצלמנו כדמותנו וירדו בדגת הים ובעוף השמים ובבהמה ובכל הארץ ובכל הרמש הרמש על הארץ [27] ויברא אלהים את האדם בצלמו בצלם אלהים ברא אתו זכר ונקבה ברא אתם [28] ויברך אתם אלהים ויאמר להם אלהים פרו ורבו ומלאו את הארץ וכבשה ורדו בדגת הים ובעוף השמים ובכל חיה הרמשת על הארץ [29] ויאמר אלהים הנה נתתי לכם את כל עשב זרע זרע אשר על פני כל הארץ ואת כל העץ אשר בו

---

[112] ויקוו המים מתחת השמים אל מקויהם ותרא היבשה: reconstructed according to LXX and 4QGen^k.

[113] ועץ: reconstructed according to SP and LXX.

[114] ולשנים: reconstructed according to 4QGen^k and LXX.

פְּרִי עֵץ זֶרַע זֶרַע לָכֶם יִהְיֶה לְאָכְלָה ³⁰ וּלְכָל חַיַּת הָאָרֶץ וּלְכָל עוֹף הַשָּׁמַיִם וּלְכֹל רוֹמֵשׂ עַל
הָאָרֶץ אֲשֶׁר בּוֹ נֶפֶשׁ חַיָּה אֶת כָּל יֶרֶק עֵשֶׂב לְאָכְלָה וַיְהִי כֵן
²:¹ וַיַּרְא אֱלֹהִים אֶת כָּל אֲשֶׁר עָשָׂה וְהִנֵּה טוֹב מְאֹד וַיְהִי עֶרֶב וַיְהִי בֹקֶר יוֹם הַשִּׁשִּׁי וַיְכֻלּוּ
הַשָּׁמַיִם וְהָאָרֶץ וְכָל צְבָאָם ² וַיְכַל אֱלֹהִים בַּיּוֹם הַשְּׁבִיעִי מְלַאכְתּוֹ אֲשֶׁר עָשָׂה וַיִּשְׁבֹּת בַּיּוֹם
הַשְּׁבִיעִי מִכָּל מְלַאכְתּוֹ אֲשֶׁר עָשָׂה ³ וַיְבָרֶךְ אֱלֹהִים אֶת יוֹם הַשְּׁבִיעִי וַיְקַדֵּשׁ אֹתוֹ כִּי בוֹ שָׁבַת
מִכָּל מְלַאכְתּוֹ אֲשֶׁר בָּרָא אֱלֹהִים לַעֲשׂוֹת ⁴ אֵלֶּה תוֹלְדוֹת הַשָּׁמַיִם וְהָאָרֶץ בְּהִבָּרְאָם

1.3.9 Characteristics of the Proto-Priestly Creation Account (Gen 1:1–2:1*)

A particularity of the word account is the careful structuring and classification of the world into different living spaces, living beings, and species. The created world consists of eight works in total: light, sky, sea and earth, vegetation, heavenly bodies, sea animals and birds, land animals, and humans. Accordingly, the narrative is divided into eight parts, which are introduced by a description of the preexisting primordial world (1:2) and which conclude with the climactic approbation formula and the summary final sentence (1:31–2:1).

The interest in diversity and classification of the animals is also found in the Priestly strand of the flood story (Gen 6–9), which emphasizes the preservation of all animal species during the flood; after the catastrophe, the animals are also included in God's covenant (9:10, 12, 15, 16). The specific vocabulary of the animals' enumeration is very similar but not identical in Gen 1 and in the Priestly flood narrative.[115] A comparable interest is visible in the Priestly laws on edible and nonedible animals in Lev 11 too. As will be shown below, however, perception and categorization of the animal world in Lev 11 differ from Gen 1.[116]

A related theme to the diversity of species in Gen 1 is the goodness of the created world, which finds expression in the repeated approbation formula, "and God saw that it was good." The creation of man constitutes the climax of the creation. Correspondingly, the last extended approbation formula, subsequent to the creation of humans, constitutes a culmination ("and God saw all that he had made, and behold, it was very good," Gen 1:31). It is possible that the description of God's creation of the world reflects a utopian "golden age," as do other myths of "beginning" from antiquity.[117] The peculiar delimitation of the sea to one place by God in Gen 1:9–10 in particular seems to be a utopian element (as stated above, Judeans and Israelites knew several

---

[115] See further in the analysis of Gen 6–9 P, below (II.3.7.2).

[116] See II.10.6.2 (d). Lev 11 divides the animals into four main categories rather than three as in Gen 1; the systematization is also more detailed. Moreover, the characterization of certain animals as "abomination" (שֶׁקֶץ) for the Israelites is in tension with the general esteem for all creatures in the word account of Gen 1.

[117] In Mesopotamia and in Greece (Hesiod, Homer); see WESTERMANN, *Genesis 1–11*, 225–27; SEEBASS, *Genesis I*, 84–86.

seas). This motif should be understood in the context of the sea's mythological association with chaos and its real, threatening power in antiquity.[118]

The themes of creation's goodness and diversity in the word account are reflected in certain creation psalms, which give insights into the diversity of the creation, express its beauty and goodness, and invite praise for the creator (see Pss 8, 19, 33, 104, 136, 148). These psalms are further connected to Gen 1:1–2:1* through shared vocabulary and motifs.[119] Psalms 33 and 148 emphasize creation by God's word,[120] and Psalm 8 highlights the importance of humans in God's creation.[121]

The references to Gen 1 in these psalms mostly concern the word account.[122] Allusions to the first Priestly redaction (deed account) appear in Ps 136:7–9[123] and Ps 148:5, 7.[124] Significantly, neither of these Psalms alludes to the seven-day scheme, which might hint at a rather late date for the redactional introduction of the latter (see above).

These manifold correspondences between Psalms and Gen 1:1–2:1* (word account) suggest that at least some of the psalms presuppose the latter composition.[125]

From a religio-historical point of view, it is noteworthy that the word account, as the assumed source text, is less theocentric than the Priestly redaction and not strictly monotheistic. The fact that certain creatures function as the grammatical subjects of creative acts expresses the idea *that they participate in these acts*. Most evident is the participation in the case of the creation of the sea and land animals: sea and earth

---

[118] See J. HUTZLI, "Überlegungen zum Motiv der Ansammlung der Wasser unterhalb des Himmels an einem Ort (Gen 1,9)," *TZ* 62 (2006): 10–16. The provision of vegetarian food for humankind and animals (see Gen 1:28–29) is another element hinting at the utopian character of the creation of the world; however, because of its distinct language, it should be assigned to the Priestly redaction (see above, II.1.3.6 [a]).

[119] Ps 19:2 shares the common expressions רקיע, שמים; Ps 33 shares the common motif of creation by word (cf. vv. 6, 9) and the common expressions עשה, כל צבאם, "all their host"; Ps 104:8, 19 shares the common motifs of a special place (מקום) that is established for the waters and the luminaries determining the seasons (מועדים); Ps 136:7–9 shares the creation of the luminaries to rule by day and night and the expression ממשלת; Ps 148:5, 7 shares creation by word, mention of the primordial sea, and the expressions תהום and תנינים, the sea monsters.

[120] Cf. 33:6: "By the word of YHWH the heavens were made, and by the breath of His mouth all their host"; 33:9: "For He spoke, and it was; He commanded, and it stood fast"; 148:5: "For He commanded and they were created."

[121] Cf. M. OEMING, *Das Buch der Psalmen: Psalm 1–41*, NSKAT 13.1 (Stuttgart: Katholisches Bibelwerk, 2000), 82–89.

[122] Ps 8: importance of humans in God's creation, order to rule; Ps 19:2: שמים, רקיע; Ps 33: creation by word (cf. vv. 6, 9), עשה, כל צבאם, "all their host"; Ps 104:8, 19: a special place (מקום) established for the waters, the luminaries determine the seasons (מועדים).

[123] Creation of the luminaries to rule by day and night; shared expression ממשלת.

[124] V. 5: use of the lexeme ברא; v. 7: mention of the "sea monsters" (תנינין).

[125] For Ps 33, cf. OEMING, *Das Buch der Psalmen*, 192; for Ps 104, see F.-L. HOSSFELD and E. ZENGER, *Psalmen: 101–150*, HThKAT (Freiburg im Breisgau: Herder, 2008), 88–89; for Ps 136, see HOSSFELD and ZENGER, *Psalmen*, 679; for Ps 148, see HOSSFELD and ZENGER, *Psalmen*, 842. Pss 136 and 148 may presuppose the reworked composition of the Priestly redaction (see the preceding footnotes). More uncertain is the relationship to Pss 8 and 19.

bring forth the various beings belonging to their respective living spaces. The three-fold use of the first-person plural in the announcement sentence of 1:26 also indicates that the conception of God in the ancient word account deviates from a strictly mono-theistic theology.

In this respect, the chosen designation for the creative deity – אלהים – also deserves attention. The term is commonly understood in the context of the supposed Priestly document with its concept of a three-stage revelation of God by means of three dis-tinct designations (אלהים, אל שדי, יהוה). This concept reflects an inclusive monothe-ism.[126] Yet considered in the context of Gen 1 (word account) alone, the designation should be understood differently: the author of Gen 1 chose the term אלהים because of its morphological specificity – the noun is a plural but is consistently used as a singu-lar. In light of the allusion to the plurality of God in 1:26, the expression might convey the idea that the deity is simultaneously one and multiple.[127] The plural in 1:26 and the emphasis on the goodness of the creation show that Gen 1 has its own theological specificities that do not find resonance in the comprehensive Priestly composition. It is remarkable that the key word טוב, which is used seven (MT, SP) or eight (LXX) times in Gen 1,[128] does not appear again in P; noticeably, is its absence from the report of the erection of the tabernacle (Exod 39–40), which is commonly considered to form an *inclusio* with Gen 1. Similarly, the allusion to God's supposed plurality in Gen 1:26 is difficult to explain in the context of the theonym theology of the Priestly composition.[129] Given its regular structure, including redundancies and climactic development, and its marked positive theology (positive ontology), the proto-Priestly creation account may have been composed as an independent and self-contained unit, not necessarily

---

[126] Concerning the concept of אלהים in P^G/P^C in general, cf. A. DE PURY, "Gottesname, Gottesbezeichnung und Gottesbegriff: 'Elohim als Indiz zur Entstehungsgeschichte des Penta-teuch," in *Abschied vom Jahwisten: Die Komposition des Hexateuch in der jüngsten Diskussion*, ed. J. C. Gertz, K. Schmid, and M. Witte, BZAW 315 (Berlin: de Gruyter, 2002), 25–47; E. BLUM, "Der vermeintliche Gottesname 'Elohim,'" in *Gott nennen: Gottes Namen und Gott als Name*, ed. I. U. Dalferth and P. Stoellger, Religion in Philosophy and Theology 35 (Tübingen: Mohr Siebeck 2008), 97–119.

[127] אלהים, without the article ה, is frequently used in the Hebrew Bible as a designation for the God of Israel or for a personal god (cf. Gen 30:2, 6, 8, 17, 18, 20, 22 [2×], 23; 31:7, 9, 16 [2×], 24, 42, 50; 1 Sam 23:14 [MT]; 26:8; 28:15; 2 Sam 14:13, among others; see K. SCHMID, "Differenzierun-gen und Konzeptualisierungen der Einheit Gottes in der Religions- und Literaturgeschichte Is-raels," in *Der eine Gott und die Götter: Polytheismus und Monotheismus im antiken Israel*, ed. M. Oeming and K. Schmid, ATANT 82 [Zurich: TVZ, 2003], 34, with n. 74; BLUM, "Der vermeint-liche Gottesname," 117–18). Some of the texts in question may predate Gen 1*. In some of the ex-amples, the designation אלהים presumably is used in a monolatric – but not in a monotheistic – sense (the referent of אלהים is YHWH). In ancient Egypt the term *ntr*, "god" (sing.), might have had a similar function; cf. E. HORNUNG, *Der Eine und die Vielen: Ägyptische Gottesvorstellungen* (Darmstadt: Wissenschaftliche Buchgesellschaft, 1973), 30–49.

[128] See above, II.1.2.2 (c).

[129] See K. SCHMID, *Schöpfung*, TdT 4 (Tübingen: Mohr Siebeck, 2012), 90–91. For Schmid, who interprets Gen 1 strictly in the context of P^G, the use of the plural form remains "enigmatic" ("sein Gebrauch [i.e., of the plural form] bleibt rätselhaft" [91]).

as a component of a more comprehensive and continuous work comprising several parts.

1.3.10 Characteristics of the Redaction Layers

As for the supposed Priestly redaction, it aims to correct the theological conception of its source. The redactor maintains a strict monotheistic theology. God is the only creator, and statements about the creation activities of other entities and about God's asserted plurality are supplemented with correcting assertions. Important elements of this layer are the combined motifs of divine blessing and order of procreation and multiplication, which are addressed to sea animals, birds, and humans. The blessing of mankind implies the nonblessing of the land animals. The redactor alludes to a relationship of coexistence between humans and land animals, who have to share the same living space, but humans find themselves in a privileged position. The characteristic motifs (blessing), lexemes (ברא, פרה, רבה), and ideological features (theocentrism, demarcation between animals and humans and between different nations) of this layer occur in other Priestly texts as well.

A second redactor introduced the Sabbath theme (by adding 2:2–3) and the seven-day scheme (by attributing the eight works to six days). The vocabulary and theology of these texts point to an author close to H and the tabernacle account.[130]

1.4 Tradition-Historical Background of the Primary Account

As in earlier research, more recent interpretations of Gen 1 pay considerable attention to the ancient Near Eastern context. Current scholarship reckons with both Mesopotamian (Enuma Elish) and Egyptian (Hermopolitan Ogdoad, Theology of Memphis, Teaching for King Merikare) influences.[131] In the past, scholars particularly emphasized the dependence of the creation account in Gen 1 on the Babylonian epic Enuma Elish. The formation of the heavens played an important role in their argumentation, as the relevant passages in the two stories share certain common points. The Hebrew expression for תהום, "primordial sea," is often compared with the designation of the sea goddess Tiamat (*tiamtu*), who plays a major role in Enuma Elish.[132] She is defeated by Marduk, who divides her into two parts, one part forming the sky. Marduk also stretches Tiamat's skin to prevent the water from flowing across and installs a guard

---

[130] See already above II.1.3.6 (c) and below III.1.3.

[131] Cf., among others, W. H. Schmidt, *Die Schöpfungsgeschichte*, 21–39; Bauks, *Die Welt*, 147–310; Keel and Schroer, *Schöpfung*, 170–84.

[132] Whether the expression תהום is an allusion to the mythological being Tiamat in Enuma Elish is disputed in research (see for instance the divergent views in Schüle, *Der Prolog*, 72 on the one hand, and in Gertz: *Das erste Buch Mose*, 41–42 on the other). The conceptual proximity between Gen 1 and the Mesopotamian creation myth concerning the creation of the sky, as well as the articleless use of the term תהום suggest this assumption.

over it.[133] Beside this strong conceptual similarity between the two compositions, however, there are also differences. Whereas Marduk violently cuts Tiamat in two after a battle, in the biblical story the separation of the waters is achieved peacefully: God speaks and the firmament emerges from the midst of the waters. In addition, according to the Babylonian tradition the upper waters are retained by a skin[134] and not by a plate or firm vault (Heb. רקיע).[135] These differences suggest that the author of Gen 1:1–2:1* was referring critically to Enuma Elish.

On the whole, Gen 1:1–2:1* seems to share more similarities and points of contact with Egyptian cosmologies. The concept of creation by divine word, expressed in the word account, is central to the theology of Memphis as it is attested in the engraved text on the seventh century BCE Shabaka Stone.[136] Remarkably, the Egyptian material depicts the heavens as a metallic firmament, too. The Egyptian term bjꜣ refers both to the heavens ("sky pool") and to the metal iron,[137] leading M. Görg to conclude that the conception of the sky (רקיע, "plate, firmament") in Gen 1:6–8 is influenced by the Egyptian term bjꜣ.[138] In Mesopotamian literature this concept is not attested.[139] Moreover, the concept of the relationship between the primordial world and the creator God of Gen 1:1–2:1* is closer to Egyptian conceptions insofar as the latter do not contain the motif of a fight between the sea (*Nun*) and the emerging god (sun, *Rê*). The primordial world and creation are not seen in diametric opposition as they are in Enuma Elish: in many Egyptian creation myths, the same god who preexists in indetermination and latency afterward manifests himself in his determined form.[140]

---

[133] Thus the translation of the Akkadian term *PAR-ku-lu maš-ku* in J. Bottéro, *Mythes et rites de Babylone* (Paris: H. Champion, 1985), 132; B. R. Foster, "Epic of Creation," *COS* 1:390–402, particularly 398 ("hide"); *CAD* 17.1:22. Others have proposed the reading *per-ku*, "lock"; see P. Talon, *The Standard Babylonian Creation Myth Enuma Eliš*, SAACT 4 (Helsinki: Neo-Assyrian Text Corpus Project, 2005); E. A. Speiser, "Akkadian Myths and Epics: The Creation Epic," *ANET* 67 ("bar"). Yet the meaning of the verb preceding the noun, *šadādu*, "to pull taut, to stretch" (cf. *CAD* 17.1:21–22), supports the first understanding. I thank J.-M. Durand for his helpful comments concerning this question.

[134] See Enuma Elish IV 139.

[135] רקיע is derived from רקע and denotes a beaten metal plate or bow (vault); see *HALOT* 1290; T. H. Gaster, "Heaven 1," *ABD* 3:551; M. Görg, "רָקִיעַ *rāqîaʿ*," *TDOT* 13:646–53.

[136] Yet the tradition may date back to the time of the Ninetheenth Dynasty (2500 BCE). See J. P. Allen, "From the Memphite Theology," *COS* 1:21–23.

[137] Cf. E. Graefe, *Untersuchungen zur Wortfamilie bj3* (Cologne: University of Cologne, 1971), 40–66; J. P. Allen, "The Cosmology of the Pyramid Texts," in *Religion and Philosophy in Ancient Egypt*, ed. W. K. Simpson (New Haven: Yale University Press, 1989), 9.

[138] Görg, "רָקִיעַ *rāqîaʿ*," 673; cf. V. Notter, *Biblischer Schöpfungsbericht und ägyptische Schöpfungsmythen*, SBS 68 (Stuttgart: Katholisches Bibelwerk, 1974), 74–75.

[139] The motif is also found in Zoroastrian literature (cf. M. L. West, *The East Face of Helicon: West Asiatic Elements in Greek Poetry and Myth* [Oxford: Clarendon, 1997], 140) and in Greek poetry (Homer mentions χάλκος, "copper," and σιδήρος, "iron," as sky materials; for χάλκος, cf. *Iliad* 17:425; for πολύχαλκος, *Iliad* 5:504; *Odyssey* 3:2; σιδήρος, *Odyssey* 5:303).

[140] Cf. especially the conceptions of the Hermopolitan cosmogony, according to which the sun was born from the lotus or from the original egg; cf. S. Sauneron and J. Yoyotte, "La

Genesis 1:2 expresses a similar concept, if we understand the term רוח אלהים as "spirit of God" or "wind of God" and identify it with the creator god (1:3).[141] The latter is present but inactive in the primordial world before he begins to act by his word. Another striking similarity lies in the fact that God first creates the light in the biblical account, parallel to the first stage of the Egyptian cosmogony, the emergence of the sun.

Another important Egyptian parallel is the idea that man is the image of God, attested in the Teaching for King Merikare (P 132).[142] Still more frequent is the motif that the king is the image of a deity.[143] In some Mesopotamian texts, the expression ṣalmu (cf. צלם in Gen 1:26–27) is used for the king (but not for a common man) as the "image" of a deity too. In this respect, A. Schellenberg's observation that the expression is used only in (a few) casual texts is important; the contention that the Assyrian king's godlikeness was a "dogma" is unfounded.[144]

Given these various commonalities and parallels, it is likely that the author of Gen 1:1–2:1* (primary account) was familiar with both Egyptian and Babylonian creation traditions but was influenced more by the former than by the latter. Yet, the fact that the biblical account has its own characteristics and differs in some aspects from both of these other traditions shows that its author wanted to develop his own original conception,[145] such as the high value of humans and the emphasis on the goodness of the creation.

1.5 Relationship to Other Biblical Compositions, Time Setting (Primary Account)

In addition to Egyptian and Babylonian influence, we must also reckon with the impact of other Israelite traditions on Gen 1:1–2:1*. The peculiar motif of the gathering of the waters "into *one* place" (אל מקום אחד) appears in the creation of the sea (Gen 1:9).[146] It may express the utopian idea that in the creation the sea – the embodiment of

---

naissance du monde selon l'Égypte ancienne: La naissance du monde," in *Sources Orientales I: La naissance du monde* (Paris: Éditions du Seuil, 1959), 51–62.

[141] Some translators and commentators prefer to render רוח אלהים as "a terrible wind" or "a divine wind"; see, e.g., NJB; WESTERMANN, *Genesis 1–11*, 147–50. But the verb רחף *piel*, which refers to a rather quiet movement ("hover and tremble"; see *HALOT* 1219–20 and Deut 32:11), supports the translation "breath of God" or "spirit of God"; see, among others, SEEBASS, *Genesis I*, 60–61.

[142] M. LICHTHEIM, "I. Instructions. Merikare," *COS* 1:65; KEEL and SCHROER, *Schöpfung*, 178–79.

[143] See KEEL and SCHROER, *Schöpfung*, 178–79.

[144] A. SCHELLENBERG, *Der Mensch, das Bild Gottes? Zum Gedanken einer Sonderstellung des Menschen im Alten Testament und in weiteren altorientalischen Quellen*, ATANT 101 (Zurich: TVZ, 2011), 106–13.

[145] See also WESTERMANN, *Genesis 1–11*, 150.

[146] Or, according to 4QGen[h1], LXX, "to one gathering" (אל מקוה אחד); see the discussion of the textual difference above, II.1.2.2 (d).

frightful and chaotic powers – was restricted to one unique place.[147] Perhaps the creation account also alludes to the "cast sea" (ים המצוק) in Solomon's Temple (see 1 Kgs 7:23–26, 44; 2 Kgs 25:16; Jer 52:20; and 2 Chr 4:2–6). The parallels and commonalities between Gen 1:1–2:1* and these texts are remarkable:[148] In 1 Kgs 7:23–26, the repeated designation for the basin is "sea" (ים, 3×; 2 Chr 4:2–6, 4×). At several additional points the temple basin is further specified as "the *one* sea" (הים האחד, 1 Kgs 7:44; 2 Kgs 25:16; הים אחד, Jer 52:20). It seems that the notion of "*one* unique sea" was also significant for the authors of the texts 1 Kings 7:23–26, 44; 2 Kgs 25:16 (and parallels).

The idea of the delimitation of the sea by God in Gen 1:9–10 can be compared with the particular design of the basin in the temple: the twelve bulls carrying (holding) the basin represent the supporting and limiting force of the weather god (YHWH).[149] The molten sculpture does not show any signs of a struggle between the deity and the sea and resembles the peaceful limitation of the waters by God in Gen 1:9–10. This concept differs from that of the violent *Chaoskampf* found in Enuma Elish (see above), in the Ugaritic Baal Yam myth, and also in certain biblical passages dealing with the confrontation between YHWH and the chaos power of the sea.[150]

Like other installations in the Solomonic Temple, the design of the molten sea evidences Phoenician and Egyptian influence. The basin's "brim was made like the brim of a cup, as a lotus blossom" (שפת כוס פרח שושן; 1 Kgs 7:26). The particular shape of the bronze basin fits well with the two pillars, Jachin and Boaz, whose tops were lotus designs as well (1 Kgs 7:22). The lotus, having important symbolic value in Egyptian mythology, often appears in ancient Egyptian and Phoenician decorations (ninth–eighth century BCE). It is attested as an ornament in wall paintings (Kuntillet 'Aǧrûd) and ivories (Samaria) in Palestine as well (eighth century BCE). The report of the temple's construction is often dated to the Neo-Assyrian period (eighth or seventh century BCE).[151]

This complex tradition-historical background and proposed influences may give some hints as to the time of the composition of Gen 1:1–2:1*. Given the parallels with the Babylonian epic Enuma Elish, which are frequently emphasized, and the undifferentiated classification of Gen 1 as a composition of P^G/P^C, scholars have often taken (and continue to take) a setting in the late Neo-Babylonian or early Persian period for granted. Yet, the affinities to Egyptian cosmology and to an architectural element of

---

[147] See above, II.1.3.3, II.1.3.9.

[148] See HUTZLI, "Überlegungen zum Motiv," 10–16.

[149] Cf. O. KEEL and C. UEHLINGER, *Göttinnen, Götter und Göttersymbole: Neue Erkenntnisse zur Religionsgeschichte Kanaans und Israels aufgrund bislang unerschlossener ikonographischer Quellen*, 5th ed. (Freiburg im Breisgau: Herder, 2001), 192: the bulls belong to the sphere of the weather god.

[150] Isa 27:1; 51:9–10; Pss 74:13–14; 89:10–11; 104:7–9; Job 9:13; 26:12.

[151] Cf. I. FINKELSTEIN and N. A. SILBERMAN, *David and Solomon: In Search of the Bible's Sacred Kings and the Roots of Western Civilization* (New York: Free Press, 2006), 157–58; A. MAZAR, "The Search for David and Solomon: An Archaeological Perspective," in *The Quest for the Historical Israel: Debating Archaeology and the History of Early Israel*, ed. I. Finkelstein, A. Mazar, and B. B. Schmidt, ABS 17 (Atlanta: SBL Press, 2007), 129.

the preexilic temple suggest that an earlier setting – in the monarchic era – should be considered for the primary composition of Gen 1:1–2:1* (word account).

1.6 Relationship between Genesis 1 and Genesis 2–3

In the past, the two creation accounts in Gen 1:1–2:4a and Gen 2:4b–3:24 have primarily been compared by means of their differences. This trend was certainly the result of the assignment of the two accounts to two different sources in the framework of the Documentary Hypothesis. But in recent years, some studies have highlighted the commonalities and similarities between the two compositions.[152] Most important among these common points and parallels are the resemblance of man to God;[153] the reference to the plurality of God;[154] shared expressions such as אלהים,[155] פרי, עץ, עשׂב, נפשׁ חיה, אדם; and the importance of animals (also with similar terminology).[156] Though it is unsurprising that some of the expressions are used in both stories, given that they are generally frequent terms, it is particularly striking that in the entire Hebrew Bible, נפשׁ חיה occurs only in Priestly texts, Gen 2–3, and once in Ezekiel.[157] Yet there are also important conceptual differences between the two accounts. Notably, the sequence of works is different; in Gen 1 man is created as the last of God's creatures, whereas in Gen 2–3 man is first. Taken together, the linguistic and thematic points common to both units are remarkable and may favor the idea that one composition depends on the other.[158] Treatment of the question of direction of dependence must consider the redactional growth of both stories, and the point of departure for the investigation is the two primary accounts. As in Gen 1:1–2:4a, there are also indications that Gen 2:4b–2:24was reworked.[159]

---

[152] Cf., among others, OTTO, "Die Paradieserzählung"; SCHELLENBERG, Der Mensch, 238–43; R. HECKL, "Die Exposition des Pentateuchs: Überlegungen zum literarischen und theologischen Konzept von Genesis 1–3*," in Ex oriente Lux: Studien zur Theologie des Alten Testaments; Festschrift für Rüdiger Lux zum 65. Geburtstag, ed. A. Berlejung and R. HECKL (Leipzig: Evangelische Verlagsanstalt, 2011), 3–37; BÜHRER, Am Anfang, 275–375.

[153] Cf. Gen 1:26–27 and 3:5, 22.

[154] Gen 1:26–27 and 3:22.

[155] See below, n. 161.

[156] Gen 1: חית הארץ; עוף השמים/עוף; Gen 2–3: חית השדה; עוף השמים. Gen 1, in contrast to Gen 2–3, also mentions the sea animals.

[157] See Gen 1:20, 21, 24, 30; 2:7, 19; 9:10, 12, 15, 16; Lev 11:10, 46; Ezek 47:9.

[158] This question becomes increasingly important in the analyses of both texts. See the cited literature above, n. 152.

[159] Concerning the following consideration, see the detailed argument in J. HUTZLI, "Transgression et initiation: Tendances idéologiques et développement littéraire du récit de Genèse 2–3," in Tabou et Transgressions: Actes du colloque organisé par le Collège de France, Paris, les 11 et 12 avril 2012, ed. J.-M. Durand, M. Guichard, and T. Römer (Fribourg: Presses Universitaires; Göttingen: Vandenhoeck & Ruprecht, 2015), 124–27.

Interpreters generally agree that the story in Gen 2:4b–3:24 is connected to several J (non-P)[160] narratives in the primeval history. In addition to the use of the Tetragram as the designation for God, a common characteristic of these stories is the strong opposition between YHWH as a harsh deity on one hand and disobedient and transgressing humankind on the other. However, the analysis of important motifs in Gen 2–3 leads to the conclusion that this story differs theologically in important ways from the postulated J texts in Gen 1–11, indicating that it was not composed as an integral part of that narrative. Important in this respect is the observation that the transgression is not seen negatively in the primary account of Gen 2–3. Both the man's praise of Eve (3:20) and the fact that the serpent's prediction in 3:4–5 is proven correct (3:22) hint at a more positive perception of the first couple's act. Certain ideological features and linguistic elements of Gen 2–3 are typical for the J stratum as well, but they are all concentrated in the section on the couple's investigation and punishment by YHWH God (3:8–19, 24). Since this passage stands in tension with its context, it should be assigned to a redactional layer (J). The unusual double name יהוה אלהים alongside the single אלהים may also hint that only אלהים was used as the designation of God in the primary account of Gen 2–3* – another reason to dissociate the primary story from the J strand.[161]

The narrative in its present, enlarged form probably belongs to a larger J narrative comprising the subsequent stories of fratricide (Gen 4) and of the tower of Babel (Gen 11:1–9). Concerning its ideology, the supposed addition in Gen 3:8–19 fits well with these stories.[162]

(a) Relationship between the Two Primary Accounts (Genesis 1:1–2:1*; Genesis 2:4b–3:24)

It is interesting that in both units these commonalities and pointed conceptual differences belong to the ostensible primary account. If in fact the two texts are genetically related to one another, it seems more probable that Gen 2:4b–3:24* depends on Gen 1:1–2:1* than the other way around. There are indeed indications that the author of Gen 2–3 was interacting with the creation story in Gen 1. One such hint is the introduction in 2:4b, through which the author sets the story in the context of the creation of the world ("earth and heaven").

---

[160] Since in the primeval narrative the non-P units share several linguistic and ideological characteristics and are mutually interconnected, I prefer the conventional sigla J and Jˢ as designations for these texts (in the section Gen 1–11). See above I.2.7.

[161] According to a theory espoused by the majority of scholars, the particular double designation יהוה אלהים functioned to facilitate the transition between Gen 1 (P), where אלהים is used consistently, and Gen 2–4, where יהוה originally stood alone. The element אלהים would have been added by a later redactor after P and J/non-P were combined. However, one might wonder why the redactor did not continue his harmonizing revision in Gen 4 (where, except for 4:25, only the Tetragram is used). Furthermore, the fact that אלהים always appears as an element of the designation of God in Gen 2–3, whereas יהוה is absent in a few places (Gen 3:1, 3, 5 [2×]), suggests that the single designation אלהים was used in the primary (pre-J) account; see EERDMANS, *Alttestamentliche Studien*, 78–79; LEVIN, *Der Jahwist*, 82–83; and HUTZLI, "Transgression," 116–17.

[162] On this supposedly oldest layer of the J texts, see SCHMID, *Literaturgeschichte*, 153–56, and below, II.2.5.

Genesis 2:4b–5a

[4b] At the time when YHWH God made earth and heaven, [5a] there was as yet no wild bush on the earth nor had any wild plant yet sprung up.

The statement in v. 4b should be considered the opening of the Gen 2–3 account. The following verses (Gen 2:5–6) cannot have this function; the passage depends on 2:4b.[163] It is tempting to interpret the given setting "in the time" (literally, "in the day"[164]) as a reference to the creation story of Gen 1:1–2:1* (in particular when compared with Gen 2:1, 4a).[165] The deviation from Gen 1 in the wording of Gen 2:4b can be explained as follows: The inverse order of the two nouns might reflect the author's application of Seidel's law.[166] Furthermore, the fact that earth precedes heaven in 2:4b (cf. Gen 2:1, 4a and Gen 1:1) is due to the importance of the earth in the plot of Gen 2–3; man, trees, and animals are shaped "from the soil of the ground" (2:7; cf. 2:19 and 3:19).[167] The heavens do not play any role in Gen 2–3.[168]

Genesis 3 could also be understood as a midrash on the more concise statement of Gen 1:26 (and 27) where the resemblance of humankind to God is concerned,[169] demonstrating concretely how humans are godlike (humankind participates in wisdom and is able to discriminate between what is useful and what is useless; they own a sense of shame) and how their relationship to God is ambiguous and even problematic (the first couple loses the intimate proximity to God).

A further indication of the priority of Gen 1:1–2:1* is its reception in biblical

---

[163] Cf. W. Gross, *Die Pendenskonstruktion im biblischen Hebräisch*, ATSAT 27 (St. Ottilien: EOS Verlag, 1987), 54.

[164] The time indication "the day," which stands in tension with the creation being accomplished in seven days according to Gen 1:1–2:4a, might reflect an early stage in the literary development of Gen 1, before the insertion of the seven-day formulary. According to our analysis, the six/seven-day schema belongs to the second Priestly redaction. See above, II.1.3.6 (c) and II.1.3.10.

[165] Thus Otto, "Die Paradieserzählung," 188 (who, however, considers 2:4a and 2:4b to be unified).

[166] I thank S. Shectman for pointing to this argument.

[167] Cf. Bosshard-Nepustil, *Vor uns die Sintflut*, 287.

[168] The term שׁמים, "heaven," appears only in the designation of the birds ("birds of the heaven"; cf. Gen 2:19, 20).

[169] Cf. de Pury, "P^G as the Absolute Beginning," 28–30.

compositions like Second Isaiah;[170] Deut 4;[171] and Pss 33, 104, 136, 148 (see above, II.1.3.9). The relationship of Gen 1 to some of these biblical compositions is disputed, and the results of the present analysis, which reckons with two different layers, render evaluation of the relationship even more complicated. Nevertheless, each of these texts bears indications that at least some of the statements in question presuppose the word account as the original composition of Gen 1. This evidence contrasts with the absence of clear literary echoes of Gen 2–3* in the Hebrew Bible. Texts like Job 15:7 and, in particular, Ezek 28 share motifs and themes with Gen 2–3, but because of the conceptual differences between these texts, scholars are reluctant to assume direct dependence of one text on the other.[172] Similarly, linguistic and thematic commonalities with late sapiential literature are not specific enough to assume a direct dependence between these texts and Gen 2–3*.[173] The first explicit references to Gen 2–3

---

[170] As highlighted by M. WEINFELD, "God the Creator in Genesis 1 and in the Prophecy of Second Isaiah," *Tarbiz* 37 (1968): 105–32 (Hebrew), and B. D. SOMMER, *A Prophet Reads Scripture: Allusion in Isaiah 40–66*, Contraversions: Jews and Other Differences (Stanford: Stanford University Press, 1998), 142–45, several texts in Second Isaiah share motifs and expressions with Gen 1. The two authors interpret the commonalities as polemical allusions to the Priestly creation account. Weinfeld's and Sommer's studies have not found much positive resonance in European scholarly research. This may be due to the fact that they do not pay enough attention to the immediate context, which is partly a polemic against idolatry (cf. T. LINAFELT, review of *A Prophet Reads Scripture: Allusion in Isaiah 40–66*, by B. D. Sommer, *JQR* 90 [2000]: 501–4). Nevertheless, Weinfeld's and Sommer's argument is convincing for the following two texts: Isa 45:7 states that YHWH created everything, not only the "good" but also the "evil." Shared expressions with Gen 1:2–3 are אור, "light," and חשך, "darkness." Furthermore, the expression רע, "evil," opposes the term טוב, "good, beautiful," a key word in God's repeated approbation of his own work in Gen 1. Second Isaiah's statement in 45:18–19 seems to be formulated with regard to both Isa 45:7 and Gen 1:2. The statement that God did not create the world as chaos (תהו, Isa 45:18) can be understood as a certain distinction regarding the assertion in Isa 45:7. Even if it is true that YHWH created everything – even darkness and evil – he did not create the earth as a waste place (תהו), and he does not reside in the dark (חשך, v. 19). The situation seems to be similar to many other passages in which Second Isaiah interacts with biblical texts and is dependent on them. Thus it is probable that the two statements (Isa 45:7, 18–19) were written with Gen 1 as reference text. The idea that the elaborate conception of the primordial world and the first creation act in Gen 1:2–3 would depend on the two *single and rather disparate* statements in Second Isaiah is less probable. For this direction of dependence between the two texts, see also R. ACHENBACH, "Das Kyros-Orakel in Jesaja 44,24–45,7 im Lichte altorientalischer Parallelen," *ZABR* 11 (2005): 181; J.-D. MACCHI, "'Ne ressassez plus les choses d'autrefois': Esaïe 43,16–21, un surprenant regard deutéro-ésaïen sur le passé," *ZAW* 121 (2009): 231.

[171] Deut 4:32 presupposes Gen 1:26–27. Deut 4:16b–19 may depend on Gen 1:14–27, as M. FISHBANE, *Biblical Interpretation in Ancient Israel* (Oxford: Oxford University Press, 1985), 321–22; and E. OTTO, *Deuteronomium 1–11*, 2 vols., HThKAT (Freiburg im Breisgau: Herder, 2011–12), 1:534–35, 564–66, argue, although the terminologies of the two passages are quite different. For instance, the expressions מים מתחת לארץ, צפר כנף אשר תעוף, בהמה אשר באדץ do not appear in Gen 1 (against E. OTTO, *Deuteronomium 1–11*, 534).

[172] For a useful overview of the scholarly discussion of the relationship between the three texts, see BÜHRER, *Am Anfang*, 355–69.

[173] On these commonalities and parallels, see, among others, OTTO, "Die Paradieserzählung";

appear in early Jewish literature from the second and first centuries BCE (Sir 25:24; Wis 2:23–24).[174] Taken together, these observations favor the idea that the primary composition in Gen 2–3 depends on Gen 1 (the recognizable primary kernel in Gen 1:1–2:1*) and interacts with it.

(b) Relationship of Genesis 2:4b–3:24 (Final Form) to Genesis 1

When considering Gen 2–3 in its present form, that is, the reworked composition by J, one is aware of further elements of the story interacting with the Priestly creation account. The added negative view of the transgressive act, visible in the drastically and uniformly negative description of the consequences of the latter (3:8–19, 24), reveals that the redactor (J) set the story of Gen 2–3 in contrast to the positive image of humankind and the world expressed in Gen 1. In a more general way, one might define the task that the author of Gen 2:4b–3:24 set himself as explaining "how evil could insinuate itself into a creation declared redundantly (seven times) to be good."[175]

K. Schmid, "Die Unteilbarkeit der Weisheit: Überlegungen zur sogenannten Paradieserzählung und ihrer theologischen Tendenz," *ZAW* 114 (2002): 21–39.

[174] Cf. K. Schmid, "Loss of Immortality? Hermeneutical Aspects of Genesis 2–3 and Its Early Receptions," in *Beyond Eden: The Biblical Story of Paradise and Its Reception History*, ed. K. Schmid and C. Riedweg, FAT II/34 (Tübingen: Mohr Siebeck, 2008), 65.

[175] Blenkinsopp, "Post-Exilic Lay Source," 54.

2. The Genealogy in Genesis 5

2.1 Introduction

Except for two short passages, 5:1b–2 and 5:29aβb, the genealogy of Gen 5 is commonly ascribed to the Priestly composition. Scholars often argue that the peculiar opening phrase, "this is the record of the descendants of Adam" (זה ספר תולדת אדם, 5:1a), presupposes a "book" or "record" of *tôlĕdōt*, the ostensible source of Gen 5 and other P genealogical texts as well.[1] In addition to these questions concerning the unity of Gen 5 and its presumed *tôlĕdōt*-record *Vorlage*, scholarship dealing with Gen 5 often focus on three further problems: the discrepancies between the main text witnesses (MT, SP, LXX) with regard to the ages of various ancestors, the relationship of the genealogy to the Sumerian King List, and the relationship to the genealogies in Gen 4, with which Gen 5 shares several names.

This chapter will address these questions and will deal with the composition of the genealogy as a whole, which is crucial for the treatment for the aforementioned problems. It will describe the global scheme of the genealogy of Gen 5 and list some striking alterations of it.[2]

2.2 Significant Textual Variants

The problem of the various textual differences has been extensively dealt with in scholarship on this unit. Most striking are the numerous discrepancies in the characters' ages in three main textual witnesses. A minor difference concerns the etiology of Noah's name.

(a) Age Indications

Most scholarly evaluations of the differences between the three main textual witnesses have mainly been in service of the quest for a "system" or rationale for the numbers given in Gen 5 and 11:10–26 and other Priestly texts. For instance, some have tried to connect the numbers to Babylonian mathematics and astronomy.[3] Others have argued

---

[1] Eerdmanns, *Alttestamentliche Studien*, 4–5; G. von Rad, *Die Priesterschrift*, 35; Cross, *Canaanite Myth*, 301; Weimar, "Die Toledot-Formel," 84–87; Blum, *Die Komposition*, 451–52, n. 29; Carr, *Reading*, 71–73.

[2] The present discussion of Gen 5 is a thoroughly reworked version of J. Hutzli, "The Procreation of Seth by Adam in Gen 5:3 and the Composition of Gen 5," *Sem* 54 (2012): 147–62.

[3] See Barnouin, "Recherches numériques," 347–65.

that they are part of an overall chronology covering several parts of the Hebrew Bible and directed toward important events and dates in the biblical narrative and in the real history of postexilic Judah and Samaria.[4] For methodological reasons, it seems more appropriate to limit analysis to the data in Gen 5,[5] and we must consider the possibility that Gen 5 forms a system in its own right, conceived independently of remote Priestly texts in the ancestral narrative, in Exodus and beyond that also provide chronological information.

(1) Tendency of Diminishment in the Three Main Textual Witnesses

The point of departure for the treatment of this complex problem is table 1 outlining a tendency toward steady decrease expressed through the chosen numbers in SP. This tendency is only partly visible in the MT and in LXX.

In SP, the patriarchs' ages at the procreation of their firstborn and at their death diminish evenly from generation to generation.[6] There are three exceptions to note: Kenan's life span (910) surpasses that of his father Enosh (905); Enoch, holding the seventh position in the genealogy, has the shortest life span (365 years); and Noah, the last patriarch in the list, lives longer as all his predecessors.

In contrast, in MT and LXX this steady diminishment is observable only in the first half of the genealogy (though Kenan's long life span, when compared to that of his father, forms an exception in both MT and LXX).

MT agrees with SP for the first five patriarchs and for Enoch and Noah. In the second half of the genealogy, however, MT has much higher numbers for Jared, Methuselah, and Lamech; in particular, the patriarch's age at the birth of the first child is much higher than in SP (+ 100, + 120, and + 129, respectively).

LXX agrees with SP only for Noah. As for the other nine patriarchs, the first indicated age (age when the first child is born) is greater by 100 or 135 (Lamech). The numbers of the remaining years are correspondingly reduced by 100, except those of Jared, Methuselah, and Lamech. The overall effect is similar to MT: the life spans of Jared, Methuselah, and Lamech are massively increased (in comparison with SP).

(2) What Could Be the Rationale behind the Three Texts?

Samaritan Pentateuch

As for SP, the steady diminishment in the men's ages, with the two exceptions of Enoch (extremely low age) and Noah (extremely high age), may correspond to the decrease in morality and justice and the increase of violence that is explicitly described in the subsequent unit of the Priestly strand (Gen 6:11–12).[7] The negatively connoted names

---

[4] See above, I.2.5.

[5] See above, I.2.5.

[6] See DILLMANN, *Die Genesis*, 123; RÖSEL, *Übersetzung als Vollendung*, 130.

[7] Similarly, K. BUDDE, *Die biblische Urgeschichte (Gen 1–12, 5)* (Giessen: J. Ricker, 1883),

Table 1.   The ages of the antediluvian ancestors according to Genesis 5; 7:6, 11; 9:28–29

	MT				SP				LXX			
	a	b	c	d	a	b	c	d	a	b	c	d
Adam	130	800	930	*930*	130	800	930	*930*	230	700	930	*930*
Seth	105	807	912	*1042*	105	807	912	*1042*	205	707	912	*1142*
Enosh	90	815	905	*1140*	90	815	905	*1140*	190	715	905	*1340*
Kenan	70	840	910	*1235*	70	840	910	*1235*	170	740	910	*1535*
Mahalalel	65	830	895	*1290*	65	830	895	*1290*	165	730	895	*1690*
Jared	162	800	962	*1422*	62	785	847	*1307*	162	800	962	*1922*
Enoch	65	300	365	*987*	65	300	365	*887*	165	200	365	*1487*
Methuselah	187	782	969	*1656*	67	653	720	*1307*	167	802	969	*2256*
Lamech	182	595	777	*1651*	53	600	653	*1307*	188	565	753	*2207*
Noah	500	*450*	950	*2006*	500	*450*	950	*1657*	500	*450*	950	*2592*
Year of flood				*1656*				*1307*				*2242*

a: Age when first child is born
b: Remaining years
c: Ancestor's age at death
d: Date of ancestor's death (in relation to the *anno mundi*)
italics: Derived data (not explicitly stated in the text)

of three patriarchs Jared, Methuselah, and Lamech, who belong to the second half of the genealogy, who have the lowest ages (when disregarding Enoch), and who die in the year of the flood, indicate that this rationale is inherent to the composition of Gen 5 (independent of the specific text form):

Jared: Different suggestions are offered: *yrd*, "to descend," as an element of a personal name appears in West Semitic. R. S. Hess supposes "a shortened form of a name with a divine element (which would request or give thanks for a heavenly deity descending to aid)."[8] Other suggested meanings are "slave" (< Akk. *wardu*)[9] and "rose" (< Arab. *ward*),[10] but these are less probable: *wardu* as an element of a name never appears in West Semitic (it is replaced by the root *ʿbd*), and ורד, "rose," does not occur in Classical Hebrew.[11] If the name does in fact derive from West Semitic *yrd*, "to descend," then the artificial character[12] of the genealogy suggests that it is metaphoric, meaning "decline" or "descent (to Sheol)."[13] In the Hebrew Bible, the lexeme ירד may indicate social decline (Deut 28:43; Jer 48:18; Lam 1:9).[14] This meaning seems fitting insofar as

89–130; SEEBASS, *Genesis I*, 181; BÜHRER, *Am Anfang*, 333–35.
    [8] R. S. HESS, *Studies in the Personal Names of Genesis 1–11*, AOAT 234 (Kevelaer: Butzon & Bercker; Neukirchen-Vlujn: Neukirchener Verlag, 1993), 69–70.
    [9] *HALOT* 435.
    [10] M. NOTH, *Die Israelitischen Personennamen im Rahmen der gemeinsemitischen Namengebung*, BWANT 3 (Stuttgart: Kohlhammer, 1928), 231.
    [11] HESS, *Studies*, 69.
    [12] On the differentiation between "primary" (authentic) and "secondary" (artificial) genealogies, cf. M. NOTH, *A History of Pentateuchal Traditions*, trans. B. W. Anderson (Englewood Cliffs, NJ: Prentice Hall, 1972), 214–19.
    [13] Thus BUDDE, *Die biblische Urgeschichte*, 100; SEEBASS, *Genesis I*, 181; BÜHRER, *Am Anfang*, 334.
    [14] See BUDDE, *Die biblische Urgeschichte*, 100.

the name opens this second half of the genealogy and precedes two other names with possible negative meanings (see below). Furthermore, the manifold connections between Gen 5 and the Sumerian King List suggest that Jared might be compared with Dumuzi the shepherd, who holds the fifth or sixth position in the Sumerian King List and whose name alludes to Dumuzi's fate: having been murdered, the latter descended (Akk. *arādu*) to the netherworld.[15]

Methuselah: The name מתושלח contains two elements: *mt*, "man, husband," and *šlḥ.* The meaning of the second element is disputed: it is identified as a weapon, a canal, or a divine name ("man of the God Selah").[16] The first meaning ("weapon") should be preferred to the others,[17] as it is attested in several biblical texts.[18] This interpretation may gain further support from the fact that in the Sumerian King List (postdiluvian section), the expression "weapon" ($^{giš}tukul$) appears regularly in the stereotyped phrase evoking the martial conflict causing the fall of a city and its dynasty ("the city A was smitten with weapons; its kingship was carried to the city B").[19] One may conclude that Methuselah's name probably means "man of the weapon." Again, the manifold parallels and shared motifs with the Sumerian King List suggest that Gen 5 was influenced by it.[20]

Lamech: As will be shown below, there are strong indications that the genealogy of Gen 5 depends on genealogical lists in Gen 4. If correct, the name Lamech certainly recalls the violent character of his namesake in the Cainite genealogy (see the "bragging" sword song 4:23).[21]

In contrast to these three "negative" names in the second half of the genealogy, no "negative" names appear in the first half of the list, and one name is obviously "positive": *Mahalalel* means "the praise of God" or "God is shining."[22] *Kenan* is also reminiscent of Cain from Gen 4. However, the fact that the names Cain and Kenan differ from each other – in contrasts to the case of Lamech – may indicate that the author of Gen 5 intended to disassociate the two.[23]

Two positive figures belonging to the second, negative half of the SP genealogy contrast the otherwise visible tendency of decline: Enoch and Noah. Both must be saved

---

[15] See below, II.2.4.1.

[16] Cf. HESS, *Studies*, 70–71.

[17] Thus also BUDDE, *Die biblische Urgeschichte*, 99; SEEBASS, *Genesis I*, 181–82; BÜHRER, *Am Anfang*, 334.

[18] The meaning "weapon" is attested in Joel 2:8; Neh 4:11; 2 Chr 23:10; 32:5. The understanding as divine name is highly speculative; neither of the supposed deities is attested in the ANE ("man of the God Selah," cf. M. TSEVAT, "The Canaanite God Šalaḥ," *VT* 4 [1954]: 41–49, and "man of the God Laḥ," cf. A. VAN SELMS, "A Forgotten God: LAḤ," in *Studia Biblica et Semitica Theodoro Christiano Vriezen*, ed. W. C. van Unnik and A. S van der Woude [Wageningen: H. Veenman, 1966], 318–26).

[19] Cf. T. JACOBSEN, *The Sumerian King List*, AS 11 (Chicago: University of Chicago Press, 1939), 85–125: col. II, 45–47; col. III, 37–39; col. IV, 5–7, 17–19, 36–38, 43–44; col. V, 1–2, 15–16, 21–22, *et passim.*

[20] See below, II.2.4.1.

[21] Similarly BUDDE, *Die biblische Urgeschichte*, 102, n. 1; SEEBASS, *Genesis I*, 181; BÜHRER, *Am Anfang*, 334.

[22] Cf. *HALOT* 553.

[23] As will be shown below, all numbers attributed to the name of Kenan, and its spelling as well, have an affinity with the number seven (see II.2.4.2 [a]). This probably points to Gen 4:15: YHWH promises Cain that in order to protect him he would be willing to avenge him seven times. Understood in this way, the name's connotation is rather positive.

by the deity from the upcoming catastrophe. Noah nevertheless fits the general correlation between age and moral behavior. The fact that he reaches the highest age among the patriarchs corresponds to his characterization in the flood story as the (most) "blameless and righteous man in his generations" (Gen 6:9). Enoch's exceptional case should be explained by the fact that the author of Gen 5 closely follows the Mesopotamian tradition of the antediluvian patriarchs. Enoch, the seventh patriarch, corresponds to Enmeduranki, who holds an exceptional and positive position in the Sumerian king list because of his privileged contact with the divine world (Šamaš and Adad). That Enoch is modeled on this figure is suggested by the choice of the symbolic number 365 for the years of his lifespan – with its connection to the sun – and by the detail that he "walked with" (had intimate contact with) the deity (5:22, 24); see further below 2.4.1.

Masoretic Text

In contrast to SP, MT seems to intentionally break the correlation between life span and moral state. The author's (scribe's) intention is clearly expressed by the fact that the patriarch attaining the greatest age here, Methuselah, is the only one who dies in the flood; he belongs to the unrighteous "generations" living at the time of Noah (see 6:9). Significantly, his life span surpasses that of righteous Noah (in SP it is Noah who attains the greatest age). The case of Methuselah suggests that MT contests the equation of (extremely) long life with goodness and agreeableness to God.

Septuagint

Providing a unique rationale, LXX prolongs of the entire period of the antediluvian patriarchs, which is effected by the massive lengthening of the patriarchs' ages at the birth of the first child. The flood happens in *anno mundi* 2242 (SP: 1307; MT: 1656). As in MT, the correlation between life span and moral state is disturbed by the abrupt increase in age for Jared and Methuselah. This massive increase creates a problem in relation to the subsequent flood story, because Methuselah survives the flood.

(3) Which Text Is More Original?

The fact that the life spans in SP fit the negative connotations of the names of the three patriarchs Jared, Methuselah, and Lamech may hint at the originality of the numbers in SP as an expression of regular decline and an allusion to the death of these three figures in the flood.

Furthermore, there is a strong indication that the deviating data in MT (and similarly in LXX) is secondary and depends on SP. In the three cases where MT deviates from SP, the age of the relevant ancestor (Jared, Methuselah, Lamech) at the birth of the firstborn *abruptly* rises by 100 or more years (Jared's age) compared with the steadily diminishing numbers found in SP. This irregularity in MT smacks of a deliberate modification of the numbers by a scribe of proto-MT. The deviation in LXX is analogous and should be explained in the same way.

(4) Klein's and Hendel's Explanation

A different explanation of the differences between the three main textual witnesses is offered by R. W. Klein and Hendel.[24] The starting point for their discussions is the observation that the differences between the primary witnesses mainly concern the second half of the genealogy and, furthermore, that in LXX Methuselah survives the flood. From these particularities they deduce that in the original text Jared, Methuselah, and Lamech survived the flood, so that in all three of the extant primary textual traditions scribes modified the numbers in order to avoid a clash between the deaths of these patriarchs and the date of the flood's onset. Thus, according to Klein and Hendel, none of the existing textual traditions preserve the original data concerning these three specific patriarchs. But by evaluating all the existing textual differences, both scholars are confident in their ability to reconstruct the original text. The guiding criteria for this evaluation are, first, the premise that each of the three patriarchs survived the flood (see above) and, second, the quantitative criterion that prioritizes agreement between two main witnesses against a third that deviates. However, there are certain difficulties with Klein's and Hendel's argument. First, the accumulation of differences between the main textual witnesses in the passages about Jared, Methuselah, and Lamech does not necessarily point to an original text form in which the three patriarchs survived the flood. (Klein's and Hendel's confidence in reaching this conclusion is in fact astonishing.) The concentration of disagreements between the witnesses in these three entries may be due to the scribes' interest in the question of who among the three patriarchs died before or during the onset of the deluge and, furthermore, in the question of the correlation between age and moral behavior (see above). Second, since Gen 5 culminates in Noah and his procreation of Shem, Ham, and Japheth, it probably presupposes the subsequent flood story, which reports the exclusive salvation of Noah, his wife, his three sons, and his three daughters-in-law.[25] It is therefore problematic to assume that the author of the primary text would have let the data about the patriarchs clash with the date for the beginning of the flood.

(b) Etiology of Noah's name: Genesis 5:29

MT: זה ינחמנו ממעשנו
SP: זה ינחמנו ממעשינו
LXX: οὗτος διαναπαύσει ἡμᾶς ἀπὸ τῶν ἔργων ἡμῶν
       זה יניחנו ממעשינו =

In the name's etiology offered in MT and SP, the lexeme נחם *piel* does not match well

---

[24] R. W. KLEIN, "Archaic Chronologies and the Textual History of the OT," *HTR* 67 (1974): 255–63; HENDEL, *Text of Genesis 1–11*, 61–71; IDEM, "Hasmonean Edition," 448–64.

[25] On the relationship between Gen 5 and the Priestly flood story, see below, II.2.4.2 (b).

with the name of Noah and its association with נוח, "to rest."[26] But the name's explanation is, as often in the Hebrew Bible, a popular etymology based on assonance. The
piel of נחם, "to comfort, to give consolation," probably alludes to Noah's invention of
viticulture. This makes good sense in the context of the reference to the curse of the
land and the pain of labor (Gen 3:17).

Since LXX renders נחם in the *niphal* (with the sense "to be comforted") and *piel*
("to comfort") four times in Genesis with appropriate equivalents,[27] the translator
most probably read not ינחמנו but a form of נוח, presumably יניחנו (< נוח *hiphil*), "(this
one) will cause us to cease (from our works)."[28] The explanation fits with the name's
supposed etymology; yet since the prediction will not be fulfilled in the subsequent
narratives dealing with the famous patriarch, the reading does not match the broader
literary context. For this reason, the variation in LXX's *Vorlage* should be considered
secondary; probably it constitutes a correction with regard to the meaning of the
name נח.

2.3 The Question concerning the Unity of the Composition: The Threefold Scheme of Genesis 5 and Some Alterations of It

The genealogy of Gen 5 is characterized by a regular structure with a three-part
scheme that is repeated for each patriarch. There are nevertheless several striking
and subtle deviations from this scheme. According to the predominant scholarly view,
some or most of the deviating passages are due to secondary redactional activity.

The genealogy contains nine passages concerning the first nine patriarchs (Adam–
Lamech). They are followed by a tenth passage concerning Noah which begins in 5:32
and continues in and after the flood story (7:6 and 9:28–29). The first nine passages
each display a three-part scheme consisting of the following elements:[29]

    I: *a* lived *x* years, and begot *b*,
   II: *a* lived after he begot *b y* years, and he begot sons and daughters,
  III: all the days of *a* were *z* years; then he died.

A shared characteristic of the passages is the omnipresent and dominant indication
of the patriarchs' ages and life phases, which is firmly anchored in the syntax of the
phrases. However, here and there this regular structure is disturbed. The deviations
are as follows:

---

[26] See *HALOT* 684–85.
[27] Gen 24:67 (παρακαλεῖν); 37:35 (παρακαλεῖν); 38:12 (παρακαλεῖσθαι); 50:21 (παρακαλεῖν).
[28] See Rösel, *Übersetzung als Vollendung*, 128.
[29] For a similar description of the scheme, cf. T. Hieke, *Die Genealogien der Genesis*, HBSt
39 (Freiburg im Breisgau: Herder, 2003), 70.

(a) After the title "This is the record of the descendants of Adam" (5:1a), before the first passage talking about Adam's offspring (5:3), a passage referring back to the creation of Adam in Gen 1:26–27 is inserted (5:1b–2).

(b) In the passage on Adam, element I is expanded (5:3b), and the naming of Seth is mentioned. Furthermore, the beginning of element II (ויהי ימי) constitutes a minor modification of the regular introductory form (ויחי).

(c) In the passage on Enoch, elements II and III are altered (5:22–24), the text reporting that Enoch walked with God and, at the end, that God "took him."

(d) In the passage on Lamech, element I of the scheme (concerning the birth of Noah) is expanded (5:28–29); 5:28–29aα contains an insertion, similar to the one in the passage on Adam (see b, above), mentioning the naming of Noah.

(e) The continuation of the verse, v. 29aβb, alludes to the invention of wine by Noah (Gen 9:20) and the curse of the earth by YHWH (Gen 3:17).

(f) In the passage about Noah (5:32), the way in which his age is indicated at the moment of his first procreation (element I) differs from the other passages. Noah is a "son" (בן) of 500 years (in the other passages the verb חיה is used). The verses containing elements II and III are split off from chapter 5, appearing in (7:6) or after (9:28–29) the flood story and explicitly referring to the flood.

In the following examination of each passage containing a deviation, special attention will be given to the question of the literary-historical relation of each deviation to the overall composition of Gen 5.

(a) Deviation a: The Retrospective on Genesis 1 in Genesis 5:1b–2

Scholars often attribute the first modification, the retrospective in Gen 5:1b–2, to a harmonizing redactor.[30]

Genesis 5:1b–2

¹ᵇביום ברא אלהים אדם בדמות אלהים עשה אתו ² זכר ונקבה בראם ויברך אתם ויקא
את שמם אדם ביום הבראם

¹ᵇ In the day that God created humankind, in the likeness of God made he him;
² male and female created he them; and blessed them, and called their name humankind, in the day when they were created.

The passage shows striking parallels to Gen 1:27–28 (identical or similar expressions include the verb ברא, the term בדמות אלהים, the phrase זכר ונקבה בראם, and the benediction expressed by the lexeme ברך *piel*). Naming (cf. 5:2), however, does not occur in the creation of man/Adam in Gen 1. In 5:1b–2, *ʾādām* is a generic term just as in Gen 1:26–28: the suffix of *ʾōtām* refers to a plurality of individuals (men and women).

---

[30] H. HOLZINGER, *Genesis*, KHC 1 (Freiburg im Breisgau: J. C. B. Mohr, 1898), 58–59; SKINNER, *Genesis*, 130; WESTERMANN, *Genesis 1–11*, 480; WENHAM, *Genesis 1–15*, 122; J. A. SOGGIN, *Das Buch Genesis* (Darmstadt: Wissenschaftliche Buchgesellschaft, 1997), 114.

In this respect, 5:1b–2 differs from v. 3, where ʾādām is a personal name, as it is also in the title of the chapter ("This is the record of the descendants of Adam," 5:1a). This is the main reason that this passage (5:1b–2) is often attributed to a secondary redaction linking this text to Gen 1.[31] The motivation for linking back to Gen 1 was to recall the generic meaning of אדם in Gen 1:26–28 and to mitigate the contradiction between Gen 1 and Gen 5 regarding the understanding of אדם. This need for an explicit link to the opening story in Gen 1 was perhaps felt only after the combination of the Priestly with the non-Priestly strand. (Read within a separate Priestly or proto-Priestly document, 5:1b–2 – which would follow shortly after the statement of 1:26–28 – would be oddly redundant.)[32]

(b) Deviation b: The Procreation of Seth by Adam (5:3)

In Gen 5:3–5, on Adam, element I of the scheme is specified in few words (highlighted):

Genesis 5:3

³ ויחי אדם שלשים ומאת שנה ויולד בדמותו כצלמו ויקרא את שמו שת

³ And Adam lived a hundred and thirty years, and begot <u>in his own likeness, after his image; and called his name</u> Seth

The particular form בדמותו כצלמו corresponds, with a slight variation (inverted word order), to the term בצלמנו כדמותנו in 1:26.[33] Furthermore, this verse presents a philological difficulty, which is mentioned or discussed in commentaries but which has never been solved. It relates to the fact that the phrase "and begot in his own likeness, after his image" (ויולד בדמותו כצלמו) is not followed by an accusative object (see the literal translation above). Commentators usually deal with the difficulty by arguing that the sentence presupposes the direct object בן, "son,"[34] or that the expression was omitted accidentally.[35] But both explanations lack conviction. Elsewhere, I have sug-

---

[31] Cf. the scholars mentioned in the previous footnote.

[32] See R. Rendtorff, "L'histoire biblique des origines (Gen 1–11) dans le contexte de la rédaction 'sacerdotale' du Pentateuque," in Le Pentateuque en question: Les origines et la composition des cinq premiers livres de la Bible à la lumière des recherches récentes, ed. A. de Pury (Geneva: Labor et Fides, 1989), 83–94; Soggin, Das Buch Genesis, 114.

[33] A remarkable number of manuscripts of the MT family, however, contain a form analogous to 1:26 (בצלמו כדמותו). This reading is clearly harmonistic.

[34] Dillmann, Die Genesis, 125; L. Pirot and A. Clamer, La Sainte Bible, I: Genèse (Paris: Letouzey et Ané, 1953), 166; Speiser, Genesis, 40; U. Cassuto, A Commentary on the Book of Genesis, Part I, 277; Wenham, Genesis 1–15, 119–20; Westermann, Genesis 1–11, 469–70; L. Ruppert, Genesis: Ein kritischer und theologischer Kommentar, 4 vols., FB 70 (Würzburg: Echter, 1992–2008), 1:240; Soggin, Das Buch Genesis, 114; Seebass, Genesis I, 178, n. b.

[35] Holzinger, Genesis, 59; Gunkel, Genesis, 135; Skinner, Genesis, 130, n. 3; G. von Rad, Das erste Buch Mose: Genesis, 11th ed., ATD 2–4 (Göttingen: Vandenhoeck & Ruprecht, 1981), 53. Numerous scholars insert the word son in their translations without justifying the change: J. Chaine, Le livre de la Genèse, LD 3 (Paris: Cerf, 1947), 85, 87; W. Zimmerli, 1. Mose 1–11, 4th

gested that the author deliberately omitted the word *son*.[36] He may have done so to indicate that Adam fathered not a male but an asexual or androgynous being. That Seth is the image of Adam and the latter is, according to 1:26, the image of Elohim (God) may provide more support for this interpretation. There is no reason to imagine the god of Gen 1 as a sexual being, and as a prototype for humans (אדם) we should consider him an asexual or androgynous being.[37] If this is the case, then Adam and Seth, who are based on the "image prototype" of the creator, must also be asexual or androgynous beings.[38] Furthermore, according to Gen 5:1a, 3, Adam has no wife. The author seems to have had in mind that Adam realized the procreation alone, as a "self-procreation." This interpretation proceeds from the assumption that the author of Gen 5* is not the same as that of Gen 1 (and that of 5:1b–2, see above). In his understanding of *ʾādām* as a proper name, this author, perhaps drawing on Gen 4 (see 4:25), deliberately deviates from the use of *ʾādām* as a generic term in Gen 1:27–28.

What, then, is the function of this verse with regard to the larger genealogy? Are the following patriarchs also androgynous beings? Or is it assumed that after Adam and Seth, Enosh opens the series of explicitly masculine descendants? After the section on Adam, element I of the scheme, "x lived y years and he begot z," is consistently used until the passage on Lamech, the ninth patriarch (v. 28). However, the specification בדמותו כצלמו is not. Moreover, after the procreation of the first child, all patriarchs – from Adam on – procreate "sons and daughters." This provides the prerequisite for ordinary sexual reproduction from the time of Seth on. These observations suggest that among the ten antediluvian patriarchs, only Adam procreates "in his own likeness, after his image"; the following members of the genealogy all just "father."[39]

The godlikeness expressed in Gen 5:3 is understood differently by other scholars. G. J. Wenham, for instance, states: "This verse makes the point that the image and likeness of God which was given to Adam at creation was inherited by his *sons*."[40] The

---

ed., ZBK 1.1 (Zurich: TVZ, 1984), 247–48; N. Sarna, *The JPS Torah Commentary: Genesis* (Philadelphia: Jewish Publication Society, 1989), 42; V. P. Hamilton, *The Book of Genesis, Chapters 1–17*, NICOT (Grand Rapids: Eerdmans, 1990), 246; A. Schüle, *Die Urgeschichte (Genesis 1–11)*, ZBK 1.1 (Zurich: TVZ, 2009), 104.

[36] Hutzli, "Procreation."

[37] In Egypt, certain ancestral (creator) gods were conceived as androgynous (cf. W. Westendorf, "Götter, androgyne," *ÄL* 2:633–35; S. Sauneron, "Le créateur androgyne," *Mélanges Mariottes* 32 [1961]: 242–44). In Mesopotamian tradition, the Sumerian high gods are considered father and mother, husband and wife in one person; Ishtar could have been considered feminine and masculine (see E. Ebeling, "Androgyn," *RlA* 1:106–7).

[38] However, as for the verb ילד hiphil, "to procreate," which in most cases is related to the act of procreation *by a man*, one may ask if the occurrence of this verb does not necessarily presuppose the masculine sexuality of its subject. The lexeme is not always used in a sexual sense but sometimes also means "produce, bring forth" (cf. Job 38:28: God makes the dew; Isa 59:4: men bring forth evil; cf. also Sir 11:33; 41:9 and Gesenius 18th ed. 2.465).

[39] In Hutzli, "Procreation," I argue with regard to the occurrences of the noun *son* in Gen 5:28–29aα, 32 that all listed ancestors who precede Noah are androgynous beings.

[40] Wenham, *Genesis 1–15*, 127 (emphasis mine).

godlikeness is considered a gift to all the patriarchs in Gen 5 and, by extrapolation, to *all* humans. This commonly accepted interpretation certainly depends on 1:26–27, which is understood in this general, "democratic" sense (in contrast to Mesopotamian and Egyptian royal ideology). However, other statements belonging to passages that deviate from the normal pattern in Gen 5 concern only a specific patriarch and should not be generalized. The information concerning Enoch and that concerning Noah distinguish them from the other patriarchs. This point may speak for the proposal made here and against the common interpretation of godlikeness in Gen 5:3.[41]

(c) Deviation c: Enoch Walks with God and Doesn't Die (5:22, 24)

In the passage on Enoch, elements II and III are altered. The expression ויתהלך את האלהים, "and he walked with God," replaces "he lived" (5:22, element II) and "he died" (5:24, element III). At the end of the passage, the narrator reports that Enoch disappeared "because God took him." Later, in the story of the flood, the expression "to walk with God" appears again as an attribute of Noah. Both Enoch and Noah are acquainted with particular knowledge from the divine realm. As will be shown below, the biblical figure Enoch is shaped after the Babylonian antediluvian hero Enmeduranki.[42] Since several common features connect Gen 5 to Mesopotamian traditions about the antediluvian epoch,[43] the shared motif of Enoch and Enmeduranki – an ancestor/king in intimate contact with a god – should be assigned to the author of Gen 5 rather than to a later redactor.

(d) Deviations d and e: Lamech's Procreation of Noah (5:28–29)

Element I of the scheme is altered for Lamech in Gen 5:28, 29aα, much like Gen 5:3 with its derivation of the global scheme (see above, deviation b). In both verses, an insertion occurs in exactly the same place, referring to naming ("and he called"). This similarity between Gen 5:3 and 5:28–29aα should be attributed to the same literary level. Both passages may be later additions, though there is no clear indication that this is the case.

What about v. 29aβb, then, the assertion concerning Noah's wine production and YHWH's curse of the earth? The name of YHWH and the explicit recourse to J (non-P) texts in this verse lead scholars to agree that it represents a non-P (J) insertion.[44] To

---

[41] Should the motif of godlikeness, as in Gen 1:26, be understood in a broader sense, that is, in the sense that it refers not only to physical form and neutral gender but also to function and task? According to a common interpretation of the statement in 1:26 that man is made in (like the) divine image, man is God's personal representative on earth (see, for instance, VON RAD, *Das erste Buch*, 46–47, and WENHAM, *Genesis 1–15*, 30–31). If godlikeness in Gen also 5 has an ethical dimension, it would be tempting to correlate the fact that godlikeness ends after Seth with the general tendency of decline expressed by the numbers and certain names in the genealogy.

[42] Cf. below, II.2.4.1.

[43] Cf. below, II.2.4.1.

[44] Against this, one may argue that the composition interacts extensively with other non-P

this we may add that the etymology for Noah does not have a parallel either in Gen 5:3 or in Gen 5 in general. For these reasons, 5:28 (with 29aα) on the one hand and the reference to two J motifs in 29aβb on the other probably do not belong to the same literary layer. Originally, element I of the scheme included only vv. 28–29aα and was immediately followed by element II (v. 30):

> Genesis 5:28–29aα, 30
> [28] And Lamech lived a hundred and eighty and two years, and begot a son. [29aα] And he called his name Noah. [30] And Lamech lived after he begot Noah five hundred and ninety-five years, and begot sons and daughters.

A reassessment of the tendency and aim of the secondary, "J-like" statement in v. 29aβb is needed. Theologically, it clearly deviates from the J story of Gen 4. An interesting structural parallel between both compositions is that Lamech is the only patriarch to whom a saying is attributed. In Gen 4, Lamech's sword song constitutes the climax of the violence's increase. In Gen 5, however, Lamech ostensibly is interested in the well-being of humanity and thus expresses an attitude of philanthropy.[45] A possible reason for Lamech's positive image in this secondary passage might be his fatherhood of Noah.

(e) Deviation f: Noah's Procreation of Three Sons (5:32)

Noah's entry at the end of the genealogy in Gen 5 is incomplete (5:32). It comprises only element I of the scheme, reporting the procreation of three sons. Elements II and III are split off from the composition in Gen 5 and are found in (7:6) or after (9:28–29) the flood story. Both explicitly refer to the flood. Strikingly, element I reports the procreation of three main descendants rather than only one. Furthermore, the formulation of element I deviates from the general pattern: instead of the expected formulation "Noah lived x years," we find "Noah was x years old" (lit., "was a 'son' of x years"). How to deal with these deviations from the global scheme?

The differences are mainly due to the plot of the following Noah narrative, in which Noah's three sons are important figures (they are mentioned twice by name, in 6:10; 7:13). This means that the composition of Gen 5 presupposes the flood narrative and is conceived in relation to it. The deviation concerning the formulation of the age is peculiar. One might ask whether the author intends to underline that Noah begot the three sons at the same time (that is, that they are triplets). As for the main deviation – the procreation of three sons – it leads the genealogy toward its climax, a high point that is also underlined by the naming of Noah by Lamech (see above, deviation d). Its function as a fitting climax suggests that 5:32 (together with 7:6 and 9:28–29) should be considered an original part of the composition.[46]

(J) texts, in particular with Gen 4, and is dependent on them (see below, II.2.4.2). However, the allusions are never so explicit as in the case of v. 29aβb.

[45] SEEBASS, *Genesis I*, 184.

[46] *Contra* SEEBASS, *Genesis I*, 185, who argues that 5:32 would be a later redactional insertion.

(f) Summarizing Remarks

In sum, we can conclude that most of the modifications (a–f) to the global scheme of the genealogy of Gen 5 belong to the original composition; exceptions are the retrospective to Gen 1:26–27 in 5:1b–2 and the "J"/non-P element in 5:29aβb. The composition of Gen 5 is characterized by a regular structure, every passage including the same three elements. However, in certain places one or two elements are varied. These formal characteristics – rigid structure and redundancy on the one hand and sudden aberration and specification on the other – are present in related Mesopotamian genealogical lists and chronicles as well.[47]

2.4 Literary Connections of Genesis 5

Obviously, Gen 5 positions itself as a continuation of the Priestly creation story in Gen 1 and as the starting point of the flood story. In comparison to Gen 1, however, it is noticeable that the author of Gen 5 changes the generic term ʾādām = "human(s)" to the proper name Adam. As mentioned above, because of this difference, it must be assumed that the two compositions are the work of two different authors. Gen 5 shares the use of ʾādām as a proper name with the genelaogy in Gen 4 (cf. 4:1, 25). Since the two lists have other names in common, it will be important to examine the literary relationship between the two compositions. Does Gen 5 depend on Gen 4, or is the opposite direction of dependence to be assumed? Or are the two units independent of each other, as many think (see 2.4.2 below)? In terms of its genre and structure, however, Genesis 5 is closer to the Mesopotamian tradition about the antediluvian kings. Again, the question arises whether Gen 5 is directly influenced by this tradition (see 2.4.1).

2.4.1 Dependence on Mesopotamian Traditions about the Antediluvian Era

Several scholars have observed that the genealogy of Gen 5 shares several common features with Mesopotamian traditions on the antediluvian era. Similarities appear in the lists of antediluvian kings[48] and certain texts about antediluvian sages.[49] Scholars agree on a number of correspondences:

---

[47] In WB 444 (Extended Sumerian King List; cf. Jacobsen, *Sumerian King List*; J.-J. Glassner, *Mesopotamian Chronicles*, SBLWAW 19 [Atlanta: SBL Press, 2004], 117–27), the determinative *dingir* precedes certain royal names ("the divine Dumuzi," "the divine Gilgamesh"). The motif of elevation to the heavens also appears. For certain kings, a profession, an important deed, or their fate is indicated.

[48] WB 62, WB 444 (Extended Sumerian King List), Ni 3195, UCBC 9 1819, Dynastic Chronicle (Babylonian Chronicle), Berossos, W 20 030:7 (Uruk tablet); cf. H. S. Kvanvig, *Primeval History: Babylonian, Biblical, and Enochic; An Intertextual Reading* (Leiden: Brill, 2011), 90–99.

[49] Lists of the Seven Apkallus, cf. Kvanvig, *Primeval History*, 107–17; Adapa, cf. Kvanvig, *Primeval History*, 117–29; Enmeduranki and the Diviners, cf. W. G. Lambert, "The Qualifications

– The extremely long reigns of the kings and the extraordinarily old ages of the patriarchs.
– The number of individuals mentioned in the list (kings and patriarchs). There are, however, several variations of the Sumerian King List, the number of the kings listed being either eight, nine, or ten.
– In both the Sumerian King List and Gen 5, one member is related to the sun god/sun. Enmeduranki, sometimes in seventh place in the list, is associated with Sippar, the center of the sun god.[50] According to Enmeduranki and the Diviners, Šamaš and Adad introduce Enmeduranki to the divine assembly and initiate him in the secrets of divination.[51] As for Enoch, the seventh patriarch of the genealogy of Gen 5, the number of years of his life (365, corresponding to the number of days in a year) points to the sun as well. Furthermore, he is in close contact with God (see the repeated phrase "and Enoch walked with God," 5:22, 24).[52] The 365 years of Enoch's life may indicate the author's interest in the calendar, with a preference for the sun and the solar year.[53] Alternately, this number might have been chosen just to interact with Enmeduranki. Enoch's being taken up to heaven is unparalleled in any statement about Enmeduranki. Rather, this motif is influenced by the immortality of the flood hero (Utnapishtim) in the Gilgamesh Epic. As John Days notes, in both traditions the taking-up is expressed by the same verb, "to take" (Hebrew לקח and Akkadian *leqû*).[54]
– In Gen 5, as in most extant versions of the Sumerian King List, the individual mentioned last is the surviving hero of the flood (Ziusudra, Noah).[55]

In addition to these acknowledged commonalities between Gen 5 and the Sumerian

---

of Babylonian Diviners," in *Festschrift für Rykle Borger zu seinem 65. Geburtstag am 24. Mai 1994*, ed. S. M. Maul, CM 10 (Groningen: Styx, 1998), 141–58; KVANVIG, *Primeval History*, 101–5.

[50] Sippar was a center of the sun god; cf. P. BIENKOWSKI, "Sippar," in *Dictionary of the Ancient Near East*, ed. P. Bienkowski and A. Millard (Philadelphia: University of Pennsylvania Press, 2010), 274.

[51] W. LAMBERT, "Qualifications," 141–58.

[52] GUNKEL, *Genesis*, 132, 135–36; SKINNER, *Genesis*, 132; BARNOUIN, "Recherches numériques," 348; and KVANVIG, *Primeval History*, 251–58, underline these common traits of Enoch and Enmeduranki of Sippar.

[53] Cf. KVANVIG, *Primeval History*, 254. In the P version of the flood story, one of the precise dates (2/27/601; Gen 8:14) alludes to the solar calendar (see below, II.3.2 [c]).

[54] See J. DAY, "The Flood and the Ten Antediluvian Figures," in *On Stone and Scroll: Essays in Honour of Graham Ivor Davies*, ed. J. K. Aitken, K. J. Dell, and B. A. Mastin, BZAW 420 (Berlin: de Gruyter, 2011), 218 (n. 31). See also GUNKEL, *Genesis*, 135. For the text of Gilgamesh (11:206), see A. R. GEORGE, *Gilgamesh: The Babylonian Epic Poem and Other Texts in Akkadian and Sumerian* (London: Penguin Books, 2003), 95: "And they took me and settled me far away, at the mouth of the rivers."

[55] Ziusudra is mentioned in all antediluvian king lists where the last part is preserved. In the Extended Sumerian King List, WB 444, however, he is not included; cf. KVANVIG, *Primeval History*, 99–100.

King List, further parallels and commonalities are not mentioned in recent commentaries and treatments of Gen 5:

- Jared (sixth position in Gen 5) may be compared with Dumuzi the shepherd (mostly fifth position in the Sumerian list of antediluvian kings, sixth position according to Berossos' *Babyloniaca*). As with its Akkadian cognate *arādu*, the Hebrew verb ירד is often used for descent into Sheol.[56] For this reason, the name Jared might allude to Dumuzi's tragic and violent destiny (he is murdered). As mentioned above, Jared is the first of three "negative" patriarchs in the second half of the genealogy whose names allude to violence and who will die in the flood.
- The name Methuselah ("man of the weapon"), which probably alludes to the violence causing the flood, might have been influenced by the Sumerian King List too: the expression "weapon" (*ᵍⁱˢtukul*) is used in the stereotyped phrase about the fall of a city of Sumer and its dynasty (in the postdiluvian section).[57]
- Finally, there is a "forgotten" correspondence. In the early twentieth century, the similarity of the name of the third antediluvian king in Berossos' list, Ἀμήλων (*amelōn*), to the Akkadian noun *amēlu* "man," was considered to hint at the dependence of the name Enosh, "man," in third position, and of Gen 5 more generally, on the Mesopotamian antediluvian tradition.[58] The discovery of older versions of the Sumerian King List made clear that the names in the lists were not Akkadian but Sumerian, and this argument was abandoned. Nevertheless, the coincidence remains striking, all the more so since the Greek spelling found in the *Babyloniaca* corresponds to the phonetic cuneiform spelling found in several Mesopotamian texts (*Am-me-lu-an-na*). According to J. J. Finkelstein, instead of the formally correct spelling *En-me-en-lú-a-na*, several texts have the identical or very similar "purely phonetic spelling" *Am-me-lu-an-na* (*Am-me-lú-an-na, Am-me-lú-a-n-na; Am-i-lu-a-n-na*).[59] Thus it cannot be ruled out that Enosh in Gen 5 is related to a Mesopotamian tradition that playfully connected the third king in the Sumerian King List with the Akkadian noun "man." Berossos's rendering Ἀμήλων might reflect such a tradition, which might have influenced the sequence Adam–Seth–Enosh (containing two names with the meaning "man") in Gen 5:1–11. In this case, the genealogy in Gen 4:25–26 would depend on Gen 5:3–11. Given certain linguistic differences between Gen 4:1–24 and 4:25–26, some ascribe the latter passage to a later redaction

---

[56] For Akk. *arādu*, cf. *CAD* 1.2:216.

[57] See above, II.2.2 (a) (2), with bibliographical references.

[58] Cf. H. ZIMMERN, "Urkönige und Uroffenbarung," in *Die Keilinschriften und das Alte Testament*, ed. E. Schrader, 2 vols. (Berlin: Reuther & Reichard, 1902–3), 2:531–32; GUNKEL, *Genesis*, 132; SKINNER, *Genesis*, 137.

[59] J. J. FINKELSTEIN, "The Antediluvian Kings: A University of California Tablet," *JCS* 17 (1963): 41–42. Cf. also JACOBSEN, *Sumerian King List*, 73, n. 18.

layer.[60] Genesis 5 would nevertheless remain dependent on the Cainite genealogy in Gen 4:17, 19–24 (see further below).

These commonalities (parallels), both the well-established and the less certain ones, clearly indicate the dependence of Gen 5 on Mesopotamian traditions.[61] Apart from these striking commonalities, Gen 5 has its own *propria*: it deals with patriarchs instead of kings. The biblical genealogy emphasizes the motif of godlikeness for Adam and Seth. A characteristic of the biblical genealogy is the steady decrease in the men's ages, with the two exceptions of Enoch and Noah (possibly corresponding to the decrease in morality and justice and the increase of violence as described in the subsequent Priestly flood story).

The visible structure of the Priestly primeval history (antediluvian patriarchs–flood–Table of Nations/postdiluvian patriarchs) might also have been inspired by Mesopotamian traditions (i.e., the Dynastic Chronicle).[62]

2.4.2 Relationship with Texts from the Biblical Primeval History

(a) The Relationship with Genesis 4 and with Other J (J^s) Texts in the Primeval History

Most of the names in Gen 5 are found in the genealogies of Gen 4:1, 17–26, some in a slightly different form; the arrangement differs as well. In addition, two names with the meaning "man, mankind" occur in close proximity in both Gen 5:1–11 and Gen 4:25–26 (Adam in first position and Enosh in third position). Many scholars deny the (direct) dependence of one text on the other.[63] However, the number of contacts between the two compositions favors the explanation that one version is a creative reworking of the other.

Two questions are relevant to the literary-historical relationship between shared (or similar) names in the two texts: (1) Which of the two contexts better fits the name in question? (2) Which name can be explained as a secondary development of the other? For certain similar or identical names, it seems likely that Gen 5 borrowed from the genealogy of Gen 4: Kenan, קינן, is the enlarged form of קין, Cain. Of the two names, only the latter is frequently attested as a personal name in Old South Arabian

---

[60] See below II.2.4.2 (a), with n. 81.

[61] With KVANVIG, *Primeval History*, 243, against, among others, WESTERMANN, *Genesis 1–11*, 199–201; RUPPERT, *Genesis*, 1:246–50.

[62] For the Dynastic Chronicle, cf. GLASSNER, *Mesopotamian Chronicles*, 119–27; KVANVIG, *Primeval History*, 91–92, n. 25.

[63] Among others, CARR, *Reading*, 68–69 (in Carr's view, the two texts "appear to be parallel versions" [69]); SEEBASS, *Genesis I*, 186; SCHÜLE, *Der Prolog*, 209; J. C. GERTZ, "Genesis 5: Priesterliche Redaktion, Komposition oder Quellenschrift?" in *Abschied von der Priesterschrift? Zum Stand der Pentateuchdebatte*, ed. F. Hartenstein and K. Schmid, VWGT 40 (Leipzig: Evangelische Verlagsanstalt, 2015), 82.

inscriptions (first millennium BCE);[64] it also occurs elsewhere in the Hebrew Bible (Num 24:21–22; Judg 4:11, associated with the Kenites). As a personal name, Kenan is attested only in (late) Safaitic idiom (first century BCE–fourth century CE) (*qnn*).[65] This favors the conclusion that Kenan is derived from Cain.[66]

Interestingly, Kenan's entry in the genealogy has an affinity to the number seven:[67] in all three main text witnesses (MT, SP, LXX), Kenan's age at death, 910, is divisible by seven. According to MT and SP, all three given numbers can be divided by seven.[68] Furthermore, the gematrial sum of the letters of Kenan's name, קינן, is divisible by seven as well (210). If not coincidental, this striking convergence may point to Gen 4:15, where YHWH, in order to protect Cain, is willing to avenge him seven times.[69]

Like Cain's name, two names that Gen 5 shares with Gen 4 – Enoch and Lamech – seem to fit a genuine Kenite genealogy as well and thus to be at home in the genealogy of Gen 4:17–24. Further biblical occurrences of the name Enoch point to a Transjordanian/Arabian provenance: bearers of this name are the firstborn of Reuben (Gen 46:9; Exod 6:14; Num 26:5; 1 Chr 5:3) and a son of Midian (Gen 25:4). Linguistically it is probably to be connected with Arabic *ḥnk*, "to be clever," or with Hebrew *ḥnk*, "to dedicate."[70] If the proposed derivation of Lamech from Arabic *yalmak* "young, powerful man"[71] is correct, the name fits well with the poem attributed to Lamech (4:23–24), which praises violent strength and disproportionate vengeance.[72]

The name Enosh (אנוש) seems more at home in Gen 4:25–26 than in 5:3–11. Crucial for this question is the presence of two names with the meaning "man, mankind" in close proximity (first and third position) at the beginning of Gen 5. This detail seems to be best explained as the result from the combination of the two genealogies in Gen 4:1–24 and 25–26 by the author of Gen 5.[73] In contrast to the odd sequence of the three first entries in Gen 5, the name of Enosh in Gen 4:26 in close vicinity to Adam makes good sense and serves an ideological function, pointing to the genesis

---

[64] Cf. Hess, *Studies*, 25–26.

[65] Cf. *HALOT* 1098.

[66] Concerning the name Cain, cf. Hess, *Studies*, 24–27, 37–39.

[67] Barnouin, "Recherches numériques," 352; Ziemer, "Erklärung," 12–13.

[68] Age at procreation of Mahalalel: 70; total of subsequent years: 840.

[69] Against the argument concerning the numbers, one might argue that the indication of age for Kenan is due to later redactional activity. However, the gematrial sum of the letters of Kenan's name seems to confirm at least the numbers for Kenan.

[70] Arabic *ḥnk*, "to be clever"; cf. W. F. Albright, "The Babylonian Matter in the Predeuteronomic Primeval History (JE) in Gen 1–11," *JBL* 58 (1939): 96.

[71] Cf. *HALOT* 523; Seebass, *Genesis I*, 168 ("possible").

[72] Another proposed derivation is Sumerian *lumga*: this name serves as the title of the deity Ea as patron of music. This association also fits with the genealogy of Gen 4:1, 17–24 rather than that of Gen 5. Lamech's son Jubal is the "father of those who play the lyre and pipe" (Gen 4:21). See Westermann, *Genesis 1–11*, 446.

[73] Cf. Wellhausen, Prolegomena zur Geschichte, 309; Kratz, *Composition*, 234; Hutzli, "Procreation," 148–49.

of a new (better) generation of humankind, as compared to the line Adam–Lamech: Enosh is a second Adam.[74]

Another possible (but less probable) explanation for the sequence Adam–Seth–Enosh in Gen 5:3–11 was mentioned above: the third member of the genealogy in Gen 5, Enosh, may be related to the name of the third king in the Sumerian Kings List, Enmenlúana. The phonetic spelling *Am-me-lu-an-na* is frequently attested for this name. The latter's proximity to the Akkadian noun *amēlu*, "man," may have provided the impetus for a tradition of interpretation that associated the third antediluvian ancestor with "man" (despite the fact that the names of the list are Sumerian). This tradition would then have influenced the author of Gen 5 in choosing the name אֱנוֹשׁ for the third member of his genealogy.[75]

Are there shared names (or name "pendants") in the two genealogies for whom the inverse direction of dependence seems more probable? E. Bosshard-Nepustil argues that the names Mehujael (מחייאל/מחויאל) and Methushael (מתושאל) in Gen 4 are dependent on the names Mahalalel (מהללאל) and Methuselah (מתושלח) in Gen 5.[76] In both names he sees allusions to all creatures being wiped out by YHWH in the flood (expressed by the root מחה, "to wipe out," in 7:23* non-P) and dying (cf. the occurrence of מתו, "[all] died," in 7:22 non-P). מְחוּיָאֵל) מחויאל) indeed can be read as "smitten by El."[77] The author of Gen 4:17–24 would have taken up the names Mahalalel and Methuselah in Gen 5 and modified them slightly. Commonly Mehujael is explained as meaning "God gives life,"[78] and Methushael is explained as "man of God."[79] Yet the second interpretation is not without difficulties,[80] and the possible affinities of the names with the non-P flood story that Bosshard-Nepustil points to are striking.

It is more difficult to determine the direction of dependence for the other name pairs (Seth/Seth; Jared/Irad) shared by Gen 4 and Gen 5.

How might Bosshard-Nepustil's considerations concerning the names Mehujael and Methushael, if correct, withstand the previous observations pointing to a dependence of Gen 5 on Gen 4? Two observations hint at a possible answer. First, the genealogy in Gen 4:1–2, 17–24 makes no other allusions to the flood narrative. Second, a closer look at the genealogy in Gen 4:1–2, 17–22, 25–26 reveals certain differences in the representation of the events of procreation and birth.

---

[74] Contrary to the genealogy of Adam–Lamech, which contains two gloomy tales, the line of Adam–Enosh clearly expresses hope. Cf. the explanation of Seth's name and the beginning of men calling on the name of YHWH; see DILLMANN, *Die Genesis*, 117; WENHAM, *Genesis 1–15*, 115; and in particular HESS, *Studies*, 67: "[Enosh's] obvious Hebrew etymology serves a literary function as the beginner of a new line of the descendants of Shet; i.e., as a second Adam."

[75] See the detailed discussion above, II.2.4.1.

[76] BOSSHARD-NEPUSTIL, *Vor uns die Sintflut*, 198.

[77] Cf. *HALOT* 586.

[78] מַחְיִיאֵל or מְחִיָּאֵל, (חיה participle, *piel* or *hiphil*); cf. *HALOT* 586; Gesenius 18th ed. 3.656–57; and HESS, *Studies*, 41–43.

[79] מת + שֶׁ + אֵל, cf. *HALOT* 654; Gesenius 18th ed. 3.763. Differently, HESS, *Studies*, 43–45 ("man of the god Shael").

[80] See HESS, *Studies*, 43–45.

Genesis 4:1–2, 17–22, 25–26

[1] Now the man knew [וידע] his wife Eve, and she conceived [ותהר] and gave birth to [ותלד את] Cain, and she said, "I have gotten a man-child with the help of YHWH." [2] And again, she gave birth to [ותלד את] his brother Abel. And Abel was a keeper of flocks, but Cain was a tiller of the ground.

[17] And Cain knew [וידע] his wife and she conceived [ותהר], and gave birth to [ותלד את] Enoch; and he built a city, and called the name of the city Enoch, after the name of his son. [18] Now to Enoch was born [ויולד ל] Irad; and Irad became the father [ילד] of Mehujael; and Mehujael became the father [ילד] of Methushael; and Methushael became the father [ילד] of Lamech. [19] And Lamech took to himself two wives: the name of the one was Adah, and the name of the other, Zillah. [20] And Adah gave birth to [ותלד את] Jabal; he was the father of those who dwell in tents and have livestock. [21] And his brother's name was Jubal; he was the father of all those who play the lyre and pipe. [22] As for Zillah, she also gave birth to [ותלד את] Tubal-cain, the forger of all implements of bronze and iron; and the sister of Tubal-cain was Naamah.

[25] And Adam knew [וידע] his wife again; and she gave birth [ותלד] to a son, and named him Seth, for, she said, "God has appointed me another offspring in place of Abel; for Cain killed him." [26] And to Seth, to him also a son was born [ילד ל]; and he called his name Enosh. Then men began to call upon the name YHWH.

The pattern וידע (ותהר), ילדה את/ותלד את is consistently used in 4:1–2 (with the subjects Adam and Eve); 4:17 (subjects Cain and his wife); 4:20 (subject Lamech's wife Adah); and 4:22 (subject Lamech's wife Zillah). In v. 18, however, which reports four births in a very concentrated form, this pattern is abandoned and, instead, other patterns are used (ויולד ל; 3× ילד with the father as subject).[81] For this reason, one should consider the possibility that v. 18 (except ויולד לחנוך) was inserted secondarily. Originally, Lamech would have been born to Enoch's wife. If correct, this would mean that Irad, too, was part of the secondary insertion (Irad would depend on Jared). What supports the reconstruction of this shorter genealogy is the fact that the references to Cain in the name Tubal-cain and in Lamech's song and the cultural achievements in vv. 20–22, an important goal of the genealogy, would be less remote from Cain's entry. If this reconstruction is correct, the genealogy in Gen 5 would depend on a more primary version of Gen 4, rather than its actual form.[82] The sequence Irad–Mehujael–Methushael would belong to a secondary redaction of Gen 4, reacting to the Priestly genealogy in Gen 5 and preparing for the non-Priestly flood story.[83]

---

[81] In the passage about Seth's and Enosh's births (4:25–26) the pattern is also slightly changed, but the difference is smaller (cf. ותלד and ילד *pual*, with the object בן).

[82] See the displayed text above: the passage that was presumably added secondarily is highlighted.

[83] Arguing for the dependence of Gen 5 on Gen 4 are WELLHAUSEN, *Prolegomena zur Geschichte*, 309; KRATZ, *Composition*, 234; HUTZLI, "Procreation," 148–49; WESTERMANN, *Genesis 1–11*, 473 (dependence on a tradition close to Gen 4). Arguing for the opposite direction of

The pattern masculine subject + יָלַד (= *w-x-qatal*) occurs often in the non-P genealogies that classical source division assigns to J (10:8–19, 21, 24–30; 22:20–24; 25:1–6).[84] According to Hendel, יָלַד *qal* with a masculine subject (with the meaning "to beget") constitutes an older form than יָלַד *hiphil*, which, at a certain time, would have replaced it (יָלַד *hiphil* is regularly used in Priestly genealogies).[85] Hendel cautiously argues that the evidence would support the diachronic priority of J in comparison to P.[86] However, the evidence is not as clear as Hendel makes it out to be. Epigraphically the lexeme יָלַד *qal* with a masculine subject is not attested. From all occurrences found in the Hebrew Bible eleven are found in the J/non-P passages in Genesis; the remaining five occurrences of יָלַד *qal* with masculine subject are found in late texts (see Zech 13:3; Dan 11:6)[87] or texts whose dating is disputed (Prov 17:21; 23:22, 24).[88] It is possible that יָלַד *qal* with a masculine subject constitutes an older form than יָלַד *hiphil*; but one should reckon with the possibility that later redactors used archaizing language.[89] As will be shown below, there are strong arguments that Gen 10 non-P, which contains several examples of the pattern masculine subject + יָלַד, should be classified as post-P (in agreement with several recent studies).[90] The texts with the pattern masculine subject + יָלַד (= *w-x-qatal*) in Genesis (4:18aβb; 10:8, 13, 15, 24, 26; 22:23; 25:3) should probably be assigned (at least some of them) to a common secondary stratum within the J strand of the primeval narrative (= J^s).

(b) Relationship with Priestly Texts in Genesis 6–11

The end of the genealogy mentioning Noah and his three sons (Gen 5:32) might lead one to conclude that Gen 5 is connected with the flood story and the Table of Nations in Gen 10 as well.[91] As seen above, three names in the second half of the genealogy probably allude to the flood: Jared ("descent, decline"), Methuselah ("man of the weapon"), and Lamech (recalls the sword-song of his namesake in Gen 4:23).[92] Methuselah's and Lamech's names hint at violence as the cause of the flood (Gen

---

dependence, see BLENKINSOPP, "Post-Exilic Lay Source," 55; BOSSHARD-NEPUSTIL, *Vor uns die Sintflut*, 197–99.

[84] Cf. all occurrences of the pattern masculine subject + יָלַד (*w-x-qatal*) in the book of Genesis: 4:18aβb (3×); 10:8, 13, 15, 24 (2×), 26; 22:23; 25:3.

[85] See HENDEL, "'Begetting,'" 39–42.

[86] See HENDEL, "Begetting," 46: "These data would seem to support the classical view that the J source is earlier than the P source (…). While the linguistic data for 'begetting' and 'being born' may not be sufficient to confirm any particular source-critical model, they do constitute data that require reckoning in any coherent source-critical argument of this type." See also HENDEL and JOOSTEN, *How Old Is the Hebrew Bible?*, 19, and R. S. HENDEL, "How Old Is the Hebrew Bible? A Response to Konrad Schmid," *ZAW* 133 (2021): 361–70.

[87] In Zech 13:3 father and mother together are the grammatical subject.

[88] Hendel is aware of Dan 11:6 but prefers to replace והילדה (MT: vocalized וְהַיֹּלַדְתָּהּ, "and who begot her") by וילדה (vocalized וְיַלְדָּהּ, "her child," conjecture), see HENDEL, "Begetting," 41, n. 6. As for Prov 17:21; 23:22, 24, he considers the possibility that these texts should be dated early (HENDEL, "Begetting," 42, n. 15).

[89] See above, I.2.6.2.

[90] See below, II.4.4 and II.4.5.

[91] Concerning Gen 5:32, see above, II.2.3 (e).

[92] See above, II.2.2 (a) (2).

6:11–13). According to the numbers provided by SP (the preferred reading), these three antediluvian patriarchs are killed by the flood. According to MT, Methuselah is the only antediluvian patriarch who is killed by the flood. These observations hint at a dependence of Gen 5 on the Priestly flood story. The former composition is directed to the latter.

Finally, let us note the great similarity in structure and vocabulary to the genealogy of Gen 11:10–26.[93] This genealogy links the biblical prehistory with the stories of the patriarchs. The fact that both genealogies lead up to an important patriarch in tenth position (Noah, Abraham[94]) illustrates their schematic and artificial character. Possibly both genealogies, Gen 5 and Gen 11:10–26, were inserted to link different parts (creation story, flood story, ancestral narrative) of the P strand. In my opinion, it is more likely that they constitute redactional elements that connect the somewhat disparate proto-P units (Gen 1*; Gen 6–10 P*; Priestly Abraham narrative) rather than stemming from an ancient source (a "book").

2.5 Conclusion:
The Literary Profile, Aim and Possible Chronological Setting of Genesis 5

With the two exceptions of the retrospective to Gen 1:26–27 in 5:1b–2 and of the supposed non-P element 5:29aβb, the genealogy in Gen 5 is a unified composition. Its structure and certain motifs demonstrate that it is dependent on Mesopotamian traditions. At the same time, the composition strongly interacts with other biblical texts, in particular Gen 4, which it contradicts. The title "This is the record of the *tôlĕdōt* " is – probably deliberately – misleading,[95] and its usage should be seen in the light of competition with the genealogy of the J strand. The author pretends to rely on an ancient and reliable tradition[96] (which is true in some sense because he is inspired by the Sumerian King List), but in reality Gen 5 is a young, redactional composition that aims to link the creation story with the flood story. This becomes apparent from several subtle hints at the continuing decline of antediluvian humanity. With regard to its transitional function, it raises the question whether the genealogy originally bridged solely the Priestly (or proto-Priestly) texts (creation story, flood narrative [P], Table of Nations [P]) or a fusion of P and J texts. The fact that the composition Gen 5* parallels

---

[93] Cf. below, II.5.

[94] However, the structure is not identical: whereas Noah marks the end of the genealogy in Gen 5, in 11:10–26 Abraham appears as one of the three sons of Terah, the ninth and last member of this genealogy.

[95] The existence of an originally independent and ancient "book of *tôlĕdōt* " was suggested by EERDMANNS, *Alttestamentliche Studien*, 4–5, and VON RAD, *Die Priesterschrift*, 35. The idea found great resonance in scholarship (see above, n. 1).

[96] In the Hebrew Bible, the term ספר frequently designates a historical record (diverse chronicles in 1–2 Kgs and 1–2 Chr; cf. also the "book of the upright" [Josh 10:13] and the "book of YHWH's wars" [Num 21:14]).

and contradicts[97] the two genealogies in Gen 4 (genealogy of Cain, genealogy of Seth) favors the first possibility. The composition Gen 1; 5; 6–10 may have constituted a counterconcept to the primeval narrative of J (Gen 2:4b–3:24; 4*; 11:1–9).

Certain indications favor the idea that the earliest J stratum in the primeval narrative once ran directly from Gen 2–4 to Gen 11:1–9.[98] (1) The following chapter on the flood story will show that the J layer (=Jˢ) of the flood narrative is fragmentary and depends on the Priestly strand (primary stratum). Jˢ takes up typical Priestly vocabulary, imitates Priestly style, and is influenced by Priestly theology.[99] The profile of the Jˢ passages strongly deviates from that of the J texts Gen *2:4b–3:24; 4*; 11:1–9, which constitute self-contained units and do not complement Priestly texts. (2) Gen *2–4 seems to be connected to the story of the tower of Babel (Gen 11:1–9). The beginning of the latter ties in with Gen 4:16 (by taking up the key word *east*).

Perhaps Gen 4:25–26 constitutes a later addition to the unit *4:1–24.

A characteristic of the primary J primeval story is the opposition between disobedient and transgressing humankind on the one hand and YHWH as a harshly punishing deity on the other.[100] Besides the main purpose of Gen 5 to fill the gap between the era of the (good) creation and the time of the flood, an important aim of its author was to correct the negative depiction of humans, in particular the image of Adam's firstborn in Gen 4.

The related genealogy of Gen 11:10–26 aims to connect the Priestly flood story and the Priestly patriarchal narrative. Because of certain differences in form (the absence of major deviations and the bipartite scheme of Gen 11:10–26), it is not sure that the two genealogies in Gen 5 and Gen 11:10–26 stem from the same author.[101]

Is the term ספר, "record, writing," in the superscription of Gen 5:1 to be understood in the sense of a relatively comprehensive writing including several tôlĕdōt (the tôlĕdōt of Noah, the tôlĕdōt of Noah's sons, and the tôlĕdōt of Terah, in addition to Gen 5), or was it intended to refer only to the list of the first nine descendants of Adam in Gen 5?[102] Either way, the particular deviation of the title ("this is the book of the tôlĕdōt" instead of "these are the tôlĕdōt") may hint at a distinct composition for Gen 5 when compared with the other (proto-)Priestly texts in Gen 1–11.

It is noteworthy that Gen 5 was open to and inspired by such a variety of traditions. In general, the assumed sexual neutrality or androgyny of the first individuals mentioned in the genealogy (alluded to in 5:3) is a rare motif in written ancient Near

---

[97] In the present arrangement, Gen 5 could be read as a resumption and continuation of the preceding genealogy in 4:25–26. The use of the same (or slightly modified) names in places other than Gen 4:1, 17–23, however, shows that the composition of Gen 5 represents a counterconcept with regard to the genealogy in Gen 4.

[98] For a good summary of the arguments, see SCHMID, *Literaturgeschichte*, 153–56.

[99] See below, II.3.6.

[100] See below, II.3.6 (b).

[101] See below, II.5.

[102] ספר can refer to a short deed, certificate (see Jer 32:10; Isa 50:1), or letter (2 Sam 11:14; 1 Kgs 21:8; 2 Kgs 5:5) or to an extensive document, such as a chronicle (*passim* in 1–2 Kings and 1–2 Chronicles); see *HALOT* 766–67.

Eastern sources about primordial history. Notable exceptions are a few writings from Persian, Hellenistic, and Roman times.

An example is Berossos, who mentions androgynous beings in his description of the primordial world in the first book of his *Babyloniaca* (I F1).[103] Berossos refers to a "time when the universe was only darkness and water," antemundane state of the world. The idea is similar to the motif of androgyny as it appears in Plato's *Symposium*, 189d–193d. Whereas Plato describes primordial beings as having one body but two heads – one male and the other female – Berossos refers to beings with two faces of different sex. Compared with these texts, Gen 5 is much less concrete. In Genesis Rabbah 8:1 (related to Gen 1:27 and 5:2), one finds the idea that the first man, Adam, is androgynous. This interpretation is due to the expression זכר ונקבה בראם, "male and female created he them" (Gen 5:2). However, as shown above, the suffix of *'ōtām* refers to a plurality of individuals (men and women). For this reason, this rabbinic interpretation has not found support in biblical scholarship.

Because Gen 5 was probably conceived for a separate proto-Priestly document, before the fusion of the P and J primeval narratives (see above), and given that the arrangement of P's primeval history is known and adopted by the Chronicler (see 1 Chr 1:1–27), one should not assume too late a date for its origin. A setting in the early or middle Persian period seems probable.[104]

---

[103] See G. VERBRUGGHE and J. M. WICKERSHAM, *Berossos and Menetho, Introduced and Translated: Native Traditions in Ancient Mesopotamia and Egypt* (Ann Arbor: University of Michigan Press, 1996), 45.

[104] Current scholarship on Chronicles has put forward several arguments for a setting in the (early) Hellenistic period; cf. H.-P. MATHYS, "Die Ketubim," in *Die Entstehung des Alten Testaments*, ed. W. Dietrich et al., Theologische Wissenschaft 1 (Stuttgart: Kohlhammer, 2014), 591–92.

3. The Priestly Flood Account in Genesis 6–9

3.1 Issues in Scholarly Debate

In the biblical flood story, the Priestly narrative thread is interwoven with the J or non-P stratum. Whereas the former represents a self-contained narrative, the latter is fragmentary, lacking an announcement of the flood, the order to build the ark, and the departure of the passengers from the ark. The literary-historical relationship between the two strata is controversial. Traditionally, the J or P passages are considered to represent independent sources (or parts of them), the two strata having been put together by a redactor. Analyzed that way, the biblical flood story served for a long time as a "prime example" of a biblical text composed of two identifiable, independent sources (J and P).[1]

This classical "two sources" model still has its adherents,[2] and it has been further developed: D. Carr and in particular M. Witte reckon with a more important contribution by the redactor who would have combined the two sources.[3] At the same time, alternative models have been proposed: P is a layer that complements non-P/J,[4] or, to the contrary, the non-P/J passages are an expansion of the Priestly "ground layer."[5] Moreover, scholars like C. Levin and J. Van Seters challenge the common verse-distribution between the two strands.[6] With regard to the complete and self-contained nature of P, the opinion of several scholars that the P text is the original kernel, with the J passages added secondarily, seems appropriate *prima facie*. However, this view is sometimes refuted by the argument that certain assertions in J (non-P) simply double

---

[1] Cf. CARR, *Reading*, 46. For decades, this model remained nearly unchallenged in scholarship.

[2] Cf. LEVIN, *Der Jahwist*, 103–17; J. VAN SETERS, *Prologue to History: The Yahwist as Historian in Genesis* (Louisville: Westminster John Knox, 1992), 160–65; SEEBASS, *Genesis I*, 199–241, in particular 228–40; N. C. BAUMGART, *Die Umkehr des Schöpfergottes: Zu Komposition und religionsgeschichtlichem Hintergrund von Gen 5–9*, HBSt 22 (Freiburg im Breisgau: Herder, 1999), 389–418.

[3] Cf. CARR, *Reading*, 57–60; IDEM, *Genesis 1–11*, IECOT (Stuttgart: Kohlhammer, 2021), 236; WITTE, *Die biblische Urgeschichte*, 74–77, 333–34.

[4] Cf. BLUM, *Studien*, 280–85; VAN SETERS, *Prologue*, 160–64.

[5] BLENKINSOPP, *Pentateuch*; J.-L. SKA, "The Story of the Flood: A Priestly Writer and Some Later Editorial Fragments," in *The Exegesis of the Pentateuch: Exegetical Studies and Basic Questions*, FAT 66 (Tübingen: Mohr Siebeck, 2009), 1–22 = IDEM, "El relato del diluvio: Un relato sacerdotal y algunos fragmentos redaccionales posteriores," *EstBib* 52 (1994): 37–62; KRÜGER, "Das menschliche Herz und die Weisung Gottes," 73–76; BOSSHARD-NEPUSTIL, *Vor uns die Sintflut*; ARNETH, *Durch Adams Fall*.

[6] Cf. LEVIN, *Der Jahwist*, 103–17; VAN SETERS, *Prologue*, 160–65.

material found in P.[7] In order to make any progress in this discussion, the literary character of the alleged doublets must be analyzed, to determine whether one of the texts is indeed repeating the content of the other or if it instead is interpreting and correcting the latter.

The dispute concerning the literary-historical relationship between P and J often pushes aside the problem of the unity of each of the two strands. Although the non-P passages are not all ascribed to the same literary level (7:7–9 is often considered a later addition to non-P/J),[8] P is often (tacitly) considered to be a unified composition. A few scholars propose an older written tradition behind P, but most renounce such a reconstruction.[9] An important problem concerning the unity of P is that its chronology partly contradicts or stands in tension with itself. The times and dates provided in the text obviously belong to distinct chronological systems (calendars) and should be ascribed to different Priestly (or post-Priestly) strata.[10] The following analysis will show that in several episodes the Priestly strand contains two distinct layers. Yet, a precise delimitation of these strata does not seem possible.

The relationship to Mesopotamian flood traditions is also much debated. Scholars compare the biblical account with three cuneiform flood-narrative traditions: Axtraḫasis, the Sumerian Eridu Genesis, and the eleventh tablet of the Gilgamesh Epic. Recently, J. Day pointed to several similarities and parallels between the Priestly flood narrative and Berossos's *Babyloniaca*, which partly seem to have been overlooked in scholarship. According to Day, the Priestly flood story is influenced by a forerunner of Berossos.[11]

The following discussion will address all these questions, along with a few differences between the main textual witnesses (MT, SP, LXX) that are relevant to the issue of content.

---

[7] Cf. CARR, *Reading*, 49ff.

[8] According to CARR, *Reading*, 57–60; WITTE, *Die biblische Urgeschichte*, 74–77, 333–34, more texts commonly ascribed to J/non-P are attributed to the redactor combining the two strands.

[9] Cf. BLUM, *Die Komposition*, 282–83; ZENGER, *Gottes Bogen*, 31, n. 13. KRATZ, *Composition*, 237, reconstructs a more primitive text consisting of P^G and P^S.

[10] Cf. WESTERMANN, *Genesis 1–11*, 594, 597, 603–4; KRATZ, *Composition*, 235–37. For BOSSHARD-NEPUSTIL, *Vor uns die Sintflut*, 91, however, the existence of different calendars does not preclude the unity of the Priestly stratum. Some commentators ignore the tensions and contradictions among the numerous statements; cf., for instance, S. E. McEVENUE, *The Narrative Style of the Priestly Writer*, AnBib 50 (Rome: Pontifical Biblical Institute, 1971), 54–56, with the comprehensive n. 45, 64–65; WITTE, *Die biblische Urgeschichte*, 130–46, esp. 141.

[11] DAY, "Flood," esp. 223.

3.2 Significant Differences between the Main Textual Witnesses

(a) Genesis 6:19, 20

MT, SP: שנים
LXX (δύο δύο), Syr. (ܬ̈ܪܝܢ ܬ̈ܪܝܢ):   שנים שנים

In MT and SP, which have the single number "two," the distributive idea has to be deduced from the context. In contrast, LXX and Syr., in accordance with the wording in 7:9 and 7:15, have the specific distributive number formed by repetition ("two of every kind").[12] This textual difference is only rarely dealt with in commentaries, though it may be significant for the literary history of the Priestly stratum. BHS and C. Westermann follow LXX, Syr.; Westermann justifies his preference by pointing to the wording of 7:9 and 7:15.[13] Hendel, however, considers LXX, Syr. a harmonizing plus.[14]

Which reading is more original? If it were a single occurrence, one might conjecture a parablepsis due to homoioteleuton in MT, SP. But since this difference occurs twice in the passage in question, and a third time in the non-P section (7:2),[15] an accidental loss of text is to be excluded. Therefore, on text-critical grounds, one should clearly adopt the reading of MT, SP as more original.

The difference between the wording in 6:19, 20; 7:2 (שנים) on the one hand and in 7:9 and 7:15 (שנים שנים) on the other probably indicates a literary development in the Priestly strand: the repetition of a noun or a number to express the distributive idea is a typical feature of Late Biblical Hebrew and is often found in Priestly texts in Exodus (tabernacle account), Leviticus and Numbers.[16] Since the short form (without repetition) is used twice in the instruction report (Priestly stratum) and the distributive number appears twice in sentences expressing the divine order's execution (also P), one may conclude that the latter stems from a later redactor (see further below).

(b) Genesis 7:9

MT, LXX (θεος):   אלהים
SP, Vulg. (MSS):   יהוה

Concerning the use of theonyms in Genesis, SP usually agrees with MT. In the flood narrative, SP nevertheless deviates twice from MT (a second deviation is found in 7:1 [non-P]: SP reads אלהים instead of יהוה [MT]). In Gen 6–9 only MT seems to be in complete agreement with the source-critical pattern of divine names; therefore it is generally considered the most reliable witness in regard to the different divine names.[17]

---

[12] On the construction, see *GKC* §134q; Joüon-Muraoka §142p.

[13] Cf. WESTERMANN, *Genesis 1–11*, 527.

[14] See HENDEL, *Text of Genesis 1–11*, 90.

[15] Here, only MT has the single שנים. SP, LXX, and Syr. have (or reflect) שנים שנים.

[16] See POLZIN, *Late Biblical Hebrew*, 47–51; *GKC* §123c, d, with n. 2, §134q.

[17] See HENDEL, *Text of Genesis 1–11*, 38: "The (...) argument – that a scribe in the proto-M tradition created the consistent source-critical pattern of divine names in M from the pattern

The difference in 7:9, however, is distinctive insofar as it is found in a section whose literary classification is disputed (see below); it should therefore be evaluated without "prejudice." Probably a scribe in the tradition of SP harmonized the text in 7:9 (...·"as God > YHWH had commanded Noah") with the similar statement a few verses before: "... according to all that YHWH had commanded him" (Gen 7:5). There is no visible motive for a deliberate modification from יהוה to אלהים in MT.

(c1) Genesis 7:11

MT, SP, Jub. 5:23:	שבעה עשר יום
4QCommGenᵃ:	שבעה עשר בו
LXX:	שבעה עשרים

(c2) Genesis 8:4

MT, SP:	שבעה עשר יום
4QCommGenᵃ:	שבעה עשר בחודש
LXX:	שבעה עשרים

(c3) Genesis 8:14

MT, SP:	שבעה עשרים יום
LXX:	שבעה עשרים
4QCommGenᵃ, Jub. 5:31:	שבעה עשר יום

Taken as a whole, the readings of MT and SP reflect the idea that the flood lasted exactly one solar year; the calculation is based on a lunar calendar: The third of the three dates (2/27/601),[18] in relation to the date of the onset of the flood (2/17/600), indicates the fulfillment of an entire solar year comprising twelve precise lunar months (29.5 days) plus eleven intercalated days (a total of 365[19] days).[20] The data in 4QCommGena and Jub. on the one hand and in LXX on the other use different means to express a duration of exactly one unspecified year for the flood.

Which textual witnesses provide more credible readings? Since the readings of MT and SP alluding to the exact lunar calendar conflict with the data in Gen 7:11, 24; 8:3, 4, which are based on a schematic lunar calendar (the ark came to rest on 7/17 of the six-hundredth year of Noah, exactly five months after the flood's beginning on 2/17 of the six-hundredth year, i.e., 150 days), the precise lunar readings of MT and SP should

---

preserved in G – is implausible. Such an event, like the hypothetical monkeys typing Hamlet, is an astronomical improbability."

[18] Chronological indications ("dates") are expressed in relation to Noah's birth (month/day/year).

[19] According to an inclusive counting (2/27 is included in the counting).

[20] See, for instance, CASSUTO, *Commentary on the Book of Genesis*, 113; WESTERMANN, *Genesis 1–11*, 603; J. VANDERKAM, *Calendars in the Dead Sea Scrolls: Measuring Time* (London: Routledge, 1998), 32–33.

be preferred as the *lectio difficilior*.[21] The alternative readings in 4QCommGena, Jub., and LXX, which are compatible with Gen 7:11, 24; 8:3, 4, are probably harmonizations with a calendar without intercalated days.[22]

(d) Genesis 9:1

MT, SP: ורבו ומלאו את הארץ

LXX: καὶ πληρώσατε τὴν γῆν καὶ κατακυριεύσατε αὐτῆς
= ורבו ומלאו את הארץ וכבשה

This plus in LXX has not garnered much attention in scholarship. As for the question of its Hebrew equivalent, Hendel opts for ורדו, "and have dominion." As his short comment reveals, this choice is probably due to the frequent reconstruction of the LXX (MSS) variant in 9:7 (see below).[23] However, the equivalent of κατακυριεύειν in the Pentateuch is predominantly כבש, "to subdue," (three out of four occurrences) and never רדה, "to have dominion."[24] For the only other occurrence of כבש in Genesis, the translator chose κατακυριεύειν (1:28). Another hint that the Hebrew *Vorlage* had the verb כבש is the fact that the verb makes the wording of LXX's *Vorlage* identical to the blessing in 1:28a.[25]

The few commentators treating this difference prefer MT, SP. The reading of LXX is considered a harmonizing plus.[26]

(e) Genesis 9:7

MT: שרצו בארץ

SP: ושרצו בארץ

LXX: καὶ πληρώσατε τὴν γῆν
= ומלאו את הארץ

Whereas MT, SP vary the blessing compared to v. 1, LXX is "consistent" (see further below).

---

[21] See also BOSSHARD-NEPUSTIL, *Vor uns die Sintflut*, 202. Concerning these two calendars, see below, II.3.4 (a).

[22] In the case of the book of Jubilees, the motive of avoiding allusion to the precise lunar calendar is evident; see VANDERKAM, *Calendars*, 32–33.

[23] HENDEL, *Text of Genesis 1–11*, 92.

[24] Gen 1:28 (כבש *qal*); Num 21:24 (ירש *qal*); 32:22 (כבש *niphal*), 29 (כבש *niphal*).

[25] WESTERMANN, *Genesis 1–11*, 616, and SOGGIN, *Das Buch Genesis*, 152, reconstruct וכבשה too.

[26] WESTERMANN, *Genesis 1–11*, 616; HENDEL, *Text of Genesis 1–11*, 92; PRESTEL and SCHORCH, "Genesis," 175; hesitating, SOGGIN, *Das Buch Genesis*, 152.

(f) Genesis 9:7 (end)

MT, SP: ורבו בה

LXX^{MSS}:   καὶ κατακυριεύσατε αὐτῆς[27]

       = וכבשה

According to some scholars, the repetition of ורבו, "and multiply!" twice in the same verse in MT and SP "leads to serious doubts regarding its originality."[28] Pointing to the reading κατακυριεύσατε of several Greek minuscule manuscripts, they consider the reading ורדו, "and have dominion," which is graphically similar to MT, instead of the second ורבו as the original reading.[29] However, as shown above, αὐτῆς probably renders וכבשה, "and subdue it." On the condition that the inner-Greek variant κατακυριεύσατε is the original LXX reading, 9:7 LXX reflects a precise *Wiederaufnahme* of its extended blessing in 9:1 and corresponds to the wording of 1:28a.[30]

Regarding LXX's tendency to harmonize, one is tempted to see in its readings in both v. 1 and v. 7 an adaptation to the fuller blessing of 1:28.[31] Nevertheless, MT's difficult reading in v. 7 may be secondary as well. Even if P is known for a repetitive style, one should consider that repetition in P is usually part of a concentric or symmetric construction. Here the case is different: in a row of four imperatives, the second and fourth are identical. Therefore, one may wonder whether ורבו is a substitute for another verbal form that a scribe of MT considered problematic (כבש).[32] With regard to the meaning of כבש ("subdue, violate"), this does not seem impossible (compare the assumed imperative, "and subdue it [the earth]," with God's promise, "never again shall there be a flood to destroy the earth," in close proximity [9:11]).

3.3 The Assignment of the Text to P and Non-P: Disputed Cases

In general, scholars agree on the differentiation between two textual strata and on their attribution to P or J (non-P). More controversial is the discussion of the contribution of a redactor who would have combined the two strata or harmonized them. Some of the texts that Carr and Witte assign to a post-P/post–non-P redaction are

---

[27] LXX reading here according to diverse minuscules, see J. W. Wevers, *Genesis* (Göttingen: Vandenhoeck & Ruprecht, 1974), 127. Most important among the MSS attesting the variant reading are the manuscript families b and d (see Hendel, *Text of Genesis 1–11*, 57).

[28] Tal, *Biblia Hebraica Quinta: Genesis*, 101, and see n. 19.

[29] Many scholars follow the (alleged) variant reading of LXX, ורדו בה; see, among others, Skinner, *Genesis*, 171; Gunkel, *Genesis*, 150; Westermann, *Genesis 1–11*, 460; Hendel, *Text of Genesis 1–11*, 56–57; Carr, *Genesis 1–11*, 230.

[30] For a cautiously positive evaluation of the inner-Greek variant αὐτῆς, see Hendel, *Text of Genesis 1–11*, 56–57.

[31] Rösel, *Übersetzung als Vollendung*, 197; Seebass, *Genesis I*, 226; and Gertz: *Das erste Buch Mose*, 222, n. 23 (among others), maintain the reading of MT.

[32] *Contra BHS*, which corrects ורבו to ורדו, and Hendel, *Text of Genesis 1–11*, 56–57. Rösel, *Übersetzung als Vollendung*, 197, and Seebass, *Genesis I*, 226, maintain the reading of MT.

classified as non-P (J) by other scholars.[33] For one of these passages, Gen 7:7–9, there is a tendency to consider it to belong (partially) to the Priestly stratum (see below, [a]). The arguments adduced by Carr and Witte do not seem persuasive; in none of the texts in question (except perhaps for Gen 7:7–9; see below) are clear literary critical signals visible that would permit an inner differentiation of the J strand. For instance, the absence of the article in אדם, "humankind," in the expression "from humankind to animals to creeping things and to birds of the sky" (6:7aβ), which contrasts the preceding האדם (6:7aα), does not hint at redactional activity but can instead be explained by the particular style of such enumerations (cf. the formulae with very similar shape in 1 Sam 15:3; 22:19, in which the article is never used). Likewise, Noah's attribute צדיק, "righteous," in 7:1 is not in tension with the statement that he found favor in "the eyes of YHWH" (6:8 J). As will be shown below, the affinity for Priestly vocabulary and style is not only found in these alleged redactional insertions; it appears in J passages in general.[34]

(a) Genesis 7:7–9

Genesis 7:7–9 is often ascribed to a harmonizing post-Priestly/post–non-P redaction.[35] In recent studies, however, 7:7 or the bulk of the passage 7:7–9 is assigned to P.[36]

Prima facie, the assignment to a post-P and post-J redaction seems appropriate. The motive of the redactor might have been to harmonize P and J. According to Bosshard-Nepustil, the redactor was also troubled by the fact that according to 7:13–16a the passengers entered the ark only after the onset of the flood. By using the expression מפני מי המבול (understood by Bosshard-Nepustil as "*before* the waters of the flood"), he would have corrected this detail.[37]

Arguments that favor the attribution of v. 7 to P are as follows: The expression "because of the water of the flood" (מפני מי המבול) in v. 7 matches well with the P strand (see מפני with the meaning "because" in 6:13 and the combination of מים and מבול in 6:17; 7:6; 9:11, 15). Genesis 7:7 in general fits with the preceding v. 6, which is

---

[33] According to the delimitation of WITTE, *Die biblische Urgeschichte*, 74–77, the redactor would have composed Gen 6:7aβ; 7:1b, 3a, 8–9, 23 [the catalogue of animals]; similarly CARR, *Reading*, 57–60; IDEM, *Genesis 1–11*, 236 (Gen 6:7aβ; 7:3a, 8–9, 23 [the catalogue of animals]; 8:13a). In contrast, SKA, "Story of the Flood," and BOSSHARD-NEPUSTIL, *Vor uns die Sintflut*, 72–73, assign all these texts except 7:7–9 to the same literary stratum as the other non-P passages (J/non-P).

[34] See below, II.3.6 (a).

[35] Among others, SEEBASS, *Genesis I*, 215; WITTE, *Die biblische Urgeschichte*, 77; BOSSHARD-NEPUSTIL, *Vor uns die Sintflut*, 72–73.

[36] RUPPERT, *Genesis*, 1:342–44; KRATZ, *Composition*, 236–37; and S. SHECTMAN, *Women in the Pentateuch: A Feminist and Source-Critical Analysis*, HBM 23 (Sheffield: Sheffield Phoenix, 2009), 135, assign Gen 7:7 to P. LEVIN, *Der Jahwist*, 111–12; SKA, "Story of the Flood," 3–5; and ARNETH, *Durch Adams Fall*, 62–66, assign the bulk or the entirety of the passage to P.

[37] See BOSSHARD-NEPUSTIL, *Vor uns die Sintflut*, 72.

commonly ascribed to P. But an assignment to a post-Priestly/post-J redaction seems equally possible.

As for the passage reporting that Noah and all the passengers entered the ark (Gen 7:8–9), this shares more common expressions with P than with J. At the same time, we note some discrepancies with both strands:

"P-like"	"J-like"
– אלהים[38]	– sequence עוף, בהמה (cf. 7:2–3)
– זכר ונקבה (cf. 6:19; 7:16)[39]	– distinction between clean and unclean
– רמש על האדמה (cf. 6:20; 9:2)	animals (cf. 7:2)

Discrepancy with P	*Discrepancy with J*
– distinction between clean and unclean	– clean animals and birds: only one pair
animals	instead of seven pairs (cf. 7:2–3)
– sequence עוף, בהמה (cf. 6:20)	

The mixture of affinities to and discrepancies with both strands favors the idea that this passage stems from a redactor reworking both layers. An assignment to P is less likely because of the distinction between clean and unclean animals and the sequence בהמה, עוף; both features are found in J (see 7:2–3).

Concerning v. 7, assignment to P raises the question of its original continuation. A possibility is that the (proto-)Priestly strand goes on with the passage 7:14–16, which reports the entrance of the animals into the ark. It shares the organizing term מין with the corresponding instruction in 6:20. Another question concerns the relationship of 7:7 to the Priestly 7:13, which shares the same content (Noah's entrance into the ark). Which statement predates the other? (See further 3.4.[c].)

(b) The Sending-out of the Raven: Genesis 8:6–7

A minority of scholars ascribe the first bird passage (sending out of the raven, 8:6–7) to P rather than to J (so the majority of scholars).[40] The following arguments may be advanced in favor of this attribution. Ascribing both bird passages (raven, dove) to J has the difficulty that the first attempt is successful, so that a second attempt in the same compositional layer seems redundant. Let us note furthermore that the style of the raven sequence is more sober and has certain distinct linguistic features when compared with that of the dove. They may point to the P provenience of the passage.

---

[38] On the alternative reading יהוה in SP and Vulg. (several MSS), see the discussion above, II.3.2 (b).

[39] J has איש ואשתו (cf. 7:2) and זכר ונקבה (cf. 7:3).

[40] F. Delitzsch, *A New Commentary on Genesis* (Edinburgh: T&T Clark, 1888), 274–75; Procksch, *Die Genesis*, 474; von Rad, *Das erste Buch*, 106; Schüle, *Der Prolog*, 255.261; L. Schrader, "Kommentierende Redaktion im Noah-Sintflut-Komplex der Genesis," in *ZAW* 110 (1998): 494–95.

The rather rare expression מקץ, "at the end of," + indication of time (see v. 6) occurs in the P texts Gen 8:3;[41] 16:3; Exod 12:41; Num 13:25. The root יבש, "to dry up," (see יבשת in v. 7) occurs in several P texts (Gen 1:9, 10; 8:14; Exod 14:16, 22, 29; 15:19). Finally, the verb יצא, "to go out," (see v. 7) is used several times in the P section reporting the humans and animals leaving the ark (see 8:16, 18, 19). Remarkably, this verb occurs only in the section about the raven and not in that of the dove, and it is not used in the J stratum at all. In contrast, the author of Gen 8:6–7 mentions a window (חלון), which does not appear – at least not under this designation[42] – in the instruction concerning the ark's construction (P stratum; 6:14–16).

3.4 Inner Differentiation of the Priestly Flood Narrative

(a) The Flood's Schedule and Date in P

P uses various time indications and calendrical systems, mentioning the period of the water's increase (150 days, see 7:24; 8:3) and several dates related to the six-hundredth year of Noah. As an ensemble, these elements do not fit well with the plot of the story. According to the narrative, after the beginning of the flood (7:6, 11) the waters grew constantly (see 7:18–20, 24), until God caused a wind to pass over the earth and the water subsided (8:1; see the *wayyiqtol* וישכו).[43] Afterward (*wayyiqtol* וישבו), the water receded steadily from the earth (8:3) and then (*wayyiqtol* ותנח) the ark came to rest on the mountains of Ararat (8:4). The framework of time designations for these events in 7:11, 24; 8:3, 4 does not fit this outline: the ark rested exactly five months after the flood's beginning (from 2/17 to 7/17 in the six-hundredth year of Noah), namely, 150 days calculated according to a schematic monthly calendar (every month containing 30 days). This would mean that the landing of the ark happened exactly at the moment of the peak of the flood! The statement concerning the height of the waters above the (highest) mountains (fifteen cubits) in 7:20 indicates that this is indeed the author's (redactor's) intention, preparing for and explaining the report in 8:4 that the 30-cubit-high ark landed on the mountains of Ararat just at the moment of the water's peak (the ark being immersed to half of its height).[44] Yet this sophisticated framework of time designations does not take into account the statements concerning the water's decline

---

[41] Reading attested in SP (cf. מקץ חמשים ומאת ימים). MT has מקצה חמשים ומאת ים. Probably a false word separation occurred and one should read מקץ החמשים ומאת ים (cf. *BHS*).

[42] The hapax legomenon צהר, for which two different meanings are proposed ("roof" or "skylight, hatch"), appears in the instruction in Gen 6:16; cf. *HALOT* 1008.

[43] According to 8:1b–2a (P), the flood stops for two different reasons (God causes a wind to pass over the earth; sources and heavenly windows are closed). It is possible that the first of the two statements (8:1b) reporting God's direct intervention is a secondary addition; see below, (d).

[44] Cf. also GUNKEL, *Genesis*, 145 ("eine überaus ausgeklügelte Theorie"); WESTERMANN, *Genesis 1–11*, 594. It seems that the redactor was playing with the numbers 15 (cubits), 30 (cubits, days), and 150 (days).

before the ark's landing on the mountain (see above).[45] Because of this conceptual difference, the framework of time designations, as an ensemble (see 7:11, 24; 8:3, 4), should not be assigned to the ground layer of the Priestly account.

There is another inconsistency: the last absolute dating, found in 8:14 (2/27/601) is obviously based on the exact lunar calendar and alludes to the completion of a solar year as a sum of 12 lunar months (354 days) and 11 days. The earth was dry exactly one year after the beginning of the flood on 2/17 of the six-hundredth year (see above, II.3.2 [c]). Yet this conflicts with the duration of the water's increase (150 days) and the absolute dates given in 7:11 for the beginning of the flood (2/17) and 8:4 for the land-ing of the ark (7/17). Calculated according to the exact lunar calendar, the water would have steadily increased until the nineteenth or twentieth of the seventh month, that is, two or three days *after* the ark's coming to rest on the mountains of Ararat.[46] With regard to these inconsistencies, one might be inclined to assign all the time indications to a secondary layer.[47] Yet the single statements, considered in isolation, do not con-tradict the plot, and thus there is no sure basis for the general conclusion that every dating is secondary.

What is the meaning of the "pedantically" precise datings? R. Kratz suggests that the date of 2/17 in 7:11 would have been inspired by the time indications of J. This date indicating the beginning of the flood hints at a 47-day period beginning with the New Year that would result from combining the lengths of the two periods found in the J layer: the seven-day span for entering the ark after YHWH's announcement on the one hand and the duration of the rain (forty days) on the other.[48] As Kratz himself admits, the redactor's calculation does not fit the narrative sequence because the rain begins just at the relevant date (see 7:11–12). However, one might speculate that the redactor originally placed v. 11 after the statement of the forty-day period of rain (v. 12). What may hint at this sequence being more original is the fact that the following v. 13 harks back to the date in 7:11 (2/17, cf. "that very day") and forms the latter's natural contin-uation; v. 12 seems to be in the wrong place.

Genesis 7:10–13 (Reconstructed Sequence)

[10] And it came about after the seven days, that the water of the flood came upon the earth. [12] And the rain fell upon the earth for forty days and forty nights. [11] In the six hundredth year of Noah's life, in the second month, on the seventeenth day of the month, on the same day all the fountains of the great deep burst open, and the floodgates of the sky were opened. [13] On the very same day Noah and Shem and

---

[45] SEEBASS, *Genesis I*, 219, also sees this difficulty.

[46] Cf. SEEBASS, *Genesis I*, 219.

[47] Cf. KRATZ, *Composition*, 235–37.

[48] Cf. KRATZ, *Composition*, 235–36. DAY, "Flood," 212–13, points to the similarity of the date of the beginning of the flood to that found in Berossos (fifteenth day of the month Daisios, the second month in the Macedonian calendar); see below, II.3.7.1.

Ham and Japheth, the sons of Noah, and Noah's wife and the three wives of his sons with them, entered the ark.

If this reconstruction is correct, how should we understand the statement in 7:11, 13? The redactor probably wanted to differentiate between a period of forty days of natural rain and the subsequent cosmic event of the opening of the heavenly windows and the fountains' bursting. His intention was to underline that מבול, "celestial sea," is more than a simple rain – rather, it is a cosmic event – and thus to correct J's interpretation of the flood as a long and constant rain. Afterward, a still-later redactor would have rearranged the sequence (the forty-day rains should follow the gate's opening on heaven and on earth).

As for the second absolute date, 7/17 (in 8:4), for the landing of the ark on the mountains of Ararat, the only ancient Near Eastern historical record from the second or first millennium BCE that gives some importance to it is, to my knowledge, the cuneiform inscription on the Harran Stele from the reign of Nabonidus.

The latter reports that the Neo-Babylonian king Nabonidus chose Tašrītu 17 as the date for his return to Babylon after his long stay in Teman.[49] That this day was considered favorable is corroborated by hemerological texts, which present it as a day upon which "Sin is merciful to mankind."[50] Perhaps the seventeenth of Tašrītu was the date of the Akītu festival in Harran.[51] This coincidence of the date for landing of the ark with the Harran inscription, if not accidental, is intriguing and recalls several probable allusions to the Sîn tradition in the Priestly Abraham narrative.[52]

To sum up, there is strong evidence suggesting that at least some of the chronological indications found in the Priestly strand belong to a secondary layer (or layers). Not

---

[49] See P.-A. BEAULIEU, The Reign of Nabonidus, King of Babylon, 556–539 B.C., YNER 10 (New Haven: Yale University Press, 1989), 150–54 ("[After] ten years the appointed time arrived, fulfilled were the days which Nannar, the king of the gods, had said. On the seventeenth day of Tašrītu, 'a day [upon which] Sin is propitious,' is its [ominous] meaning," 153). H. SCHAUDIG, *Die Inschriften Nabonids von Babylon und Kyros' des Grossen*, AOAT 256 (Münster: Ugarit-Verlag, 2001), 491. I thank Jan Rückl, Prague, for having drawn my attention to this parallel.

[50] See BEAULIEU, Reign of Nabonidus, 150–54; SCHAUDIG, *Die Inschriften Nabonids*, 20, with n. 84, 491.

[51] See BEAULIEU, *Reign of Nabonidus*, 152: "According to Neo-Assyrian sources, the *akītu* festival of Sîn in Ḥarran started on the seventeenth day of an unspecified month (....). Since *akītu* festivals generally took place in Nisanu or Tašrītu (spring and fall festivals), there is a probability that that of Sîn at Ḥarran started on Tašrītu 17." For Beaulieu, the choice of this propitious date by Nabonidus for his return to Babylon would be even more understandable if it were the date of the Akītu festival of Sîn in Harran (see BEAULIEU, *Reign of Nabonidus*, 152). See also SCHAUDIG, *Die Inschriften Nabonids*, 20, with n. 84.

[52] See below, II.6.5.2, II.6.7 (b). Note, however, that whereas in the present instance the allusion to the Sîn tradition seems positive, the allusions in the Priestly Abraham narrative are rather polemical. Another tentative interpretation of the precise date would be as follows: one might wonder whether the date's proximity to the Day of Atonement (7/10) – precisely one week after the latter – is not accidental. Might the author (redactor) have thought that God's remembering Noah and the beginning of the water's decline happened on the Day of Atonement?

all statements are compatible with each other, and some of them seem to be driven by different motivations. One important date, that of the beginning of the cosmic flood, probably presupposes the J stratum. Yet, as most commentators note, a precise and secure differentiation of literary strata on the basis of the observed inconsistencies between the various time designations is not possible.[53]

(b) Indications of Noah's Age and Death (Genesis 7:6, 11; 9:28–29)

The statements in 7:6, 11; 9:28–29 (cf. also 8:13) are connected to the characteristic age designations in Gen 5. One among these is part of the exact indication in Gen 7:11, which should probably be ascribed to a secondary redaction (see above). As for the two others, do they belong to the ground layer of the Priestly flood narrative or to a secondary redaction layer? The latter possibility is supported by the fact that the notice concerning Noah's procreation of three sons (6:10) at the beginning of the narrative does not contain any statement of age.

Furthermore, the Table of Nations (basic composition, proto-P), which constitutes a natural continuation of the Priestly flood story,[54] does not provide the ages of the patriarchs and national eponyms either.[55]

(c) Two Passages Reporting the Beginning of the Flood and Noah's Entering into the Ark (Genesis 7:6–7 * // 7:11, 13)

Two distinct Priestly layers are perceptible in 7:6–16. The beginning of the flood and Noah's entering into the ark are reported twice (in 7:6–7* and in 7:11, 13).[56]

Genesis 7:6–7
[6] And Noah was six hundred years old, then the flood of water came upon the earth. [7] Then Noah and his sons and his wife and his sons' wives with him entered the ark because of the water of the flood.

Genesis 7:11, 13
[11] In the six hundredth year of Noah's life, in the second month, on the seventeenth day of the month, on the same day all the fountains of the great deep burst open, and the floodgates of the sky were opened. [13] On the very same day Noah and Shem and Ham and Japheth, the sons of Noah, and Noah's wife and the three wives of his sons with them, entered the ark.

---

[53] Cf. M. Rösel, "Die Chronologie der Flut in Gen 7–8: Keine neuen textkritischen Lösungen," ZAW 110 (1998): 593; Baumgart, Die Umkehr, 64; Bosshard-Nepustil, Vor uns die Sintflut, 92.

[54] Shared motifs are the number of Noah's sons, their names, and the geographical affinity (Ararat–Japheth); see below, II.3.5.

[55] However, the lack of ages given in the Table of Nations might be explained by the multitude of names in this composition.

[56] See also Kratz, Composition, 236–37.

This evidence is difficult to interpret. The fact that the wording of 7:6b matches the flood announcement in 6:17 (see the explanatory apposition מים, "water," following the term מבול, "celestial sea," in both verses) better than the one in 7:11 may indicate that 7:6 should be attributed to a previous layer and 7:11 to a secondary stratum. Moreover, the term מבול in its only occurrence outside of the flood story (Ps 29:10) refers only to the *celestial* sea and not to both the celestial and the underground ocean, as implied by the two statements in 7:11 and 8:2 (opening and closing the terrestrial sources and the heavenly windows).[57] The idea that God assembles the clouds in order to make it rain, present in the establishment of the covenant with Noah (Gen 9:8–17; see v. 14), reinforces the understanding of מבול as celestial sea.

(d) Two Causes for the Waters' Decline

According to 8:1–2a, the waters begin to subside for two different reasons (God causes a wind to pass over the earth; the terrestrial sources and heavenly windows are closed):

Genesis 8:1
[1] But God remembered Noah and all the beasts and all the cattle that were with him in the ark; and God caused a wind to pass over the earth, and the water subsided.

Genesis 8:2a, 3b
[2a] And the fountains of the deep and the floodgates of the sky were closed [3b] and at the end of one hundred and fifty days the water decreased.

An older version likely mentioned only one cause. With regard to the tentative assignment of the opening of the terrestrial fountains and heavenly windows to a secondary Priestly stratum (see above, [a], [c]), possibly only the first of the two statements (8:1) should be considered to belong to the original account.[58]

(e) Blessing and Dietary Law (Genesis 9:1–7)

The Priestly flood narrative contains two concluding passages, each one focusing on a central motif: blessing (9:1–7) and establishment of the covenant (9:8–17). Scholars have pointed out the similar structure, with *inclusio* (9:1//7; 9:8//17), of the two passages, regarding the two themes as fitting with one another. Thus most scholars consider 9:1–17 to be a unified, elaborate epilogue to the Priestly flood narrative.[59]

Yet, others have observed that the two passages have two different orientations:[60] the second one corresponds much more to the preceding sections of the Priestly flood account. Verses 8–17 are strongly linked to the introduction of the Priestly flood

---

[57] See also *HALOT* 541. For the motifs of bursting fountains and heavenly windows opening, see below, II.3.8 (3).

[58] See also KRATZ, *Composition*, 236–37.

[59] Thus with much emphasis WESTERMANN, *Genesis 1–11*, 617–18.

[60] GUNKEL, *Genesis*, 141, 148–50; EERDMANS, *Alttestamentliche Studien*, 29, 90, 93; RUPPERT, *Genesis*, 1:377–79.

narrative: the solemn self-commitment in 9:11, 12, 15 takes up several expressions of God's announcement to "bring the flood to destroy all flesh" in 6:13, 17, 18 (i.e., לשחת, "to destroy"; כל בשר, "all flesh"; מים, "water"; מבול, "flood"; ברית, "covenant"). As for 9:1–7, it is tightly connected to the creation account in Gen 1 by several shared expressions – in particular the motifs of blessing and multiplication belonging to the Priestly redaction layer – and it reformulates the dietary law in 1:29–30, which we assigned to P^c as well. In contrast to the latter stipulation, 9:1–7 permits the consumption of meat under a special premise: blood as seat of the soul is accounted sacred and cannot be eaten. The section 9:1–7 furthermore distinguishes itself within the Priestly strand of the flood narrative through the marked opposition between humans and animals. According to 9:1–7, only the former – and among them only men – receive God's blessing (see 9:1, 7); all animals are put under "the fear and the terror" of the humans and "given in their hands" (see 9:2). Both syntagmata are predominantly used in late Dtr texts dealing with the "war of yhwh."[61] None of them occur in any Priestly texts. In the other parts of P's flood narrative, humans and animals are seen through a common lens: they share not only in the general destruction caused by the flood (majority of humans and animals) but also in salvation from the flood and in protection through God's covenant (the representatives of every species). In the following passage the being together of humankind and animals is underlined (see v. 9–10: "Now behold, I myself do establish my covenant with you, and with your descendants after you; and with every living creature *that is with you*"). The blatant language of holy war in 9:2 may point to a distinct author in 9:1–7, as compared with the unit narrating God's covenant with all creatures and his renunciation of violence (9:8–17). As for its form, 9:1–7 is marked by the repetition at beginning and end of the order to Noah and his sons to be fruitful and multiply; this may also be an indication of a composition *à part* that was inserted by a later redactor. Alternatively, one might consider the blessing of Noah and his sons in 9:1 an original part of the primary Priestly stratum; 9:7, in contrast, would form a *Wiederaufnahme* of v. 1 at the end of the insertion vv. 2–7.[62]

As already mentioned before, the obvious motivation of the redactor inserting 9:1–7 (or 9:2–7) was to link the flood story more tightly with the Priestly creation account; yet a few linguistic and conceptual differences hint at different authors of the respective texts.[63]

Scholars often see 9:1–7 as connecting thematically to the beginning of the Priestly

---

[61] For the first motif, see Deut 2:25; 11:25; Josh 2:9, and for the second Exod 23:31; Deut 2:24; 2:30; Josh 6:2; 8:1. See McEvenue, *Narrative Style*, 68; L. Lohfink, "Die Schichten des Pentateuch und der Krieg," in *Studien zum Pentateuch*, SBAB 4 (Stuttgart: Katholisches Bibelwerk, 1988), 255–315. See, however, the relativizing view in Neumann-Gorsolke, *Herrschen*, 254–60.

[62] The following scholars consider Gen 9:1–7 a distinct literary unit within the Priestly strand: Eerdmans, *Alttestamentliche Studien*, 29, 90, 93; Fishbane, *Biblical Interpretation*, 318–21; Levin, *Der Jahwist*, 99–100. According to Eerdmans, *Alttestamentliche Studien*, 90, 93, the passage is linked to the "monotheistic" redaction of Gen 1 through the פרו ורבו order. Fishbane, *Biblical Interpretation*, 318–21, considers Gen 9:1–7 an aggadic interpretation of Gen 1:26–28.

[63] See Eerdmans, *Alttestamentliche Studien*, 90, 93, and below, II.3.8 (4).

flood account (6:9–13), where the motif of violence as the cause for the flood plays an important role. Genesis 9:1–7 answers the question of how a renewed increase of violence can be avoided.[64] However, it is noteworthy that there is no terminological correspondence between the two passages; the specific vocabulary of Gen 6:11–13 referring to violence (חמס, "violence," שחת niphal, "to be corrupt," שחת hiphil, "to destroy") is absent from Gen 9:1–7.[65] Therefore, the two passages probably do not stem from the same author.[66]

(f) Designation and Enumeration of the Animals in the Various Sections

The striking differences and incoherences in designation and enumeration of the animals in the various sections of the flood story (cf. the listings in 6:19–20; 7:14–16, 21; 8:1, 17, 19; 9:2, 10) contrast with the stereotypical designation of Noah and his family ("Noah …, and his sons and his wife and his sons' wives with him"; see 6:18; 7:7, 13; 8:16, 18). This hints at the presence of different Priestly strata.

One notices several general designations for the animals in the different sections of the flood story: כל בשר, "flesh" (in the sense of all creatures, 6:19; 7:15, 21); כל החי, "all living beings" (6:19); כל החיה, "all animals" (8:17, 19); and כל רמש, "every moving thing" (9:3). The distributive idea is expressed by the simple cardinal number שנים, "two (of every kind)," (6:19, 20)[67] or by the distributive number שנים שנים, "two of every kind" (7:9, 15). Certain designations are used with different meanings within the Priestly stratum: Whereas the expression בהמה in 6:20 and 8:17 refers to both wild and domestic animals (the specific expression for wild animal, חיה, is absent[68]), other sections differentiate between wild (חיה) and domestic animals (בהמה; see 7:14, 21). The listings in 8:19 and 9:2 mention only חיה and not בהמה. In the case of 9:2 this choice seems deliberate; the author excludes the domestic animals from the species that will have to live in "fear and terror." In 8:19, however, the reference to חיה certainly also includes domestic animals.

Is it possible to assign the differing assertions to different literary strata? One inference is as follows: the use of the single number שנים in 6:19, 20 in the instruction report probably hints at a more original literary stage in comparison to the execution statements in 7:9 and 7:15, which have the distributive number (שנים שנים). It seems

---

[64] O. H. STECK, "Der Mensch und die Todesstrafe," *TZ* 53 (1997): 120–21; BAUMGART, *Die Umkehr*, 199, 338; BOSSHARD-NEPUSTIL, *Vor uns die Sintflut*, 202; NEUMANN-GORSOLKE, *Herrschen*, 252–53.

[65] Notably, the vocabulary of the interdiction of homicide (Gen 9:5–6, with the key words שפך דם, אדם) is completely different from that of the passage dealing with violence (6:11–13, with the key words שחת חמס, niphal, hiphil, בשר).

[66] Apparently, the author of the primary Priestly composition was not concerned with this question of preventing accumulated violence, or he saw in Noah's integrity and righteousness a good precondition for the development of a better humanity.

[67] For a discussion of the variant reading of LXX, see above, II.3.2 (a).

[68] In 8:17, חיה is an umbrella term ("animals").

more likely that the author of the latter passages was keen to impose the expression that was grammatically correct in Late Biblical Hebrew than that the author of 6:19, 20 would have decided to deviate from the grammatically correct form in 7:9 and 7:15.[69] Furthermore, the more detailed character of the listing in 7:14–16 may hint at the secondary nature of that passage. As for 7:9, above we assigned this verse to a post-P/J redaction. Perhaps in the primary account, Noah's fulfillment of the divine order was expressed only through the general statement of 6:22 ("Thus Noah did; according to all that God had commanded him, so he did").

(g) Conclusion

The aforementioned observations suggest an inner differentiation between at least two Priestly layers. They concern doublets, conflicting time designations, and terminological differences within the Priestly strand. We distinguish between a Priestly ground layer and several redactional Priestly elements. The question of how the latter are linked among themselves and with other redactional elements within the P strand will be addressed below.[70]

However, important to note is that classification is not possible for several elements (e.g., statements with dating); in general, the assignments are more tentative than in other sections.

3.5 Characteristics of the Priestly Flood Narrative (Primary Stratum): Its Beginning and Its End

A particularity of the presumably original flood composition is the soberness of the report. No details concerning certain circumstances (storm, rain, etc.) of the flood's outbreak are given. The terminology used for the outbreak and the continuance of the flood (water, *mabbul* [celestial ocean]) is consistent.[71] The concretizing statements about the opening and closing of the terrestrial sources and heavenly windows are probably secondary.

The story has a well-marked beginning with a title ("These are the *tôlĕdōt* of Noah") and Noah's introduction. The end consists of the passage about God's covenant. The mention of Noah's three sons by name (6:10) suggests that the genealogy of Gen 10 (Priestly [= proto-Priestly] stratum), which bases itself on these three ancestors, constitutes the "natural" continuation of the Priestly flood story (primary stratum).

A (seeming) difficulty is the inverted order of the three sons in the Table of Nations: Japheth comes first, and Ham and Shem follow. Yet the same feature is also observable in the

---

[69] See above, II.3.2 (a).

[70] II.3.8.

[71] Cf. 6:17; 7:6, 7; 9:11 (2×), 15.

Terah-Abraham narrative: after the statement about Terah's three procreations, the focus moves to Haran, the youngest son. A reason for Japheth's first position in the Table of Nations could be the ark's landing in Ararat (which is located in the area of Japheth).[72] Another reason might be that this sequence was already in place in the tradition in which the Table of Nations originated.[73]

A further shared element of Gen 6–9 P and Gen 10 P is the categorizing expression מִשְׁפָּחָה, "family." In the flood story, it is used in the passage about the animals leaving the ark (8:19). In Gen 10 P, it is used frequently (for humans; see Gen 10:5, 20, 31, 32).[74] It seems that the author of Gen 6–9 P, by using this atypical expression for the subdivision of the animals in 8:19, was preparing for the transition to the Table of Nations (Gen 10 P).[75]

As for its theological tendency, the Priestly flood story presents the flood as a divine judgment resulting from the world's corruption and predominant violence. Remarkably, God's intervention corresponds precisely to the corrupted state of the world (see the fourfold use of the root שׁחת in 6:11–13, twice as a *niphal* ["to be corrupt"] and twice as a *hiphil* ["to destroy"]; additionally, 6:17 uses the *piel* ["to destroy"]). However, at the end, God himself corrects his retaliatory judgment, concluding a covenant with all creatures and promising never again to destroy (שׁחת *piel*, see 9:11, 15) them. As confirming sign, he puts his warrior's bow in the sky, the rainbow.[76] God's covenant with Noah and all surviving humans and animals should be considered the central motif of the narrative (see 6:18; 9:9, 11, 12, 13, 15, 16, 17).

3.6 The Literary-Historical Relationship between P (Primary Stratum) and J

(a) Priestly Language, Style and Motifs in the J Stratum (J^s)

Perhaps the most important clue for J's dependence on the Priestly strand (primary stratum) is the fact that J uses both linguistic and theological features typical of Priestly literature.[77] As for vocabulary, we must mention the verb ברא (Gen 6:7), the Priestly terms for the designation of animals,[78] and the cultic expression רֵיחַ הַנִּיחֹחַ, "soothing aroma," (8:21)[79] which occurs only in P, H, and Ezekiel. A *stylistic feature* is the typi-

---

[72] For this argument, cf. Bosshard-Nepustil, *Vor uns die Sintflut*, 202.

[73] There are indications favoring the idea that the Priestly Table of Nations in Gen 10 is built on an elaborate list of commerce partners of the Phoenicians nations; see below, II.4.8.

[74] See also the occurrences in other Priestly texts: Gen 36:40; Exod 6:14, 15, 17, 19, 24, 25.

[75] Concerning the cataphoric function of מִשְׁפָּחָה, cf. also Bosshard-Nepustil, *Vor uns die Sintflut*, 112.

[76] U. Rüterswörden, "Der Bogen in Genesis 9: Militärhistorische und traditionsgeschichtliche Erwägungen zu einem biblischen Symbol," *UF* 20 (1988): 248–63.

[77] See Schmid, *Literaturgeschichte*, 154–55.

[78] See 6:7: מֵאָדָם עַד בְּהֵמָה עַד רֶמֶשׂ וְעַד עוֹף הַשָּׁמָיִם, "from humankind to animals to creeping things and to birds of the sky"; cf. also 7:2–3 and 7:23 (for the assignment of this expression to the J stratum, see above, II.3.3).

[79] Exod 29:18, 25, 41; Lev 1:9, 13, 17; 2:2, 9, 12; 3:5, 16; 4:31; 6:8, 14; 8:21, 28; 17:6; 23:13, 18;

cal Priestly correspondence between order and fulfillment found in 7:5 ("And Noah did according to all that YHWH had commanded him"; cf. 6:22 P). A *theological theme* with great importance in P, is the distinction between clean and unclean animals (see 7:2; 8:20).[80] Interestingly, neither this theme nor the noted linguistic and stylistic features are present in other J texts (Gen 2:4b–4:25; 11:1–9). This particularity of the J texts in the flood narrative probably suggests a diachronic differentiation between the J texts in the primeval narrative. The earliest J strand in the primeval narrative once ran directly from Gen 2–4 to Gen 11:1–9.[81] Therefore, the J stratum of the flood narrative is labeled Jˢ (J secondary stratum).

There is no cogent evidence suggesting influence of the J parts on P. One expression in the P strand, אדמה, "ground," which occurs in 6:20; 7:8 and 9:2,[82] is a key word in Gen 2–4 and other J texts in the primeval narrative.[83] However, this term occurs in the P section only as an element of the term "creeping thing" and in the expression "everything that creeps on the ground," and it has precisely this meaning in Gen 1:25 (Pᶜ) and in Ezek 38:20.

(b) J Interprets P

Scholars insisting that the J/non-P stratum is a source and that it is independent from P argue that certain assertions in J (non-P) simply double material found in P.[84] However, in the following it will be shown that with regard to certain distinctive elements these alleged doublets in the J strand may be read as theological reinterpretations of the older P layer by J.

(1) *Image of humankind:* While P describes the "corruption of all flesh" and the omnipresent violence in the world without blaming any species in particular, Jˢ stresses the wickedness of mankind as cause of the flood (see 6:5–8 and 8:21). Significantly, humankind's nature will not change after the flood (see 8:21). This motif fits the emphasis put on human's disobedience and their disposedness to transgressions found elsewhere in J's primeval story: The primordial man and his wife eat of the forbidden fruit, and the primordial couple is punished (cursed) by YHWH and cast out of the garden (Gen 2:4b–3:24). Cain kills and is cursed and expelled by YHWH (Gen 4). Angels and women marry, and YHWH

26:31; Num 15:3, 7, 10, 13, 14, 24; 18:17; 28:2, 6, 8, 13, 24, 27; 29:2, 6, 8, 13, 36; Ezek 6:13; 16:19; 20:28, 41.

[80] See in particular Lev 11; cf. also Deut 14 and Ezek 4:14.

[81] See above, II.2.5. For arguments favoring the idea that the earliest J strand in the primeval narrative once ran directly from Gen 2–4 to Gen 11, cf. SCHMID, *Literaturgeschichte*, 153–56.

[82] מכל רמש האדמה, "every creeping thing of the ground," and בכל אשר תרמש האדמה, "with everything that creeps on the ground."

[83] See all occurrences of the term אדמה in Gen 2:4b–4:26 and in other parts of the primeval narrative of J: Gen 2:5, 6, 7, 9, 19; 3:17, 19, 23; 4:2, 3, 10, 11, 12, 14; 5:29; 6:1, 7; 7:4, 23; 8:8, 13b, 21; 9:20.

[84] Cf. CARR, *Reading*, 49–56.

limits human lifespan (Gen 6:1–4). Ham sees his father, Noah, naked, and Noah curses Canaan, Ham's son (Gen 9:20–27). The tower of Babel is built out of overweening ambition, and people are dispersed by YHWH (Gen 11:1–9).

(2) *Image of YHWH:* In contrast to the primary Priestly stratum, in J^s YHWH's image is strikingly anthropomorphic. His actions are described plastically: YHWH closed the ark (7:16); YHWH smelled the pleasant odor (8:21). Furthermore, YHWH *"wiped out* [מחה] from the face of the land every living thing that he had made." The concrete expression מחה, "to wipe out," with YHWH as subject is used three times (6:7; 7:4, 23).[85] Similar anthropomorphisms occur elsewhere in J's primordial history. The deity is author of concrete actions in the world (YHWH acts as a potter [2:7]; he walks daily in the wind in Eden's garden [3:8]; he undertakes inspection visits on earth [11:5]; he chases the man and his wife [3:24] and Cain [4:10–12]). In P (primary stratum), God is also considered author of the world's destruction, but the chosen verbs are less plastic: God will let the flood come (6:17: הנני מביא את המבול); he will destroy the "world with them" (6:13). Three times the flood (מבול) is the subject of the destruction (6:17; 9:11, 15).

(3) *"'Israelization' of the plot":* In comparison with the 150-day period of P,[86] J^s introduces two typically biblical periods into the narrative: a seven-day span for the passengers entering into the ark and a forty-day period of rain. Even if a seven-day (or six-day/seven-night) span is also known from Mesopotamian flood accounts (for the duration of the heavy rain, see the Sumerian Eridu Genesis, Atraḥasis, and the eleventh tablet of the Gilgamesh Epic), the combination of the seven-day and forty-day periods is striking and might be considered an attempt to introduce typical time spans from Israelite/Judahite literature into the flood account.[87] Furthermore, Noah is the first to observe the distinction between clean and unclean animals and thus anticipates correct Israelite Priestly commitment.[88] Another example of this tendency is the selection of the dove for the bird experiment. In contrast to the raven,[89] the dove is considered a clean animal in Israelite cultic legislation. It is prominently mentioned in the book of Leviticus as an animal of sacrifice[90] and is connoted positively elsewhere in the Hebrew Bible.[91] Such "nationalization" of the story matches other theological

---

[85] See this concrete meaning of the verb מחה in Prov 30:20; Isa 25:8; 2 Kgs 21:13; Num 5:23.

[86] Assuming that this time specification belongs to the base layer; see above, II.3.4 (a).

[87] Yet, if the attribution of the passage reporting the raven experiment (Gen 8:7) to P is correct (see above, II.3.3 [b]), a forty-day period also appears in the P strand.

[88] The distinction between clean and unclean animals is known in cultic legislation elsewhere in the ANE; but in view of the tendency of other J passages, the above interpretation nevertheless seems justified (see also above, II.3.6 [a], with n. 80).

[89] See Lev 11:15 MT, SP; Deut 14:14 MT, SP.

[90] Lev 5:7, 11; 12:6, 8; 14:22, 30; 15:14, 29.

[91] See the noun's frequent occurrences in Song of Songs and the fact that the expression serves as the prophet Jonah's name.

features of J in the primeval narrative. The deity's name (YHWH) is that of the national god. In Gen 2–3, the J redaction subtly inverts the geography of the primary layer in order to assimilate God's garden into Jerusalem.[92] A further example is found in the J additions of the Table of Nations.[93]

Considering all these features together, it seems that the author of J[s] interpreted the Priestly account (primary stratum) by including his own distinct theological accents. Accordingly, in the parallel passages (so-called doublets) J[s] does not simply renarrate P's content but alters the latter in a significant manner. In the announcement of the flood, J[s] aims to specify the cause for the flood (humanity's evil). Similarly, the reformulation of God's order to enter the ark gives the redactor the occasion to introduce the distinction between clean and unclean animals into the plot. For a similar reason, the sending out of the raven has been "corrected." At the end, in God's promise that the flood will not return again (Gen 8:21–22), J[s] once more emphasized humanity's wickedness. The characterization of the J[s] passages as a redaction layer thus seems justified.

3.7 Parallels of the Priestly Account (Primary Stratum) with the Flood Narratives of the Levant and Biblical Texts

As shown above, the Priestly ground layer constitutes a coherent, self-contained narrative that is independent of the J passages. Yet it shares several commonalities with neighboring proto-Priestly and Priestly texts[94] and with Mesopotamian traditions. The following discussion will list similarities and differences between these texts and traditions and draw tentative conclusions for the literary-historical relationship between these units. Important and constitutive for this comparison is the diachronic differentiation of the Priestly stratum (the distinction between primary stratum and secondary Priestly elements). The manifold correspondences with other Priestly texts are reassessed under this rubric.

---

[92] Cf. H. Gese, "Der bewachte Lebensbaum und die Heroen: Zwei mythologische Ergänzungen zur Urgeschichte der Quelle J," in *Wort und Geschichte: Festschrift für Karl Elliger zum 70. Geburtstag*, ed. H. Gese and H. P. Rüger, AOAT 18 (Kevelaer: Butzon & Bercker, 1973), 82; J. C. Gertz, "Von Adam zu Enosch: Überlegungen zur Entstehungsgeschichte von Gen 2–4," in *Gott und Mensch im Dialog: Festschrift für Otto Kaiser zum 80. Geburtstag*, ed. M. Witte, BZAW 345 (Berlin: de Gruyter, 2004), 235; Hutzli, "Transgression," 121–23; idem, "J's Problem with the East: Observations on the So-Called Yahwist Texts in Genesis 1–25, in *The Social Groups behind the Pentateuch*, ed. by J. Jeon, AIL 44 (Atlanta: SBL Press, 2021), 99–120.

[93] See below, II.4.4.2, II.4.5.

[94] This section examines relationships with the Priestly units Gen 1, 5, 10, and 11:10–26. For the relationship with the Priestly Abraham narrative, see below, II.6.7 (a).

3.7.1 Relationship with the Flood Traditions of the Levant

Genesis 6–9* P shares several commonalities with Mesopotamian flood traditions. There were at least three different cuneiform flood-narrative traditions: Atraḫasis,[95] the Sumerian Eridu Genesis,[96] and the eleventh tablet of the Gilgamesh Epic.[97] A late oeuvre, which has several affinities with the biblical flood narrative, is Berossos's *Babyloniaca*.[98]

Common elements shared by these traditions and the Priestly flood story include the announcement of the flood by a/the deity, the instruction to build an ark, the meticulous fulfillment of the order, the preservation of the animals, and the landing of the ark on a mountain. There is also a striking terminological commonality: the word for *pitch*, כֹּפֶר (Gen 6:14), a *hapax legomenon* in the Hebrew Bible, is probably a loanword from Akkadian *kupru*.[99] The corresponding verb *to pitch* (כפר in Gen 6:14, related to Akkadian *kapāru*, "to pitch") was apparently preferred over the Hebrew synonyms חמר, "to pitch" (Exod 2:3), חֵמָר, "asphalt" (Gen 11:3; 14:10; Exod 2:3), and זֶפֶת, "pitch" (Exod 2:3; Isa 34:9).[100] Both *kupru* and *kapāru* are attested in existing versions of Atraḫasis and Gilgamesh.[101]

In addition to these commonalities, the Priestly flood narrative includes some important specifics, such as a monotheistic conception of deity, the name of the flood hero (Noah is not derived from any of the Mesopotamian names [Ziusudra, Atraḫasis, Utnapishtim, Xisouthros]), the name of the region where the ark landed (Ararat [Urartu] instead of Mount Niṣir[102]), the long duration of the flood (150 days,[103] versus seven days in the Mesopotamian traditions[104]), and the absence of sacrifices by the

---

[95] W. G. LAMBERT and A. R. MILLARD, *Atra-Ḥasis: The Babylonian Story of the Flood*, repr. ed. (Winona Lake, IN: Eisenbrauns, 1999), 42–121; W. VON SODEN, "Der altbabylonische Atramḫasis-Mythos," in *Texte aus der Umwet des Alten Testaments, III: Weisheitstexte, Mythen, Epen, 3.1, Weisheitstexte*, ed. O. Kaiser (Gütersloh: Mohn, 1990), 612–45.

[96] LAMBERT and MILLARD, *Atra-Ḥasis*, 138–45; T. JACOBSEN, "The Eridu Genesis," *JBL* 100 (1981): 513–29.

[97] J. BOTTÉRO, *L'Épopée de Gilgamesh: Le grand homme qui ne voulait pas mourir* (Paris: Gallimard, 1992); R.-J. TOURNAY and A. SHAFFER, *L'Épopée de Gilgamesh*, LAPO 15 (Paris: Cerf, 1998); A. R. GEORGE, *The Babylonian Gilgamesh Epic*, 2 vols. (Oxford: Oxford University Press, 2003); S. M. MAUL, *Das Gilgamesch-Epos: Neu übersetzt und kommentiert* (Munich: Beck, 2005).

[98] See S. M. BURSTEIN, *The Babyloniaca of Berossus*, SANE 1.5 (Malibu, CA: Undena, 1978); VERBRUGGHE and WICKERSHAM, *Berossos*, 13–94.

[99] See *HALOT* 495.

[100] See BAUMGART, *Die Umkehr*, 527–28.

[101] Old-Babylonian Atrahasis III, col. I 33; II 13, 51; Gilgamesh XI 54, 65.

[102] With the exception of Berossos (book 2 of *Babyloniaca* F4a): "in the mountains of the Korduaians of Armenia"; see below.

[103] Provided that this time indication belongs to the ground layer; see above, II.3.4 (a).

[104] Sumerian Eridu Genesis: seven days and seven nights; Atraḫasis III, col. IV 24–25: seven days and seven nights; Gilgamesh XI 126–31: seven days. In Berossos (book II of *Babyloniaca*), the duration of the flood is not specified.

hero of the flood.[105] As for the central theme of the conversion of God in Gen 6–9 P (primary stratum), it appears to be an adaptation of the conflicting positions of the gods toward humans in the Mesopotamian tradition and Enlil's final acceptance of the flood hero's salvation to the monotheistic conception. Within an innerbiblical discourse, the aim of this adaptation is to respond to the prophets' and Deuteronomist's conception of YHWH as a God of definitive judgment.

The relationship of the Priestly primeval history to Berossos's *Babyloniaca* (dated to the early third century BCE) deserves particular attention.[106] There are some striking similarities between the second book of the *Babyloniaca* and the (proto-) Priestly units that are not or are only partly shared by other Mesopotamian flood traditions.[107]

Parallels

List of Antediluvian Kings/Patriarchs

(a)   number of the members of the king list/of the genealogy of Adam (ten members)[108]

(b)   seventh position of Enmeduranki/Enoch[109]

Flood Story

(c)   beginning of the flood: precise and similar date (fifteenth day of second month/ seventeenth day of second month)[110]

(d)   landing of the ark in the mountains of Armenia[111]

(e)   rectangular form of the ark[112]

(f)   mention of provisions[113]

---

[105] See the useful overview in Ruppert, *Genesis*, 1:306–7.

[106] For the possible setting of the *Babyloniaca*, cf. G. De Breucker, "Berossos: His Life and His Work," in The World of Berossos: *Proceedings of the 4th International Colloquium on "The Ancient Near East between Classical and Ancient Oriental Traditions," Hatfield College, Durham 7th–9th July 2010*, ed. J. Haubold et al., Classica et Orientalia 5 (Wiesbaden: Harrassowitz, 2013), 15–18.

[107] See also Day, "Flood," 211–23.

[108] See *Babyloniaca* II F3. The list of WB 62 also contains ten members in total.

[109] See *Babyloniaca* II F3. The seventh position of Enmeduranki is also attested in WB 444.

[110] See *Babyloniaca* II F4a: "on the fifteenth day of the month Daisios" (the second month in the Macedonian calendar); Day, "Flood," 212, with n. 7.

[111] See *Babyloniaca* II F4a 20–21: "It also said that the land in which they found themselves was Armenia," and II F4b: "A portion of the ship ... still remains in the mountains of the Korduaians of Armenia." See also Day, "Flood," 214, with n. 17.

[112] See *Babyloniaca* II 4a: "he built a boat five stades in length and two stades in breadth." One should note, however, that the measures are completely different from those of Gen 6:15. In the Gilgamesh Epic the form is cubic. In Atraḫasis and the Sumerian Eridu Genesis the form is not specified.

[113] See *Babyloniaca* II F4a: "Food and drink should be placed in it."

Postdiluvian Patriarchs

(g) correspondence of a wise man in tenth generation with Abraham, the firstborn of Terah, the ninth member in the genealogy of Gen 11:10–26[114]

In contrast, certain similarities between Gen 5; 6–9* P and Mesopotamian traditions are not shared by Berossos. Unlike the other Mesopotamian traditions, Berossos does not localize Enmeduranki in Sippar, the city of the sun god, but rather in Pautibiblon (= Badtibira, see *Babyloniaca* II F3). Thus in his account there is no link between Enmeduranki and the sun god. The biblical patriarch Enoch, however, is clearly shaped after the "solar" figure Enmeduranki.[115] A further particularity of Berossos, as compared with Gen 6–9* P and Gilgamesh, is the fact that Xisouthros sends the birds out before the ship lands on the mountain.[116]

Based on the multiple similarities between P and Berossos, J. Day concludes that P (as a unified document) and Berossos "shared a common knowledge of certain late Babylonian traditions."[117] However, following modern commentators on Berossos, we should also consider the possibility that some of the shared motifs in the *Babyloniaca* were inserted later by Jewish or (and) Christian transmitters.[118] In particular, this could be the case for correspondences a) and g) mentioned above. Scholars believe that the tradition in Berossos's list that there were ten antediluvian kings is not original, as a total of ten antediluvian kings is alien to the Mesopotamian tradition (originally there were no more than nine[119]). The fourth king in Berossos's list, Ammenon, has no equivalent in the older forms of the antediluvian kings' names; perhaps it corresponds to the postdiluvian king Enmenuanna. The fact that the duration of his reign (twelve *sar*, i.e., 43,200 years) comes close to that of his predecessor, Ammelon (thirteen *sar*, i.e., 46,800 years) might favor the idea that this name is a secondary doublet (thus T. Jacobson, who points to the similarity of ἀμμελων and ἀμμενων)[120] or that it was invented in order to bring the number of kings in the list up to the biblical number ten (thus G. De Breucker[121]). Moreover, one cannot exclude the possibility that Berossos himself was acquainted with the biblical tradition and influenced by it.

---

[114] See Josephus, *Ant.* I:158.

[115] See above, II.2.4.1. Concerning this discrepancy between Gen 5 and Berossos, see also Day, "Flood," 218.

[116] See *Babyloniaca* II F4.

[117] Day, "Flood," 223.

[118] Thus De Breucker, "Berossos," 21–22, and P. Schnabel, *Berossos und die babylonisch-hellenistische Literatur* (Leipzig: Teubner, 1923), 155–62.

[119] See De Breucker, "Berossos," 22. In the case of WB 62, which also lists ten antediluvian kings, the number ten seems to be achieved in an artificial manner: the fact that Larsa is included as the second city "seems to be a sort of local patriotism" (Finkelstein, "The Antediluvian Kings," 46).

[120] Jacobsen, *Sumerian King List*, 73, n. 18.

[121] Scholars believe that the total of ten antediluvian kings in Berossos's list is not original. Either it arose from a dittography by Berossos himself or by later transmitters (cf. Jacobsen,

The close parallels between Gen 6–9* P and Mesopotamian flood tradition(s) render it likely that the former was composed in view of the latter. However, the dissimilarities probably point to an additional background tradition. For instance, Gen 6–9* P may depend on a Hurrian or Urartian tradition; the location of the ark's landing place (Ararat) and Noah's name point in this direction. In a Hurrian fragment of the Gilgamesh Epic (K.Bo. vi, 33), the flood hero apparently has the name *ᵈna-aḫ-mu-ú(?)-li-el*.[122]

3.7.2 Relationship with Biblical Texts

Recent treatments of Gen 6–9 P have revealed numerous intertextual contacts with other biblical texts, in particular with other Priestly texts.[123] Most scholars, due to their commitment to the theory of a unified Priestly document, see in these commonalities a confirmation of the theory of a coherent, homogeneous Pᴳ (Pᶜ). Since the present approach reckons with both literary pre-states and redactional reworking of the Priestly texts, the diachronic relationship between Gen 6–9 P and the Priestly texts in question should be reassessed.

Regarding the story's climactic finale, the passage about the covenant with Noah, scholars see in the Priestly flood account an answer to both the prophetic theology of judgment and the Deuteronomistic theology of covenant. The author of Gen 6–9 P maintains that prophecy about the "end" (קץ, see Amos 8:2; Ezek 7:2–6) addressed to Israel by its prophets was already formulated in the primeval history.

Genesis 6:13

¹³ויאמר אלהים לנח קץ כל בשר בא לפני כי מלאה הארץ חמס מפניהם והנני משחיתם את הארץ

¹³ Then God said to Noah, "The end of all flesh has come before me; for the earth is filled with violence because of them; and behold, I am about to destroy them with the earth."

Amos 8:2b

²ᵇויאמר יהוה אלי בא הקץ אל עמי ישראל לא אוסיף עוד עבור לו

²ᵇ Then yhwh said to me, "The end has come for my people Israel. I will spare them no longer."

Sumerian King List, 73, n. 18.; G. De Breucker, "Berossos," 22): The fourth king, Ammenon, has no equivalent in the older forms of the antediluvian kings; perhaps the name corresponds to the postdiluvian king Enmenuanna. This might suggest that this name is a doublet (cf. Jacobsen, *Sumerian King List*, 73, n. 18, who points to the similarity of ἀμμελων and ἀμμενων) or was invented in order to bring the number of kings in the list up to the biblical number ten (cf. De Breucker, "Berossos," 22).

[122] Cf. E. Burrows, "Notes on Harrian," *JRAS* 2 (1925): 281–82, and Hess, *Studies*, 29. Yet this identification is not beyond doubt; see Bosshard-Nepustil, *Vor uns die Sintflut*, 146.

[123] Pola, *Die ursprüngliche Priesterschrift*, 339–40, 286–90; Baumgart, *Die Umkehr*, 187–201, 252–89, 531–42; Bosshard-Nepustil, *Vor uns die Sintflut*, 110–43.

Ezekiel 7:2

‎² ואתה בן אדם כה אמר אדני יהוה לאדמת ישראל קץ בא הקץ על ארבעת כנפות הארץ

² "And you, son of man, thus says YHWH God to the land of Israel, 'An end! The end is coming on the four corners of the land.'"

Yet here, in the Priestly flood story, the logic of God's retribution is broken by God himself: God solemnly vows never again to destroy the world (Gen 9:8–17).[124] Furthermore, unlike the breakable covenant of the Deuteronomists, the covenant given to Noah and to postdiluvian humanity is eternal. Moreover, this covenant is universal rather than limited to only one nation (Israel).[125]

The Priestly flood narrative (proto-Priestly stratum) has several similarities to and affinities with other Priestly texts. The statement that "God looked at the earth, and behold: it was corrupt" (6:12a) interacts with the frequently used approbation formula of Gen 1:1–2:1*, the "bad" condition of the world, and juxtaposes it with the good or very good creation at the beginning, without explaining the massive decline. The author might have intended to leave this question open.[126] The specific vocabulary of the mentioned animals has several commonalities with those of Gen 1:1–2:1* (common designations: ‎עוף, "birds," ‎בהמה, "cattle," ‎רמש, "creeping things.") There are several other similarities of vocabulary and motif with Gen 1, but according to our analysis the passages in question probably belong to the later Priestly redaction, which aimed to reinforce the relatedness of the two texts. In contrast, the primary Priestly stratum has its own specific vocabulary. The expressions ‎חי, "living thing," ‎בשר, "flesh," ‎מבול, "celestial sea," and ‎משפחה, "family" (as a categorizing expression for animals[127]), for instance, do not occur in Gen 1.

Genesis 6–9 P (primary stratum) shares certain common points with the genealogy of Adam in Gen 5 as well. The beginning of the narrative, Gen 6:9–10, uses the verb ‎ילד hiphil and the noun ‎תולדות, both important elements of the composition in Gen 5. Furthermore, the expression ‎ויתהלך את האלהים, "he walked with God," occurs in both sections, attributed to Enoch (5:22, 24) and to Noah (6:9). In both contexts, this term expresses intimacy and a privileged relationship with God: Enoch and Noah are acquainted with particular knowledge from the divine realm.[128] Nevertheless, a

---

[124] Cf. Knauf, "Die Priesterschrift," 102–4; E. Otto, *Das Gesetz des Mose: Eine Literatur- und Rechtsgeschichte der Mosebücher* (Darmstadt: Wissenschaftliche Buchgesellschaft, 2007), 190; Schmid, *Literaturgeschichte*, 146.

[125] Cf. Knauf, "Die Priesterschrift," 102–104.

[126] See Otto, *Das Gesetz*, 190: "Die Frage, wie das Böse in die Welt gekommen sei (Gen 6,12), läßt die Priesterschrift unbeantwortet, was keineswegs Ausdruck eines theologischen Unvermögens sein muß, sondern eher einer theologischen Weisheit, die um die Grenzen unserer Erkenntnis weiß."

[127] Cf. Gen 8:19. See also above, II.3.5.

[128] In Gen 6–9 P, Noah's intimacy with God is perceptible, concrete; he receives insight into Elohim's plan to bring a catastrophic flood; furthermore, this intimacy is expressed through the fact that Elohim speaks to him in a direct, immediate manner (see Gunkel, *Genesis*, 141). It is a traditional motif, borrowed from Mesopotamian epic (Ziusudra, the flood hero, has intimate

clue favors the idea that both Gen 5 and Gen 6–9 P are not naturally connected with one another. The statement that Noah bears three sons in Gen 5:32 does not really fit its context. Since the latter statement is linked to the statement of Noah's age, the reader gets the impression that Noah's sons are triplets or that they stem from three different mothers. This difficulty can be explained by the assumption that the genealogy of Gen 5 presupposes the flood story. The former's author, composing a "bridge" between Gen 1:1–2:1* and the flood story, was confronted with the difficulty of connecting his unilinear genealogy with a narrative dealing with a father and his three sons.[129]

Genesis 6–9* proto-P has also several similarities and common points with the Abraham narrative. In both narratives, the covenant plays a central role. The attributes "complete" (תמים) and "walking with/before God" (הלך *hitpael* עם / לפני) appear in both stories (cf. Gen 6:9 with 17:1). As will be shown below, the theological tendency of the proto-Priestly Abraham narrative greatly resembles that of Gen 6–9* P.[130]

The Priestly flood story (primary stratum) shares lexical commonalities with additional Priestly texts. The word זכר, "to remember," (Gen 8:1) is an important theological term in Priestly texts in Genesis–Exodus.[131] This, however, does not mean that all these texts belong to the same literary layer. R. Rendtorff correctly points to a conceptual difference between Gen 8:1 and 19:29 (both generally assigned to P[G]/P[C]).[132] In 8:1, God instantaneously remembers those he wants to rescue (including the animals and not only Noah [and his family[133]], with whom he concluded a covenant). In 19:29, however, God remembers Abraham (because of the covenant concluded with him) and, as a consequence, rescues Lot. The logic of the latter statement comes closer two other Priestly texts, Exod 2:24; 6:5, where God remembers his covenant with Abraham, Isaac, and Jacob and promises to free the Israelites (Exod 6:5). This observation reminds us to be cautious about assigning the statements in Gen 8:1 (primary Priestly stratum) on the one hand and Gen 19:29; Exod 2:24; 6:5, on the other, to the same literary layer.

Theologically, the Priestly Noah story (primary stratum) does not match the Priestly exodus narrative, in particular the plague narrative and the story of the parting of the sea. YHWH's violent intervention against Pharaoh and the Egyptians is hard to reconcile with God's striking conversion and his symbolically underlined renunciation of violence as presented in Gen 6–9* P. This discrepancy is even more evident

---

contact with Ea [Enki]). In Enoch's case this knowledge remains less concrete: his position (seventh) in the genealogy and the number of years of his life are comparable to the Babylonian sage Enmeduranki, who had access to the gods Hadad and Shamash (see above, II.2.4.1).

[129] Because of this difficulty, SEEBASS, *Genesis I*, 185, assumes that Gen 5:32 would be a later redactional insertion.

[130] See below, II.6.7 (a).

[131] See Gen 19:29; Exod 2:24; 6:5; Lev 26:42, 45.

[132] RENDTORFF, *Problem*, 153.

[133] Noah's wife, his sons, and his sons' wives are not mentioned but are probably subsumed under Noah and included in God's remembering.

in Exod 14 P, where destruction by God is accomplished by the element of water, as in Gen 6–9* P. Note furthermore that in Exod 6–11 P and 14 P it is the deity who "hardens the heart" of Pharaoh (see Exod 9:12; 11:10; 14:4, 8, 17). Linguistically, the destruction by water is described similarly (cf. the use of כסה *piel*, "to cover," with the subject "water" in Exod 14:28 with that of כסה *pual*, "to be covered [by the water]" in Gen 7:19, 20). As for the shared expression בקע *niphal* in 7:11 on the one hand and that of בקע *qal* and *niphal* in Exod 14:16, 21 on the other, its use differs in the two contexts: whereas the "breaking-up of the fountains" in 7:11 initiates the flood, the splitting of the sea in Exod 14:16, 21 opens a way for the Israelites.[134] Scholars point out other striking motifs and lexical correspondences shared between Gen 6–9 P and Exod 14 P (announcement of God's intervention: ואני הנני + ptcpl. in Gen 6:17 and Exod 14:17; God's instruction: אתה + imp. in Gen 6:21 and Exod 14:16; and the use of the verb יבש in Gen 8:7, 14 and the noun יבשה in Exod 14:16, 22, 29). What conclusions can be drawn from this comparison between the two texts? The linguistic commonalities are not proof of common authorship. With regard to the remarkable theological "shift" between the two texts, the parallels should instead be explained by the dependence of one text on the other.[135] What is the direction of dependence? This question is difficult to answer on the basis of the noted parallels and shared expressions. In favor of the dependence of Exod 14 on Gen 6–9 P (primary stratum), however, are the respective literary profiles and contexts of the two texts: Gen 6–9 P, a self-contained and well-marked unit having a beginning and an end, is linked with units of similar profile (in particular with the subsequent Priestly Table of Nations in Gen 10), which bear signs of independence from the comprehensive Priestly composition. Like these units, Gen 6–9 P (primary layer) probably should be assigned to a proto-Priestly level. In contrast, Exod 14 P, though it has a few linguistic and thematic particularities, is conceptually connected to the preceding Priestly texts in Exodus and shares the profile of a redaction with them.

Certain scholars emphasize the correspondences between the Priestly flood story and the tabernacle account.[136] The ark would represent a sanctuary, a prototype of the Sinai tabernacle. However, there is little to suggest that the author intended such prefiguration. Scholars point to the correspondence between construction order and

---

[134] Gen 7:11, however, should be assigned to the second Priestly layer (P^C), see above II.3.4 (c).

[135] For the classification of Exod 14 P, see below, II.8 (it is commonly assigned to P^G/P^C). Assigning both stories to the same author would only be possible if the flood story's final passage about God's conversion was added secondarily to the primary Priestly account. However, there is no cogent argument favoring this solution; on the contrary, since the central idea of the conclusion of the covenant with Noah is developed in this final passage (the statement in Gen 6:18 by itself would seem isolated), the latter should be considered an integral part of the Priestly flood narrative (primary stratum).

[136] See B. JACOB, *Das Buch Genesis*, repr. ed. (Stuttgart: Calwer, 2000), 187; POLA, *Die ursprüngliche Priesterschrift*, 286–90, 367; BAUMGART, *Die Umkehr*, 531–42; BOSSHARD-NEPUSTIL, *Vor uns die Sintflut*, 127–30.

execution (in similar formulation[137]) and the common location of the "sanctuary" on a mountain. But in the case of the first argument, again one text might depend on the other – specifically, the former's author might have taken up the formulation of the latter. The fact that both the ark and the sanctuary are located on a mountain (Ararat/ Sinai) is not in itself significant; in both cases, this location is predetermined by the tradition (Mesopotamian flood tradition;[138] non-P Sinai tradition). Furthermore, the scholarly discussion overlooks the fact that the representation of the ark and of the sanctuary, respectively, in the two accounts have nothing in common. The measurements of the ark (300 × 50 × 30 cubits) and those of the tabernacle (30 × 10 × 10 cubits) are completely different.[139] Remarkably, the dimensions of the ark have elements in common with Solomon's (secular) House of the Forest (100 × 50 × 30 cubits; see 1 Kgs 7:2). Specific architectural and sacral terms of Exod 25–40 are absent from Gen 6–9 P.[140] The term for the designation of the ark (תבה) occurs only once more in the Hebrew Bible, in the non-Priestly text Exod 2.

Summing up this section on the relationship between the Priestly flood narrative (primary stratum) and the Priestly texts in Genesis–Exodus, we note, alongside shared linguistic and thematic features, a few important theological and linguistic differences. The central motif of God's conversion seems to be disregarded in the Priestly story of the miracle at the sea. The important lexeme זכר, "to remember," with God as subject is used differently in Gen 6–9 P than in certain other texts in P[c]. For these reasons, Gen 6–9 P originally probably did not belong to the same literary stratum as the abovementioned Priestly texts in Genesis–Exodus.

3.8 Literary Connections of the Secondary Additions in P

The following conceptional and ideological concerns are perceptible behind the various redactional additions.

---

[137] Gen 6:22; Exod 39:32; 40:16.

[138] See above, II.3.7.1.

[139] The measurements of the tabernacle can be inferred from Exod 26:15–30. Scholars believe that the ground plan of the Priestly tabernacle is half that of the Solomonic temple according to 1 Kgs 6:2 and influenced by the latter. See below II. 10.7.2.

[140] A closer look at the comparison between the two accounts by Baumgart, *Die Umkehr*, 532–33, shows, in my opinion, that the parallels are insignificant. The subordinate concept of a "house" would be the *tertium comparationis* of ark and tabernacle (see also Pola, *Die ursprüngliche Priesterschrift*, 287). But in none of the two narratives does the expression בית, "house," appear! In both units, the building material is wood. However, the terminology is different: עצי גפר, "gopher wood," in Gen 6–9 P; קרשים, "boards"; עצי שטים, "acacia wood," in the tabernacle account. Both "houses" have an inventory: food (מאכל) in Gen 6–9 P and sacred utensils (כלים) in the tabernacle account. Obviously, these inventories are very different from one another!

(1)   The statements of Noah's age (in 7:6, 11 and 9:28–29), attributed to the second-ary Priestly layer, depend on the given ages for the patriarchs in Gen 5. Perhaps they stem from the author of the latter.

(2)   The author of the redaction layer was obviously interested in recording accurate absolute dates for reported events. Such an interest is also discernible in certain Priestly texts in the books of Exodus and Numbers; absolute datings were con-sidered important for the flood incident and for key events in the exodus-Sinai pericope. In other important sections – for instance in the Abraham narrative and in the revelation of YHWH's name to Moses – however, precise dates are lacking. The flood, exodus, and Sinai narratives are set in relation to each other by the attributed absolute dating. There is a striking parallelism between the New Year, which marks the end of the flood (Gen 8:13), the beginning of the exodus (Exod 12:1), and the erection of the tabernacle (Exod 40:2, 17).

(3)   In the secondary Priestly stratum, the outbreak and the end of the flood are de-scribed more concretely and in more specific terms related to the flood under-stood as a cosmic event. Though the primary account presents the event as a depletion of the celestial ocean (מבול) by rain, the redaction layer refers to an inundation *by both celestial and underground waters*. In doing so, this redaction picks up traditional motifs and expressions – bursting fountains (מעינת),[141] the great deep (תהום רבה),[142] and opening heavenly windows (ארבת)[143] – that all appear several times in the Hebrew Bible. Interestingly, the key word מבול of the primary account is not used. Furthermore, the redactor relies on the cosmic geography of Gen 1:1–2:1*, which distinguishes between the waters above and the waters under the firmament (see Gen 1:6–8).[144]

However, the cosmological terms used in Gen 7:11; 8:2 are not exactly the same as those in Gen 1:1–2:1*. These differences seem meaningful and intended. As in Gen 1:6–8, the sky forms a sort of plate or firm vault that retains the waters of the abyss.[145] However, new information is given that goes beyond Gen 1. The sky has windows (ארבת), through which the cosmic rains fall. Similarly, foun-tains (מעינת) on the earth function like gates, which burst at the beginning of the flood and give way to the waters of the "great deep." At the end of the flood, the upper and lower windows are closed: Concerning the two expressions that also appear in Gen 1 (תהום, "primordial sea, abyss, deep," and שמים, "sky"),

---

[141] For "bursting fountains," see Ps 74:15 (identical formulation with בקע and מעין) and Isa 48:21; Hab 3:9; Ps 78:15.

[142] Appears in Isa 51:10; Amos 7:4; Pss 36:7; 78:15.

[143] The expression *'ărubbâ* (*'ărubbôt*) is used in 2 Kgs 7:2, 19; Isa 24:18; Mal 3:10 and is also known in Ugarit (in the Baal Cycle, the expression *'urbt* together with *ḥln* designates a heavenly window through which Baal thunders; cf. KTU 1.4 V 61–62; VI 5–6; VII 17–18, 25–27).

[144] See J. HUTZLI, "La conception du ciel dans la tradition sacerdotale de la Bible hébraïque," *JA* 300 (2012): 595–607.

[145] See above, II.1.4.

their usage in the flood story is strikingly different. In Gen 1, תהום is used only in the passage describing the primordial world (1:2). After sky and sea have been created, the water is never again called תהום, "primordial sea." In addition, the expression רקיע, "firmament," a key term in the creation of the sky (Gen 1:6–8), is missing in Gen 6–9. Indeed, after Gen 1 this term never again appears in Priestly texts. These differences are probably not coincidental. In choosing the term תהום, "primordial sea, abyss," the author of the Priestly flood account (Priestly redaction) alludes to the unstructured, "chaotic" world before creation described in Gen 1. Furthermore, this redactor avoids the expression רקיע, "firmament," which connotes firmness, hardness, and stability. In doing so, he shows that at the beginning of the flood the sky is no longer the firm bulwark that it was when the world was created. If this interpretation is correct, it is with great subtlety that the Priestly redactor refers to the text of Gen 1 and highlights the destabilization of the cosmos at the onset of the flood.

(4)   Genesis 9:1–7, likewise attributed to the secondary redaction, is tightly connected to the creation account in Gen 1 by several shared expressions, in particular those that are related to blessing and multiplication.[146] At the same time, there are several meaningful deviations from the creation story. Genesis 9:3–4 reformulates the dietary law in 1:29–30. In contrast to the latter stipulation, the stipulation in Gen 9 permits the consumption of meat under a special premise: blood as seat of the soul is accounted sacred and cannot be eaten. Furthermore, the humans' obligation "to have dominion, to rule" (רדה)[147] over the animals (Gen 1:26, 28) does not seem to be valid anymore. The striking repetition of the lexeme רבה ("to multiply") in 9:7 MT and SP, though perhaps erroneous, should not be corrected to רדה (since the latter verb is not presupposed by LXX).[148] The absence of the lexeme רדה might be interpreted to mean that "fear and terror" on the part of animals (Gen 9:2) replaces active government of the animals by humans (רדה, "to have dominion, to rule"). Probably the latter was considered utopian and unrealistic by the author/redactor.

In giving a new food law and reformulating the constitutional relationship between humans and animals, Gen 9:1–7 answers the question of how another

---

[146] ברך *piel*, מלא את, רבה, פרה.

[147] The meaning of the verb is disputed: cf. *HALOT* 1190; U. Rüterswörden, *Dominium terrae: Studien zur Genese einer alttestamentlichen Vorstellung*, BZAW 215 (Berlin: de Gruyter, 1993), 81–130; M. Weippert, "Tier und Mensch in einer menschenarmen Welt: Zum sogenannten *dominium terrae* in Genesis 1," in *Ebenbild Gottes – Herrscher über die Welt: Studien zu Würde und Auftrag des Menschen*, ed. H.-P. Mathys, Biblisch-theologische Studien 33 (Neukirchen-Vluyn: Neukirchener Verlag, 1998), 35–55; W. Gross, "Gen 1,26.27; 9,6: Statue oder Ebenbild Gottes? Aufgabe und Würde des Menschen nach dem hebräischen und dem griechischen Wortlaut," *Menschenwürde*, ed. B. Hamm, JBTh 15 (Neukirchen-Vluyn: Neukirchener Verlag, 2001), 21–38; Neumann-Gorsolke, *Herrschen*, 207–23.

[148] See above, II.3.2 (f).

increase in violence can be avoided.[149] According to the redactor, the vegetarian law of 1:29–30 was ineffective for peaceful cohabitation between humans and animals. Living together is only possible through a clear "natural" barrier between the animals and the humans: fear and dread of humans is put on the animals (Gen 9:2). As in Gen 1, God's blessing has a selective function, showing God's preference for the humans – over the land animals in Gen 1 and over all species of animals in Gen 9.

The observations assembled here point to a systematic adaptation of the proto-Priestly flood story to the Priestly units in Gen 1, Gen 5, and Exod 14 P. References and allusions to these texts are manifold. In general, the elements in question match well with the linguistic and ideological profile of the Priestly composition (P^c), although there is vocabulary typical of other literary corpora (Deuteronomistic History, Psalms) too. In addition, the secondary passages reveal the redactor's (or redactors') great interest in cosmic geography, calendars, and perhaps even specific dates (the seventeenth day of the seventh month).

There are clues hinting at redactional development in several stages (allusion to different calendars [schematic moon calendar, exact moon calendar combined with solar calendar] and striking differences in the designation and enumeration of the animals).

---

[149] See above, II.3.4 (e).

4. The Priestly Table of Nations in Genesis 10

4.1 Introduction: Issues in Scholarly Discussion

The so-called Table of Nations consists of a segmented genealogy of Noah's three sons. As in the previous section, the flood story, two literary strata are interwoven here. Both strata are easily differentiable and identifiable by their distinct style and vocabulary. The passages of the first stratum, which are assigned by most scholars to P, consist of verbless lists; they contain repetitive structuring elements (see Gen 10:31: "according to their families, according to their languages, by their lands, according to their nations"; cf. also 10:5, 20) and are marked by systematization. The passages belonging to the other stratum and ascribed by most scholars to J (non-P) have three striking characteristics: they use the pattern "x begot (ילד *qal*) the a, the b, and the c"; the nations cited often appear as gentilics (10:13–14, 16–19); and the list is interspersed with sporadic notes and legends concerning some of the nations (10:8b–9, 19, 25b). Among these three features of the J passages, the first and the third are also features of the genealogical composition Gen 4:17–26 (J).[1]

The literary classification of the first, "Priestly-like" layer, traditionally assigned to P, is not univocal. Since it has a similar position and function within P as does the genealogy of Gen 11:10–26 (transitioning between the flood account and the ancestral narrative) and since it contradicts that text at certain points, a few scholars ascribe it either to J or to a post-Priestly redaction.[2]

Likewise disputed is the literary-historical relationship between the two strata of Gen 10. Traditionally, the J and P passages are considered to belong to independent sources (or to parts of them), the two strata having been combined by a redactor. The J texts are considered to predate P.[3] This theory is increasingly contested; several scholars see the primary kernel of the chapter in the Priestly composition.[4]

---

[1] In Gen 4, the first element, which is restricted to 4:18, should be assigned to a second J layer (Jˢ), see above II.2.4.2.

[2] Levin, *Der Jahwist*, 121–26; Carr, *Reading*, 99–101; Kratz, *Composition*, 237. See also Eerdmans, *Alttestamentliche Studien*, 4.

[3] See, for instance, Gunkel, *Genesis*, 86; Westermann, *Genesis 1–11*, 498–501; Van Seters, *Prologue*, 174–76.

[4] See, among others, Wenham, *Genesis 1–15*, 215; I. Knohl, "Nimrod and the Dates of P and J," in *Birkat Shalom: Studies in the Bible, Ancient Near Eastern Literature, and Postbiblical Judaism Presented to Shalom Paul on the Occasion of His Seventieth Birthday*, ed. C. Cohen et al., 2 vols. (Winona Lake, IN: Eisenbrauns, 2008), 1:45–52; Witte, *Die biblische Urgeschichte*, 110–16; Nihan, "L'écrit sacerdotal," 180–82.

4.2 Significant Differences between the Main Textual Witnesses and Further Textual Problems

(a) Genesis 10:1

MT, LXX (ἐγενήθησαν), Syr. (ܐܬܝܠܕܘ):   ויולדו
SP: ויולידו

The ancient translations take the verb as a *niphal* and render it in the passive voice, which is in accordance with the spelling in MT. The multiple sons of Shem, Ham, and Japheth, on whom the following Table of Nations is centered, are the subject of the sentence ("and sons were born to them"). By contrast, in SP the verb appears in the active (causative) voice (ויולידו, "they begot"), and consequently the following suffixed preposition להם should be understood as the reflexive element "to themselves." Accordingly, Noah's sons are the subject of the sentence.[5]

SP is probably harmonizing with the consist use of *hiphil* in the Priestly genealogies in Gen 5 and 11. ילד *niphal* is absent there (although it is found in other Priestly texts; cf. Gen 17:17; 21:3, 5; 46:20; 48:5; Num 26:60).

(b) Genesis 10:2

MT, SP, Vetus Latina (MSS):   ויון
LXX (MSS):   καὶ Ιωυαν καὶ Ἐλισά
                               ויון ואלישה =

In LXX Ἐλισά (Elisha) is found in the list of Japhet's sons as a plus when compared with MT, SP, which raises their number to eight. Probably one should follow Tal's interpretation, according to which the toponym was erroneously interpolated from v. 4, where it also follows Ἰωυάν (יון, Jawan) but designates one of the latter's sons.[6]

(c) Genesis 10:4

MT: ודדנים
MT^MS, SP, LXX (Ῥόδιοι) 1 Chr 1:7: ורודנים

The reading of MT, which is supported by Ezek 27:15 MT (but not by LXX of that text), perhaps presupposes the identification of the name with the population of Dodona in Greece.[7] The alternative reading refers to the inhabitants of Rhodes.

One may imagine that one of the two readings emerged from scribal confusion between two similar letters, ד and ר.[8] Which reading is original? Since the names of

---

[5] See TAL, *Biblia Hebraica Quinta: Genesis*, 781, and Joüon-Muraoka §133d.
[6] TAL, *Biblia Hebraica Quinta: Genesis*, 781.
[7] Thus P. R. BERGER, "Ellasar, Tarschisch und Jawan, Gn 14 und 10," *WdO* 13 (1982), 60–61.
[8] Thus TAL, *Biblia Hebraica Quinta: Genesis*, 781.

the three other sons of Jawan (Elisha, Tarshish, and Kittim) each designates an island or a coastal area,[9] the reading Rhodians seems preferable.[10]

(d) Genesis 10:5

conjecture: אלה בני יפת בארצתם איש ללשנו למשפחתם בגויהם
MT, SP, LXX: בארצתם איש ללשנו למשפחתם בגויהם

The second and third parts of the tripartite composition each conclude with an almost identical postscript (see v. 20, "These are the sons of Ham, according to their families, according to their languages, by their lands, by their nations," and v. 31, "These are the sons of Shem, according to their families, according to their languages, by their lands, according to their nations"). This formula is partly found at the end of the first part of the composition, in 10:5, too (בארצתם איש ללשנו למשפחתם בגויהם, "by their lands, each with its language, their clans and their nations"). What is absent, however, is the introduction of the postscript, "these are the sons of Japheth," without which the conceptual logic of the text is disturbed. The first part of v. 5, מאלה נפרדו איי הגוים, refers back to the sons of Javan, while the second half of v. 5 concerns all the sons of Japheth.[11]

Apparently the first part of the postscript had already been accidentally left out early in the history of the transmission of the text.

(e) Genesis 10:22

MT, SP: וארם
LXX: καὶ Αραμ καὶ Καιναν
= וארם וקינן

The plus of LXX probably is related to 11:12–13 LXX in the genealogy of Gen 11:10–26, which adds a supplementary generation by inserting Kenan between Arpachshad and Shelah (see below, II.5.2 [b]).[12] Note, however, that the two plusses are not in precise accord. In 10:22 LXX Kenan is Arpachshad's brother rather than his son as he appears in 11:12–13 LXX. Another supplementary mention of Kenan in 10:24 LXX fits better with the additional entry in Gen 11:12–13 LXX.

The shorter reading of MT, SP is to be preferred.

---

[9] Although the identifications are disputed, for each name the association with the sea is confirmed by other biblical texts (see Ezek 27:7 ["isles of Elisha"]; Jona 1:3 ["ship going to Tarshish", cf. Isa 23:6]; Ezek 27:6 ["isles of Kittim", cf. Num 24:24]).

[10] Most scholars follow the reading of SP, LXX: SKINNER, *Genesis*, 199; SPEISER, *Genesis*, 66; WESTERMANN, *Genesis 1–11*, 665, 678; GERTZ: *Das erste Buch Mose*, 296, n. 2. Supporting MT: P. R. BERGER, "Ellasar, Tarschisch und Jawan, Gn 14 und 10," *WdO* 13 (1982), 60–61.

[11] Thus HENDEL, *Text of Genesis 1–11*, 58–59. Differently, W. HOROWITZ, "The Isles of the Nations: Genesis X and Babylonian Geography," in *Studies in the Pentateuch*, ed. J. A. Emerton, VTSup 41 (Leiden: Brill, 1990), 35–43.

[12] See also TAL, *Biblia Hebraica Quinta: Genesis*, 789.

4.3 The Classification of the "Priestly-Like" Layer

Since the two compositions Gen 10 and Gen 11:10–26 both contain a genealogical chain departing from Shem, scholars such as Levin, Carr, and Kratz argue that only one of the two texts can belong to P.[13] They also point to the problem of the immediate sequence of 10:32–32 and 11:10, which constitute a doublet, in an independent P document.

> Genesis 10:31–32
> [31] These are the sons of Shem, according to their families, according to their languages, by their lands, according to their nations. [32] These are the families of the sons of Noah, according to their procreations, by their nations; and out of these the nations were separated on the earth after the flood.

> Genesis 11:10
> [10] These are the descendants of Shem. Shem was one hundred years old, and he fathered Arpachshad two years after the flood.

The aforementioned scholars also see contradictions between the two compositions. Whereas Gen 10 begins with the genealogy of Japheth, Gen 11:10–26, along with 5:32; 6:10; 7:13; 9:18–27; and 10:1 consider Shem to be Noah's firstborn. Furthermore, in Gen 10:22 Elam opens the list of the descendants of Shem; 11:10, on the other hand, seems to consider Arpachshad Shem's firstborn.[14] These difficulties and (alleged) contradictions cannot easily be passed over. It seems obvious that the two texts stem from different hands. If so, which of the two texts constitutes the original continuation of the Priestly (proto-Priestly) flood story? Levin, Carr, and Kratz ascribe Gen 11:10–26 to P[G] and the Table of Nations (primary stratum) either to J or to a post-Priestly redaction. They point to the similarity of Gen 11:10–26 to the genealogy in Gen 5 (whose ascription to the primary strand of P remains unquestioned by these scholars).[15] Carr emphasizes the reference to the flood in 11:10b (which, according to him, would show that Gen 11:10–26 once stood closer to the end of the Priestly flood story).[16] Kratz, furthermore, points to the fact that Gen 11:10–26 presupposes the same order for the three sons of Noah as is found in the flood story (in the Table of Nations this order is reversed).[17] Yet these arguments in favor of the "displacement" of the Table of Nations from P does not stand up to close scrutiny. First, Carr's argument concerning the reference to the flood in 11:10 is not pertinent; this reference after the intermediate Table of Nations is by no means impossible. Second, the inverted sequence of the three sons of Noah expressed by *the structure* of the Table of Nations (Japheth, the youngest son

---

[13] See CARR, Reading, 99–101; KRATZ, Composition, 237; LEVIN, *Der Jahwist*, 121–26.

[14] Cf. also BLUM, *Studien*, 279, n. 187.

[15] See above, n. 13. LEVIN, *Der Jahwist*, 123–24, ascribes the basic framework of Gen 10 to a pre-Yahwist source, arguing that Gen 10* predates Gen 11:10–26 (P).

[16] CARR, *Reading*, 100, with n. 44. Cf. also LEVIN, *Der Jahwist*, 124.

[17] KRATZ, *Composition*, 237.

comes first; Shem, the firstborn, concludes) should not necessarily be considered a contradiction when compared with the order in 5:32, in the flood story, and in other texts. In the context of this question, it is important to note that in the introduction to the Table of Nations (10:1 P), the order is the same as in the flood story (Shem–Ham–Japheth). The inversion of this order in the subsequent genealogy should probably be explained by the fact that the (proto-)Priestly composition relies here on a source text and was willing to preserve its structure intact.[18] Third, neither the assignment of Gen 10* (primary tripartite composition) to J nor its attribution to a post-Priestly redaction layer is convincing. The Table of Nations shows no sign of Yahwistic style. Rather, as mentioned above, it features typical characteristics of Priestly texts (repetitive structuring elements and systematization).[19] Even if it is true that ילד *niphal* does not appear in the Priestly genealogies in Gen 5 and 11, it is found in several Priestly texts (Gen 17:17; 21:3, 5; 46:20; 48:5; Num 26:60).[20] Fourth, and most important, the theory according to which Gen 10* would belong to a post-Priestly redaction cannot explain why here, in the allegedly later composition, some features contradict the genealogy of Gen 11:10–26, as in the statement that Elam (rather than Arpachshad, who appears in the third position in Gen 10*) was Shem's firstborn or the remarkable absence of Eber. No ideological device is detectable behind these two deviations in Gen 10*. In contrast, the deviations in Gen 11:10–26 from the Table of Nations – Arpachshad's status as firstborn, Eber's appearance, and the direct guidance to Abraham – are well explained in view of the continuation of P's narrative (focus on Abraham, Isaac, and Jacob [Israel]). Finally, as will be shown in the next paragraph, the name Shem gets its meaning ("reputation") in the context of the names of Noah's other two sons. Within the genealogy of Gen 11:10–26 this sense is less evident. That means that Shem's literary origin lies in Gen 10* rather than in Gen 11:10–26.

On the whole, it seems more likely that within the Priestly strand the "cumbersome" Table of Nations forms the older part (perhaps a proto-Priestly unit) and that the bridging and harmonizing genealogy in Gen 11:10–26 was added by a Priestly redactor.

---

[18] There are other possible explanations for the inversion of this order in the genealogy of Gen 10: According to BOSSHARD-NEPUSTIL, *Vor uns die Sintflut*, 202, the inverted order in Gen 10 might be due to the landing area of the ark in the flood story (land of Ararat, located in the region of Japheth). Perhaps the inverted order aims further to prepare for the following Terah-Abraham story (located in the region of Shem; see further below, II.4.6).

[19] See above, II.4.1. Cf. also NIHAN, "L'écrit sacerdotal," 180–81.

[20] See above, II.4.2 (a). Thus Levin's contention (cf. LEVIN, *Der Jahwist*, 124) that ילד *niphal* would "contradict Priestly language" is unfounded.

4.4 Content and Profile of the Two Layers

4.4.1 Priestly Stratum

As in the flood narrative, the Priestly stratum represents a self-contained and rather homogeneous composition; it lists the descendants of Noah's three sons up to the third (Japheth, Shem) or to the fourth (Ham) generation. The tripartite division of the world seems to be made according to the two criteria of geographical position and significance of names. First, they stand for the three regions of the world: north (Japheth), south (Ham), and east (Shem).[21] Only one nation, Lydia (לוד, Gen 10:22), does not match its geographical affiliation (it should be ascribed to the north, to Japheth); likely the significance of the designation שֵׁם (see below) is more important for its classification. Second, each name, through its meaning, seems to allude to a characteristic of the relevant nation. Ham (חָם) can be associated with "heat" (חֹם) and "hot" (חַם),[22] and Ham indeed encompasses nations that are located in the hot regions of the south. Shem's name (שֵׁם) may have the meaning "(great) name, reputation" (שֵׁם),[23] which makes good sense insofar as Shem is considered to be the ancestor of five nations (regions) of great importance in the Levant during the first half of the first millennium BCE: Elam, Assyria, Arpachshad (Babylonia), Lydia (in western Anatolia), and Aram.[24] The name Japheth (יֶפֶת) is more difficult to interpret. One possibility seems to be an association with "beautiful, nice" (root יפי), referring to the much-appreciated art and handcrafts that came from this area.[25] This interpretation is based on the observation that Gen 10 P has several commonalities with the poem of Tyre's decline in Ezek 27, in which the beauty (יפי) of Tyre is a key motif (see 27:3, 4, 11).[26] Tyre's splendor derives from the magnificent products typically associated with the city's international trade partners. It is striking that among the latter, several "sons" of

---

[21] Cf. E. LɪᴘɪŃsᴋɪ, "Les Sémites selon Gen 10,21–30 et 1 Chr 1,17–23," *ZAH* 6 (1993): 213; Lᴇᴠɪɴ, *Der Jahwist*, 123. Concerning the absence of the cardinal point *west*, see further below, II.4.8. According to other scholars, the three sons represent the three world regions *north*, *south*, and *middle*; cf. G. Höʟsᴄʜᴇʀ, *Drei Erdkarten: Ein Beitrag zur Erderkenntnis des hebräischen Altertums*, Sitzungsberichte der Heidelberger Akademie der Wissenschaften 3 (Heidelberg: Winter, 1948), 45–56; Soɢɢɪɴ, *Das Buch Genesis*, 166.

[22] For חֹם, "heath," see Gen 8:22; 18:1;1 Sam 11:9, 11; 21:7; 2 Sam 4:5; Neh 7:3; Isa 18:4; *KAI* 200:10f.; for חַם, "hot," see Josh 9:12; Job 37:17. See also E. LɪᴘɪŃsᴋɪ, "Les Chamites selon Gen 10, 6–10 et 1 Chr 1, 8–16," *ZAH* 5 (1992): 135; Soɢɢɪɴ, *Das Buch Genesis*, 166.

[23] It is of interest that שֵׁם, "reputation," plays an important role in the J strand of the book of Genesis (6:4; 11:4; 12:2); see further below, II.4.7.

[24] The inclusion of Aram among the nations of "renown" is due to its political importance, as is attested also in historical reports elsewhere in the Bible (for Aram-Damascus, see 1 Kgs 11:25; 15:18; 19:15; 20 *passim*; 22 *passim*; 2 Kgs 5:1–5; 6 *passim*; 7 *passim*; 8–13 *passim* [Hazael]; 15–16 *passim* [Rezin]).

[25] Scholars often connect Japheth with the Greek titan Ἰαπετός (son of Uranos and Gaia, mentioned by Homer and Hesiod); cf. Soɢɢɪɴ, *Das Buch Genesis*, 165–66.

[26] See also below, II.4.8, on the possible historical location.

Japheth are mentioned: the coastlands of Cyprus (Kittim, v. 6), Elishah (v. 7), Tarshish (v. 12), Jawan (v. 13), Tubal (v. 13), Meshech (v. 13), and Beth-togarmah (v. 14).

What favors the interpretation of the names of Shem, Ham, and Japheth as artificial and evocative names is, first, that none of them are attested elsewhere as designations for the three regions of the world and, second, that the three suggested meanings fit the three "world regions." The three names are almost completely absent from the *onomasticon* of the ANE. There are two attestations of *šēm* as a short or hypocoristic form of a personal name;[27] Ham occurs in three late psalms as a designation for Egypt (Pss 78:51; 105:23, 27; 106:22).

In contrast, most of their "descendants," that is, the nations mentioned in the Priestly (proto-P) strand, are attested literarily and can be identified with some certainty.[28] Exceptions are the names of three sons of Aram (Hul, Gether, and Mash, Gen 10:23) and the cryptic name Arpachshad (ארפכשד, 10:22). The latter probably alludes to Ur-Chasdim (אור כשדים, Gen 11:28, 31) and designates Babylonia.[29]

The almost-accurate tripartite geographical division of the enumerated nations suggests that the (proto-)Priestly composition depicts a plausible literary world map.[30] In this regard, the text is unique within the Bible and the literature of the ancient Near East. The absence of the western cardinal point might be explained by the provenance of the text in a region facing the Mediterranean Sea in the west (see below).

4.4.2 Non-Priestly Stratum

In opposition to the Priestly stratum, J does not constitute a self-contained composition but supplements the framework of the Priestly composition. In doing so, however, it deals only with the descendants of Ham and Shem but not with those of Japheth. As for the descendants of Ham and Shem, the two layers – P (=proto-P) on the one hand and J (=Jˢ) on the other – disagree on several points.

1. P associates Havilah and Sheba with Ham (Gen 10:6–7). J lists these figures among the sons of Shem (10:28–29).
2. According to P, Assyria and probably also Babylonia (see Arpachshad) are attributed to Shem. However, J assigns Assyria and Babylonia to Ham (10:8–12).

---

[27] See N. AVIGAD and B. SASS, *Corpus of West Semitic Stamp Seals* (Jerusalem: Israel Academy of Sciences and Humanities, 1997), 536; F. L. BENZ, *Personal Names in Phoenician and Punic Inscriptions* (Rome: Biblical Institute Press, 1972), 180; *HALOT* 1551.

[28] See, for instance, SIMONS, *Geographical and Topographical Texts*, §§150–51; SEEBASS, *Genesis I*, 256–58, 263; E. LIPIŃSKI, "Les Chamites"; IDEM, "Les Sémites." For Gomer, Madai, and Lud, see also below, II.4.8.

[29] See below, II.4.6.

[30] See T. STAUBLI, "Verortungen im Weltganzen: Die Geschlechterfolgen der Urgeschichte mit einem ikonographischen Exkurs zur Völkertafel," *BiKi* 58 (2003): 25; D. JERICKE, *Die Ortsangaben im Buch Genesis: Ein historische-topographischer und literarisch-topographischer Kommentar* FRLANT 248 (Göttingen: Vandenhoeck & Ruprecht 2013), 72.

The reason for this "faulty" attribution in J remains somewhat obscure. In light of other J texts in close proximity, we might see an association between Assyria and Babylonia on the one hand and Noah's son Ham, who has a negative image in the story in Gen 9:18–27 (J), on the other.[31] Indeed, Assyria and Babylonia are often depicted negatively in the Hebrew Bible (for a negative depiction of Babylonia see, e.g., Gen 11:1–9). According to J, Ham's offspring comprise several other traditional enemies of Israel, another fact favoring this interpretation (see 10:13–19: Egyptians, Philistines, and numerous Canaanite peoples).[32]

3. According to P, Lud belongs to Shem (10:22; in this context, Lud is generally identified with the Lydian kingdom in Asia Minor, which played an important role in the seventh–sixth century BCE).[33] In contrast, J associates the Ludians (לודים) with Egypt and Ham. A precise location (in Africa?) is not possible.

4. The names of Shem's offspring in P on the one hand and in J on the other differ completely from one another (cf. 10:22–23 [P] with 10:21, 24–30 [J]). In P, most of Shem's sons correspond to the great nations of the Levant in the second half of the first millennium BCE.[34] As noted above, the name of their eponym, Shem, "name, reputation," may allude to the political or cultural importance of these nations. In contrast, in J Shem's line leads through Arpachshad and Shelah to Eber, Peleg, and Joktan. The only name the two lists have in common is Arpachshad. Shem is explicitly declared Noah's firstborn (v. 21). Eber – whose affiliation with Shem is emphasized (v. 21) – should be identified with the so-called Hebrews.[35] Since J's Shem lacks the negatively depicted Babylonia and Assyria (see above, 2.) but includes Eber, Shem is the "good seed" of the two Noahide lines in J.

4.5 The Literary-Historical Relationship between the Two Layers

As in the flood story, the literary-historical relationship between the two strata in this chapter is a subject of scholarly controversy. According to the traditional view of the Documentary Hypothesis, the J and P passages belong to independent sources, the two strata having been combined by a redactor. The J texts are considered to predate P. This explanation relies on the assumption that much of the J material (for instance,

---

[31] Cf. KNOHL, "Nimrod," 48–49.

[32] Cf. KNOHL, "Nimrod," 49.

[33] Cf., for instance, SIMONS, *Geographical and Topographical Texts*, §§150–51; LIPIŃSKI, "Les Sémites," 198; SEEBASS, *Genesis I*, 263; NIHAN, "L'écrit sacerdotal," 182–83, with n. 104.

[34] See above, II.4.4.1.

[35] See GUNKEL, *Genesis*, 91; RUPPERT, *Genesis*, 1:474 (but see 477); SOGGIN, *Das Buch Genesis*, 174; WITTE, *Die biblische Urgeschichte*, 105–6.

the entire lineage of Japheth) was – perhaps because of its similarity to the corresponding P parts – left out.[36]

Yet this theory remains speculative and, as in the previous section of the flood story, here also the *prima facie* impression is rather that the self-contained P (proto-P) composition constitutes the old kernel of the chapter; only later on were punctual J passages added. Recently, more and more scholars have come to adopt this view.[37] The fact that some features of the J passages can be explained *by the wish to rearrange the P plot and its structure* supports the idea that J depends on the Priestly composition. J ascribes many of Israel's traditional enemies to Ham, whose line is cursed in 9:18–27 (J). In contrast, Shem's importance is underlined (he is Noah's firstborn) and he is, through his "fatherhood" of Eber, put in relationship to Israel (see above, II.4.4.2.2 and II.4.4.2.4). A similar "national" tendency is observable in the J texts (in Gen 2–4, 6–8 J).[38]

4.6 The Table of Nations (P) as Transition between the Flood Narrative (P) and the Ancestral Narrative (P)

Given that it is the Table of Nations (primary stratum) rather than Gen 11:10–26 that functioned to link the flood narrative and the ancestral narrative at an early stage in the formation of the Priestly writings, one should expect certain connections between Gen 10* and the latter two compositions. There are indeed a few subtle ties between them. As shown above, the Table of Nations is finely connected with the proto-Priestly flood narrative. The tripartite structure has its basis in the three sons of Noah, who are mentioned in the proto-Priestly flood story. The categorizing expression מִשְׁפָּחָה, a key word in the segmented genealogy of Gen 10, is used at the end of the flood narrative for the enumeration of the animals (in 8:19).[39] Since the proto-Priestly flood narrative is firmly oriented toward the Priestly Table of Nations as its natural continuation, that latter should probably be assigned to a proto-Priestly layer too.

The Priestly Table of Nations is subtly linked with the Priestly ancestral narrative too. The spelling of the name Arpachshad (אַרְפַּכְשַׁד) in Gen 10:22 is similar to that of Ur-Chasdim (אוּר כַּשְׂדִּים, Gen 11:28, 31). By using the cryptic name Arpachshad, the author of Gen 10 P probably meant to allude to Terah's initial place of residence and Abraham and his brothers' birthplace. Thus Arpachshad presumably designates Babylonia. According to E. Lipiński, the name's first element *ʾrp* (< *ʾrb*) refers to Arabs or

---

[36] See, for instance, GUNKEL, *Genesis*, 86; WESTERMANN, *Genesis 1–11*, 498–501; S. TENGSTRÖM, *Die Toledot-Formel und die literarische Struktur der priesterlichen Erweiterungsschicht im Pentateuch*, ConBOT 1.7 (Lund: Gleerup, 1982), 21–25; VAN SETERS, *Prologue*, 174–76.

[37] See WENHAM, *Genesis 1–15*, 215; KNOHL, "Nimrod," 47–48; WITTE, *Die biblische Urgeschichte*, 110–16; NIHAN, "L'écrit sacerdotal," 180–82.

[38] See above, II.3.6 (b).

[39] See above, II.3.7.2.

Bedouin.[40] Thus the name Arpachshad might allude to a Babylonian kingdom marked by Arabic influences.[41] Since Shem, the firstborn, follows in third (last) position in the Table of Nations, the transition to the Terah-Abraham narrative is smooth.

4.7 The Relationship to Genesis 11:1–9 (J)

The Priestly Table of Nations shares certain commonalities with the J story about the tower of Babel. Common points include the shared expression (name) שֵׁם, "renown, reputation" (10:22 and 11:4) and the theme of humanity's dispersal and its ethnic ramifications.

However, the two accounts also contradict one the other. The cause of humanity's spreading over the world and of the inner differentiation in nations, tribes, and languages is different. According to Gen 10, this development seems neutral or positive. In Gen 11:1–9, however, it results from humans' hubris, namely, the attempt to reach the divine realm, to "make themselves a name," and from God's countermeasure, confusing their language and scattering them over the whole world.

What is the literary-historical relationship between the two compositions? Does one of them depend closely on the other and react to it? The question is only rarely put forward in scholarship, because the two accounts are predominantly interpreted in their own respective contexts, J and P, whereupon the former is considered to be presupposed by the latter.[42] But treating the texts individually allows us to reexamine the question of their relationship. The few scholars who deal with this relationship believe that the story Gen 11:1–9 is a response to the Table of Nations (Gen 10):[43] In fact, it is imaginable that the author of Gen 11:1–9, by taking up and reinterpreting certain motifs found in Gen 10 (diversity of human languages and their spreading over the world), casts the development of humanity and its ethnic ramifications in Gen 10* in a negative light.[44] What appears as a neutral or positive characteristic of humanity in the Table of Nations becomes a mark of hubris and dissent between God and people.

---

[40] See Lipiński, "Les Sémites," 193–94. According to Lipiński, the evolution of *ʾrp* (< *ʾrb*) is reflected in Neo-Assyrian spelling ("les lettres de Ṭab-ṣill-Ešarra, gouverneur d'Ashour au temps de Sargon II, nomment les Arabes ᵏᵘʳ*Ar-pa-a-a* ou ᵏᵘʳ*Ár-pa-a-a* en se servant du signe cunéiforme *pa*" [193]).

[41] See also Seebass, *Genesis I*, 263 ("Bezeichnet vielleicht Arpakschad ein arabisiertes Chaldäa [Nabonid]?"). In Gesenius 18th ed. 1.101, the name is explained as "district of the Chaldeans" ("Gebiet der Chaldäer") with reference to Arabic *ʾurfa*, "borderland, border."

[42] See Schüle, *Der Prolog*, 382–83.

[43] Witte, *Die biblische Urgeschichte*, 90; Bosshard-Nepustil, *Vor uns die Sintflut*, 210–12; Schüle, *Der Prolog*, 402–3; de Pury, "P^G as the Absolute Beginning," 30–32.

[44] Instead of the neutral פרד *niphal* (see Gen 10:5, 32), the verb פוץ (*qal* "to spread, to be scattered"; *hiphil* "to disperse") is used (see 11:4, 8, 9); this verb often appears in the context of forced exile (for Israel's exile, see 1 Kgs 22:17 = 2 Chr 18:16; Isa 11:12; Jer 40:15, Ezek 11:17; 20:34, 41; 28:25; 34:6, 12 [*niphal*] and Deut 4:27; 28:64; Jer 9,15; Ezek 11:16; 12:15; 20:23; 22:15; 36:19; Neh 1:8 [*hiphil*]). See Witte, *Die biblische Urgeschichte*, 90.

The shared motif שֵׁם, "name, renown, reputation," also conveys a different estimation of the peoples of the east. Whereas in Gen 10 their "reputation" and "renown" seem to be a fact described in a neutral way, in Gen 11:1–9 "reputation" and "renown" appear to be values that Babylonia's ancestors unsuccessfully attempted to achieve. Read in the context of the text's possible continuation in 12:1–3 (in the J strand), it becomes clear that "renown" and "reputation" are not the fruit of human effort but are given by YHWH to whomever he has chosen, for example, Abraham (12:3: "And I will make you a great nation, and I will bless you, and make your name [שְׁמֶךָ] great; and so you shall be a blessing").

Other J texts (the earliest strand, Gen 2:4b–4:26; 11:1–9)[45] are marked by a similar ideological device: the primeval history appears as a sequence of inequities committed by humans (first couple, Cain, entire humanity), who attempt to become like God and contest the will of God.

In view of these points, it seems likely that the text of Gen 11:1–9 belongs to a larger narrative that contains at least the texts Gen 2–3 and 4 and seems to react to certain Priestly (proto-Priestly) texts, for instance Gen 1 and the Table of Nations (Gen 10*). By reshaping already existing compositions and composing new texts, the author(s) of this redaction (J) responded to the "positive" theology and anthropology of the proto-Priestly texts, confronting them with a "dialectical" theology of sharp opposition between YHWH and humankind.[46] In particular, Gen 11:1–9 constitutes a counterstory to the segmented genealogy of Gen 10*. The author interpreted the ethnic and linguistic diversity of humanity as a consequence of human hubris. Furthermore, through the motif of "making a name (שֵׁם) for oneself" (11:4), the author/redactor alluded to Shem and his region in Gen 10, giving it a negative connotation.

4.8 Possible Historical Location

European and American scholars predominantly ascribe the Priestly Table of Nations to the Persian period. This dating is certainly due to P^C's placement in this era by a majority of scholars. But scholars advocating this setting often argue with special regard to the genealogy of Gen 10 P. For them, the composition reflects the Persian *oikumene*; it corresponds neither to Neo-Assyrian nor to Neo-Babylonian but rather to Persian imperial policy.[47] However, we should ask whether Israelite (Judean) scribes in the more nationalist Neo-Assyrian and Neo-Babylonian Empires might

---

[45] See above, II.2.5.

[46] See above, II.1.6, II.2.5, II.3.6 (b).

[47] Cf. J. G. VINK, "The Date and the Origin of the Priestly Code in the Old Testament," in *The Priestly Code and Seven Other Studies*, ed. J. G. Vink et al., OTS 52 (Leiden: Brill, 1969), 61; M. KÖCKERT, "Das Land in der priesterlichen Komposition des Pentateuch," in *Von Gott reden: Beiträge zur Theologie und Exegese des Alten Testaments; Festschrift für Siegfried Wagner*, ed. D. Vieweger and E.-J. Waschke (Neukirchen-Vluyn: Neukirchener Verlag, 1995), 150, n. 16; NIHAN, *From Priestly Torah*, 383; IDEM, "L'écrit sacerdotal," 185–86.

nevertheless have had an interest in the *oikumene* and expressed a multiethnic view or an interest in world geography by composing a text like the Table of Nations. Certain scholars compare the Priestly Table of Nations with the enumeration of nations in the monumental inscriptions of the Persian kings Darius I and Xerxes.[48] But a close comparison of these lists with the biblical account shows that both in form and in content the Table of Nations clearly distinguishes itself from the enumeration of the nations in the inscriptions, which has its own characteristic sequence.[49] Whereas the form of the Table of Nations is tripartite, the enumeration of the nations in the Persian lists is linear. In Gen 10 P, Persia and Arabia are absent; the Medes and Elam, which in the Persian lists are almost always mentioned one after the other, are assigned to two different ancestors (Japheth and Shem, respectively). Finally, whereas the order in the Persian lists reflects relative importance (Persia, Media, and Elam stand at the beginning), in the Table of Nations there is no visible hierarchy.

What speaks *prima facie* against a setting in the Persian era is the fact that Persia is not mentioned in the composition, though the name appears frequently in late biblical writings.[50] Concerning this argument, some have maintained that the author passed over the Persians because he considered the emergence of the Persian Empire too recent a development.[51] In this respect, however, the occurrence of Jawan (Greece) in Gen 10 P, mentioned mostly in postexilic texts of the Hebrew Bible, must be taken into consideration.[52] Moreover, Gen 10 P mentions other nations that became important regional powers a few decades before the emergence of Persia (in the eighth–early sixth century BCE): the Cimmerians (Gomer, Gen 10:2),[53] the Medes (Madai, Gen

---

[48] See KÖCKERT, "Das Land," 150–51, n. 16; NIHAN, *From Priestly Torah*, 383; IDEM, "L'écrit sacerdotal," 185–86. The enumerations of nations are found in inscriptions of Darius I (Behistun, Naqš-e Rustam, Persepolis, Susa) and Xerxes (Persopolis); see P. LECOQ, *Les inscriptions de la Perse achemenide: Traduit du vieux perse, de l'élamite, du babylonien et de l'araméen* (Paris: Gallimard, 1997), 188, 219–20, 228, 232–33, 257 (see also the commentary on 130–49).

[49] All Persian lists have in common that Persia, the Medes, and Elam appear at the enumeration's beginning. For the subsequent nations the sequence is from east to west or inverse; see LECOQ, *Les inscriptions de la Perse*, 134. See, for instance, the inscription of Persepolis (DPe §2): "By the favor of Ahuramazda these are the countries which I got into my possession along with this Persian people, which felt fear of me and bore me tribute: Elam, Media, Babylonia, Arabia, Assyria, Egypt, Armenia, Cappadocia, Lydia, the Greeks who are of the mainland and those who are by the sea, and countries which are across the sea, Sagartia, Parthia, Drangiana, Aria, Bactria, Sogdia, Chorasmia, Sattagydia, Arachosia, Hinduš, Gandara, Sacae, Maka." On the organization of the list, see also G. AHN, *Religiöse Herrscherlegitimation im Achämenidischen Iran: Die Voraussetzungen und die Struktur ihrer Argumentation*, AcIr 33 (Leiden: Brill; Leuven: Peeters, 1992), 267–68.

[50] In total thirty-four occurrences in Esther, Daniel, Ezra, and 2 Chronicles.

[51] Cf. NIHAN, "L'écrit sacerdotal," 185, n. 116.

[52] 1 Chr 1:5, 7; Isa 66:19; Ezek 27:13; Joel 4:6, Zech 9:13; Dan 8:21; 10:20; 11:2. For a useful overview of these texts, see GONZALEZ, "Jawan," 1–2.

[53] Attested in cuneiform records, in Homer (*Odyssey* 11:13), and in Herodotus, *Persian Wars* 4:11–12 (κιμμεροι). Stemming from the northern coast of the Black Sea, they immigrated into

10:2), and Lydia (Lud, Gen 10:22).[54] These observations favor the idea that the author of Gen 10* mentioned nations without any regard to the relative time of their appearance in history. The absence of Persia therefore points to a setting *before* the Persian era.[55] The absence of the name Arabia (ערב), which appears in exilic and postexilic biblical writings, may also be significant.[56]

It is also worth considering W. Spiegelberg's suggestion to take the particular sequence of the Hamites as an indication for the setting: Kush precedes Egypt (see Gen 10:6). This may point to the era of Kushite hegemony in Egypt (Twenty-Fifth Dynasty, 727–673 BCE), especially the rule of Taharqa at the end of this dynasty.[57]

As for the question of the geographical provenance of the composition, the above-mentioned commonalities with Ezek 27, the lament about Tyre's decline, may be significant.[58] This text mentions various tradeware and products connected with the city-state's trade partners. Among the latter one finds several of Japheth's descendants listed in Gen 10: Cyprus (Kittim, 27:6), Elishah (v. 7), Tarshish (v. 12), Jawan (v. 13), Tubal (v. 13), Meshech (v. 13), and Beth-togarmah (v.14). A key word in this composition is "beauty" (יפי): it appears as an attribute of Tyre (27:3, 4, 11), but the beautiful artifacts mentioned in the poetic composition stem mainly from nations of the northern Mediterranean Sea, that is, the region of Japheth.

The question of how Ezek 27 was formed is disputed. A list detailing commerce with a multitude of trade partners is integrated into the poem about Tyre's decline (27:12–24). Generally, this list is considered to derive from an independent document.[59] Yet poem and list seem to be harmonized with one another. W. Zimmerli has observed that the list of trade partners and the poem are mutually exclusive; Kittim (Cyprus, v. 6), Elishah (Crete?, v. 7), and Egypt (v. 7) are mentioned in the poem but

---

Asia Minor and settled in the direction of Armenia (eastern Anatolia). They lost their importance at the beginning of the sixth century BCE.

[54] Lud is mostly identified with the Lydian kingdom in Asia Minor (playing an important role in the seventh–sixth century BCE). Cf., for instance, Simons, *Geographical and Topographical Texts*, §§150–51.

[55] Arguing for a setting before the Persian era are Gunkel, *Genesis*, 154; Eerdmans, *Alttestamentliche Studien*, 9, 91; Noth, *Überlieferungsgeschichtliche Studien*, 254, n. 619; Ruppert, *Genesis*, 1:460; Seebass, *Genesis I*, 267; see also Soggin, *Das Buch Genesis*, 169 (though he hesitates in this).

[56] Thus Gunkel, *Genesis*, 154. The name ערב is found in Isa 21:13; Jer 25:24; Ezek 27:21; 2 Chr 9:14; see also the occurrences of the gentilic ערבי, "Arabian," in Neh 2:19; 4:1; 6:1; 2 Chr 17:11; 21:16; 22:1; 26:7.

[57] W. Spiegelberg, *Ägyptische Randglossen zum Alten Testament* (Strasbourg: Schlesier & Schweikhardt, 1904), 9–11. See also E. A. Knauf, "Ishmael (Son of Abraham and Hagar)," *EBR* 13:352–55.

[58] See above, II.4.4.1.

[59] Cf. K.-F. Pohlmann, *Das Buch des Prophet Hesekiel (Ezechiel) Kapitel 20–48*, ATD 22.2 (Göttingen: Vandenhoeck & Ruprecht, 2001); M. Saur, *Der Tyroszyklus des Ezechielbuches*, BZAW 386 (Berlin: de Gruyter, 2008), 66–74.

are lacking in the list.[60] Ezekiel 27 may be built on an elaborate list of nations with whom the Phoenicians maintained trade relations, and the author of Gen 10 perhaps also made use of such a list (or lists).[61] In support of this view concerning the Phoenician provenance of Gen 10 in proto-P is the fact that neither of the Phoenician cities (Tyre, Sidon) is mentioned and, furthermore, Canaan is attributed to the south (Ham). A striking particularity of the Table of Nations is the absence of the western cardinal point. Lipiński's explanation seems appropriate: the geographical list stems from a region localized at the Mediterranean Sea. From the perspective of a city located on the Phoenician coast, the west is in fact occupied by the sea.[62] In this respect, Phoenicia also fits well as the place of a supposed list that may have served as a source text for the proto-Priestly composition of Gen 10.

It remains to answer how the authors of both texts, Ezek 27 and Gen 10 P, accessed the presumed source.[63]

---

[60] Cf. W. ZIMMERLI, *Ezechiel 25–48*, BKAT 12.2 (Neukirchen-Vluyn: Neukirchener Verlag, 1969), 659.

[61] According to ZIMMERLI, *Ezechiel 25–48*, 659, the list behind Ezek 27 was "a matter-of-fact enumeration stemming from a great commercial house or from a government agency." With regard to the absence of Egypt in Ezekiel's list, G. FOHRER, *Ezechiel, mit einem Beitrag von K. Galling*, HAT I/13 (Tübingen: J. C. B. Mohr, 1955), supposed an Egyptian origin. But M. GREENBERG, *Ezekiel 21–37: A New Translation with Introduction and Commentary*, AB 22A (New York: Doubleday, 1997), 569, raised an important counterargument: "but would Tyre be omitted from a list of Egypt's trade?" Thus Zimmerli's explanation of the absence of important trade partners from the list seems preferable.

[62] LIPIŃSKI, "Les Sémites," 214.

[63] If the authors were priests, we may assume that they had access to the temple archive (cf. GREENBERG, *Ezekiel 21–37*, 569).

5. The Genealogy in Genesis 11:10–26

5.1 Features of the Scholarly Discussion and Important Questions

The Priestly origin of Gen 11:10–26 is undisputed in scholarship. However, the preceding analysis has shown that this unit performs a transitional function in P similar to the Priestly Table of Nations – both texts link the primeval narrative and the ancestral story – and that the two texts contradict each other in certain details, so that they should not be assigned to the same literary layer. We argued that, within the Priestly strand, the Table of Nations forms the older part and the bridging and harmonizing genealogy in Gen 11:10–26 was added by a (or the) Priestly redactor.[1] In general, the relationship of Gen 11:10–26 to all adjacent Priestly texts should be investigated. In this respect, the short specification "two years after the flood," which appears at the beginning of the entry about Shem, is of particular interest, as it contradicts the age designations in the preceding Priestly units (Gen 5:32; 7:6, 11; 9:28–29). Furthermore, the relationship to the similar genealogy in Gen 5 must also be examined. Besides the striking similarities between the two compositions, some differences should also be taken into account.

Genesis 11:10–26 shares certain names with the non-Priestly Gen 10:21, 24–30 in the Table of Nations. The question of the literary-historical relationship between these two texts will be addressed too.

Scholars dealing with the genealogy in Gen 11:10–26 are confronted with significant differences between the main textual witnesses. First, the characteristic tripartite scheme underlying the genealogy of Gen 5 appears in Gen 11:10–26 only in SP and LXX. The MT provides a bipartite scheme and thus deviates from the scheme of the genealogy in Gen 5. Second, the number of the genealogy's entries is different: LXX lists ten instead of nine entries (MT, SP). Third, as in Gen 5, important disagreements between the three primary textual witnesses concern the patriarchs' life spans.

5.2 Textual Differences

(a) Two-Part versus Three-Part Scheme

The genealogy of Gen 11:10–26 resembles that of Gen 5 in having a regular structure and being marked by redundancy. Yet in MT the conformity with Gen 5 is less close:

---

[1] See above, II.4.3.

according to this text, each passage displays a two-part scheme consisting of the same elements:

I: *a* lived *x* years and begot *b*
II: *a* lived after he begot *b y* years, and he begot sons and daughters

What is missing in Gen 11:10–26 MT is the third element of Gen 5 (which, compared to the two preceding statements, does not present any new information). Yet according to SP, the third element is present in each passage of Gen 11:10–26. In the LXX, element 3 is reduced to the statement "and he died." This discrepancy between the main textual witnesses is probably due to a more (SP) or less (LXX) consequent assimilation of Gen 11:10–26 to the composition of Gen 5.

(b) Additional Entry about Kenan (Καιναν) in the Septuagint (Gen 11:12–13) and in Jubilees 8:1

A striking "plus" of the LXX version is the additional entry about Kenan (Καιναν) between the passages concerning Arpachshad and Shelah. Thanks to this "plus," the LXX contains ten passages instead of only nine, as found in MT and SP. The fact that the genealogy in Gen 5 comprises ten entries as well favors the idea that a scribe of the *Vorlage* of LXX (and Jubilees) wanted to harmonize the number of entries in the two genealogies.[2] A further indication for the secondary nature of the plus in LXX may be seen in the agreement of the two time indications (130: age when first child is born; 330: remaining years) with those of the subsequent entry for Shelah (see the table below). Significantly, Kenan is not mentioned in the parallel text of 1 Chr 1:24–25, either in MT or in LXX.[3]

The fact that LXX shares this plus with the Hebrew book of Jubilees hints at a modification on the level of the Hebrew *Vorlage* of LXX, rather than that of the Greek translation, by a scribe of the Hebrew Vorlage rather than by the translator.

(c) Age Indications

As in Gen 5, the three main textual witnesses differ one from the other concerning the patriarchs' ages and life phases. In general, a rather regular diminishment of the patriarchs' life spans from the first to the ninth entry is observable in all textual witnesses, with the exception of Eber in MT and LXX, which in both witnesses is higher than that of his father, Shelah. In MT Terah also lives longer than his father, Nahor.

J. Hughes and M. Rösel consider the MT in general more reliable than SP and LXX because of the realistic patriarchal ages at the birth of the first child (much less than a hundred years, except for Shem). The readings in MT match well with the Priestly

---

[2] See GUNKEL, *Genesis*, 155; RUPPERT, *Genesis*, 1:518; SEEBASS, *Genesis I*, 289; SOGGIN, *Das Buch Genesis*, 186.

[3] See SEEBASS, *Genesis I*, 289. In 1 Chr 1, the LXX (G^B) has a shorter text (running from 1:17 directly to 1:24).

Table 2. Age indications in Genesis 11:10–26

	MT				SP				LXX			
	a	b	c	d	a	b	c	d	a	b	c	d
Year of flood				*1656*				*1307*				*2242*
Shem	100	500	*600*	*2158*	100	500	*600*	*1909*	100	500	*600*	*2744*
Arpachshad	35	403	*438*	*2196*	135	303	*438*	*1747*	135	430	*565*	*2809*
Kenan	–	–	–	–	–	–	–	–	130	330	*460*	*2839*
Shelah	30	403	*433*	*2126*	130	303	*433*	*1877*	130	330	*460*	*2969*
Eber	34	430	*464*	*2187*	134	270	*404*	*1978*	134	370	*504*	*3143*
Peleg	30	209	*239*	*1996*	130	109	*239*	*1947*	130	209	*339*	*3112*
Reu	32	207	*239*	*2026*	132	107	*239*	*2077*	132	207	*337*	*3242*
Serug	30	200	*230*	*2049*	130	100	*230*	*2200*	130	200	*330*	*3365*
Nahor	29	119	*148*	*1997*	79	69	*148*	*2248*	79	129	*208*	*3373*
Terah	70	135	*205*	*2083*	70	75	*145*	*2324*	70	135	*205*	*3449*

a: Age when first child is born
b: Remaining years
c: Ancestor's age at death
d: Date of ancestor's death (in relation to the *anno mundi*)
italics: Derived data (not explicitly stated in the text)

text Gen 17:17, which sees the age of one hundred years (and ninety years, respectively) for expectant parents as unrealistic. In contrast, SP and LXX, which share the same numbers in this "category" (age when the first child is born), have seven numbers that surpass one hundred or more.[4] Hughes's and Rösel's argument is not compelling, the lower numbers of MT might also be considered the *lectio facilior*, a harmonizing attempt to solve the tension with Gen 17:17.

There is another argument against a "general" preference for MT: the fact that in MT and LXX Eber's significance is underlined probably hints at secondary reworking in these two textual witnesses (see further below).

5.3 Characteristics of the Presumably Original Composition

The presumably original composition of Gen 11:10–26 has the following characteristics:

– Genesis 11:10–26 contains nine instead of ten entries, as in the related composition of Gen 5.
– Each entry is marked by a twofold scheme.
– The scheme is consistently carried out; nevertheless, a few rather small deviations are perceptible; they are less prominent than the alterations in Gen 5. The most important of these is the short specification "two years after the flood," which is found

---

[4] J. HUGHES, *Secrets of the Times: Myth and History in Biblical* Chronology, JSOTSup 66 (Sheffield: Sheffield Academic Press, 1990), 85, 11; RÖSEL, *Übersetzung als Vollendung*, 132.

at the beginning of the entry of Shem (11:10b). Furthermore, in the passages on Ar-pachshad and Shelah, once in each entry the *w-x-qatal* חֵי replaces the *wayyiqtol-x* וַיְחִי (both for "and X lived"), which appears in all other passages of Gen 11:10–26 (and regularly in Gen 5).

– By trend, the numbers from the first to the ninth entry decrease in all textual wit-nesses.

– The three names Serug, Nahor, and Terah can be associated with *toponyms* referring to towns in the region of the city of Harran.[5] Furthermore, H. Seebass considers three of the preceding four names meaningful, alluding to Mesopotamia (Shelah, "water canal"; Eber, "across [the Euphrates]"; Peleg, "water canal") and matching the three names Serug, Nahor, and Terah, which perhaps allude to the region of Harran.[6] The name found between the two series, Reu, cannot be attributed to one of the two groups. Seebass tentatively adopts the (unattested) variant reading רְעִי, "pasture" (instead of רְעוּ),[7] arguing that the "artificial" list points to the route from Babylonia to northern Mesopotamia and thus would anticipate Terah's journey from Ur to Harran.[8]

If Seebass's suggestive interpretation is correct, the name Eber, in contrast to 10:21, 24–25,[9] is not used as an eponym of the so-called Hebrews. In the context of Gen 11:10–26 (SP) there is indeed nothing to suggest this association; Eber, together with the neighboring names Shelah and Peleg, hints rather at the geographical area of Mes-opotamia. In the MT and the LXX, however, the situation is different: here Eber's sig-nificance seems to be emphasized through the strikingly advanced age[10]). The only visible reason I can see for Eber's significance is his possible identification with Israel. This may point to the secondary influence of Gen 10:21, 24–25 (J[s]) on MT and LXX. The text of SP, in which Eber's number are inconspicuous, better matches Eber's meaning in Gen 11:10–26.

---

[5] See HESS, *Studies*, 85–89. The proposed identifications are Serug < *URU sa-ru-gi* (appear-ing in texts from the region to the west of Harran, stemming from the seventh century BCE); Nahor < *na-ḫu-ur* or *na-ḫur* (situated to the east of the city of Harran, on the western branches of the river Ḥabur; appearing only in Old and Middle Babylonian and Middle Assyrian texts); and Terah < *til ša turaḫi*, a site situated on the river Balikh in the region of Harran (attested in Neo-Assyrian texts of the mid-ninth century). See also WESTERMANN, *Genesis 1–11*, 746–50; SEEBASS, *Genesis I*, 291. For Terah, see also E. G. KRAELING, "Terach," *ZAW* 40 (1922–23): 153–54. Nahor is also attested as a personal name (see HESS, *Studies*, 86–87).

[6] See SEEBASS, *Genesis I*, 291.

[7] SEEBASS, *Genesis I*, 291. E. G. KRAELING, "Geographical Notes," *AJSL* 41 (1925): 193–94, who identified the name with a toponym *Ru-gu-li-ḫi* (cf. also *HAL* 900), has not found support in scholarship. According to *HALOT* 1264, רְעוּ is a short form of the personal name רְעוּאָל.

[8] SEEBASS, *Genesis I*, 291.

[9] See above, II.4.4.2 and II.4.5.

[10] In MT, it is the highest age after Shem; in LXX, it is the third-highest age. See the table above (II.5.2 [c]).

5.4 Literary-Historical Relationship of Genesis 11:10–26 to Adjacent Texts

(a) Relationship to Genesis 5 and Other Texts Containing Age Indications

Genesis 11:10–26 is tightly connected with the genealogy of Gen 5 and shares with the latter the literary function of bridging different parts in the Priestly narrative strand in Genesis (creation–flood story; flood story–ancestral narrative). Because of the aforementioned differences in form (the absence of major deviations and the bipartite scheme of Gen 11:10–26), it is not certain that the two genealogies are by the same author.

The short specification "two years after the flood" as an indication of Shem's procreation of Arpachshad, combined with the preceding indication of his age at this moment (see Gen 11:10), contradicts the previous age designations in P (Gen 5:32; 7:6, 11; 9:28–29). The latter texts state that at the beginning of the flood Noah was six hundred and Shem one hundred years old, respectively, and after the flood Noah lived another 350 years, with a total lifetime of 950 years. This information suggests that the flood lasted much less than one year (it "counts" for zero years in this chronology) and that at the end of the flood Shem was one hundred years old. The number given in 11:10b can hardly be reconciled with those numbers that, given in isolation, are coherent.[11] On a diachronic level, we should assume the secondary nature either of verse 5:32 or of the statement in 11:10b.[12] The second option makes more sense: 11:10b ("two years after the flood") constitutes a later gloss. Genesis 11:10a ("These are the descendants of Shem: Shem was a hundred years old, and he begot Arpachshad"), considered in isolation, is compatible with 9:28–29; both presuppose a duration of less than a year (five months) for the מבול, "flood."[13] According to Gen 5:32; 7:6, 11; 9:28–29; and 11:10a, Arpachshad is born in the year of the flood (i.e., during or shortly after the מבול).[14] The glossator who added 11:10b apparently felt the need to make sure that Arpachshad was clearly born after the flood. After all, Shem and his wife should have been given a bit time for their first procreation after the terrifying flood.[15] Given that Gen 11:10b is a later gloss, Gen 11:10–26 can be assigned to the same literary stratum as the diverse Priestly age indications in Gen 5–9.

---

[11] See the somewhat forced and unconvincing explanations in JACOB, *Das Buch Genesis*, 306–8, and WITTE, *Die biblische Urgeschichte*, 115–16.

[12] See KRATZ, *Composition*, 234.

[13] Cf. SEEBASS, *Genesis I*, 250. Alternately, one may see in the term *mabbul* a reference to the *beginning* of the flood.

[14] According to BUDDE, *Die biblische Urgeschichte*, 109, and HENDEL, "Hasmonean Edition," 11, the author wanted to prevent Arpachshad from being born during the flood.

[15] Thus BLENKINSOPP, *Pentateuch*, 92; RUPPERT, *Genesis*, 1:522; WITTE, *Die biblische Urgeschichte*, 116, n. 147.

(b) Relationship to the Priestly Terah-Abraham Narrative

The immediate continuation of Gen 11:10–26 is the Priestly Terah-Abraham narrative. The opening passage 11:27–32 shares certain personal names and vocabulary with the preceding genealogy (use of the verb ילד *hiphil*; the personal names Terah, Abram, and Nahor). The transition between the two units is marked by a repetition (11:27 repeats Terah's procreations):

> Genesis 11:26–27
> [26] And Terah lived seventy years, and begot Abram, Nahor, and Haran. [27] Now these are the descendants of Terah: Terah begot Abram, Nahor, and Haran; and Haran begot Lot.

There are indications favoring the idea that the genealogy of Gen 11:10–26 is built on the following Terah-Abraham narrative. As we will see below, the Terah-Abraham narrative has its own distinct literary profile. Important in this respect is the fact that the indications of the patriarchs' ages, which are also found in the Terah-Abraham narrative, are not anchored in the narrative's plot. In certain instances they obviously depend on the non-P context and do not match well with the plot of the Priestly strand; they should accordingly be ascribed to a secondary redactional layer.[16] In Gen 11:10–26, however, the age and time designations form a central and indispensable element. Moreover, as argued above, the proto-Priestly Abraham narrative has some subtle ties to the Table of Nations, which is anterior to Gen 11:10–26.[17]

For these reasons, the genealogy of 11:10–26 on the one hand and the Terah-Abraham narrative on the other probably did not belong to the same literary layer originally. Shared motifs and linguistic elements should be explained by the influence that the Terah-Abraham narrative had on 11:10–26. Assuming this genetic relationship between the two compositions, the striking twofold use of the personal name Nahor in Gen 11:10–26, which creates a papponymy, might be explained as follows: the use of this name for the second son of Terah (11:26) was given by the earlier Terah-Abraham narrative; its reuse for Terah's father (11:22–25) permitted the author of 11:10–26 to create the sequence of the three toponyms Serug–Nahor–Terah (designating cities in the region of Harran; see above). What might suggest such a "redaction-historical" explanation for the repetition of Nahor's name is the fact that it is the only case of papponymy in Genesis.[18]

(c) Relationship to Genesis 10:21, 24–30

The genealogy in Gen 11:10–26 shares certain members with the redactional J texts of the Table of Nations. The first four members are indeed identical with the patriarchs listed in 10:21, 24–30 (Arpachshad–Shelah–Eber–Peleg). This cannot be accidental;

---

[16] See below, II.6.4 (a).
[17] See above, II.4.6.
[18] See Hess, *Studies*, 86.

it is a clear sign that one text depends on the other.[19] In which of the two compositions is the sequence Arpachshad–Shelah–Eber–Peleg more at home? Since the three
names Shelah, Eber, and Peleg probably allude to Mesopotamia, this triad fits well
with 11:10–26, which functions as a bridge to the part of the Terah-Abraham narrative that is located in Mesopotamia.[20] Therefore, the sequence of three names seems
to have been invented by the author of Gen 11:10–26; later, this sequence was reused
by the author of 10:21, 24–30 (J^s), who partially gave them another meaning (Eber as
the eponym of the Hebrews).[21]

---

[19] See SEEBASS, *Genesis I*, 29. WESTERMANN, *Genesis 1–11*, 746–47, mentions the possibility
that both texts rely on a common source, but the fact that both genealogies show clear signs of
artificial composition pleads rather for the "dependence" model.

[20] See above, II.5.3.

[21] See SEEBASS, *Genesis I*, 291.

6. The Priestly Ancestral Narrative in Genesis 11:27–50:13

6.1 Introduction

The P and non-P strands alternate one with one another in the ancestral narrative. With the exception of a few disputed cases, the strands are easily differentiable. Some among the Priestly texts are assigned to secondary Priestly layers (P[s], H[-like]) by some scholars.

This section plays an important role in the debate over the literary profile of P[G]/P[C]. Scholars advocating the redaction model base their argument in particular, although not exclusively, on observations related to the ancestral narrative.[1] Others admit that P, though elsewhere having the profile of a source, in this section is a redaction.[2] In the ancestral narrative the Priestly texts are indeed sparser than in other sections, and at several points they seem fragmentary and dependent on the non-P narrative. However, one should be aware that the literary profile of the Priestly strand is not uniform in the different sections of the ancestral narrative.[3] In Gen 11:27–25:9, which concerns Abraham, P forms a continuous narrative thread that is framed by notices of Abraham's birth, death, and burial. In contrast, in the sections concerning Jacob, Esau, and Joseph, the thin Priestly stratum seems to be fragmentary and dependent on the non-P narrative. Since this difference concerning P's literary profile in the ancestral narrative is mostly overlooked by scholars, the present study will put a special focus on this question and examine P's profile(s) in the two sections. Furthermore, it will ask whether this disparity – if confirmed by the present investigation – is relevant to the question of the inner differentiation of P.

While the few Priestly texts in the Jacob-Esau and Joseph sections are generally considered to presuppose and postdate the neighboring non-Priestly texts, the literary-historical relationship between P and non-P in the Abraham section is controversial. In view of the great number of texts involved in this large section, an overarching, systematic assessment of the question is not possible. Nevertheless, the present study will pay special attention to the intriguing question concerning the relationship between P and non-P in the Abraham narrative (Gen 11:27–25:9).

---

[1] Cf. Cross, *Canaanite Myth*, 301–22; Van Seters, *Abraham*, 279–85; Rendtorff, *Problem*, 136–70.

[2] R. Pfeiffer, "Non-Israelite Source," 67; Blum, *Studien*, 229–85; idem, "Noch einmal," 32–64; Gertz, *Tradition*, 390–91; idem, "Genesis 5," 90–91; Wöhrle, *Fremdlinge*, 147–60.

[3] See Römer, "Der Pentateuch," 105; Blum, *Studien*, "Noch einmal," 52.

<h2 style="text-align:center">6.2 Significant Textual Differences</h2>

(a) Genesis 11:28, 31

MT, SP: אור כשדים
LXX: χώρᾳ τῶν Χαλδαίων

Two additional texts in the LXX render אור by χώρᾳ (see Gen 15:7; Neh 9:7). This raises the question whether the Greek term χώρᾳ, "region, land," presupposes the Hebrew reading ארץ as a substitute for the graphically similar אור. χώρᾳ, "region, land," is a frequent translation of ארץ in LXX and in particular in the book of Genesis (see Gen 10:20, 31; 41:57; 42:9). Nevertheless, in the preceding assertion ארץ is rendered by γῇ, which instead speaks against this possibility.[4] The consistent deviation in LXX indicates an intentional change, either in MT (and SP) or in the LXX. Since the more specific reading of MT is geographically more difficult, and there is no visible motive for a deliberate modification from ארץ, מקום, or מדינה (possible Hebrew equivalents for χώρᾳ) to אור in MT, the second possibility seems more probable.[5] A change in LXX could have been motivated as follows: The translator (rather than a scribe of the LXX *Vorlage*) did not know the toponym Ur-Chasdim and thought that instead of the obscure first element of the toponym an appellative with the meaning "region, land" would be more appropriate. Apparently, archaeological and epigraphic records for Ur (Tall al-Muqayyaren) cease in the Seleucid period;[6] the location of the translator in Egypt (Alexandria), far away from Mesopotamia, may also favor this hypothesis.[7] Perhaps, the choice of the Greek rendering χώρᾳ was influenced by the phonetic proximity to Hebrew אור.[8]

(b) Genesis 11:32

MT, LXX: 205 years
SP: 145 years

According to the statement of 11:32a (MT, LXX), Terah was 205 years old when he died in Harran. The SP offers an alternative number (145 years). At first sight, with respect to the events' sequence in the Priestly narrative, the reading of SP seems preferable.

---

[4] Note that the translator has no problem translating a Hebrew term occurring twice in close proximity with the same Greek expression (for ארץ, see Gen 1:26; 12:5; 17:8; 31:13; 34:21; 36:6; 37:1; 41:34, 36; 47:1, 11, 13, 14, 15, 27; 50:24).

[5] Thus explicitly SOGGIN, *Das Buch Genesis*, 187. Many scholars prefer the reading of MT/SP without giving any argument; so C. WESTERMANN, *Genesis 12–36*, BK 1.2 (Neukirchen-Vluyn: Neukirchener Verlag, 1981), 151–52; LEVIN, *Der Jahwist*, 140–41; VAN SETERS, *Prologue*, 202–3; WÖHRLE, *Fremdlinge*, 25–30, 177–78. H. SEEBASS, *Genesis II/1: Vätergeschichte (11,27–22,24)* (Neukirchen-Vluyn: Neukirchener Verlag, 1999), 2–3, supports the reading of LXX.

[6] See STRECK, "Ur," *NBL* 3:975; J. A. BRINKMANN, "Ur. A. III. Philologisch. Mitte 2.–1. Jahrtausend," *RlA* 14:366–67 ("The last known local documents date from year 12 of Alexander the Great (325) and year 7 of Philip Arrhidaeus (317)," see p. 367).

[7] See also KEPPER, "Genesis," 114.

[8] Thus PRESTEL and SCHORCH, "Genesis," 179–80.

According to P (11:32; 12:5), Abraham left Harran after the death of his father (cf. *wayyiqtol* ויקח in 12:5). The number in SP fits this sequence (Terah was 71 at Abraham's birth; Abraham left Harran in the age of 75, i.e., one year after his father's death). As for the reading of MT and LXX, it might have been composed in response to non-P Gen 12:1, relating YHWH's order to Abraham to "go forth from your country, and from your relatives and from your father's house," a text that seems to presuppose that Terah was still alive when YHWH addressed his order to Abraham.

Scholars generally prefer the reading of MT, LXX. The SP variant is considered a harmonization with the immediate context of P.[9] A few scholars believe that a scribe of MT (LXX *Vorlage*) modified the number in view of the non-P statement in 12:1.[10] Since there are indications that the statements about the patriarchs' ages were composed in view of the sequences of events in the combined non-P/P strand (see further below, II.6.4 [a]), the reading of MT, LXX *Vorlage* might be more original. If this was the case, then the reading of SP indeed should be considered harmonistic.

(c1) Genesis 17:16

MT, LXX:	וברכתיה
SP, LXX[MSS], Syr.:	וברכתיו

(c2) Genesis 17:16

MT, SP:	והיתה
Syr. ܘܢܗܘܐ (*peal* 3rd m.s. impf.):	והיה
LXX: καὶ ἔσται (the gender is not specified)	

(c3) Genesis 17:16

MT, SP, LXX:	ממנה
LXX[MSS] (ἐξ αὐτοῦ), Syr. (ܡܢܗ, 3rd m.s. suff.):	ממנו

As for the difference, MT and LXX (according to the Göttingen edition[11]) may appear redundant (God blesses Sarah twice). SP reads the pronominal suffix as masculine; the latter refers to Isaac. The second half of the verse contains a promise that, according to MT and SP, is related to Sarah. In a less important Greek manuscript and the Peshitta (Syriac translation) the promise concerns Isaac. What favors the reading of

---

[9] DILLMANN, *Die Genesis*, 226; SEEBASS, *Genesis II/1*, 3. Many commentators and translations follow MT without pointing to the textual difference.

[10] BUDDE, *Die biblische Urgeschichte*, 429–30; GUNKEL, *Genesis*, 158. Budde points to an important aspect of this case: Gen 11:32 is not significant for the chronological system of either SP or MT. The textual difference is certainly due to the discrepancy between the close narrative contexts of P and non-P, respectively.

[11] The text of the Göttingen edition is based, among others, on the old papyrus called Berlin Genesis (911).

MT and SP in v. 16b is that "the passage is concerned with Sarah, whereas her son is as yet incidental."[12]

(d) Genesis 36:6

MT: וילד אל ארץ מפני יעקב אחיו

SP, LXX (καὶ ἐπορεύθη ἐκ γῆς Χανααν ἀπὸ   וילד מארץ כנען מפני יעקב אחיו
προσώπου Ιακωβ τοῦ ἀδελφοῦ αὐτοῦ):

LXX agrees with the reading of SP; most probably its model had the same reading as SP. The MT of Gen 36:6 is quite enigmatic: "Then Esau took his wives and his sons and his daughters ... and all his goods which he had acquired in the land of Canaan and went *to a land away* from his brother Jacob." Considered in isolation, one might understand MT in the sense that Esau settled in a country distinct from that of Jacob but that is nevertheless part of the "land of Canaan" (although the wording of 36:6 seems to set Esau's new land in opposition to the land of Canaan, where he had acquired all his goods). The SP and LXX are clearer: "and he left the land of Canaan away from his brother Jacob." Assessed in the broader context of P, however, the sense of the two readings seems the same. In view of Gen 37:1 (P, וישב יעקב בארץ מגרי אביו בארץ כנען, "And Jacob settled in the land of the sojournings of his father, in the land of Canaan"), 36:6 MT should also be understood in the sense that Esau left the land of Canaan in order to live "in a land away from his brother Jacob."

Which reading is more ancient? Probably SP and LXX *Vorlage* intended to clarify the sense of MT.

6.3 The Assignment of the Text to P and Non-P: Disputed Cases

(a) Genesis 11:28–30

With regard to its vocabulary, many scholars ascribe Gen 11:28–30 to non-P or J;[13] others consider the entirety of 11:27–32 to belong to P.[14] This involves the question concerning the literary coherence and unity of the introduction in 11:27–32 as well.

---

[12] SPEISER, *Genesis*, 125. Scholars generally follow the readings of MT, LXX (and SP); see, among others, WESTERMANN, *Genesis 12–36*, 305; SEEBASS, *Genesis II/1*, 97. Differently SHECTMAN, *Women*, 139, who argues that "annunciation scenes usually follow the announcement of the son with predictions or statements about the son, and not the mother." A middle course is taken by SPEISER (*Genesis*, 125): the second occurrence of the verb "to bless" has Isaac as its object (cf. SP), while the following promise again refers to Sarah (as in MT and SP).

[13] Cf. ELLIGER, "Sinn," 121; LOHFINK, "Die Priesterschrift," 198, n. 29; GUNKEL, *Genesis*, 162–63; VON RAD, *Das erste Buch*, 129; WESTERMANN, *Genesis 12–36*, 134; VAN SETERS, *Prologue*, 202; CARR, *Reading*, 110–11; KRATZ, *Composition*, 238; SHECTMAN, *Women*, 80.

[14] DILLMANN, *Die Genesis*, 222; BLUM, *Die Komposition*, 441–42; SCHMID, *Genesis and the Moses Story*, 94, with n. 266; J.-L. SKA, "The Call of Abraham and Israel's Birth-Certificate (Gen 12:1–4a)," in *The Exegesis of the Pentateuch*, FAT 66 (Tübingen: Mohr Siebeck, 2009), 48–49, with n. 14; WÖHRLE, *Fremdlinge*, 25–30.

Genesis 11:27–32

²⁷ Now these are the descendants of Terah. Terah became the father of Abram, Nahor, and Haran; and Haran became the father of Lot. ²⁸ And Haran died in the presence of [על פני] his father Terah in the land of his birth [ארץ מולדתו], in Ur of the Chaldeans. ²⁹ And Abram and Nahor took wives for themselves. The name of Abram's wife was Sarai; and the name of Nahor's wife was Milcah, the daughter of Haran, the father of Milcah and Iscah. ³⁰ And Sarai was barren [עקרה]; she had no child. ³¹ And Terah took Abram his son, and Lot the son of Haran, his grandson, and Sarai his daughter-in-law, his son Abram's wife; and they went out together from Ur of the Chaldeans in order to enter the land of Canaan; and they went as far as Harran, and settled there. ³² And the days of Terah were two hundred and five years; and Terah died in Harran.

Scholars who attribute 11:28–30 to non-P (J) point first to the expression מולדת (11:28; here "nativity, birth"), which appears in 12:1 (non-P) in close proximity and which generally occurs more frequently in non-P than in P.[15] Second, they note the term עקרה ("barren," 11:30), which appears twice in non-P texts but nowhere else in P.[16] However, on the whole, these linguistic arguments are not convincing.

As for the term מולדת, it is used differently in 11:28 and 12:1 (non-P). First, the grammatical construction is different (genitival group in 11:28: בארץ מולדת; two independent nouns in 12:1: מארצך ומולדתך). Second, with regard to the motif of Haran's procreation (ילד hiphil) in 11:27, מולדת in 11:28 means "nativity," rather than "relatives" as in 12:1 (non-P). The meaning "nativity, birth" for מולדת is evident in Jer 22:10; 46:16; Ezek 16:3, 4; 23:15.[17] Furthermore, 11:28 contains the typical Priestly term על פני, "before, in presence of" (see Num 3:4b and Gen 23:19; 25:9, 18) and the toponym Ur of the Chaldeans, which is found also in Gen 11:31 (P). These observations taken together render the assignment of 11:28 to the Priestly strand probable.

Concerning the expression עקרה (v. 30), we should take into account that this expression is the common designation of barrenness and that the Abraham narrative is the only Priestly text dealing with the problem of childlessness and sterility. The singularity of the expression within P should therefore not be considered a problem. The tension with Abraham's objection in Gen 17:17 concerning Abraham's and Sarah's old age should be explained by the secondary origin of the age indications and of the passage containing the motif of the couple's old age (which is borrowed from the non-P strand).[18]

---

[15] Non-P: Gen 12:1; 24:4; 31:3; 32:10; 43:7; P: 48:6.

[16] Cf. Gen 25:21; 29:31.

[17] Cf. *HALOT* 556; *KAHAL* 284, and most translations (for instance, KJV, NASB, NJB, NJPS) translate "nativity" or "birth" in 11:28 and in all the above-mentioned texts. As for the occurrence of מולדת in 12:1, the sense "kindred, relatives" is undisputed.

[18] See below, II.6.4 (a), (b).

Summing up, there is no cogent linguistic argument to disconnect vv. 28–30 from the Priestly passage Gen 11:27–32, which seems coherent in itself.

(b) Genesis 16:1a

The current scholarly classification of this half verse is controversial. Traditionally, v. 1a is assigned to P.[19] The specification "Abram's wife" after "Sarai" is considered typically Priestly (see v. 3); however, Carr calls this argument into question. If P contained both statements in v. 1a and v. 3, it would "doubly identify" Sarai in two consecutive phrases (within an independent P document).[20] Note furthermore that since Sarai's barrenness was already noted in 11:30, 16:1a is not an indispensable element for a continuous Priestly thread.[21] Nevertheless, repetition and redundance are typical features of the Priestly narrative (cf. Gen 16:15; 21:2–3; see below).

(c) Genesis 16:15; 21:2–3

The statements of Ishmael's and Isaac's birth and naming (16:15; 21:2–3), tradition- · ally ascribed to P, are considered to belong to non-P by a few scholars.[22] However, the redundant structure of the sentences with the relative clause (the structure of the two texts is very similar) and the close vicinity of an undisputed P verse in each case (16:16; 21:4) favor their attribution to P. Furthermore, the use of the expression הרה, "to conceive, to get pregnant" (21:2; lacking in 16:15), which is unique in P – but the common designation for conception in the Hebrew Bible! – is well explained by Sarah's former barrenness, which is an important motif of the plot.[23] Moreover, we should also take into consideration the possibility that P relies on a proto-Priestly story having its own linguistic and thematic characteristics.

---

[19] See GUNKEL, *Genesis*, 158 (v. 1a), 264; NOTH, *Überlieferungsgeschichtliche Studien*, 17; ELLIGER, "Sinn," 121 (v. 1); SPEISER, *Genesis*, 116; KRATZ, *Composition*, 231 (v. 1a). For the assignment of the verse to non-P, see WELLHAUSEN, *Die Composition*, 15; DILLMANN, *Die Genesis*, 264; WESTERMANN, *Genesis 12–36*, 405; E. A. KNAUF, *Ismael: Untersuchungen zur Geschichte Palästinas und Nordarabiens im 1. Jahrtausend v. Chr.*, 2nd ed., ADPV (Wiesbaden: Harrassowitz, 1989), 25; I. FISCHER, *Die Erzeltern Israels: Feministisch-theologische Studien zu Genesis 12–36*, BZAW 222 (Berlin: de Gruyter, 1994), 260–61; CARR, *Reading*, 111, n. 69.

[20] CARR, *Reading*, 111, n. 69.

[21] See DILLMANN, *Die Genesis*, 264.

[22] Assigning Gen 16:15; 21:2–3 to P are ELLIGER, "Sinn," 121; LOHFINK, "Die Priesterschrift," 198, n. 29; DILLMANN, *Die Genesis*, 267, 294–95; GUNKEL, *Genesis*, 264, 272; NOTH, *Überlieferungsgeschichte*, 13; VON RAD, *Das erste Buch*, 147–48, 182; W. ZIMMERLI, *1. Mose 12–25*, ZBK 1.1 (Zurich: TVZ, 1976), 60, 99; SEEBASS, *Genesis II/1*, 91, 183; RUPPERT, *Genesis*, 2:298, 460; KRATZ, *Composition*, 238–40. Ascribing these verses to a non-P layer are RENDTORFF, *Problem*, 124–25; BLUM, *Die Komposition*, 316; WÖHRLE, *Fremdlinge*, 42–44, 55.

[23] *Contra* WÖHRLE, *Fremdlinge*, 55.

(d) Genesis 21:1b

The statement about YHWH's intervention for Sarah in Gen 21:1b ("and YHWH did for Sarah as he had spoken") is often ascribed to the Priestly strand.[24] The doubling of the fulfillment statement certainly indicates the presence of two different literary layers. What favors the assignment of 21:1b to P is that it fits nicely with the promise in 17:15–16 (YHWH will bless Sarah and will give Abraham a son by her). Furthermore, it employs typical linguistic and theological features of P (use of עשׂה with YHWH/God as subject; correspondence of YHWH/God's act with its announcement).[25] In addition, the following passage reporting the birth of Isaac stems from P.[26] The use of the theonym YHWH led Wöhrle to ascribe 21:1b to non-P.[27] However, the Tetragram also appears in Gen 17:1, an undisputed P text. The twofold use of the theonym YHWH in close vicinity in this section of P is striking; it will be discussed below.[28]

6.4 Inner Differentiation of the Priestly Ancestral Narrative in Current Scholarship

This section will discuss all cases where the unity of a Priestly text is disputed in scholarship. In the subsequent sections, this study will propose a further differentiation within the P stratum based on the differences observed in the literary profile of the Priestly texts in the Abraham section on the one hand and in the Isaac, Jacob-Esau, and Joseph sections on the other (see below, II.6.5–6).

(a) Statements about the Patriarchs' Ages

The Priestly ancestral narrative contains a total of seventeen statements about the patriarchs' ages.[29] Despite minor formal differences, the statements share important commonalities and are coherent.[30]

---

[24] See, among others, DILLMANN, *Die Genesis*, 295; ELLIGER, "Sinn," 121; SPEISER, *Genesis*, 153–54; LOHFINK, "Die Priesterschrift," 198, n. 29; POLA, *Die ursprüngliche Priesterschrift*, 124, 129, 132; CARR, *Reading*, 97–98, with n. 36; KRATZ, *Composition*, 238–40. According to other scholars, P's account of Isaac's birth begins only in 21:2; see WELLHAUSEN, *Die Composition*, 15; WESTERMANN, *Genesis 12–36*, 405, WÖHRLE, *Fremdlinge*, 54.

[25] See Gen 1:7, 16, 25; 8:1–2. See also the correspondence between YHWH's oral order, his *word*, and Moses and the people's execution in the Tabernacle account (Exod 35:4, 29; 39:1, 5, 7, 21, 26, 29, 31, 43; 40:19, 21, 23, 25, 27, 29, 32).

[26] See the preceding paragraph (c).

[27] WÖHRLE, *Fremdlinge*, 54.

[28] See II.6.6.4.

[29] See Gen 11:32a; 12:4a; 16:16; 17:1; 17:24, 25; 21:5; 23:1; 25:7, 17, 20, 26; 26:34; 35:28; 37:2; 41:46; 47:28. In the exodus section, chronological information is given only in Exod 12:40, 41.

[30] In some of the statements the order of numbers is ascending (e.g., 12:4: five years and seventy years), for others descending (e.g., 16:16: eighty years and six years).

In one group of examples, the statement begins with the *wayyiqtol* of היה, followed by the personal name and the indication of age.[31] The second group has the sequence PN – indication of age (with the element בֶן) – infinitive construct with בְ (expressing a subordinate sentence).[32] The former figure refers to upcoming events, the latter to an episode reported in a preceding passage.[33] A striking particularity shared by all examples is the repetition of the expression "year/years" (שׁנה/שׁנים) after each digit.[34]

All examples are commonly assigned to P^G/P^C. A few scholars, however, recognize that some of these notes (Gen 12:4b; 17:1a) do not fit the intimate (proto-)Priestly context.[35] Furthermore, as shown above in the methodological introduction, it seems that these statements belong to a comprehensive chronological network including data from outside the Pentateuch.[36] This referential chronology raises the question of the classification of these chronological notes. Are they unified among themselves? Do they belong to a Priestly layer (proto-P, P^C, P^S) or should they rather be ascribed to a comprehensive late P or post-P redaction? An initial clue to answer these questions is the fact that several of the age statements do not fit well with the immediate P (proto-P) context and partly depend on non-P. Significantly, all statements that stand in tension with the P context belong to the Priestly Abraham narrative:

(1) The half verse Gen 12:4b, about Abraham's age at his departure from Harran, which is commonly ascribed to P, presupposes the late non-P context of Gen 12:1–4a. Furthermore, Gen 12:4b *doubles* the following verse, v. 5 (P). This is a sure sign that the two verses (4b and 5) do not belong to the same literary layer.[37]

> Genesis 12:4–5
> [4a] (*non-P*) *So Abram went forth as* YHWH *had spoken to him; and Lot went with him.* [4b] (P) Abram was seventy-five years old when he departed from Harran. [5] And Abram took Sarai his wife and Lot his nephew, and all their possessions which they had accumulated, and the persons which they had acquired in Harran, and they set out for the land of Canaan; thus they came to the land of Canaan.

(2) Concerning the age indication at the beginning of God's revelation to Abraham (Gen 17:1a), R. Rendtorff argues that normally the verb "appear" (ראה *hiphil*) stands at the beginning of a statement about God's revelation.[38]

---

[31] See Gen 11:32a; 17:1, 23:1; 25:7, 26:34; 35:28; 47:28.

[32] See Gen 12:4a; 16:16; 17:24, 25; 21:5; 25:26; 41:46. The classification of 25:17, 20; 37:2 is unclear.

[33] Wöhrle, *Fremdlinge*, 35.

[34] This peculiar spelling with the repetition of the expression שׁנה occurs only in texts commonly assigned to the Priestly stratum. For the exception, 1 Kgs 6:1, see below, III.1.2.2 (b) (3).

[35] For Gen 12:4b, see Kratz, *Composition*, 238–39; for 17:1a, see Rendtorff, *Problem*, 159.

[36] See above, I.2.5, and the more detailed argument below, III.1.2.2 (b) (3).

[37] See also Kratz, *Composition*, 238–39.

[38] See Rendtorff, *Problem*, 159.

Genesis 17:1

¹And Abram was ninety-nine years old, and YHWH appeared to Abram (ויהי אברם
בן תשעים שנה ותשע שנים וירא יהוה אל אברם) and said to him, "I am El Shaddai." ...

In addition to the statement about YHWH's revelation appearing only in the second
sentence, the name of Abram is repeated. Both features may indicate that the notice
concerning Abram's age is secondary.

(3) Abraham's argument in 17:17 concerning his and Sarah's advanced age (they are
one hundred, and ninety, respectively) is surprising given the earlier mention of Sarah's barrenness (11:30; cf. 16:1a, 3³⁹). The preceding episode in Gen 16 P gives no indication of Sarah's old age, and assuming that her old age (76 years) was presupposed
by the P plot, one would wonder why she would not have given her maidservant to
Abraham long before. Abraham's reasoning is probably influenced by the non-P story
in Gen 18. Here, the couple's old age as an obstacle to having children is an important
theme (see 18:11). Genesis 17:17–22 is influenced by non-P stories concerning Abraham in other instances as well.⁴⁰ All other indications of Abraham's and Sarah's ages
are aligned with the assertion in 17:17, i.e., those for Abraham in 12:4b (75 years), 16:15
(86 years), 17:1a (99 years), 21:5 (100 years), 25:7 (175 years), and that for Sarah in 23:1
(127 years).

(4) Genesis 25:8 mentions Abraham's (natural) advanced age at his death in a
three-part expression (he died "at a ripe old age, an old man and satisfied [with life]");
following the precise indication of his age in 25:7 (the unnaturally high number of
175), this assertion seems awkward.

Genesis 25:7–8

⁷And these are all the years of Abraham's life that he lived, one hundred and
seventy-five years. ⁸And Abraham breathed his last and died at a ripe old age, an
old man and satisfied (with life); and he was gathered to his kin.

The presence of the two statements dealing with Abraham's age is best explained by
assuming that v. 8 belongs to the original story and v. 7 was inserted secondarily.

As for the remaining statements of age in the ancestral narrative, there are no signs
of incoherence in their Priestly contexts.⁴¹ Notably, however, the five statements of
age in the Isaac, Jacob-Esau, and Joseph sections are better embedded in their intimate Priestly contexts. In the first example, the age indication is formulated as the
main clause while the relevant Priestly content follows within the subordinate clause
(25:20aβγ, b):

---

³⁹ As shown above, it is not certain that Gen 16:1a belongs to P (see above, II.6.3 [b]).

⁴⁰ See below, (b).

⁴¹ See Gen 11:32a; 16:16; 21:5; 23:1; 25:17, 20, 26; 35:28; 37:2; 41:46; 47:28.

Genesis 25:20

²⁰ ויהי יצחק בן ארבעים שנה בקחתו את רבקה בת בתואל הארמי מפדנארם אחות לבן
הארמי לו לאשה

²⁰ And Isaac was forty years old when he took [בקחתו] Rebekah, the daughter of Bethuel the Aramean of Paddan-aram, the sister of Laban the Aramean, to be his wife.

Here, the Priestly context (25:20aβγb) visibly *depends on the age statement*, which favors the idea that it stems from the same author as the latter.

The following four age statement in the Jacob-Esau and Joseph sections likewise fit their immediate Priestly contexts. As some indications in the Abraham section, they partly depend on information of the non-Priestly plot. At the same time, however, there is no sign of disruption, tension or repetition in relation to neighboring Priestly texts.

To sum up: several age indications belonging to the Priestly Abraham narrative do not fit with their Priestly contexts. Regarding these examples, one should ask whether all age indications belong to a redaction, which secondarily complemented the primary stratum. By contrast, in the Isaac, Jacob-Esau, and Joseph sections, no tensions or incoherence with other Priestly statements are visible. On the contrary, at least one age statement seems to be a necessary element of the Priestly plot. How to explain this contrasting evidence? The observed discrepancy probably points to different Priestly contexts in the Abraham section on the one hand and in the subsequent sections on the other. The following paragraphs will further support this tentative hypothesis. There are several reasons to conclude that the Priestly passages in the Abraham section originally formed a self-contained narrative (a proto-Priestly unit) that predated the Priestly stratum in the Isaac, Jacob-Esau, and Joseph sections (see further II.6.5–6). The age indications seem to be an integral part of the latter.

(b) Inner Differentiation of Genesis 17

Scholars are unanimous in assigning Gen 17 to the Priestly strand. As for the question of the chapter's unity, however, they are divided. Many, relying partly on the influential study of S. McEvenue, defend the unity of the composition.[42] Others point to linguistic differences and conceptual tensions in this unit, suggesting an inner, diachronic differentiation. In particular, the passages containing the order for circumcision (17:9–14) and its execution (17:23–27) are often ascribed to a late (or post-) Priestly layer.[43] In the first half of twentieth century, scholars often differentiated between several layers.[44]

---

[42] See McEvenue, *Narrative Style*, 145–78, and the positive recourse on his analysis in Van Seters, *Abraham*, 279ff.; Westermann, *Genesis 12–36*, 305–6; Blum, *Die Komposition*, 420–22.

[43] See Levin, *Der Jahwist*, 157; Seebass, *Genesis II/1*, 111; Wöhrle, "Integrative Function," 74–84; idem, *Fremdlinge*, 46–50.

[44] C. Steuernagel, "Bemerkungen zu Genesis 17," in *Beiträge zur alttestamentlichen Wissenschaft (Festschrift K. Budde)*, ed. K. Marti, BZAW 34 (Giessen: Töpelmann, 1920), 172–79;

More recently, Weimar has argued for a differentiation between four different literary strata, identifying a pre-Priestly kernel in Gen 17:1–4a, 6, and 22.[45] The present study likewise sees indications of incoherence in the composition, in particular in what concerns the conception and the addressee of the covenant.

(1) Covenant: Conditional or Unconditional?

As some scholars have noted, Gen 17:1–4 contains both a conditional and an unconditional statement about the covenant. Both refer to the promise of abundant offspring.

Genesis 17:1b–2
[1b]And YHWH appeared to Abraham and said, "I am El Shaddai. Walk before me, be blameless, [2]that I might give my covenant [ואתנה בריתי] between me and you [ביני ובינך], and that I will multiply you exceedingly."

Genesis 17:4
[4]"As for me, behold, my covenant is with you [בריתי אתך], And you shall be the father of a multitude of nations."

According to both statements, God's covenant consists in providing Abraham a rich, multiethnic offspring. Yet the mode of the two statements is different. In the center of the first statement is a cohortative (volitive) form (ואתנה); since it follows two imperatives, it must be understood as a final or as a consecutive clause.[46] This means that the promise expressed in 17:2 is conditioned on Abraham's obedience to the command to "walk before YHWH and to be blameless."[47] In contrast to this, in v. 4 the covenant appears as gift given to Abraham (in the nominal clause "behold, my covenant is with you"). Furthermore, in 17:2, as in 17:7, 10, 11, the bilateral character of the covenant seems to be underlined by the phrase ביני ובינך, "between me and you." Some scholars compare this feature to the emphasis on strict observance of YHWH's commandments in P.[48] Interestingly, the formulation of 17:4 also deviates from 17:2 ("my covenant is *with you* [אתך]") in this respect. These discrepancies are rarely considered by scholars, who tend to place the different assertions about the covenant in Gen 17 on the same literary level; the discussion focuses in a general way on the question whether

---

M. Löhr, *Untersuchungen zum Hexateuchproblem, I: Der Priestercodex in der Genesis*, BZAW 38 (Giessen: Töpelmann, 1924), 11–14; von Rad, *Die Priesterschrift*, 20–25.

[45] Weimar, *Studien*, 185–225.

[46] See *GKC* §108d; Joüon-Muraoka §116bl; McEvenue, *Narrative Style*, 162; W. Gross, "Bundeszeichen und Bundesschluss in der Priesterschrift," *TTZ* 87 (1978): 111, n. 27; Knohl, *Sanctuary*, 138, 141, n. 66; Weimar, "Gen 17," 39.

[47] For the signification of this expression, see below, II.6.7 (a).

[48] Knohl, *Sanctuary*, 141–42; J. Joosten, *People and Land in the Holiness Code: An Exegetical Study of the Ideational Framework of the Law in Leviticus 17–26*, VTSup 67 (Leiden: Brill, 1996); J. Milgrom, *Leviticus 23–27: A New Translation with Introduction and Commentary*, AB 3B (New York: Doubleday, 2001), 2339–42.

the covenant in Gen 17 is conditional or unconditional.[49] How should we understand the sequence in 17:1–4, containing as it does both a conditional and an unconditional statement about the covenant? To my knowledge, among scholars dealing with Gen 17, only Weimar addresses this question. He considers 17:1–4 to be coherent and unified. According to him, Abraham's prostration before the deity (v. 3) constitutes the fulfillment of God's order (v. 1b), afterward which the covenant is implemented (v. 4).[50] Yet this argument is not convincing. Abraham's punctual act corresponds in no way to the deity's order, which is directed toward existential, continuous behavior.[51] Hence it seems difficult to reconcile the two statements (17:1b–2 and 4) with one another. This suggests that they do not belong to the same literary level. Which statement is more original? A clue to the answer may be found in the progress of the argument in chapter 17. A first indication is the *immediate* implementation of the change of Abram's name (see Gen 17:15). Second, the statement concerning Sarai's future offspring in Gen 17:15–16, an indispensable element of YHWH's promise, uses an indicative formulation:

Genesis 17:15–16

[15] Then God said to Abraham, "As for Sarai your wife, you shall not call her name Sarai, because Sarah is her name (כי שרה שמה). [16] And I will bless her, and indeed I give (וגם נתתי) you a son by her. Then I will bless her, and she shall be a mother of nations; kings of peoples shall come from her."

Given the indicative mood in v. 15b and in v. 16aβ (*perfectum declarativum*, performative perfect[52]), the phrasing of 17:15–16 gives the impression of an unconditional promise. A further indication favoring the idea that the statement expressing the unconditional character of the covenant in v. 4 is more original than v. 2 is the fact that only the former is connected with the central promise of being father of multiple nations (cf. 17:4–6). In the context of the following promise, 17:4–6, the two imperatives in 17:1 should not necessarily be understood as an "order" in the strict sense but rather as an invitation addressed to Abraham to live in the presence of the deity.[53]

The following passages contain two further statements related with the deity's establishment of the covenant.

---

[49] With regard to construction in 17:1–2 and the phrase ביני ובניכם / ביני ובניך, several scholars consider the Abrahamic *běrît* conditional (see, among others, KNOHL, *Sanctuary*, 138, 141, n. 66; JOOSTEN, *People*; MILGROM, *Leviticus 23–27*, 2339–42). Still, a majority of scholars follow Zimmerli (see ZIMMERLI, "Abrahambund und Sinaibund") in regarding the covenant as unconditional (see the instructive summary of different scholarly views in NIHAN, "Priestly Covenant," 91–103).

[50] WEIMAR, "Gen 17," 39–40.

[51] See, for instance, WESTERMANN, *Genesis 12–36*, 311: "Mit dem התהלך לפני gebietet Gott dem Abraham … ein Leben im Gegenüber zu Gott." For the interpretation of the two imperatives, see also below, II.6.7 (a).

[52] See *GKC* §106m; Joüon-Muraoka §112g.

[53] Similarly NIHAN, "Priestly Covenant," 99 ("the demands on Abraham are expectations rather than conditions strictly speaking").

Genesis 17:7

[7] "I will establish (והקמתי) my covenant [ברית] between me and you and your descendants after you throughout their generations for an everlasting covenant [לברית עולם], to be God to you and to your descendants after you."

Genesis 17:19b, 21a

[19b] "I will establish [והקמתי] my covenant [בריתי] with him [Isaac] for an everlasting covenant [לברית עולם] for his descendants after him. [21a] But I will establish [והקמתי] my covenant [בריתי] with Isaac."

The statements are formulated for the future, including all of Abraham's descendants (v. 7) or only one of his descendants (Isaac, vv. 19b, 21a; at the expense of Ishmael, vv. 20–21a; see below). They stand in tension with the concept of the unconditional and instantly operative covenant of v. 4. This seems to be the reason that certain translations render the lexeme קום *hiphil*, which appears in all three texts (17:7, 19, 21), with "to maintain (my covenant)," which is linguistically possible.[54] However, the idea that the deity would maintain or keep the covenant established in 17:4 seems difficult because of the different contents of the covenant found in 17:4 (promise of multiple offspring) on the one hand and in 17:7 (promise "to be God to you and to your offspring after you"), 19, 21 (related uniquely to Isaac) on the other. Moreover, in the flood narrative קום *hiphil* (cf. Gen 9:9, 11, 17) necessarily has the meaning "to establish (a covenant)."[55]

The evidence adduced here regarding different articulations of the covenant in Gen 17 suggests that only the statement in 17:4 likely belonged to the primary Abraham narrative.[56] This covenant is unconditional and consists of the promise that Abraham will be a "father of a multitude of nations." Tied to the promise is the proclamation of the change of name (Abram – Abraham) with the fitting etiology of the name (see 17:5). Possibly, the promise of the land in 17:8 also belongs to the original kernel of the chapter.

The proclamation of the change of name contains a secondary addition in v. 6: The sentence in v. 6a (והפרתי אתך במאד מאד ונתתיך לגוים, "And I will make you exceedingly fruitful, and I will make nations of you") was probably inserted later and belongs to the "fruitfulness and multiplication" redaction (based on the roots פרה, "to be fruitful" and רבה, "to multiply") which is part of P^c (visible in Gen 1:22, 28; 9:1,

---

[54] See NJB; NJPS; W. R. GARR, "The Grammar and Interpretation of Exodus 6:3," *JBL* 111 (1992): 403–4; K. SCHMID, "Gibt es eine 'abrahamitische Ökumene' im Alten Testament? Überlegungen zur religionspolitischen Theologie der Priesterschrift in Genesis 17," in *Die Erzväter in der biblischen Tradition: Festschrift für Matthias Köckert*, ed. A. C. Hagedorn and H. Pfeiffer, BZAW 400 (Berlin: de Gruyter, 2009), 75, n. 47.

[55] It is not appropriate to translate קום *hiphil* twice as "to establish" (9:9, 17) and once as "to maintain" (9:11) in one and the same passage (*contra* NJB and NJPS).

[56] WEIMAR, "Gen 17," 38–42, ascribes the two first statements to the pre-Priestly ground layer. This primary kernel would contain 17:1–4a, 6, 22.

7; 28:3; 35:11; 48:4; Exod 7:1, see further below, III.1.2.2 [a] [1]). This consideration is supported by the fact that the second part of the expression in question (v. 6aβ ונתתיך לגוים, "and I will make nations of you") may be considered a *Wiederaufnahme* of the statement at the end of v. 5 (כי אב המון גוים נתתיך, "for I make you a father of a multitude of nations"). The "fruitfulness and multiplication" redaction seems to have left its mark also in v. 2b (וארבה אותך במאד מאד, "and I will multiply you exceedingly"); as shown above, the entire v. 2 should be considered secondary.

(2) The Order of Circumcision and Its Execution (Genesis 17:9–14, 23–27)

Because of their distinct vocabulary, the passages containing the order of circumcision (vv. 9–14) and its execution (vv. 23–27) are ascribed to a secondary layer by several scholars.[57] The expression שמר ברית, "keeping the covenant" (vv. 9–10), is not found in other Priestly texts. The term "breaking the covenant" (הפר *hiphil*) occurs only in H. The two designations for slave – יליד בית, "slave born in the house(hold),"[58] and מקנת כסף, "slave bought with money"[59] – do not occur in P.[60] In addition, vv. 15–16 (dealing with the name change of Sarai) have no link with vv. 9–14 but follow "naturally" on vv. 4–8 (or vv. 4–6).

(3) Genesis 17:17–22

Linguistic evidence suggests the differentiation of this passage from the primary kernel in Gen 17. Genesis 17:17–22 contains an idiomatic expression found only in late Priestly texts. The motif of Abraham's "falling on his face" (ויפל אברהם על פניו, v. 17), appears already in 17:3. The expression נפל על פניו, is frequently used in the Priestly texts of the book of Numbers but is never found in (other) Priestly texts of Genesis and Exodus.[61] Furthermore, the passage contains several expressions found in the non-P stories in Gen 16 and 18:[62] Genesis 17:17–19 is comparable to the wordplay on Isaac's name in 18:12–15 and 21:6; the wordplay on Ishmael's name in 17:20 is similar to that in Gen 16:11; 17:21; finally, the indication of the time until Isaac's birth (17:21) is formulated like that in 18:14. This striking accumulation of expressions shared with the two non-P units in the short section 17:17–22 makes it likely that the passage in question

---

[57] LEVIN, *Der Jahwist*, 157; SEEBASS, *Genesis II/1*, 111; WÖHRLE, "Integrative Function," 74–84; IDEM, *Fremdlinge*, 46–50. K. GRÜNWALDT, *Exil und Identität: Beschneidung, Passa und Sabbat in der Priesterschrift*, BBB 85 (Frankfurt: Anton Hain, 1992), 42–46, considers only the order secondary.

[58] Occurrences in Gen 14:14; 17:12, 13, 23, 27; Lev 22:11; Jer 2:14.

[59] Occurs only in Gen 17:12, 13, 23, 27; Exod 12:44.

[60] Significantly, 12:5 (P) uses a different expression for an acquired slave: ואת הנפש אשר עשו, "the persons which they had acquired."

[61] The occurrences of נפל על פניו in P and H are as follows: Gen 17:3, 17; Lev 9:24; Num 14:5; 16:4, 22; 17:10; 20:6.

[62] See McEVENUE, *Narrative Style*, 153.

is influenced by the former texts. (In this respect, the remarkable absence of common points with non-P in other parts of the Priestly Abraham narrative should be noted.)

As for its content, in light of the central promise of Gen 17:1, 4–6 concerning Abraham's future "multinational" offspring, the sudden transfer of the covenant to Isaac and Ishmael's exclusion from it are astonishing. Genesis 17:17–22 pursues a different ideology than does the primary kernel of the chapter. It prepares for the limitation of Abraham's covenant to Israel alone, as is expressed in subsequent sections of the Priestly narrative. There, the covenant with Abraham is directed explicitly to Israel; it is referred to as God's "covenant with Abraham, Isaac, and Jacob" (Exod 2:24; cf. 6:4–5) and is seen as the basis for God's intervention in favor of Israel in Egypt (God remembers his covenant).

(4) Conclusion

We may conclude from the above redaction-critical considerations on chapter 17 that the latter originally contained only the passages about YHWH's revelation, the promise of multiplication and of becoming "a father of a multitude of nations," the announcement of the name changes (Abram–Abraham, Sarai–Sarah), the promise of the land, and the promise that Sarah would give birth and become a "mother of kings." The primary composition of Gen 17 may have read as follows:

Genesis 17:1b, 4–5, 6b, 8a, 15aβγb–16

וירא יהוה אל אברם ויאמר אליו אני אל שדי התהלך לפני והיה תמים אני הנה הנה בריתי אתך והיית לאב המון גוים ולא יקרא עוד את שמך אברם והיה שמך אברהם כי אב המון גוים נתתיך ומלכים ממך יצאו ונתתי לך ולזרעך אחריך את ארץ מגריך את כל ארץ כנען לאחזת עולם שרי אשתך לא תקרא את שמה שרי כי שרה שמה וברכתי אתה וגם נתתי ממנה לך בן וברכתיה והיתה לגוים מלכי עמים ממנה יהיו

(c) Genesis 19:29 (God's Destruction of the "Cities of the Plain")

Because of its vocabulary (use of אלהים, זכר), the short notice about God's destruction of the cities of the plain in Gen 19:29 is generally assigned to the Priestly strand. But scholars often consider its position in P inappropriate and secondary; initially, the statement would have followed the Priestly passage Gen 13:6, 11–12*(13*).[63] Nevertheless, the actual placement of the statement is preferable;[64] Elohim's intervention, which is motivated by his remembering Abraham, obviously presupposes God's covenant with Abraham in Gen 17.

However, Gen 19:29 does not fit well with the literary profile of the other passages

---

[63] WELLHAUSEN, *Die Composition*, 15; GUNKEL, *Genesis*, 263; NOTH, *Überlieferungsgeschichte*, 13; LEVIN, *Der Jahwist*, 103; CARR, *Reading*, 57–60; J. BADEN, "The Original Place of the Priestly Manna Story in Exodus 16," *ZAW* 122 (2010): 501.

[64] See also WÖHRLE, *Fremdlinge*, 52–53, who argues that Gen 19:29 was modeled for its context in Gen 19.

of P's Abraham narrative. While the latter constitute a self-contained and autonomous strand (see below), the statement in 19:29 obviously depends on the non-Priestly narrative in Gen 18–19 (the Sodom and Gomorrah incident is not mentioned elsewhere in the Priestly Abraham account).

(d) Genesis 21:2b (Chronological Notice)

Since the chronological notice in 21:2b depends on the secondary passage in Gen 17:17–22, it must be considered secondary as well.

(e) Genesis 21:4 (Isaac's Circumcision)

The statement about Isaac's circumcision is said to be a (further) execution of the instruction given by Elohim in 17:9–14. Accordingly, it should be assigned to the same secondary literary stratum.

(f) Genesis 23; 25:9–10; 49:29–32; 50:12–13

Because of its distinct, elaborate style and particular vocabulary, many scholars consider Gen 23 to belong to a late Priestly or post-Priestly layer.[65] Central expressions in this unit, such as גר ותושב, "stranger and sojourner" (23:4), and עם הארץ, "the people of the land" (23:7, 12, 13), are not used in the Priestly texts of Genesis and Exodus. These terms, however, do occur in the so-called Holiness Code.[66] The topic of the preservation of Israelite ownership over the land is vital to the Holiness Code. Given these commonalities with H, one might assume that Gen 23 (and the related passages in Gen 25:9–10; 49:29–32; 50:12–13) is by the same author or stems from the same milieu. Conspicuously, יש with infinitive ("it is possible to [...]") as found in 23:8 appears frequently in Chronicles and other late biblical texts but never in Pᶜ.[67] However, Gen 23 also shares connections with the burial formulae for the patriarchs in the Priestly strand (Gen 25:9–10; 49:29–32; 50:12–13),[68] which mention the Machpelah cave and repeat information given in Gen 23 as well. Yet the redundant and overloaded nature of the burial formulae has led some scholars to suggest that the formation of the texts took place in stages:[69]

---

[65] Among others, BLUM, *Die Komposition*, 441–46; KRATZ, *Composition*, 239; WÖHRLE, *Fremdlinge*, 58–63.

[66] גר ותושב: Lev 25:23, 35, 47 (2×), outside of H only in Gen 23:4 and Num 35:15; עם הארץ: Lev 20:2, 4; cf. furthermore Lev 4:27; Num 14:9.

[67] On this construction, see S. R. DRIVER, *Notes*, §202.1.

[68] Cf. NIHAN, *From Priestly Torah*, 67, n. 242.

[69] Among others: R. SMEND, *Die Erzählung des Hexateuch: Auf ihre Quellen untersucht* (Berlin: Reimer, 1912), 10–11, with n. 1; BLUM, *Die Komposition*, 444–46; WÖHRLE, *Fremdlinge*, 60–63. BLUM, *Die Komposition*, 444–46, reckons with secondary additions in 25:9b–10; 49:29b, 30b–32.

Genesis 25:9–10 (parts referring to Gen 23 are underlined)

⁹ ויקברו אתו יצחק וישמעאל בניו אל מערת המכפלה <u>אל שדה עפרן בן צהר החתי אשר
על פני ממרא</u> ¹⁰ <u>השדה אשר קנה אברהם מאת בני חת שמה קבר אברהם ושרה אשתו</u>

⁹ Then his sons Isaac and Ishmael buried him in the cave of Machpelah, <u>in the field
of Ephron the son of Zohar the Hittite</u>, before Mamre, ¹⁰ <u>the field which Abraham
purchased from the sons of Heth; there Abraham was buried with Sarah his wife.</u>

This consideration seems correct. The burial notice for Abraham (Gen 25:9–10) offers
several pieces of information concerning Abraham's burial site, among other things
the former owner of the field (v. 9b: "the field of Ephron the Hittite") and Abraham's
purchase (v. 10: "the field which Abraham purchased from the sons of Heth"). The
latter statements share vocabulary with Gen 23.

Jacob's instruction concerning his own burial (Gen 49:29–33) contains the same
two assertions (about the former owner of the field and about Abraham's purchase;
see 49:29–30, 32). The same information is found in the notice of the fulfillment of
Jacob's commission by his sons (in 50:13b). The clumsiness of the relevant phrases and
the terminological correspondences with the late composition Gen 23 suggest that
the information about the (former) owner of the cave and about Abraham's purchase
should be attributed to a late redaction connected to Gen 23. Apparently, the author
(redactor) of these texts was interested in emphasizing Abraham's (Israel's) ownership of the cave of Machpelah. This is the purpose of Gen 23 and of the related back-
references in Gen 25:9–10; 49:29–30, 32; and 50:13b as well.

(g) Inner Differentiation of Genesis 36

The history of the formation of Gen 36, which consists in total of seven genealogical lists and lists of rulers (kings), is a matter of debate. A striking particularity is the
repetition of the *tôlĕdōt*-formula (ואלה תולדת עשו, "And these are the *tôlĕdōt* of Esau";
vv. 1, 9). In addition, the title "these are the names of the chiefs descended from Esau"
in 36:40 appears as the third heading in the unit. Most scholars assign 36:1–8 (or parts
of it) to P^G/P^C on the basis of several typical Priestly expressions (v. 2: "daughters of
Canaan"; v. 5: "land of Canaan"; v. 6: "all his household, and his livestock and all his
cattle and all his goods which he had acquired in the land of Canaan"; v. 7: "for their
property had become too great for them to live together"). However, there is a massive contradiction between the statement in Gen 36:2–3 and that of Gen 26:34–35,
which is commonly assigned to P^G/P^C too. In the latter text, Esau's wives are called
"Judith the daughter of Beeri the Hittite, and Basemath the daughter of Elon the Hittite." In 36:2–3, however, Esau's wives bear other names: "Adah the daughter of Elon
the Hittite, and Oholibamah the daughter of Anah and the granddaughter of Zibeon
the Hivite, and also Basemath, Ishmael's daughter, the sister of Nebaioth." Scholars
believe either that the Priestly author relied on different traditions or that one of the
two statements stems from a later redactor (P^s).

The assignment of 36:9–43 is matter of controversy: do these lists (some of them) stem from a pre-Priestly tradition, should they (some of them) be ascribed to P^C, or should they be attributed to post-Priestly authors? Some scholars believe that 36:9–43 includes pre-Priestly traditions. M. Noth, for instance, considers 36:9–14 an ancient tradition stemming from the supposed "toledot book."[70] M. Weippert and J. R. Bartlett recognize in 36:9–14, 20–28 the two most original nuclei of the text.[71] In contrast to this, a recent tendency is to regard vv. 9–43 in general as a later insertion, consisting of different parts subsequently added to the original 36:1–8, stemming from the Priestly author.[72] The first redaction-critical option seems more convincing. Genesis 36:9–19 shares formal and conceptual commonalities with the genealogical list of Ishmael (25:12–18*) and with that of Jacob (35:22b–26a); all three texts may stem from a pre-Priestly or proto-Priestly tradition (see further below). Speaking against the second explanation is the fact that it explains neither (1) the insertion of considerable genealogical material for Esau nor (2) the striking repetition of the introductory formula, "And these are the *tôlĕdōt* of Esau." (1) What reason would there have been to integrate these lists, which give dense and detailed information, in a rather late – i.e., Persian – period? Knauf argues that the Priestly additions (P^s) were influenced by certain Dtr ideas, such as the idea that Edom was formerly populated by an indigenous, ethnically distinct population, the Horites (cf. 36:20–28, 29–30 with Deut 2:12, 22).[73] Yet, in contrast to Deut 2:12, 22, the passages about Horites in Gen 36 do not hint at a conflict between Horites and Esavites; on the contrary, shared names seem to allude to a family relation between the two tribes (cf. the personal names צבעון in 36:14, 24, 29, תמנע in 36:12, 22, and ענה in 36:14, 18, 20, 24, 25, 29). In the other lists, ideological concerns are not perceptible either. According to Weippert, the notices in 36:10–14 and 20–28 (in particular the information about marriages between Esavites and Horites) evidence the peaceful coexistence of two distinct ethnic groups, the Esavites and the Horites.[74] (2) A further argument against the theory of the secondary insertion of 36:9–43 is the question why the later (P^s) redactor would repeat the *tôlĕdōt* heading (cf. v. 9) and the information concerning Esau's sons (vv. 10, 14), which are already given in 36:1–8, instead of simply listing Esau's grandsons (sons of Eliphas and Reuel; cf. 36:11–13). With regard to the repetition, it is more plausible to imagine that the author of 36:1–8 inserted his composition before the previously existing unit in vv. 9–43*, which was introduced by the heading "and these are the *tôlĕdōt* of Esau." The latter, a compilation of lists, was part of the proto-Abraham narrative, together with

---

[70] Noth, *Überlieferungsgeschichte*, 18, n. 51.

[71] M. Weippert, "Edom: Studien und Materialien zur Geschichte der Edomiter auf Grund schriftlicher und archäologischer Quellen" (Ph.D. diss., Tübingen, 1971), 437–58; J. R. Bartlett, *Edom and the Edomites*, JSOTSup 77 (Sheffield: Sheffield Academic Press, 1989), 86–90.

[72] See Westermann, *Genesis 12–36*, 684; Kratz, *Composition*, 241; Wöhrle, *Fremdlinge*, 95–98; E. A. Knauf, "Genesis 36,1–43," in *Jacob: Commentaire à plusieurs voix de Gen. 25–36; Mélanges offerts à Albert de Pury*, ed. J.-D. Macchi and T. Römer [Geneva: Labor et Fides, 2001], 291–300.

[73] See Knauf, "Genesis 36,1–43," 297–300.

[74] See Weippert, "Edom," 446–47.

other genealogical lists (of Ishmael and Jacob; see below, II.6.5 [b]). In this respect, it should be noted that 36:9–19 shares striking commonalities with the genealogical list of Ishmael (25:12–18*) and with that of Jacob (35:22b–26a): the consequent mention of the sons' mothers (lacking in Ishmael's genealogy) and the indication of the first-born by an explicit designation (cf. 25:13; 35:23; 36:15). The first aspect is emphasized by S. Shectman, who argues that the similarities between the list of Jacob's sons and that of Esau's sons perhaps indicate "that P perceived the Israelites and the Edomites as so closely related that they shared a similar social structure, in which tribal and family groups were affiliated by matrilineage."[75]

These observations and considerations on Gen 36 favor the conclusion that its primary kernel lies within 36:9–43 and that 36:1–8 constitutes a later introduction inserted by the Priestly redactor.[76]

(h) Priestly Texts in the Joseph Narrative

(1) Did P[C] Contain a Joseph Story?

With regard to the paucity of P texts in the Joseph narrative and their dependence on the non-Priestly stratum, Schmid and Römer consider the possibility that P – which they consider a source (P[G]) – did not contain a Joseph story at all.[77] They ascribe the allusions to Joseph and to the non-P story about him that are commonly attributed to P[G]/P[C] to a secondary Priestly or post-Priestly layer. In Schmid's and Römer's reconstruction, Jacob and his clan's move to Egypt (46:6) follows directly on the notice of Jacob's settling down in the land of Canaan in 37:1(–2aα1).[78]

Genesis 37:1–2aα1
[1] Now Jacob settled in the land where his father had sojourned, in the land of Canaan. ([2aα1] These are the descendants of Jacob.)

Genesis 46:6
[6] And they took their livestock and their possessions which they had accumulated in the land of Canaan, and came to Egypt, Jacob and all his descendants with him.

---

[75] S. Shectman, "Women in the Priestly Narrative," in *The Strata of the Priestly Writings: Contemporary Debate and Future Directions*, ed. S. Shectman and J. Baden, ATANT 95 (Zurich: TVZ, 2009), 178.

[76] Similarly, Noth, *Überlieferungsgeschichte*, 18, n. 51, and Weippert, "Edom," 437–58, see 36:9–14 as the primary kernel of the composition.

[77] K. Schmid, "The So-Called Yahwist and the Literary Gap between Genesis and Exodus," in *A Farewell to the Yahwist? The Composition of the Pentateuch in Recent European Interpretation*, ed. T. B. Dozeman and K. Schmid (Atlanta: Society of Biblical Literature, 2006), 46–47; T. Römer, "The Joseph Story in the Book of Genesis: Pre-P or Post-P?," in *The Post-Priestly Pentateuch: New Perspectives on Its Redactional Development and Theological Profiles*, ed. F. Giuntoli and K. Schmid, FAT 101 (Tübingen: Mohr Siebeck, 2015), 198.

[78] Schmid, "So-Called Yahwist," 46–47; Römer, "Joseph Story," 198. In his reconstruction Römer leaves 37:2aα1 out.

However, the absence of any motivation for Jacob's move to Egypt (see 46:6), far away from the land of Canaan *promised to him by God* (see 17:8; 28:3–4, 35:12), seems odd. At other points in P's ancestral narrative, similar moves are explained (see Gen 13:6 and 36:7). The change in the subject's number in 46:6 (pl., unspecified), in comparison to 37:1 (sing.), is also noteworthy. For these reasons, it seems probable that the Priestly texts in 37:1(–2) and 46:6 presuppose some of the non-P text between, in particular Joseph's being sold into Egypt by his brothers and his rise in the Egyptian court. This is confirmed by the following observations: The unspecified subject in 46:6 ("they") reveals that this Priestly statement depends on the preceding non-Priestly text.

> Genesis 46:5–6
> [5] *(non-P) And Jacob arose from Beersheba; and the sons of Israel carried their father Jacob and their little ones and their wives, in the wagons which Pharaoh had sent to carry him.* [6] (P) And they took their livestock and their possessions which they had accumulated in the land of Canaan, and came to Egypt, Jacob and all his descendants with him.

Note furthermore that two other of the texts traditionally assigned to the Priestly stratum in the Joseph section refer explicitly to the Joseph story as literary background. The statement in 37:2 alludes to the conflict between Joseph and his brothers; it should be understood to hint at a (further) cause of conflict between them, namely, the bad behavior of Jacob's brothers and Joseph's "service" in advising Jacob (see below).[79] The second text is the statement concerning Joseph's service before the Pharaoh in Gen 41:46a P. The fact that this assertion depends syntactically on the typically Priestly indication of age (see above, II.6.4 [a]) pleads for its assignment to P[C].

To conclude, there are clear indications that the Priestly strand (P[C]) referred to the Joseph-story.

Nevertheless, the classification of a few elements in this section that are generally assigned to the Priestly strand is also a matter of dispute among scholars who reckon with a Priestly Joseph "narrative" (episode). They are discussed in the following paragraphs:

(2) Gen 37:2αγδ

Many scholars assign Gen 37:2 in its entirety to P[G]/P[C], although the specification that Joseph was "still a youth with the sons Bilhah and the sons of Zilpah, his father's wives"

---

[79] According to an alternative interpretation offered by KRATZ (*Composition*, 241), Joseph's brothers are responsible for an evil report about the land of Canaan. The statement would shed new light on Jacob's decision to leave the land of Canaan: he was influenced by the bad report about the land. As in the spy story (cf. Num 13–14), a gossip (cf. Num 13:32; 14:36, 37: דבתם רעה) negatively influences the addressee of the land promise and makes him deviate from this promise. However, the lack of a specific "(report) about the land" in 37:2 (as is found in Num 13–14) renders Kratz's interpretation rather unlikely.

is considered a secondary insertion by some.[80] A few scholars ascribe the mention of Joseph's bad report about his brothers to a secondary layer as well.[81]

Genesis 37:2

[2] (a) These are the descendants of Jacob. Joseph, when seventeen years of age, was pasturing the flock with his brothers while he was still a youth, along with the sons of Bilhah and the sons of Zilpah, his father's wives. (b) And Joseph brought back a bad report about them to their father.

There is no apparent reason to detach the statement about Joseph's report concerning his brothers (v. 2b). As for the specification concerning Joseph's brothers (v. 2aβ), however, it is a little surprising after the general reference to "his brothers" (אחיו) in v. 2aα2. Perhaps it should be assigned to a late Priestly or post-Priestly redaction. The differentiation between Jacob's sons may be understood in light of P's interpretation of the Jacob-Esau story: Jacob initially acted according to the instruction of his father (see Gen 28:1–5) and married two daughters of his uncle Laban. Yet, in addition, he also took two unrelated maidservants as wives (see Gen 30:1–13 [non-P] and 35:22b–26a [P]). P[C] (or a later redactor) illustrates the negative consequences of Jacob's deviation from his parents' will, the "bad" behavior of the maidservants' sons causing serious conflict among Jacob's sons.

(3) Gen 47:7–11

The assignment of 47:7–11 is also disputed. The indication of age and the appearance of vocabulary typical of P (מגור and אחזה) cause some scholars to ascribe it to P[G]/P[C].[82] Many others, however, consider this passage non-Priestly.[83] There are indications favoring the second option. Negative (or positive) evaluation of lifetime, such as in 47:9, does not appear in any other Priestly text. The form of the age indication in the same verse distinguishes itself in an important detail from the age indications of the Priestly strand: the repetition of the noun *year*, which is almost consistently used for multiunit numbers in most Priestly texts, is absent.[84] Finally, the argument concerning

---

[80] Assigning 37:2 in its entirety to P[C]: GUNKEL, *Genesis*, 492; ELLIGER, "Sinn," 121; LOHFINK, "Die Priesterschrift," 198, n. 29; VON RAD, *Das erste Buch*, 285–86; C. WESTERMANN, *Genesis 37–50*, BK 1.1 (Neukirchen-Vluyn: Neukirchener Verlag, 1982), 26 (among others). Considering v. 2aγ a secondary insertion: LEVIN, *Der Jahwist*, 272; KRATZ, *Composition*, 241; H. SEEBASS, *Genesis III: Josephsgeschichte (37,1–50,26)* (Neukirchen-Vluyn: Neukirchener Verlag, 2000), 27 (hesitating); WÖHRLE, *Fremdlinge*, 101–2 (among others).

[81] SEEBASS, *Genesis III*, 27 (hesitating); WÖHRLE, *Fremdlinge*, 101–2.

[82] GUNKEL, *Genesis*, 495; VON RAD, *Das erste Buch*, 255; SEEBASS, *Genesis III*, 134; WÖHRLE, *Fremdlinge*, 116–18 (among others).

[83] ELLIGER, "Sinn," 121; LOHFINK, "Die Priesterschrift," 198, n. 29; LEVIN, *Der Jahwist*, 304–6; KRATZ, *Composition*, 241 (among others).

[84] Chronological indications with multiunit numbers appear in about forty Priestly texts. In all instances, the term שנה / שנים appears twice or three times (after each digit). See below, III.1.2.2 (b) (3). The peculiar spelling with the repetition of the noun *year* is shared by SP but

the vocabulary is not conclusive; אחזה is used in many late (post-)Priestly texts too.[85] It raises the question of whether the use of the expression אחזה here (for a territory at Ramses attributed to the Israelites by Joseph) is compatible with its usage in 17:8 (אחזה refers to the the term is assigned to the specific land in which a people [Israel, Edomites] traditionally lives or is supposed to live according, see Gen 17:8)

(4) Gen 48:3–6

A majority of scholars assign Gen 48:3–6 to P[G]/P[C].[86] A few critics, however, recognize traits of a post-Priestly origin in this passage and refrain from ascribing it to P[G]/P[C].[87] Although this pericope shares commonalities with other Priestly texts in the Jacob-Esau section ("assembly of peoples" [קהל עמים], theonym El Shaddai), it deviates in two respects from the parallel Priestly text in Gen 35:9–13: instead of Bethel, the toponym Luz is used, and YHWH's order "to be fruitful and multiply" is replaced by YHWH's promise that he will make Jacob fruitful and numerous; fecundity and multiplication are declared a gift from YHWH. A further theological particularity can be seen in the marked interest in the two northern tribes of Ephraim and Manasseh (Jacob updates the status of Joseph's two sons who are born in Egypt, Ephraim and Manasseh, by adopting them and giving them the same rank as his two firstborns, Reuben and Simeon).[88]

6.5 Literary Profiles of the Priestly Texts

The literary profile of the Priestly Abraham narrative and that of the Priestly texts concerning Jacob, Esau, and Joseph differ significantly from each other. In the following, I will first describe the profile of the Priestly texts in the Jacob-Esau and Joseph sections. Its fragmentary character is obvious and undisputed. More effort and space is needed to deal with the distinct profile of the Priestly texts in the Abraham section; the latter form a self-contained and autonomous stratum. The observations below will lead to the conclusion that the Priestly texts in the ancestral narrative, which are commonly assigned to P[G]/P[C], do not form a diachronically monolithic layer; the texts related to Abraham predate those belonging to the following sections.

---

is consistently absent in LXX. The deviation in LXX should most probably be assigned to the translators, who chose not to do a literal translation in this case.

[85] As admitted by WÖHRLE, *Fremdlinge*, 117.

[86] GUNKEL, *Genesis*, 496; ELLIGER, "Sinn," 121; LOHFINK, "Die Priesterschrift," 198, n. 29; VON RAD, *Das erste Buch*, 339; WESTERMANN, *Genesis 37–50*, 207–9; SEEBASS, *Genesis III*, 159; WÖHRLE, *Fremdlinge*, 120–23 (among others).

[87] LEVIN, *Der Jahwist*, 311; KRATZ, *Composition*, 241.

[88] For the interpretation of detail, see below, II.6.9 (b).

6.5.1 Profile of the Jacob-Esau and Joseph Narratives

(a) Jacob-Esau Narrative

The Priestly account about Jacob and Esau contains neither an account of the twins' birth nor a report of Jacob's stay in Paddan-aram. The few Priestly texts clearly presuppose the non-P accounts relating to those themes and respond to them.[89] For example, since P is silent about Jacob's prosperous sojourn in Paddan-aram, Gen 31:18 presupposes the non-P stories about Jacob's accumulation of livestock in the homeland of Rebecca's family. Furthermore, it is striking that 31:18 lacks the explicit subject (Jacob) and is syntactically tightly connected to the immediately preceding verse, 31:17 (non-P, text highlighted in italics):

Genesis 31:17–18

‏וַיָּקָם יַעֲקֹב וַיִּשָּׂא אֶת בָּנָיו וְאֶת נָשָׁיו עַל הַגְּמַלִּים‏ 18 ‏וַיִּנְהַג אֶת כָּל מִקְנֵהוּ וְאֶת כָּל רְכֻשׁוֹ‏ 17
‏אֲשֶׁר רָכָשׁ מִקְנֵה קִנְיָנוֹ אֲשֶׁר רָכָשׁ בְּפַדַּן אֲרָם לָבוֹא אֶל יִצְחָק אָבִיו אַרְצָה כְּנָעַן‏

[17] (non-P) *Then Jacob arose and put his children and his wives upon camels;*
[18] (P) and he drove away all his livestock and all his possessions which he had accumulated, his acquired livestock which he had accumulated in Paddan-aram, to go to the land of Canaan to his father Isaac.

Significantly, the preceding passage in the Priestly strand, 28:8–9, focuses on Esau and does not mention Jacob.

Moreover, it is noteworthy that the brief Priestly statement contains the same terminology to designate the livestock acquired as the non-Priestly strand (‏מִקְנֶה‏) in addition to the typical Priestly expression (‏רְכֻשׁ‏).[90]

These observations suggest that P is a redaction layer supplementing the older non-P stratum.

However, an argument advanced in favor of the source theory is the fact that the Priestly strand takes up and "doubles" a central aspect of the pre-Priestly texts, namely the theophany at Bethel. The appearance and self-introduction of El Shaddai at this place in 35:9–15 parallels the Bethel etiology in 28:10–22. For Carr and other scholars, it is inconceivable that P would have composed his account to be integrated into a literary context already containing similar content.[91] Yet, one may reply, with Blum, that in this as in other cases the Priestly author is supplementing the pre-Priestly tradition in order to interpret and correct it. Blum's careful analysis of 35:9–15 demonstrates the likelihood that the pericope is reacting to the Bethel etiology in Gen 28 and reformulating Bethel's status as a place of revelation. Through the motif of YHWH's *departing* from the place of revelation (35:13), the Priestly author insinuates that Bethel is not the place where God dwells (cf. 28:16–17: "In this place YHWH is there! ... This is

---

[89] See Gen 25:20, 26b; 31:18; 35:9.
[90] See further below, II.6.6.1.
[91] Cf. CARR, *Reading*, 88–90.

nothing other than the house of God") but rather a place where "ʏʜᴡʜ had spoken with him" (cf. the repeated phrase in vv. 13, 14, 15), comparable to other places where God communicated with a human (as for instance the place in Gen 17).[92] The expression עוֹד, "again," reveals that the author is complementing rather than replacing the pre-Priestly Bethel etiology (Gen 28:10–22).[93] Additionally, Jacob's name change in Gen 35:9–10 is often considered a doublet of the name change in the non-P story of the battle at the Jabbok in Gen 32:23–33. Recent analyses, however, show that the short passage related to the name change (32:28–29) might be a late – post-P? – insertion.[94] Even if, on the contrary, this text predates Jacob's name change in P, the latter's nature as a doublet may be explained by the author's intention to correct the theologically objectionable name etiology in 32:23–33 (which is based on Jacob's struggle with a deity).

(b) Joseph Narrative

As in the Jacob-Esau narrative, only brief, isolated Priestly texts occur in the Joseph narrative. These short Priestly passages are dependent on the non-P Joseph narrative, being incomprehensible without them.

– As shown above, the dependence of Priestly texts on the non-Priestly Joseph story is essential: Jacob's move to Egypt needs a motivation, which is only given by the plot found in Gen 37–50. Moreover, the statement reporting Jacob and his sons' move depends syntactically on the preceding non-Priestly context.[95]
– The Priestly statement that "Joseph was thirty years old when he began to serve Pharaoh" (Gen 41:46a) depends on the previous non-P statements about Joseph's stay in Egypt.
– The allusion to Jacob's bed in 49:33a depends on Gen 47:31 (non-P); 48:2 (non-P).[96]

Furthermore, there are indications that the Priestly passages in the Joseph narrative also presuppose the non-P Jacob-Esau story. By passing over Rachel in the enumeration of the ancestors buried in the cave of Machpelah, the author of Gen 49:29–33 reveals his knowledge of the account of Rachel's death and burial on the way to Ephrath (Gen 35:16–20, non-P[97]).

In general, the profile of the Priestly strand in the Joseph narrative resembles the one in the Jacob-Esau narrative. In both parts, P's plot contains considerable lacunae and depends on the non-P narrative. At the same time, the Priestly layer adds new and

---

[92] Cf. Blum, *Die Komposition*, 265–70; idem, "Noch einmal," 47–50.
[93] See also Wöhrle, *Fremdlinge*, 66; differently Blum, "Noch einmal," 47, n. 57.
[94] See below, II.6.6.3.
[95] See above, II.6.4 (h) (1).
[96] See below, II.6.6.2.
[97] See below, II.6.6.2.

similar interpretive elements to the different sections. These will be explored in the following paragraphs.[98]

6.5.2 Profile of the Abraham Narrative

A close reading of P's Abraham narrative reveals that P here forms not only an uninterrupted thread but also a self-contained and fairly coherent entity. At its beginning, the narrative presents Abram's genealogical, geographical, and religious origins (11:27–32). Abram is the firstborn among three sons of Terah. The youngest, Haran, marries first and has a child, Lot. It is only after Haran's premature death that Abram and Nahor, his older brothers, marry. Nahor's wife, Milcah, is a daughter of his brother Haran. The only information given about Abram's wife, Sarai, is that she is barren (11:30). Since such information is absent for Milcah, one should conclude that she is fecund. Then Terah decides to leave his hometown, Ur "of the Chaldeans," together with Abram, Sarai, and Lot, in order to go to the land of Canaan (v. 31).

With regard to the arguments in favor of the passage's unity noted above, we should understand v. 31 in relation to the preceding statements of vv. 27–30. A possible motive for Terah's decision to leave Ur may be deduced from the fact that Terah takes Abram, Sarai, and Lot but not Nahor and Milcah on his journey. What the childless couple and fatherless Lot[99] have in common is that they are not favored by fate. Presumably, Terah departs from Ur because he hopes to find better living conditions for them in another land.[100]

The emigrants stop in Harran, where they settle down (11:31) and where Terah dies (11:32).[101] In this place, Abraham and Loth acquire great possession. The narrative continues, reporting Abram and Lot's move to the land of Canaan (12:5). Scholars often wonder about the described itinerary Ur-Chasdim–Harran–Canaan,[102] which apparently is chosen by Terah (see 11:31) but which geographically is a detour. The direct itinerary would lead via Mari through Aleppo.[103] A frequent explanation for the deviation from the direct route is that the Priestly author would depend on non-P texts and take up the localization of Rebecca's family in Harran (see Gen 27:43; 28:10;

---

[98] See II.6.6.1–6.

[99] The reader is not given any information about Lot's mother.

[100] As far I can see, scholars never discuss Terah's motivation to leave Ur (v. 31). This may be due to the frequent source-critical severing of vv. 28–30 from 11:27–30.

[101] On the question of literary unity and classification of the passage 11:27–32, see above, II.6.3 (a).

[102] According to MT and SP. For the alternative reading of LXX, see above, II.6.2 (a).

[103] See WÖHRLE, *Fremdlinge*, 29. Note, however, that leaders of military campaigns apparently often preferred the northern route, via Harran, to the one traversing the Euphrates and the desert, see L. MARTI, "From Ur to Harran: History of Origins or Late Rewriting," in *The Historical Location of P*, ed. J. Hutzli and J. Davis (forthcoming).

29:4).[104] Yet this explanation is doubtful.[105] It is more probable that Terah (or rather, the author) chose the route for a theological reason.[106] Ur and Harran were the most important centers of the moon god (Sîn) in Mesopotamia in the first half of the first millennium BCE. The theological motive for the author's choice of these toponyms seems to be confirmed by other affinities to the moon cult. Soggin considers Sarah's name, and its Akkadian equivalent *šarratu(m)* "queen, princess" a translation of Ningal's, Sîn's wife's, Sumerian name ("the great Lady").[107] Milcah may be associated with *malkatu* (princess), which is used as an epithet of Ishtar, daughter of Sîn.[108] Terah's name (תרח), too, has been linked with the moon (ירח).[109] This accumulation of possible allusions to the moon cult is probably not accidental, hinting at the religious and spiritual "home" of Terah's family. Thus it seems that Terah's choice of itinerary is dictated by his religious allegiance.[110]

---

[104] WESTERMANN, *Genesis 12–36*, 159; BLUM, *Die Komposition*, 143, n. 11; WÖHRLE, *Fremdlinge*, 29.

[105] The argument concerning P's dependence on Gen 27:43; 28:10; 29:4 is questionable. Since the toponym Harran, as a designation of the big city in northern Syria, does not fit well with the context of the Jacob-Laban narrative, several scholars believe that the toponym was secondarily inserted in the aforementioned texts (cf. SKINNER, *Genesis*, 334; NOTH, *Überlieferungsgeschichtliche Studien*, 110, with n. 294, 218; BLUM, *Die Komposition*, 164–66; I. FINKELSTEIN and T. RÖMER, "Comments on the Historical Background of the Abraham Narrative: Between 'Realia' and 'Exegetica,'" *HBAI* 3 [2014]: 3–23). However, scholars wonder about the motivation for this insertion. In my opinion, one should consider the possibility that the insertion aimed to reinforce the connection of the Jacob-Laban story with the Priestly Abraham narrative, where the toponym is firmly anchored. If so, this redaction layer would depend on the (proto-)Priestly Abraham narrative.

[106] See also M. KÖCKERT, *Abraham: Ahnvater – Vorbild – Kultstifter*, Biblische Gestalten (Leipzig: Evangelische Verlagsanstalt, 2017), 54.

[107] See SOGGIN, *Das Buch Genesis*, 189–90. However, the use of the Akkadian term *šarratu(m)* for Ningal seems rare (for an example from the Neo-Babylonian era, see *CAD* 17.2:75); more often the expression is applied to Ishtar (see *CAD* 17.2:74–75). Pointing to this and other allusions to the moon cult (see below) are GUNKEL, *Genesis*, 162–63; P. DHORME, "Abraham dans le cadre d'histoire," *RB* 37 (1928): 367–85, 481–511; WESTERMANN, *Genesis 12–36*, 158.

[108] *CAD* 10.1:166.

[109] Cf. *HAL* 1041; R. DUSSAUD, "Les Phéniciens au Négeb et en Arabie d'après un texte de Ras Shamra," *RHR* 108 (1933): 33–34; according to Dussaud, Terah's name would be connected with ירח as תימן (תמן) is with ימין (33–34). Similarly SOGGIN, *Das Buch Genesis*, 189 ("offensichtlich mit dem Mond verbundener Name, hebr. *jārēăḥ* mit Prefix /t/"). Both explanations are hypothetical; however, regarding the other allusions to the moon god, the similarity of the consonants in the two nouns is hardly coincidental.

[110] The remaining question is why Terah chose the land of Canaan as his final destination. The move to Harran can be explained as follows: Because of the problems encountered in Ur (see above), Terah wanted to live with part of his family in the region of another manifestation of Sîn, namely, Harran. Did the "land of Canaan" have a reputation for widespread veneration of the mood god in the eyes of the author and his audience? For iconographic and epigraphic evidence for the veneration of the moon god in Israel/Palestine in the late monarchic period, see O. KEEL and C. UEHLINGER, *Göttinnen, Götter und Göttersymbole*, 340–69; G. THEUER, *Der Mondgott in den Religionen Syrien-Palästinas: Unter besonderer Berücksichtigung von KTU*

Interestingly, current scholarship pays little if any attention to the above-mentioned allusions to the moon cult.[111] They are played down or ignored, likely because most scholars attribute the location in Harran to non-P/pre-P tradition. As for interpretation of the Priestly narrative, only Ur-Chasdim attracts attention. The choice of this city by the Priestly writer is explained by its geographical proximity to the location of the Judean *golah* and by its general importance.[112] However, even if the toponym Harran was borrowed from a pre-Priestly tradition (which is doubtful[113]), the choice of two centers of the moon god (Sîn) as key toponyms of the plot is striking. This and the presence of personal names with possible connections to the moon cult in this Priestly passage deserve an explanation.

In Canaan, Abram and Lot separate from each other because the land "could not sustain them." Afterward, the reader learns about a first solution of the problem of Sarai's barrenness: Sarai gives her Egyptian servant Hagar to her husband Abram as wife. She will give birth to a son, Ishmael. Then the narrative reaches its climax, which consists of YHWH's revelation to Abram by the name of El Shaddai and the establishment of his covenant with Abram. Concretely, the covenant is God's granting of a rich and abundant offspring and Sarai's giving birth. The covenant's importance is underlined by the name changes of the two protagonists: from now on, they are called Abraham and Sarah, respectively. Then the promise begins to come true, Sarah becoming pregnant and bearing Isaac. The narrative proceeds immediately to Abraham's death and burial (Gen 25:8–9*). This episode might be considered the end of the story; the plot would thus reach from Abraham's birth to his death. Yet at this point one should consider that there are four similar genealogies for Abraham's descendants (Ishmael, 25:13–16, 18[?]; Isaac, 25:19; Esau/Edom, 36:10–43; Jacob/Israel, 35:22b–26[114]), all of which are ascribed to the Priestly strand. These genealogies nicely illustrate the fulfillment of the promise that Abraham will be a "father of a multitude of nations." Perhaps this explanation (popular etymology) of the name Abraham is based on Arab. *ruhām*, "multitude."[115] In the present arrangement of the book of Genesis, the combination of

---

1.24 (Fribourg: Presses Universitaires; Göttingen: Vandenhoeck & Ruprecht, 2000), 514–39; O. Keel, *Die Geschichte Jerusalems und die Entstehung des Monotheismus*, 2 vols., Orte und Landschaften der Bibel 4.1–2 (Göttingen: Vandenhoeck & Ruprecht, 2007), 1:484–88. For the importance of the moon and its phases in ancient (Yahwistic) Israel, as reflected in the feast calendar, in narrative texts, blessings, etc., see Theuer, *Der Mondgott*, 539–60. In the preexilic period, Sabbath probably referred to the celebration of the full moon; see A. Lemaire, "Le sabbat à l'époque royale israélite," *RB* 80 (1973): 161–85; idem, "Sabbat," *NBL* 3:388–91; E. Otto, "Sabbat," *RGG* 7:712–13.

[111] Exceptions are Westermann, Soggin, and Köckert (see the immediatly preceding notes). However, these scholars content themselves with the mention of some of these allusions and with the remark that they have lost their significance in the context of P (thus explicitly Westermann, *Genesis 12–36*, 158, and Soggin, *Das Buch Genesis*, 189).

[112] See Blum, *Die Komposition*, 344, n. 11; Wöhrle, *Fremdlinge*, 176–77.

[113] See above, n. 105

[114] Or Gen 46:8–27* or Exod 1:1–5*.

[115] This suggestion is made by I. Eitan, "Two Onomatological Studies," *JAOS* 49 (1929): 30–33, and Gesenius 18th ed. 1.10–11. In ancient Islamic tradition (hadith), the personal name

the Abraham narrative with the non-P Jacob, Esau, and Joseph narratives separates some of the genealogies from the Abraham story. Nevertheless, their relatedness to the Abraham narrative is obvious. In the narrower context of the Abraham narrative, the genealogies' function becomes more visible.[116] They should probably be considered the final part of the plot. Sarah's promised status as a "mother of kings" (her new name is *śārâ*, "ruler, mistress"[117] whose Akkadian equivalent is "queen"[118]) is also alluded to in the introduction of Esau's king list (cf. Gen 17:15–16 with 36:31).

The development from Sarah's infertility to her status as a mother of peoples and kingdoms should be seen as the punchline of the story. The fact that it is the deity El Shaddai/YHWH rather than Sîn, the moon god, who allows Sarah to conceive is significant. Among Israel's neighbors, the moon cult was relevant to fertility and procreation;[119] the moon god could positively influence the woman's menstrual cycle.[120] But, apparently, neither Sîn of Ur nor Sîn of Harran were able to solve Sarah's infertility. Another interpretation would be to see El Shaddai/YHWH in continuity with Sîn of Ur and Sîn of Harran rather than in opposition to them.[121]

Another important theme that comes up several times is the internal solidarity of Terah's and Abraham's families. Nahor marries his deceased brother's daughter Milcah; Terah cares about the childless couple Abram and Sarai and the fatherless grandson Lot. After Terah's death, Abraham takes over this protective role toward Lot. Sarah gives her servant Hagar to her husband Abram as wife in order to offer to the family the possibility of procreation.

P's Abraham narrative is also homogeneous where vocabulary is concerned. The acts of departing, moving, arriving, and settling at a certain place are expressed

---

Abū-Ruhām is attested. See also H.-P. MATHYS, "Künstliche Personennamen im Alten Testament," in *"... der seine Lust hat am Wort des Herrn!": Festschrift für Ernst Jenni zum 80. Geburtstag*, ed. J. Luchsinger, H.-P. Mathys, and M. Saur, AOAT 336 (Münster: Ugarit-Verlag, 2007), 218–49.

[116] Concerning the formation and literary classification of the complex composition Gen 36, see above, II.6.4 (g).

[117] *Śārâ* as personal name is not attested. According to NOTH, *Die Israelitischen Personennamen*, 10, the name is a literary creation. Even if the literary function the name seems evident, it is not necessary to consider it an ad hoc invention (cf. J. J. STAMM, "Hebräische Frauennamen," in *Hebräische Wortforschung: Festschrift zum 80. Geburtstag von Walther Baumgartner*, ed. B. Hartmann et al., VTSup 16 [Leiden: Brill, 1967], 326). Milcah's name is attested, see Num 26:33; 27:1; 36:11; Josh 17:3.

[118] See *CAD* 17.2:72–75.

[119] B. B. SCHMIDT, "Moon," *DDD* 587–88; M. GROSS, "Ḥarrān als kulturelles Zentrum in der altorientalischen Geschichte und sein Weiterleben," in *Kulturelle Schnittstelle. Mesopotamien, Anatolien, Kurdistan. Geschichte. Sprachen. Gegenwart*, ed. L. Müller-Funk, S. Procházka, G. Selz, and A. Telič, Vienna: Selbstverlag des Instituts für Orientalistik der Universität Wien, 149–50.

[120] This aspect is well documented for the Hittite religion; cf. V. HAAS and D. PRECHEL, "Mondgott A. II Bei den Hethitern," *RlA* 8:370–71.

[121] For affinities of ancient Yahwistic Israel with the cult of the moon god, see above n. 110 (lit.).

consistently with the same vocabulary. Terah and Abraham both are the initiators of a "multipart" movement: they take (לקח) their family and their possessions, they go forth (יצא) to go (הלד) into the land of Canaan, they come (בוא) to Harran/the land of Canaan, and they settle (ישב) there.[122] Likewise, Abraham's naming of his sons Ishmael and Isaac is expressed in an almost identical manner.

Genesis 16:15b
[15b] And Abram called the name of his son, whom Hagar bore, Ishmael.

Genesis 21:3
[3] And Abraham called the name of his son who was born to him, whom Sarah bore to him, Isaac.

These stylistic features do not appear in subsequent sections concerning Jacob, Esau, and Joseph.

The Abraham narrative also contains certain texts that are dependent on non-P and interact with it, thus deviating from the profile of an independent, self-contained narrative. These match well with the "dependent" texts in the subsequent Jacob-Esau narrative. We have already discussed the frequent statements about the patriarchs' ages, which depend partly on the non-Priestly context. At least some of these statement should be ascribed to a secondary, Priestly layer (P[C]), which presupposes the combination of Priestly and non-Priestly strands.[123] Another example is the short notice about God's destruction of the cities of the plain and Sodom (19:29), which was discussed above as well. Disregarding these secondary, "dependent" Priestly texts, P's Abraham narrative is, in comparison to the subsequent "deficient" P sections, continuous and self-contained to a significant degree.

Nevertheless, it must be admitted at this point that there are few punctual problems concerning the coherence of the supposed narrative. These concern a certain inconsistency in the use of toponyms and the absence of a genealogy for Isaac.

In P's Abraham narrative, toponyms play an important role from beginning to end. The list includes Ur, Harran, the land of Canaan, the "cities of the plain," and the burial place of Machpelah, in or near Mamre where Abraham is buried. The land of Canaan, mentioned as the destination of Terah's and Abraham's journeys (see Gen 11:31; 12:5), is evidently a key toponym. However, the juxtaposition of this toponym with the "cities of the plain," Lot's residence mentioned in 13:12, seems strange. First, one may ask whether the "plain" (ככר), usually identified with the southern part of the Jordan valley, should not be part of the land of Canaan.[124] Second, in view of Gen 12:5 (P), which states that Abraham and Lot "arrived in the land of Canaan," one would

---

[122] All four verbs are used together in 11:31 (subject Terah) and three of them appear in 12:5 (subject Abraham).

[123] See above, II.6.4 (a). For the literary classification of this layer, see below, III.1.2.2 (b) (3).

[124] See SEEBASS, *Genesis II/1*, 36; A. DE PURY, T. RÖMER, and K. SCHMID, *L'Ancien Testament commenté: La Genèse* (Paris: Bayard; Geneva: Labor et Fides, 2016), 78.

expect a verb expressing Lot's departure to precede the statement about his settling in the "plain" ("Lot *departed and* settled in the cities of the plain"), but such a verb is absent. Therefore, I am inclined to consider the statement in Gen 13:12abα ("Abram settled in the land of Canaan; Lot settled in the cities of the plain") a secondary addition (P^c), influenced by the non-Priestly strand, according to which Lot took up residence in Sodom (see 13:12bβ non-P). As will be shown below, the redactor (P^c) is keen to limit the land of Canaan in the Jacob-Esau section as well and to exclude certain nations, by their eponyms, from the right of usufruct.[125] If so, then Abraham and Lot separated in the primary account (see 13:11b: "Thus they separated from each other"), but nevertheless both remained in the land of Canaan.[126] Their specific domiciles would not have been mentioned, because the author would have sought to avoid associating either protagonist with a concrete place (for a possible reason, see below, II.6.7 [a], [b]).[127]

A second problem is that in P genealogies are preserved for Ishmael, Jacob, and Esau but not for Isaac. There is a sort of beginning of a genealogy for the latter, yet the expected short enumeration of descendants is missing; what follows is instead a second statement of Isaac's provenance (Gen 25:19: "Now these are descendants of Isaac, Abraham's son: Abraham begot Isaac"). This particular genealogical phrase is followed by the non-P birth story of Esau and Jacob. It seems possible that P originally contained a short genealogy for Isaac, perhaps in the form, "Now these are the descendants of Isaac, Abraham's son: Isaac begot Esau and Jacob." Later, in the course of the narrative's connection to the non-P birth story, this sentence would have been altered in order to avoid an odd repetition.

Notwithstanding these two problems, the fact remains that P's Abraham narrative is, in comparison with the following "deficient" P sections, continuous, self-contained, and highly coherent.

With regard to its distinct literary profile, one should ask whether the P stratum in Gen 11:27–25:9 – perhaps together with the genealogies that complete it – was composed independently of the following Priestly texts in the Jacob-Esau and Joseph sections. Did they once form an autonomous, self-contained narrative, a *proto-Priestly* Abraham narrative? Lending support to this assumption are several striking linguistic, thematic, and theological differences between P's Abraham narrative and the following P sections. These are presented in the following sections (6.6.1–6).

---

[125] See below, II.6.6.6 and II.6.8 (b).

[126] This is the understanding of SEEBASS, *Genesis II/1*, 36; A. DE PURY, T. RÖMER, and K. SCHMID, *L'Ancien Testament commenté: La Genèse* (Paris: Bayard; Geneva: Labor et Fides, 2016), 78.

[127] Alternately, one may speculate that 13:12 was modified by the redactor (P^c): a specific home (Mamre?) was replaced with "the land of Canaan" in the course of redactional reworking, in order to associate Abraham with the whole land instead of just one city.

6.6 Linguistic and Theological Differences between the Abraham Section and the Other Sections

A striking feature of P's ancestral narrative is the fact that several motifs in the Abraham section reappear in the Isaac, Jacob-Esau, and Joseph narratives. These motifs are (1) the motif of accumulation of property; (2) the death and burial notices; (3) the deity's revelation and the related name changes; (4) El Shaddai as intervening deity; (5) the diversity of the promised offspring; and (6) the promise of the land. On the one hand, there are striking correspondences in content and linguistic formulation of these motifs in the different sections, but on the other hand, there are important deviations from the Abraham section in the Isaac, Jacob-Esau, and Joseph sections. In the first three cases (1–3), the deviation concerns linguistic and formal particularities; the formulations in the Isaac, Jacob-Esau, and Joseph sections seem to be influenced in part by the non-P context. The last three examples (4–6) involve important theological shifts.

6.6.1 Accumulation of Possessions

In several instances, P mentions the accumulation of possessions by the patriarchs. The rather rare and general expression רכוש, "possession, good," is used. In some texts, however, all of which belong to the Jacob-Esau and Joseph sections, other specifying expressions occur in addition to רכוש.[128]

Genesis 12:5
[5] And Abram took Sarai his wife and Lot his nephew, and <u>all their possessions which they had accumulated</u> [ואת כל רכושם אשר רכשו], and the persons which they had acquired in Harran, and they set out for the land of Canaan; thus they came to the land of Canaan.

Genesis 13:6
[6] And the land did not sustain them while dwelling together; for <u>their possessions</u> [רכושם] were so great that they were not able to remain together.

Genesis 31:18
[18] And he drove away <u>all his livestock</u> [את כל מקנהו] <u>and all his possessions which he had accumulated</u> [ואת כל רכש אשר רכש], <u>his acquired livestock</u> [מקנה קנינו] which he had <u>accumulated</u> [רכש] in Paddan-aram, to go to the land of Canaan to his father Isaac.

Genesis 36:6–7
[6] Then Esau took his wives and his sons and his daughters and all his household, <u>and his livestock</u> [ואת מקנהו] <u>and all his cattle</u> [ואת כל בהמתו] <u>and all his goods</u> [ואת כל קנינו] which he had <u>accumulated</u> [רכש] in the land of Canaan, and went

---

[128] The specified expressions are highlighted by double underlining in the following.

to a land away from his brother Jacob. [7] For their possessions [רכושם] had become too great for them to live together, and the land where they sojourned could not sustain them because of their livestock [מקניהם].

Genesis 46:6
[6] And they took their livestock [את מקניהם] and their possessions which they had accumulated [ואת רכושם אשר רכשו] in the land of Canaan, and came to Egypt, Jacob and all his descendants being with him.

The accumulation of property is expressed differently. In the two texts belonging to the Abraham section, Gen 12:5 and 13:6, the term רכוש refers in a general manner to possessions acquired by Abraham. No further specifying expression is used. In a second statement the acquisition of humans (slaves) is mentioned. The use of two different verbs shows that the author distinguishes between two different kind of acquisitions. In Gen 31:18; 36:6; and 46:6 (belonging to the Jacob-Esau and Joseph narratives), however, the term רכוש never occurs alone but is always accompanied by the specifying term מקנה, "livestock," קנין, "goods," and (or) בהמה, "cattle." The author intends to identify the acquired property with cattle. As Wöhrle shows, the expression מקנה, "livestock as property" is often used in non-P texts of the ancestral narrative (above all in the Jacob-Esau section) in order to indicate possession of (numerous) cattle.[129] This consistent difference between P's Abraham narrative on the one hand and the sections concerning Jacob, Esau, and Joseph on the other hints at different authors in the respective sections. Whereas the P narrative in the Abraham section has its own language and is independent from the non-P stratum, the later author of the P passages in the Jacob-Esau and Joseph sections combines the vocabulary found in the Abraham narrative with certain expressions borrowed from the non-P strand.

6.6.2 Death and Burial Notices

In P's ancestral narrative, Abraham, Isaac, and Jacob are each given a combined death and burial notice. For Ishmael, there is only a death notice. The first death and burial notice appears in Gen 25:8–9, the end of the Abraham narrative:

Genesis 25:8–9abβ
[8] ויגוע וימת אברהם בשיבה טובה זקן ושבע ויאסף אל עמיו [9abβ] ויקברו אתו יצחק
וישמעאל בניו אל מערת המכפלה אשר על פני ממרא
[8] And Abraham breathed his last and died in a ripe old age, an old man and satisfied (with life); and he was gathered to his people. [9abβ] And his sons Isaac and Ishmael buried him in the cave of Machpelah, which is before Mamre.

---

[129] Wöhrle, *Fremdlinge*, 83–84. In the non-P sections, מקנה is found in Gen 13:2, 7 (2×); 26:14 (2×); 29:7; 30:29; 31:9; 33:17; 34:5, 23; 46:32, 34; 47:6, 16 (2×), 17 (4×), 18; קנין occurs in Gen 34:23; בהמה in 34:23; 47:18.

Abraham's death and burial formula is carefully composed. As the analyses of B. Alfrink and N. Artemov show, the three verbs used in v. 8 express a distinct aspect of the process of dying: the first verb (גוע) probably means "breathed his last" (< "gasped for breath").[130] The second verb, מות, "to die," has the complement "in a ripe old age, an old man and satisfied [with life]."[131] The expression refers to the end of earthly life. The third verb, אסף *niphal*, "to be gathered with his kin," points to the realm of the afterworld.[132] The following verse reports the burial (with the verb קבר).[133]

In comparison with Abraham's death formulary, the notices for Ishmael, Isaac, and Jacob have several minor deviations. The death formula for Ishmael (25:17) depends on the statement about his age. The same three verbs that were used in 25:8 are used here; the burial notice, however, is lacking. As for the notice for Isaac (Gen 35:29), the differences are more numerous.

Genesis 35:29

29 ויגוע יצחק וימת ויאסף אל עמיו זקן ושבע ימים ויקברו אתו עשו ויעקב בניו

29 And Isaac <u>breathed his last</u> and <u>died</u>, and <u>was gathered to his people</u>, an <u>old man satisfied with days</u>; and his sons Esau and Jacob buried him.

In contrast to the formula in Gen 25:8–9, the expression "in a ripe old age" (בשיבה טובה, 25:8) is absent here, and the word order is not the same: זקן ושבע ימים, "an old man satisfied with days" follows ויאסף אל עמיו, "and was gathered to his people" instead of וימת, "and died" (cf. the more natural sequence in Gen 25:8). The elliptical expression "satisfied (with life)" in 25:8 (MT) is rendered more explicitly: "satisfied

---

[130] Cf. G. R. Driver, "Resurrection of Marine and Terrestrial Creatures," *JSS* 7 (1962): 12–22; *HALOT* 184.

[131] The elliptical phrasing שבע "satisfied" (with life) is attested in MT. SP and LXX read שבע ימים ("satisfied with days").

[132] B. Alfrink, "L'expression נֶאֱסַף אֶל עַמָּיו," *OTS* 5 (1948): 128, and N. Artemov, "Belief in Family Reunion in the Afterlife in the Ancient Near East and Mediterranean," in *La famille dans le Proche-Orient ancien: Réalités, symbolismes, et images; Proceedings of the 55th Rencontre Assyriologique Internationale at Paris, 6–9 July 2009*, ed. L. Marti (Winona Lake, IN: Eisenbrauns, 2014), 29–30, convincingly argue that the reference of the idiom אסף *niphal* + אל עמיו in Gen 25:8 and parallel texts must be distinguished from the death of the person (expressed by the preceding lexemes גוע and מות) on the one hand and from his burial (referred to in the subsequent v. 9 by the verb קבר) on the other. Thus the action described with the expression אסף *niphal* + אל עמיו should refer "to something which ... immediately follows the death of a person and ... precedes his or her burial." (Artemov, "Belief," 29). With regard to the adverbial complement אל עמיו, "to his kin," one must understand the idiom as referring to the reunion with the ancestors in the afterlife. The interpretation according to which the term would refer to the reunion with the deceased family members *in the tomb* (cf. E. Bloch-Smith, *Judahite Burial Practices and Beliefs about the Dead*, JSOTSup 123 [Sheffield: Sheffield Academic Press, 1992], 110) is contradicted by three of the four death and burial notices using the expression אסף *niphal* + אל עמיו: they all contain an explicit reference to the burial too (cf. Gen 25:8–9; 35:29; 49:33; 50:12–13; only in Gen 25:17, the notice of Ishmael's death, is a burial statement lacking).

[133] The information about the former owner and about Abraham's purchase of the land (v. 10) should be ascribed to a secondary layer (cf. below, II.6.4 [f]).

with days." The most striking difference is the missing burial location. The death notice for Jacob is combined with a long instruction by the patriarch for his sons and is followed by a burial notice (Gen 49:29–33; 50:12–13):

Genesis 49:29–33* *Jacob's death*

[29abα] Then he [Jacob] charged them and said to them, "I am about to be gathered to my people [נאסף אל עמי]; bury [קברו] me with my fathers in the cave [30*] which is before Mamre, in the land of Canaan. [31] There they buried Abraham and his wife Sarah, there they buried Isaac and his wife Rebekah, and there I buried Leah." [33] When Jacob finished charging his sons, he gathered up his feet into the bed [ויאסף רגליו אל המטה] and breathed his last [ויגוע], and was gathered to his people [ויאסף אל עמיו].

Genesis 50:12–13abβ *Jacob's burial*

[12] And his sons did for him as he had charged them; [13abβ] and his sons carried him to the land of Canaan, and buried [ויקברו] him in the cave of the field of Machpelah before Mamre.

As for the death notice, the verb מות is notably absent. A new element appears, using the motif of the gathering-up "of his [Jacob's] feet into the bed." The author playfully takes up the verb אסף from the traditional death and burial formula for a second time, but he uses it in another sense. Since Jacob's bed (מטה) is mentioned twice in the preceding non-P narrative,[134] the P passage must have been influenced by this text.[135] Likewise, the fact that the author of this passage does not include Rachel in the enumeration of ancestors buried in the cave of Machpelah shows that P here depends on the non-P narrative (see Gen 35:16–20). The reports on Jacob's death and burial are more elaborate than the others. Furthermore, Wöhrle has observed that Gen 49:31 contradicts the passage concerning Isaac's burial.[136] Whereas Gen 35:29 reports that Esau and Jacob buried Isaac, Jacob refers to anonymous subjects (3rd-person pl.) performing the burial act in 49:29–33. Furthermore, the fact that 35:29 is lacking a burial notice possibly indicates that its author did not expect Jacob to be buried in the cave of Machpelah. Therefore, the two passages probably do not belong to the same literary stratum.

In comparison with the other death and burial formulae, the statement in Gen 25:8–9 seems to be the most compact and complete, standing out in its careful structure and alignment of four verbs. In contrast, the other death (and burial) formulae lack one or more elements, they change the latter's sequence, and one among these texts depends on the non-P context (Gen 49:29–33). The formula in 25:8–9, the particular motif "gathered to one's people," and the indication of a concrete burial place

---

[134] Cf. Gen 47:31; 48:2.

[135] Cf. Wöhrle, *Fremdlinge*, 127–28.

[136] See Wöhrle, *Fremdlinge*, 127.

("in the cave of Machpelah") may point to a proto-Priestly tradition.[137] The latter may have served as a model for the phrases in 25:17; 35:29; and 49:29–33, 50:12–13 (which again differ among themselves, Gen 49:29–33, 50:12–13 standing out for its length and showing signs of secondary expansion.)[138]

6.6.3 Changes of Personal Names

In the ancestral narrative of P, El Shaddai/YHWH reveals himself twice, once to Abraham and once to Jacob. On the occasion of these revelations, the deity announces a total of three name changes: Abram–Abraham (Gen 17:5); Sarai–Sarah (17:15–16); and Jacob–Israel (35:9–10).

In the case of Abraham and Sarah, these changes are explained by etiologies. The extension of Abraham's name (Abra-*ha*-m) is explained by the promise that Abram would become a "father of a multitude (*hāmôn*) of nations."[139]

Genesis 17:5
[5] "No longer shall your name be called Abram, but your name shall be Abraham; for I will make you the father of a multitude of nations."

Also Sarah's new name (*sārâ*, "mistress, ruler") is explained by a promise: kings of peoples will go out from her.

Genesis 17:15–16
[15] Then God said to Abraham, "As for Sarai your wife, you shall not call her name Sarai, but Sarah shall be her name. [16] And I will bless her, and indeed I will give you a son by her. Then I will bless her, and she shall be a mother of nations; kings of peoples shall come from her."

The idea seems to be that her "royal" offspring will justify her new name.[140]

As for the passage containing the statement of Jacob's new name (Israel), however, no explanation for the name change is given.

Genesis 35:10
[10] And God said to him [Jacob], "Your name is Jacob; You shall no longer be called Jacob, But Israel shall be your name." Thus he called him Israel.

The absence of an etiological explanation for the name change is striking. Furthermore, Jacob's name change is not anchored in the subsequent parts of the Priestly strand. P goes on to use the name Jacob (see Gen 35:14, 15, 23, 27, 29; 36:6; 37:1 and *passim*). In contrast, Abraham's and Sarah's changed names are used consistently

---

[137] See further below II.6.7 (b).
[138] See also above, II.6.4 (f).
[139] Cf. also above, n. 115.
[140] Cf. also above, n. 117.

throughout the remainder of the Priestly Abraham narrative.[141] These differences may indicate that Gen 35:10 does not belong to the same literary layer as Gen 17:5, 15–16.

Generally, scholars believe that the renaming of Jacob in P depends on the motif of the name change found in the non-P section of the Jacob narrative (in the story of the battle at the Jabbok in Gen 32:23–33). Yet, recently scholars have put forward some arguments favoring the idea that the non-P name change (32:28–29) should be considered a secondary insertion into the story of the nighttime fight.[142] If these analyses are correct, perhaps one might determine the direction of dependence between the two texts differently: Gen 35:10 would predate 32:28–30a.[143] Accordingly, the motif of Jacob's name change would be inspired uniquely by the name change in Gen 17.

6.6.4 Theonyms: Two Occurrences of the Tetragram in the Priestly Abraham Narrative

In all sections of the ancestral narrative presenting a revelation of the deity, the latter introduces himself as El Shaddai (cf. Gen 17:1; 28:3; 35:11; 48:3; Exod 6:3). This designation fits well with the theonym system of the Priestly composition. According to P's theology, the name Elohim is used in the story of origins (Gen 1–11 P). El Shaddai is the name of the deity who appears to Abraham and Jacob. Finally, the deity reveals his genuine name, YHWH, to Moses (Exod 6:2); from now on, the deity will use this name in his interaction with the people of Israel. Yet this consistency is disturbed by two occurrences of YHWH as designation of God in the Priestly Abraham narrative (Gen 17:1b and 21:1b). El Shaddai is equated with YHWH. In the context of P^C, in which the theology concerning the deity's name occupies an important place, these two occurrences of YHWH are difficult to explain.

Genesis 17:1b

וירא יהוה אל אברם ויאמר אליו אני אל שדי התהלך לפני והיה תמים ^1b

[1b] And YHWH appeared to Abram and said to him, "I am El Shaddai; walk before me, and be blameless!"

---

[141] To the divergence concerning the name changes between the two revelation passages (Gen 17 and 35:9–10), one may add the difference of the designation of the revealing deity (YHWH in 17:1 and Elohim in 35:9). See below, II.6.6.4.

[142] The use of the lexeme שׂרה, "to strive," in the etiological explanation, which matches the name ישׂראל, contrasts with the twofold occurrence of אבק, "to wrestle," in the battle story (see WESTERMANN, *Genesis 12–36*, 631–32; LEVIN, *Der Jahwist*, 250–51; KRATZ, *Composition*, 269, 274). Furthermore, the statement that Jacob prevailed against both God and men departs from the scope of the story and overlooks the entire Jacob cycle, which reports that first Esau and then Laban have been outplayed by Jacob. Moreover, a discrepancy consists in the fact that whereas (cf. v. 25) the battle ends in a draw in the primary story, v. 29 declares Jacob the winner (cf. WESTERMANN, *Genesis 12–36*, 632).

[143] Cf. WÖHRLE, *Fremdlinge*, 89–90, with n. 63, and WESTERMANN, *Genesis 12–36*, 632 (hesitating).

Genesis 21:1b

1bויעש יהוה לשרה כאשר דבר

[1b]YHWH did for Sarah as he had spoken.

Genesis 17:1b is generally considered a P text, and verse 21:1b is often ascribed to P as well. As shown above, this classification is justified.[144]

It is striking to see that both verses, 17:1b and 21:1b, mark key events in the plot of P's Abraham narrative: the revelation of the deity on the one hand and the conception and birth of Isaac by Sarah on the other. How can we explain the use of the Tetragram in these texts? Following T. Römer, one might argue that the narrator uses the Tetragram at these important points in the plot "in order to inform the reader about the identity of El Shaddai."[145] It is true that in none of these narratives is the name YHWH revealed to Abraham. Nevertheless, this argument raises the question why the author would use the Tetragram only in these two cases and not also in his revelation to Jacob, Israel's eponym. For this reason, we tentatively envisage another explanation: the author of the comprehensive Priestly layer found the Tetragram in its source and decided to preserve the name despite the fact that it stood in tension with his concept of a three-stage revelation of God with three distinct designations. According to the argumentation outlined above, the supposed source would have been a proto-Priestly Abraham narrative. Because the Tetragram occurs in the pivotal texts of this narrative, we may ask whether YHWH, in addition to El Shaddai, was originally the main designation for God in the proto-Priestly Abraham narrative. The fact that the designation Elohim occurs frequently in 11:27–25:18 would at first seem to contradict such a conclusion. However, the distribution of Elohim in this section is strikingly uneven: in the passages before Gen 17 the deity is *never* (!) mentioned. A massive concentration of occurrences of is found in the long chapter Gen 17 (9×), and it is found in a few other texts, most of which have been assigned to redactional Priestly (or H-like) strata (Gen 19:29 [2×]; 21:2b, 4; 23:6; and 25:11) as well (see above, II.6.4). This overview shows that in some texts and subsections of P's Abraham account, the deity is only sporadically mentioned, if at all. Looked at that way, the designation of God as YHWH in two central passages gains significance. We might even go a step further and raise the question whether the designation Elohim was absent from the proto-Priestly Abraham narrative and was introduced into the narrative only at a later stage by the Priestly redactor.[146]

---

[144] See above, II.6.3 (d).

[145] RÖMER, "Exodus Narrative," 162, n. 23.

[146] At least some of the relevant passages should be ascribed to a secondary layer. (1) As for the strikingly comprehensive chapter Gen 17, where the designation Elohim occurs several times, there are indications favoring the idea that the chapter is not unified and originally was much shorter. As shown above, certain passages are probably secondary insertions, including the order of circumcision in 17:9–14 and its execution in 17:23–27, and the passage 17:17–22. In the tentatively reconstructed text, the sole designation of the deity is YHWH (see above, II.6.4 [b]). (2) In the passage on Isaac's birth, the two statements containing the name Elohim

According to Gen 17, the revealing deity introduced himself as El Shaddai (v. 1b). Yet the author identifies the deity as YHWH. Such a juxtaposition of YHWH and El Shaddai also occurs in the Balaam story and in the book of Job.[147] In a certain respect, YHWH, in company with El Shaddai, makes better sense than the universal and "neutral" Elohim as a designation for the intervening deity in the context of the supposed proto-Priestly Abraham narrative. The author aimed to show how YHWH brought salvation to Sarah and Abraham, a couple coming from Mesopotamia to the land of Canaan and suffering childlessness. As mentioned above, two toponyms and perhaps also certain personal names in the story's introduction allude to the moon cult.[148] The fact that it is the local deity El Shaddai/YHWH rather than Sîn, the moon god, who is able to bring fecundity to Sarah and Abraham may be considered a fine point of the story. Fertility and procreation fell under the purview of the ancient Near Eastern moon cult.[149] In this respect, we should also note that in some traditions in the Hebrew Bible, YHWH is connected with fertility and procreation, too.[150]

6.6.5 Diversity of the Offspring

A particularity of the Priestly Abraham narrative is its "internationality": Abraham's route begins in Ur in Mesopotamia and leads via Harran in northern Syria to Mamre, in the south of the "land of Canaan." Abraham's first child is borne by the Egyptian servant Hagar. The narrative's internationality culminates in the promise of Gen 17, which depicts the patriarch as a "father of a multitude of nations."

> Genesis 17:4–5, 6b
> [4] "As for me, behold, my covenant is with you, and you shall be the father of a multitude of nations. [5] No longer shall your name be called Abram, But your name shall be Abraham; For I will make you the father of a multitude of nations, [6b] and kings shall come forth from you."

– a chronological notice (21:2b) and Isaac's circumcision (21:4) – are dependent on secondary passages in Gen 17 (17:9–14, 17–22); see II.6.4 (d), (e). (3) Two further occurrences of Elohim appear in the short notice about God's destruction of the cities of the plain and Sodom (19:29). This verse clearly should also be considered a later insertion (6.4.[c]). (4) The texts containing the two remaining occurrences of Elohim (23:6; 25:11) seem secondary as well. Due to its linguistic and stylistic particularities, Gen 23 is rightly ascribed to a secondary P layer (6.4.[f]). As for 25:11, its statement about Isaac's blessing by Elohim is quite astonishing; Abraham, the central narrative figure, does not receive any blessing (see Gen 17). Thus the attribution of 25:11(a) to the original Priestly Abraham narrative seems doubtful. This overview of texts containing the designation אלהים does not pretend to answer the question conclusively, but the evidence is suggestive nevertheless.

[147] Cf. H. PFEIFFER, "Gottesbezeichnungen/Gottesnamen (AT), 3: El Schaddaj/Schaddaj ('Allmächtiger'?)," WIBILEX, https://www.bibelwissenschaft.de/stichwort/19928/.

[148] See II.6.5.2.

[149] See II.6.5.2.

[150] Cf. Gen 29:31–30:16; 1 Sam 1–2.

Several of Abraham's descendants indeed become eponyms of important peoples, namely, the Ishmaelites, Edomites, and Israelites, a fact evidenced by the extensive genealogies attributed to these descendants. Tensions or conflicts between these peoples (or representatives of these peoples) are not alluded to at all. This focus on "internationality" in the short Priestly Abraham narrative is striking and should be considered an intentional device by the author.

In the section following the Abraham narrative, however, the atmosphere changes, and relations between the eponymous characters are not as harmonious as in the previous section. Here, the reader is told that Esau took two Hittite women as wives and that they are despised by Rebecca and Isaac (26:34–35; 27:46–28:9). Esau's act is seen in a negative light; it seems to be the reason for Isaac's preferential treatment of Jacob, whom Isaac blesses instead of Esau (28:1). According to most scholars, the author of this passage puts forward the principle of Israel's separation from the autochthonous, unrelated population,[151] reflecting a line of thought that became dominant in the time of Ezra and Nehemiah. Yet, the author's critique of Esau's behavior stands in tension with the importance given to Esau in the comprehensive genealogy Gen 36.[152] As shown above, the genealogies of Ishmael, Esau, and Jacob can be read as fulfilling of the promise of Gen 17 that Abraham will become a "father of a multitude of nations."

Significantly, the motif of diversity of promised offspring also appears in the Jacob-Esau section but in peculiar transformation: like Abraham, Jacob will also become an "assembly of nations":

Genesis 28:3–4
[3] And may El Shaddai bless you and make you fruitful and multiply you, that you may become an assembly of peoples (קהל עמים). [4] May he also give you the blessing of Abraham, to you and to your descendants with you; that you may possess the land of your sojournings, which God gave to Abraham.

Genesis 35:11
[11] God also said to him, I am El Shaddai; Be fruitful and multiply; A nation (גוי) and an assembly of nations (וקהל גוים) shall come from you, and kings shall come forth from you.

The repeated promise to Jacob (Israel) that he will be an assembly of nations (גוים) parallels Abraham's prospective designation as "father of multiple nations [גוים]" in the (proto-)Priestly Abraham narrative (Gen 17:4–5). As in other examples, it seems that

---

[151] See GUNKEL, *Genesis*, 386; VON RAD, *Das erste Buch*, 227; SPEISER, *Genesis*, 216; WESTERMANN, *Genesis 12–36*, 546; BLUM, *Die Komposition*, 263; RUPPERT, *Genesis*, 3:158. Differently SHECTMAN, *Women*, 144–45, who argues that P does not forbid exogamy but simply emphasizes the importance of the Bethuelite lineage (in doing so, P would rely on a received tradition).

[152] Among the genealogies, those concerning Esau especially stand out in their extent (Gen 36), even if some parts of the complex composition seem to have been accumulated secondarily. On the history of the formation of Gen 36, see above II.6.4 (g).

the author of the former "Israelizes" a central motif of the latter. Whereas the promise to Abraham concerns both Israel and ethnically related nations in the Abraham narrative, the promise in the Esau-Jacob and Joseph sections includes only Israelite "nations." Who, concretely, are these "nations" within Jacob (Israel)? Since the promise is addressed to Jacob, the referents of the terms *peoples* and *nations* are probably the later kingdoms of Israel and Judah and their legal successors in the Persian era. The term קהל stresses the religious unity of the two nations ("cultic assembly, congregation"). The kings mentioned in Gen 35:11 are the later Israelite and Judean kings.[153] The promise of kings already present in the (proto-)Priestly Abraham narrative (see Gen 17:6, 16) has also been taken up by the Priestly author and applied to Israel alone.

The motif of multiple offspring fits well with the plot of the Priestly Abraham narrative insofar as it contrasts with Abraham's and Sarah's long-lasting childlessness. The etiology of Abraham's name hints at the centrality of this theme in the Abraham story as well. There is no such contrast in the Jacob narrative, and the equation of Jacob's sons with "nations" (peoples) is somewhat surprising (one would instead expect the expression *tribes*). These are indications that the motif and the associated terms are anchored in the Priestly Abraham narrative rather than in the Jacob-Esau one; the author of the latter borrowed it from the former and transformed it.

6.6.6 Promise of the Land

The promise of the land appears in all sections of the Priestly ancestral narrative and in Exod 6. The vocabulary of the promise, related to the question of being a sojourner and having the right of usufruct of the land (or owning it), includes the terms גר / גור / מגור (sojourner/to sojourn/sojourning), אחזה (right of usufruct), and ירש (to take possession; become heir, owner).[154] Recent scholarship has tended to consider the land promise to be fulfilled during the lifetime of the patriarchs.[155] This understanding seems confirmed by the statements that the land of Canaan *was given* to Abraham and Isaac (formulated in the perfect [*qatal*] conjugation; see Gen 28:4 and 35:12).[156] This has implications for the interpretation of the expression אחזה used in the central statement in 17:8: since neither Abraham nor Isaac possessed the land but rather lived as sojourners in it, אחזה should be understood as "right of usufruct"

---

[153] So BLUM, *Die Komposition*, 457. – For a more detailed analysis see below, II.6.8 (b) and III.1.2.2 (a) (4).

[154] גר / גור / מגור: Gen 17:8; 23:4; 28:4; 36:7; 37:1; 47:9 (2×); Exod 6:4 (2×); אחזה: Gen 17:8; 23:4, 9, 20; 36:43; 48:4; 49:30; 50:13; ירש / מורשה: Gen 28:4; Exod 6:8.

[155] See KÖCKERT, "Das Land," 153; BLUM, *Die Komposition*, 443; WÖHRLE, *Fremdlinge*, 194–95; T. RÖMER, "La construction d'Abraham comme ancêtre œcuménique," *RSR* 26 [2014]: 16–17.

[156] See WÖHRLE, *Fremdlinge*, 194–95.

rather than "possession" or "property."[157] This meaning of אחזה seems evident in Gen 47:11 (post-P: Joseph attributes land in Ramses to the Israelites).[158]

What is not considered in scholarship, however, is that apart from the passage 17:8 (assigned to proto-P in the present study), the expression אחזה occurs in P^C in at most one other passage, 48:4 (which often is attributed to P^S or post-P).[159] In light of this, the fact that in the context of the land promise the Priestly author twice uses an expression derived from the root ירש (Gen 28:4; Exod 6:8) becomes significant: the verb ירש, qal, "to take possession of, inherit, become owner of" (Gen 28:4), and the noun מורשה, "acquisition, ownership" (Exod 6:8). In the present context of P, however, scholars often understand מורשה (and ירש) in the same sense as אחזה.[160] Nevertheless, the difference of vocabulary is striking, and one should ask whether the Priestly author has not differentiated purposefully between אחזה and מורשה. Significantly, מורשה and ירש, are both used in the land promise to Jacob/Israel.[161] This may indicate that Gen 28:4 and Exod 6:8 allude to the non-Priestly account of Israel's conquest of the land, in which the verb ירש, "to take possession (of the promised land)," plays an important role.[162] It is significant that YHWH's promise in Exod 6:8 is phrased in terms of an oath that recalls formulations in Deut 10:11; 11:9, 21; 31:7 and Ezek 20, which are all texts that refer to the conquest of the land.[163] It is also noteworthy that the expression מורשה, which is used predominantly in the book of Ezekiel, does not seem to have the specific meaning "right of usufruct of the land."[164]

The concept of the land promise in P's Abraham section differs from that in the subsequent Priestly sections in another important respect: the beneficiary of the promise and the extent of the promised land. Who are the beneficiaries of these various sections? Explicitly mentioned are Abraham (Gen 17:8; 28:4; 35:12; Exod 6:4, 8; in Gen 17:8 Abraham's descendants are included), Isaac (Gen 35:12; Exod 6:4, 8), and Jacob and his descendants (Gen 28:4; 35:12; 48:4; in the latter text the land is promised only to Jacob's offspring). Traditionally, all these texts are assigned to P^G/P^C. In the first promise, in the Abraham section, the particular formulation ("*all* the land of Canaan" and explicit mention of Abraham's descendants; 17:8a) and Abraham's characterization as "ancestor of a multitude of nations" (17:4; cf. also v. 6) indicates that

---

[157] See Köckert, "Das Land," 153; Blum, *Die Komposition*, 443; Wöhrle, *Fremdlinge*, 194–95; T. Römer, "La construction d'Abraham," 16–17.

[158] Concerning literary classification, see above, II.6.4 (h) (3).

[159] For the classification of this text, see above II.6.4 (h) (4).

[160] See, for instance, M. Bauks, "Die Begriffe מורשה und אחזה in P^G: Überlegungen zur Landkonzeption der Priestergrundschrift," *ZAW* 116 (2004): 172–74, 183–85; Wöhrle, *Fremdlinge*, 198, n. 24; Römer, "From the Call of Moses," 135–36.

[161] For a distinction between the two terms, see also Albertz, *Exodus 19–40*, 126.

[162] The lexeme ירש *qal*, "to take possession of," with the complement "land," occurs more than fifty times in the books of Deuteronomy and Joshua.

[163] See Römer, "From the Call of Moses," 136.

[164] Ezek 11:15; 25:4, 10; 33:24; 36:2, 3, 5. In most cases, the term refers to property acquired through military conquest.

not only Abraham but *all* his sons and *all* his grandsons should be considered beneficiaries of the promise.[165]

Genesis 17:8a

[8a]"And I will give to you and to your descendants after you the land of your sojournings, all the land of Canaan, for everlasting usufruct."

Accordingly, "all the land of Canaan" encompasses a good part of the Levant; in particular, it comprises the territories of Israel, Judah, the Ishmaelites, and Edom, as A.
de Pury has suggested forcefully.[166]

In the subsequent Priestly sections, namely those of Jacob-Esau, Joseph, and Exod
1–6 P, however, the group of beneficiaries becomes restricted: it consist only of Abraham, Isaac, and Jacob (Israel). Here, the relevant Priestly texts in Gen 28:4; 36:7; 35:12
and 37:1 establish a dichotomy between Jacob, to whom the land of Canaan is given
(cf. 37:1), and Edom's descendants, for whom the mountain of Seir is destined.

Genesis 28:4

[4]"May he (YHWH) also give you the blessing of Abraham, to you and to your descendants with you; that you may possess the land of your sojournings [ארץ
מגריך], which God gave to Abraham."

Genesis 35:12

[12](God said to Jacob:) "And the land which I gave to Abraham and Isaac, I will give
it to you, And I will give the land to your descendants after you."

Genesis 36:6–8

[6]Then Esau took his wives and his sons and his daughters and all his household,
and his livestock and all his cattle and all his goods which he had acquired in the
land of Canaan, and went to another land away[167] from his brother Jacob. [7]For
their property had become too great for them to live together, and the land of their
sojournings [ארץ מגוריהם] could not sustain them because of their livestock. [8]So
Esau lived in the hill country of Seir; Esau is Edom.

Genesis 37:1

[1]Now Jacob lived in the land of his father's sojournings [בארץ מגרי אביו], in the
land of Canaan.

In addition, in Exod 6:4, 8 the land of Canaan, which is called "the land of the sojournings" of the three patriarchs, is said to be promised to the latter and to Israel.

---

[165] See DE PURY, "Abraham," 80, with n. 30.

[166] DE PURY, "Abraham," 80, with n. 30, even speaks of "nearly the whole of the Levant." According to Gen 13:6, 11b–12bα, the Jordan valley (the area in which Lot settled) is excluded
from the land of Canaan; however, this statement should perhaps be assigned to the secondary
Priestly redaction (P[c]); see above II.6.5.2.

[167] Concerning the textual difference, see above, II.6.2 (d).

Exodus 6:4

[4] And I (YHWH) also established my covenant with them, to give them the land of Canaan, the land of their sojournings [ארץ מגוריהם], in which they sojourned.

Exodus 6:8

[8] And I will bring you to the land which I swore to give to Abraham, Isaac, and Jacob, and I will give it to you for a possession; I am YHWH.

Significantly, in all these texts the (multiple and multiethnic) descendants of Abraham are no longer mentioned in a general sense. Genesis 28:4 states that the land was given to Abraham (uniquely). According to 35:12, the land was given to Abraham and Isaac. In light of these texts, it becomes clear that not only Esau but also Ishmael is excluded from the promise (the latter is never mentioned as a beneficiary of the promise of the land). Only one line among Abraham's offspring – that of Isaac and Jacob – will have the right to the land.

Accordingly, the extent of the promised land of Canaan in the Jacob-Esau and Joseph sections is reduced in comparison to the Abraham section. The territories of Ishmael and Esau are not included in it. This conclusion seems confirmed by the fact that the author of the Priestly texts in the Jacob-Esau section is anxious to show which places should be considered to belong to "the land of Canaan," adding the specification "in the land of Canaan" to certain Judean or Israelite toponyms (see 23:2, 19: "Hebron in the land of Canaan"; 33:18: "Shechem, which is in the land of Canaan"; cf. also 35:6: "Luz, which is in the land of Canaan").[168] Significantly, such specifications for toponyms in the Priestly ancestral narrative are restricted to place names in the territories of the later kingdoms of Israel and Judah. Yet it is remarkable that such additional information never appears in the "core" of the Priestly Abraham narrative (cf. the toponyms "Machpelah before Mamre" in 25:9 and Beer El Roi in 25:11, which lack the aforementioned specification).

To conclude, the promise of the land in the Priestly Abraham narrative is conceived of differently than it is in the subsequent Priestly sections. In the former, the land of Canaan is destined for Abraham and all his descendants. In the Priestly texts of the Jacob-Esau, Joseph, and exodus sections, the group of beneficiaries is limited to the line Isaac-Jacob (Israel) alone. While the promise to Abraham visibly concerns the right of usufruct of the land, the later promises refer to a more secure, long-term ownership of land. Since these conflicting statements can hardly be reconciled with one another, they should be evaluated diachronically. As with other themes analyzed in this section, so here it appears that the author(s) of the Priestly texts in the Jacob-Esau, Joseph, and exodus sections took up an important theme of the (proto-)Priestly Abraham narrative, reformulated it and restricted it to Israel alone.

---

[168] Since the specification "in the land of Canaan" for certain Judean or Israelite toponyms also appears in texts in Joshua and Judges, some of these occurrences may belong to a post-Priestly layer. See below, III.1.3.

6.6.7 Conclusion: Evidence for an Independent Proto-Priestly Abraham Narrative

The assembled observations in the previous sections show that the Priestly ancestral narrative has two different literary profiles: an old kernel, which constitutes a self-contained, independent story, is perceptible in the Abraham section (Gen 11:27–25:18; 35:22b–29; 36*). In contrast, elements depending on the non-P strand and belonging to wide-ranging redaction layers are found in all sections of the ancestral narrative (Gen 11:27–50:13) and beyond. One observation on its own would not allow for such a conclusion. For instance, the striking linguistic differences between the statements concerning the accumulation of possessions (in the Jacob-Esau and Joseph narratives the expressions מקנה, "livestock," קנין, "goods," and [or] בהמה, "cattle," are used in addition to the lexemes רכשׁ, "to accumulate," and רכושׁ, "possession")[169] could be interpreted as an intentional device by an apparent single Priestly author, whose intention would have been to allude to the increase of Jacob's property in comparison with that of Abraham. However, the multitude of instances in the Jacob-Esau and Joseph sections in which the P narrative repeats and slightly alters certain motifs of the previous Abraham section is striking. The fact that several of these deviations seem to be influenced by the parallel non-P narrative strand favors the conclusion that the authors of these Priestly passages were later *redactors* and were not identical with the author of the proto-Priestly Abraham narrative. As additional evidence, these "copying" texts in the Jacob-Esau and Joseph sections reflect an obvious theological interest. Motifs which in the Abraham narrative are associated with Abraham (God's revelation, the burial site in Mamre, wealth, the promise of the land) are also ascribed to Jacob, Israel's eponym, in order to enhance the latter's importance.

This proposed literary-historical reconstruction – which builds on the "traditional" delimitation of the supposed Priestly layer[170] – is confirmed by the fact that it is able to explain certain motifs that remain blind in a theory that posits a "monolithic" P. The motif of Abraham the father of a multitude of nations and the promise of Edom, Israel, and Judah's future do not play any role in the following episodes of the Priestly stratum. Similarly, the striking allusions to the moon cult in geographical and personal names[171] make better sense in the context of the reconstructed proto-Priestly Abraham narrative (with YHWH/El Shaddai as intervening deity) than in a comprehensive Priestly document covering texts in Genesis–Exodus at a minimum.

---

[169] Cf. II.6.6.1.

[170] Scholars dispute the classification of Gen 11:28–30; 21:1b; and 23; see above, II.6.3 (a), (d), and II.6.4 (f).

[171] See above, II.6.5.2.

6.7 The Nature and the Setting of the Proto-Priestly Abraham Narrative

(a) Commonalities with Other Proto-Priestly Accounts

The proto-Priestly Abraham narrative shares certain linguistic and theological commonalities with the other proto-Priestly units of the primeval history (the creation account in Gen 1, the flood story, and the Table of Nations). All four accounts are connected to one another through the common title "these are the descendants of."[172] A further shared feature is the narratives' universal or multiethnic scope.

As demonstrated in the preceding chapter, the Abraham narrative is subtly connected with the previous proto-Priestly composition, the *Table of Nations*, Gen 10*,[173] which concludes with Shem and the nations of the east in preparation for the Abraham narrative, which likewise begins in the east, in Mesopotamia. Furthermore, the name ארפכשד, Arpachshad, can be connected to the toponym אור כשדים, Ur of the Chaldeans. We may now add another common point: Noah and Terah both have three sons. After the statement about their births (procreations), the story's focus immediately moves to the youngest son (Japheth, Haran) and the descendant(s) of the latter (see 10:1–2; 11:27–28).

A central motif shared with the *Priestly flood story* (Gen 6–9 P) is that of the covenant (ברית). An important commonality is that in both narratives the covenant is unconditional and is concluded between the deity and a non-Israelite. There is nevertheless a terminological difference: in the flood narrative, the establishment of the covenant is expressed by the lexeme קום *hiphil* ("I establish my covenant with you" [Gen 9:11]); in the Abraham narrative (primary layer), a nominal sentence with the subject בריתי is used ("my covenant is with you" [Gen 17:4]).

As will be shown below, the understanding of the covenant in the two (proto-) Priestly accounts may be understood as a response to the Deuteronomic/Deuteronomistic conception of the covenant idea.[174] Whereas the Deuteronom(ist)ic ideology emphasizes fulfillment of the covenant and obedience to the law, in Gen 6–9* P and the proto-Priestly Abraham narrative, the fulfillment of the covenant by Israel is not an issue at all.[175]

Another commonality, which the proto-Priestly Abraham narrative shares with the proto-Priestly flood story, is the double motif "to be blameless" and "to walk with/ before God" (see 6:9 and 17:1). The two protagonists, Noah and Abraham, are associated with honor. Yet a certain gradation is visible: for Noah, contact with the deity

---

[172] For the formula in Gen 2:4a, see above, II.1.3.6 (b) and II.1.3.7.

[173] See II.4.6.

[174] See, III.1.1.3–5.

[175] There are several indications that the command of circumcision (17:9–14) and the report of its fulfillment by Abraham belong to a secondary layer (see above II.6.4 [b]). As for the Priestly flood account, the dietary laws (Gen 9:1–7), which are not directly connected with the establishment of the covenant (9:8–17), probably should be ascribed to a secondary stratum too (see above, II.3.4 [e].)

seems more intimate and close (use of הלך *hitpael* + את instead of הלך *hitpael* + לפני). Interestingly, תמים, "complete, without blemish," as an attribute of a person appears often in Job, Psalms, and Proverbs and once in Deuteronomy and Ezekiel but is not used elsewhere in P.[176] In several contexts, the term stands in opposition to "sinful, iniquitous."[177] However, the expression תמים is frequently used in Priestly legislative texts concerning sacrifice, where it designates the required undamaged, intact state of the animal.[178] The expression הלך *hitpael* + לפני can also be connected with the cultic sphere ("to be in service of YHWH") but is not found in Priestly legislative texts at all.[179]

How to interpret this evidence? As is often observed, a striking particularity of both the flood story and the Abraham narrative consists in the absence of any cultic actions (sacrifices) by the main protagonists (Noah, Abraham). The lack of animal sacrifice in Priestly texts before the Sinai pericope is commonly explained by the exclusive validity of YHWH worship constituted at Sinai. Sacrifices are not mentioned in Genesis because God has not yet revealed his holy, solely adequate name for the cult and the procedures for how to perform them.[180] However, this particular feature of both the flood story and the Abraham narrative may be interpreted in a different way: the emphasis on the qualities "blameless" and "walking before YHWH" on the one hand and on the motif of the covenant on the other may point to a model of allegiance to YHWH that does not include the traditional animal sacrifice. Complete allegiance to God (YHWH) is possible without a particular sanctuary and without cultic duties. What is required of Noah and Abraham is a life "without blemish" before God rather than the sacrifice of animals "without blemish." Similar claims appear in several other texts of the Hebrew Bible.[181] Furthermore, nowhere is a concrete domicile for Abraham mentioned (only his place of burial is indicated), a striking fact that fits nicely with this feature of the narrative. The proto-Priestly Abraham narrative is apparently focused not on a particular place as sanctuary but on a large area (the land of Canaan). No place is privileged; permanent presence before the deity everywhere in the promised land is important instead.

---

[176] See Pss 15:2; 18:24, 26; 37:18; 119:80; Job 12:4; 36:4 (besides תם in Job 1:1, 8; 2:3; 8:20; 9:20–22); Prov 2:21; 11:5; 28:10, 18; Deut 18:13; Ezek 28:15.

[177] See Deut 18:13 (cf. 18:9–12); Ezek 28:15; Pss 15:2 (cf. 15:3); 18:24 // 2 Sam 22:24; 101:2 (cf. 101:3); 101:6 (cf. 101:7); 119:1 (cf. 119:3); Job 12:4 (cf. 12:6); Prov 2:21 (cf. 2:22); 11:5; 28:10, 18.

[178] Half of all occurrences (45) of תמים have this meaning and are found in legislative texts (cf. *HALOT* 1448–50).

[179] See 1 Sam 2:30 (cf. 2:35). Other occurrences of הלך *hitpael* + לפני + reference to YHWH/ God: Gen 24:40 (depends on 17:1); 2 Kgs 20:3//Isa 38:3; Pss 56:14; 116:9.

[180] Cf. WELLHAUSEN, *Prolegomena zur Geschichte*, 38; W. K. GILDERS, "Sacrifice before Sinai and the Priestly Narratives," in *The Strata of the Priestly Writings: Contemporary Debate and Future Directions*, ed. S. Shectman and J. Baden, ATANT 95 (Zurich: TVZ, 2009), 57–72; C. LEVIN, "Die Priesterschrift als Quelle. Eine Erinnerung," in *Abschied von der Priesterschrift? Zum Stand der Pentateuchdebatte*, ed. F. Hartenstein and K. Schmid, VWGT 40 (Leipzig: Evangelische Verlagsanstalt, 2015), 29.

[181] Cf. also Hos 6:6; Amos 5:21–25; Micah 6:8; Ps 50:7–15, 23; 1 Sam 15:22.

The fact that the specific terminology in question (הלך *hitpael* + לפני; תמים in the ethical sense) is absent from the Priestly sections in Exodus and Leviticus casts doubt on the common view that these texts stem from the same author. The dissimilarity between the two proto-Priestly narratives on the one hand and the Priestly Sinai section on the other suggests that their literary-historical relationship should be defined differently. The former units probably first existed independently of the latter; only later did Priestly authors integrate them into a much more comprehensive composition, in order to give them a new goal: Abraham's covenant with YHWH/El Shaddai was now directed to Israel.

(b) Purpose and Setting of the Abraham Narrative

Regarding the central motif of Abraham's abundant and international offspring, a primary aim of the author was presumably to foster a multiethnic tradition about a famous patriarch who was honored as an ancestor by different tribes in the southern Levant. In so doing, he probably intended to counter a nationalistic Deuteronomistic agenda. The related motif of the promise of the land, that is, the "eternal" right of Abraham's descendants to live in Canaan, is probably directed against the Deuteronomistic ideology of Israel's loss of the land. The emphasis on the permanence of right of usufruct of the land (cf. עולם) insinuates that Jerusalem's fall and the Neo-Babylonian pillaging of the temple could not affect the validity of the promise addressed to Abraham. The promise of abundant offspring and land is formulated in terms of a covenant (ברית), a motif also present in the proto-Priestly flood story. The recourse to this motif may again be understood as a response to Deuteronomistic ideology, namely, the concept of covenant. A subtle point of the narrative is that it is the local deity El Shaddai/YHWH rather than Sîn, the moon god, who brings fertility and posterity to Sarah and Abraham. This assertion is probably a polemic directed against the Sîn tradition. Alternatively, one might propose that the author wanted to depict El Shaddai/YHWH in the tradition of the moon god.

Since most of the key motifs mentioned above seem to polemicize against Deuteronomistic judgment theology, the Neo-Babylonian era would be a fitting historical setting. The allusions to the moon cult fit the period of Nabonidus, who promoted the moon cult, particularly well. Another important feature noted above, the absence of cultic actions (sacrifices) by the main protagonists (Noah, Abraham) and "cultless" allegiance to God (YHWH), would seem to match the situation of the Judeans in the Neo-Babylonian era nicely: performance of the regular cult at the looted Jerusalem temple was no longer possible; many Judeans lived abroad, without access to a Yahwistic sanctuary.

Are there clues hinting at the geographical setting? In the land of Canaan, Abraham is linked to one specific geographical place: Mamre, the place of his burial, in vicinity of Hebron. This may point to the region of Hebron as the place of origin of the narrative. The specification "in the cave of Machpelah" (Gen 25:9) enhances the impression of a genuine tradition.[182] Mamre is also known from the non-P stratum, in relation to Abraham's home (the "oak of Mamre"). The toponyms lead scholars to conclude that the Abraham tradition (either the oldest stratum of the non-P narrative, as the majority of scholars argue, or the Priestly stratum as the first literary layer, following de Pury) originally stemmed from the region of southern Judah. As for the Priestly narrative, however, it is worth noting that Mamre is mentioned only at the end of the narrative (in Gen 25:9). The place name is absent from other important points of the narrative (e.g., Ishmael's birth, the deity's revelation, Isaac's birth). In contrast, the designation of Canaan as the land of Abraham's residence seems to play a much more important role (five mentions) in the plot. Thus it seems that the author sought to avoid focusing too much on the presumably geographical center of the tradition. His interest, rather, was supraregional and aimed toward the figure of Abraham as the common ancestor of several ethnic groups in the southern Levant. The striking absence of the toponym Hebron in the primary stratum of the Priestly narrative may be explained similarly. Only the non-Priestly and later Priestly texts localize Mamre in the vicinity of Hebron (see Gen 13:18 non-P; 23:2 P[s], 19 P[s]; 35:27). For this reason, one should not necessarily conclude that the proto-Priestly Abraham narrative originated in southern Judah (in the region of Hebron), although certain elements of the plot probably stem from there. Where should one geographically locate the proto-Priestly Abraham narrative instead? At first sight, the story's exposition of Abraham's origins in Mesopotamia and his itinerary from Ur through Harran to Palestine might be considered indications of the narrative's setting in the Judean *golah* in Mesopotamia. Many scholars see Abraham's journey from Ur to Canaan as an allusion to the exiles' return from Babylon to Judah. They understand the literary figure Abraham to serve as a model for the Judeans who should leave their Mesopotamian homes.[183] However, such a conclusion is not necessary either, or at least it is not the only possible one. It is also imaginable that this exposition was meant to support the claim of those who remained in the land, that they were the heirs of Abraham and hence the land had been given to them. Giving the eponymous father Babylonian roots, and locating those roots in the two centers of the moon cult, was intended to attract the favor of Neo-Babylonian authorities (in particular during the reign of Nabonidus). A few prophetic texts referring to Abraham and possibly stemming from this period (Jer 33:23–24; Isa 41:8–9; 51:1–3) may favor such an idea (see further below, II.6.10.6). It is then possible that

---

[182] The tradition about Abraham's burial place in the cave of Machpelah might be reflected in the peculiar passage Isa 51:1b–2, which refers in parallel statements first to a cave (cistern) as the "origin" of Israel and then to Abraham and Sarah as its parents. See B. Duhm, *Das Buch Jesaja*, 2nd ed., HKAT III/1 3.1 (Göttingen: Vandenhoeck & Ruprecht, 1902), 344–45; A. de Pury, "Genèse 12–36," in *Introduction à l'Ancien Testament*, ed. T. Römer et al., 2nd ed. (Geneva: Labor et Fides, 2009), 233–34.

[183] J. Blenkinsopp, "Abraham as Paradigm in the Priestly History in Genesis," *JBL* 128 (2009): 225, 233–35; Wöhrle, *Fremdlinge*, 176–77.

this exposition was, from the beginning, an integral part of the authentic plot of the Abraham tradition stemming from Judah.

6.8 The Nature of the Redaction Layer (Priestly Composition)

Most of the redactional texts of the Priestly stratum in the ancestral narrative contain features that are typically attributed to the supposed comprehensive Priestly composition. Principally, these texts have two functions: First, in complementing the pre-Priestly strand, they interpret and correct this stratum (cf., for instance, Gen 35:11–15). Second, they simultaneously take up and reuse certain motifs and themes of the proto-Priestly Abraham tradition and adapt them to the context of the Isaac, Jacob, and Esau narratives. Theologically, the Priestly texts are marked by the intention to whitewash Jacob's image of the pre-Priestly tradition and to "Israelize" motifs and themes of the proto-Priestly Abraham narrative.

There are indications that not all of these redactional Priestly texts belong to the same stratum. For instance, certain elements of the burial notices contradict one another.[184] Moreover, certain passages have distinct linguistic features that they share with texts commonly attributed to the Holiness school. These presumably later elements are treated in a separate paragraph (II.6.9).

(a) Reinterpretation of the pre-Priestly Jacob-Esau Narrative

In the Priestly presentation of the Jacob-Esau story, the redactor passes over Jacob's problematic behavior (his deception of his brother Esau) found in the non-P strand. Jacob, Israel's eponym, is free of any reproach. The reason for Jacob's departure from the land of Canaan is not the fear of the revenge by his deceived brother but his parents' will that he should marry a daughter from his mother's family. According to the inserted Priestly passages, Jacob's behavior is preferable to that of his brother because he heeds his parents' wishes. In emphasizing this point, the Priestly redactor puts forward the principle of Israel's separation from the autochthonous population ("Hittites"). This shift goes along with the establishment of Jacob's preferential status in comparison to Esau. The reader learns that Esau took two Hittite women as wives and that they brought grief to Rebecca and Isaac (26:34–35; 27:46–28:9). Esau's act is seen in a negative light; it seems to be the reason for Isaac's privileging Jacob, whom he blesses instead of Esau (28:1).[185] Many scholars believe that the author of this passage was promoting Israel's separation from the autochthonous, unrelated population (i.e., the Judean population who had remained in the land), reflecting a line of thought that became dominant in the time of Ezra and Nehemiah.[186]

---

[184] See above, II.6.6.2.

[185] This ideological device also seems to be perceptible in a Priestly passage in the Joseph story (Gen 37:2aγδ). See above, II.6.4 (h) (2).

[186] See above, II.6.6.5.

As shown above, the Priestly Gen 35:9–15 is reacting to the Bethel etiology in Gen 28 and modifying Bethel's status as a place of revelation. Through the motif of Elohim's *departing* from the place of revelation (35:13), the Priestly author asserts that Bethel is not the place where God dwells (as Gen 28:10–22 claims) but just a place of temporary encounter with God, equivalent to other places where such encounters happen (cf. Gen 17:22).[187] Also, Jacob's name change in Gen 35:9–10, which duplicates the name change in the non-P story of the battle at the Jabbok (Gen 32:23–33), might be explained by the author's intention to correct the non-P etiology (although it is not certain that the latter really predates the former).[188]

(b) "Israelization" of the Plot of the Abraham Narrative

Certain motifs originally belonging to the Abraham narrative (covenant, name change, burial site in Mamre, wealth) are assigned to Jacob, Israel's eponym, as well. Under the influence of non-P texts, they have been slightly modified. In particular, the promises addressed to Abraham in Gen 17 were enlarged and redirected to Jacob.

Furthermore, the consistent use of Elohim and the five occurrences of El Shaddai (Gen 17:1b; 28:3; 35:11; 48:3 [P^s]; Exod 6:3) as designations for the deity are related to the theonym ideology of P, which makes clear that YHWH made himself known by his name only to Israel from its stay in Egypt onward. In contrast, in the proto-Priestly Abraham narrative the two names are simply juxtaposed; here the Tetragram does not stand out from the name El Shaddai.

The Priestly passages in the Jacob-Esau and Joseph sections stress Israel's diversity. The recipient of the promise is told that Israel will constitute an "assembly [קהל] of peoples" (Gen 28:3; 35:11; cf. 48:3–4). This promise probably envisages the later kingdoms of Israel and Judah and perhaps their legal successors in the Persian era, Yehud and Samaria, as well.

An important theme in the Jacob-Esau and Joseph sections and in Exod 6 is the motif of the possession of the land. Whereas in the proto-Priestly Abraham narrative the land of Canaan includes the areas of Israel, Judah, the Ishmaelites, and Edom, in the Priestly texts of the subsequent sections, the group of beneficiaries becomes restricted: it consists only of Abraham, Isaac, and Jacob (Israel). Accordingly, in P^c the promised land of Canaan comprises the northern and southern parts of Palestine but neither Edom and the adjoining Arab territories nor the Transjordan. This conception agrees with the late Priestly Num 34, which outlines the boundaries of the land of Canaan more precisely, insofar as both texts exclude Edom and Transjordan (for the exclusion of the Transjordan, see also Num 32). As shown above, the land promise seems to have already been fulfilled during the lifetime of the patriarchs.[189] The latter do not own the land but rather have the right to sojourn in it. Nevertheless, the use

---

[187] See above, II.6.5.1 (a).
[188] See above, II.6.5.1 (a).
[189] See above, II.6.6.6.

of the verb ירשׁ, "to take possession, become heir, owner" (Gen 28:4), and later, of the noun מורשׁה (Exod 6:4) in the case of Jacob (Israel) shows that the author alludes to the ownership of the land of Canaan by the later Israelites too. If this interpretation is correct, how can we explain these two land concepts appearing side by side in P^C? The author retained the idea that the patriarchs owned the land in the form of usufruct, but at the same time shared with the non-P tradition the promise of full and permanent ownership of the land. The author of P^C is also a "historian" and alludes to the historical military conquest reported by non-P. A clue to P^C's interest in Israel and Judah's history is the reference to the Israelite and Judean kingdoms in 35:11.

In several instances, the narrative contains chronological statements and indications of age that are not always well integrated in the plot of proto-P. They are linked, as recent studies have shown, with similar age designations found in Exod 12:40, 41; 1 Kgs 6:1 and other texts and thus constitute elements of a comprehensive framework. Abraham's birth is linked to the construction of the First Temple in Jerusalem by the round number of years (1200) between the two events. Possibly most indications of age and chronological statements belong to the supposed wide-ranging framework.

6.9 Late Priestly Supplements (P^s, H)

(a) Passages Sharing Characteristics of Texts Belonging to the So-Called Holiness Redaction

The vocabulary and style of Gen 23 are distinct when compared to the other Priestly texts in the ancestral narrative. The central expressions גר ותושׁב, "stranger and sojourner" (23:4), and עם הארץ, "the people of the land" (23:7, 12, 13), are absent from the Priestly texts of Genesis and Exodus but do occur in the so-called Holiness Code.[190] The theme of Gen 23, Abraham's acquisition of a grave site for his wife, matches a vital topic of the Holiness Code: the preservation of Israelite ownership of the land. With regard to these commonalities with the Holiness Code, Gen 23 and the related passages in Gen 25:9–10; 49:29–32; 50:13 should be assigned to the same author or to the same milieu as H.

Similarly, the passages containing the command of circumcision and its execution in 17:9–14, 23–27; 21:4 share vocabulary with "H" or "H-like" texts. They probably stem from an author close to H.[191]

(b) Texts Expressing Interest in the North

A special interest in the north is also perceptible in a P-like text of the Joseph narrative. Jacob improves the status of Joseph's two Egyptian-born sons, Ephraim and

---

[190] See above, II.6.4 (f).
[191] See above, II.6.4 (b), (e).

Manasseh, by adopting them and assigning them the same rank as his two firstborn (Reuben and Simeon).

Genesis 48:3–6

[3] Then Jacob said to Joseph, "El Shaddai appeared to me at Luz in the land of Canaan and blessed me, [4] and he said to me, 'Behold, I will make you fruitful and numerous, and I will make you an assembly of peoples, and will give this land to your descendants after you for an everlasting usufruct.' [5] And now your two sons, who were born to you in the land of Egypt, before I came to you in Egypt, are mine; Ephraim and Manasseh shall be mine, as [כְּ] Reuben and Simeon are. [6] But your offspring that have been born after them shall be yours; they shall be called by the names of their brothers in their inheritance."

Concerning the classification of this text, one should note that the passage deviates in two important points from the Priestly stratum: the place of El Shaddai's revelation to Jacob is called Luz instead of Bethel (cf. 48:3 with 35:14–15), and fertility and increase are promised rather than "ordered" (cf. 48:4 with 35:10).[192] For this reason, we can conclude that this passage probably stems from a different author than that of P[c].

For what reason does Jacob adopt his grandsons? Two possible motives suggest themselves. First, the adoption act was intended to enhance the position of the "north." In the book of Samuel, Joseph and Ephraim are designations for the Northern Kingdom. According to E. Speiser, a second possible motivation can be located in the fact that the mother of the two boys was an Egyptian: Jacob wanted to protect the boys from the influence of their Egyptian mother.[193] A detail that is often overlooked in commentaries is that Ephraim and Manasseh not only acquire equal status to Jacob's sons but are *put on a par with Reuben and Simeon,* Jacob's oldest sons. According to the Chronicler's interpretation, Jacob's act of adoption implies the transfer of the right of the firstborn to Joseph's sons (see 1 Chr 5:1–2). S. Japhet sees in Joseph's double portion the double portion destined for the firstborn (see Deut 21:17).[194] However we interpret this text, it is clear that its intention is to enhance the position of Joseph and the region of the former Northern Kingdom and possibly its legal successors in postexilic eras.[195]

---

[192] See above, II.6.4 (h) (4).

[193] SPEISER, *Genesis*, 358.

[194] S. JAPHET, *I and II Chronicles: A Commentary*, OTL (Louisville: Westminster John Knox, 1993), 133.

[195] See above, II.6.4 (h) (4).

6.10 The Literary Historical Relationship between P and Non-P in the Abraham Section: Preliminary Remarks

In the preceding paragraphs we assembled arguments favoring the idea that the ancestral narrative of P represents two different literary profiles. In 11:27–25:18, the P stratum is continuous, self-contained, and highly coherent. In the passages concerning Esau, Jacob, and Joseph, the narrative thread of P is very fragmentary and clearly builds on non-P. In these sections, the Priestly texts postdate a continuous non-Priestly strand.

This leads to the crucial question concerning the relationship between P and non-P in the Abraham section (11:27–25:18): which strand depends on the other? Although observations concerning its profile suggest that the Priestly strand was composed without being in "contact" with non-P, many scholars still consider the P strand in general to presuppose most non-P entities in this section.[196] This estimation is certainly due to the adherence of some of these scholars to the classical Documentary Hypothesis and its fixed relationship between J and P (the former predating the latter). Nevertheless, since the 1990s, scholars have developed new views of certain non-P units (Gen 15; 20; 21:8–21; 22:1–19), leading them to the opposite view concerning the relationship between these texts and P (namely, that non-P depends on P). Investigations of the literary-historical relationship between the two covenant texts in Gen 15 and 17 are illustrative. For a long time, most scholars pleaded for the dependence of the latter on the former.[197] Today, however, an increasing number of scholars see the relationship between the two texts the other way around.[198] Their main arguments concern the following particularities in Gen 15: (1) the presence of typical Deuteronomistic (ירש) and Priestly (P-Abraham narrative: שיבה טובה, רכוש) language in Gen 15; (2) a link to the Priestly chronology of 430 years until the exodus in the prediction of 400 years of exile in v. 13; and (3) the tight connection with the preceding late composition in Gen 14. One among these scholars, de Pury, went a step further, arguing that most non-P texts in Gen 12–25 depend on P.[199] In what follows, I do not intend to answer the question in a conclusive way; rather, I would like to add some observations and considerations, based on the above analyses, to the discussion.

The previous investigation of the ancestral narrative has shown that key data from

---

[196] See, most influentially, WELLHAUSEN, *Prolegomena zur Geschichte*, 322–47.

[197] Cf., for instance, MCEVENUE, *Narrative Style*, 152–53; VAN SETERS, *Abraham*, 281–82; WESTERMANN, *Genesis 12–36*, 306; BLUM, *Die Komposition*, 423; ZIEMER, *Abram–Abraham*.

[198] Among others, T. RÖMER, "Gen 15 und Gen 17: Beobachtungen und Anfragen zu einem Dogma der 'neueren' und 'neuesten' Pentateuch-kritik," *DBAT* 26 (1989–90): 32–47; IDEM, "Genèse 15 et les tensions de la communauté juive postexilique dans le cycle d'Abraham," *Transeu* 7 (1994): 107–21; J. HA, *Genesis 15: A Theological Compendium of Pentateuchal History*, BZAW 181 (Berlin: de Gruyter, 1989); SCHMID, *Genesis and the Moses Story*, 158–71; IDEM, "So-Called Yahwist," 29–50; DE PURY, "Abraham," 88.

[199] DE PURY, "P^G as the Absolute Beginning," 32–37; IDEM, "Genèse 12–36," 217–38; DE PURY, RÖMER, and SCHMID, *L'Ancien Testament commenté: La Genèse*, 104–6. In de Pury's view, texts like Gen 16 and 18–19, usually considered "old," could be in fact also be "late" and depend on P. See further below.

the Abraham narrative are found in P rather than non-P. (1) It is the P thread that provides information about the birth (Gen 11:27) and death and burial of Abraham (25:8–9). (2) The central theme of sterility on the one hand and promise of offspring and reproduction on the other hand is organically developed in P (Gen 11:30; 16:1a, 3, 15; 17*). My analyses above hinted at the idea that certain distinct elements of the P strand – for instance, the statement concerning the patriarchs' ages – depend on non-P texts (they are assigned to the redaction layer [P^C]). However, for the bulk of the Priestly texts, which form the sober but continuous and self-contained backbone of the Abraham narrative, such indications are lacking.

In contrast, the units and passages of the non-P strand are often more elaborate[200] but lack the cited "key data." Most important, non-P does not provide a satisfying opening text; Gen 12:1–4a, which does not offer an introduction of the protagonist, cannot have this function; it depends on the Priestly introductory passage in 11:27–32a (see below).[201] Noth was aware of the very fragmentary plot of the non-Priestly strand. Nevertheless, he defended the presence of non-Priestly sources in the Abraham section and their anteriority (with regard to P). He conjectured that in the final redactor's arrangement the four Priestly "key texts," Gen 12:4b–5 (Abram and Lot's departure from Harran); 16:1a, 3, 15–16 (birth of Ishmael); 21:1b–5 (birth of Isaac); and 25:7–11a (death of Abraham) displaced similar key texts in the non-P strand.[202] Of course, this theory cannot be disproved, but it seems forced. *Prima facie*, it seems more probable that the alleged key texts in the non-P strand never existed and that the proto-Priestly narrative generally constitutes the older layer.

Further suggesting this literary development from P to non-P, Abraham and Sarah's name changes, introduced in Gen 17:5 and 17:15 are consequently implemented not only throughout the P narrative strand but also throughout the non-P stories. Non-P texts that precede Gen 17 contain the name forms Abram and Sarai, respectively; in the chapters following Gen 17, only Abraham and Sarah occur. The consistent implementation of the name change makes the assumption of a global development from non-P to P problematic, as it would imply a systematic redactional adjustment of the older non-P texts by the alleged late P redaction (thus explicitly Ziemer[203]) or post-P redaction.[204] However, such a systematic intervention is contraindicated by the fact that (otherwise) the non-P section shows no visible traces of such a systematic adaptation to the Priestly narrative. Therefore, this literary development seems implausible

---

[200] Cf., for instance, 12:6–9; 13 (non-P); 16:2, 4–13; 18–19; 22.

[201] See Blum, *Die Komposition*, 343, n. 11; Schmid, *Genesis and the Moses Story*, 94–95; Ska, "Call of Abraham," 46–66; de Pury, "Genèse 12–36," 234; M. Köckert, "Wie wurden Abraham- und Jakobüberlieferung zu einer 'Vätergeschichte' verbunden?" *HBAI* 3 (2014): 49–50. *Contra* Van Seters, *Abraham*, 224; Kratz, *Composition*, 262–63.

[202] Noth, *Überlieferungsgeschichte*, 13.

[203] Ziemer, *Abram–Abraham*, 308–26.

[204] See, for instance, Levin, *Der Jahwist*, 140–41, 145, 150: his "Endredaktion" changed Abraham to Abram and Sarah to Sarai systematically in the non-P texts preceding Gen 17.

to me. More probable is the idea that the authors of the non-P texts were aware of the name changes in 17:5 and 17:15, respected it, and thus followed the P framework that is very consistent in this regard. This possibility is confirmed by the fact that precisely this attitude of awareness and respect toward the name change of Abraham is attested for late biblical and postbiblical books like 1–2 Chronicles, Nehemiah, and Jubilees, which consistently reflect the name change as it is introduced in Gen 17:5.[205]

These more general *prima facie* arguments favoring non-P's dependence on P raise the question of whether the analyses of individual chapters permit classifying them, or some of them, as post-Priestly. In current European scholarship, Gen 14; 15; 20; 21:8–21; 22:1–19; 24 are often considered post-Priestly.[206] However, according to most – also European – scholars, Gen 12:10–20; 13*; 16*; 18–19 would predate the Priestly narrative.[207] These scholars nevertheless admit that the passages in question cannot be read as continuous and cohesive narrative(s). In the following, I will focus on these latter chapters and their literary relationship to the Priestly strand. I will also discuss Gen 12:1–4a, which is traditionally assigned to the Yahwist and considered to predate P.

6.10.1 Genesis 12:1–4a // Genesis 11:27–31, 32b; 12:5

Since the first verses in the non-P strand (Gen 12:1–4a) do not provide a satisfying opening text, it is tempting to consider this passage dependent on the fitting and self-contained introduction of the Priestly Abraham story (see above). As both Crüsemann and Ska have observed, Gen 12:1–4a shares its vocabulary not only with

---

[205] Cf. Neh 9:7; 1 Chr 1:27–28; Jub. 15:7. In the preserved text of the Genesis Apocryphon corresponding to Gen 12:1–15:4, only the names Abram and Sarai occur (in accordance with the onomastic device of Gen 17). With regard to these texts, ZIEMER, *Abram–Abraham*, 323, also acknowledges that the latter "lassen die prägende Wirkung der Namensänderung von Gen 17,5 erkennen."

[206] Gen 14: VAN SETERS, *Abraham*, 296–308; BLUM, *Die Komposition*, 462–64 (n. 5); DE PURY, RÖMER, and SCHMID, *L'Ancien Testament commenté: La Genèse*, 79–82; Gen 20–22: M. KÖCKERT, "Gen 20–22 als nachpriesterliche Erweiterung der Vätergeschichte," in *The Post-Priestly Pentateuch: New Perspectives on Its Redactional Development and Theological Profiles*, ed. F. Giuntoli and K. Schmid, FAT 101 (Tübingen: Mohr Siebeck, 2015), 157–76; O. LIPSCHITS, T. RÖMER, and H. GONZALEZ, "The Pre-Priestly Abraham Narratives from Monarchic to Persian Times," *Sem* 59 (2017): 265–67; Gen 24: B. J. DIEBNER and H. SCHULT, "Alter und geschichtlicher Hintergrund von Genesis 24," *DBAT* 10 (1975): 10–17; A. ROFÉ, "La composizione de Gen 24," *BeO* 129 (1981): 161–65; IDEM, "An Enquiry into the Betrothal of Rebekah," in *Die Hebräische Bibel und ihre zweifache Nachgeschichte: Festschrift für Rolf Rendtorff zum 65. Geburtstag*, ed. E. Blum (Neukirchen-Vluyn: Neukirchener Verlag, 1990), 27–39.

[207] I. FISCHER, *Erzeltern*, 338–74; M. KÖCKERT, "Die Geschichte der Abrahamüberlieferung," in *Congress Volume: Leiden, 2004*, ed. A. Lemaire, VTSup 109 (Leiden: Brill, 2006), 120–21; IDEM, "Wie wurden Abraham- und Jakobüberlieferung zu einer 'Vätergeschichte' verbunden?" *HBAI* 3 (2014): 63; SCHMID, *Literaturgeschichte*, 91–93, 124–26; LIPSCHITS, RÖMER, and GONZALEZ, "Pre-Priestly Abraham Narratives." Only A. de Pury considers these accounts post-Priestly (see DE PURY, "P^G as the Absolute Beginning," 32–37; DE PURY, RÖMER, and SCHMID, *L'Ancien Testament commenté: La Genèse*, 75–112).

non-Priestly but also with Priestly texts.[208] The classificatory terms *nation* (גוי), *clan* (משפחה), and *country* (ארץ) are all found in the Priestly part of the Table of Nations (see 10:5, 20, 31, 32). The expression מולדת is also used in a Priestly text in a close context (although the meaning is different: "nativity" or "birth" in 11:28; "kindred" or "relatives" in 12:1).[209] Genesis 12:1–4a most probably presupposes theses texts.

Further favoring this direction of dependence is the fact that 12:1–4a may be read as a theological reinterpretation of the older proto-P layer. As de Pury states, it is conceivable that the statement that YHWH "will make" Abraham "a great nation" (cf. v. 2) is revising the promise in Gen 17:4–5 (proto-P): "YHWH will make Abraham a father of a multitude of nations."[210] Abraham is the ancestor specifically of Israel, rather than of several nations. Nevertheless, the stature of this "Israelite" Abraham exceeds that of the Priestly protagonist: in him "all the families of the earth will be blessed" (12:3). A further theological motivation is also probable: the author of Gen 12:1–4a wanted to correct the proto-Priestly tradition that Abraham departed from Harran on his own initiative (see 12:5, cf. also 11:31). According to non-P, it is YHWH who gives Abraham the order to leave his country, his relatives, and his father's house. This matches the ideology of the Yahwistic primeval narrative, according to which acts undertaken by humans on their own initiative lead to fiasco (see Gen 3; 4:3–16; 11:1–9, and, formulated in a programmatic way, Gen 6:5; 8:21a). Evidence for this intertextual connection appears in the shared motif "making a name for oneself/making someone's name [שם] great" (cf. Gen 11:4 with 12:2).

6.10.2 Genesis 12:10–20 // Genesis 16 P

The story in Gen 12:10–20 about Abraham's stay in Egypt is generally considered a coherent and unified unit, but scholars disagree over relationship to two other non-P units dealing with the abandonment of the wife by her husband (Gen 20 and 26:1–11). Genesis 12:10–20 contains a motif that can be linked with the Priestly strand, in the statement that "because of her [Sarai], it went well with Abram; he acquired sheep, oxen, asses, male and female servants [שפחת], she-asses, and camels" (v. 16). In Gen 16:1b (non-P), 3 (P), Hagar is described as an Egyptian servant (שפחה). In a synchronic reading, Hagar should be identified with one of the female servants (slaves) whom Abram received as a gift from the Pharaoh.[211] On a diachronic level, it

---

[208] See F. CRÜSEMANN, "Die Eigenständigkeit der Urgeschichte. Ein Beitrag zur Diskussion um den 'Jahwisten,'" in J. Jeremias and L. Perlitt (eds.), *Die Botschaft und die Boten: Festschrift für Hans Walter Wolff zum 70. Geburtstag* (Neukirchen-Vluyn: Neukirchener Verlag, 1981), 29; SKA, "Call of Abraham," 56–57.

[209] See above II.6.3 (a).

[210] DE PURY, "Genèse 12–36," 234; DE PURY, RÖMER, and SCHMID, *L'Ancien Testament commenté: La Genèse*, 71, cf. also IDEM, "PG as the Absolute Beginning," 32.

[211] A recent joint article by Lipschits, Römer, and Gonzalez sees in Hagar's designation as an Egyptian servant in Gen 16 an indication (in addition to others) favoring common authorship

is tempting to see dependence of one text on the other. Given the tentative assessment concerning Gen 16 below (P predates non-P), the following question arises: Is the Priestly Hagar episode in Gen 16 inspired by the story of Gen 12:10–20? Or, on the contrary, does the latter depend on the statement of Gen 16:3? What speaks against the former option is first that neither the formulation in 16:3 nor formulations in other Priestly texts contain elements hinting at the motif of Abraham's stay in Egypt. Second, it is striking that in 16:3 Hagar is called Sarah's maidservant rather than Abraham's. Therefore, we should also consider the possibility that Gen 12:10–20 was composed in view of Gen 16 proto-P. Dependence on the proto-Priestly narrative in Gen 13:6, 11b; 16:3, 15 might explain the curious position of the unit 12:10–20 so close to the beginning of the Abraham narrative: the story about Abram's lucrative stay in Egypt not only gives an explanation for his riches in the following episode (Gen 13:6, 11b) but also prepares the reader for the sudden appearance of an *Egyptian* slave in his family (Gen 16).

6.10.3 Genesis 16 Non-P // Genesis 16 P

In Gen 16, the few proto-Priestly verses (vv. 1a[?], 3 and v. 15) are well identifiable by their repetitive style and by the fact that they contradict their context. In v. 2 (non-P), Sarai demands that her husband "go into" her servant so that she might obtain children by her. According to 16:3 (P), however, Sarai gave her maid to Abram *as wife*.[212] The second divergence concerns the naming of the newborn child: according to Gen 16:11 (non-P), Hagar should name the son; 16:15, however, states that Abraham named the boy (P). The statements of the P strand match the theology of the proto-Priestly account. Both Hagar (as second wife) and Ishmael (as a son named by his father) belong "close" to Abraham. The birth and naming of Isaac are formulated with almost the same wording (21:2a, 3, proto-Priestly). The two brothers together will bury their father (25:9). In contrast to the short proto-Priestly text, the comprehensive non-P story is marked by conflicts between the three protagonists. The reader is told that the pregnant Hagar looks down on Sarai (Gen 16:4). Pressured by his wife, Abram hands Hagar over to her (16:6a). Sarai mistreats her servant, which provokes the latter's escape (16:6b). Furthermore, a contentious future is foretold for the newborn Ishmael (see 16:12: "And he will be a wild donkey of a man, his hand will be against everyone, and everyone's hand will be against him; and to the face of all his brothers he will set his dwellings."). This concentration of "conflict" motifs in the non-Priestly story about Ishmael's birth is striking. Commonly, the non-P narrative is considered more ancient; this assessment is often due to the classical attribution of the two strands to the younger P on the one hand and to the older J on the other.[213] In P, a harmonizing

---

for the stories in Gen 12:10–20 and Gen 16 non-P (which they consider pre-Priestly). LIPSCHITS, RÖMER, and GONZALEZ, "Pre-Priestly Abraham Narratives," 292.

[212] See SEEBASS, *Genesis II/1*, 91; WÖHRLE, *Fremdlinge*, 25–30, 39–40.

[213] See, among others, LEVIN, *Der Jahwist*, 147–52; BADEN, *Composition*, 69–70.

tendency would be at work. However, regarding the concentration of conflict motifs, de Pury's observation that the non-Priestly presentation of the plot "smacks of reaction" against the Priestly pacifistic standpoint is worth considering. According to de Pury, the non-Priestly story insinuates in a subtle and polemical manner that peaceful relationships in Abraham's pluriethnic family are not possible and that Ishmael will never be a peaceful neighbor.[214] Another hint of such an ideological agenda behind the text is that the conflict begins with the misconduct of Hagar the Egyptian (when she had conceived, she looked down on Sarah, v. 4).[215] In addition, the non-Priestly story of Gen 16, like the Abraham-Lot narrative, lacks a fitting conclusion (Ishmael's birth is not related),[216] suggesting that the non-Priestly text is an interpretive redaction of the sober proto-Priestly account.

6.10.4 Genesis 13 Non-P; 18–19 // Genesis 17

Among the non-P units in question, Gen 13; 18–19 are distinguished from the others insofar as they are connected among themselves. H. Gunkel was the first to consider them an initially independent and cohesive composition (an Abraham-Lot story), and many scholars still adhere to this idea:[217] Gen 13 and Gen 18–19 have in common the two protagonists Abram/Abraham and Lot and the toponyms "oak of Mamre" and Sodom.[218] The plot seems coherent: at its beginning, the narrative deals with the separation between Lot and Abram and their settlement in Sodom and Mamre, respectively. In chapters 18–19, which are located in Mamre and in Sodom, respectively, the reader is told how Abraham and Lot acquire offspring. The Abraham-Lot story highlights the origins of the three neighboring nations of Israel, Moab, and Ammon, the

---

[214] DE PURY, "Abraham," 87–88. The motif that he has taken the bow into his hands might well be a polemical allusion to the Priestly imagery of pacifism in the flood story (God placed his war bow in the clouds).

[215] This relativizes the parallelization of the plot in Gen 16 with the exodus narrative, as is pointed out by LIPSCHITS, RÖMER, and GONZALEZ, "Pre-Priestly Abraham Narratives," 292–93: "There is a similar theme in the story of Ishmael's birth in Genesis 16*: Hagar, the Egyptian, is here oppressed by her Hebrew mistress (וַתְּעַנֶּהָ, cf. Exod 1:11–12; Deut 26:6 and Gen 15:13). And, in the same way as the children of Israel escape (בָּרַח, Exod 14:5) from Egypt, Hagar flees (וַתִּבְרַח) from her oppressor (Gen 16:6)." What "disturbs" the parallel is that Hagar's disrespect toward Sarai causes the oppression she suffers from her mistress. According to the biblical exodus narrative, the Israelites do not have any responsibility for their misery and suffering in Egypt. Another difference is that according to Gen 16:9, the angel of YHWH gives Hagar the order to return to her mistress and to "submit" (*hitpael* of ענה, coming from the same root as "oppress" in v. 6 [ענה *piel*]).

[216] With GUNKEL, *Genesis*, 190; ZIMMERLI, *1. Mose 12–25*, 64; WESTERMANN, *Genesis 12–36*, 297–98; and against KNAUF, *Ismael*, 31–32.

[217] See GUNKEL, *Genesis*, 159–61, 173; BLUM, *Die Komposition*, 280–89; I. FISCHER, *Erzeltern*, 339; RÖMER, "Genese 15 et les tensions," 111; SCHMID, *Genesis and the Moses Story*, 96.

[218] The singular preserved in the LXX should be preferred to the plural of MT, SP ("grove"). Gen 18:4, 8 presuppose an individual tree. See J. HUTZLI, "Interventions présumées des scribes," 320–28.

eponymous offspring of Abraham and Lot. In view of its thematic scope and aim, the combined Gen 13; 18–19 is comparable with the proto-Priestly Abraham narrative, which depicts Abraham as the "father of multiple nations" and illustrates the origins of Ishmael, Israel, and Edom. In contrast to the proto-Priestly account, the non-P narrative has something of a polemical undertone: Lot, the father, begot his children when drunk, with no consciousness of his act. Moab and Ammon stem from an incestuous relationship.[219] The depiction of Moab and Ammon's origins is often seen in relation to the hostile stance toward these nations in Deut 23:4–9. However, the interpretation of the story as a polemic is disputed; several scholars believe that the author values the role of Lot's daughters, who assure their father's posterity in an unconventional manner.[220]

The strong cohesion between Gen 13 and 18 is indicated by the opening verse of Gen 18, in which Abraham is referred to only with a suffix. Genesis 18:1a seems to depend on the final statement of the story of Gen 13 (13:18a), which is also localized in Mamre. However, the supposed pre-Priestly Abraham-Lot story has no satisfying beginning, as is admitted by scholars arguing for such a composition. In its actual form, the beginning of Gen 13 (13:1) depends on the story about Abram and Sarai's stay in Egypt (12:10–20), but the latter text is clearly a distinct composition: first, Lot, who plays an important role in Gen 13, is not mentioned in Gen 12:10–20; and second, silver and gold, mentioned in the description of Abram's wealth in 13:2, do not appear in the list of gifts that Abram received from Pharaoh (see 12:16). Genesis 12:1–4a would make a more fitting beginning (though it does not itself constitute a satisfying opening either; see above), followed by 12:6–8. However one reconstructs the narrative's beginning, it depends on the Priestly introduction of Abraham and Lot in Gen 11:27–31, 32b. As for the end of the supposed Abraham-Lot narrative, it seems to be lost. The statement in 18:14 that yhwh will again visit Abraham at the same time in the following year, when Sarah will have a son, remains unfulfilled.

Recent treatments see in Gen 13; 18–19 an early pre-Priestly Abraham narrative from the time of the monarchy, which (perhaps) was itself based on originally independent individual stories (in particular Gen 18* and 19*).[221] However, this theory seems doubtful to me because all three units have traits of artificial and relatively late compositions (see the short overviews in the following paragraphs).

---

[219] DILLMANN, *Die Genesis*, 287; ZIMMERLI, *1. Mose 12–25*, 94; SOGGIN, *Das Buch Genesis*, 290 (mentioned as one possible interpretation); SEEBASS, *Genesis II/1*, 2–3; DE PURY, RÖMER, and SCHMID *L'Ancien Testament commenté: La Genèse*, 111–12.

[220] GUNKEL, *Genesis*, 218; WESTERMANN, *Genesis 12–36*, 282; SHECTMAN, *Women*, 100.

[221] See BLUM, *Die Komposition*, 280–89; I. FISCHER, *Erzeltern*, 339; RÖMER, "Genese 15 et les tensions," 111; SCHMID, *Genesis and the Moses Story*, 96, with n. 278; LIPSCHITS, RÖMER, and GONZALEZ, "Pre-Priestly Abraham Narratives," 284–91.

(a) Genesis 13 Non-P

At the center of the narrative in Gen 13 is a territorial conflict that leads to Abraham and Lot's separation. However, no reason for the conflict is mentioned. The motif of the quarrel between servants of rival territorial chiefs also appears in Gen 21 (servants of Abraham and Abimelech) and 26 (Isaac and Abimelech); these stories are more concrete; the conflicts concern water wells (cf. 21:22–34; 26:12–33). Thus it is imaginable that the author of the non-P narrative took up the Priestly motif concerning Lot and Abraham's separation and explained it with the motif of struggle between the protagonists' servants, which he borrowed from one of the two aforementioned non-Priestly stories.

(b) Genesis 18:1–15

The story in Genesis 18 shares important linguistic commonalities with several other texts. Like the preceding composition in Gen 17, it contains the theme of the promise of a son for Sarah and the identical opening statement about YHWH's revelation ("YHWH appeared to him/YHWH appeared to Abraham," use of ראה *niphal*, cf. 17:1b with 18:1a). This may support the idea that one of these neighboring units depends on the other and "competes" with it. As for the introductory sentence in Gen 18:1, it is striking that it is followed not by a verbal address by God, as with most other examples of this opening formulation,[222] but by the elaborate story developing the theme of theoxenia.[223]

It is through the latter theme, hospitality toward God, that the story in Gen 18 is closely connected to the following episode in Gen 19. As is often observed, the acts of Abraham and Lot are similar and expressed in equal terms. Abraham and Lot are both sitting (ישׁב) when they see (ראה, cf. 18:1b with 19:1a) the travelers arriving. Both rise to meet them (לקראתם) and bow down (חוה *hishtaphel*) before them (compare Gen 18:2 with 19:1). Both express hope that they will "find favor in the sight" of the visitors (compare Gen 18:3 with 19:19). Although both Abraham and Lot perform exemplary hospitality, Abraham visibly outmatches Lot: Abraham not only rises up but runs to meet the foreigners, his speech is more polite and subservient than Lot's,[224] the festive meal he prepares is described in much more detail than is Lot's, and the quantities of food are extremely generous.[225] Several scholars believe that the more elaborate scene in Gen 18 depends on that of Gen 19.[226] With regard to the verbal similarities and

---

[222] See Gen 12:7; 17:1; 20:3; 26:2, 24; 31:24; 35:9.

[223] SARNA, *Genesis*, 128; B. T. ARNOLD, *Genesis*, NCBC (Cambridge: Cambridge University Press, 2009), 193.

[224] Compare the formulation in Gen 18:3 with that of 19:19.

[225] Since a seah of fine meal corresponds to fifteen liters (see *HALOT* 737; *KAHAL* 284), three seahs would make a great quantity of bread, "while to kill 'a bull' for just three visitors shows royal generosity: a lamb or a goat would have been more than adequate" (G. J. WENHAM, *Genesis 16–50*, WBC [Waco, TX: Word, 1994], 46.)

[226] R. KILIAN, *Die vorpriesterlichen Abrahamüberlieferungen* (Bonn: Hanstein, 1966), 152;

conceptual correspondences, Van Seters concludes that both stories stem from the same author.[227]

The story in Gen 18 has a further striking parallel with the story of YHWH's revelation to Jacob in Gen 28:10–22: just as YHWH "stands before" (נצב על) Jacob in his dream, the three travelers "stand before" (נצבים על) Abraham (cf. Gen 18:2 with 28:13).[228]

Moreover, Gen 18 shares the theme of the unexpected promise of birth and several additional expressions with the story in 2 Kgs 4:8–17. The promise is formulated almost identically (cf. "At the appointed time I will return to you, at this time next year, and Sarah shall have a son" [למועד אשוב אליך כעת חיה ולשרה בן; Gen 18:14] and "At the appointed time, at this time next year you shall embrace a son" [למועד הזה כעת חיה אתי חבקת בן; 2 Kgs 4:16]); the husbands of both the Shunamite woman and Sarah are "old" (זקן; compare Gen 18:12 with 2 Kgs 4:14); and both women are standing "at the door" when listening to the promise (בפתח; compare 18:10 with 2 Kgs 4:15).[229]

Finally, the idiom "is anything too difficult for YHWH?" (היפלא מיהוה דבר; Gen 18:14) has close parallels in Jer 32:17, 27: "Nothing is too difficult for you (YHWH)" (לא יפלא ממך כל דבר; Jer 32:17); "is anything too difficult for me (YHWH)?" (הממני יפלא כל דבר; Jer 32:27).[230]

The number of linguistic commonalities with other units is impressive. In any individual case, considered in isolation from the others, it would be difficult to determine the direction of dependence between the two texts in question. The quantity of striking parallels with several texts found in different parts of the Hebrew Bible, however, suggests that the author of Gen 18 composed the story by borrowing formulations from other texts sharing the same theme or a similar motif.[231] It is possible that a few of the aforementioned texts (Gen 19*; 28:10–17) stem from the same author as Gen 18.[232]

Would it be possible to consider the present shape of Gen 18:1–15 to be the result of a later reworking of an earlier form that did not yet have the previously mentioned parallels? Scholars sometimes express doubts about the unity of the story in Gen 18:1–15 on the basis of the variation in the number and identity of the invited guests in the story.[233] However, the change in number cannot be resolved by distinguishing between different literary strata. As Kratz has argued, the inconsistency in the number seems to have been produced purposefully by the author. On the one hand, the speech

---

LEVIN, *Der Jahwist*, 155–56; KRATZ, *Composition*, 271.

[227] See VAN SETERS, *Abraham*, 215–16.

[228] YHWH stands either "over him," i.e., Jacob, or "over it," i.e., the ladder (staircase); see WESTERMANN, *Genesis 12–36*, 554; WENHAM, *Genesis 16–50*, 222.

[229] See also LEVIN, *Der Jahwist*, 155, with n. 9.

[230] See also LEVIN, *Der Jahwist*, 155, with n. 10.

[231] It is less likely that all the mentioned parallel texts would depend on Gen 18. For instance, neither the Elisha stories in 2 Kgs nor Jer 2 has, to my knowledge, intertextual contacts with the Abraham texts of Genesis.

[232] Traditionally they are ascribed to the "Jahwist." See LEVIN, *Der Jahwist*, 155.

[233] VAN SETERS, *Abraham*, 210–11.

of YHWH in the singular in vv. 10 and 13–14 is, as to content, an indispensable part of the story; on the other hand, v. 10 depends on v. 9, which is formulated in the plural.[234] The shifting between one and three guests might be explained by the influence of the Greek Hyrieus myth, which presents a similar plot.[235] In this legend, which is first documented in Pindar's work, old King Hyrieus, a widower, is visited by the three gods Zeus, Poseidon, and Hermes, who promise him a son.[236] Such a borrowing from Greek mythology would lend further support to the idea that the story is a relatively late, learned scribal composition. Interestingly, YHWH's internal plurality is expressed in other texts in Genesis that share commonalities and are traditionally assigned to "J" (Gen 3:22; 11:7; 19 and cf. 6:1–4).[237] Thus the allusion to YHWH's plurality in Gen 18, often considered an archaic feature, seems to belong to a late literary stratum. It is probably a reaction to strict monotheism becoming dominant in late biblical texts.

(c) Genesis 19

The story in Gen 19 can be read as a fitting continuation of Gen 18:1–15 even though a few differences between the two plots cannot be overlooked. In contrast to the story in Gen 18:1–15, only two divine protagonists are mentioned; in addition to the dominant designation of these figures as men (אנשים), they are also called angels (מלאכים). YHWH seems separate from them (see 19:13b). These tensions may find an explanation in the redactional development of Gen 18–19. The passage reporting the negotiation between Abraham and YHWH in 18:22b–33a was probably inserted secondarily. The motif of the two angels in 19:1 (which presumably replaced "the three men" or "the men") and in vv. 13b and 15 is connected to this redactional text.[238] Once these texts have been recognized as later additions, the story in Gen 19 follows seamlessly from that in 18:1–22a. The intermediate passage in 18:16–22a recounts the divine travelers' trip from Mamre to Sodom. YHWH's intention is to check whether the inhabitants of Sodom "have done entirely according to its outcry, which has come to (him)." The

---

[234] See KRATZ, *Composition*, 271.

[235] This parallel is pointed out by A. de Pury (DE PURY, RÖMER, and SCHMID, *L'Ancien Testament commenté: La Genèse*, 102–3) and T. Römer (T. RÖMER, "The Hebrew Bible and Greek Philosophy and Mythology: Some Case Studies," *Sem* 57 [2015]: 193–96).

[236] F. GRAF, "Hyrieus," in *Brill's New Pauly*, 2006, http://dx.doi.org/10.1163/1574-9347_bnp_ e520260.

[237] According to T. Römer, there may be other reasons for the appearance of three visitors. The three prehistoric figures Ahiman, Sheshai, and Talmai, associated with Hebron in Num 13:22, Josh 15:13–14, and Judg 1:10, might stand behind the three travelers (as deified ancestors). See RÖMER, "Die politische Funktion der vorpriesterlichen Abrahamtexte," in F. Neumann, M.G. Brett, J. Wöhrle (eds.) *The Politics of the Ancestors: Exegetical and Historical Perspectives on Genesis 12–36*, FAT 124 (Tübingen: Mohr Siebeck, 2018), 123–24; LIPSCHITS, RÖMER, and GONZALEZ, "Pre-Priestly Abraham Narratives," 289–90.

[238] See WELLHAUSEN, *Die Composition*, 25–26; KRATZ, *Composition*, 297, n. 38. Similarly LEVIN, *Der Jahwist*, 168–70.

subsequent narrative in Gen 19 reports the result of YHWH's inquiry. As in Gen 18, the author shifts between plural (three) and singular (= YHWH) divine protagonists.

There are several indications of artificial elaboration in the story in Gen 19. The motif of a divine judgment on Sodom (and Gomorrah) is strikingly frequent in the Hebrew Bible. But in all these occurrences, God's intervention is neither connected to the motif of theoxenia nor provoked by sexual violence.[239] The causes of punishment are corruption of justice (Isa 1:9–10; 3:9); arrogance, abundant food, careless ease, and lack of care for the poor (Ezek 16:46–50); and adultery, false dealing, and support of evildoers (Jer 23:14). Moreover, none of these texts mention Lot. The absence of any literary echoes of Gen 19 in these – mainly late, that is, exilic or postexilic – texts and in the Hebrew Bible in general is significant for the former's dating. If the plot of Gen 19 were an ancient tradition stemming from the time of the monarchy, one would expect the texts stemming from a later period to allude at least sporadically to these motifs.[240]

Furthermore, scholars have observed many commonalities with the story of the rape of the Levite's wife in Judg 19, which most recent treatments consider a late polemical composition. The parallels and common points between the stories are impressive: Hospitality offered for a traveler in a "corrupted" city; menacing of the guests by the inhabitants of the town; "offering" of two women to the besiegers by the host. There are also many shared expressions: לין ברחב, "to spend the night in the square" (Gen 19:2; Judg 19:20); פצר, "to urge" (Gen 19:3; Judg 19:7); סבב niphal, "to surround" (Gen 19:4; Judg 19:22); יצא hiphil, "bring out" (Gen 19:5; Judg 19:22); and ידע, "have intercourse with" (Gen 19:5; Judg 19:22). In addition, Gen 19:8 and Judg 19:24 are strikingly similar. One story is surely dependent on the other, but it is difficult to determine the direction of dependence. Since in Judg 19 the outrage is executed and the motif of the shocking "infamy" (נבלה, Judg 19:23, 24; 20:6, 10) is firmly anchored in the narrative, it is more probable that the author of Gen 19 borrowed the motif from Judg 19.[241] Remarkably, Judg 19–21 together with the preceding chapters 17–18 are assigned to the latest layers of the book and are often considered an "appendix."[242]

Like Gen 18, Gen 19 shares a rare expression with a legend from the Elisha cycle.

---

[239] See all occurrences in Deut 29:22; 32:32; Isa 1:9–10; 3:9; 13:19; Jer 23:14; 49:18; 50:40; Ezek 16:46–50, 55–57; Amos 4:11; Zeph 2:9; Lam 4:6. Cf. further the occurrences of Admah and Zeboiim in Gen 10:19; 14:2, 8; Deut 29:22; Hos 11:8. See also ZIMMERLI, *1. Mose 12–25*, 90–91; SOGGIN, *Das Buch Genesis*, 284–85.

[240] See also VAN SETERS, *Abraham*, 210.

[241] Similarly WESTERMANN, *Genesis 12–36*, 366 (cautiously); SOGGIN, *Das Buch Genesis*, 284; SEEBASS, *Genesis II/1*, 150.

[242] See WELLHAUSEN, *Die Composition*, 229–33; W. JÜNGLING, *Richter 19: Ein Plädoyer für das Königtum; Stilistische Analyse der Tendenzerzählung Ri 19,1–30a; 21,25*, AnBib 84 (Rome: Pontifical Biblical Institute, 1981); Y. AMIT, *Hidden Polemics in Biblical Narrative*, trans. Jonathan Chipman, BibInt 25 (Leiden: Brill, 2000), 178–84; E. A. KNAUF, *Richter*, ZBAT 7 (Zurich: TVZ, 2016), 155–71.

According to 19:11, the angels "struck the men with a sudden blindness." The word for "blindness" (סנורים, related to Akk. *sinlurmā/sinnūru*, "day- or night-blindness") occurs only once more in the Hebrew Bible, in 2 Kgs 6:18, where the context is similar and the noun is used with the same verb, נכה *hiphil* (YHWH struck the Arameans "with blindness according to the word of Elisha").

Again, one should ask whether some of the noted parallels might belong to a secondary redaction layer, so that the latter would not have any impact on the setting of the original story. Despite the multiplicity of themes and climaxes within Gen 19, it seems impossible to isolate preexisting literary traditions; the story should be considered unified.[243] As Van Seters and Blum have shown, the different parts of the narrative depend on one another.[244] On the one hand, the stage is set for the episode of Lot's incest with his daughters by the motif of the daughter's separation from their spouses in the part of the story about the angels' visit and by the sudden death of Lot's wife in v. 26. On the other hand, the aforementioned elements seem firmly anchored in the plot of the relevant parts.

A striking parallel in Greek mythology is also noteworthy in the context of the literary-historical classification of the narrative.[245]

The story of Philemon and Baucis, in its transmission by Ovid, tells how an old peasant couple, Philemon and Baucis, are the only inhabitants in their region who welcome the disguised gods Zeus and Hermes. The two gods tell them that they will destroy their city, exhorting the couple to leave the town with them and climb the mountain. After reaching the top of the mountain, they look back and see that everything except their own house has vanished.[246]

Parallels with this story include the offer of hospitality by one couple and the rejection of hospitality by all others, the divine judgment, the salvation of the pious couple, and the mountain refuge.

The existence of a close parallel in Greek mythology for each of the two stories in Gen 18–19 is remarkable, all the more so because there is no evidence for comparable plots in ANE traditions.

6.10.5 Conclusion

Summing up this reassessment of the literary relationship between the non-P stories in Gen 12; 13; 18–19 and the proto-Priestly Abraham narrative, we can conclude that several observations favor the idea that the non-Priestly elements were composed as

---

[243] The story contains three distinct aetiologies as climaxes: an aetiology of place for the desert landscape of the Dead Sea with pillar-like salt formations (19:25–26), an aetiology for the city of Zoar, and, at the end, an etymological explanation of the names of Moab and Ammon.

[244] VAN SETERS, *Abraham*, 217–21; BLUM, *Die Komposition*, 287–88.

[245] DE PURY, RÖMER, and SCHMID *L'Ancien Testament commenté: La Genèse*, 104–6; RÖMER, "Hebrew Bible," 193–96.

[246] R. BLOCH, "Baucis," in *Brill's New Pauly*, 2006, http://dx.doi.org/10.1163/1574–9347_bnp_e214090.

redactional additions to the Priestly strand. The key data of Abraham's "biography" are all found in the Priestly strand rather than in the non-Priestly texts. Furthermore, the absence of any suitable beginning or ending in the non-P stories is striking. Some of these texts (Gen 18:1–15; 19) seem to have been composed in view of a number of biblical texts found outside of the Pentateuch and, at the same time, to have been influenced by legends from Greek mythology as well. The polemical undertone that runs through some of them (Gen 16; 19) gives a particular impression that they are inserted *interpretive* units (in relation to the proto-P stratum).

6.10.6 Possible Resonance of the Proto-Priestly Abraham Narrative in Texts outside of Genesis

Texts outside of Genesis that provide specific information on Abraham may also be relevant to the question of the relationship between the proto-Priestly and non-Priestly strata and the question of the most ancient Abraham tradition. They attest that the latter was understood as a figure with whom Judeans could identify. The texts presumed to be the oldest traditions about Abraham outside of the Pentateuch are found in Ezekiel and Second Isaiah. They stem from the exilic or early postexilic period. Do they reflect the proto-Priestly plot, certain non-Priestly stories, or yet another (now-lost) Abraham tradition instead?

   An important text that is often discussed in relation to our question is Ezek 33:23–24.

> Ezekiel 33:23–24
> [23] Then the word of YHWH came to me saying, [24] "Son of man, they who live in these ruins in the land of Israel are saying, 'Abraham was only one, yet he possessed the land; so to us who are many the land has been given as a possession.'"

Ezekiel 33:24 cites the argumentation of nonexiled Judeans: the latter appeal to Abraham, who, as an individual, "inherited the land, and we are many." Although Abraham is not referred to as an autochthonous figure, Matthias Köckert and Thomas Römer infer that, as a figure with whom the remainees in the land identified, he was probably indigenous.[247]

   Nevertheless, one should not exclude the possibility that the saying of the remainees in the land in Ezek 33:23–24 might rely on the proto-Priestly narrative, including its exposition localizing Abraham's birth in Ur. The combination of the themes of being alone/multiplication on the one hand and the gift of the land on the other appears in Gen 15 (non-Priestly) and Gen 17 (Priestly). As shown above, there are

---

[247] KÖCKERT, "Die Geschichte der Abrahamüberlieferung," 106; T. RÖMER, "Abraham Traditions in the Hebrew Bible outside the Book of Genesis," in *The Book of Genesis: Composition, Reception, and Interpretation,* ed. C.A. Evans, J.N. Lohr, and D.L. Petersen, VTSup 152 (Leiden: Brill, 2012), 163.

valuable arguments for classifying Gen 15 as post-Priestly.[248] Thus, the reference text of Ezek 33:23–24 might well be Gen 17 and the proto-Priestly narrative.[249] This would mean that both the author of the passage in Ezekiel and the exilic community, as well as their contemporaries in Judah, were familiar with the proto-Priestly narrative tradition. Köckert and Römer, however, deny such a tight connection between Ezek 33:23–24 and the Priestly (and non-Priestly) narrative in Genesis, arguing that the Judahites would not refer to a divine promise.[250] Nevertheless, the passive formulation "the land has been given" may imply the notion of a donation by YHWH. Furthermore, Köckert and Römer's argument disregards the fact that the quotation is part of *a polemic addressed against the remainees in the land*; the author might have intended to avoid explicit reference to the promise and its giver. Moreover, Gen 17 fits as the background of Ezek 33:23–24 insofar as it foretells that a "multitude" will possess the land (Gen 17:4–6, 8). Abraham's origins in Mesopotamia in the Priestly story's exposition should not necessarily be linked with the claim of the exiles to possess the land, as Römer, Köckert, and others do. More generally, it fits with a setting of the story in the Neo-Babylonian era. By suggesting a Mesopotamian origin for the people's eponym, the author may have aimed to attract the benevolence of the Neo-Babylonian authorities.

Ezekiel 33:23–24 has several similarities with a passage in Second Isaiah: Isa 51:1–3.

Isaiah 51:1–3

[1] Listen to me, you who pursue righteousness,
    who seek YHWH:
Look to the rock from which you were hewn,
    and to the quarry from which you were dug.
[2] "Look to Abraham your father,
    and to Sarah who gave birth to you in pain;
when he was one I called him,
    then I blessed him and multiplied him."
[3] Indeed, YHWH will comfort Zion;
    he will comfort all her ruins.
And her wilderness he will make like Eden,
    and her desert like the garden of YHWH;
joy and gladness will be found in her,
    thanksgiving and sound of a melody.

---

[248] See the beginning of this section.

[249] Regarding the term מורשה, which also occurs in Exod 6:8, one might even ask whether the author of Ezek 33:23–24 was acquainted with the latter text (and, if so, with an early form of the comprehensive Priestly composition). Most scholars, however, believe that the Priestly text in 6:2–8 presupposes and responds to the passage in Ezekiel.

[250] KÖCKERT, "Die Geschichte der Abrahamüberlieferung," 106; RÖMER, "Abraham Traditions in the Hebrew Bible outside the Book of Genesis," 163.

Abraham appears in both texts as "one," which contrasts with his "many" descendants. Both texts use the expression "ruins" (חרבות) as a designation for the desolated city of Jerusalem during the exile. In addition to the "one"/"many" contrast, another motif is reminiscent of P: Abraham and Sarah's depiction as father and mother of the addressee (cf. Gen 17:4–5, 16). The importance of the "father" metaphor for Abraham is confirmed by the polemical reaction to it in Isa 63:16, which claims that only YHWH can be considered Israel's father. Obviously, there was a debate about Abraham's role as Israel's father; the reference in Trito-Isaiah aims to downplay this function of Abraham. Outside of Isaiah, Josh 24:4 names Abraham as Israel's father as well. Most probably the "father" metaphor depends on Gen 17:4–6.

Abraham appears in another text in Second Isaiah:

Isaiah 41:8–9
[8] But you, Israel, my servant,
    Jacob whom I have chosen,
    descendant of Abraham my friend,
[9] you whom I have taken from the ends of the earth (מקצות הארץ),
    and called from its remotest parts (ומאציליה),
    and said to you, "You are my servant,
    I have chosen you and not rejected you."

Commentators such as Köckert and Lena-Sofia Tiemeyer maintain that this text alludes to the specific geographical localization of Abraham's birthplace at the beginning of the Priestly narrative (Gen 11:27–31, 32b): the "most remote" place possible (Isa 41:9) is a city very far away from Judah. Ur, in southern Mesopotamia (see Gen 11:28, 31), indeed fits perfectly with this expression.[251] Several non-Priestly texts refer explicitly to Mesopotamia as Abraham's native land (Gen 15:7; Neh 9:7; Jos 24:2). Furthermore, when considering the Abraham narrative, it is striking that the first non-Priestly text following just after the Priestly exposition, Gen 12:1–4, 6–9, agrees with the latter in the detail that Abraham has left his native land (v. 1) before journeying through Palestine. With regard to these various passages referring or alluding to Mesopotamia (or at least to a foreign country [in the case of Gen 12:1–4, 6–9]) as Abraham's native land, it is worth noting that not a single text in the Hebrew Bible explicitly refers to Judah as Abraham's country of origin.

Despite this negative evidence, scholars believe that the earlier strand of the tradition portrayed Abraham as an autochthonous figure, whereas only afterward did the Priestly and post-Priestly authors transform the protagonist into an immigrant coming from Mesopotamia. The argument is based in particular on the two non-Priestly stories in Gen 16 and 18 and furthermore on Ezek 33:24 (see above).[252] The two allegedly old accounts in Gen 16 and 18 have in common that they

---

[251] L.-S. TIEMEYER, *For the Comfort of Zion: The Geographical and Theological Location of Isaiah 40–55*, VTSup 139 (Leiden: Brill, 2011), 133; KÖCKERT, "Die Geschichte der Abrahamüberlieferung," 111.
[252] See KÖCKERT, "Die Geschichte der Abrahamüberlieferung," 106, 121, and in particular

are located in Southern Judah. This is taken as an indication that the Abraham figure originated in this region. With regard to this theory, however, it is important to note that none of the three texts refer or even allude to Palestine or Judah as Abraham's place of origin or birth.

Does Isa 41:8–9 belong to the same literary stratum as the other Abraham pericope in Second Isaiah, which should be assigned to the exilic period? In the framework of this study, this question must be remain open. All three texts mentioned here have elements that resemble motifs in the proto-Priestly Abraham narrative. The strong commonalities suggest that the authors of the former texts were familiar with the proto-Priestly Abraham narrative, although the possibility of influence by an unknown and unpreserved tradition cannot be excluded.

LIPSCHITS, RÖMER, and GONZALEZ, "Pre-Priestly Abraham Narratives," 271–74.

7. The Priestly Texts in Exodus 1–12:
Israel's Stay in Egypt and Exodus

7.1 Issues in Scholarly Discussion

Scholars are generally unanimous in identifying the Priestly strand in this section (in its differentiation from the non-P strand). Yet, attribution to a secondary Priestly or "H" redaction layers is proposed for several of these texts, and for a few texts a post-Priestly (or late Priestly) origin is suggested. The questions of the literary profile of P (source or redaction?) and of the literary-historical relationship between P and non-P in the subsections of the narrative are controversial. The latter question is treated extensively in scholarship, in particular for the Priestly texts in Exod 1, which form a transition between the Joseph story and the Exodus narrative. Several European scholars currently consider P to be the first source to combine the ancestral narrative and that of exodus.

The following paragraphs will address the aforementioned questions. They are preceded by a discussion of the most important textual variants (including an overview of characteristic features of the main textual witnesses in the whole book of Exodus).

7.2 Significant Textual Variants

7.2.1 Introduction

Striking characteristics of the main textual witnesses in the book of Exodus are as follows. SP shows an expansionistic tendency in comparison with MT and LXX, which it shares with one of the Dead Sea Scrolls (4QpaleoExod[m]).[1] Furthermore, in several instances SP harmonizes with its immediate context. In the tabernacle account, SP tends to adapt the language of the instruction section to that of the fulfillment section.

The LXX translation of Exodus is considered to be freer and more elegant than those of the other books of the Pentateuch. Some of its readings are theologically or philosophically influenced. A well-known example is the rendering of the particular "theonym" in Exod 3:14 (ἐγώ εἰμι ὁ ὤν "I am the existing one" for אהיה אשר אהיה, "I will be who I will be"). In Exod 4:6–7 the translator probably sought to deliberately conceal the notion of Moses's (temporary) leprosy present in MT and SP by skipping the expression מצרעת, "leprosy," in v. 6 and adding χρόαν ("to the color") in v. 7. What

---

[1] J. SANDERSON, *An Exodus Scroll from Qumran: 4QpaleoExod[m] and the Samaritan Tradition*, HSS 30 (Atlanta: Scholars Press, 1986), 28–35.

happens to Moses is only a change of complexion.[2] Because of the relative freeness of the translation, it is often more difficult to decide whether a deviation in the LXX derives from a divergent *Vorlage* or should be attributed to the translator.[3] A striking feature of the LXX translation in Exodus is that the Greek translation of the fulfillment section of the tabernacle account (Exod 35–40) distinguishes itself in several respects from that of the first section (25–29) and that of Exod 1–34 in general (see below, II.10.2).

The LXX *Vorlage* has a reputation for being expansionistic, but it nevertheless contains minuses and variants, some of which are considered more original when compared with MT and SP.[4] In Exod 35–40, the LXX and Vetus Latina (according to Codex Monacensis) distinguish themselves considerably from MT and SP in terms of the internal organization of the account; the former texts are considerably shorter than the latter in these sections. Such a great number of sizable literary (editorial) variants does not appear elsewhere in the Pentateuch. Scholars do not agree on the question whether the deviations in LXX and Vetus Latina should be assigned to the translators or to a Hebrew *Vorlage* that was (mostly) distinct from MT and SP.[5] Some scholars believe that the LXX of the fulfillment report reflects a Hebrew *Vorlage* that is not only different from but also older than MT. Nevertheless, the evaluation of the variants in LXX and VT in Exod 35–40 is complicated by the noted peculiarity that the Greek translation in this section is different from that of the first section. Moreover, given important differences in lexical choices, scholars suggest that Exod 35–40 (or its core, 36:8–38:20) was translated at a later time than Exod 1–34.[6] If this were the case, one could possibly conclude that the first translator's Hebrew *Vorlage* did not contain a fulfillment account.

---

[2] Thus A. Le Boulluec and P. Sandevoir, *La Bible d'Alexandrie, I: L'Exode; Traduction du texte grec de la Septante; Introduction et Notes* (Paris: Cerf, 1986), 97, who think that the translator responded to the polemic of Manetho according to whom Moses, leprous, would have led a great leprous crowd out of Egypt. See also P. Schwagmeier, "Exodos, Exodus, Das zweite Buch Mose," in *Einleitung in die Septuaginta: Handbuch zur Septuaginta/Handbook of the Septuagint*, ed. M. Karrer, W. Kraus, and S. Kreuzer, JSCS 49 (Gütersloh: Gütersloher Verlagshaus, 2016), 129.

[3] See the hesitation and balanced assessment in Schwagmeier, "Exodos, Exodus, Das zweite Buch Mose," 131.

[4] See Schwagmeier, "Exodos, Exodus, Das zweite Buch Mose," 130–31. The text-critical value of the LXX is evidenced by the text-critical investigation of Bénédicte Lemmelijn on the Plagues Narrative (B. Lemmelijn, *A Plague of Texts? A Text-Critical Study of the So-Called Plagues Narrative in Exodus 7:14–11:10*, OtSt 56 [Leiden: Brill, 2015]). In her evaluation of the text-relevant variants, she offers good arguments that the LXX reflects the text-critically preferable reading in seven cases (see ibid., 165–66, 172–73, 174, 176, 185–86, 190).

[5] See below, II.10.2.

[6] See J. Popper, *Der biblische Bericht über die Stiftshütte: Ein Beitrag zur Geschichte der Composition und Diaskeue des Pentateuch* (Leipzig: Heinrich Hunger, 1862), 172–76, followed by several scholars. See further below, II.10.2.

7.2.2 Textual Differences

(a1) Exodus 1:3

MT, SP, LXX: —
4QExod[b]:   יוסף

(a2) Exodus 1:5

MT, SP, 4QGen–Exod[a],   ויוסף היה במצרים (position at the end of v. 5)
4QpaleoGen–Exod[l]:
4QExod[b]:   —
LXX: Ιωσηφ δὲ ἦν ἐν Αἰγύπτῳ
        = ויוסף היה במצרים (position at the end of v. 4)

According to 4QExod[b], Joseph goes to Egypt together with his father and his brothers; Joseph's previous stay, as it is reported in the Joseph narrative, is ignored. All other
textual witnesses exclude Joseph from Jacob's migration and, in agreement with Gen
37–50, state that "Joseph was already in Egypt" at the moment of Jacob and his others
sons' migration (see Exod 1:5). Because of the preceding statement that "all the souls
that came out of the loins of Jacob were seventy souls," the text of MT, SP, and their
congeners may give the impression that Joseph does not belong to the seventy descendants of Jacob. In LXX, however, this difficulty does not exist because the sentence
"Joseph was already in Egypt" precedes the statement of the counting of Jacob's clan.

How to explain these differences? The only coherent reading is that of LXX. In
contrast, the readings of MT and its congeners on the one hand and that of 4QExod[b]
on the other both seem difficult, the former when examined in their immediate environment and the latter when considered in its larger context (it contradicts the Joseph
story). Which one among the two *lectiones difficiles* should be preferred? What may
help to answer this question is the insight that Exod 1:1–5 constitutes a late redactional
text whose function is to smooth the transition between the book of Genesis and that
of Exodus.[7] If correct, the reading of 4QExod[b], which ignores Joseph's stay in Egypt
(and thus implicitly the Joseph story), can hardly be original. For these reasons, MT,
SP, 4QGen–Exod[a], 4QpaleoGen–Exod[l] should be preferred.[8] The difficulty of Joseph's
exclusion from the seventy descendants of Jacob was probably felt in both 4QExod[b]
and LXX and led to the respective changes in the two texts (inclusion of Joseph in the
listing of Jacob's sons and omission of the sentence "Joseph was already in Egypt" in
4QExod[b]; transposition of the latter sentence in LXX).

---

[7] See below, II.7.3 (a).
[8] See ALBERTZ, *Exodus 1–18*, 131. Commentators generally prefer the reading of MT and its
congeners. For an alternative view, see RÖMER, "Joseph Story," 199–200, who assigns Exod 1:1–5a
to P[G]; since Römer's view is that P[G] does not mention Joseph's stay in Egypt, the reading of
4QExod[b] is fitting in this reduced context, and accordingly, Römer considers it the original
reading.

(b) Exodus 1:5

MT, SP: 70 descendants
4QExod[b], 4QGen-Exod[a], LXX: 75 descendants

Whereas the reading of MT and SP agrees with Gen 46:27 (MT, SP) and Deut 10:22 (MT, SP, LXX), the variant reading of 4QExod[b], 4QGen–Exoda, LXX conforms with Gen 46:27 LXX.

The round number seventy appears in ANE literature in similar contexts: in particular, one is reminded of the seventy sons of the Ugaritic goddess 'Aṯiratu and the seventy sons of Gideon (Judg 8:30) and Ahab (2 Kgs 10:1).[9] W. H. C. Propp notes, "If the tally of Hebrew immigrants to Egypt is based in legend rather than fact, we should expect such a round number."[10] This argument is comprehensible but not cogent. One might be inclined to consider the reading of MT and SP secondary, influenced by Deut 10:22, Judg 8:30 or 2 Kgs 10:1. Nevertheless, MT and SP should be preferred because seventy-five most likely constitutes a secondary development connected with the LXX pluses in Gen 46:20, 27 (inclusion of five sons and grandsons of Manasseh and Ephraim), which may have been motivated in turn by Num 26:28–37.[11]

(c) Exodus 2:25

MT, SP: וידע אלהים
LXX: καὶ ἐγνώσθη αὐτοῖς
           = וידע אליהם

The two readings are graphically similar. The usage of ידע qal without object ("knew, noticed"), as it appears in MT, is considered problematic by certain scholars.[12] However, it is also attested in Gen 18:21. The reconstructed reading of LXX *Vorlage* ("and he made himself known to them") is fitting, insofar as ידע niphal also appears in the following P text, Exod 6:3.[13] Nevertheless, at first sight, the plural of the suffix in אליהם, "to them," does not match the close context; the addressee of God's (yhwh's) revelation is Moses and not the Israelites.

It is difficult to decide between the variants. For both readings, one might argue that it has resulted from the attempt to resolve a difficulty present in the *Vorlage*: a scribe of MT may have felt the observed difficulty of LXX (the addressee of the revelation is in the plural) and changed the text. Alternately, a scribe of LXX *Vorlage* may have intended to harmonize the text with the immediately following context; through

---

[9] See W. H. C. PROPP, *Exodus 1–18: A New Translation with Introduction and Commentary*, AB 2 (New York: Doubleday, 1999), 121.

[10] PROPP, *Exodus 1–18*, 121.

[11] See PROPP, *Exodus 1–18*, 121; PRESTEL and SCHORCH, "Genesis," 247. Differently, SCHWAGMEIER, "Exodos, Exodus, Das zweite Buch Mose," 130–31.

[12] Cf. W. H. SCHMIDT, *Exodus*, BKAT 2.1 (Neukirchen-Vluyn: Neukirchener Verlag, 1988), 79; RÖMER, "From the Call of Moses," 130.

[13] ידע niphal, which expresses a cognitive aspect of the reception of the revelatory act, seems to be opposed to ראה niphal, which is consistently used in the Priestly texts of Genesis.

minor modifications, he thus created a statement that is related to the following revelation of YHWH in Exod 3. As for the "difficult" plural, he chose it because of the similarity of אליהם to אלהים. (As for contents, the plural can be explained by the fact that
Moses will report the deity's message to the Israelites after YHWH's revelation.)

A clue to the grammatical correctness of the reading of MT, SP is the fact that ידע
qal with YHWH/God as subject also appears in two thematically similar texts (Gen
18:20–21 and Exod 3:6–7). In both texts, the deity examines a peculiar situation on
earth.

(d) Exodus 6:2

MT, Cairo Genizah, LXX:	אלהים
SP, LXX (minuscules), Vetus Latina, Targum	יהוה
Onkelos, Targum Pseudo-Jonathan:	

Strikingly, this textual difference is only rarely dealt with in commentaries. The reading of MT fits well with the theonym concept of P. In a synchronistic reading, however, it stands in tension with the preceding verse, Exod 6:1 (non-P), where the Tetragram appears. Most likely, the alternative reading of SP and its congeners harmonizes
with this latter text.[14]

(e) Exodus 12:40

MT, 4QExod^a:	בני ישראל
SP:	בני ישראל ואבותם
cf. LXX^{MSS}:	αὐτοὶ καὶ οἱ πατέρες αὐτῶν
	המה ואבותם =

This difference is connected with the next one. In contrast to MT, the chronological
indication in SP and LXX includes the era of the ancestors (see the following textual
note).

(f) Exodus 12:40

MT:	במצרים
4QExod^c:	בארץ מצרים
SP:	בארץ כנען ובארץ מצרים
LXX:	ἐν γῇ Αἰγύπτῳ καὶ ἐν γῇ Χανααν
	בארץ מצרים ובארץ כנען =

The SP and LXX agree against MT in relating the 430 years not exclusively to Israel's stay in Egypt but also to Israel's previous sojourn in Canaan. The reading of MT
is considered more original by most scholars. Indeed, MT's reference solely to Israel's stay in Egypt better fits the context reporting Israel's exodus from Egypt. The
reading of SP (to which the LXX[-*Vorlage*] was probably secondarily adapted)[15] can

---

[14] See W. H. SCHMIDT, *Exodus*, 286; PROPP, *Exodus 1–18*, 263.

[15] Indicating the secondary nature of the plus in LXX (in comparison with the two plusses

be explained as a harmonization with the information in Exod 6:16–25 (P[s]), which reckons with only tree generations between Jacob and Moses.[16] The small deviation of 4QExod[b] is a minor problem; the expansion should probably be considered secondary.

7.3 Literary Classification of the (Putative) Priestly Texts: Disputed Cases

The following presents the scholarly discussion on all (putative) Priestly texts whose literary classification is disputed and, wherever possible, draws conclusions.

(a) Exodus 1:1–5, 7

The classification of the opening passage, Exod 1:1–5, 7, is disputed. In the past, the latter was generally attributed to P[G]/P[C].[17] Today, 1:1–5 is often considered a post-Priestly redactional text composed in view of the existing separation of the books of Genesis and Exodus.[18] The fact that three similar genealogies are integrated into the Priestly strand (Gen 35:23–26; 46:8–27; Exod 1:1–5) may indeed indicate that the three genealogies do not all stem from the same hand. Since Exod 1:1–5 is the opening text of the book of Exodus, it is tempting to consider the passage a secondary, post-Priestly transitional text.

Verse 7, however, should be treated separately. The verse contains the two lexemes פרה and רבה, which frequently occur in P. Moreover, the statement according to which the people increased and filled the land forms an inclusion with the order in Gen 1:28 to fill the earth.[19] The problem of cohabitation as a result of increased population might be compared with a recurrent motif in the Priestly ancestral

---

of SP) is, first, the sequence Egypt – Canaan, and second, the insertion of "their fathers" after the pronoun "they" instead after "the Israelites" at the beginning of the statement (see the translation of the entire v. 40: "And the sojourning of the children of Israel, while they sojourned in the land of Egypt *and the land of Canaan, they and their fathers,* was four hundred and thirty years.") The reviser has put the two plusses in SP together into one (see the part in italics in the above translation).

[16] See, for instance, KOENEN, "1200 Jahre," 498–99; SCHMID, *Genesis and the Moses Story*, 90, n. 245. See also PROPP, *Exodus 1–18*, 365.

[17] For the classical view, see, among others, ELLIGER, "Sinn," 121; LOHFINK, "Die Priesterschrift," 198, n. 29; M. NOTH, *Das zweite Buch Mose: Exodus*, ATD 5 (Göttingen: Vandenhoeck & Ruprecht, 1958), 10 (1:1–4, 5, 6–7 belong to P); B. S. CHILDS, *The Book of Exodus*, OTL (Louisville: Westminster John Knox, 1974), 2 (P in 1:1–5, 7); W. H. SCHMIDT, *Exodus*, 26–31 (P in 1:1a, 2–4, 5b, 7*); BLUM, *Studien*, 241 (P in 1:1–5, 7); ALBERTZ, *Exodus 1–18*, 41–43 (P in 1:1a, 2–5a, 7), RÖMER, "Joseph Story," 199–200 (P in 1:1–5a, 7).

[18] Cf., among others, LEVIN, *Der Jahwist*, 315; PROPP, *Exodus 1–18*, 3; KRATZ, *Composition*, 243; GERTZ, *Tradition*, 352–57; BERNER, *Die Exoduserzählung*, 38–41, IDEM, "Der literarische Charakter," 96–97. See also SCHMID, *Genesis and the Moses Story*, 62.

[19] However, one should note the different use of the expression ארץ (Gen 1:28: "earth"; Exod 1:7: "land") in the two texts.

narrative: the difficulty of living together because of the accumulation of property (livestock). However, the fact that the verb עָצַם, "to become mighty," is never used in P but appears several times in non-P (J) texts creates a problem for attributing Exod 1:7 to P. The root עצם (verb עצם and adjective עָצוּם, "mighty") is used twice in the close non-P context (Exod 1:9 [עָצוּם], 20 [וַיַּעַצְמוּ]). J. Van Seters and T. Dozeman ascribe the verse to so-called J, but this is not convincing.[20] With the exception of the verb עצם, the vocabulary is typically Priestly. Other scholars ascribe 1:7, like 1:1–5, to a late Priestly or post-Priestly redaction that would combine elements of both the P and the non-P strata. However, when considering P[C] (texts belonging to the comprehensive Priestly composition) a redactional layer building on non-P (see below), the argument for assigning 1:7 to a post-Priestly layer loses its weight. The use of non-P vocabulary finds sufficient explanation in P's nature as a redaction layer. The use of the lexeme עצם in 1:7 can thus be explained as P picking up the "alien" root from its close context. The analysis of the Priestly texts of the Jacob-Esau narrative demonstrated a similar "borrowing" by P (P taking up the noun מקנה, "livestock").[21]

(b) Exodus 6:6–8

The passage concerning YHWH's revelation to Moses (Exod 6:2–9) contains a report about Moses being commissioned to speak to the Israelites, the execution of the commission, and its failure (6:6–9). Because of its distinct conception of land possession (see 6:8, with the "non-Priestly" term מוֹרָשָׁה, "acquisition, property"[22]) and language use (the expressions מִתַּחַת סִבְלֹת מִצְרַיִם, "out from under the burdens of Egypt," נצל hiphil, "to pull out, deliver," גאל, "to redeem," בִּזְרוֹעַ נְטוּיָה, "with an outstretched arm," נשׂא יד, "to express an oath"), Otto considers vv. 6–8 a secondary insertion that would presuppose Deuteronomy and the Holiness document and stem from his supposed *Pentateuchredaktion*.[23] However, without the following verses (6:6–8), the passage 6:2–5, which lacks Moses's commission to speak to the Israelites, hangs in the air. Exodus 6:2–9 in its entirety seems to form a well-composed unity.[24]

Nevertheless, the peculiar vocabulary is striking and will be discussed further in the section concerning P's literary profile. Some of the expressions that are not

---

[20] J. Van Seters, *The Life of Moses: The Yahwist as Historian in Exodus–Numbers* (Kampen: Kok Pharos, 1994), 20; T. B. Dozeman, *Commentary on Exodus* (Grand Rapids: Eerdmans, 2009), 68.

[21] Cf. II.6.6.1.

[22] See above, II.6.6.8 (b).

[23] Cf. Otto, "Forschungen zur Priesterschrift," 10, n. 45. Otto refers to Kuenen, *Historisch-kritische Einleitung*, 1.1:315–16, and B. Baentsch, *Exodus–Leviticus–Numeri*, HKAT I/2 (Göttingen: Vandenhoeck & Ruprecht, 1903), who assigned vv. 6–8 to a secondary Priestly tradtition or to R[P].

[24] Cf. Gertz, *Tradition*, 249–50; Römer, "Exodus Narrative," 161.

typical of P appear in the book of Ezekiel. In addition, the key term expressing YHWH's self-presentation (ידע *niphal*) occurs frequently in the book of Ezekiel.[25]

(c) Exodus 6:13, 14–27

The Priestly passage describing YHWH's self-presentation to Moses and their dialogue concerning Moses's commission to the Israelites and Pharaoh (6:2–12) is followed by a long genealogy in Exod 6:14–27 (after the proleptic 6:13). This very selective genealogy of Jacob's sons is clearly centered on the Levites, who form the third and most extensive entry after the entries of Reuben and Simeon. The genealogy leads to figures who play important roles in certain Priestly texts in Leviticus (10:4: Mishael and Elzaphan) and Numbers (16: Korah; 25; 31: Phinehas). This concentration of allusions to different texts in the Priestly strand favors the idea that the genealogy presupposes these late texts.[26] The expression בית אבות (6:14, 25) appears predominantly in postexilic texts.[27] The statement in v. 13 concerning Moses and Aaron's charge to speak with the Israelites and Pharaoh seems precipitous compared with 7:1, which forms a fitting continuation of 6:12. It is probably a secondary addition too. Moreover, vv. 28–30, following immediately after the genealogy in vv. 14–27 and providing a short summary of vv. 1–12, seem to be a "classic *Wiederaufnahme*."[28] Finally, the name of Amram's wife, Jochebed (יוכבד, 6:20), with its theophoric element *yô*, seems to presuppose pre-Mosaic acquaintance with YHWH, which contradicts the preceding Priestly passage on the revelation of YHWH's name (6:2–3).[29] Taken together, these observations make it likely that Exod 6:13, 14–30 was inserted secondarily into the P context.[30]

As for the tendentiousness of this passage, most commentators detect a particular interest in the Aaronides, who are clearly contrasted with Moses, who in turn is listed without wife and without descendants. This silence concerning Moses's family is certainly meaningful. In addition, the fact that the genealogy leads to the birth of

---

[25] ידע *niphal*: Ezek 20:5, 9; 35:11; 36:32; 38:23; בזרוע נטויה: Ezek 20:33, 34; מורשה: Ezek 11:15; 25:4, 10; 33:24; 36:2, 3, 5; יד נשא to express an oath: Ezek 20:6. See GERTZ, *Tradition*, 248–49, and JEON, "Source of P?," 82–84.

[26] Recent analyses favor a late date for each of these texts. For Lev 10, see R. ACHENBACH, *Die Vollendung der Tora: Studien zur Redaktionsgeschichte des Numeribuches im Kontext von Hexateuch und Pentateuch*, BZABR 3 (Wiesbaden: Harrassowitz, 2003), 93–110; NIHAN, *From Priestly Torah*, 148–50; for Num 16, see NIHAN, *From Priestly Torah*, 582–86; for Num 25, cf. J. HUTZLI, "La fureur divine et son détournement en Nb 25," in *Colères et repentirs divins: Actes du colloque organisé par le Collège de France, Paris, les 24 et 25 avril 2013*, ed. J.-M. Durand, L. Marti, and T. Römer, OBO 274 (Fribourg: Presses Universitaires; Göttingen: Vandenhoeck & Ruprecht, 2015), 177–99.

[27] Exod 6:14; 12:3; 37× in Num; Josh 22:14; Ezra 10:16; Neh 2:3; 7:61; 10:35; 24× in 1–2 Chr. The elliptical use (> אָבוֹת) occurs in Exod 6:25; Num 31:26; Josh 14:1; 1 Kgs 8:1; Ezra 1:5; 1 Chr 8:6; 26:32; 29:6; 2 Chr 5:2. See *HALOT* 125 and ACHENBACH, *Die Vollendung*, 110–12.

[28] PROPP, *Exodus 1–18*, 267; ALBERTZ, *Exodus 1–18*, 131 ("eine klassische Wiederaufnahme"); RÖMER, *Moïse*, 159.

[29] PROPP, *Exodus 1–18*, 276.

[30] WELLHAUSEN, *Die Composition*, 62; ALBERTZ, *Exodus 1–18*, 128–32.

Phinehas as its climax demonstrates the importance of this figure and of the event reported in Num 25, where Phinehas, Aaron's grandson, overtakes Moses as a rigorous and successful leader.[31] Furthermore, 6:26 mentions Aaron before Moses, in a statement about YHWH's instruction to lead the Israelites out of Egypt. Aaron's marriage to Elisheba, which makes him a brother-in-law of Nahshon the son of Amminadab (see Exod 6:23), should be considered an allusion to David's genealogy found in Ruth 4:18–22: Aaron is thereby linked to the Davidic line.[32] The links to late Priestly texts and to the book of Ruth favor a late date, and the entire passage should be assigned to a late Priestly redactional layer.

R. Achenbach offers a different interpretation of Exod 6:14–27, arguing that the entire line of Levi is cast in an ambiguous light by a late pro-Zadokite "Torah-redaction."[33] In the reference to Jacob's three oldest sons, Achenbach sees a polemical allusion to Gen 49:3–7, where these sons all are criticized or cursed. However, this interpretation is not necessary. The author of Exod 6:14–27 may have focused only on the three oldest sons of Jacob because Levi, who appears in the third position in the genealogy, was the center of his interest. Perhaps he wanted to establish a correspondence between Levi's and Eleazar's position as third in their respective families. Another argument put forward by Achenbach concerns the specification of Amram's wife, Jochebed, as "his aunt" (דדתו) in Exod 6:20. Achenbach emphasized the fact that in Lev 18:14; 20:20 the expression דודה refers to the wife of the father's brother. However, the author hardly alludes to the prohibition of illicit incest in Lev 18:12; 20:20. It is true that Amram's marriage to his aunt contradicts the prohibition of Lev 18:12. But nothing in the text favors the interpretation of Exod 6:20 as a polemic. On the contrary, the positive-sounding name of Amram's wife, Jochebed, with its associations with the Tetragram and with YHWH's *kābôd*, suggests that the author is reporting Amram's act in a sympathetic manner.

Allusions to certain problematic or scandalous episodes in the history of the Levites can be explained by the author's desire to oppose the competing clans among Levi's descendants in order to highlight and set apart the winning line of Eleazar and especially Phinehas.

(d) Exodus 7:3 (7:2–8 and 6:12bγ)

The passage Exod 7:1–7, which introduces the miracle report, is traditionally assigned to P^G/P^C. V. 3 is often considered a secondary insertion.[34] Scholars arguing for this redaction-historical option point first to the term קשה *hiphil*, "to harden," which never occurs in P (P uses חזק *hiphil* instead) but which appears in Exod 13:15 (non-P, with

---

[31] See D. A. BERNAT, *Sign of the Covenant: Circumcision in the Priestly Tradition* (Atlanta: Society of Biblical Literature, 2009), 83–96; ALBERTZ, *Exodus 1–18*, 128–32.

[32] Cf. BERNAT, *Sign*, 84; ALBERTZ, *Exodus 1–18*, 130. Perhaps Elisheba recalls Batsheba, David's wife and Solomon's mother.

[33] ACHENBACH, *Die Vollendung*, 110–23.

[34] See SMEND, *Die Erzählung*, 125, 129, n. 1; L. SCHMIDT, *Studien zur Priesterschrift*, BZAW 214 (Berlin: de Gruyter, 1993), 3–4; GERTZ, *Tradition*, 252–54; F. KOHATA, *Jahwist und Priesterschrift in Exodus 3–14*, BZAW 166 (Berlin: de Gruyter, 1986), 34–36 (only 3b is an addition); BERNER, *Die Exoduserzählung*, 163; IDEM, "Der literarische Charakter," 103.

Pharaoh as subject) and twice in Deuteronomy,[35] and second to the double expression "signs and wonders" (see את אתתי ואת מופתי), which again is lacking in P but is frequent in the book of Deuteronomy.[36]

However, there are hints of a non-P or late P provenience in other parts of the introductory passage as well. The combination of the two designations עם and בני ישראל for the people of Israel in 7:4 appears elsewhere only in non-Priestly texts.[37] Furthermore, 7:3 and 7:4 fit well together insofar as they anticipate God's twofold judgment over Egypt as it is reflected in subsequent Priestly texts: the miracles (alluded to by 7:3) and the striking of the firstborn (referred to in 7:4).

> Exodus 7:3–4
> [3] But I will harden Pharaoh's heart that I may multiply my signs and my wonders in the land of Egypt. [4] And Pharaoh will not listen to you, then I will lay my hand on Egypt, and bring out my hosts, my people the Israelites, from the land of Egypt by great judgments.

The introductory passage also seems to be unified in terms of its theology, which distinguishes it from the following miracle report. Aaron plays the role of a "word prophet"[38] (in the miracle report, he acts as a magician), and much emphasis is placed on YHWH's authorship of the "great judgments" (whereas Aaron and Moses's activity, which is emphasized in the miracle story, is not mentioned at all).[39] For these reasons, the question arises as to the literary relationship of this introductory passage to the Priestly account of the five miracles, on the one hand, and to the Priestly composition (P^C) in general, on the other. The discrepencies between Exod 7:1–7 and the Priestly miracles narrative are also pointed out by Christoph Berner.[40] In view of these differences, he excludes the Priestly plagues account from the primary stratum of P. His argument is that the latter would depend on the introduction in 7:1–7. However, if we look closely, the narrative of the five miracles does not depend on the entire text 7:1–7, but only on v. 1, which fits it better than the following verses. The prophetic role assigned to Aaron in 7:1 can be understood in the sense of Elijah's and Elisha's roles as charismatic prophets who possess magical abilities.[41] An indication that 7:1 originally ran to v. 9 is as follows: the latter, in which YHWH addresses Moses alone, works better as the continuation of 7:1 – much better than it does as the continuation of v. 8,

---

[35] Deut 2:30; 10:16; cf. also the frequent Dtr expression קשה ערף (Exod 32:9; 33:3, 5; 34:9; Deut 9:6, 13; 31:27).

[36] Cf. Deut 4:34; 6:22; 7:19; 13:2, 3; 26:8; 28:46; 29:2; 34:11.

[37] The only other three occurrences are found in Exod 1:9; 3:10; 1 Kgs 20:15.

[38] Aaron's prophetic function, matches well with the Deuteronomic prophetic ideal (cf. Deut 18:9–22, in particular v. 18).

[39] Note the contrast with the summarizing statement in 11:10, according to which Moses and Aaron performed the miracles (ומשה ואהרן עשו את כל המפתים האלה לפני פרעה).

[40] BERNER, "Der literarische Charakter," 103–4.

[41] The author's terminological choice in 7:1 may be due to the Deuteronomic doctrine in Deut 18:9–18 (among the mantic practices, only the prophetic one is permitted).

in which YHWH addresses both Moses and Aaron (and which seems influenced by vv. 1–7):

Exodus 7:1–9 [secondary material underlined]

[1] And YHWH said to Moses, "See, I make you as God to Pharaoh, and your brother Aaron shall be your prophet. [2] You shall speak all that I command you, and your brother Aaron shall speak to Pharaoh that he let the Israelites go out of his land. [3] But I will harden Pharaoh's heart that I may multiply my signs and my wonders in the land of Egypt. [4] When Pharaoh will not listen to you, then I will lay my hand on Egypt, and bring out my hosts, my people the Israelites, from the land of Egypt by great judgments. [5] And the Egyptians shall know that I am YHWH, when I stretch out my hand against Egypt and bring out the Israelites from their midst." [6] So Moses and Aaron did it; as YHWH commanded them, thus they did. [7] And Moses was eighty years old and Aaron eighty-three, when they spoke to Pharaoh.

[8] And YHWH spoke to Moses and Aaron, saying, [9] "When Pharaoh speaks to you, saying, 'Work a miracle,' then you shall say to Aaron, 'Take your staff and throw it down before Pharaoh, that it may become a serpent.'"

What further supports this diachronic differentiation – the assignment of Exod 7:2–8 to a secondary layer – is the fact that in P[c] Aaron never plays the role of Moses's "mouthpiece"; on the contrary, *in all Priestly texts (P[c]) he remains silent!*[42] Moreover, this motif appears neither in the following non-P context (plagues narrative, killing of the firstborn, miracle of the sea). The following theological motive might explain the insertion of this passage: The author of 7:2–8 aimed to correct the narrative of the miracle theologically. Aaron should be given the more accepted role of a word prophet rather than that of a magician.

The introductory passage in 7:2–8 might be correlated with the motif of Moses's "foreskinned lips" (inept speech) in Exod 6:12bγ; Aaron's introduction as "word prophet" depends on the latter. Strikingly, this motif contrasts with the statement in 6:9, which gives another cause for the failure of Moses's mission to the Israelites (the latter's "anguish of spirit and cruel bondage"). Therefore, one should ask whether the motif of Moses's incompetent speech belongs to the primary Priestly stratum or whether it was inserted secondarily into its context.

EXCURSUS II: Was the Motif of Moses's Inept Speech Inserted Secondarily?

In Exod 6:12bγ, the author lets Moses refer to his "foreskinned lips" (see also the secondary *Wiederaufnahme* in 6:30). Why does the author use the expression "fore-skinned" (עָרֵל), which used metaphorically ("unskilled, inept") always has a negative connotation (Lev 26:41; Deut 10:16; Jer 4:4; 6:10; Ezek 44:7.9)?[43] Is the author fore-

---

[42] The only text attesting the "mouthpiece role" of Aaron is Exod 16 (see vv. 6, 9, 10), which, however, belongs to a secondary Priestly (P[s]) or post-Priestly stratum (see below, II.9.3.2).

[43] As PROPP, *Exodus 1–18*, 273, points out, the motif of uncircumcised organs is uniquely

shadowing some episode where Moses uses his lips in an inappropriate manner? In Exod 14:15 (commonly assigned to P[G]/P[C]), yhwh indeed rebukes Moses for crying to him. And in Num 20:10 (traditionally assigned to P[G]/P[C]; classification now disputed), Moses addresses himself in an inappropriate way to the Israelites (or so it seems in light of yhwh's reaction in 20:12). These statements contrast with the generally positive image of Moses presented in the Priestly strand and the "ideal anthropology" attributed to P[G]/P[C] by scholars.[44] For instance, it is noteworthy that at the climax of the miracle account, it is Moses and not Aaron who accomplishes the last miracle (see Exod 9:10). Regarding the two striking statements of Exod 6:12bγ and 14:15, it is significant that neither of them seems to be well anchored in its context: The last part of Exod 6:12, Moses's argument concerning his "foreskinned lips," follows rather abruptly on the rest of the verse:

Exodus 6:12
[12] But Moses spoke before yhwh, saying, "Behold, the Israelites have not listened to me; how then will Pharaoh listen to me, *and I am of uncircumcised lips* [ואני ערל שפתים]?"

As nentioned above, the motif of Moses's "uncircumcised lips" is absent from 6:9, which reports the failure of Moses's mission to the Israelites:

Exodus 6:9
[9] So Moses spoke thus to the Israelites, but they did not listen to Moses for anguish of spirit, and for cruel bondage.

According to this verse, the cause for the commission's failure has nothing to do with any defect of Moses.

Aaron's role in fulfilling the miracle further favors the assignment of Moses's inept speech to a secondary layer, as it gives the clear impression that Aaron assisted Moses because of his magical abilities rather than his eloquence.

As for yhwh's rebuke of Moses (Exod 14:15), it matches neither the preceding Priestly context (14:10) nor the previous non-P passage (Exod 14:11–14). The Priestly story reports the Israelites' crying out to yhwh in 14:10, but there is no mention of Moses's crying out.

Remarkably, all other Priestly texts in Exodus and Lev 1–16* depict Moses positively.

---

found in biblical texts. Further parts of the human body qualified as *ʿārēl* ("uncircumcised") are the ear (Jer 6:10) and the heart (Lev 26:41; Jer 9:25; Ezek 44:7, 9; cf. Deut 10:16; 30:6; Jer 4:4), "both associated with communication and understanding. In these passages, at issue is neither deafness nor a cardiac condition, but moral imperviousness to the divine word." (Propp, *Exodus 1–18*, 273). According to Propp, the author "probably invented the image of an 'uncircumcised' (....) mouth, in order to denigrate Moses" (see Propp, *Exodus 1–18*, 274). Bernat, *Sign*, 86, similarly detects a hidden polemic against Moses, wondering why the Priestly author uses such "a heavily laden term in the Priestly lexicon."

[44] See Pola, *Die ursprüngliche Priesterschrift*, 145.

(e) Exodus 7:8–11:10 (Priestly Miracle Account)

Concerning the Priestly account of the miracles, most scholars ascribe five miracles of similar structure to the primary stratum of P: the rod's transformation into a snake (Exod 7:8–13), the transformation of all water into blood (7:19–22*), the "invasion" of frogs (8:1–3), the plague of gnats (8:12–15), and the plague of boils with sores (9:8–12). The plague report concludes with a fitting summary (11:10). Regarding the literary classification, however, Kratz and Berner deviate from the *communis opinio*.[45] Because of its (alleged) breadth and the fact that it slows down the action, Kratz assigns the miracle report to a secondary Priestly layer. Another reason for him is that the exclusion of the Priestly plague account and the Passover instruction (see below) from the primary Priestly layer provides a sequence in which Aaron does not yet appear. In this reconstructed stratum Aaron would be introduced only in the tabernacle account, where he is more at home. As for the first argument, it is not compelling. When compared with the non-P plagues account, the Priestly miracle account is short; its sobriety and regular, redundant structure rather advocate for Priestly provenience (note also the emphasis on the correspondence between YHWH's commandment and its accomplishment by Moses and Aaron). The second argument, referring to P's conception, is worth considering, although it should be noted that there are no literary-critical reasons suggesting this option; furthermore, the narrative thread reconstructed by Kratz (running from Exod 6:1–8 directly to 12:41–42) seems thin and incomplete. P would, in any case, presuppose the non-P plague narrative (including the killing of the firstborn).

(f) Exodus 12:1–14, 15–20

Most scholars assign the Passover instruction and the announcement of the killing of the firstborn in 12:1–13 to P^G/P^C.[46] There are exceptions, however.[47] Because of the absence of a corresponding fulfillment account, Kratz considers this passage to

---

[45] KRATZ, *Composition*, 242–43; BERNER, "Der literarische Charakter," 103–4. Berner's argument is discussed above, (d).

[46] See for instance, ELLIGER, "Sinn," 121; GERTZ, *Tradition*, 31–37; BERNER, *Die Exoduserzählung*, 278–93, IDEM, "Der literarische Charakter," 118–23; DOZEMAN, *Commentary on Exodus*, 270–71; ALBERTZ, *Exodus 1–18*, 199.

[47] LOHFINK, "Die Priesterschrift," 198, n. 29; KRATZ, *Composition*, 242–43; J.-L. SKA, "Les plaies d'Égypte dans le récit sacerdotal (P^G)," *Bib* 60 (1979): 23–35. The reason for Ska's exclusion of the Passover instruction and the announcement of the killing of the firstborn is the "program speech" in Exod 7:1–5 which would aim to the account of the magicians' competition and that of the miracle at the sea rather than to the Passover prescription and the proclamation of the killing of the firstborn. However, the intertextual contacts mentioned by Ska are rather few and not close. The announcement that "the Egyptians shall know that I am YHWH" (Exod 7:5) is never fulfilled in the Priestly account (see below II.8.5); the particular assertion that YHWH will lay his hand upon Egypt (7:4) remains unparalleled in the subsequent Priestly sections. As shown above, there are several indications that the "program speech" in Exod 7:2–5 belongs to a secondary redaction.

be a secondary addition.[48] Yet this lacuna, like others in the Priestly strand, can be explained by P's nature as a redaction layer. In connection with this question, it is also necessary to point out a peculiarity of the vocabulary used in this passage. The term עֵדָה, "congregation," which occurs in Exod 12:3, 6, no longer is found in the texts undisputedly assigned to P[G]/P[C], but is frequent in later Priestly texts, in particular in Numbers.[49] One might assume that the term is used in view of the enactment of the first cultic law for Israel (i.e., the Passover prescription in Exod 12:1–8). Yet it is surprising to see that the term עֵדָה is absent from the main parts of the tabernacle account, appearing only in Exod 35:4, 20; 38:25 and lacking in the central chapters, Exod 25–29 and 40. It should be noted, however, that such peculiarities of vocabulary occur in other Priestly units as well (see above on Exod 6:6–8 and further below below, II.7.4 [a]). The section 12:1–14 is not unified. The statement in 12:14, which concludes the Passover provision, contradicts it: According to the latter, passover is celebrated in every "house" (בַּיִת, 12:3, 4), that is, within the limited circle of the family. Exodus 12:14, however, declares the feast to be a pilgrimage festival (חַג). Possibly, the assertion in v. 14 refers also to the Feast of Unleavened Bread (Mazzoth) in the passage 12:15–20 and belongs to the same redactional layer as the latter.[50]

Looking at the stipulation concerning Mazzoth, we note that it does not match the preceding instructions on the Passover. Whereas the latter is based on the guiding idea that Israel has to leave Egypt *in a hurry* (בְּחִפָּזוֹן, v.11), Exod 12:14, 15–20 prescribes a seven-day feast that begins on the evening of Passover (1/14). Another discrepancy concerns the characterization of the two feasts: Passover is celebrated in every "house" (בַּיִת, 12:3, 4), that is, within the limited circle of the family. According to Exod 12:14, however, Mazzoth should be celebrated as a pilgrimage festival (חַג). A third indication favoring the attribution of the two texts to two different layers is the following: whereas Exod 12:1–13 does not specify who is allowed or obligated to participate in the Passover, 12:19 makes clear that both the alien and the native-born Israelite must observe the festival of Mazzoth. However, it is possible that the subsection 12:18–20, which specifies the beginning and the end of the feast at the evening, is a later addition to Exod 12:14–17.

Furthermore, it is noteworthy that several expressions found in Exod 12:14–20 are frequently used in the Holiness Code and related texts, especially in Lev 23:5–8:[51]

– חֲגַג חַג לַיהוה ("celebrate it as a feast to YHWH," 12:14; cf. Lev 23:39, 41; Num 29:12)

---

[48] KRATZ, *Composition*, 242–43.

[49] The expression עֵדָה occurs in the manna story in Exod 16 and in the framing itinerary notices in 16:1, 17:1, which however should not assigned to primary Priestly stratum (see below, II.9.3.1–2.)

[50] PROPP, *Exodus 1–18*, 402; DOZEMAN, *Commentary on Exodus*, 270–71.

[51] See J. A. WAGENAAR, *Origin and Transformation of the Ancient Israelite Festival Calendar*, BZABR 6 (Wiesbaden: Harrassowitz, 2005), 94–95; NIHAN, *From Priestly Torah*, 564–65; ALBERTZ, *Exodus 1–18*, 199–200, with n. 4.

– לדרתיכם חקת עולם ("throughout your generations as a permanent ordinance," 12:14, 17; cf. Lev 23:14, 21, 31, 41)

– ונכרתה הנפש ההיא מישראל ("that person shall be cut off from Israel," 12:15, 19; cf. Lev 18:29; 19:8; 22:3 and Gen 17:14; Exod 31:14)

– כל מלאכה לא יעשה ("no work at all shall be done," 12:16; cf. Lev 23:3, 7, 8, 21, 25, 28, 31, 35, 36 and Lev 16:29; Num 29:7)

– מקרא קדש ("a holy announcement" [or "a holy convocation"], 12:16*bis*; cf. Lev 23:2, 3, 4, 7, 8, 21, 24, 27, 35, 36, 37 and six times in Num 28–29)

– בכל מושבתיכם ("in all your settlements," 12:20; cf. 23:3, 14, 21, 31)

As Wagenaar and Nihan show, Exod 12:14–20 probably revises the law of Lev 23:5–8.[52] The passage adopts the Mazzoth feast from the H law but envisages a simultaneous beginning of the celebration of the two feasts of Passover and Mazzoth (evening on the fourteenth of the first month). Furthermore, the ban on "day-to-day" work (Lev 23:7–8) is extended to the more severe prohibition in 12:16.

(g) Itinerary Notices in Exodus 12:37a; 13:20

A minority of scholars assign the two related itinerary notices in 12:37a and 13:20 to P.[53] Most scholars, however, agree on the non-Priestly (pre-Priestly) identity of these texts.[54] In fact, 12:37a is naturally connected to the preceding and subsequent non-Priestly material (12:31–36, 37b–39). Furthermore, if we consider 12:37a to be an integral part of P^c, this text and 12:40–41 would form a doublet, insofar as both report Israel's departure from Egypt. Additionally, it is significant that the two itinerary notices in question have nothing in common with the typical Priestly itinerary phrases in Exod 16:1aβγb; 17:1a; and 19:1, which are built on the more original non-P itinerary notices in Exod 16:1aα; 17:1b; and 19:2 (see further, below).[55] Typical Priestly language is absent from these texts, the only exception being בני ישראל in Exod 12:37a (which, however, appears also in non-Priestly texts[56]).

---

[52] See WAGENAAR, *Origin*, 93–96; NIHAN, *From Priestly Torah*, 564–65.

[53] WELLHAUSEN, *Die Composition*, 72, 76; CROSS, *Canaanite Myth*, 310; LOHFINK, "Die Priesterschrift," 198, n. 29; and more recently A. R. ROSKOP, *The Wilderness Itineraries: Genre, Geography, and the Growth of Torah*, History, Archaeology, and Culture of the Levant 3 (Winona Lake, IN: Eisenbrauns, 2011), esp. 136–218.

[54] ELLIGER, "Sinn," 121; NOTH, *Das zweite Buch Mose*, 72; LEVIN, *Der Jahwist*, 335; GERTZ, *Tradition*, 203, with n. 62.; KRATZ, *Composition*, 294; PROPP, *Exodus 1–18*, 380, 461; DOZEMAN, "The Priestly Wilderness Itineraries and the Composition of the Pentateuch," in *The Pentateuch: International Perspectives on Current Research*, ed. T. B. Dozeman, K. Schmid, and B. J. Schwartz, FAT 78 (Tübingen: Mohr Siebeck, 2011), 262–66; ALBERTZ, *Exodus 1–18*, 216, 237; BERNER, "Der literarische Charakter," 121; UTZSCHNEIDER and OSWALD, *Exodus 1–15*, 270, 294–97.

[55] See below, II.9.3.1, 3. Characteristic Priestly elements are עדה, "congregation" (16:1aβγb; 17:1a), בוא in itinerary notices (16:1aβγb; 19:1), and datings (16:1aβγb; 19:1).

[56] See the following non-P texts: Gen 32:33; Gen 42:5; 45:21; 46:5; 50:25; Exod 1:9, 12; 4:29,

(h) Exodus 12:43–51

This passage regulates the participation of different groups of alien persons in Passover. The passage distinguishes between persons living temporarily (בן נכר, "foreigner"; תושב, "alien client"; שכיר, "day laborer") and those living permanently (מקנת כסף, "purchased slave"; גר, "resident alien") in the land. Only the latter are allowed to participate in the Passover festival, and only on the condition that they are circumcised.

Among scholars, it is widely accepted that the passage was inserted secondarily.[57] It shares several commonalities with the prescriptions of the Holiness code (see especially Lev 22:10–11[58]), on the one hand, and with Gen 17:10–14,[59] dealing with circumcision (which is also close to H), on the other.[60]

7.4 The Literary Profile of the Priestly Texts

(a) Source or Redaction?

Extensive Priestly portions of Exod 1–11 texts can be read as a continuous strand. They first report Israel's stay in Egypt, their growth into a numerous people, and their oppression by the Egyptians. God's awareness of and compassion for the Israelites marks the narrative's turning point, which leads to the deity's self-presentation to Moses and the latter's commissioning to speak to his people, who do not listen. Afterward, he is sent to Pharaoh. But Moses, citing the people's refusal objects to YHWH's directive. As a consequence, Aaron is appointed by YHWH to be Moses's "prophet." Together, Moses and Aaron accomplish five miracles, which, however, do not change Pharaoh's mind. YHWH's announcement that he will strike the Egyptian firstborn and his instructions for the celebration of Israel's first Passover follow. There is no report of these being accomplished, however. P mentions Israel's "exodus" only briefly.

31; 5:14, 15, 19; 9:4, 6, 26, 35; 10:20, 23; 11:7; 12:31, 35; 13:2, 18, 19; 17:7; 19:3, 6; 20:22: 24:5, 11 (among others).

[57] See, among others, NOTH, *Das zweite Buch Mose*, 72, 78; CHILDS, *Exodus*, 200; GRÜNWALDT, *Exil und Identität*, 71; KRATZ, *Composition*, 242; ALBERTZ, *Exodus 1–18*, 199–200, 218–19; WÖHRLE, "Integrative Function," 71–87, esp. 81–84.

[58] According to Lev 22:10–11, of alien persons only purchased slaves of the priests are allowed to eat the "holy things"; alien clients (תושב) and daily laborers (שכיר) are forbidden. Further common expressions with H are בן נכר (Exod 12:43; Lev 22:25); the combination גור and גר (Exod 12:48–49; Lev 17:8, 10, 12, 13; 18:26; 19:33, 34; 20:2); and the combination אזרח and גר (Exod 12:49; Lev 17:15; 18:26; 19:34).

[59] Common expressions include מקנה כסף (Exod 12:44; Gen 17:12, 13, 23, 27; does not occur elsewhere in HB); בן נכר (Exod 12:43; Gen 17:12, 27; only one other occurrence in HB, in Lev 22:25).

[60] See ALBERTZ, *Exodus 1–18*, 199–200, 218–19, and especially WÖHRLE, "Integrative Function," 81–84. See the analysis of Gen 17:9–14 in II.6.4 (b).

Afterward, P can be identified again only beginning in Exod 14, where the Priestly layer relates Israel's (YHWH's) ultimate victory over the Egyptians at the Sea of Reeds.

Since P partly constitutes an uninterrupted literary strand in Exod 1–12, the Priestly layer is often considered an independent source. But this is problematic because P contains some lacunae. First, Moses's appearance is unannounced, so that there is no adequate introduction of the story's main protagonist.

Some scholars see in the LXX reading of Exod 2:25 ("he made himself known, revealed himself to them") a confirmation of an original direct consecutive to 2:23aβ–25 and 6:2–9.[61] It can not to be ruled out that LXX reflects the original text.[62] ידע niphal, "to make oneself know, reveal," also appears in Exod 6:3. However, the direct transition between 2:23aβ–25 and 6:2–9 in this reconstructed text is awkward too, owing to the absence of an appropriate introduction for Moses. It seems more plausible that these Priestly passages were composed as redactional supplements to an already-existing non-P text in which Moses was properly introduced (Exod 2:1–10).

Second, as already mentioned, YHWH's striking of the Egyptian firstborn and the celebration of Israel's first Passover are not reported.

In these cases, P must be dependent on the adjacent non-P passages, unless we are to assume the loss of similar text sequences in P during the process of combining P and non-P. An indication favoring the redaction hypothesis is the fact that in the passage about YHWH's self-presentation, P refers to the preceding (or subsequent) non-Priestly texts by taking up certain motifs and specific expressions (סבלות, "burden bearing, compulsory labor";[63] נצל hiphil, "to pull out, deliver"[64]) that occur often but do not appear elsewhere in the Priestly strand.[65] As already shown above, P also takes up an expression in Exod 1:7 (the verb עצם, "to become mighty") that is used in adjacent non-Priestly texts.

Scholars defending the source model also note the (alleged) redundancy of certain units of the Priestly account. The short passage Exod 1:13–14, reporting Israel's forced labor, shares similar content with the preceding vv. 11–12, creating a doublet and at first sight supporting the idea that it was composed for an independent document. Nevertheless, these verses are also understandable as a redactional complement to the non-Priestly strand, in that they either point out a further dispersion and intensification of the forced labor (cf. Albertz)[66] or "explore the legal background of the Egyptian oppression" (Dozeman).[67] The specific legal term בפרך, "with force, violence," is also used in the legislation of Lev 25:35–55 on slavery and its termination.

---

[61] Cf., for instance, W. H. SCHMIDT, *Exodus*, 79; RÖMER, "From the Call of Moses," 132.

[62] See above, II.7.2 (c).

[63] Cf. Exod 1:11; 2:11; 5:4, 5 (all texts belong to non-P strands).

[64] Cf. Exod 2:19; 3:8; 5:23 (2×); 12:27; 18:4, 8, 9, 10 (2×) (all texts belong to non-P strands).

[65] Cf. BLUM, *Studien*, 234–35; RÖMER, *Moïse*, 151.

[66] See ALBERTZ, *Exodus 1–18*, 48. According to Albertz, the specification "at all kinds of labor in the field" (Exod 1:14) indicates that in addition to public projects the Israelites were also enslaved in the private sector.

[67] See DOZEMAN, *Commentary on Exodus*, 72.

God's self-presentation (Exod 6:2–9) is another allegedly redundant account, read in relation to the preceding non-Priestly story in Exod 3. Read synchronically, one might get the impression that Exod 6 doubles Moses's calling and the statement of YHWH's revelation of his name (Exod 3:15–16). Since the non-P account of YHWH's revelation in Exod 3 is considered to predate the Priestly episode in Exod 6 by the majority of scholars, many argue that the Priestly account is only understandable as part of an *autonomous source text*, which was later combined with an older non-P report.[68] However, first it is worth noting that Exod 6:2–9 is not a report of Moses' call but rather an account on YHWH's self-presentation. As Utzschneider and Oswald show, the characteristic elements of the "vocation schema" are absent from Exod 6:2–9.[69] Furthermore, it is striking that the passage is introduced not with the verb "to reveal," as in Exod 3:2 (ראה *hiphil*) and in the Priestly texts Gen 17:1; 35:9 (in all these cases, ראה *niphal* is used), but simply with "he spoke" (דבר *piel*).[70] In addition, there are good arguments for considering the alleged pre-Priestly account Exod 3 a post-Priestly insertion.[71]

Scholars advocating the source model also point to the regular structure and elaborate character of a particular Priestly composition belonging to this section: the Priestly miracle account (Exod 7:1–11:10 P).[72] This unit resembles the "autonomous" and self-contained Priestly units in Genesis. J. Reindl argues that P would have integrated an independent, "single" story that originated in the Judean Egyptian diaspora.[73]

What are the outline and structure of the Priestly miracle narrative?

P[C] reports five miracles within Exod 7–11: transformation of the staff into a serpent (Exod 7:8–13), transformation of all water into blood (7:19–22*), the "assault" of frogs (8:1–3), the plague of gnats (8:12–15), and the plague of boils with sores (9:8–12). The end consists of a resumptive statement (11:10). In this presentation, competition between magicians plays a dominant role. Gertz rightly argues that the Priestly stratum deals primarily with miracles (*Schauwunder*) rather than plagues (as in the non-P passages).[74] Aaron's role is likely parallel to that of his Egyptian competitors, who are constantly called by the Egyptian loanword חרטמים, "soothsayer priests, magicians." The latter's identity as magicians also becomes clear through the fact that they act בלהטיהם, "with their enchantments" (7:11, 22; 8:3, 14).[75] The competition between

---

[68] Cf., among others, NOTH, *Das zweite Buch Mose*, 42; KOCH, "P – kein Redaktor!," 462–67; RÖMER, *Moïse*, 151.

[69] UTZSCHNEIDER and OSWALD, *Exodus 1–15*, 161; the main elements of the vocation schema are "mission and sending – objection – assurance of support – sign."

[70] See UTZSCHNEIDER and OSWALD, *Exodus 1–15*, 161–62.

[71] See below, II.7.5 (b).

[72] See J. REINDL, "Der Finger Gottes und die Macht der Götter: Ein Problem des ägyptischen Diasporajudentums und sein literarischer Niederschlag," in W. Ernst et al. (eds.), *Dienst der Vermittlung: Festschrift zum 25-jährigen Bestehen des Priesterseminars Erfurt*, ETS 37 (Leipzig: St. Benno Verlag, 1977), 49–60; BLUM, *Studien*, 250–52 (who nevertheless does not support the source model); RÖMER, "From the Call of Moses," 139–44.

[73] REINDL, "Der Finger Gottes," 49–60.

[74] GERTZ, *Tradition*, 82, with n. 24.

[75] RÖMER, *Moïse*, 164–65.

Hebrew and Egyptian magicians consists in each case first of a miracle accomplished by Aaron or (and) Moses and second of the Egyptian magicians' attempt to reproduce the miracle. This structure implies that the magical transformation for each miracle is brief; in each case, the return to the natural state is implicit, as the Egyptian magicians could not "repeat" the miracle performed by Moses and Aaron otherwise. The Egyptian magicians succeed in reproducing the first three wonders. As for the fourth and the fifth miracles, however, the Egyptian magicians fail: after the fourth wonder they are forced to acknowledge the superiority of their adversaries, and after the fifth they are themselves afflicted with boils, the result of the miracle accomplished by Moses. This paraphrasing shows that the Priestly account has a clear, sober structure with an inherent climax. Strikingly, all five miracles have a goal that is negative or dangerous for Egypt. The results of the first three actions have considerable potential for danger: emergence of a snake (or rather, a crocodile), complete destruction of water resources, and an invasion of frogs. The two final miracles are factually disastrous for the Egyptians, who are afflicted by gnats (fourth miracle; 8:14) and boils (fifth miracle; 9:11). The idea that the Egyptian magicians imperil their people every time they copy a miracle performed by Moses and Aaron should be considered a polemical feature. The magician-priests are not only inferior to Aaron and Moses but also silly.[76]

When compared with the self-contained proto-Priestly compositions in Gen 1–25, it appears that the miracle account is not a well-marked unit having a clear beginning and end. The beginning of the episode lacks exposition. Furthermore, its conclusion in Exod 11:10 seems preliminary: The fact that Pharaoh's heart is again hardened by YHWH at the end, after the fifth miracle, indicates that the story was conceived *as having a continuation*, namely the Priestly Passover episode. These details weaken Reindl's theory that the report of the five miracles was a single and self-contained story. (Reindl includes the motif of Pharaoh's hardened heart in his reconstruction of the assumed Egyptian diaspora story.)[77]

Furthermore, even if this Priestly text was composed as a short, single document, its literary character makes it likely that its author knew and had in mind the presupposed non-P texts. As will be shown below, the Priestly composition depends on the exposition (introduction) of the older non-P strand (Exod 7:14–18), which locates the plot on the shore of the Nile, and was composed in view of the latter.[78] The regular structure and elaborate character of the story may be explained by assuming the following compositional procedure: first the unit was composed as a separate text, and then it was integrated into the non-P narrative strand.[79] Further indicating such a procedure is that the five Priestly miracles are very brief and schematic in structure; they lack any concretization, as for example the localization of the protagonists or chronological indications. This striking feature can be explained by the author's intention to provide the simplest possible form for each element, to make it easily combinable with the more ancient non-P plague narrative, which provides some concretization (see Exod 7:14–15; 8:16).

---

[76] Cf. also BERNER, "Der literarische Charakter," 116–17.

[77] REINDL, "Der Finger Gottes," 49–60.

[78] See the detailed argument below, II.7.5 (c).

[79] ALBERTZ, *Exodus 1–18*, 122, 141–42.

(b) One or Several Priestly Authors?

An additional argument against the theory of a unified P source is the difference in vocabulary, style, and motif between the various Priestly accounts. For instance, as mentioned above, the expression עֵדָה, "congregation," appears several times in the Priestly texts of Exod 12 but never in the miracle account or in Exod 14.[80]

Similarly, the term צָבָא, "host," which in the book of Numbers frequently depicts Israel as an organized army, appears in the Priestly texts of Exodus sporadically in this sense and always in the plural ("regiments"): in the introduction to the miracle narrative (6:26; 7:4) and in the notice concerning Israel's exodus (12:41, 51).[81] It is absent from the story of the miracle at the sea, the manna story and the tabernacle account.

Strikingly, one pericope, Exod 6:2–9, is much more influenced by the book of Ezekiel than are the other Priestly units, sharing a significant number of linguistic commonalities.[82]

These linguistic and also at times conceptual differences between the Priestly texts in Exod 1–14 (and beyond), which nevertheless go hand in hand with a generally observable conceptual and ideological coherence, seem to be overlooked in current scholarship. They speak against the general understanding of the Priestly texts as a unified strand in this section.[83] The evidence instead favors the idea that the Priestly texts were written by a number of distinct authors who may also have collaborated together.

7.5 The Literary Relationship between the P and the Non-P Strata

The examination in the preceding section made it likely that the Priestly stratum depends on and complements a preexisting non-Priestly stratum. However, as in other sections, the question of the relationship between neighboring Priestly and non-Priestly strata is complex. The non-Priestly strand probably also contains some post-Priestly texts. Yet, in the framework of the present study on Priestly texts, it is not

---

[80] Cf. Exod 12:3, 6, 19, 47.

[81] The expression is used predominantly in the Priestly texts of Numbers: Num 1–10 (61×); 26:2; 31 (13×); 32:27; 33:1. In Gen 2:1 (proto-P), צָבָא has a different sense ("host [of beings]"); see above, I.2.3 (a).

[82] See above, II.7.3 (b). JEON, "Source of P?," 90, sees an "indirect" influence by Ezekiel on the Priestly miracle accounts, especially in what concerns the תַּנִּין imagery.

[83] Pᴳ/Pᶜ is considered a "monolithic" block by most scholars (see above, I.1.1 [3]), expressed in the use of the singular "the Priestly author" by these critics. There are nevertheless some exceptions: J. Wellhausen contests the conceptual coherence of P (see WELLHAUSEN, *Die Composition*, 72–73: "Es ist übrigens, was wir als Q bezeichnen, hier schwerlich als ein schriftstellerisches Ganzes von einheitlicher Conception"). I. Knohl, J. Milgrom, and E. Blum propose that Pᶜ (in their terminology, "Priestly Torah," "P," and "Kompositionsschicht," respectively) was composed by a group or a "school" (see KNOHL, *Sanctuary*, 220–22; MILGROM, *Leviticus 1–16*, 2; BLUM, "Noch einmal," 53, n. 67); see further below, III.1.2.1.

possible to give a detailed and conclusive analysis of all non-Priestly texts. Nevertheless, the following paragraphs will present some preliminary observations and considerations. This investigation is important for the question of the literary "origin" of certain key motifs that appear in both strands, for instance, Israel's move from Canaan to Egypt, YHWH's revelation (or self-presentation), and Aaron's assistance to Moses. We must ask for each one of these motifs whether it was initially introduced by a Priestly or a non-Priestly author.

(a) Exodus 1:7, 13–14 and Adjacent Non-Priestly Texts

Exodus 1:7 plays a central role in the question of the relationship between the Priestly and the non-Priestly strand at the beginning of the book of Exodus. Its connection to its nearer non-P context is a matter of controversy.

Exodus 1:7

⁷ ובני ישראל פרו וישרצו וירבו ויעצמו במאד מאד ותמלא הארץ אתם

[7] But the Israelites were fruitful and increased greatly, and multiplied, and became exceedingly mighty, so that the land was filled with them.

K. Schmid argues that Pharaoh's statement about Israel's strength and greatness in 1:9 depends on 1:7 and therefore cannot be older than this text.[84]

Exodus 1:9

⁹ ויאמר אל עמו הנה עם בני ישראל רב ועצום ממנו

[9] And he said to his people, "Behold, the people of the Israelites are too numerous and mighty for us [or: Israel are more and mightier than we]."[85]

It is striking that the expressions בני ישראל and רב and the root עצם also appear in the Priestly text 1:7. However, it is noteworthy that all these terms also appear in non-P texts in the exodus narrative and in the Joseph story as well.[86] Thus, it is no surprise that others see the dependence the other way round, taking the occurrence of the verb עצם, "to become mighty," in 1:7 as an indication that v. 7 is dependent on non-P. Indeed it is striking that the root עצם (both the verb עצם and the adjective עצום, "mighty") appears twice in the close non-P context (in Exod 1:9, 20) but is absent elsewhere in P.[87] Therefore it is probable that the author of 1:7 (P) picked up עצם from the non-P context (see above).[88]

---

[84] Cf. Schmid, *Genesis and the Moses Story*, 63–65.

[85] For the preferred translation, see below.

[86] The designation בני ישראל, "the children of Israel, the Israelites," in 1:9, which is characteristic of Priestly texts, appears frequently in non-P texts of both the Joseph story and the exodus narrative (for a list of such texts, see above in n. 56). For עצום and רב in non-P, cf. below.

[87] Besides the texts mentioned, the root appears in Genesis–Numbers only in Gen 18:18; 26:16; Num 14:12.

[88] Thus Albertz, *Exodus 1–18*, 42. Differently Römer, *Moïse*, 44–45, who considers the lexeme ויעצמו a harmonizing addition.

The comparative רב ועצום ממנו in v. 9 can be understood either as "more and mightier than we"[89] or as "too many and too mighty for us."[90] Grammatically, both readings are possible, as both are attested elsewhere in the Hebrew Bible.[91] At first sight, the second understanding seems to fit the context better and to be more "realistic." In contrast to the first interpretation, it does not imply the argument that the Israelites are more numerous than the Egyptians.[92] Nevertheless, as part of a despot's propaganda, such a statement is possible.

If Exod 1:9 does not presuppose 1:7, then what other texts reporting Israel's growth might it depend on? Given the understanding of the comparative רב ועצום ממנו in v. 9 ("too many and too mighty for us") proposed above, two statements in the Joseph story that evoke Israel's development into a "great people" may have served as preparation for the assertion in Exod 1:8–9.

Genesis 45:7

[7] [Then Joseph said to his brothers:] "And God sent me before you to preserve for you a remnant on the earth, and to keep alive for you a great group of survivors [לשום לכם שארית בארץ ולהחיות לכם לפליטה גדלה]."

Genesis 50:20b

[20b] [And Joseph said to them:] "But God meant it for good in order to bring about this present result, to preserve a great people alive [עם רב]."

Genesis 50:20 is often considered the end of the original Joseph narrative.[93] Genesis 45:7 is usually assigned to the original stratum of the Joseph story. The statements depicting Israel as a "great group of survivors" (לפליטה גדלה) and a "great people" (עם רב) allude to Israel's growth and thus develop "a national perspective for Israel."[94] Thus, it seems possible that these passages in the Joseph story look head to the expression in Exod 1:9 of Israel's magnitude and strength. It is striking that one of these two texts, Gen 50:20, has two expressions in common with Exod 1:9 (עם רב); this points to the relatedness of at least these latter texts.[95] Yet, according to Schmid, Gen 45:7 and

---

[89] Cf., among others, KJV, NASB, Nouvelle Edition de Genève, and Einheitsübersetzung.

[90] Cf., among others, RSV, NJPS, TOB, and Neue Zürcher Übersetzung. For the construction, see *GKC* §133c; Joüon-Muraoka §141i.

[91] For the first understanding, cf. Num 14:12; Deut 4:38; 7:1; 9:14; 11:23; 20:1; for the second understanding, cf. Gen 26:16; Exod 18:18; Num 11:14; Deut 1:17; Ps 38:5.

[92] See C. Houtman, *Exodus*, 4 vols., HCOT (Kampen: Kok, 1993–2002), 1:236.

[93] See von Rad, *Das erste Buch*, 378; Blum, *Die Komposition*, 255, Schmid, *Genesis and the Moses Story*, 95. The question is controversial, and a number of scholars consider Gen 50:15–21a to be a secondary conclusion of the Joseph story (cf., among others, D. B. Redford, *A Study of the Biblical Story of Joseph [Genesis 37–50]*, VTSup 20 [Leiden: Brill, 1970], 163–64; C. Westermann, *Genesis 37–50*, BK I.3 [Neukirchen-Vluyn: Neukirchener Verlag, 1982], 230–31; Van Seters, *Prologue*, 323).

[94] Cf. Schmid, *Genesis and the Moses Story*, 54; see also 64, n. 87.

[95] For רב, cf. also Exod 5:5 (non-P). Beside Schmid (*Genesis and the Moses Story*, 54, see the preceding footnote), L. Schmidt, *Literarische Studien zur Josephsgeschichte*, BZAW 167 (Berlin: de Gruyter, 1986), 216 and H. Seebass, *Genesis III: Josephsgeschichte (37,1–50,26)*

50:20 "do not originally have the exodus event in view"[96] but should rather be seen in relation to the theme of the deliverance from famine. However, it seems that at least the striking expression, עַם, "people," cannot be explained by the narrow context of the Joseph story. It is more probable that the author used the term to allude to Jacob/Israel's growth into a veritable people, to prepare for the transition to the exodus narrative. One may even go further: the use of the term עַם, "people," may be considered a clue that the author did not know the Priestly assertion about multiplication and growth in Exod 1:7 (or any other statement containing this motif at the beginning of the Exodus story[97]): If he presupposed this statement, the choice of the peculiar expression עַם, "people," in Gen 50:20 would not be necessary.

On the whole, it is more likely that Exod 1:7 presupposes an existing transition between the Joseph story and the exodus narrative beginning in Exod 1:8.

The relationship of the following Priestly passage, Exod 1:13, 14, to non-P seems to be similar. As argued above, the two Priestly verses may complement the non-P context (1:8–12, 15).[98]

(b) Exodus 2:23aβ–25; 6:2–9 and Adjacent Non-Priestly Texts

The discussion above (II.7.4 [a]) revealed strong indications that the Priestly texts Exod 2:23aβ–25 and 6:2–9 presuppose adjacent non-Priestly texts (i.e., in Exod 1:8–2:23aα; 4:19–6:1). Exodus 6:2–12 takes up certain motifs and expressions found in the non-P texts of Exod 2 and 5 (סבלות, "burden bearing, compulsory labor"; נצל hiphil, "to pull out, deliver") that do not appear elsewhere in the Priestly strand.[99] It is uncertain whether P also presupposes the comprehensive insertion in Exod 3:1–4:18. Traditionally, Exod 3* is thought to predate Exod 6 P. Recently, however, Otto and K. Schmid have put forward several arguments favoring the opposite direction of dependence, meaning that the Priestly account of yhwh's revelation would predate Exod 3:1–4:18.[100] The starting point of this consideration is the observation of J. Wellhausen and others that Exod 3:1–4:18 interrupts the sequence of 2:1–23aα and 4:19ff., which

---

(Neukirchen-Vluyn: Neukirchener Verlag, 2000), 200, also point to this correspondence and interpret 50:20 as an allusion to the Israelites in Egypt.

[96] SCHMID, *Genesis and the Moses Story*, 54; see also 64, n. 87.

[97] Some scholars reckon with the suppression of such a statement in non-P in the course of the insertion of the Priestly text 1:7. Cf. BLUM, "Die literarische Verbindung von Erzvätern und Exodus: Ein Gespräch mit neueren Forschungshypothesen," in *Abschied vom Jahwisten: Die Komposition des Hexateuch in der jüngsten Diskussion*, ed. J. C. Gertz, K. Schmid, and M. Witte, BZAW 315 (Berlin: de Gruyter, 2002), 147; ALBERTZ, *Exodus 1–18*, 42.

[98] See the preceding section (II.7.4 [a]).

[99] See above, II.7.4 (a).

[100] E. OTTO, "Die nachpriesterliche Pentateuchredaktion im Buch Exodus," in *Studies in the Book of Exodus: Redaction – Reception – Interpretation*, ed. M. Vervenne, BETL 126 (Leuven: Leuven University Press, 1996), 108–111; SCHMID, *Genesis and the Moses Story*, 172–93. They are now also followed by BERNER, "Der literarische Charakter," 106–7.

locate the story in the land of Midian.[101] There are indeed indications that 3:1–4:18 constitutes a secondary insertion. Interestingly, the LXX in 4:19 takes up the statement of 2:23aα concerning the death of the Egyptian king. It is tempting to see in it a *Wiederaufnahme* following the insertion of 3:1–4:18. In MT, the phrase would have been omitted. Otherwise, the repetition of this statement in LXX is difficult to explain. A rather late setting for this unit is suggested by the fact that it alludes to several themes found in the broader context: revelation of the law at Horeb, conquest of the land, and plagues (miracles). Interestingly, besides the name Horeb, which is mentioned explicitly in 3:1, the toponym Sinai is perhaps alluded to by the designation for the thornbush (סנה; see 3:2–4).[102] This may point to a late composition that aimed to harmonize the two toponymic traditions.[103] The use of different theonyms ("messenger of YHWH," YHWH, Elohim, "God of your father, God of Abraham, God of Isaac, God of Jacob") might have a similar integrative function. The fact that God refuses to reveal his name in his dialogue with Moses (see 3:13–14) can indeed be read as a reaction against the theonym theory of P, which emphasizes the importance of God's names, in particular that of YHWH (see Exod 6:2–3). According to the non-Priestly author, the essential idea is not God's name but his decision "to be with Moses (Israel)" see אהיה in 3:12, 14), as was experienced also by Moses's father and ancestors and as is reported from generation to generation.[104] As for Exod 4:1–18, certain indications favor the idea that this passage depends on the Priestly miracle account and aims to correct it. Aaron's role is limited to a mouthpiece of Moses and the staff miracles are transmitted from Aaron to Moses.[105] Summing up, it is tempting to see in Exod 3:1–4:18 a late redactional and possibly post-Priestly insertion.[106] Nevertheless, it cannot be ruled out

---

[101] Cf. WELLHAUSEN, *Die Composition*, 71; W. RUDOLPH, *Der "Elohist" von Exodus bis Joshua*, BZAW 68 (Berlin: Töpelmann, 1938), 6–7; NOTH, *Überlieferungsgeschichtliche Studien*, 31–32, n. 103.

[102] Whereas the name Horeb is explicitly mentioned (cf. 3:1), the toponym Sinai is presumably alluded to by the motif of the burning thornbush (סנה); cf. SCHMID, *Genesis and the Moses Story*, 185–86.

[103] BLUM, *Die Komposition*, 28, n. 85, however, believes that the name Horeb in 3:1 is a late substitution by a Dtn/Dtr redaction for the original toponym, Sinai.

[104] The argument is put differently by OTTO, "Die nachpriesterliche Pentateuchredaktion," 108–11, according to whom the author of Exod 3–4, i.e., his Pentateuch redactor, aimed to level out P's purposeful differentiation between theonyms.

[105] See Excursus III at the end of the following section.

[106] Other arguments by Schmid and Otto seem less conclusive. They argue that a secondary relocalization of YHWH's revelation in Egypt (instead of Sinai) by P is more difficult to imagine than a correction toward Horeb/Sinai in Exod 3 (in agreement with Exod 19–24) (see OTTO, "Forschungen zur Priesterschrift," 10–11; SCHMID, *Genesis*, 186). With regard to the lack of any toponym in Exod 6:2–9, this argument loses its weight (see J. JEON, *The Call of Moses and the Exodus Story: A Redactional-Critical Study in Exodus 3–4 and 5–13*. FAT 60 [Tübingen: Mohr Siebeck, 2013], 193–94). Furthermore, Schmid points out several motifs and expressions in Exod 3:6–7 that occur in the preceding Priestly text Exod 2:24–25 (צעקה, "screaming"; שמע; ראה; ידע) and would depend on the latter. For a different evaluation of this intertextual context, see JEON, *Call*, 191–92.

that the narrative in Exod 3 is built on an old tradition, although there is no sure indication favoring such a theory.[107]

What must be considered, however, is that without Exod 3:1–4:18 the non-Priestly strand remains incomplete. The narrative in Exod 5*, which deals with Moses' conversation with Pharaoh, and which is presupposed in the Priestly 6:2–9 (see above), needs an introduction including the commission to Moses to speak to Pharaoh. Such an introduction might originally have been included in Exod 4–5*, but would later have been replaced by the secondary introduction of Aaron and the commission to Moses and Aaron (cf. the present text in Exod 4).[108]

(c) The Priestly Miracle Account (Exodus 7:1–11:10) and Adjacent Non-Priestly Texts

Several scholars take the even and regular structure of the Priestly stratum of the plague account in Exod 7–11 as an indication that it was originally an autonomous miracle or plague account (see above II.7.4 [a]). However, there are indications that the Priestly miracle account depends on the non-P plague narrative and was composed in view of it. A first argument is as follows: only the non-P report of the Nile's pollution contains a fitting introduction (7:14–16 non-P, which is the continuation of Exod 5:1–6:1*, non-P). It relocates the plot on the shore of the Nile.[109] As noted above, the thin and sober structure of the Priestly composition, which lacks any chronological indications or localization for its protagonists, might have been chosen by the Priestly author in order to better embed the five miracles in the non-Priestly thread.[110] Furthermore, it seems more likely that the fantastical Priestly motif of the transformation of all Egyptian water into blood originated from the simple transformation of the Nile to blood (found in the non-P strand; see Exod 7:17–18), rather than tracing a literary evolution in the opposite direction.[111] The author of the pre-Priestly text might have been influenced by the Admonitions of Ipu-wer, which used the motif of the transformation of the Nile's water into blood as well.[112]

---

[107] The distinct name of Moses's father-in-law, Jethro (cf. Exod 3:1; 4:18 [Jether]; 18:1–2, 5–6, 9–10, 12), when compared with Reuel in Exod 2:18, might support the thesis of an old, independent tradition. It is, however, not to be excluded that the name is an invention to avoid the name Reuel, whose possible meaning "friend (confident) of God" (see NOTH, *Die Israelitischen Personennamen*, 153–54) was perhaps felt to be inappropriate because it conflicts with the role of Moses in the story of Exod 3.

[108] BLUM, *Die Komposition*, 27–28 and ALBERTZ, *Exodus 1–18*, 88, with n. 25, suggest that the original commission would have been given to Moses and the elders (according to Exod 3:16–20).

[109] Cf. GERTZ, *Tradition*, 105; BERNER, *Die Exoduserzählung*, 169–70; UTZSCHNEIDER and OSWALD, *Exodus 1–15*, 198–99, n. 2.

[110] See above, II.7.4 (a).

[111] There is no literary-critical argument for the exclusion of the blood motif from the non-Priestly stratum; see ALBERTZ, *Exodus 1–18*, 144, *pace* NOTH, *Das zweite Buch Mose*, 55; BERNER, *Die Exoduserzählung*, 174–75 and others.

[112] Admonitions 2:10. See A. H. GARDINER, *The Admonitions of an Egyptian Sage* (Leipzig: J.

EXCURSUS III: The Emergence of the Motif of Aaron as Moses's Assistant

Aaron is only rarely mentioned in the pre-Priestly plague narrative (fish dying, frogs, flies, pestilence on livestock, death of the firstborn). As the dialogue partner and adversary of Pharaoh, only Moses is firmly anchored in the plot.[113] Most scholars agree that references to Aaron are secondary and that the primary version of the pre-Priestly narrative had Moses negotiating with Pharaoh and announcing the plagues without Aaron's assistance.[114]

Aaron is first introduced in the non-Priestly strand of the previous chapters (Exod 1–5) in 4:14–17, which is often considered post-Priestly.[115] In 4:14, Aaron is explicitly called a Levite. Blum detects here a pro-Levite perspective. He points to the particular spelling לֵוִי instead of בֶּן לֵוִי in the sentence in 4:14 ("Aaron is also a Levite"). More specifically, one might see in this designation an attempt to gloss over the privileged position of the Aaronides among the Levites in the Priestly conception (Aaron is a Levite – and no more!).[116] Aaron's relegation to Moses's mouthpiece (compared with his role in the Priestly miracle account, where he fulfills the role of magician) also gives the impression that Exod 4:1–9 is reacting to the Priestly miracle story.[117] Moreover, the fact that Moses performs miracles with his staff instead of Aaron (see Exod 4:1–9) points to the assumed polemical (anti-Priestly) tendency of the whole passage of Exod 4:1–17.

In the following non-P texts (4:27–31; 5:1–21), Aaron appears several times. Many scholars believe that all mentions of Aaron in these texts are secondary, too.[118] Indications of redaction-critical differentiation are as follows: 5:23a ("Ever since I came to Pharaoh to speak in your name, he has done harm to this people") hints at a more primary version of the text in which only Moses negotiated with Pharaoh.[119] Furthermore, the beginning of the first non-Priestly plague, which in 7:14–16 explicitly harks

---

C. Hinrichs, 1909), 27; N. SHUPAK, "The Admonitions of an Egyptian Sage: The Admonitions of Ipuwer (1.42)," *COS* 1:94.

[113] Aaron is mentioned, always together with Moses, only in Exod 8:4, 8, 21; 12:31. Moses appears as Pharaoh's unique counterpart in 7:14, 26; 8:5, 9, 16, 22, 25, 26, 27; 9:1, 13, 22, 23, 29, 33.

[114] See, among others, NOTH, *Das zweite Buch Mose*, 57; BLUM, *Die Komposition*, 255, n. 95; ALBERTZ, *Exodus 1–18*, 142, 156, 173, 202; UTZSCHNEIDER and OSWALD, *Exodus 1–15*, 160, 195, 212, 217, 226, 284.

[115] ALBERTZ, *Exodus 1–18*, 91–93; RÖMER, *Moïse*, 130–31.

[116] BLUM, *Studien*, 362.

[117] ALBERTZ, *Exodus 1–18*, 93; RÖMER, *Moïse*, 130–31. It is also imaginable that the non-Priestly author was acquainted with the secondary Priestly passage in Exod 7:2–8, which presents Aaron as a "word prophet" and as Moses's "mouthpiece" too (see above, II.7.3 [d]), and influenced by it. If this is the case, the non-P author has accentuated Aaron's role as mouthpiece to the point that he may speak only those words that Moses "has put in his mouth" (Exod 4:15). See ALBERTZ, *Exodus 1–18*, 93.

[118] WELLHAUSEN, *Die Composition*, 71–72; NOTH, *Das zweite Buch Mose*, 33–37; BLUM, *Die Komposition*, 27–28; UTZSCHNEIDER and OSWALD, *Exodus 1–15*, 159–60.

[119] UTZSCHNEIDER and OSWALD, *Exodus 1–15*, 160, focus on this argument.

back to Moses's first encounter with Pharaoh, alludes to a dialogue scene with Moses as the only counterpart of the Egyptian king (see 7:16).

The collected evidence from all references to Aaron in Exod 1–12 suggests that the motif of Aaron's assistance to Moses during the confrontation with Pharaoh was introduced by the author of the Priestly miracle account (see Exod 7:1, 9).[120] Only later was the motif taken up by non-Priestly authors and inserted in both the non-Priestly plague narrative in Exod 7–11 and the non-Priestly strand of Exod 4–5.

Interestingly, Aaron and his sons are never called Levites in the Priestly texts of Exodus and Leviticus. Nevertheless, Moses's Levite parentage, mentioned in Exod 2:1, is presupposed in Exod 7:1. By calling Aaron Moses's brother, the Priestly author provides Aaron with Levite ancestry. Aaron is called Moses's brother also in Exod 28:1, 2, 4, 41 (P^C). But it is clear that P^C generally emphasizes Aaron's position as high priest rather than his Levite parentage. The latter is explicitly mentioned only in the secondary genealogy in Exod 6:14–27.[121]

---

[120] ALBERTZ, *Exodus 1–18*, 91–93; RÖMER, *Moïse*, 130–31. For the reconstruction of the primary Priestly stratum, see above, II.7.3 (d), Excursus II.

[121] See above, II.7.3 (c).

8. The Priestly Story of the Miracle at Sea in Exodus 14

8.1 Issues in Scholarly Discussion

In older research, the existence of P in this unit was sometimes denied or assumed to be limited.[1] Today, this view has largely been abandoned; current scholarship agrees in assigning roughly half of the chapter to P.

Priestly and non-Priestly material is interwoven in Exod 14, the narrative reporting the miracle at the sea. Whereas scholars generally agree on the outline of the Priestly parts of the story, the content of the non-Priestly texts (primary stratum) is a matter of greater dispute. The Priestly and non-Priestly passages constitute two distinct stories, each of which seems to be – according to the various scholarly views – complete or almost complete in its present configuration.

However, the literary-historical relationship between the two strata is controversial. Traditionally, J, E, or P passages are considered to represent independent sources (or parts of them), the two or three strata having been put together by a redactor. Like the biblical flood story, Exod 14 served for a long time as a "prime example" of a biblical text composed of two or three identifiable sources. Recent treatments reckon with only two sources (P and J [non-P]) and with an important contribution by the redactor who would have combined the two sources.[2] In addition, alternative models have been proposed: P is a layer that complements non-P/J,[3] or, to the contrary, the non-P/J passages are an expansion of the Priestly "ground layer."[4]

The present study primarily aims to determine the content and profile of the Priestly strand. The difficult issues of the precise demarcation of the non-P narrative

---

[1] O. Eissfeldt, *Hexateuch-Synopse* (Leipzig: J. C. Hinrichs, 1922), 35–37, 134–35; Smend, *Die Erzählung*, 125, 129. Assuming a limited contribution: Wellhausen, *Die Composition*, 75–77 (P is found in Exod 14:1, 2, 4*, 8b, 9*, 10*, 16*).

[2] Cf. T. Krüger, "Erwägungen zur Redaktion der Meerwundererzählung (Exodus 13:17–14:31)," *ZAW* 108 (1996): 519–33; Gertz, *Tradition*, 189–232; idem, "The Miracle at the Sea: Remarks on the Recent Discussion about Origin and Composition of the Exodus Narrative," in *The Book of Exodus: Composition, Interpretation, and Reception*, ed. T. B. Dozeman, C. A. Evans, and J. N. Lohr, VTSup 164 (Leiden: Brill, 2014), 93–120.

[3] Cf. Van Seters, *Life of Moses*, 128–39; Blum, *Studien*, 256–62; M. Vervenne, "The 'P' Tradition in the Pentateuch," in *Pentateuchal and Deuteronomistic Studies*, ed. C. Brekelmans and J. Lust, BETL 94 (Leuven: Peeters, 1990), 67–90.

[4] H.-C. Schmitt, "'Priesterliches' und 'prophetisches' Geschichtsverständnis in der Meerwundererzählung Ex 13,17–14,31," in *Textgemäss; FS E. Würthwein*, ed. A. H. J. Gunneweg and O. Kaiser (Göttingen: Vandenhoeck & Ruprecht, 1979), 139–55; C. Berner, "Gab es einen vorpriesterlichen Meerwunderbericht?," *Bib* 95 (2014): 1–25; idem, "Der literarische Charakter," 123–31.

(primary stratum) and of later redactional elements are beyond the scope of this investigation. As a consequence, the relationship between the P layer and the non-P stratum (strata) cannot be determined conclusively.

Recently, R. Albertz assigned Exod 15:19–21 to the Priestly composition (his "Priesterliche Bearbeitung 1").[5] The question of the literary classification of this text will also be addressed in a short section.

8.2 Significant Textual Differences

(a) Exodus 14:17

MT, SP:	לב מצרים
4QReworked Pentateuch[c]:	לב פרעה ולב מצרים
LXX:	τὴν καρδίαν Φαραω καὶ τῶν Αἰγυπτίων πάντων
	לב פרעה וכל בני מצרים =

The *lectio brevior* in MT, SP is also the *lectio difficilior*: elsewhere in the Priestly strand in Exodus, Pharaoh's rather than the Egyptians' heart is "hardened" (חזק, cf. 7:13, 22; 8:15; 9:12; 10:20, 27; 11:10; 14:4, 8). Therefore, it is tempting to see both LXX ("the heart of Pharaoh and all the Egyptians") and 4QReworked Pentateuch[c] ("Pharaoh's heart *and* Egypt's heart") as harmonistic expansions.[6] A *parablepsis* due to *homoioteleuton* in MT, SP (לב מצרים > לב פרעה ולב מצרים) cannot be excluded, but the fact that the alternative readings of 4QReworked Pentateuch[c] and LXX deviate from each other renders this explanation rather unlikely.[7]

8.3 Outline of the Two Main Literary Strata and Their Classification

Most scholars agree on the rough separation between a Priestly and a non-Priestly stratum within Exod 14. The two strands are interwoven and constitute two distinct, nearly coherent, and self-contained stories.

The outline of the Priestly story is as follows: At its beginning yhwh gives Moses the instruction that Israel, just after having escaped from Egypt, should turn back. As a second step, the deity hardens Pharaoh's heart to continue Israel's persecution. This allows yhwh to confront Pharaoh and his army and to defeat him decisively. From the outset of the narrative, it is made clear that the purpose of this maneuver is the glorification of yhwh and recognition of his power by the Egyptians (see Exod 14:4, and cf. v. 18). The miracle happens immediately after the Egyptians have approached

---

[5] See ALBERTZ, *Exodus 1–18*, 253–55.

[6] Giving preference to the reading in MT, SP: NOTH, *Das zweite Buch Mose*, 81; DOZEMAN, *Commentary on Exodus*, 315; ALBERTZ, *Exodus 1–18*, 226.

[7] This explanation is offered by PROPP, *Exodus 1–18*, 468 (referring to a private conversation with D. N. Freedman).

the Israelites. Moses splits the waters by stretching out his hand over the sea (Exod 14:16, 21*), permitting the Israelites to pass through the sea. The Egyptians, attempting to follow them, are covered by the returning waters. A particularity of the Priestly account is Moses's role as miracle worker; YHWH gives Moses the instructions but does not intervene directly in the plot.

Today current scholarship roughly agrees in assigning to P Exod 14:1–4, 8–9, 10abβ, 15–18, 21aαb, 22–23, 26–27aα1, 28–29.[8]

The identification of the Priestly thread in 14:8–10 is more disputed than in the other sections of Exod 14. Possible Priestly elements are as follows: 14:8a reports the fulfillment of the first of YHWH's announcements in v. 4, namely, the hardening of Pharaoh's heart by YHWH and Pharaoh's pursuit of the Israelites (expressed with the same terms: חזק piel; לב; רדף). As a consequence, this half verse is mostly attributed to P. The assignment of 14:8b, with the motif "with a high hand" (ביד רמה, possibly meaning "boldly" or "confidently"), is doubtful, as this motif does not appear in other texts of Pᶜ. Verse 9 reports the Egyptian approach toward the Israelites and takes up the motif of Israel's encampment before Baal Zaphon given in 14:2, which generally fits well with the Priestly strand. The only uncertainty is in v. 9aα, which repeats Israel's pursuit (רדף, with the Egyptians instead of Pharaoh as subject, cf. v. 8). This part of the verse is often assigned to non-P. However, the repetition is not really disturbing, and without v. 9aα, the shift to the plural in the subsequent parts of this verse would be abrupt. The assignment of v. 10a, which again focuses on Pharaoh and his drawing near, is also doubtful. The language of v. 10bα ("to raise the eyes"; "to fear greatly") is non-Priestly.[9] The motif of Israel's crying out in v. 10bβ appears elsewhere in P (cf. 2:23, MT זעק and in 14:15 [Pˢ], צעק) but is much more frequent in non-P.[10]

What were the arguments in older research for classifying the outlined "Priestly-like" text as non-Priestly? Eissfeldt observed that 14:1–4 depends on the non-Priestly itinerary notice in 13:20 and therefore excluded it from P.[11] This observation is important; however, this relatedness can be explained by P's nature as a redaction layer.[12] Wellhausen pointed out Aaron's absence and the lack of such typical Priestly vocabulary as קהל, "cultic assembly," and עדה, "congregation."[13] Nevertheless, certain typical Priestly expressions and motifs render the assignment to a Priestly stratum likely (בני ישראל, חזק piel, with accusative לב; ויעשו כן, יבשה, and the dividing of the sea). Another argument favoring the attribution to P is the precise correspondence between YHWH's order and Moses's (the people's) fulfillment in 14:4, 21, 27, which is likewise a

---

[8] See NÖLDEKE, *Untersuchungen*, 45–46; ELLIGER, "Sinn," 121; LOHFINK, "Die Priesterschrift," 198, n. 29; KRÜGER, "Erwägungen zur Redaktion der Meerwundererzählung," 520, n. 9. On disputed texts, see below, II.8.4.2.

[9] See PROPP, *Exodus 1–18*, 478.

[10] See Gen 4:10; 18:21; 19:13; 27:34; 41:55; Exod 3:7, 9; 5:8, 15; 8:8; 11:6; 12:30; 15:25; 17:4 and PROPP, *Exodus 1–18*, 478.

[11] EISSFELDT, *Hexateuch-Synopse*, 35–36.

[12] See below, II.8.5. As for Exod 14:8b, it is assigned to non-P by ELLIGER, "Sinn," 121; KRÜGER, "Erwägungen zur Redaktion der Meerwundererzählung," 521 (among others).

[13] WELLHAUSEN, *Die Composition*, 76.

dominant feature of other Priestly texts.[14] The observation about the unit's specificities (in particular Aaron's absence) is important, but linguistic and at times conceptual differences between the Priestly texts in Exod 1–40 are observable in general.[15]

The non-Priestly story begins with the flight of the Israelites from slavery. Israel's escape causes Pharaoh to immediately react and pursue the Israelites. The latter are delivered by YHWH: having driven the sea back with a strong east wind during the night, the deity troubles the Egyptians and, as a consequence, the latter run straight into the returning sea. In contrast to the Priestly narrative, here YHWH alone causes the miracle; Moses and the Israelites are passive. The miracle happens during the night and early the following morning.

Scholars do not agree on the precise identification of the non-Priestly story. For instance, Levin attributes to his "Jahwist" 14:5a–6, 10b, 13–14, 19b–20aαb, 21a*, 24–25b, 27*, 30, whereas Albertz assigns to his "Exodus-Komposition" Exod 14:5–7, 9aα, 10bα, 11–13, 19b–20, 21a*, 24–25, 27*, 30.[16] More complex reconstructions are offered by scholars who reckon with two non-Priestly sources (J and E) or with a major addition by the redactor who combined the two strata.[17] According to the classical view, the outlined non-P story is part of the "Yahwistic" source; it harks back to the itinerary notices in Exod 12:37a; 13:20, which are traditionally assigned to "J" as well.[18] Today this classification is doubted or rejected by many. For instance, the narrative's connection to the itinerary notices and to the non-Priestly plague story does not seem evident. The motif of the Israelites' flight (14:5a, ברח) does not appear elsewhere in Exodus. According to some scholars, this statement would form the fragment of a relatively ancient tradition, which would have been lost in the course of redaction.[19] T. Krüger, however, defends the classical view and rightly argues that Pharaoh's statement in 14:5a can be understood in the sense that the Israelites used the holidays granted them (see 12:31–32) to flee (ברח) and to leave Egypt definitively.[20] A few

---

[14] See Gen 6:22; 7:9, 16; Exod 7:6; 14:4, 21, 27; several occurrences in the fulfillment report of the tabernacle account (see below, II.10.4.2). See further Lev 8:4; Num 17:26; 27:22.

[15] See above, II.7.4 (b).

[16] See ALBERTZ, *Exodus 1–18*, 253–55, LEVIN, *Der Jahwist*, 341–44.

[17] See, for instance, PROPP, *Exodus 1–18*, 461–63, 476–81 (reckoning with J, E, P, and a redactor [R]), and KRÜGER, "Erwägungen zur Redaktion der Meerwundererzählung," 522–23, 531–33 (reckoning with "J," P, and a redaction).

[18] See, among others, NOTH, *Das zweite Buch Mose*, 80–95; WEIMAR, *Die Meerwundererzählung*, 86–104; LEVIN, *Der Jahwist*, 341–47; VAN SETERS, *Life of Moses*, 131; KRÜGER, "Erwägungen zur Redaktion der Meerwundererzählung," 521. – Concerning the classification of 12:37a and 13:20, see above, II.7.3 (g).

[19] See, NOTH, *Das zweite Buch Mose*, 88 (assigning the passage to E); ALBERTZ, *Exodus 1–18*, 233; GERTZ, "Miracle at the Sea," 106.

[20] KRÜGER, "Erwägungen zur Redaktion der Meerwundererzählung," 521.

scholars consider Exod 14 non-P to be a rather late, post-Priestly addition.[21] According to Berner, its language and style share commonalities with late Deuteronomistic texts.[22]

8.4 Inner Differentiation of the Priestly Stratum

8.4.1 Is There a Proto-Priestly Vorlage behind the Priestly Account?

According to Blum, the aforementioned singularities of Exod 14 P point to a distinct *Vorlage* lying behind the Priestly stratum. Blum explicitly mentions the use of כבד *niphal*, "to appear in one's glory," and Moses's staff (which contrasts with Aaron's staff in Exod 7–9 P). Furthermore, he refers to the apparent gap in 14:15 (the previous Priestly context does not report *Moses's* crying-out), which would be the result of P's reworking of a preexisting *Vorlage*. Blum is nevertheless skeptical about the possibility of a detailed reconstruction of the latter.[23] Weimar attempts to do precisely this. Weimar's reconstructed *Vorlage* (Exod 14:8b, 15aα, 16, 21aαb, 22, 23aαb, 28a*, 29) does not contain the introductory 14:1–4, the motifs of the hardening of Pharaoh's heart and of YHWH's glory.[24] His analysis is based on observations of a few alleged incoherences within the Priestly stratum. For instance, the very short fulfillment statement in 14:4 contrasts with the more detailed and accurate execution reports in vv. 21aαb, 22 and 27aα1, 28.[25] However, this difference can be explained by the author's intention to highlight the accurate accomplishment of the miracle that is at the center of the narrative. Additionally, Weimar points to the fact that vv. 15–16 contain two orders by YHWH, one following immediately after the other,[26] and to an assumed tension between the statements in 14:8a and 14:8b.[27] In both cases, the sequence is not really disturbing.

The toponyms at the narrative's beginning in 14:2 and 14:9 are noteworthy too; toponyms do not appear in the previous Priestly texts in Exod 1–12 at all.[28] Another particularity concerns the motif of the hardening of the heart. Whereas in the Priestly miracles-plagues narrative YHWH hardens only the heart of the Pharaoh, in Exod 14:17 P (according to MT, SP[29]) the Egyptians in general (and in particular the Egyptian sol-

---

[21] H.-C. Schmitt, "'Priesterliches' und 'prophetisches' Geschichtsverständnis," 139–55; Berner, "Der literarische Charakter," 123–31.

[22] Berner, "Gab es?," 1–25.

[23] See Blum, *Studien*, 260–61, with notes 120 and 121.

[24] See P. Weimar, *Die Meerwundererzählung: Eine redaktionskritische Analyse von Ex 13,17–14,31*, ÄAT 9 (Wiesbaden: Harrassowitz, 1985), 175–99.

[25] See Weimar, *Die Meerwundererzählung*, 175–76, with n. 26.

[26] See Weimar, *Die Meerwundererzählung*, 177–78.

[27] See Weimar, *Die Meerwundererzählung*, 178–79.

[28] See also above, II.7.4 (b).

[29] See the discussion above, II.8.2.

diers) are YHWH's targets. Another distinctive feature: Aaron, who plays an important role in P's narrative of the miracles-plagues, is absent from Exod 14 P.

However, as noted above, differences in vocabulary, style, and motif are observable between various Priestly accounts (which may hint at different authors who may also have collaborated with each other).[30] The In general, the language, style, and motifs of Exod 14 P are typically Priestly.[31]

8.4.2 Possible Secondary Elements in the Priestly Stratum

The classification of a few elements that are generally assigned to the Priestly strand is a matter of dispute:

(a) Exodus 14:2bβ (נכחו תחנו על הים)

Krüger and Gertz see 14:2bβ as a secondary insertion.[32] Gertz offers the following detailed argument: in the direct speech in 14:2, 4, the Israelites are consistently addressed in the third-person plural, except in the last colon of v. 2, where the author shifts to the second-person plural; Moses is included in the direct address. Gertz supposes that the (repeated) mention of Israel's encampment (חנה) was probably "motivated by the non-priestly text that several times mentions such an encampment of the Israelites (13:20; 14:9*)."[33] The shift to the second person is striking; nevertheless, one might consider it a deliberate device by the Priestly author in order to highlight the precise location of the miracle. The repetition of the lexeme חנה, "to encamp," may have the same function. Furthermore, Gertz' argument concerning v. 4 is not sound: the situation is different from that of v. 2 (which is part of an instruction), insofar as the Israelites are the subject in a indicative sentence (the fulfillment assertion "and they did so").

(b) Exodus 14:15aβ (מה תצעק אלי)

YHWH's rebuke of Moses (Exod 14:15) does not form a smooth continuation either of the previous Priestly (v. 10abβ) or of the preceding non-Priestly (v. 11–14) context. The Priestly story reports the Israelites crying out to YHWH in 14:10abβ, but there is no mention of Moses crying out.

> Exodus 14:10abβ, 15
> [10abβ] And as Pharaoh drew near, the Israelites cried out to YHWH. [15] And YHWH said to Moses, "Why do you cry out to me? Tell the Israelites to go forward."

---

[30] See above, II.8.3, and in particular II.7.4 (b).
[31] See the examples in II.8.3.
[32] See KRÜGER, "Erwägungen zur Redaktion der Meerwundererzählung," 521; GERTZ, "Miracle at the Sea," 102.
[33] GERTZ, "Miracle at the Sea," 102.

However, YHWH's focus on Moses alone in v. 15 can be explained by YHWH's conversation with Moses and that the statement presupposes that Moses cried out together with the Israelites (cf. v. 10).[34] Nevertheless, the reproach appears isolated in its context; the story continues with two other orders that fulfill important functions in the plot. Another clue favors the idea that v. 15aβ might have been inserted secondarily: remarkably, all other Priestly texts in Exodus depict Moses positively (P^C);[35] and in particular Moses plays an important and positive role in Exod 14 P.[36]

(c) Exodus 14:16aα (הרם את מטך)

YHWH's command to Moses to lift his staff is without correspondence in the fulfillment report (v. 21aαb). The order and execution of the flowing-back of the waters in vv. 26–27 do not include the motif either. For this reason, most scholars assign the short order in 14:16aα to a post-Priestly redactor.[37] According to Gertz, this redactor would have been influenced by the non-Priestly episodes about hail and locusts in the plague cycle.[38]

8.5 The Literary Profile of the Priestly Layer and Its Relationship to the Non-P Stratum

In the sea-miracle narrative, in contrast to the flood story in Gen 6–9, the two identified strata constitute two (almost) complete and self-contained stories. Therefore, the question of the literary-historical relationship between these two texts is difficult to answer. In principle, the possibility should also be considered that a redactor might have put together two originally independent stories.

The following observation leads to the tentative conclusion that the Priestly narrative, though nearly coherent and self-contained, nevertheless is dependent on the larger non-Priestly context. The detailed itinerary notice in Exod 14:2 is not visibly connected with the end of the Priestly Passover account (Exod 12:41, 51), which relates Israel's exodus without reference to toponyms. At the same time, as some scholars have observed, the statement is dependent on the non-P itinerary in 13:20, according to which the Israelites "camped in Etham on the edge of the wilderness."[39] According

---

[34] See NOTH, *Das zweite Buch Mose*, 90 ("...damit wird Mose als der Sprecher der 'schreienden' Israeliten angeredet"); KRÜGER, "Erwägungen zur Redaktion der Meerwundererzählung," 521. See, however, BLUM, *Studien*, 266, n. 90, who argues that wilderness and exodus texts would usually emphasize the differences between Moses and the people.

[35] See above, II.7.3 (d), Excursus I.

[36] WELLHAUSEN, *Die Composition*, 76–77, also excludes the element מה תצעק אלי from P (he assigns it to E).

[37] Exceptions are NOTH, *Das zweite Buch Mose*, 81, 90; DOZEMAN, *Commentary on Exodus*, 317.

[38] GERTZ, "Miracle at the Sea," 103.

[39] See VAN SETERS, *Life of Moses*, 131; ALBERTZ, *Exodus 1–18*, 233.

to Exod 14:2–3, the Israelites gave Pharaoh the impression that they could not enter the wilderness and would have to return to Egypt, i.e. in the inhabited region of Pi-hahiroth, Migdol, and Baal and Baal Zaphon (cf. Exod 14:2).[40]

> Exodus 14:2–3
> ² "Tell the Israelites to turn back [שׁוב] and camp before Pi-hahiroth, between Migdol and the sea; you shall camp in front of Baal Zaphon, opposite it, by the sea. ³ For Pharaoh will say of the Israelites, 'They are wandering aimlessly in the land; the wilderness has closed against them.'"

The meaning of Exod 14:3 is controversially. With regard to the movement of return (cf. שׁוב) in v.2, the phrase סגר עליהם המדבר should be rendered "the wilderness has closed against (before) them."[41] However, the understanding adopted by most scholars is "the wilderness closed them in." But since the Israelites in fact *return* to the inhabited area of Egypt (cf. the toponyms Pi-hahiroth and Migdol in 14:2), the latter understanding does not make sense.

Most scholars see Exod 13:20 as the beginning of the non-Priestly ("J") sea-miracle story (see above). If so, at this point P would be dependent on the non-Priestly sea-miracle narrative.[42] If, however, 13:20 has its direct continuation in 15:22aβ, thereby forming a coherent pre-Priestly itinerary sequence,[43] the dependence would not be relevant to the question of the literary relationship between the two sea-miracle accounts.[44] In this latter case, the Priestly stratum would nevertheless depend on the larger non-P context.

The relationship of the P story with the near non-Priestly context (the non-P story) is more difficult to establish. A possible argument for P's dependence on non-P is as follows. YHWH's announcement that he will "be honored through Pharaoh and all his army" and that the Egyptians will know that he is YHWH (Exod 14:4; cf. 14:17–18) is never fulfilled in the Priestly account: the Egyptians – that is, the chariots and the horsemen, Pharaoh's entire army – are covered by the sea; "not even one of them remained" (14:28). Given the emphasis on YHWH's motivation (see the statement's repetition in 14:17–18), the absence of any fulfillment of the announcement in P is striking. According to Vervenne, the Priestly narrative, read on its own, is "ineffective" because the "miracle seems unsuccessful. It is not told that the Egyptians finally ידעו

---

[40] Migdal is attested in Jer 44:1; 46:14; Ezek 29:10; 30:6; in Jer 44:1 it appears as a place of residence for Judean refugees. Scholars agree on the Israelites' movement "back" to Egypt (see PROPP, *Exodus 1–18*, 491; DOZEMAN, *Commentary on Exodus*, 311; IDEM, "Priestly Wilderness," 263; ALBERTZ, *Exodus 1–18*, 239, among others).

[41] See PROPP, *Exodus 1–18*, 461, 491, and SMEND, *Die Erzählung*, 139, with n. 2; EISSFELDT, *Hexateuch-Synopse*, 35, 134; U. CASSUTO, *A Commentary on the Book of Exodus* (Jerusalem: Magnes, 1967), 160.

[42] See, for instance, NOTH, *Das zweite Buch Mose*, 83; VAN SETERS, *Life of Moses*, 131; KRÜGER, "Erwägungen zur Redaktion der Meerwundererzählung," 522–23; GERTZ, *Tradition*, 209.

[43] See BERNER, "Der literarische Charakter," 129.

[44] For arguments against the assignment of 13:20 to P, see above, II.7.3 (g).

יהוה‏.‏"[45] Thus, it seems tempting to relate YHWH's promise to the statement in the non-P strand of the Egyptians' recognition that YHWH is fighting against them (see 14:25b: "And the Egyptians said, 'Let us flee from the Israelites, for YHWH is fighting for them against Egypt'").[46]

Yet, in the context of this question, it is important to note a possible intertextual contact between the immediately preceding v. 25a and the Priestly stratum.[47] The expression כבדת, "heaviness, difficulty," in this part of the verse ("he [YHWH] made them [the chariots of the Egyptians] drive with difficulty"; v. 25a) may be linked with the motif that YHWH would "be honored" (כבד niphal) through Pharaoh and all his army. How to interpret this correspondence? It is possible that the term כבדת inspired the Priestly redactor to introduce the motif of YHWH's being honored (although the latter might have been motivated by YHWH's כבוד in the Priestly tabernacle account). Conversely, however, one might see in 14:25 a post-Priestly insertion aiming to fill in the lacuna of the "unrounded" Priestly plot by introducing the motif of the Egyptians' recognition of YHWH and that of the difficulty of their movement (as an intertextual link to the root כבד in the P story).[48] Thus at this point the assessment is inconclusive. Attention should be focused therefore on the literary character of the non-Priestly passages.

The non-Priestly story does not offer a geographical localization of the event and seems to depend on P in this respect. The non-P stratum contains some motifs and specifics that are classified as late by scholars, such as the murmuring and faith of the Israelites, the angel of YHWH, the proximity to the deuteronomic and deuteronomistic texts dealing with the "war of YHWH," the simultaneous mention of the pillar of cloud and the pillar of fire. Scholars that hold to a pre-Priestly sea miracle narrative exclude some of these motifs from the non-Priestly basic narrative.[49] C. Berner, on the other hand, classifies all of these motifs and the non-Priestly narrative in general as post-Priestly.[50] According to him, the YHWH-centeredness of the non-P stratum (YHWH intervenes on his own) is a reaction to the P narrative, in which the deity delegates the salvation act to Moses.[51]

Summing up this section, we state that the Priestly sea story depends on the

---

[45] VERVENNE, "'P' Tradition in the Pentateuch," 79.

[46] See ALBERTZ, *Exodus 1–18*, 244–45.

[47] Pointing to the connection between כבדת and כבד *niphal* are G. FISCHER and D. MARKL, *Das Buch Exodus*, NSKAT 2 (Stuttgart: Katholisches Bibelwerk, 2009), 162; UTZSCHNEIDER and OSWALD, *Exodus 1–15*, 310.

[48] A few scholars see in 14:25a a secondary insertion in this non-Priestly passage interacting with the Priestly motif of YHWH's aim to glorify himself. According to them, the motif of the "heaviness" and deceleration of the Egyptian chariots would not fit the following non-Priestly context (cf. v. 27: the confused Egyptians flee right into the water). See H. HOLZINGER, *Exodus*, KHC 2 (Freiburg im Breisgau: J. C. B. Mohr, 1900), 44; LEVIN, *Der Jahwist*, 345; KRÜGER, "Erwägungen zur Redaktion der Meerwundererzählung," 523, n. 26, 533.

[49] LEVIN, *Der Jahwist*, 345 and GERTZ, "Miracle at the Sea," 109–17, exclude the motif of the murmuring and faith of the Israelites and that of the angel of YHWH (among others) from the base layer.

[50] C. BERNER, "Gab es einen vorpriesterlichen Meerwunderbericht?," 1–25.

[51] C. BERNER, "Gab es einen vorpriesterlichen Meerwunderbericht?," 20–25.

itinerary notices in the more remote non-Priestly context (12:37a; 13:20). But at the same time, the Priestly account seems to have constituted the diachronically primary base stratum on which the non-Priestly story was built, although this conclusion remains uncertain.

8.6 The Literary Classification of Exodus 15:19–21

The introduction of the so-called Song of Miriam recalls the Priestly story of the miracle at the sea; it shares various motifs (parting of the sea, the Israelites' walking on dry land through the midst of the sea) and vocabulary (בוא, רכב, פרש, שוב hiphil, בני ישראל, יבשה, בתוך הים). For this reason, R. Albertz assigns the passage to the Priestly ground layer (his "Priesterliche Bearbeitung 1").[52] However, at the same time, certain characteristic motifs of the Priestly account are absent (the splitting of the sea, the wall of waters) or modified (it is YHWH rather than Moses who causes the waters to come back [שוב hiphil]). In general, the passing-over of Moses throughout the passage is striking; Miriam appears as the sister of Aaron rather than Moses and Aaron (see Exod 15:20). Exodus 15:19–21 should therefore probably be attributed to a post-Priestly author. Further favoring such a classification is the fact that the author borrows a motif from the Former Prophets (1 Sam 18:6–7; Judg 11:34), integrating it with nearly identical wording (see the common expressions יצא, "to go out" with subject נשים, "women," בטפים, "with trimbels," במחלת, "with dancing," ענה, "to chant," שיר, "to sing"). This is rather unusual for the Priestly strand. As Utzschneider and Oswald convincingly point out, the "drum-dance-song" genre is typically "connected with the 'Sitz im Leben' of victorious troops returning home" (see Judg 11:34; 1 Sam 18:6 and Jer 31:4), and thus does not fit well with the situation at the Sea of Reeds described in Exod 14; here it is YHWH who defeats the Egyptians and there are no Israelite troops returning home.[53] With regard to the surprising detail that Miriam is presented as Aaron's sister only, certain scholars see here an "ancient" piece of tradition, albeit hesitantly.[54] Nevertheless, in light of the artificial character of the passage, it seems more likely that this specification is a late polemical point in favor of Aaron and against Moses.

It is imaginable that this author was responsible for the song's attribution to Miriam. This would mean that the song about YHWH's victory at the sea, found in Exod 15, was given a subscript similar to the introduction in Exod 15:1 and competing with the latter. It was reinserted into Exod 15 at a late stage of the literary development of this unit.

---

[52] See ALBERTZ, Exodus 1–18, 253–55.

[53] UTZSCHNEIDER and OSWALD, Exodus 1–15, 338.

[54] NOTH, Überlieferungsgeschichte, 197–98, with n. 506; KRATZ, Composition, 288, n. 55.

9. The Priestly Texts in Exodus 16–20: Israel Moves to Sinai

9.1 Outline of the Priestly Texts and Issues in Scholarly Discussion

According to the Priestly conception, the miracle at the sea happens while the Israelites are still in Egypt (cf. Exod 14:1–2), and Israel's passage through the wilderness begins only afterward.[1] Thematically, the Priestly units in Exod 16–40 (and beyond) belong together insofar as they deal with Israel's passage through the wilderness. The present section focuses on the few Priestly texts reporting Israel's move to Sinai, short itinerary notices, and the manna story.

For some of these texts (or parts of them), which are traditionally assigned to P, the literary classification is now disputed. For instance, the base layer of Exod 16 was generally attributed to P[G]/P[C]; only a few isolated verses and passages were thought to belong to the pre-Priestly strand. The tendency of recent treatments, however, is to assign the non-Priestly passages to post-Priestly redactions. A few authors consider the entire unit a post-Priestly composition. The section Exod 16–19 contains a few itinerary notices, most of which were commonly assigned to P (16:1; 17:1; 19:1–2a). Several recent treatments, however, assign parts of these notices to non-P (pre-P). A few scholars who consider the Priestly ground layer a redaction rather than a source assign the justification for the Sabbath instruction in the Ten Commandments (Exod 20:11) to P[C].

9.2 Significant Textual Variants

(a) Exodus 16:6

MT, SP: כל בני ישראל
MT (MS Kennicott), LXX: πᾶσαν συναγωγὴν υἱῶν Ισραηλ
= כל עדת בני ישראל

The reading "all the congregation of the Israelites," attested in LXX and one Hebrew manuscript, is in line with the wording of 16:1, 2, 9, 10. Since there is no visible cause (*homoioarkton* or *homoioteleuton*) for an unintentional textual omission (*parablepsis*) in MT and SP, one should rather consider the "inconsistent" reading of MT and SP

---

[1] Cf. Dozeman, "Priestly Wilderness," 263–65; R. Albertz, "Wilderness Material in Exodus (Exodus 15–18)," in *The Book of Exodus: Composition, Interpretation, and Reception*, ed. T. B. Dozeman, C. A. Evans, and J. N. Lohr, VTSup 64 (Leiden: Brill, 2014), 158.

original; LXX and Kenn. 196 are probably harmonizing with the elaborate designation predominantly used in late Priestly texts.[2]

(b) Exodus 16:8

MT, SP: עָלָיו
LXX: καθ᾽ ἡμῶν
        = עָלֵינוּ

It is difficult to decide between these two variants, because both may have resulted from an attempt to harmonize with the larger context. The reading of LXX fits with statements in 16:2, 7b, 8b and may have been adjusted toward them. The reading of MT and SP goes well with the statements in 16:7a and may be the result of a harmonization with them.

9.3 Literary Classification of the (Putative) Priestly Texts

9.3.1 Itinerary Notices in 16:1, 17:1

Traditionally, the two verses were assigned in their entirety to P.[3] However, recent treatments point to the composite character of the notices to argue for redaction-critical differentiation.[4] Both itinerary notices seem indeed to be overloaded. The fact that the subject in 16:1 follows only the second verbal form (instead of the first one, denoting Israel's departure) is a sign of reworking.[5] Since the beginning of 16:1 and the end of 17:1 contain typical elements of the pre-Priestly itinerary notices (ויסעו, ויחנו), some scholars assume a primitive form of the notice ויסעו מאילם ויחנו ברפידים (16:1aα; 17:1bα: "And they set out from Elim and they camped at Rephidim"). This reconstructed notice also matches well with the preceding and subsequent pre-Priestly itinerary notices in 12:37a; 13:20; 15:22, 27; and 19:2.[6] According to this more original itinerary notice, Israel went directly from Elim to Rephidim (see the unhighlighted text below). The parts between (Exod 16:1aβγb; 17:1a, highlighted text) are considered secondary; since they comprise typical Priestly components (i.e., the expressions עדה, "congregation," and למסעיהם, "by stages," and the dating in Exod 16:1aβγb; 17:1a), they

---

[2] See also PROPP, *Exodus 1–18*, 585.

[3] See WELLHAUSEN, *Die Composition*, 78–79; NOTH, *Das zweite Buch Mose*, 101, 106, 110–11; V. FRITZ, *Israel in der Wüste: Traditionsgeschichtliche Untersuchung der Wüstenüberlieferung des Jahwisten*, MarbTSt 7 (Marburg: Elwert, 1970), 8–10; G. W. COATS, "The Wilderness Itinerary," *CBQ* 34 (1972): 143, 146, 148; ROSKOP, *Wilderness Itineraries*, 136–218, esp. 178, 182, 188–89.

[4] See L. SCHMIDT, "Die Priesterschrift in Exodus 16," *ZAW* 119 (2007): 483–98; DOZEMAN, "Priestly Wilderness," 266–73; ALBERTZ, "Wilderness Material in Exodus," 155–56; C. BERNER, "Das Wasserwunder von Rephidim (Ex 17,1–7) als Schlüsseltext eines nachpriesterschriftlichen Mosebildes," *VT* 63 (2013): 193–209.

[5] See L. SCHMIDT, "Die Priesterschrift in Exodus 16," 484–86.

[6] See above, II.7.3 (g).

should be considered Priestly (P^C or P^S). The older notice was reworked in order to give a location and a dating for the quail-manna story.[7]

Exodus 16:1

¹ וַיִּסְעוּ מֵאֵילִם וַיָּבֹאוּ כָל עֲדַת בְּנֵי יִשְׂרָאֵל אֶל מִדְבַּר סִין אֲשֶׁר בֵּין אֵילִם וּבֵין סִינָי בַּחֲמִשָּׁה
עָשָׂר יוֹם לַחֹדֶשׁ הַשֵּׁנִי לְצֵאתָם מֵאֶרֶץ מִצְרָיִם

¹And they set out from Elim, and all the congregation of the Israelites came to the wilderness of Sin, which is between Elim and Sinai, on the fifteenth day of the second month after their departure from the land of Egypt.

Exodus 17:1

¹ וַיִּסְעוּ כָּל עֲדַת בְּנֵי יִשְׂרָאֵל מִמִּדְבַּר סִין לְמַסְעֵיהֶם עַל פִּי יהוה וַיַּחֲנוּ בִּרְפִידִים וְאֵין מַיִם
לִשְׁתֹּת הָעָם

¹And all the congregation of the Israelites set out by stages from the wilderness of Sin, according to the command of YHWH, and they camped at Rephidim, and there was no water for the people to drink.

The twofold use of the expression כל עדת בני ישראל, "all the congregation of the Israelites," may point to a secondary Priestly layer (P^S, see the following section) rather than P^C.

9.3.2 Exodus 16:2–36: Manna Story

The bulk of Exod 16 is marked by Priestly vocabulary and Priestly motifs (בני ישראל, "the Israelites," עדה, "congregation," כבוד יהוה, "the glory of YHWH," בין הערבים,[8] "twilight," rationing of food,[9] prohibition against conserving food until the following day,[10] Sabbath theme[11]). The following statement by A. Kuenen is representative of older scholarship: "Niemand leugnet, dass in bei weitem dem grössten Teile von Ex. 16 der Sprachgebrauch und die Schreibweise von P herrschen."[12] Until today, a majority of scholars assign the main part of the unit, roughly covering 16:1*, 2–3, 6–26, 33–35, to

---

[7] Cf. Dozeman, "Priestly Wilderness," 260–73; Albertz, "Wilderness Material in Exodus," 155–56. Cf. also L. Schmidt, "Die Priesterschrift in Exodus 16," 484–86.

[8] See the further occurrences of בין הערבים in Exod 12:6; 29:39, 41; 30:8; Lev 23:5; Num 9:3, 5, 11; 28:4, 8.

[9] Cf. Exod 16:16, 18, 21 with 12:4. See Albertz, *Exodus 1–18*, 262.

[10] Cf. Exod 16:19 with 12:10. See Albertz, *Exodus 1–18*, 262.

[11] Emphasizing the connection between Exod 16:22–26 and the allusion to the Sabbath in Gen 2:2–3: T. Römer, "Israel's Sojourn in the Wilderness and the Construction of the Book of Numbers," in *Reflection and Refraction: Studies in Biblical Historiography in Honour of A. Graeme Auld*, ed. R. Rezetko et al., VTSup 113 (Leiden: Brill, 2007), 431; idem, *L'Ancien Testament commenté: L'Exode* (Paris: Bayard; Geneva: Labor et Fides, 2017), 91. However, the language of the passage dealing with the Sabbath favors the idea that the latter stems from H (see below).

[12] See A. Kuenen, "Beiträge zur Hexateuchkritik, VII: Manna und Wachteln (Ex. 16.)," in *Gesammelte Abhandlungen zur biblischen Wissenschaft: Aus dem Holländischen übersetzt von K. Budde* (Freiburg im Breisgau: Herder, 1894), 287.

P[G]/P[C].[13] According to the classical view, some of the non-P passages would be part of the pre-Priestly "Yahwistic" source.[14] A recent tendency, however, is to regard these non-Priestly texts as post-Priestly Deuteronomistic (or D-like) additions.[15] Another recent trend in European scholarship is to contest the assignment of the story's bulk to P. Several arguments are put forward in favor of its attribution to a late Priestly (P[s]) or a post-Priestly author.[16]

Scholars assigning the main parts of the story to P disagree about the demarcation and the unity of the Priestly stratum. The passage in Exod 16:13b–15[17] and the conclusion in vv. 33–35,[18] which are assigned to non-P by some, are the subject of some dispute. However, more recently, the diversity of themes (feeding the Israelites quails and manna; prohibition of hoarding provisions; discovering the Sabbath) and differences in vocabulary has led certain scholars to make more far-reaching redaction-critical proposals. In particular, several treatments assign the Sabbath theme developed in 16:22–26 to a secondary redaction; the original kernel of the composition would limit itself to the first part of the actual text (16:1–15* or 16:1–21*).[19] What may favor

---

[13] NÖLDEKE, *Untersuchungen*, 48–49; WELLHAUSEN, *Die Composition*, 78–79; NOTH, *Das zweite Buch Mose*, 103–9; G. W. COATS, *Rebellion in the Wilderness: The Murmuring Motif in the Wilderness Traditions of the Old Testament* (Nashville: Abingdon, 1968), 83–127; CHILDS, *Exodus*, 274–92; E. RUPRECHT, "Stellung und Bedeutung der Erzählung vom Mannawunder," *ZAW* 86 (1974): 269–307; BLUM, *Studien*, 146–48; PROPP, *Exodus 1–18*, 585, 588–601; L. SCHMIDT, "Die Priesterschrift in Exodus 16"; DOZEMAN, *Commentary on Exodus*, 374–87; ALBERTZ, *Exodus 1–18*, 261–65; IDEM, "Wilderness Material in Exodus," 155–56; BOORER, *Vision of the Priestly Narrative*, 54–58; RÖMER, *L'Ancien Testament commenté: L'Exode*, 91.

[14] For some of the scholars mentioned in the previous note (WELLHAUSEN, *Die Composition*, 78–79; CHILDS, *Exodus*, 274–92; PROPP, *Exodus 1–18*, 585, 588–601; DOZEMAN, *Commentary on Exodus*, 374–87), the "J" (or "JE") strand is continuous and self-contained. See further LEVIN, *Der Jahwist*, 352–55; VAN SETERS, *Life of Moses*, 185–88. According to NOTH, *Das zweite Buch Mose*, 103–9, and COATS, *Rebellion*, 83–127, however, the J part would have been fragmentarily preserved, containing only vv. 4–5 and 29–30.

[15] NÖLDEKE, *Untersuchungen*, 48–49; RUPRECHT, "Erzählung vom Mannawunder," 269–307; BLUM, *Studien*, 146–48; L. SCHMIDT, "Die Priesterschrift in Exodus 16"; ALBERTZ, *Exodus 1–18*, 261–65; IDEM, "Wilderness Material in Exodus," 156; RÖMER, *L'Ancien Testament commenté: L'Exode*, 91.

[16] See POLA, *Die ursprüngliche Priesterschrift*, 134–43; KRATZ, *Composition*, 291; E. OTTO, *Das Deuteronomium im Pentateuch und Hexateuch: Studien zur Literaturgeschichte von Pentateuch und Hexateuch im Lichte des Deuteronomiumrahmens* (FAT 30; Tübingen: J. C. B. Mohr [Paul Siebeck], 2000), 37–38, n. 111; ACHENBACH, *Die Vollendung*, 232–35.

[17] Assigning 16:13b–15 to non-P: CHILDS, *Exodus*, 274–92; PROPP, *Exodus 1–18*, 585, 588–601; L. SCHMIDT, "Die Priesterschrift in Exodus 16," (according to Schmidt 16:16–20 is also secondary); DOZEMAN, *Commentary on Exodus*, 374–87.

[18] Assigning 16:33–35 to non-P: NOTH, *Das zweite Buch Mose*, 103–9; RUPRECHT, "Stellung und Bedeutung" (within Exod 16:33–35 only 16:35a belongs to P[G]); L. SCHMIDT, "Die Priesterschrift in Exodus 16" (only 16:35a belongs to P[G]); ALBERTZ, *Exodus 1–18*, 161–64 (only 16:35a belongs to P[C] ["Priesterliche Bearbeitung 1"]); BOORER, *Vision of the Priestly Narrative*, 58.

[19] P. MAIBERGER, *Das Manna. Eine literarische, etymologische und naturkundliche Untersuchung*, ÄAT 6 (Wiesbaden: Harrassowitz, 1983), 141; FREVEL, *Mit Blick*, 118, n. 164; NIHAN, *From Priestly Torah*, 568, n. 666; BOORER, *Vision of the Priestly Narrative*, 57.

the latter redaction-critical differentiation is first the author's emphasis on God's wise provision – his perfect attribution of the "right" portion for everybody (recalling the Priestly instruction for the Passover; see 12:10) – which constitutes the climax of the primary story (and as such competes with the Sabbath theme), and second the central expression שבתון שבת קדש ליהוה ("a strict sabbath consecrated to YHWH") in the passage dealing with the Sabbath (Exod 16:23), which is reminiscent of the language of H.[20]

Regarding certain anticipatory Priestly motifs in Exod 16 – YHWH's *kābôd* appearing before Sinai; YHWH seeming to have a precise locus in Israel's camp (as indicated by the location "before YHWH"); the mention of "testimony" (עדת) – critics such as B. Baentsch, A. Dillmann, C. Westermann, and more recently J. Baden have argued that this chapter originally had its place in P[G] after the account of the construction of the tabernacle.[21] However, the "displacement theory" does not apply for the following reason: providing that the story originally was placed after the tabernacle account, one would expect the mention of the tent of meeting (in episodes reporting YHWH's revelation, the tent of meeting is regularly mentioned; see Exod 40:34–35; Lev 9:23; Num 14:10; 16:19; 17:7; 20:6). But in Exod 16 the location "before YHWH" (לפני יהוה) is not further specified. The author does not mention the ark either: among the sacred articles belonging to the tabernacle, only the "testimony" (עדת) is mentioned (in 16:34). Might the reason for this exception be that, though the fabrication of the ark and tent is reported in the tabernacle account, the manufacturing of the "testimony" is never stated, so that the author imagined that it already existed before the Sinai revelation? In any case, even if the motifs in question appear anticipatory, the author, being obviously considerate of the tabernacle account in the subsequent Priestly context, is deliberately "moderate" in his anticipation. This means that the unit was conceived for its present placement before the tabernacle account. The anticipatory Priestly motifs are nevertheless striking and deserve an explanation (see below).

The arguments of scholars who favor the assignment of the unit's main part to a post-Priestly author are as follows: The complaint motif would be alien to P[G] and contradict its "positive" or "ideal" anthropology.[22] The lack of food and famine would be in tension with the Israelites' comfortable economic situation, reflected in the tabernacle account (possession of luxury goods such as precious stones and curtains; possession of sufficient cattle and flocks for the sacrificial cult is presupposed as well).[23] The basis for Otto's classification of the unit as "post-Priestly" is the aforementioned

---

[20] Cf. the other occurrences in Exod 31:15; 35:2; Lev 16:31; 23:3, 24, 32, 39 (2×); 25:4, 5. Supposing the influence of H: KNOHL, *Sanctuary*, 17–18 (assigning Exod 16* entirely to H), and NIHAN, *From Priestly Torah*, 568, n. 666.

[21] See BAENTSCH, *Exodus–Leviticus–Numeri*, 144–45 (after Num 10); A. DILLMANN and A. W. KNOBEL, *Die Bücher Exodus und Leviticus* (Leipzig: S. Hirzel, 1880), 181 ("zum Beispiel hinter Nu 10"); WESTERMANN, *Exodus*, 203; BADEN, "Original Place."

[22] POLA, *Die ursprüngliche Priesterschrift*, 145–46.

[23] POLA, *Die ursprüngliche Priesterschrift*, 136–37.

anticipatory emergence of YHWH's *kābôd*. Otto interprets the fact that it appears before Sinai and thus independently of the tent of meeting as a critique of the cultic *kābôd* conception in P (the *kābôd* appears only in the tent of meeting).[24] To Otto's observation one may add the peculiar location לפני יהוה (16:9, 33), which in the context of P suggests a position before the tent of meeting (see above).[25] The assumed Priestly passages in Exod 16 have also some linguistic singularities: J. Jeon points out that 16:6–8 shares stylistic figures with the Korah story in Num 16.[26] They have in common a peculiar rhetorical question: "What are we?" (מה נחנו; Exod 16:8b) and "What is Aaron?" (ואהרן מה הוא; Num 16:11b). Similarly, the syntactic structure of the assertions in v. 6b and v. 7a, in each case beginning with an adverbial expression of time (ערב, "at evening," and בקר, "tomorrow morning") and being followed by a subordinated sequence with a relative ו-construction, appears also in Num 16:5a:

Exodus 16:6–7

⁶ויאמר משה ואהרן אל כל בני ישראל ערב וידעתם ... ⁷ובקר וראיתם

⁶ So Moses and Aaron said to all the Israelites, "At evening you will know ... ⁷ and in the morning you will see ..."

Numbers 16:5

⁵וידבר אל קרח ואל כל עדתו לאמר בקר וידע יהוה ...

⁵ So he (Moses) spoke to Korah and all his company, saying, "Tomorrow morning YHWH will let you know ..."

Whereas the first stylistic figure seems unique in the Priestly texts of Genesis–Leviticus, the second is also found in Exod 12:3 (mostly assigned to P^G/P^C).[27] A further singularity are references to instructions of YHWH ("This is the thing which YHWH has commanded," see Exod 16:16, 32) which however are mentioned nowhere in the preceding Priestly context. Such references, in identical formulation, appear only in late Priestly texts (P^S, H).[28] A last example: The expression כל עדת בני ישראל, "all the congregation of the Israelites," appearing four times in Exod 16 "P," is frequent in late Priestly texts but is not found in texts unanimously assigned to P^G/P^C.[29] Regarding these thematic and linguistic singularities, I am inclined to assign Exod 16* to P^S

---

[24] OTTO, *Das Deuteronomium im Pentateuch und Hexateuch*, 37–38, n. 111.

[25] See above.

[26] J. JEON (oral communication).

[27] בעשר לחדש הזה ויקחו להם איש שה לבית אבת שה לבית ("On the tenth of this month they are each one to take a lamb for themselves, according to their fathers' households, a lamb for each household").

[28] In total eight occurrences: Exod 16:16, 32; 35:4; Lev 8:5; 9:6; 17:2; Num 30:2; 36:6. As for the classification of Lev 8:5 and 9:6 see below, II.10.6.2 (b). Because of this stylistic figure S. Boorer considers Exod 16:16–20 a later expansion and excludes it from P^G (see BOORER, *Vision of the Priestly Narrative*, 57).

[29] Cf. all occurrences: Exod 16:1, 2, 9, 10; 17:1; 35:1, 4, 20; Lev 16:5; 19:2; Num 1:2, 53; 8:9, 20; 14:5, 7; 15:25, 26; 25:6; 26:2; 31:12; Josh 18:1; 22:12.

rather than to P^C. Regarding the wording of the Priestly parts of the itinerary notices in 16:1 and 17:1 (containing the element כל עדת בני ישראל, see above), it is probable that the reformulated itinerary notice stems from the same author as Exod 16* (P^S). This author, by reworking the itinerary notices in 16:1 and 17:1 and inventing the wilderness of Sin, "created space in which he could insert his Manna story into the non-priestly context."[30]

The passage about the Sabbath might constitute even a later insertion influenced by H (see above) and thereby be comparable to the additions in Exod 12:14–20 and 12:43–51.[31]

9.3.3 Itinerary Notice in Exodus 19:1–2

Traditionally the entire itinerary notice in 19:1–2a is assigned to the Priestly strand (P^G/P^C).[32] However, the itinerary seems to be overloaded. The arrival at the wilderness of Sinai is reported twice:

Exodus 19:1–2a

¹בחדש השלישי לצאת בני ישראל מארץ מצרים ביום הזה באו מדבר סיני ²ªויסעו מרפידים ויבאו מדבר סיני ויחנו במדבר

¹ In the third month after the Israelites had gone out of the land of Egypt, on that very day they came into the wilderness of Sinai. ²ª And they set out from Rephidim, came to the wilderness of Sinai, and camped in the wilderness.

The second part of the notice (19:2a) matches the pre-Priestly notices in Exod 12:37a; 13:20; 16:1aα; 17:1bα (with the common terms ויסעו, "and they set out," ויחנו, "and they camped"; see above). For this reason, several scholars rightly ascribe 19:2a to non-P (pre-P).[33] As for 19:1, it is commonly assigned to P^G/P^C. It contains typical Priestly motifs and terms, such as the date and the expressions בני ישראל and ביום הזה.

---

[30] ALBERTZ, "Wilderness Material in Exodus," 155. Albertz assigns these texts to his "PB1" (first Priestly redactor).

[31] According to ROSKOP, *Wilderness Itineraries*, 164, the given date in the Priestly itinerary notice (according to our analysis P^S) – 2/15 – would allude to the Sabbath because, according to the ideal 364-day solar calendar, the fifteenth day of the second month would fall on the sixth weekday. However, this is not the only explanation for the concrete temporal setting in 16:1. The Israelites arrive in the desert of Sin exactly one month after having left Egypt. Furthermore, it seems that the Priestly author(s) had an affinity for settings at the new moon and full moon (see Exod 12:6, 12; 16:1; 19:1; 40:17).

[32] NOTH, *Das zweite Buch Mose*, 124–25; ELLIGER, "Sinn," 121; LOHFINK, "Die Priesterschrift," 198, n. 29; COATS, *Rebellion in the Wilderness*, 145; CHILDS, *Exodus*, 274–92; BLUM, *Studien*, 155, n. 235; DOZEMAN, *Commentary on Exodus*, 438–39. WELLHAUSEN, *Die Composition*, 96, assigned 19:2a to P but considered Exod 19:1 to be a later addition ["Nachtrag"]).

[33] P. WEIMAR, "Sinai und Schöpfung: Komposition und Theologie der priesterschriftlichen Sinaigeschichte," *RB* 95 (1988): 359, n. 78; POLA, *Die ursprüngliche Priesterschrift*, 112, 264–65, 268–69; LEVIN, *Der Jahwist*, 364–65; KRATZ, *Composition*, 152, n. 44, 282–83; ALBERTZ, *Exodus 19–40*, 38–39 (who nevertheless assigns 19:2aβ to his first Priestly redactor ["PB1"]).

It is striking that the date appears first and is set apart and further emphasized by the specification ביום הזה, in contrast to the P^s notice in Exod 16:1. Furthermore, the lack of a *wayyiqtol* form (e.g., ויהי) may be interpreted, with Propp, as rendering the following sequence – the report of YHWH's revelation at Sinai and instructions for the tabernacle and their fulfillment – independent of what precedes and thus giving it a particular significance.[34] The specification "on this day" probably points to the first day of the month; if so, *ḥōdeš*, often used for "month" in P, here bears the more original sense of "new moon."[35]

9.3.4 Exodus 20:11: Justification of the Sabbath Commandment

A few scholars who consider P a redaction also assign the justification for the Sabbath instruction in the Ten Commandments (Exod 20:11) to P^c,[36] given the reference to God's rest following his six-day work according to Gen 2:2–3.

It is noteworthy, however, that the notion of the Sabbath in Exod 20:11 differs slightly from the seventh day in Gen 2:2–3. Whereas the former refers to God's rest (cf. נוח, "to rest"), the latter evokes the notion of the cessation of work (cf. מן שבת, "to cease, stop").[37] But perhaps one should not put too much weight on this difference in formulation; the author of Gen 2:2–3 probably used שבת in order to allude to the Sabbath (without mentioning it explicitly); the sense of "rest" may nevertheless be involved.[38] Furthermore, the fact that Exod 20:11 takes up terminology and phrasing from Gen 1:1–2:4a hints at the relatedness of the passages (see the sequence heaven, earth, and sea in Exod 20:11a and the similarity of Exod 20:11b to Gen 2:3a, and further the common expressions ברך *piel*, "to bless" and קדש *piel*, "to make holy").

According to our analysis of Gen 1:1–2:4a, however, the section relating to the seventh day (2:2–3) and the six/seven-day schema should be assigned to the second Priestly redactor (H) rather than to P^c.[39]

---

[34] See W. H. C. PROPP, *Exodus 19–40: A New Translation with Introduction and Commentary*, AB 2A (New York: Doubleday, 2006), 134.

[35] See, among others, NOTH, *Das zweite Buch Mose*, 124; PROPP, *Exodus 19–40*, 134; FISCHER and MARKL, *Das Buch Exodus*, 211.

[36] BLUM, *Studien*, 230; ALBERTZ, *Exodus 19–40*, 64–65.

[37] See KNOHL, *Sanctuary*, 67; J. STACKERT, "Compositional Strata in the Priestly Sabbath: Exodus 31:12–17 and 35:1–3," *JHS* 11, art. 15 (2012): 1–20, https://doi:10.5508/jhs.2011, 13–14, n. 49. Stackert refers to a paper by B. J. SCHWARTZ, "The Sabbath in the Torah Sources," presented at the Annual Meeting of the Society of Biblical Literature, San Diego, California, November 19, 2007.

[38] *HALOT* 1408 proposes the meaning "to rest, to celebrate" for Gen 2:2–3. See also *THAT* 2:863.

[39] See above, II.1.3.6 (c).

9.4 The Profile of the Priestly Texts

The Priestly units in Exod 16–20 are neither well connected to each other nor to the preceding story of the miracle at the sea (Priestly stratum). The late Priestly itinerary notices in 16:1 and 17:1 and the manna story (all P^s) depend on the pre-Priestly itinerary notices in 16:1aα and 17:1bα. A genuine Priestly connection back to the story of the parting of the sea does not exist. At the beginning of the Sinai pericope (Exod 19:1), P^c harks directly back to Israel's exodus in Exod 12:40–41.

10. The Priestly Texts in Exodus 24:15b–40:38: The Tabernacle Account

10.1 Outline of the Priestly Texts and Issues in Scholarly Discussion

The large unit dealing with the construction of the tabernacle (Exod 25–31, 35–40) is held to be the core text of P^G/P^C. The tabernacle account is introduced by the short passage in Exod 24:15b–18, which reports Moses's ascent of Mount Sinai and the appearance of the cloud and the glory of YHWH on the mountain. This unit is traditionally ascribed to the Priestly strand too. A few modern critics, however, question the unity of this unit and (or) its assignment to P^G.

Scholarly debate related to the tabernacle account focuses on several issues. First, there are important differences between the main textual witnesses, especially in the second section (Exod 35–40), the fulfillment account. Here, LXX and, in particular, a manuscript of the Vetus Latina, the Codex Monacensis, have a distinct and shorter text when compared with MT and SP. For instance, in several instances where MT mentions the golden incense altar, the LXX and, to a greater extent, the Vetus Latina (according to Codex Monacensis) omit it. Scholars are divided on the question whether the deviations in LXX and Vetus Latina should be attributed to the translators or to a *Vorlage* distinct from MT and SP. Some scholars believe that the LXX of the fulfillment report reflects a different Hebrew *Vorlage* that predates MT.

Much research on the redaction history of the tabernacle account assigns the last part of the instruction section, Exod 30–31, to a secondary redaction because of several tensions with the preceding chapters. Furthermore, since the fulfillment account in Exod 35–40 includes motifs that appear only in the presumably secondary part of the instruction section in Exod 30–31, many scholars assign most parts of Exod 35–40 to a later redactor as well. A small minority of scholars take the opposite view of the literary-historical relationship between the two sections of the tabernacle account (namely, that Exod 35–40 predates 25–31). In general, scholars are cautious about the possibility of a detailed reconstruction of the complex formation process. However, an engaged examination of the latter nevertheless provides some significant insights.

A further important question in the scholarly investigation of the tabernacle account concerns the relationship of the tabernacle account to the sacrificial legislation in Lev 1–16. One trend in current European research is to consider Exod 40* the end of the Priestly *Grundschrift*; Lev 1–16 would therefore constitute a secondary addition. Other scholars emphasize the connection between Exod 25–29* and Lev 1–16*. Precise conclusions concerning the relationship between the tabernacle account and sacrificial legislation, however, go beyond the framework of the present investigation, which is focused on the Priestly texts in Gen 1–Exod 40.

Other questions pertain to the tradition-historical background of the tabernacle account and its aim (purpose), milieu, and setting. In European research in particular, the tabernacle is often considered to be closely connected to the rebuilding of the (second) temple in Jerusalem after the exile. Today, the unilateral focus on the Jerusalem temple is questioned by scholars who assume instead that the tabernacle account may have been conceived as a model for several sanctuaries in the Persian era. Some scholars see the tabernacle account as utopian literature that takes a critical position against the preexilic temple in Jerusalem.

10.2 The Main Textual Problems in the Tabernacle Account

10.2.1 Introduction

While in the section of the instruction (Exod 25–31) the main textual witnesses mostly agree (but nevertheless differ in a few important differences), the LXX and Vetus Latina (according to Codex Monacensis) distinguish themselves considerably from MT and SP in the fulfillment narrative, in terms of the internal organization of the account. On the whole, LXX and Codex Monacensis both have a considerably shorter text than MT and SP. The concentration of sizable literary (editorial) variants in one specific pericope is unique in the Pentateuch. An important question in this respect pertains to the text-critical value of the fragmentary Codex Monacensis.[1] According to M. Bogaert, this Latin translation relies on a Greek version of Exodus that is older than any other preserved Greek translation of this book.[2] Because of its fragmentary nature, its variant readings are difficult to evaluate. Recently, J. Rhyder has pointed out a possible recensional development in the tradition of Codex Monacensis.[3] According to the report of the construction of the inner sanctum in Monacensis (Ziegler, p. 22, col. 2, line 26, corresponding to Exod 37:2 LXX), the latter is adorned with two seraphim. This variant certainly aims to align the tabernacle with Isa 6:2. Note

---

[1] For the edition of Exod 36–40, see L. Ziegler, *Bruchstücke einer vorhieronymianischen Übersetzung des Pentateuch aus einem Palimpseste der k. Hof- und Staatsbibliothek zu München* (Munich, 1883); A. Dold, "Versuchte Neu- und Erstergänzungen zu den altlateinischen Texten im Cod. Clm 6225 der Bayer. Staatsbibliothek," *Bib* 37 (1956): 39–58.

[2] P.-M. Bogaert, "L'importance de la Septante et du 'Monacensis' de la Vetus Latina pour l'exégèse du livre de l'Exode (chap. 35–40)," in *Studies in the Book of Exodus: Redaction – Reception – Interpretation*, ed. M. Vervenne, BETL 126 (Leuven: Leuven University Press, 1996); idem, "La construction de la Tente (Ex 36–40) dans le Monacensis de la plus ancienne version latine: L'autel d'or et Hébreux 9,4," in *L'enfance de la Bible hébraïque: Histoire du texte de l'Ancien Testament*, ed. A. Schenker and P. Hugo, MdB 52 (Geneva: Labor et Fides, 2005), 63–64.

[3] J. Rhyder, *Centralizing the Cult: The Holiness Legislation in Leviticus 17–26*, FAT 134 (Tübingen: Mohr Siebeck, 2019), 50–51.

furthermore that Codex Monacensis shares with LXX the midrash-like allusion to the Korahites' rebellion (see Num 16–17) in Exod 38:22 that forms a plus when compared with MT.

Commentators are divided in their evaluations of the textual differences in the fulfillment account. Scholars have long thought that these divergences were due to a different Hebrew *Vorlage*.[4] Because the LXX differs more substantially from the instruction section than do MT and SP, some consider LXX (and the Vetus Latina) to have preserved the more original text form, MT and SP having been adjusted to Exod 25–29.[5] Others attribute the deviations in LXX to the translator or to a later reviser who would have rearranged the Greek text independently from the Hebrew.[6]

Specialists in LXX studies note a further question related to the LXX translation: in several respects the translation of the fulfillment account (of its mayor part) distinguishes itself from that of the first section and of Exod 1–34 in general.

There are striking differences in the lexical choices between the translations of the two sections of the tabernacle account. To give an example: the first tabernacle account renders Hebrew בד, "pole, stave," in a systematic manner with three different terms. The poles of the ark and the table are named ἀναφορεύς (see Exod 25:13, 14, 15, 27, 28), those of the bronze altar φορεύς (27:6, 7), and those of the incense altar σκυτάλη (30:4, 5). The translator of the second account, however, uses ἀναφορεύς only once, namely for the first mention of the poles of the ark (35:12); afterward he prefers διωστήρ for the poles of the ark and those of the table (37:14, 15 [LXX 38:10, 11]; 39:35 [LXX 14]; 40:20) and μοχλός for the poles of the bronze altar (38:5 [LXX 24]).[7] Another example pertains to the designation of the compass points in the sections on the construction of the courtyard.[8] The translator of the second account chose two different renderings for the Hebrew terms, as compared to the first account.[9] Furthermore, the orientation is different. Though in

---

[4] Popper, *Der biblische Bericht über die Stiftshütte*; Wellhausen, *Die Composition*, 144–47; R. D. Nelson, "Studies in the Development of the Tabernacle Account" (Ph.D. diss., Harvard University, 1987); A. Aejmelaeus, "Septuagintal Translation Techniques: A Solution to the Problem of the Tabernacle Account," in *Collected Essays: On the Trail of Septuagint Translators* (Kampen: Kok Pharos, 1993); Bogaert, "L'importance de la Septante et du 'Monacensis' de la Vetus Latina,"; Nihan, *From Priestly Torah*, 32–33, with n. 68.

[5] See Popper, *Der biblische Bericht über die Stiftshütte*; Aejmelaeus, "Septuagintal Translation Techniques"; Bogaert, "L'importance de la Septante"; Nihan, *From Priestly Torah*, 32–33, with n. 68. According to these scholars, neither LXX nor the Codex Monacensis of Vetus Latina reflects the original text; both are adjusted to MT.

[6] A. H. Finn, "The Tabernacle Chapters," *JTS* 16 (1914–15): 449–82; J. W. Wevers, *Notes on the Greek Text of Exodus*, SCS 30 (Atlanta: Society of Biblical Literature, 1990), 392.

[7] See M. L. Wade, *Consistency of Translation Techniques in the Tabernacle Accounts of Exodus in the Old Greek*, SBLSCS 49 (Leiden: Brill, 2003), 89–90.

[8] See P.-M. Bogaert, "L'Orientation du parvis du sanctuaire dans la version grecque de l'Exode (Ex., 27, 9–13 LXX)," *L'Antiquité classique* 50 (1981): 79–85; J. W. Wevers, *Text History of the Greek Exodus* (Göttingen: Vandenhoeck & Ruprecht, 1992), 123, 146; Wade, *Consistency of Translation Techniques*, 98–100.

[9] Whereas the instruction account designates the east ἀπηλιώτης and the north θάλασσαν ("toward the sea"), the fulfillment account uses the terms ἀνατολή (east) and βορρᾶς (north) (see the following footnote).

Exod 27 LXX the sanctuary complex is rotated 90 degrees (compared to MT), which seems to be an adaption to an Alexandrian perspective (the sea side indicates the northern compass point instead of the western cardinal point [cf. MT]), Exod 37 LXX agrees with MT's orientation. As a consequence, in Exod 27 LXX the gate of the courtyard is facing south, whereas according to Exod 37 LXX (38 MT) it is facing east (which corresponds to MT of Exod 27; 38).[10] In the re-adaptation to the Palestinian orientation in Exod 37 LXX one might see a clue to the supposed chronological order of Exod 25–29 LXX > 35–40 LXX: while current research localizes the early LXX translations, in particular those of the Pentateuch, in Egypt, more precisely in Alexandria, it views the origin of most of the later translations and revisions in Palestine.[11]

Because of these and other differences in lexical choices, some scholars suggest that Exod 35–40 (or its core, 36:8–38:20) was translated by a second translator after Exod 1–34.[12] If this is correct, it raises the question whether the second section had not yet been composed when the first section was translated.[13] This question is of great importance for the history of the formation of the tabernacle account (see below).[14]

The assumption of a second translator complicates the examination of the textual differences in the fulfillment section. The LXX's translation technique in Exod 35–40 (or 36:8–38:20) has to be evaluated independently from Exod 1–34.[15] It seems that the translator omitted either obscure or redundant words or perhaps even passages.[16] Nevertheless, a few agreements between LXX and SP against MT show that the *Vorlage* of LXX was different from that of MT (Exod 35:13, 14b; 38:25b).[17] Moreover, in her concise study of the LXX version of the tabernacle account, A. Aejmelaeus

---

[10] The renderings of the compass points in the instruction account are as follows (see Exod 27:9–15): λίψ (west) – נגב תימן (south); ἀπηλιώτης (east) – צפון (north); θάλασσαν ("toward the sea" = north) – לפאת ים (toward the sea = west); νότος (south) – קדמה מזרחה (east). In the fulfillment account the compass points are translated as follows (see Exod 37:7–11 LXX [38:9–15 MT]): λίψ (south) – נגב תימן (south); 37:9: βορρᾶς (north) – צפון (north); 37:10: θάλασσαν ("toward the sea" = west) – לפאת ים ("toward the sea" = west); 37:11: ἀνατολή (east) – קדם מזרח (east).

[11] Tov, *Text-Critical Use of the Septuagint*, 203–6.

[12] See Popper, *Der biblische Bericht über die Stiftshütte*, 172–76 (only Exod 36:8–38:20 is translated by the second translator); Wellhausen, *Die Composition*, 146–47 (Exod 35–40 is translated by the second translator); Nelson, "Studies in the Development of the Tabernacle Account" (only Exod 36:8–38:20 is translated by the second translator); Wevers, Text History of the Greek Exodus, 146 ("tentative conclusion"; Exod 35–40 is translated by the second translator); Wade, Consistency of Translation *Techniques*, 236–45 (Exod 35–40 is translated by the second translator). Differently Aejmelaeus, "Septuagintal Translation Techniques," 122–25.

[13] Assuming this, Popper, *Der biblische Bericht über die Stiftshütte*, 172–76; Wellhausen, *Die Composition*, 147; Nelson, "Studies in the Development of the Tabernacle Account."

[14] See II.10.4.2. For Wellhausen, the evidence pointing to two different translators of the tabernacle account is the most important result of Popper's thorough study of the tabernacle account (see Wellhausen, *Die Composition*, 146–47).

[15] For the classification of Exod 1–34 (relatively free, compared to the translations of the other books in the Pentateuch), see above, II.7.2.1.

[16] See Wevers, *Text History of the Greek Exodus*, 145, and case 10.2.2.(h), below.

[17] See Schwagmeier, "Exodos, Exodus, Das zweite Buch Mose," 120–45.

discusses several "samples" of LXX Exod 36–40.[18] In these examples, the text of LXX, though it distinguishes itself from MT in small details (minor pluses or minuses), nevertheless provides readings that reflect Hebrew phrasings known from other passages in MT.[19] This means that not every deviation of the LXX should be assigned to the translator. Possibly, LXX originally deviated more from MT but was later adjusted to MT, as suggested by certain variants of Codex Monacensis.[20]

10.2.2 Textual Differences

(a1) Exodus 25:6

MT, SP: שמן למאר בשמים לשמן המשחה ולקטרת הסמים
LXX: —

(a2) Exodus 35:8

MT, SP: ושמן למאור ובשמים לשמן המשחה ולקטרת הסמים
LXX: —

In the list of items for the donation offering, the LXX includes neither oil for illumination, nor fragrances for the anointing oil and for the spice incense (see Exod 25:6). The analogous minus is observable in the fulfillment report (see Exod 35:8). A few commentators suppose a deliberate or inadvertent omission in LXX. The scribe of the *Vorlage* or the translator would have considered oil and spices incongruous alongside the mentioned construction materials.[21] Others maintain that the LXX reading was caused by a *parablepsis* due to *homoioteleuton* (cf. *štym* in v. 5 to *smym* in v. 6). However, the latter explanation applies only to Exod 25:6, not to 35:8.[22] The textual difference can be clarified more convincingly in light of the absence of the incense altar in Exod 25–29* (probably constituting the primary layer of the instruction report) and its presence in the supplemental section Exod 30–31.[23] MT and SP seem to have been expanded in view of the secondary introduction of the incense altar in Exod 30; the shorter reading of LXX is preferable. Since oil is used not only for the preparation of

---

[18] See AEJMELAEUS, "Septuagintal Translation Techniques," 125–26.

[19] See also the numerous examples in M. L. WADE, *Consistency of Translation Techniques in the Tabernacle Accounts of Exodus in the Old Greek*, SBLSCS 49 (Leiden: Brill, 2003), 149–212.

[20] An intriguing variant in Codex Monacensis is the explicit attribution of certain works concerning the tabernacle (including wooden utensils such as the ark) to Oholiab. See BOGAERT, "L'importance de la Septante," 413–16; D. LO SARDO, *Post-Priestly Additions and Rewritings in Exodus 35–40: An Analysis of MT, LXX, and Vetus Latina*, FAT II/119 (Mohr Siebeck: Tübingen, 2020), 53–54, 62.

[21] DILLMANN and KNOBEL, *Die Bücher Exodus und Leviticus*, 309; WEVERS, *Notes on the Greek Text of Exodus*, 392.

[22] See PROPP, *Exodus 19–40*, 320.

[23] See below, II.10.4.1 (a).

the spice incense but also for lighting the lampstand and for the ointment, these two purposes were added in MT and SP too.

(b1) Exodus 28:23–28

MT, SP: instruction for the fabrication of golden rings to be placed on the corners of the ḥōšen and on the shoulder-pieces and for the connection of the ḥōšen with the shoulder-pieces through two golden chains and a blue cord
LXX: —

(b2) Exodus 28:29

Plus LXX (at the end of the verse): brief explanation of how the ḥōšen is fastened to the Ephod

The plus in Exod 28:29 LXX seems to compensate secondarily for the minus in 28:23–28. Its awkward position after the statement about the enrobed Aaron entering the sanctuary probably reveals its secondary character. The minus in 28:23–28 might be due to a parablepsis through homoioarkton (ועשית [beginning of v. 23] – ונשא [beginning of v. 29]) or through homoioteleuton (טהור [end of v. 22] to האפוד [end of v. 28]; resh/dalet).[24]

(c1) Exodus 28:30

SP: ועשית את האורים ואת התמים ונתתה
MT, LXX: —

(c2) Exodus 39:21

SP, 4QExod-Levᶠ: ויעשו את האורים ואת התמים כאשר צוה יהוה את משה
MT, LXX: —

In both parallel texts belonging to the instruction section and to the fulfillment account, respectively, SP has a plus related to the fabrication of the Urim and Thummim.

Prima facie, both pluses may be explained by accidental loss of text in MT and LXX. In 28:30, the missing text may have fallen out of MT and LXX *Vorlage* by *parablepsis* owing to *homoioteleuton* or *homoioarkton* (cf. ועשית, "and you shall make" with ונתת, "and you give"). The same explanation is possible in 39:21 (*homoioteleuton* or *homoioarkton*; cf. כאשר צוה יהוה את משה, "as YHWH had ordered Moses," with כאשר צוה יהוה את משה, "as YHWH had ordered Moses").[25] However, a "double" accidental loss of text related to the same motif does not seem likely.

Might one imagine a deliberate omission in MT and in LXX? Or, regarding the

---

[24] See Propp, *Exodus 19–40*, 345–46, who points to a further possibility: a skip in Greek from καὶ 'and' to καὶ 'and'.

[25] Cf. F. M. Cross, "4QExod-Levᶠ," in *Qumran Cave 4.VII*, ed. E. Ulrich et al., DJD 12 (Oxford: Clarendon, 1994), 139.

expansionistic tendency observable in SP, is it more probable that a scribe of SP wanted to assure the Urim and Thummim's fabrication at Sinai (the Urim and Thummim are one of the rare items mentioned in the tabernacle account that are not produced or worked on by the Israelites![26])? The starting point in answering this question is the observation that the case of Exod 39:21 MT, LXX is different from that of 28:30 MT, LXX insofar as the Urim and Thummim are not mentioned there at all. Moreover, the breastpiece of judgment (חשֶׁן מִשְׁפָּט), which in Exod 28 alludes to the use of the Urim and Thummim (see 28:15, 29, 30),[27] does not appear in the corresponding passage in the fulfillment section (see חשֶׁן, "breastpiece," 39:8, 9, 15, 19, 21 [2×]).[28] This makes it likely that the author of the fulfillment account *consciously left out the motif of the Urim and Thummim.*[29] Probably a scribe of SP and 4QExod-Levᶠ was bothered by this incongruency between instruction and fulfillment section and keen to supplement both a fabrication instruction (see Exod 28:30) and a realization notice (39:21).[30]

(d) Exodus 29:43

MT: וְנֹעַדְתִּי
LXX: τάξομαι
SP: ונדרשתי

In the short verse 29:43 (וְנֹעַדְתִּי שָׁמָּה לִבְנֵי יִשְׂרָאֵל וְנִקְדַּשׁ בִּכְבֹדִי), the main textual witnesses diverge twice. The first difference concerns the verb at the beginning of the sentence. דרשׁ *niphal*, "to be inquirable, to let oneself be consulted," with the deity as subject, does not appear anywhere else in P (in non-P texts, it appears in Isa 65:1; Ezek 14:3; 20:3, 31; 36:37). In contrast, יעד *niphal*, "to be meetable, to let be met," is a key word in the tabernacle account. The reading of both SP and LXX (translation) ("And I will there give orders to the Israelites") might be explained by the attempt to attenuate the theologically daring statement of MT (according to which not a single person but rather the whole nation will encounter YHWH).[31] In the case of SP, a motive might also have been to harmonize with Exod 18:15, where the Israelites inquire (דרשׁ) of Elohim through Moses.[32]

(e) Exodus 29:43

MT, SP: וְנִקְדַּשׁ בִּכְבֹדִי
LXX: καὶ ἁγιασθήσομαι ἐν δόξῃ μου
          (?) וְנִקְדַּשְׁתִּי בִּכְבֹדִי =

Since Targums Onkelos and Pseudo-Jonathan also read a first common singular

---

[26] Another example is the עֵדֻת ("testimony"; see Exod 25:16, 21–22; 40:20).
[27] SP and LXX (λογεῖον τῆς κρίσεως) agree with MT.
[28] SP and LXX (λογεῖον) agree with MT.
[29] For a possible motive, see below, II.10.4.2.
[30] See also PROPP, *Exodus 19–40*, 346–47 and 654.
[31] See ALBERTZ, *Exodus 19–40*, 227.
[32] See PROPP, *Exodus 19–40*, 355–56.

(ואתקדש ביקרי), it is possible that LXX's *Vorlage* read ונקדשתי בכבדי, "I will be sanctified in my glory." Not to be excluded, however, is an independent development in these three translations from a common exegetical tendency.

At any rate, this alternative reading of LXX/LXX *Vorlage* and Targums Onkelos and Pseudo-Jonathan most probably is caused by the ambiguity of the reading of MT, SP ("it/one will be made holy"; it is not clear which is the subject). This obscurity is probably due to the redactional insertion of the passage 29:38–42 (dealing with the תמיד sacrifice). The subject of ונקדש in 29:43 is the altar that is the focus of 29:36–37.[33] A scribe of the *Vorlage* of LXX, Targum Onkelos, and Targum Pseudo-Jonathan (or the translators of these texts) was (were) probably not aware of the statement's connection to 29:36–37 and therefore harmonized with the subject of the first half of the verse (first-person singular). The reading of MT, SP is to be preferred.

(f) Exodus 30:1–10

MT, LXX: post 29:46
SP, 4QpaleoExod[m]: post 26:35

The instruction concerning the incense altar appears in different places in MT and LXX (after Exod 29:46) on the one hand and in SP and 4QpaleoExod[m] (after Exod 26:35) on the other.[34] This divergence is certainly due to a deliberate displacement by a scribe in the textual tradition of SP and 4QpaleoExod[m] who wanted to improve the order of the various items in the instruction section in Exod 25–31:[35] the incense altar is associated with the other tabernacle furniture (table, lampstand) to be set in front of the veil. This order also appears in the fulfillment section. In several instances, SP adapts the instruction section to the fulfillment section.[36]

(g) Exodus 35–40

Different internal orders of topics in MT, SP on the one hand and LXX, Codex Monacensis on the other

All the textual witnesses reflect different internal orders for the manufactured items in the fulfillment section when compared with the order of these items in the instruction

---

[33] See further below, II.10.4.1 (b).

[34] P. W. SKEHAN, E. ULRICH, and J. E. SANDERSON, *Palaeo-Hebrew and Greek Biblical Manuscripts with a Contribution by P. J. Parsons*, DJD 9 (Oxford: Clarendon, 1992), 23.

[35] NIHAN, *From Priestly Torah*, 32, is right in seeing in the reading of SP and 4QpaleoExod[m] proof that the considerations of modern scholars related to the inappropriate place of the incense altar are "not merely a matter of modern taste" (in response to M. HARAN, *Temples and Temple Service in Ancient Israel* [Oxford: Oxford University Press, 1978], 228–29, and C. MEYERS, "Realms of Sanctity: The Case of the 'Misplaced' Incense Altar in the Tabernacle Texts of Exodus," in *Texts, Temples, and Traditions: A Tribute to Menahem Haran*, ed. M. V. Fox et al. [Winona Lake, IN: Eisenbrauns, 1996], 33–46).

[36] See POPPER, *Der biblische Bericht über die Stiftshütte*, 84–104, and WELLHAUSEN, *Die Composition*, 145–46.

section (where MT, SP, and LXX agree), but to different extents. In MT and SP, the fabrication of the tabernacle precedes the manufacture of the cultic furniture for the holy of holies (ark with cover [mercy seat], golden table, lampstand). These latter articles are mentioned first in the instruction section. For the remaining items (the court with its hangings and pillars and the priest's vestments), the order is the same as in the instruction section. In LXX, the sequence deviates much more from that of the instruction account; the making of the priestly garments appears at the beginning, preceding the fabrication of the tabernacle and the courtyard; the cultic furniture follows only afterward.[37]

In two instances, LXX's arrangement does not seem coherent and appears to depend on the order of MT. In Exod 39:10–12 LXX (38:31–39:1 MT), LXX agrees with the order of MT against the logic of its own composition: Exod 39:13 LXX (39:1 MT), dealing with the blue, purple, and scarlet material to be used for the garments of ministry for Aaron, should naturally follow 36:8 (LXX), at the beginning of the section on the vestments for the priests. Similarly, the beginning of the cost accounting in 37:19–21 LXX (38:21–23 MT) follows after 37:18 LXX (38:20 MT), although its natural place would be after the report of the accomplishment of the various works (between 38:27 LXX and 39:1 LXX). Following Wellhausen's reasoning, one might tentatively assume MT's priority.[38] Or is LXX's agreement with MT in Exod 39:10–12 LXX and in 37:19–21 LXX due to LXX's later sporadic adjustment to MT?

(h) Exodus 35–40

MT, SP: wooden boards (or frames) as interior fittings
            (קרשים; Exod 35:11; 36:20–34; 39:33 [LXX 39:13]; 40:18)
LXX Vorlage: ?

In LXX, according to Codex Vaticanus of the instruction section, the Hebrew term קרש, "wooden board,"[39] is consistently rendered by the expression στῦλος, "post."[40] στῦλος also renders עמוד, "pillar, post."[41] In the fulfillment section, στῦλος seems to

---

[37] See the figure in Aejmelaeus, "Septuagintal Translation Techniques," 119.

[38] See Wellhausen, *Die Composition*, 146–47, n. 3.

[39] The noun קרש appears only in the tabernacle account and in Ezek 27:6, where the meaning is uncertain (suggested meanings are "deck," "living room," and "post"; see HALOT 1149). For the tabernacle account, the meaning "board" is proposed by HALOT 1149, BDB 903, and most translations and commentaries. A few scholars render the term "frame" or "trellis"; see Aejmelaeus, "Septuagintal Translation Techniques," 128–29 ("frame"); Propp, *Exodus 19–40*, 410–11 ("trellis"); D. Fleming, "Mari's Large Public Tent and the Priestly Tent Sanctuary," *VT* 50 (2000): 489–90.

[40] See Exod 26:15, 16 (2×), 17 (2×), 18 (2×), 19 (3×), 20, 21 (2×), 22, 23, 25 (3×), 26, 27 (2×), 28, 29.

[41] See Exod 27:10, 11 (2×), 12, 14, 15, 16, 17.

render קרשׁ only once (Exod 38:18 LXX/36:34 MT[42]) but עמוד several times.[43] Most strikingly, the report of the fabrication of the boards (posts) in Exod 36:20–33 MT – immediately preceding Exod 38:18 LXX/36:34 MT – is absent from LXX.[44] Moreover, LXX does not have an equivalent for קרשׁ in the lists in 35:4–29 (cf. 35:11 [LXX: 35:10]); 39:33 (LXX 39:14); and 40:18. According to Aejmelaeus, who believes that the LXX reflects a Hebrew *Vorlage* distinct from MT (see below), this might indicate that the motif of the קרשׁים was absent from the original fulfillment account.[45]

P.-M. Bogaert, by contrast, points out the presence of a detailed report on the fabrication of the boards in Codex Monacensis (Exod 37:1–2 LXX[46]), which differs significantly from MT. He conjectures that there is a deliberate editorial omission of the wooden framework in LXX due to its distinct conceptualization when compared with Exod 25–29. The original LXX still reflected in Codex Monacensis would have reported the fabrication of the wooden posts (boards).[47]

Another explanation for the absence of an equivalent for קרשׁ in Exod 35–40 LXX is as follows: the translator of the fulfillment section was bothered by the presence of the two nouns קרשׁ and עמוד – which, as already mentioned, are both rendered by στῦλος, "pillar, post," in the instruction section – *in one and the same verse* (see Exod 35:11 [LXX: 35:10]; 39:33 [LXX 39:14]; 40:18).[48] He decided to translate only one of them (i.e., עמוד, because he was more familiar with this noun).[49]

Another minus in the fulfillment report might be explained similarly. As in the case of קרשׁ and עמוד, the translators "assimilated" the "tabernacle" (משכן) and the "tent of meeting" (אהל מועד), making them into two seemingly identical items by using the rendering σκηνή for both of them.[50] Even in cases where the two expressions occur together, the translator of the fulfillment section

---

[42] "He overlaid the posts (στύλους < את הקרשׁים) with silver, and cast for each post golden rings, and gilded the bars with gold; and he gilded the posts of the veil with gold, and made the hooks of gold."

[43] See Exod 35:11, 12 (LXX 17); 37:4 (LXX 36:36), 6 (36:38), 8 (38:10), 10 (38:12), 12 (38:14), 13 (38:15), 15 (38:17; 2×), 17 (38:19); 38:28 (39:6), 33 (14), 40 (20); 40:18.

[44] See BOGAERT, "L'importance de la Septante," 409.

[45] See AEJMELAEUS, "Septuagintal Translation Techniques," 128–29.

[46] Cf. the edition and the reconstruction in DOLD, "Versuchte Neu- und Erstergänzungen zu den altlateinischen Texten," 44–45.

[47] See P.-M. BOGAERT, "L'importance de la Septante," 409, and IDEM, "La construction de la Tente (Ex 36–40) dans le Monacensis de la plus ancienne version latine: L'autel d'or et Hébreux 9,4," in *L'enfance de la Bible hébraïque: Histoire du texte de l'Ancien Testament*, ed. A. Schenker and P. Hugo, MdB 52 (Geneva: Labor et Fides, 2005), 63–64.

[48] Since the three lists have no parallels in the instruction section, the latter's translator was not confronted with this problem.

[49] See also WADE, *Consistency of Translation Techniques*, 93, n. 47, who, however, also entertains the possibility that the minus was due to the abbreviation of the text by a scribe of LXX's *Vorlage*.

[50] משכן is consistently rendered by σκηνή and אהל mostly but not always so (for the latter, see Exod 26:9, 12, 13, 14; 27:21; 28:43; 29:4, 11, 30, 32, 42, 44; 30:16, 18, 20, 26, 36; 31:7 [2×]; 35:21; 37:5 [MT 36:37]; 38:26 [MT 8], 27 [MT 40:30]; 39:8 [MT 38:30], 14 [MT 39:33], 21 [MT 39:40]; 40:2, 6, 12, 19, 24, 26, 29, 34).

only rarely differentiates between them;[51] more frequently he translates both terms with σκηνή[52] or he renders only one of them.[53]

Therefore, the omission of the report of the fabrication of the "pillars" (στῦλοι < קרשׁים; Exod 36:20–33 MT) before Exod 38:18 LXX might be due the preceding report of manufacture of pillars in chapter 37 (στῦλοι < עמודים). A further reason for the omission might have been the difficulty of the meaning of στῦλος, the Greek rendering of קרשׁ, within its context:[54] The translator of the fulfillment section could not make sense of a vertical pillar of ten cubits "length" and one and a half cubits "width" (these designations match measures of horizontal articles instead), which had two tenons through which it was connected to another pillar.

(i) Exodus 35–40

Partial absence of the incense altar in LXX and in Codex Monacensis

The report of the fabrication of the incense altar (Exod 37:25–29) does not appear in either LXX or Codex Monacensis.[55] The incense altar is also absent from the list in 35:4–29 LXX (cf. 35:14–15 LXX with 35:15 MT).[56] In both witnesses, the incense altar nevertheless appears in a few summaries (Exod 39:38 [LXX 39:15][57]; 40:5); in LXX (but not in Monacensis) furthermore in 40:26–27.

Since the minuses in LXX and Codex Monacensis concerning the incense altar coincide with the awkward placement of this piece of furniture in the instruction section (see further below), scholars believe that the Greek text in Exod 35–40*, in comparison with MT, reflects a more primitive literary stage. At the point when Exod 35–40* was translated, the instruction concerning the incense altar (Exod 30:1–10) would not have existed yet.[58] Only at a later time would the text of LXX have gradually been adapted to MT. What makes me skeptical of this theory is the frequent mention of the fragrant incense in the fulfillment report (see Exod 35:12 LXX, 19 LXX; 39:15 LXX; 40:27 LXX). In Exod 35:12 LXX the reference to the spice incense obviously presupposes the altar of fragrance, which is the preceding item in the corresponding 35:15

---

[51] See Exod 35:11; 40:19.

[52] See Exod 40:22, 24, 34, 35.

[53] See Exod 39:21 (MT 40); 40:2,6, 29.

[54] See also Wevers, *Text History of the Greek Exodus*, 145.

[55] On the text of Codex Monacensis, see Bogaert, "L'importance de la Septante," and idem, "La construction de la Tente," 62–76.

[56] In this section (Exod 35) the text of Codex Monacensis is not preserved.

[57] Since the term θυσιαστήριον, "altar," is not specified, scholars do not agree on its referent. Regarding the subsequent expression "and all its furniture" (αὐτοῦ), some scholars consider θυσιαστήριον to refer to the altar of burnt offering. However, because of the subsequent mention of the fragrant incense and the anointing oil (συνθέσεως), one should think instead of the incense altar (see Bogaert, "La construction de la Tente," 70; Wade, *Consistency of Translation Techniques*, 189).

[58] Popper, *Der biblische Bericht über die Stiftshütte*; Wellhausen, *Die Composition*,139; Nelson, "Studies in the Development of the Tabernacle Account."

MT. (The fragrant incense should not be associated with the altar of burnt offering [cf. v. 16], because the accessory always follows the main item [cf. the analogous "natural" sequence in v. 14: lampstand for lighting – oil for lighting]). Moreover, there are indications that the translation of 35–40 postdates that of Exod 1–34 (see above). For these reason, one should consider the possibility that the golden altar was deliberately omitted from the fulfillment report by a later scribe of LXX *Vorlage* or by the translator. Perhaps some dispute over the legitimacy of offering incense without sacrifice led to the omission of the incense altar in the aforementioned passages of LXX.[59] This means that when dealing with the textual differences concerning the altar of fragrance one should not necessarily prospect a strict linear development (absence of the altar of fragrance – introduction of the altar of fragrance – general acceptance of it), such a view would probably be too simplistic.

10.3 The Unity and Literary Classification of Exodus 24:15b–18a (Introduction to the Tabernacle Account)

10.3.1 The Unity of Exodus 24:15b–18a

Traditionally, Exod 24:15b–18a is considered a unified unit and assigned to P^G/P^C.[60] According to a minority of scholars, however, v. 17 disrupts the internal logic of the unit and belongs to a secondary Priestly or non-Priestly layer or to a post-Priestly layer.[61]

Exodus 24:15b–18a
[15b] And the cloud covered the mountain. [16] And the glory of YHWH settled upon Mount Sinai, and the cloud covered it for six days; and on the seventh day he called to Moses from the midst of the cloud. [17] And to the eyes of the Israelites the appearance of the glory of YHWH was like a consuming fire on the mountain top. [18a] And Moses entered the midst of the cloud and he went up to the mountain.

How to understand the narrative logic of the text as it is transmitted? Exodus 24:15 states that the cloud covered the mountain. Verse 16aα refers to the dwelling of the glory of YHWH on Mount Sinai. Verse 16aβ takes up the assertion of v. 15b but specifies: the cloud covered the mountain for six days. Verse 16b adds that on the seventh day YHWH called to Moses out of the midst of the cloud. Even though, considered on its own, the statement that the mountain was covered by the cloud for six days would

---

[59] See PROPP, *Exodus 19–40*, 369.

[60] DILLMANN and KNOBEL, *Die Bücher Exodus und Leviticus*, 291; BAENTSCH, *Exodus–Leviticus–Numeri*, 268; NOTH, *Das zweite Buch Mose*, 163; ELLIGER, "Sinn," 121; LOHFINK, "Die Priesterschrift," 198, n. 29; POLA, *Die ursprüngliche Priesterschrift*, 217, 219, 266, 349.

[61] WEIMAR, "Sinai und Schöpfung," 359, n. 78; SCHMID, "Der Sinai," 114–27; Hesitating, FREVEL, *Mit Blick*, 140–41, n. 8.

imply that on the seventh day the mountain was uncovered, the subsequent assertion (v. 16b) makes clear that this is not case: the cloud remained on the mountain after the sixth day; the six-day period related to the cloud's *silent* rest on the mountain. This interpretation is also confirmed by the later v. 18a, which states that Moses entered the cloud. Verse 17, however, suggests a different understanding of the passage: since the "glory of YHWH" was visible to all the people on the seventh day, the cloud must have disappeared on that day.[62] Since such an understanding is contradicted by the context, Schmid considers 24:17 a secondary insertion.[63] He also points to certain expressions and motifs in 24:17 that are not used elsewhere in P[G] but that appear in non-Priestly texts (אש אכלת, "a consuming fire";[64] לעיני בני ישראל, "before the eyes of the Israelites";[65] ראש ההר, "summit of the mountain"[66]).[67] Taken together, Schmid's arguments seem compelling; v. 17 was probably inserted by a later redactor.

However, one should ask whether not only v. 17 but also the preceding v. 16aβ–b is secondary. It repeats the statement that the cloud covered the mountain in v. 15b (P). Furthermore, as Schmid points out, this statement establishes an inapt parallel to Gen 2:2–3 (see below). For this reason, one should consider the possibility that v.16aβ–b was – perhaps together with v. 17 – inserted secondarily. The original text would have run as follows:

Exodus 24:15b, 16aα, 18a
[15b] And the cloud covered the mountain. [16aα] And the glory of YHWH settled upon Mount Sinai. [18a] And Moses entered the midst of the cloud and he went up to the mountain.

10.3.2 The Literary Classification of 24:15b–18a*

As for the passage's relationship to the Priestly context, W. Oswald and K. Schmid have observed that two important motifs in Exod 24:15b–18a, the mountain and the cloud, are not introduced in the preceding Priestly texts.[68] When the Priestly stratum is read as source, the definite forms (ההר and הענן) come as a surprise:

---

[62] Differently Houtman, according to whom the presence of the cloud and the visibility of the glory of YHWH do not contradict each other; he argues that "presumably the light was so intensively bright that it shone through the cloud" (see HOUTMAN, *Exodus*, 2:304).

[63] SCHMID, "Der Sinai," 120–21; see also FREVEL, *Mit Blick*, 140–41, n. 8.

[64] Within the Pentateuch there are only two further attestations: Deut 4:24 (post-Priestly); 9:3.

[65] Besides Exod 24:17 there are only two occurrences, in Num 20:12; Josh 22:33.

[66] This expression does not occur elsewhere in Priestly texts. In the immediate context, it is used in two non-Priestly texts, Exod 19:20; 34:2.

[67] SCHMID, "Der Sinai," 120–21. See also WEIMAR, "Sinai und Schöpfung," 359, n. 78 who refers to the expressions אש אכלת and לעיני בני ישראל.

[68] W. OSWALD, *Israel am Gottesberg: Eine Untersuchung zur Literaturgeschichte der vorderen Sinaiperikope Ex 19–24 und deren historischem Hintergrund*, OBO 159 (Fribourg: Presses

Exodus 19:1; 24:15b–16

[19:1] In the third month after the Israelites had gone out of the land of Egypt, on that very day they came into the wilderness of Sinai. [24:15b] And *the cloud* covered *the mountain.* [16] And the glory of YHWH settled upon Mount Sinai, …

Schmid considers it unlikely that the article has a cataphoric function, particularly in the case of the mountain, which does not play an important role in P.[69]

As far I can see, cataphoric determination is rare in the Priestly texts; in the following tabernacle account, nouns designating important articles, such as the sanctuary, the ark, the cover, the table and the lampstand, do not carry the article when they are mentioned for the first time.[70] An exception is the altar for animal sacrifices.[71]

Oswald and Schmid conclude that the two motifs depend on the previous non-Priestly context, where Mount Sinai (see Exod 19:18–20) and the cloud (Exod 19:16) are mentioned.[72] Would this not suggest that P in this section is a redaction that takes up motifs from its non-P context, rather than a source? Both Oswald and Schmid reject this possibility, again because of the limited importance they assign to the mountain in P[G];[73] rather, they are inclined to ascribe Exod 24:15b–18 to a secondary Priestly (P[s]) or post-Priestly (Pentateuch redactor) stratum.[74]

Schmid sees a further problematic point hindering the passage's assignment to P[G]. At first sight, Exod 24:15b–18 contains a six/seven-day structure similar to Gen 1:1–2:4a (six workdays plus a day of rest). The cloud covers Mount Sinai for six days, and YHWH calls Moses on the seventh day. However, in Schmid's view this parallel is not really apt because the structure of Exod 24:15b–18a is the inverse of that in Gen 1:1–2:4a:[75] Mount Sinai is covered by the cloud for six days, and on the seventh day YHWH speaks to Moses. Thus it is only on the seventh day that YHWH becomes active (calling Moses), and on the same day Moses also becomes active and goes up the mountain. This does not fit with the idea of the Sabbath as a day with cessation of activity, as described in Gen 2:2–3 (after six working days, God rests on the seventh day).[76] Since

---

Universitaires; Göttingen: Vandenhoeck & Ruprecht, 1998), 205, 206; SCHMID, "Der Sinai," 115–17.

[69] SCHMID, "Der Sinai," 116. On the cataphoric use of the article, see *GKC* §126q.

[70] See Exod 25:9 (מקדש), 10 (ארון עצי שטים), 17 (כפרת זהר טהור), 23 (שלחן עצי שטים), 31 (מנרת זהב טהור).

[71] See Exod 27:1 MT (המזבח עצי שטים). SP and LXX have undetermined forms, probably for harmonistic reasons regarding the incense altar in Exod 30:1–10. The use of the article may be explained by the fact that the altar is "the sine qua non of any cult site" (A. B. EHRLICH, *Randglossen zur hebräischen Bibel 1* [Leipzig: Hinrichs, 1908], 371). In addition, the noun קרשים ("boards" or "frames") carries the article at its first occurrence in the tabernacle account (26:15).

[72] OSWALD, *Israel am Gottesberg*, 205–10; SCHMID, "Der Sinai," 116–17.

[73] OSWALD, *Israel am Gottesberg*, 208–9; SCHMID, "Der Sinai," 116, n. 14.

[74] SCHMID, "Der Sinai," 116–17, 126–27; OSWALD, *Israel am Gottesberg*, 208–9.

[75] Cf. SCHMID, "Der Sinai," 120.

[76] On God's cessation of work in Gen 2:2–3, see also above, II.9.3.4. However, despite this difficulty, Propp believes that Exod 24:15b–18a may fit with the six/seven-day schema of Gen 1.

Schmid assigns the passage Gen 2:2–3 and the six/seven-day schema to the primary
Priestly composition, according to him Exod 24:15b–18a cannot belong to the latter.

What may one conclude from this discussion? If P^C is a redactional layer building
on non-P, the motifs of the mountain and cloud can be explained as an adaptation to
the non-Priestly context.[77] Oswald and Schmid's counterargument, that the mountain motif would be marginal or nonexistent in the Priestly Sinai pericope, depends
on their redaction-critical analysis of the tabernacle account. The contention that that
all mentions of the mountain (הר) in Exod 25–29 belong to a secondary layer is not
shared by the present study. The location "on the mountain" appears three (MT) or
four (SP, LXX) times in the instruction section of the account (Exod 25–29); in these
statements, the reader is told that the model (תבנית) of the sanctuary and its utensils is shown to Moses on the mountain (see Exod 25:9 [SP, LXX], 40; 26:30; 27:8).
The three (four) statements in question are of similar form and are often considered
to form a group of structuring notices within the composition Exod 25:1–29:46.[78] In
particular, as will be shown below, Oswald's claim that all these structuring phrases
were secondary because they are absent from the fulfillment section in chapters 35–40
is not justified.[79] As for the cloud motif, it plays an important role in the conclusion
of the fulfillment report, which most scholars assign to P^G/P^C (Schmid assigns Exod
40:34–35 to P^G).[80] In other words, in the case of the cloud, the exclusion of 24:15b–
18a from the base layer of the Priestly composition does not solve the problem of the
motif's sudden appearance.

Concerning the "inversion" of the six/seven-day structure of Gen 2:2–3 in our passage, we may ask whether this ("inapt") parallel was created through the insertion of
16aβ–b, 17 by a secondary redactor (see above).[81]

10.4 The Inner Differentiation of the Tabernacle Account
(Exodus 25–31, 35–40)

Scholars agree that a complex literary history lies behind the tabernacle account.
Since Popper and Wellhausen, there has been a consistent tendency to assign the two

---

According to him, YHWH "spends six days making the model for the Tabernacle (25:9, 40), just
as he spent six days making the world" (see PROPP, *Exodus 19–40*, 299). The difficulty of this
explanation is that the conjectured six-day activity of YHWH is not mentioned in the text (which
contrasts with Gen 2:2–3).

[77] ALBERTZ, *Exodus 19–40*, 147.

[78] See further below, II.10.4.1 (b).

[79] See below, II.10.4.2.

[80] As far I can see, the only scholars who exclude Exod 40:34–35 entirely from P^G are NOTH,
Das zweite Buch Mose, 227 (the reconstructed fulfillment report consists of 39:32, 42–43; 40:17),
and OTTO, "Forschungen zur Priesterschrift," 35; IDEM, *Das Gesetz*, 179–80.

[81] See above, II.10.3.1.

comprehensive passages Exod 30–31 and 35–40 to secondary layers. More controversial is the scholarly discussion concerning the literary history of chapters 25–29.

10.4.1 The Inner Differentiation of the Instruction Account (Exodus 25–31)

(a) The Secondary Nature of Exodus 30–31

Several passages in Exod 30–31 stand in tension with certain motifs and subjects in Exod 25–29 or have other characteristics that point to their secondary nature.[82] For several reasons, the appearance of the golden incense altar at the beginning of Exod 30:1–10 seems out of place; one would expect it to be mentioned together with the other items destined for service in the inner sanctum in Exod 25:10–40 and 26:31–37. Further indications of the secondary nature of the incense altar are the fact that the bronze altar (see 27:1–8) for animal sacrifices is mentioned with the article ("the altar"); the absence of the incense altar from Lev 2 and from Ezek 40–42. Since the instruction for the sacred incense and sacred oil in Exod 30:22–33, 34–38 completes the passage concerning the incense altar, it should be considered secondary as well.

The instruction for the census and tax (Exod 30:11–16) stands in tension with the order concerning the donation offering in 25:1–7, which is a voluntary endowment.

As for the passage on the sages responsible for the construction of the tent (31:1–11), this presupposes the incense altar, the incense, and the oil of 30:22–38 and seems to contradict statements that assign the building of the sanctuary to all Israel (see, for instance, 25:10 MT; 39:42) or to Moses alone (see, for instance, 25:11, 12, 13).[83]

Scholars vividly debate the classification of the instruction on the Sabbath in 31:12–17. Given the appearance of several typically H expressions (שמר with accusative שבת, "to observe the (my) sabbath(s)," vv. 13, 14, 16; שבתי, "my sabbaths," v. 13; כי אני יהוה מקדשכם, "that I am YHWH who sanctifies you," v. 13; שבת שבתון, "a strict Sabbath," v. 15; ונכרתה הנפש ההוא מקרב מעמיה, "that person shall be cut off from among his kin," v. 14; חלל piel, "to profane," v. 14), many scholars assign the passage to H. The fact that the instruction combines phrasings found in different Sabbath texts in the Pentateuch (Gen 2:2–3; Exod 20:8, 11; Deut 5:12) further suggests that it depends on the latter.[84]

---

[82] See WELLHAUSEN, *Die Composition*, 139–41; NOTH, *Das zweite Buch Mose*, 191–98; NIHAN, *From Priestly Torah*, 31–33.

[83] Significantly, the names of Bezalel (Ezra 10:30), Uri (Ezra 10:24), and Hur (1 Chr 2:50; 4:1, 4; Neh 3:9) are predominantly attested in late postexilic texts. Oholiab and Ahisamach (Exod 31:6) are not attested elsewhere. This points to a late, postexilic origin of the text (see also NOTH, *Das zweite Buch Mose*, 197). The names Bezalel and Oholiab were probably chosen because of their meanings ("in the shadow of God" and "Father is my tent").

[84] Assigning 31:12–17 to Pˢ or H: KNOHL, *Sanctuary*, 14–17, 105; GRÜNWALDT, *Exil und Identität*, 173–77; S. OWCZAREK, *Die Vorstellung vom Wohnen Gottes inmitten seines Volkes in der Priesterschrift*, Europäische Hochschulschriften 23 (Bern: Peter Lang, 1998), 40–42; NIHAN, *From Priestly Torah*, 567. Ascribing the passage to the basis layer of P: S. OLYAN, "Exodus

The classification of Exod 31:18, which concludes the section on YHWH's instruction, is also controversial. Since the Priestly strand does not contain any (other) assertion reporting Moses's reception of the "testimony" by YHWH, and in particular given the use of the characteristically Priestly term עדת, "testimony, law"[85] in 31:18, several scholars ascribe this verse entirely or partly to the primary tabernacle account.[86] However, the motif of the two tablets (לחת), which does not appear elsewhere in the tabernacle account, renders such a classification questionable. Though the phrase "to put the *ʿēdut* [testimony] in the ark," which appears a few times in the tabernacle account (25:16, 21; 40:20), conveys the understanding of the ark as a container, it is important to note that the term *ʿēdut* here is not connected with the two tablets.[87] While these latter statements should be considered to belong to the primary composition of the tabernacle account – there are no literary-critical reasons to assign them to a secondary layer[88] – the motif of the two tablets makes the assignment of 31:18 to the Priestly tabernacle account doubtful. Since the expression שני לחת העדת, "the two tablets of the testimony," reappears in Exod 32:15 and 34:29, it is tempting to attribute this verse to the author/redactor of the Non(/post)-Priestly narrative in Exod 32–34 (see further below).

(b) The Inner Differentiation of Exodus 25–29

Scholarly opinions differ considerably on which texts in Exod 25–29 should be assigned to the most primary Priestly layer (P[G]/P[C]). Most scholars agree that Exod 29:43–46 (or 29:45–46) forms the conclusion of the instruction section because it takes up the promise in 25:8 (YHWH will dwell [שכן] among the Israelites).[89] Exceptions are Noth, Knohl, and Milgrom, who see in Exod 29:43–46 a later supplement (Knohl and Milgrom assign it to H).[90] In a very concentrated form, 29:43–46 expresses YHWH's action toward Israel in three verbs: he will meet Israel (יעד niphal; v. 43); he will sanctify

---

31:12–17: The Sabbath according to H, or the Sabbath according to P and H," *JBL* 124 (2005): 201–9, and STACKERT, "Compositional Strata" (only 31:11a, 15 belong to the basis layer of P).

[85] See below, II.10.10.1.

[86] Assigning the entire verse to P[G]/P[C]: WELLHAUSEN, *Die Composition*, 91–92, n. 1; ELLIGER, "Sinn," 121; LOHFINK, "Die Priesterschrift," 198, n. 29; B. J. SCHWARTZ, "The Priestly Account of the Theophany and Lawgiving at Sinai," in *Texts, Temples, and Traditions: A Tribute to Menahem Haran*, ed. M. V. Fox et al. (Winona Lake, IN: Eisenbrauns, 1996), 114, 126–27. Assigning v. 18a to P and v. 18b to a pre-Priestly source ("E"): BAENTSCH, *Exodus–Leviticus–Numeri*, 268; NOTH, *Das zweite Buch Mose*, 203.

[87] See also BOORER, *Vision of the Priestly Narrative*, 313, n. 260.

[88] *Pace* NIHAN, *From Priestly Torah*, 49–50, and with OSWALD, *Israel am Gottesberg*, 209–10; PROPP, *Exodus 19–40*, 376; H. UTZSCHNEIDER, "Tabernacle," in *The Book of Exodus: Composition, Interpretation, and Reception*, ed. T. B. Dozeman, C. A. Evans, and J. N. Lohr, VTSup 284 (Leiden: Brill, 2014), 283; BOORER, *Vision of the Priestly Narrative*, 313, n. 260.

[89] Among others see PROPP, *Exodus 19–40*, 372; NIHAN, *From Priestly Torah*, 34; BOORER, *Vision of the Priestly Narrative*, 60.

[90] NOTH, *Das zweite Buch Mose*, 188; KNOHL, *Sanctuary*, 18, n. 24; 81; 102, n. 145; 125, n. 102; MILGROM, *Leviticus 17–22*, 1338.

Israel's cult (קדשׁ *piel*; v. 44), and he will dwell among the Israelites (שׁכן; v. 45). The climactic character of the statements in 29:43–46 and the fact that Exod 29:45 forms an inclusion with the statement in Exod 25:8 (keyword שׁכן, "to dwell") are further arguments for the above delimitation of the instruction section (the primary composition consists of Exod 25–29*; chapters 30–31 form a supplement).

However, the unity of 29:43–46 and its original place within Exod 25–29 are disputed.

Pola and Weimar separate 29:43–44 from vv. 45–46; the former would be a secondary supplement depending on the passage 29:38–42 concerning the תמיד sacrifice (Pola).[91] Furthermore, some critics believe that Exod 29:43–46* originally followed on 26:30 ("Then you shall erect the tabernacle according to its plan which you have been shown on the mountain"), forming an appropriate conclusion of the instruction section.[92] This reconstruction remains without literary-critical arguments, and it has the difficulty that v. 44 alludes to contents of all subsections in Exod 25–29 (altar in 27 and priesthood in 28 included; cf. 29:44).

The inner organization and the literary history of 29:43–46 are difficult to elucidate. Given their different literary scopes, 29:43 and 29:44–46 should perhaps be assigned to different literary strata. In the present arrangement, v. 43 follows on the passage introducing the תמיד sacrifice (29:38–42). But contrary to Pola's opinion, it depends not on this passage but on the short section 29:36–37, which is focused on the sanctity of the altar.[93] Several scholars consider 29:38–42 to be a digression and assign it to a secondary redaction: the introduction of the daily sacrifice does in fact seem out of place in this section dealing with the consecration of the priesthood and the altar.[94] If this redaction-historical consideration is correct, the adverb שׁמה, "there," in v. 43 harks back to the altar whose holiness is pointed out in 29:36–37.[95] Once this connection is recognized, the difficulty of the expression ונקדשׁ בכבדי in the same verse is solved: its grammatical subject is the altar ("And there I will meet with the Israelites, and it [i.e., the altar] shall be sanctified by my glory").[96] After the statement in 25:22, the beginning of 29:43 again takes up the key word יעד *niphal*, "to be meetable, to let be met, to encounter," and forms a sort of inclusion: while 25:22 focuses on YHWH's encounter with Moses "from above the mercy seat" of

---

[91] WEIMAR, "Sinai und Schöpfung," 341–43; POLA, *Die ursprüngliche Priesterschrift*, 235–37.

[92] LOHFINK, "Die Priesterschrift," 198, n. 29; WEIMAR, "Sinai und Schöpfung," 341–43 (since Weimar considers 29:43–44 secondary, he connects 26:30 directly with 29:45–46); FREVEL, *Mit Blick*, 103.

[93] 29:43 (ונעדתי שׁמה לבני ישׂראל ונקדשׁ בכבדי) does not fit with the previous passage: with regard to this context, the referent of שׁמה, "there," is not clear and the expression ונקדשׁ בכבדי, "it will be sanctified by my glory" (MT, SP), remains obscure. For the textual problem (the alternative reading of LXX), see above, II.10.2.1 (e).

[94] NIHAN, *From Priestly Torah*, 36–37; PROPP, *Exodus 19–40*, 472–73; ALBERTZ, *Exodus 19–40*, 212–13, (among others). V. 42b most likely bridges the inserted passage and the concluding statement related to YHWH's encounter with Israel. See NIHAN, *From Priestly Torah*, 37; ALBERTZ, *Exodus 19–40*, 213.

[95] PROPP, *Exodus 19–40*, 356, 472–73; ALBERTZ, *Exodus 19–40*, 212–13. This reference has been rendered explicit by Jerome: "et sanctificabitur altare in gloria mea."

[96] See PROPP, *Exodus 19–40*, 472–73; ALBERTZ, *Exodus 19–40*, 212–13. NIHAN, *From Priestly Torah*, 132–34, excludes Exod 29:36–37 from the ground layer because of the absence of a corresponding passage in the compliance report of Lev 8. In so doing, however, he leaves the problem of the referent of v. 43 unsolved (Nihan includes 29:43 in P[G]).

the ark, 29:43 deals with the deity's encounter with Israel at the altar. In comparison with 29:43, the literary scope of 29:44 is much broader: whereas 29:43 is closely related to the limited passage 29:36–37, v. 44 looks back to the large complex in Exod 26–28, including the instructions for the building of the tent and the altar and for the fabrication of the Priestly vestments and for the installation of the priests. The order of consecrated items (tent, altar, priests) in v. 44 corresponds exactly to the organization of chapters 26–28. One might consider the possibility that vv. 44–45 (46) originally followed immediately after chapter 28 (28:39), forming a fitting conclusion to chapters 25–29. Exodus 29:43 would have been added later in order to bridge the supplement 29:1–37* with 44–45 (46). Alternatively, one might assign the whole of 29:43–46 to a later redaction (H), which wanted to correct 29:1–37* and ensure the priests' and the altar's consecration *by YHWH*. The assignment to H seems tempting in particular for v. 46 because of the formulaic signature אני יהוה at its end, which is typical of H.[97] (In the case of the first tentative redaction-critical reconstruction, v. 46 could also be considered a later addition by H).

In the following, the most debated questions concerning the literary unity of Exod 25–29 will be discussed. Exodus 25:2–7, on the donation offering, is considered a later addition by many of the scholars who assign Exod 30–31 to a secondary redaction.[98] The oil for illumination and the fragrances for the anointing oil and spice incense in 25:6 (which depend on the instruction for the incense altar and related passages in Exod 30–31) play an important role in such arguments. However, this statement is lacking in LXX and was probably absent from the primary version of the passage in 25:1–7* (see the text-critical analysis above).[99] Conceptually, the report of the donation offering seems to be a necessary part of the tabernacle account. Regarding the precious materials in abundant quantities used for building the tabernacle, the question of their provision arises naturally.[100] The chronicle of Solomon's reign in 1 Kgs 3–10 also gives information about the provision of the temple building project (see 1 Kgs 5:27–30; 10:14). Possibly the author of Exod 25:1–7*, by emphasizing the voluntary endowment, deliberately sought to contrast Solomon's exacted service and taxation to build the luxurious sanctuary.[101]

Pola, Weimar, and Oszcarek, among others, exclude the passage describing the fabrication of the furniture in 25:10–40 in particular for conceptual reasons (the manufacturing of the interior should follow rather than precede that of the exterior [tents]).[102]

---

[97] See MILGROM, *Leviticus 17–22*, 1338.

[98] See OWCZAREK, *Die Vorstellung vom Wohnen Gottes*, 55; NIHAN, *From Priestly Torah*, 44; BOORER, *Vision of the Priestly Narrative*, 60 (hesitating).

[99] POPPER, *Der biblische Bericht über die Stiftshütte*, 84–85, furthermore observes that in 25:6–7, in the listing of the items, the copula is absent before שמן למאר, בשמים, and אבני שהם, in striking contrast to the preceding verses (3–5), in which the copula is used. Popper concludes that in addition to v. 6, v. 7 is also secondary.

[100] Exod 25:1–7* is included in the primary tabernacle report by WELLHAUSEN, *Die Composition*, 145; NOTH, *Das zweite Buch Mose*, 163–64 (excluding 25:6–7); PROPP, *Exodus 19–40*, 372; ALBERTZ, *Exodus 19–40*, 142–43, 153–57 (among others).

[101] See PROPP, *Exodus 19–40*, 372. For a further possible motive for the voluntary character of the endowment, see further below, II.10.6.3.

[102] POLA, *Die ursprüngliche Priesterschrift*, 224–98; WEIMAR, "Sinai und Schöpfung," 349;

According to their reconstruction, the inner sanctuary, "deprived" of all furniture, would remain empty.[103] However, there are no literary-critical indications of the secondary nature of 25:10–40; the exclusion of this passage from the tabernacle account therefore seems arbitrary.[104]

A strong tendency in earlier scholarship was to believe that P combined two independent sanctuary traditions in Exod 26, one related to a fixed building (מִשְׁכָּן; see 26:1–6, 15–19) and the other to a mobile tent (אֹהֶל; see 26:7–14). The former layer was considered the older stratum while the latter, since it repeatedly refers to the "dwelling," depended on it.[105] Nihan, however, argued for the internal coherence of the chapter: the different parts (vv. 1–6, 15–19 on the one hand, 7–14 on the other) complement each other; the מִשְׁכָּן sections deal with the inner wall of the tabernacle whereas the אֹהֶל section focuses on the outer wall, which covers the former.[106]

According to A. Aejmelaeus, the motif of the wooden boards or frames (see 26:15–29), which she believes to be absent from the LXX *Vorlage* of the fulfillment account, might belong to a secondary stratum.[107] She formulated her conceptual "objection" to the wooden boards (frames) as follows: "With the wooden frames inside and the various coverings over the tabernacle, the fine woven curtains decorated with cherubim would have been invisible for the most part. … The normal way to put up a tent would have been with the aid of pillars, cords and pegs, and these are all present in the summary of Ex 39."[108] Yet there is no literary-critical reason to exclude the instruction to build wooden boards in 26:15–29 from the primary account. Moreover, is not assured that the construction report of LXX's *Vorlage* did not include the construction of the boards (posts, according to the LXX translation).[109]

As already mentioned above, some critics believe that Exod 26:30 ("Then you shall

---

OWCZAREK, *Die Vorstellung vom Wohnen Gottes*, 58–64.

[103] A radically short account is reconstructed by POLA, *Die ursprüngliche Priesterschrift*, 224–98. He classifies only Exod 25:1a, 8a, 9; 29:45–46; 40:16, 17a, 33b as belonging to P[G]. Underlying his redaction-critical differentiation are the two designations מִשְׁכָּן, "dwelling, abode" (designating the sanctuary in the primary layer) and אֹהֶל מוֹעֵד, "tent of meeting" (belonging to a secondary stratum). However, a close reading of Exod 25–26 shows that there is no tension between מִשְׁכָּן and אֹהֶל מוֹעֵד and that the two tents are instead coordinated with one another; the latter is conceived as the cover of the former. The differentiation between the two tents is further connected to the symbolic hierarchy of metals involved in the building of the sanctuary (gold is used for the מִשְׁכָּן and bronze for the אֹהֶל מוֹעֵד; cf. Exod 26:6 with 26:11, and see further below).

[104] See NIHAN, *From Priestly Torah*, 43–44; BOORER, *Vision of the Priestly Narrative*, 61.

[105] See the survey of earlier scholarship in B. JANOWSKI, *Sühne als Heilsgeschehen: Traditions- und religionsgeschichtliche Studien zur priesterschriftlichen Sühnetheologie*, WMANT 55 (Neukirchen-Vluyn: Neukirchener Verlag, 1982), 328–36.

[106] See NIHAN, *From Priestly Torah*, 35–38 who is followed by BOORER, *Vision of the Priestly Narrative*, 59–60.

[107] See AEJMELAEUS, "Septuagintal Translation Techniques," 129. For a discussion of the textual problem, see above, II.10.2.2 (h).

[108] See AEJMELAEUS, "Septuagintal Translation Techniques," 129.

[109] See above, II.10.2.2 (h).

erect the tabernacle according to its plan which you have been shown on the mountain") was originally followed immediately by 29:43 ("And I will meet there with the Israelites, and it shall be consecrated by my glory"), the two verses forming an appropriate conclusion of the instruction section.[110] This would imply the exclusion of the instructions for the altar (for animal sacrifices), the court (plaza), and the priesthood.[111] For several reasons, however, this solution is not convincing. First, the assertion in Exod 26:30 does not necessarily function as a literary-critical signal; rather, it belongs to a group of similar structuring notices (25:9, 40; 26:30; 27:8) whose last example *follows after* 26:30.[112]

The four assertions run as follows: 25:9: "Exactly as I show you[113] – the pattern [תבנית][114] of the tabernacle and the pattern [תבנית] of all its furnishings – so shall you make it." 25:40: "And see that you make them after the pattern [תבנית] for them, which was shown to you on the mountain." 26:30: "Then you shall erect the tabernacle according to its plan [משפט] which you have been shown on the mountain." 27:8: "You shall make it hollow with planks; as it was shown to you on the mountain, so they shall make it." (Almost) all statements share the motif of Moses's vision on the mountain (הר);[115] as for the noun תבנית, "model," it occurs only in the first two statements, is replaced by משפט in the third, and is omitted in the last. The notices seem to have been placed at important points in the instruction section (at the beginning; after the description of the items of the inner sanctum; after the instruction about the tent; and after the instruction concerning the altar in the outer sanctum).

Second, the altar, the division between inner and outer sanctum, and the priesthood are important elements of the concept of the ANE sanctuary and its cult. Third, the entire section Exod 25–27 gives the impression of being a carefully elaborated and coherent composition. It describes a sophisticated architecture reflecting a gradation of sanctity through the subdivision of the sanctuary area (holy of holies – the other parts of the inner sanctum – outer sanctum) and through the attribution of different metals (gold – silver – bronze).[116] Gold is typically reserved for the furniture in the holy of holies and the remaining interior, bronze for outer items (court and altar). The principle of gradation leads to sophisticated combinations of metals for the different pillars in the inner sanctum and on the plaza (the pillars for the inner veil are plated

---

[110] LOHFINK, "Die Priesterschrift," 198, n. 29; WEIMAR, "Sinai und Schöpfung," 341–43; FREVEL, *Mit Blick*, 103.

[111] G. STEINS, "'Sie sollen mir ein Heiligtum machen': Zur Struktur und Entstehung von Ex 24,12–31,18," in *Vom Sinai zum Horeb: Stationen alttestamentlicher Glaubensgeschichte*, ed. F. L. Hossfeld (Würzburg: Echter Verlag, 1989), 159–67; JANOWSKI, "Tempel und Schöpfung," 49–51 (following Steins).

[112] NIHAN, *From Priestly Torah*, 41–42.

[113] Thus MT; SP and LXX have the plus בהר, "on the mountain."

[114] For possible concrete references of the expression *tabnît*, see PROPP, *Exodus 19–40*, 376–77 (lit.): a clay model (as found throughout the ancient Near East); a heavenly tabernacle; a drawing.

[115] The specification "on the mountain" is only absent from 25:9 MT; see above n. 113.

[116] HARAN, Temples, 189–94; NIHAN, *From Priestly Torah*, 40–41.

with gold but put on silver sockets;[117] the pillars for the outer veil are plated with gold but put on bronze sockets;[118] the pillars of the outer court are plated with gold and put on bronze sockets with hooks and bands of silver[119]).

With regard to the well-structured Exod 25:1–27:19, a few scholars are inclined to read the conclusion in 29:43–46 immediately after 27:19 (the end of the instruction related to the court).[120] However, the texts dealing with the outfitting, tasks, and consecration of the high priest should be considered an indispensable part of the sanctuary conception. Furthermore, Aaron's appointment is important for P^C's conception of the priesthood, which is built on Aaron. Nihan rightly notes that without Exod 28–29, "the introduction of Aaron alongside Moses in the previous Priestly narrative in Exodus remains nothing more than a blind motif."[121]

There are nevertheless a few short assertions in Exod 27–28 and most parts of Exod 29 that should be assigned to a secondary stratum.

The short unit 27:20–21 demanding the Israelites donate "clear oil of beaten olives" for kindling the lamps of the lampstand and assuring a constantly burning light seems to be a revision of the earlier command in 25:6:[122] because of the permanent need for oil, the contribution is continual (instead of one-time) and mandatory (instead of voluntary; cf. the statement in 27:21b [חקת עולם לדרתם מאת בני ישראל, "it shall be a perpetual statute throughout their generations for the Israelites"] with the formulation in 25:2). The olive oil should be of finest quality and the light burn constantly during the night. Obviously, this specification is influenced by the nearly identical instruction in Lev 24:2–3 (H).

In Exod 28, which deals with the vestments of the priests, a few passages should be assigned to a secondary redaction. Exodus 28:1b, which repeats Aaron's name and adds those of his sons, is presumably a secondary addition.[123] The motif of the naming of Aaron's sons in 28:1b probably presupposes late Priestly texts like Exod 6:14–27 or Lev 10. Aaron's sons are not specified elsewhere in P^C. The motif of the anointing of Aaron's *anonymous* sons in 28:41, often ascribed to a secondary layer, however, may

---

[117] See Exod 26:32.

[118] See Exod 26:37.

[119] See Exod 27:10.

[120] See E. Cortese, "The Priestly Tent (Ex 25–31.35–40): Literary Criticism and Theology of P," *LASBF* 48 (1998): 14. According to Albertz, *Exodus 19–40*, 233–34, 329–30, Exod 25:12–27:19 originally constituted an independent unit, a source that was reused by the first Priestly redactor ("PB^1").

[121] Nihan, *From Priestly Torah*, 51 (quoted part in italics).

[122] See Propp, *Exodus 19–40*, 427–29; Albertz, *Exodus 19–40*, 185.

[123] See Albertz, *Exodus 19–40*, 190, 194. Noth, *Das zweite Buch Mose*, 179, and Owczarek, *Die Vorstellung vom Wohnen Gottes*, 78, assign the entirety of 28:1 to a secondary Priestly layer.

belong to the primary stratum.[124] The simultaneous mention of Aaron and his sons (without naming) in both v. 1a and v. 41 creates a fitting *inclusio* of the chapter.[125]

The passage describing the loincloths (28:42–43) betrays its secondary nature in its position after the concluding statement in 28:41.[126]

According to many scholars, the passage referring to the skilled men (28:3–5) does not fit with the remainder of the chapter, which sees Moses as executor of YHWH's order. The passage in question would presuppose the thematically similar pericope in Exod 31:1–11 and should be assigned to a secondary layer too.[127]

Concerning the classification of chapter 29, Noth's observations are still noteworthy. Pointing out a few differences between chapter 28 and chapter 29, Noth assigned only 25–28 to P^G; chapter 29 he considered a later supplement.[128] Noth mentioned in particular the different designations of Aaron's diadem (28:36: ציץ, "flower"; 29:6: נזר הקדש, "holy diadem") and the absence of the belt in the description of Aaron's garments in 29:5 (it is mentioned in 28:39b). He argued further that because it deals with the act of the consecration of the Aaronide priests, conceptually chapter 29 distinguishes itself from the previous chapters, which consist of instructions for the fabrication of the sanctuary and all its inventory needed for the cultic procedures. Nihan, in contrast, considers the priests' consecration necessary as a continuation of Exod 28.[129] However, as shown above, Exod 28:41, which contains an instruction for consecration, might function as a fitting conclusion to Exod 28.

10.4.2 The Distinctness of Exodus 35–40

The majority of scholars assign the fulfillment section in Exod 35–40 to a different author than the instruction section in 25–29.[130] There are several factors favoring this idea. First and most important in this respect are a few consistent and significant

---

[124] With NOTH, *Das zweite Buch Mose*, 179; OWCZAREK, *Die Vorstellung vom Wohnen Gottes*, 80. NIHAN (*From Priestly Torah*, 52, n. 172) also recognizes that 28:41 is a fitting conclusion to Exod 28 but nevertheless hesitates to include the anointing of Aaron's sons in the original concluding statement because he thinks that the texts referring solely to the anointing of Aaron (but not his sons) in Exod 29:7 and Lev 8:12 express the more original Priestly point of view in this matter.

[125] See also NIHAN, *From Priestly Torah*, 52, n. 172.

[126] As recognized by most scholars. See, among others, NOTH, *Das zweite Buch Mose*, 179; OWCZAREK, *Die Vorstellung vom Wohnen Gottes*, 78; ALBERTZ, *Exodus 19–40*, 189; NIHAN, *From Priestly Torah*, 52, n. 172.

[127] See NOTH, *Das zweite Buch Mose*, 179; OWCZAREK, *Die Vorstellung vom Wohnen Gottes*, 78; NIHAN, *From Priestly Torah*, 52; BOORER, *Vision of the Priestly Narrative*, 62.

[128] NOTH, *Das zweite Buch Mose*, 187–88.

[129] NIHAN, *From Priestly Torah*, 51–2, with n. 171.

[130] See, among others, POPPER, *Der biblische Bericht über die Stiftshütte*, 84–103; WELLHAUSEN, *Die Composition*, 141–47; NOTH, *Das zweite Buch Mose*, 225–26, 227; KNOHL, *Sanctuary*, 66–68; ALBERTZ, *Exodus 19–40*, 233–34, 329–30.

differences in language between the two sections.[131] Instead of the poetic expression
אשָׁה אֶל אֲחֹתָהּ and אִישׁ אֶל אָחִיו (Exod 25:20; 26:3 [2×], 5, 6, 17; literally "each to her
sister/his brother"), the fulfillment account uses אַחַת אֶל אֶחָת (36:10 [2×], 12, 13, 22;
"one another") nearly exclusively.[132] חֹבְרֹת (26:4, 10; "set, coupling") is replaced by
מַחְבֶּרֶת (36:11, 17; "set, coupling"). עֶשְׂרִים קֶרֶשׁ (26:18, 19; "twenty boards") is replaced
by עֶשְׂרִים קְרָשִׁים (36:23, 24, 25). Moreover, the fulfillment report tends to systematize
the use of the accusative particle אֵת.[133] Note, furthermore, the Aramaising pl. קְצָוֹת,
"edges," (according to the ketiv) in 37:8; 39:4 against the Classical Hebrew spelling
קְצוֹת in 25:19; 27:4; 28:7.[134] These variations, some of which render the assertions
more prosaic and grammatically correct, were probably intended to improve the language of the instruction section. Interestingly, the same "improving" variations are
found in SP of the instruction account (Exod 25–31).[135]

Second, Exod 35–40 contains several motifs that appear in the instruction section only in the presumably secondary addition Exod 30–31, for example, the artisans
Bezalel and Oholiab, the incense altar (partly absent in LXX), the copper laver (partly
absent in LXX), the census, and the tax.[136]

Third, one finds additional elements that have no equivalent in Exod 25–29 or
30–31. Cords appear as an additional element in the tabernacle architecture (see Exod
35:18 and 39:40). There are, furthermore, striking haggadic and anticipatory motifs
(the reuse of the mirrors of the women who served at the entrance to the tent of meeting [Exod 38:8]; the Levites' task as treasurers under the guidance of Ithamar [38:21];
the reuse of the brazen censers, which belonged to the Korahites [38:22 LXX]). Note
that all three elements are preserved in LXX and Codex Monacensis, which are considered by certain scholars to constitute the shorter and more original form of the
fulfillment section and to correspond closely to the instruction part. It is significant,
however, that similar haggadic elements are absent from the first account (instruction
account).

Fourth, the fulfillment report also contains certain "minuses" in comparison to the
instruction section. Absent are the motif of the model (*tabnît*) shown to Moses on the
mountain; the Urim and Thummim (according to MT, LXX in Exod 39:21);[137] and the

---

[131] See POPPER, *Der biblische Bericht über die Stiftshütte*, 89 and PROPP, *Exodus 19–40*, 368.

[132] Exod 37:9, however, has אִישׁ אֶל אָחִיו, as does 25:20, as pointed out by POPPER, *Der biblische Bericht über die Stiftshütte*, 89.

[133] Cf. Exod 37:16 with 25:29 and Exod 38:3 with 27:3; see POPPER, *Der biblische Bericht über die Stiftshütte*, 86–87, 89.

[134] See WAGNER, *Die lexikalischen und grammatikalischen Aramaismen*, 102 (§268), 134.

[135] See the "prosaic" readings of SP in Exod 25:20; 26:3 (2×), 5, 6, 17; the linguistic variations in 26:4, 10 and 26:18, 19; the addition of the copula in 25:6–7; and the addition of the accusative particle in 25:29 (in 27:3, however, the particle is not added). See POPPER, *Der biblische Bericht über die Stiftshütte*, 84–103, and WELLHAUSEN, *Die Composition*, 145–46.

[136] The accomplishment of the census and tax order is presupposed by the statement in Exod 38:26.

[137] For the variant of SP, see above, II.10.2.2 (c).

expression "breastpiece of judgment," which is replaced by the simple "breastpiece" (see 39:8, 9, 15, 19, 21 [2×], according to all textual witnesses).

What may one conclude from this evidence? Hurowitz and Milgrom, despite all these differences, believe that Exod 25–31 and Exod 35–40 stem from the same author.[138]

Their argument is first that ANE building inscriptions containing a divine prescription to construct a temple are always followed by the description of its actual erection. Second, they point to variations in style between the instruction and fulfillment accounts in these inscriptions. As for the first argument, one should note that the rare instruction reports in ANE inscriptions are much shorter than the instruction section in the tabernacle account. Furthermore, the parallels adduced by Hurowitz are too remote in time from the presumed setting of the tabernacle account to be significant.[139] Moreover, it is worth noting that the author of the (proto-)Priestly flood narrative does not follow the aforementioned pattern: The detailed prescription to build the ark (Gen 6:14–16) is *not* followed by a fulfillment account. The second argument is not sound either: the instruction and fulfillment parts of the tabernacle account are not only stylistically but also conceptually too divergent to ascribe them to one and the same author.

Apart from this rather isolated view, scholars are aware of the importance and quantity of the differences between the two sections; they draw different redaction-historical conclusions from them. Four tendencies are perceptible in current scholarship: (1) Noth, Pola, and others think that the comprehensive instruction section was followed by only a few concise fulfillment statements. Some of these scholars offer (tentative) reconstructions of this presumed short end of the tabernacle account, positing that the comprehensive remaining parts of the fulfillment report were added by later redactors.[140] (2) Others believe that Exod 35–40, in a shorter form than its present one, constituted a compliance report corresponding to 25–29 (stemming from the same author as the latter).[141] For instance, contents present in MT and SP that are absent from LXX (in some places) would not have belonged to the primary composition. (3) A minority view holds that the short construction report (Exod 35–40*) predated the instruction account.[142] (4) According to a few scholars, including Knohl, Otto, and Albertz, the original tabernacle account concluded in 29:37 (Knohl) or in 29:42–46

---

[138] Milgrom, *Leviticus 1–16*, 36–37; V. A. Hurowitz, "The Priestly Account of Building the Tabernacle," *JAOS* 105 (1985): 21–30.

[139] Cylinder of Gudea (ca. 2150 BCE); bilingual "B" inscription of Samsuiluna, king of Babylon (1749–1712 BCE).

[140] Noth, *Das zweite Buch Mose*, 225, 227 (the fulfillment report probably contained 39:32, 42–43; 40:17); Pola, *Die ursprüngliche Priesterschrift*, 224–98 (Exod 40:16–17, 33); Frevel, *Mit Blick*, 145, 183 (35:1a, 4b; 39:32, 43; 40:17, 33b, 34–35); Boorer, *Vision of the Priestly Narrative*, 66–67 (Exod 39:32, 43; 40:17, 33b, 34). See also Wellhausen, *Die Composition*, 144, who however declined to identify the concrete statements within Exod 39–40.

[141] See Popper, *Der biblische Bericht über die Stiftshütte*; Aejmelaeus, "Septuagintal Translation Techniques," 129; Bogaert, "L'importance de la Septante"; Nihan, *From Priestly Torah*, 32–33, with n. 68, 58.

[142] Nelson, "Studies in the Development of the Tabernacle Account"; Lo Sardo, *Post-Priestly Additions*, 16 (referring to Propp, who, however, labels his idea "speculation"; see Propp, *Exodus 19–40*, 368), 119.

(Otto, Albertz) without any fulfillment statement. With regard to the distinctiveness of the fulfillment account, when compared with the instruction report, they assign the former to a secondary literary layer. Knohl ascribes the instruction report to "PT" and the fulfillment account to "H."[143] Albertz puts it differently: the differences are due to the fact that the Priestly redactor (*Bearbeiter*) integrated different *Vorlagen* ("sources") in his work (i.e., Exod 25:12–27:19* and 30*) but composed the other parts – e.g., the fulfilling report in 35–40 – himself.[144] For Otto, finally, the instruction report represents the programmatic goal of the Priestly document which he dates to the exilic period. With its open-ended conclusion, P[G] would point beyond itself and promise the reconstruction of the temple for the exiled addressees.[145]

In my view, both the presence of several motifs that are missing in Exod 25–29* and the linguistic particularities that seem intended to improve the language of the instruction section strongly suggest that Exod 35–40 does not stem from the same author as 25–29*. The (partial) absence of the boards and the incense altar in LXX cannot bear the weight of the argument in favor of the relative early composition of the fulfillment account (according to the second and third explanations); as shown above, the items in question might have been omitted by the translator.[146] What speaks further in favor of the first but against the second and third theories is that LXX and Codex Monacensis contain both the abovementioned haggadic and anticipatory pluses of the fulfillment account when compared with the instruction section. A further argument in support of the first and against the second and the third explanations is the strong evidence suggesting that Exod 35–40 LXX stems from a translator other than that of Exod 1–34. The most probable reason for this seems to be the nonexistence of Exod 35–40 at the time of the first translation (covering Exod 1–34; 40*).[147]

As for the fourth theory, it seems less probable because it cannot explain the incompleteness of Exod 25–29 (which, according to that explanation, would be the only section belonging to the first redactional stage). What speaks against Otto's theory is that the tabernacle, as it will be shown below, by its dimensions and objects anticipates Solomon's temple. It not only points to the reconstruction of the Second Temple in Persian times, but more generally aims to establish the continuity of legitimate Yahwistic worship from the time of the Exodus through the time of the Judean monarchy and

---

[143] KNOHL, *Sanctuary*, 66–68.

[144] ALBERTZ, *Exodus 19–40*, 233–34, 329–30. Exod 35–40 contains typical features that appear in other Priestly texts, as for instance the correspondence between YHWH's oral order, his *word*, and Moses and the peoples' execution (see 35:4, 29; 39:1, 5, 7, 21, 26, 29, 31, 43; 40:19, 21, 23, 25, 27, 29, 32; see further below).

[145] OTTO, "Forschungen zur Priesterschrift," 35; IDEM, *Das Gesetz*, 179–80; IDEM, "Die Priesterschrift und das Deuteronomium im Buch Levitikus. Zur Integration des Deuteronomiums in den Pentateuch" in *Abschied von der Priesterschrift? Zum Stand der Pentateuchdebatte*, ed. F. Hartenstein and K. Schmid, VWGT 40 (Leipzig: Evangelische Verlagsanstalt, 2015), 166.

[146] See above, II.10.2.1 and II.10.2.2 (h), (i).

[147] See above, II.10.2.1.

into the Persian period of Judaism.[148] In light of this concept, the idea that detailed instructions would have remained unfulfilled in the original tabernacle account does not make sense.

All in all, the theory that Exod 25–29* had its conclusion in a short and general fulfillment statement (see above [1]) is probably the best explanation.[149]

Assuming that the fulfillment account was composed after the instruction, how can we explain the absence of such important elements as the Urim and Thummim (together with the related expression "breastpiece of judgment"), and the motif of the "model"? First, we should consider the possibility that these items were inserted into Exod 25–29 at a rather late point, namely after the conclusion of the original compliance account. However, there are no clues hinting at such a redactional development of these topics. Alternately, can we imagine that the author of the fulfillment account deliberately omitted these motifs? In the case of the Urim and Thummim, the absence of the expression "breastpiece of judgment" (חשן משפט) – which hints at the use of the Urim and Thummim – alongside the absence of the motif of the Urim and Thummim in the same passage indeed suggests deliberate omission (see above).[150] Instead of "breastpiece of judgment" (חשן משפט), only "breastpiece" (חשן; see 39:8, 9, 15, 19, 21 [2×]) is used.[151] The author of the passage in question may have had a theological objection to both the Urim and Thummim and the "model."[152] The Urim and Thummim and the *tabnît* (model) equally constitute means through which the will of yhwh is made known. As Oswald rightly observes, in the fulfillment report the narrator consistently refers to the correspondence between yhwh's oral order, his *word*, and Moses and the people's execution (see 35:4, 29; 39:1, 5, 7, 21, 26, 29, 31, 43; 40:19, 21, 23, 25, 27, 29, 32).[153] In so doing, he emphasizes the "directness" of yhwh's instruction, which is orally and verbally transmitted. The precise correspondence between yhwh's *word* and the people's fulfillment is likewise a dominant feature of other parts of P^C.[154] Thus, it is imaginable that the author of the fulfillment account was keen to accentuate this idea and to remove competing theological concepts (related to an "intermediary" such as the Urim and Thummim and the *tabnît*) from "his" section (Exod 35–40) of the tabernacle account.

---

[148] See below, II.10.7.2.

[149] For diverse reconstructions of these concluding statements, see above, n. 140.

[150] See II.10.2.1 (c). At first sight, the absence of the Urim and Thummim may be explained by the fact that their fabrication is not mentioned in the instruction section. However, the ʿēdut ("testimony"), for which the manufacturing is not mentioned in the instruction section either, nevertheless appears in the fulfillment account. Therefore, the absence of the Urim and Thummim from 39:1–31 should be explained differently.

[151] SP and LXX (λογεῖον replaces κρίσεων) agree with MT.

[152] For NOTH, *Das zweite Buch Mose*, 225, a possible reason for the omission of the Urim and Thummim was that they were not in use in the Second Temple (however, see Ezra 2:63 // Neh 7:65).

[153] OSWALD, *Israel am Gottesberg*, 203.

[154] See Gen 6:22; 7:9, 16; Exod 7:6; 14:4, 21, 27; Lev 8:4; Num 17:26; 27:22.

10.5 Characteristics of the Priestly Wilderness Sanctuary

According to the aforementioned analysis, the most original kernel of the tabernacle account is found in the instruction section Exod 25–29* and has found its conclusion in a short and general fulfillment statement. The particularity of the blueprint of the tabernacle as indicated in the ground layer of this section becomes evident when it is compared to the plan of Ezek 40–48. Whereas the structure of Ezekiel's sanctuary is quadratic and is centered on the altar as its only cultic object (see Ezek 40–42; neither the ark nor other holy vessels are mentioned), the Priestly tabernacle is rectangular and has two foci: the ark with the *kappōret* in the holy of holies within the sanctum on the one hand and the altar in the court on the other.[155] As will be shown below, this structure is influenced by the plan of the First Temple in Jerusalem as described in the report in 1 Kgs 6–8. Among the two foci apparent in Exod 25–29*, greater importance seems to be assigned to the ark. According to Exod 28, which deals with the clothing and consecration of the high priest, the major task of the latter consists in representing Israel before yhwh and affirming Israel's "justice" before the deity (by wearing the breastpiece "of justice" with the Urim and Thummim whenever he enters the sanctuary and stands before the deity; see Exod 28:29–30).[156] In the context of chapter 28*, the sacrifice and the altar are not mentioned. The gradation of sanctity of the two areas (sanctum – court) is also expressed through the attribution of different building materials to them (gold and precious wood for the furniture of the holy of holies and of the outer sanctuary; bronze for the altar in the court).

Since the fabrication of the altar nevertheless occupies an important place in Exod 27, one should ask about the role attributed to the sacrificial cult. This leads to the important question pertaining to the relationship between the tabernacle account in Exod 25–29*, 39–40* on the one hand and the Sinaitic sacrificial legislation in Lev 1–10, 16 on the other. Should the latter (or parts of it) be considered an integral part of the former? In the framework of this study, which is limited to the Priestly texts in Gen 1–Exod 40, this question can be treated only preliminarily (see the following section).

Another difference between Ezek 40–48 and Exod 25–29*, 39–40* concerns the protagonists playing a leading role in the sanctuary. Whereas the tabernacle account assigns a central role to the figure of the high priest, the latter is absent from both Ezek 40–48 and 1 Kgs 6–8. In contrast to those two texts, a king does not play any role in the tabernacle account in Exodus. Related to this absence is the fact that, as a few commentators have observed, Aaron's vestments and consecration in Exod

---

[155] See B. Reicke, *BHH* 3:1875: "Während der quadratische Tempelentwurf von Ez 41–42 … einseitig auf den Altar als Mittelpunkt ausgerichtet war, wird hier durch ein angereihtes zweites Quadrat ein zweiter Brennpunkt für die Lade geschaffen." Quoted in Keel, *Die Geschichte Jerusalems*, 2:930. For the plan of Ezekiel's temple, see the illustration in T. Ganzel, *Ezekiel's Visionary Temple in Babylonian Context*, BZAW 539 (Berlin: de Gruyter, 2021), 56.

[156] The influence of the Egyptian deity Maât is likely visible in this important detail (see below, II.10.7.1).

28 contain royal traits (diadem, anointment with oil, breastpiece, and majestic garments).[157] Whereas the priests of the Solomonic temple were under the supervision of the Judean king, the high priest of the tabernacle account is independent of the king and, in a certain sense, takes up the latter's role.

10.6 The Relationship to Leviticus 1–16: Preliminary Considerations

10.6.1 Scholarly Views

In the past, a majority of scholars excluded the cultic laws in Lev 1–7, 11–15 from P^G/ P^C because the latter was considered to be a historical narrative without inclusion of other literary forms. The narrative material in Lev 8–10, the consecration of Aaron and his sons, the offering of the first sacrifices, and the offense of Nadab and Abihu, however, was partly assigned to the Priestly base layer (P^G/P^C).[158] Wellhausen characterized this primary composition of the tabernacle account as an "order for the divine service in historical form."[159] The classification of Lev 8 was controversial because Lev 8, while forming the fulfillment report of Exod 29, at the same time deviates from the latter in several respects. Accordingly, Wellhausen and Kuenen concluded that Lev 8 stemmed from a later author.[160]

Recent treatments argue for the inclusion of the sacrificial *tôrôt* in Lev 1–7* and the purity laws in 11–15 in P^G/P^C, in particular for conceptual reasons.[161] An important aspect of this question pertains to the relationship between Lev 9 and the prescriptions in Lev 1–7. Wellhausen's influential classification of Lev 1–7 as a secondary insertion in the Priestly base writing was questioned by K. Koch. He has pointed out striking commonalities and parallels between Lev 8–9 and the section 1–7 in terms of vocabulary, different types of sacrifices, and the description of rituals, concluding that most parts of Lev 8–9 depend on and are later than the legislation in Lev 1–7.

---

[157] See NOTH, *Das zweite Buch Mose*, 179–86; NIHAN, *From Priestly Torah*, 393–94, n. 513.

[158] See WELLHAUSEN, *Die Composition*, 135–49, esp. 137, 144; KUENEN, *Historisch-kritische Einleitung*, 1.1:70–78; BAENTSCH, *Exodus–Leviticus–Numeri*, 342–44; K. ELLIGER, *Leviticus*, HAT 4 (Tübingen: Mohr Siebeck, 1966), 104–39; MILGROM, *Leviticus 1–16*, 61–62, 543, 1060.

[159] WELLHAUSEN, *Die Composition*, 137: "Was übrig bleibt, ist eine zusammenhängende Gottesdienstordnung in historischer Form, zerfallend in die Anweisung Exod. 25–31 und in die Ausführung Kap. 35–40. Lev. 8–10."

[160] See WELLHAUSEN, *Die Composition*, 143–44; KUENEN, *Historisch-kritische Einleitung*, 1.1:70–78. In the second half of the twentieth century, scholars also became reluctant to include Lev 10 in P^G/P^C; see, for instance, NOTH, *Das dritte Buch Mose*, 4; LOHFINK, "Die Priesterschrift," 198, n. 29; WEIMAR, "Sinai und Schöpfung," 376; and see further below, II.10.6.2 (b)

[161] See K. KOCH, *Die Priesterschrift von Exodus 25 bis Leviticus 16: Eine überlieferungsgeschichtliche und literarkritische Untersuchung*, FRLANT 71 (Göttingen: Vandenhoeck & Ruprecht, 1959), 45–46, 91–92, 98–99; BLUM, *Studien*, 312–29; KNOHL, *Sanctuary*, 59–106; NIHAN, *From Priestly Torah*, 111–382; T. RÖMER, "Der Pentateuch," 132–34; T. HIEKE, *Levitikus 1–15*, HThKAT (Freiburg im Breisgau: Herder, 2008), 65–69.

Koch assigns only the latter and Lev 9:22–24 to P[G].[162] Nihan, who emphasizes Koch's observations, nevertheless argues for the inclusion of Lev 8–9 alongside 1–3 in the "extended" tabernacle account.[163]

Furthermore, some scholars have noted that, on a narratological level, the narrative thread continues smoothly from the passage in 40:34–35, which they consider the original end of Exod 40*, to the sacrificial laws in Lev 1–7. Leviticus 1:1 is considered an appropriate continuation of Exod 40:35.[164]

Exodus 40:34–35
[34] Then the cloud covered the tent of meeting, and the glory of YHWH filled the tabernacle. [35] Moses could not enter the tent of meeting, because the cloud had settled upon it and the glory of YHWH filled the tabernacle.

Leviticus 1:1
[1] (a) Then he called [ויקרא] to Moses (b) and YHWH spoke [וידבר יהוה] to him from the tent of meeting.

This particular sequence of elements has two parallels (Exod 24:16, 18a; 25:1; and Ezek 9:3–4), which are built in precisely the same way. According to Greenberg and Rendtorff, the sequence with the explicit subject following only after the second verb should be considered an intentional device by the authors.[165] In each case the *kābôd* is the implicit subject of the verb ויקרא, "he called"; later on this subject is identified with YHWH. The reason for this peculiar syntactical figure might be that the subsequent weighty divine commands (in all three cases) should be related to YHWH in the closest possible way (Greenberg).[166] To this, we may add that the syntactical figure would fit with Exod 40:34 (instead of 40:35) as the immediately preceding assertion as well (on redaction-critical differentiation between v. 34 and v. 35, see below).

In addition, Nihan has observed that 40:35 itself cannot function as a fitting conclusion to the tabernacle account but, on the contrary, is intended as a continuation.[167] By stating that "Moses was not able to enter the tent of meeting because the cloud had settled on it" (Exod 40:35), the author hints at the incompletion of his account: the Israelites, Moses included, cannot yet approach the deity.

---

[162] KOCH, *Die Priesterschrift von Exodus 25 bis Leviticus 16*, 70–71.

[163] NIHAN, *From Priestly Torah*, 232–33.

[164] See, among others, KOCH, *Die Priesterschrift von Exodus 25 bis Leviticus 16*, 45–46, 99; BLUM, *Studien*, 312; POLA, *Die ursprüngliche Priesterschrift*, 218–22, 362; FREVEL, *Mit Blick*, 95, n. 66, 154; NIHAN, *From Priestly Torah*, 53, with n. 177, and especially 232, n. 549; ALBERTZ, *Exodus 19–40*, 379.

[165] See M. GREENBERG, *Ezekiel 1–20: A New Translation with Introduction and Commentary*, AB 22A (New York: Doubleday, 1983), 176–77; RENDTORFF, *Leviticus*, BK 3.1 (Neukirchen-Vluyn: Neukirchener Verlag, 1985), 5–7, 20–21; see also NIHAN, *From Priestly Torah*, 53, with n. 177.

[166] See GREENBERG, *Ezekiel 1–20*, 176–77.

[167] NIHAN, *From Priestly Torah*, 232–33.

How should these arguments be weighed? For conceptual reasons, I tend to include certain sacrificial *tôrôt* in P^C. The account of the construction of the sanctuary, with the cultic furnishings, including the altar, makes better sense if it is followed by a description of the sacrificial cult. Regarding the argument for the coherence of genre (the Priestly "source" is mostly considered a "narrative"), it should be noted that the tabernacle account, with its broad and detailed instructions, itself constitutes a change of style when compared with the preceding narratives.

However, certain indications raise doubts as to whether the connection between Exod 40:34–35 and Lev 8–9 belongs to the primary stratum of P^C. Several scholars exclude either both vv. 34–35 or only v. 35 from the primary stratum (P^G/P^C).[168] Verse 34, considered on its own, might have formed a fitting conclusion to the tabernacle account.[169] Exodus 40:34–35 does not necessarily constitute a unified passage. It is striking that v 35b is identical to v. 34b (וכבוד יהוה מלא את המשכן, "And the cloud covered the tent of meeting"); it could be a *Wiederaufnahme*.[170] One should note that the statement in v. 35 (Moses cannot enter the tent of meeting because of the cloud's presence upon the latter and YHWH's glory dwelling in the tabernacle) stands in tension with 24:18a (Moses is allowed to enter the cloud; he receives the tabernacle instructions while in the cloud)[171] and with 25:22:

Exodus 25:22
[22] And there I will meet [יעד *niphal*] with you; and from above the mercy seat, from between the two cherubim which are upon the ark of the testimony, I will speak to you about all that I will give you in commandment for the Israelites.

As is apparent, Exod 25:22 attributes to Moses the role of recipient of the cultic law and the privilege of encountering YHWH *within* the inner sanctum. This statement goes well with YHWH's promulgation of the cultic law and other instructions to Moses in Lev 1–15 and beyond.

Nihan and others are right to see Exod 40:35 in close connection to the inauguration of the sacrificial cult in Lev 9:23–24, when Moses and Aaron are allowed to enter the אהל מועד for the first time. According to Lev 16, access to the inner sanctum is limited to Aaron alone, on one day, namely the Day of Atonement. However, one should take into account that the instruction section of the tabernacle account does not share

---

[168] Cf. NOTH, *Das zweite Buch Mose*, 22; POLA, *Die ursprüngliche Priesterschrift*, 224–98; OTTO, "Forschungen zur Priesterschrift," 35; KRATZ, *Composition*, 134–36, 243; BAUKS, "Genesis 1," 333; BOORER, *Vision of the Priestly Narrative*, 66–67.

[169] Cf. KRATZ, *Composition*, 134–36; 243; BAUKS, "Genesis 1," 333; BOORER, *Vision of the Priestly Narrative*, 66–67.

[170] Thus M. J. RÖHRIG, *Innerbiblische Auslegung und priesterliche Fortschreibungen in Lev 8–10*, FAT II/128 (Tübingen: Mohr Siebeck, 2021), 118. See also BOORER, *Vision of the Priestly Narrative*, 67, who considers the repetition of the cloud and the glory motifs in v. 35 a literary-critical signal.

[171] FREVEL, *Mit Blick*, 155.

this scope. Possibly the restriction and refusal of access put on Moses in Exod 40:35; Lev 1:1; 8–10; 16 belongs to a secondary redaction.

Which parts of Lev 1–16 should be included in P^c? The following survey endeavors to answer that question.

10.6.2 Survey on Leviticus 1–16

(a) Leviticus 1–7

Leviticus 1–7 is a compilation of different sacrificial laws. Leviticus 1–3 outlines three main types of traditional sacrifices: the burnt offering (עלה), the grain offering (מנחה), and communal sacrifice (זבח השלמים). The addressees are the individual Israelites. Chapters 4 and 5 contain laws related to expiatory sacrifices (חטאת, "sin-offering"; אשם, "guilt-offering"). Chapters 6–7 reconsider the different types of offerings and focus especially on the theme of the disposal of the remains of the sacrificial animals and sacrificial food. Leviticus 1–3 probable once formed a single literary unit that was independent of the two other parts.[172]

Leviticus 1 and 3, which are tightly connected with one another, also share several common points with Lev 2 on the conceptual and the linguistic level. Several features indicate that the Priestly narrative framework – easily identifiable through the expressions "sons of Aaron" (accompanying "the priests") and "tent of meeting" – is secondary and that the Priestly author made use of two older documents (Lev 1, 3 on the one hand and Lev 2 on the other).[173] As for Leviticus 4, the presence of linguistic particularities and the mention of the incense altar betray its late origin. The terms נשיא, "prince" (4:22; frequent in Num 1–10); עם הארץ, "people of the land" (Lev 4:27; absent from other Priestly texts but occurring in Lev 20:2, 4 [H]); אשמה, instead of אשם for "guilt offering" (Lev 4:3; 5:24, 26; 22:16 [H]; Ezra 9:6–7, 13, 15; 10:10, 19; 1 Chr 21:3; 2 Chr 24:18; 28:10; 33:23) are atypical of P but appear in postexilic literature.[174] One particularity is the expression הכהן המשיח, "the anointed priest" (unique occurrences in the Hebrew Bible: Lev 4:3, 5, 16; 6:15), which replaces Aaron and "sons of Aaron" (only one single priest, the high priest, is mentioned in Lev 4). Leviticus 5 is a collection of single instructions related to the sin and guilt offerings whose purpose is to supplement the legislation of Lev 4. Leviticus 6–7 has a supplementary character too: the systematic recapitulation ("teaching") of all five types of offerings in this section provided the opportunity to introduce further details yet lacking in the previous chapters 1–5.[175] For instance, 6:5–6 adds an instruction for the conservation of the fire of the altar of burnt offerings, and 7:1–7 introduces the description of the ritual of the אשם offering for which Lev 5:14–26 does not provide any instruction.

In conclusion, there are indications that within the legislative texts Lev 1–7 the

---

[172] BAENTSCH, *Exodus–Leviticus–Numeri*, 308; NOTH, *Das dritte Buch Mose*, 16, 26; NIHAN, *From Priestly Torah*, 150–231.

[173] See NOTH, *Das dritte Buch Mose*, 11, 16, 26; NIHAN, *From Priestly Torah*, 198–215.

[174] See NOTH, *Das dritte Buch Mose*, 26; NIHAN, *From Priestly Torah*, 161–66.

[175] NOTH, *Das dritte Buch Mose*, 42–43; NIHAN, *From Priestly Torah*, 150–231.

prescriptions in Lev 1–3 probably form the most primary stratum and were supplemented with Lev 4–7 only at later stages in the development of Lev 1–7.

(b) Leviticus 8–9

Koch's arguments for not including Lev 8–9 in the primary Priestly Sinai narrative seem pertinent. They are supported by the observations of other scholars: As Noth pointed out, Lev 8 shares features with the secondary fulfillment account in Exod 35–40 that distinguish the latter from the instruction section.[176]

As for Lev 9, S. Boorer rightly points to the striking absence of any "preceding divine speech giving the instructions that are carried out in Lev 9 as is the consistent pattern throughout Pg."[177] Instead, v. 6, in precisely the same formulation as in Exod 16:16, 32a, refers to a divine word ("this is the thing which yhwh has commanded") that, however, has not been preceded by a corresponding concrete instruction.[178] Frevel mentions further linguistic particularities that distinguish Lev 9 from the tabernacle account, including the expression אל פני אהל מועד (v. 5)[179] and עם as the most frequent designation of the cultic "assembly" (vv. 7 [2×], 15 [2×], 18, 22, 23 [2×], 24). The latter expression clearly outclasses the typical Priestly expressions בני ישראל (v. 3) and עדה (v. 5). Worth noting in particular is the expression כל העם in the climactic statement at the end, in 9:22–24.[180] In Priestly texts in Genesis–Leviticus, עם as designation of the people of Israel is extremely rare, if not nonexistent.[181] Another striking feature is עגל, "young bull," as the designation for the animal of the sin offering in Lev 9:2, 8, which occurs neither in Exod 29:1, 10–14, 36 (where the designation is פר, "[young] bull") nor in the sacrificial *tôrôt* of Lev 1–16 (see Lev 4; 8:14–17; 16: the designation is always פר). Since according to Lev 9:2, 8, Aaron offers the young bull *as a sin offering for himself*, Frevel sees in the designation עגל an allusion to the story of the golden bull in Exod 32 (see further below).[182] Another singularity atypical of P[c] is

---

[176] While the instruction account calls the ornament on the forehead of the priest a "flower of pure gold" (ציץ זהב טהור; see Exod 28:36) and the secondary account of Aaron's consecration calls it a "holy diadem" (נזר הקדש; see 29:6), the fulfillment statements in 39:30 and Lev 8:9 both combine the two designations: "the flower of the holy diadem of pure gold" (ציץ נזר הקדש זהב טהור) and "the golden flower, the holy diadem," (ציץ הזהב נזר הקדש), respectively. See Noth, *Das dritte Buch Mose*, 56.

[177] Boorer, *Vision of the Priestly Narrative*, 68.

[178] See Boorer, *Vision of the Priestly Narrative*, 57, 68, and above, II.9.3.2.

[179] The only other occurrences in the Hebrew Bible are Num 17:8; 19:4.

[180] Frevel, *Mit Blick*, 166–80. See also Pola, *Die ursprüngliche Priesterschrift*, 172–74; 221, n. 22; E. Otto, "Das Buch Levitikus im Pentateuch," *TRu* 74 (2009): 473, n. 13. Concerning affinities to non-P language in Lev 9, see Baentsch, *Exodus–Leviticus–Numeri*, 347.

[181] According to my classification, there is only one occurrence in Exod 6:7. Interestingly, in the Priestly texts of Genesis, the plural עמים is used twice as a designation for Jacob's offspring (Gen 28:3; 48:4); it probably refers to Israel and Judah (which would create a certain tension with the use of the singular עם for all Israel!). In later Priestly texts (P[s]), עם as designation for Israel appears in Exod 16:27, 30; 36:5, 6; Lev 4:3; 10:3; 16:15, 24 (2×), 33.

[182] Frevel, *Mit Blick*, 178–79. Elliger's theory (Elliger, *Leviticus*, 122–32) that the original

the inclusion of the elders (זקנים) beside Aaron and his sons as addressees of Moses's speech (cf. 9:1). "Elders" as social group are never mentioned in Priestly texts of Genesis–Exodus.[183]

(c) Leviticus 10

The interpretation of Lev 10, its unity, and its literary classification are disputed. Traditionally, the core of the text (principally 10:1–5) was assigned, together with Lev 9, to the primary Priestly stratum (P[G]/P[C]).[184] Yet, in the course of the twentieth century, critics began to see the plot in (more or less) sharp contrast to the preceding context; the failure of Aaron's sons would oppose the celebration of Aaron in Lev 8–9. In consequence, these scholars considered the unit a later addition to P.[185] The kernel, that is, the story of Nadab and Abihu's fall in vv. 1–5, nevertheless was often thought to be based on ancient tradition.[186] A more recent tendency, however, is to stress the elaborate chiastic structure of Lev 10 as a whole and, furthermore, its connectedness with Lev 9 (in particular, Lev 10 develops vocabulary and themes present at the end of the preceding chapter).[187] A few interpreters consider the text to be a unified composition.[188]

---

composition knew only the offering of the community and not yet that of Aaron for himself is speculative. There are no literary-critical signals to dissociate the two types of sacrifices. In particular, the argument that the introduction in 9:1–2 would be secondary has the great difficulty that 9:3 depends on it syntactically (cf. v. 3a: ואל בני ישראל תדבר לאמר; see NIHAN, *From Priestly Torah*, 147). Note furthermore that according to Lev 9:3, Aaron offers another young bull (עגל) as a burnt offering accompanying the sin offering of the people. One might also see here a reference to the sin of the people in Exod 32. See further below, II.10.10.2.

[183] Is it a concession to the scribal group defending lay (i.e., non-priestly) leadership in Jerusalem? For a theory concerning this group and their literary production, see J. JEON, "The Elders Redaction (ER) in the Pentateuch: Scribal Contributions of an Elders Group in the Formation of the Pentateuch," in *The Social Groups behind the Pentateuch*, ed. J. Jeon, AIL (Atlanta: SBL Press, 2021), 73–98.

[184] KUENEN, *Historisch-kritische Einleitung*, 1.1:78–79, 82; WELLHAUSEN, *Die Composition*, 147; BAENTSCH, *Exodus–Leviticus–Numeri*, 349–53; KOCH, *Die Priesterschrift von Exodus 25 bis Leviticus 16*, 71–72; ELLIGER, *Leviticus*, 121–39; MILGROM, *Leviticus 1–16*, 595–640; KNOHL, *Sanctuary*, 106.

[185] See NOTH, *Das dritte Buch Mose*, 69; WEIMAR, "Sinai und Schöpfung," 376; and more recently FREVEL, *Mit Blick*, 178–79; R. ACHENBACH, "Das Versagen der Aaroniden: Erwägungen zum literarhistorischen Ort von Leviticus 10," in *"Basel und Bibel": Collected Communications to the XVIIth Congress of the IOSOT, Basel 2001*, ed. M. Augustin and H. N. Niemann, BEAT 51 (Frankfurt: Lang, 2004), 55–70; IDEM, *Die Vollendung*, 93–110; NIHAN, *From Priestly Torah*, 148–50.

[186] See, among others, NOTH, *Das dritte Buch Mose*, 69–70.

[187] See the following description in the present section.

[188] See A. RUWE, *"Heiligkeitsgesetz" und "Priesterschrift": Literaturgeschichtliche und rechtssystematische Untersuchungen zu Leviticus 17,1–26,2*, FAT 26 (Tübingen: Mohr Siebeck, 1999), 45–51; NIHAN, *From Priestly Torah*, 576–607; J. W. WATTS, *Leviticus 1–10*, HCOT (Leuven: Peeters, 2014), 503–52.

A *crux interpretum* of Lev 10 is the identification of the exact nature of the offense of the two first sons of Aaron. Both ancient and modern interpreters have offered a variety of explanations. The text disqualifies their act as an offering of "strange," illegitimate fire (אש זרה) and as an offering "which was not commanded by YHWH" (10:1). What is meant by "a strange fire"? Significant for this question might be the fact that the fire is called "strange" after the addition of incense (קטרת; see v. 1bγ). The incense offering appears in Leviticus only later, in Lev 16; it is performed by the high priest. With Nihan, one might see the transgression in the fact that none of the preceding laws in Lev 1–9 demand the incense offering (hence the statement in 10:1bβ).[189] In contrast, Lev 8–9 stresses the fact that the mentioned sacrifices were offered in conformity with YHWH's instruction (see the repeated formula כאשר צוה יהוה, "as YHWH commanded," in 8:4, 9, 13, 17, 21, 29, 36; 9:7, 10). Nadab and Abihu's sacrifice, "which he (YHWH) had not commanded them" (אשר לא צוה אתם; v. 10:1bβ), indeed breaks this pattern.[190]

Beside the latter correspondence, there are further expressions and motifs shared between Lev 10 and 9. In both stories "a fire comes out from YHWH and consumes" (ותצא אש מלפני יהוה ותאכל) – there the offering and here the faulty priests (compare 9:24 with 10:2). The linguistic commonalities point to the close proximity of the two texts. Furthermore, recent treatments underline Aaron's importance and the positive role he plays: for the first time, YHWH addresses himself directly to Aaron (see v. 8), and, at the end, the high priest outperforms Moses as interpreter of the *tôrâ* (see vv. 16–20). From that point of view, Lev 10 aligns well with the preceding unit (where Aaron plays a central role as well) rather than opposing it.[191] Moreover, the two units share the theological commonality of alluding in a subtle way to the story of the golden bull in Exod 32: as mentioned above, in Lev 9 the expression עגל, "young bull," which is unique in Priestly texts, is used to designate the animal of Aaron's sin offering (see Lev 9:2, 8 and cf. v. 3). In Exod 29:1, 10–14, 36 and in the sacrificial *tôrôt* of Lev 1–16, the bull of the sin-offering is always called פר (see Lev 4; 8:14–17; 16). Yet עגל is the designation of the molten bull in the story of Israel's apostasy in Exod 32 (see vv. 4, 8, 19, 20, 24, 35). Frevel argues that by presenting the young bull as a sin offering for himself, Aaron is making expiation for his own sin – namely the fabrication of the golden bull![192] As for the allusion to Exod 32 in Lev 10, it lies in the names of Aaron's two transgressing sons. Nadab and Abihu, who are strongly reminiscent of the unlucky (Abijah) and negatively connoted (Nadab) sons of Jeroboam I, visibly recall Aaron's "connection" to Bethel and the reign of Jeroboam I. What is the author's intention in doing this? Apparently, the author(s) of Lev 9 and 10 cannot help but "accept" Aaron's defamation and the Aaronides' association with Jeroboam's cult policy in Exod

---

[189] NIHAN, *From Priestly Torah*, 581–82.

[190] NIHAN, *From Priestly Torah*, 582. See also RUWE, *Heiligkeitsgesetz*, 48.

[191] See NIHAN, *From Priestly Torah*, 591–93, 598–605; WATTS, *Leviticus 1–10*, 537, 546–52.

[192] FREVEL, *Mit Blick*, 178–79. Frevel emphasizes that within the Pentateuch עגל is only used in Exod 32, Lev 9, and the parallel of the golden calf story in Deut 9 (178).

32. Accordingly, he (they) tried to integrate the "bad mark" of the past into the Priestly plot by transforming and mitigating it. In Lev 9, Aaron's offense is expiated by his sin offering. As for Lev 10, the "creation" and dismissal of Nadab and Abihu allow the author to eliminate a corrupt branch of the Aaronides and to reconceive the priestly dynasty by putting forward one particular, entirely positive line (comprising the high priests of the second and third generation, i.e., Eleazar and Phinehas).[193] Perhaps Lev 9–10 is related to a few texts "promoting" this line, such as Exod 6:14–27 or Num 25.[194]

(d) Leviticus 11–15

In general, scholars assume a complicated genesis for the Priestly laws contained in Lev 11–15, which concern different purity and impurity issues (laws on edible and nonedible animals, instructions on bodily impurities such as the *tôrôt* of birthing women, of different types of scale-disease, and of various kinds of male and female genital impurities). In the past, European scholars tended to consider the collection as it stands a secondary insertion into the Priestly stratum (independent of the presupposed antiquity of the laws).[195] Arguments for this idea are the inclusion of Aaron as an addressee of divine speech (11:1; 13:1; 14:33; 15:1, cf. also Aaron's mention in 13:2) and the direct back-reference to Lev 10 in 16:1. Koch and Nihan, however, assign Lev 11–15 to the first Priestly stratum (P^G). According to Koch, the aforementioned arguments are not conclusive, because both the mention of Aaron and the back-reference might have been added secondarily.[196] For Nihan, in contrast, Aaron's mention would hint at the Priestly author (P^G), who, according to Nihan, composed Lev 8–9. Nihan furthermore identifies alleged Priestly elements (P^G) within the narrative framework (12:1–2aα; 14:1, 34; 15:2a, 31) and beyond (the mention of the tent of meeting in 12:6; 14:11, 23; 15:14, 29 and that of the encampment [מחנה] in 13:46; 14:3).[197] Moreover, Nihan sees these laws in close connection to the beginning of the Priestly account in Gen 1–11, as an attempt at "systematic control over all major forms of biological intrusions into the social sphere" in order to assure the "process of recreation by instituting separation from phenomena regarded as contrary to the creational norm."[198] Some of Nihan's arguments are not compelling. First, the narrative framework is partly

---

[193] To be sure, Nadab and Abihu also appear in Exod 24:1, 9–11, where they play a positive role. However, because of the blatantly negative role of the two figures in Lev 10, it is likely that it was the author of Lev 10 who "invented" and introduced Nadab and Abihu as an allusion to Aaron's connection with Bethel and Jeroboam I in Exod 32. Exod 24:1, 9–11 and the genealogical notices in 6:23; 24:1, 9; 28:1 probably also presuppose Lev 10.

[194] See below, III.1.3.

[195] See WELLHAUSEN, *Die Composition*, 148–49; BAENTSCH, *Exodus–Leviticus–Numeri*, 353; ELLIGER, *Leviticus*, 12–13; NOTH, *Das dritte Buch Mose*, 4–5; LOHFINK, "Die Priesterschrift," 198, n. 29.

[196] See KOCH, *Die Priesterschrift von Exodus 25 bis Leviticus 16*, 91–92; NIHAN, *From Priestly Torah*, 269–382; see also BLUM, *Studien*, 318, with n. 119 and T. RÖMER, "Der Pentateuch," 133–34.

[197] NIHAN, *From Priestly Torah*, 270.

[198] NIHAN, *From Priestly Torah*, 339.

formulated with *late* Priestly language (see especially Lev 14:34, which resembles the H phraseology in 19:32; 23:10; 25:12 much more than the Priestly language in Exod 6:8).[199] Second, since the encampment (מחנה) does not appear elsewhere in P^C, its presence in Lev 13:46; 14:3 oddly anticipates the presentation of Israel's camp in Num 1–10.[200] Moreover, the postscript formula (זאת התורה, "this is the law," see 11:46; 12:7; 13:59; 14:32, 57; 15:32), which according to Nihan stems from an ancient tradition, also appears in the late texts Lev 7 and Num 5–6 (but nowhere else in the Priestly strand).[201] It is therefore tempting to assign it to a later Priestly author (P^S) who may, as indicated by Aaron's inclusion as an addressee, either have known Lev 8–10[202] or be identical with the latter's author.[203]

Nihan's argument about the conceptual connectedness to the Priestly story of origins is suggestive, but it does not necessitate the literary-historical conclusion of common authorship for Gen 1–11 P and Lev 11–15; the back-reference may have been intended by a later author (redactor). In the context of this question, it is important to note certain distinct features of Lev 11–15 when compared with Gen 1–11 P. For instance, perception and categorization of the animal world in Lev 11 differ from Gen 1: while the former is divided in four main categories (including also winged insects), the latter is tripartite.[204] Also, the classification of certain animals as an "abomination" (שקץ, see Lev 11:10, 11, 12, 13, 20, 23, 41, 42) for Israel stands in tension with the general appreciation of all creatures in Gen 1.[205] Nevertheless, these differences might also be explained by the assumption that the classification of the animals and the approbation formulae of Gen 1 belong to the proto-Priestly *Vorlage*.[206]

In sum, there are several indications speaking against the assignment of Lev 11–15 to the most original stratum of the Priestly Sinai legislation.

---

[199] With KNOHL, *Sanctuary*, 95, n. 119, and MILGROM, *Leviticus 1–16*, 866–86, and *pace* NIHAN, *From Priestly Torah*, 276.

[200] See WELLHAUSEN, *Die Composition*, 148; BAENTSCH, *Exodus–Leviticus–Numeri*, 353.

[201] Lev 7:37; Num 5:29; 6:21.

[202] Thus WELLHAUSEN, *Die Composition*, 148, and BAENTSCH, *Exodus–Leviticus–Numeri*, 353–54 (Lev 11–15 stem from a later author than Lev 8–10; 16).

[203] See E. OTTO, "Das Buch Levitikus zwischen Priesterschrift und Pentateuch," review of *From Priestly Torah to Pentateuch*, by C. Nihan, *TRu* 74 (2009): 474. According to Otto, "Lev 11–15 ist unlösbar mit Lev 10,10, der Beauftragung der Priester, zwischen rein und unrein zu unterscheiden, verbunden. Lev 11–15 stellt die dafür notwendigen Gesetze bereit."

[204] See P. ALTMANN, *Banned Birds. The Birds of Leviticus 11 and Deuteronomy 14*, Archaeology and Bible 1 (Tübingen: Mohr Siebeck, 2019), 145, 147.

[205] According to Gen 1, in general all beings created by God are considered "good" (טוב; see Gen 1:31), although a certain differentiation in the appreciation of the animals is visible (on the level of the Priestly redaction, P^C): while the sea animals and the birds receive a blessing from God, the land animals are bereft of the latter. As argued above (II.1.3.5, II.1.3.10), this is due to the humans' blessing by God. Since mankind and land animals have to share the same living space, they cannot both be blessed.

[206] See the analysis of Gen 1:1–2:4a, above (II.1.3).

(e) Leviticus 16

Most scholars assume an extremely complicated genesis for Lev 16; some reject the possibility of reconstructing its composition history because of this complexity.[207] Nevertheless, a few recent treatments view the bulk of the chapter, found in vv. 2–28, to be a homogeneous composition.[208] Traditionally Lev 16, or its central part, is considered to be the continuation of Lev 8–10 and to belong to the primary Priestly stratum in the Sinai pericope.[209] Recent treatments highlight the chapter's connections with the preceding ritual laws, in particular with Lev 4 and 11–15. Leviticus 16 is considered the "capstone" of the Priestly ritual legislation in Lev 1–16.[210] Some of these scholars opt for a relatively late date of composition.[211] Others among them, however, see in Lev 16 a strong connection to the tabernacle account and thus view it as the conclusion of the Priestly Sinai legislation and as part of the original Priestly layer (P^G/P^C) in general.[212] This conclusion is defended in particular by Nihan.[213] At the center of his argument are the motifs of the "cloud" (עָנָן) and the "cover" (or "mercy seat," כפרת):

> The cloud motif connects the ceremony of ch. 16 with a wider pattern rounding off Ex 24–Lev 16 through the description of the cloud's move from *Mt Sinai* (Ex 24:15b–18aα) to the *tent of meeting* (Ex 40:34–35) to the *inner-sanctum* (Lev 16). The general device underlying this pattern … *suggests that the entire Sinai account has been conceived by P on the model of ancient Near Eastern temple entrance rituals* [in particular the Babylonian *akītu* festival containing similar cleansing and purification rituals].[214]

Nihan connects the incense cloud in Lev 16 with the emergence of the divine cloud

---

[207] Baentsch, *Exodus–Leviticus–Numeri*, 369–87; Elliger, *Leviticus*, 202–18; Noth, *Das dritte Buch Mose*, 100–102; J. E. Hartley, *Leviticus*, WBC 4 (Waco, TX: Word, 1992), 219; R. Péter-Contesse, *Lévitique 1–16*, CAT IIIa (Geneva: Labor et Fides, 1993), 245–48. The latter three authors abdicate reconstruction of the unit's literary genesis.

[208] Milgrom, *Leviticus 1–16*, 1061–65; Nihan, *From Priestly Torah*, 340–70.

[209] Thus Kuenen, *Historisch-kritische Einleitung*, 1.1:79; Wellhausen, *Die Composition*, 147–48, Baentsch, *Exodus–Leviticus–Numeri*, 379–80 ("Zusammengehörigkeit zu P [im weiteren Sinn])"; Milgrom, *Leviticus 1–16*, 62, 1061.

[210] F. Crüsemann, *Die Tora: Theologie und Sozialgeschichte des alttestamentlichen Gesetzes*, 2nd ed. (Munich: Kaiser, 1997), 364; T. Seidl, "Levitikus 16 – 'Schlussstein' des priesterlichen Systems der Sündenvergebung," in *Levitikus als Buch*, ed. H.-J. Fabry and H.-W. Jüngling, BBB 119 (Berlin: Philo, 1999), 219–48; Nihan, *From Priestly Torah*, 95–97, 99–105, 340–82; Otto, "Buch Levitikus im Pentateuch," 474–76.

[211] Seidl, "Levitikus 16," 243–45; Otto, "Das Buch Levitikus im Pentateuch," 474–76. Seidl considers Lev 16 to be a late summarizing speculation of P, possibly presupposing Lev 23:26–32 and Num 29:7–11 (see Seidl, "Levitikus 16," 243–45).

[212] Crüsemann, *Die Tora*, 361–65; Nihan, *From Priestly Torah*, 95–97, 99–105, 340–82.

[213] Nihan, *From Priestly Torah*, 95–97, 99–105, 340–82. He is followed by, among others, R. Albertz, *Pentateuchstudien*, ed. J. Wöhrle, FAT 117 (Tübingen: Mohr Siebeck, 2018), 300–312; Rhyder, *Centralizing the Cult*, 156–57.

[214] Nihan, *From Priestly Torah*, 381.

in Exod 24:15b–18aα, seeing in both the expression of the deity's presence. Further-more, Nihan views the purification and cleansing rituals in Lev 16 in close connec-tion to the mention of the "cover" in Exod 25:17–22. The "enigmatic" notion of the ark's "cover" (כפרת) would thereby receive an explanation only in Lev 16, "when the *kappōret* is presented … as the focal point of the purgation rite (*kipper*) performed by Aaron inside the inner-sanctum."[215] Nihan is essentially arguing that the tabernacle account, especially 24:15b–18aα; 25:17–22, aims towards Lev 16 as the original con-clusion of P's Sinai pericope and of the Priestly composition in general. However, on close examination, this reasoning is not compelling. The identification of the cloud in Exod 24:15b–18a*, 40:34 with the human-made incense cloud of Lev 16 is not evi-dent. Furthermore, and this seems more important, neither the passage dealing with the mercy seat in Exod 25:17–22 nor any other statement in Exod 25–29*; 40* alludes or looks ahead to the purging act (כפר *piel*) of Lev 16. Significantly, Exod 25:22 asso-ciates the mercy seat with *the revelation of* YHWH's *commandments to Moses* rather than with cultic acts to be performed by the high priest. Furthermore, it is important to note that the central statement in 28:29–30, according to which Aaron, wearing the pectoral with the twelve precious stones and the Urim and Thummim, should present Israel's justice before YHWH remains without any resonance in Lev 16. The motifs of the "breastpiece of judgment" and the Urim and Thummim, which play an important role in this passage, are absent from Lev 16, although one would expect them there (related to Aaron's presence in the sanctuary) if both texts stemmed from the same author. Another tension between Lev 16 and Exod 28:29–30 pertains to the restriction that Aaron may access YHWH only once a year.[216] Aaron's obligation as expressed in 28:29–30 is without any time limitation.

How then should one classify Lev 16 literary-historically? Both the unit's strong connectedness with the late Priestly texts Lev 4–7 and the particular vocabulary choices plead for the assignment of this chapter to a late Priestly stratum. Through the dominant key word חטאת ("expiation," "sin-offering") Lev 16 is in particular linked to Lev 4 which deals with this sort of sacrifice.[217] As in Lev 9, the non-Priestly designa-tion עם, "people," for Israel appears beside בני ישראל, "the Israelites," עדה, "congrega-tion," קהל, "assembly," and עם הקהל, "all the people of the assembly."[218] Such confla-tion of different terms designating Israel is frequent in late Priestly texts such as Lev 9; 10; Num 17; 20:1–13; 25. The absence of the incense altar does not necessarily indicate

---

[215] NIHAN, *From Priestly Torah*, 382.

[216] The section 16:29–34, which fixes the date for the rituals described before, is seen as a secondary addition by most scholars. With ALBERTZ, *Pentateuchstudien*, 303–5, it should be noted, however, that this passage cannot easily be "detached" from vv. 1–28, because the nega-tive statement in v. 2 ("Tell your brother Aaron that he shall not enter at any time into the holy place inside the veil, before the mercy seat which is on the ark, lest he die") requires a positive prescription related to the suitable time (for this argument, see also ELLIGER, *Leviticus*, 203).

[217] חטאת appears in Lev 16:3, 5, 6, 9, 11 (2×), 15, 25, 27. See SEIDL, "Levitikus 16," 236–37; OTTO, "Das Buch Levitikus im Pentateuch," 474–75.

[218] עם: Lev 16:15, 24 (2×). בני ישראל: 16:5, 16, 19, 21, 34. עדה: 16:5. קהל: 16:17. עם הקהל: 16:33.

that Lev 16 predates Lev 4. The author of Lev 16 might have left this piece of cultic furniture unmentioned deliberately, because he was opposed to it.

10.6.3 Conclusion

To sum up this section on Lev 1–16, the sacrificial prescriptions in Lev 1–3 probably form the most original stratum within Lev 1–16. In terms of its concise form and content, Lev 1–3 matches the tabernacle account (Exod 25–29*, 40*) well. Because of its limitation to the three main sacrifices, Lev 1–3 appears to be a fitting complement to Exod 25–28*, 40*. Because they are voluntary (cf. the introductory formula, "When any person among you brings an offering to YHWH," in Lev 1:2; 2:1; 3:1), the described offerings nicely match the *voluntary* endowment for the building of the sanctuary by the community (see Exod 25:2–7*).

Leviticus 4–7 develop Lev 1–3 further by integrating information about concrete occasions for sacrifice and dealing with specific problems of procedure. The use of distinct vocabulary and motifs hints at their later origin in comparison to Lev 1–3.

The above overview of the narrative parts of Lev 8–10 assembled numerous indications of the interrelatedness of these chapters and their dependence on Lev 1–7. Against widespread opinion, Lev 9 should not be assigned to P^C. Affinities to language and motifs of late Priestly and non-Priestly texts suggest a late date of composition of this unit. Leviticus 8–10 postdate the tabernacle account (Exod 25–29, 40*) and the sacrificial laws in Lev 1–3. Allusions to the story of the golden bull in Exod 32 and the "background narrative" in 1 Kgs 12–15 make it likely that Lev 9–10 presuppose them and are reacting to them.

The brief assessment of the legislation in Lev 11–15 indicated several clues of late Priestly (P^s) authorship. In their present form, these units presuppose Lev 4, the narrative parts of Lev 8–10, and certain texts in Numbers as well. Similarly, the description of the atonement ritual in Lev 16 presupposes Lev 4 and the secondary passage in Exod 28:42–43.

This tentative reconstruction, which assigns Exod 25–28*, 40* and Lev 1–3 to the original kernel of the Priestly Sinai pericope, seems to reflect the socioeconomic realities of early postexilic Yehud.[219] In particular, we note the absence of stable leadership and the economic difficulties that the population was confronted with during this period, as evidenced by a number of passages in Haggai and Zechariah.[220] The

---

[219] For the early Persian era as the possible setting of the tabernacle account, see below, II.10.9.

[220] To be sure, both the author of Haggai and that of Zechariah expect important positions for the governor (Zerubbabel) and the high priest (Joshua) (see Hag 2:23; Zech 4; 6:9–15), but there is no evidence for the fulfillment of these hopes. The temple building project met inner-Judean opposition (see Hag 1:2). Economic misery is described in Hag 1:6–11 and Zech 8:10. See furthermore L. L. Grabbe, *A History of the Jews and Judaism in the Second Temple Period, Volume 1: Yehud; A History of the Persian Province of Judah* (London: T&T Clark, 2007), 279–82, 284.

voluntary form of donation in 25:1–7* may well be explained by the pressure of the economic situation in early Persian Yehud.[221] The book of Haggai shows that funding for the Second Temple was based on voluntary donations.[222] Similarly, the limitation of the sacrificial legislation to three basic *voluntary* sacrifices would fit the penurious economic situation in the early Persian era. One may wonder whether the implementation of complex legal provisions on a compulsory level, such as those found in Lev 4–7 and 11–15, which implied material tribute (i.e., sacrificial animals) to the sanctuary, would have been a conceivable objective for the Priestly authors under such difficult circumstances. Furthermore, one should consider the fact that in the early Persian period most Judeans lived far away from Palestine and did not have the option to regularly offer sacrifices at the central sanctuary. Such a situation would have required the possibility for the people to offer sacrifices on a voluntary level rather than to have regular mandatory offerings. Likewise, the programmatic extension of the high priest's powers becomes understandable in this particular context, with the Judeans predominantly residing in the diaspora: his task to present *all* Israel's justice (משפט) before YHWH in the sanctuary in order to attract the deity's propitious "remembering" (זכרן cf. Exod 28:29–30) clearly has *a compensatory function* (the high priest also represents Israelites living far away from Jerusalem, who are unable to participate in the cult) and makes best sense in that light.[223]

10.7 Tradition-Historical Background and Literary Influences

10.7.1 Alleged and Possible Influences from ANE Tent and Temple Traditions

Scholars have long held that the author of the tabernacle account was influenced by ancient tent-shrine traditions on the one hand and by temple traditions – and in particular by the tradition of the Jerusalem temple – on the other. Relatively few tent-shrine traditions are attested in ANE literature. The following parallels have been put forward by scholars.

The first is an eighteenth-century BCE tablet from Mari (M.6873), which, like the tabernacle account, refers to a large tent with ten heavy wooden *qersū*, which have to be transported by twenty men.[224] The second example is the description of

---

[221] Because of the absence of a strong indigenous authority capable of extracting taxes from the population, the temple was probably forced to rely on a system of voluntary funding and to convince the Judeans of their moral obligation toward the Jerusalem temple (see P. R. BEDFORD, "Temple Funding and Priestly Authority in Achaemenid Judah," in *Exile and Return: The Babylonian Context*, ed. J. Stökl and C. Waerzeggers, BZAW 478 [Berlin: de Gruyter, 2015], 336–51).

[222] See Hag 1:8.

[223] Similarly KEEL, *Die Geschichte Jerusalems*, 2:936.

[224] See J.-M. DURAND and M. GUICHARD, "Les rituels de Mari," *FM* 3 (1997): 65–66; FLEMING, "Mari's Large Public Tent."

El's mountain sanctuary in the Ugaritic Baal Cycle. The tent of El is called a *qrš* (see KTU 1.4 IV.24). The two parallels are remote in time from the presumed setting of the tabernacle account and do not seem strong enough to suggest the direct dependence of the biblical account on the two much-earlier traditions. The conception of El's tent, a meeting place for the gods, is very different from the intricate plan of the Priestly tabernacle.

Furthermore, the Priestly tabernacle has been compared to several Egyptian tent traditions. The closest parallel is the military camp of Ramses II at Qadesh, which is depicted on four temple reliefs in Luxor, Abu Simbel, and twice at the Ramesseum. These reliefs and accompanying inscriptions portray the camp as comprising an approximately 3:1 rectangular tent, composed of a 2:1 reception tent and the adjoining square throne tent of Ramses II, which conforms nicely with the structure of the tabernacle. Other parallels pointed out by scholars – the throne being flanked by falcon wings; the east–west orientation of the tent – seem less indicative; these elements appear frequently in Egyptian sacral architecture.[225] In any case, common points of contact between the tabernacle and the Jerusalem temple – concerning the measurements and the cherubim – seem more significant (see below).

Nevertheless, it is probable that the elaborate and complex architectural conception of the tabernacle account – as it is visible in particular in Exod 25–28* – drew on certain elements of ANE tent-shrine traditions. With regard to several motifs betraying Egyptian influence on the one hand and clues of late authorship in the Persian era on the other, one might especially infer an influence deriving from Egypt's Late Period. A. Bühler points to similarities with Amun's military tent in the Inaros Cycle.[226] Egyptian influence is visible in the particular order of the compass points, namely, south-north-west-east (see Exod 26:18–22, 35; 27:9–15; and furthermore 36:23–27; 38:9–15). The reference point of the Egyptian order was indeed the source of the Nile, in the south, instead of the east, as in other regions of the ancient Near East.[227] The motif that the high priest wears a pectoral with the inscribed gems corresponding to the twelve tribes is probably influenced by the frequent ancient Near Eastern use of seals and other objects as votives to a deity for the sake of the latter's attention and favor (זכרון).[228] What is uncommon in ANE votive practice, however, is the dedication

---

[225] See K. A. Kitchen, "The Tabernacle – A Bronze Age Artefact," *ErIsr* 24 (1993): 121*; M. M. Homan, *To Your Tents, O Israel! The Terminology, Function, Form, and Symbolism of Tents in the Hebrew Bible and the Ancient Near East*, CHANE 12 (Leiden: Brill, 2002), 89–62.

[226] For these parallels, see A. Bühler, "The Demotic Literature and the Priestly Exodus: The *Legend of Sesostris*, the *Inaros Cycle*, and the Battles of Magicians compared to the Priestly Exodus," in *The Historical Location of P*, ed. J. Hutzli and J. Davis (forthcoming). There are in particular similarities with Amun's military tent in the Inaros Cycle (see ibid., 14–15).

[227] Pointing to this parallel, see Bühler, "Demotic Literature and the Priestly Exodus." See G. Posener, *Sur l'orientation et l'ordre des points cardinaux chez les Egyptiens*, NAWG 1, Philologisch-historische Klasse (Göttingen: Vandenhoeck & Ruprecht, 1965).

[228] See W. Zwickel, "Die Edelsteine im Brustschild des Hohenpriesters und beim himmlischen Jerusalem," in *Edelsteine in der Bibel*, ed. W. Zwickel (Mainz: von Zabern, 2002), 50–70;

of an object in favor of a tribe or a territory. Nevertheless, the symbolic and continuing dedication may be compared to the Egyptian ritual of the presentation of a Maat figurine by the pharaoh.[229] In this ritual, the king presents justice and social and cosmic order in Egypt to a god (often Re). What may indeed indicate Egyptian influence on the Priestly conception is that according to late sources (Diodorus Siculus, *Bibliotheca Historica* 1.75.5; Aelian, *Varia Historia* 14.34), chief justices of high courts, as viziers of the pharaoh, wore an image set with gemstones called "Truth" (Ἀλήθεια, Maat) as a pendant whenever they officiated.[230] The expression "breastpiece of justice (חֹשֶׁן המשׁפט)" in the tabernacle account (Exod 18:15, 19, 30[2×]) recalls this Egyptian legal custom and may be a clue that the Priestly author was inspired by it (if it existed in pre-Hellenistic times).[231] In light of this parallel it is probable that in v. 30 the term משׁפט, through association with the Urim and Thummim, alludes to the concrete jurisdiction exercised by the high priest (v. 30).[232]

10.7.2 Influences from Israelite Sacral Traditions

Biblical scholars assume, furthermore, that the author of the tabernacle account was influenced by ancient Israelite tent traditions reflected in other biblical texts.[233] An ancient אהל מועד ("tent of meeting") tradition is seen to lie behind several non-Priestly texts using this term (see Exod 33:7–11; Num 11:16–17, 24–26; 12:4–5, 10). In the past, these texts were commonly considered pre-Priestly; several recent treatments, however, classify them as post-Priestly.[234] A few scholars maintain that the Priestly tabernacle reflects the premonarchic Shilo sanctuary (which they consider a tent shrine).[235] Yet their argument relies on late texts influenced by P, such as 1 Sam

---

J. TIGAY, "The Priestly Reminder Stones and Ancient Near Eastern Votive Practices," in *Shay: Studies in the Bible, Its Exegesis and Language Presented to Sara Japhet*, ed. M. Bar Asher, D. Rom-Shiloni, E. Tov, and N. Wazana (Jerusalem: Bialik, 2007), 119–38; C. NIHAN, "Le pectoral d'Aaron et la figure du grand prêtre dans les traditions sacerdotales du Pentateuque," in *Congress Volume Stellenbosch 2016*, ed. L. C. Jonker, G. R. Kotzé, and C. M. Maier, VTSup 177 (Leiden: Brill, 2017), 23–55.

[229] See O. KEEL, "Die Brusttasche des Hohenpriesters als Element priesterschriftlicher Theologie," in *Das Manna fällt auch heute noch: Beiträge zur Geschichte und Theologie des Alten, Ersten Testaments; Festschrift für Erich Zenger*, ed. F.-L. Hossfeld, and L. Schwienhorst-Schönberger, HBS 44 (Herder: Freiburg im Breisgau, 2004), 379–91; KEEL, *Die Geschichte Jerusalems*, 2:934–36; C. NIHAN, "Le pectoral d'Aaron," 23–55.

[230] See PROPP, *Exodus 19–40*, 443, 523.

[231] See also PROPP, *Exodus 19–40*, 523.

[232] For this twofold meaning of משׁפט, see NIHAN, "Le pectoral d'Aaron," 47–50.

[233] G. VON RAD, *Theologie des Alten Testaments, Band I: Die Theologie der geschichtlichen Überlieferung Israels*, 10th ed. (Munich: Kaiser, 1992), 247–54; CROSS, *Canaanite Myth*, 322; HARAN, *Temples*, 270–73.

[234] For a discussion of Exod 33:7–11 and related texts, see below, II.10.10.2 (lit.).

[235] M. HARAN, "Shilo and Jerusalem," *JBL* 81 (1962): 21–22; IDEM, *Temples*, 198–204; CROSS, *Canaanite Myth*, 73, n. 114; J. MILGROM, *Studies in Cultic Theology and Terminology*, SJLA 36 (Leiden: Brill, 1983), 26–28.

2:22 MT[236] and 2 Sam 7:6–7,[237] and it is contradicted by 1 Sam 1–3, in which the Shilo sanctuary is a permanent building (see 1 Sam 1:7, 9; 3:15).[238] F. M. Cross suggested that the tent David pitched for the ark (2 Sam 6:17; see also 7:2) was the prototype of the Priestly tabernacle. This tent would have been influenced by contemporary Canaanite architecture.[239] Cross's theory seems quite speculative, however, and goes beyond the scarce information given by the texts in question (whose settings are disputed as well).[240] One of the expressions denoting the Priestly sanctuary and often considered to be typical "tent" terminology, מִשְׁכָּן, "tabernacle, dwelling," is probably derived from the Jerusalem temple tradition and refers to the Jerusalem temple (see Pss 26:8; 46:5; 74:7; 84:2; 132:5, 7); similarly, the cognate verb שׁכן in 1 Kgs 8:12; Isa 8:18; Pss 68:17; 135:21 denotes YHWH's dwelling on Zion.[241]

Notwithstanding the question of influence by certain tent-shrine traditions, most scholars agree on the importance of numerous points of contact between the tabernacle and the Solomonic temple as it is described in the construction report in 1 Kgs 6–8.[242] In particular, recent treatments emphasize these parallels and commonalities, which are indeed numerous.[243]

---

[236] 1 Sam 2:22 MT deals with a sexual offense committed by "sons of Eli." It states that the delinquents "laid with the women who served at the entrance of the tent of meeting (פתח אהל מועד)." Given its Priestly language, its allusion to Exod 38:8, and the contradiction of architectural information given elsewhere in the Hannah-Samuel story (cf. 1 Sam 1:7, 9; 3:15), it is considered foreign "matter" in 1 Sam 1–2 and assigned to a secondary layer by most scholars. Note furthermore that the statement is absent from 4QSam[a] and LXX. Wellhausen considered it a late (proto-)"Pharisaic" gloss directed against the Priestly class (WELLHAUSEN, *Der Text der Bücher Samuelis untersucht* [Göttingen: Vandenhoeck und Ruprecht, 1871], 46).

[237] One may ask whether this passage expresses a more fundamental critique of David's temple project than in the main text of 2 Sam 7, adhering perhaps to a conservative nomadic ideal. Hinting at the secondary nature of the passage is the typical Priestly designation "the children of Israel, the Israelites" (בני ישראל), which occurs twice in 7:6–7 but is absent from all other parts of the comprehensive unit in 2 Sam 7. The double term "tent and tabernacle" (אהל ומשכן) recalls Priestly terminology of the tabernacle account. If we consider 2 Sam 7:8aα a *Wiederaufnahme* of 7:5a, then 7:8aβ becomes a smooth continuation of 7:5a. The whole of vv. 6–7 or parts of them are considered a later addition by D. KELLERMANN, "מִשְׁכָּן *miškān*," *TWAT* 5:62–69; O. SERGI, "The Composition of Nathan's Oracle to David (2 Samuel 7:1–17) as a Reflection of Royal Judahite Ideology," *JBL* 129 (2010): 275–77; T. A. RUDNIG, "König ohne Tempel: 2 Samuel 7 in Tradition und Redaktion," *VT* 61 (2011): 435; J. HUTZLI, "Priestly(-like) Texts in Samuel and Kings," in *Writing, Rewriting, and Overwriting in the Books of Deuteronomy and the Former Prophets: Essays in Honour of Cynthia Edenburg*, ed. I. Koch, T. Römer, and O. Sergi, BETL 304 (Leuven: Peeters, 2019), 229.

[238] For this reason, Cross and Haran's view remains isolated.

[239] Cross, *Canaanite Myth*, 322.

[240] See the critique of BLUM, *Studien*, 303; BOORER *Vision of the Priestly Narrative*, 300.

[241] See T. N. D. METTINGER, *The Dethronement of Sabaoth: Studies in the Shem and Kabod Theologies*, ConBOT 18 (Lund: Gleerup, 1982), 28–30, 92–97; BOORER, *Vision of the Priestly Narrative*, 305, 367–68 (lit.).

[242] WELLHAUSEN, *Prolegomena zur Geschichte*, 34–38, has been very influential in this matter.

[243] See HARAN, *Temples*, 189–94; UTZSCHNEIDER, *Das Heiligtum und das Gesetz*, 270–74;

(1) H. Utzschneider points to various linguistic and formal commonalities (vocabulary, order of listed copper vessels [cf. Exod 27:3 with 1 Kgs 7:45]).[244]

(2) The general structure, and measurements of the tabernacle correspond largely to those of the Solomonic temple. Both sanctuaries are rectangular and have an east-west orientation.[245] Both have a holy of holies (inner sanctum), holy place (outer sanctum), and courtyard. As for the dimensions of the tabernacle (a footprint of 30 × 10 cubits), these correspond to those of the Solomonic temple (whose footprint was 60 × 20 cubits, see 1 Kgs 6:2[246]), covering precisely half the area of the Jerusalem temple.[247]

(3) The tabernacle account describes important items of furniture that appear in the report of the construction of Solomon's temple (cherubim, wooden lining, ark, table, lamp[s]).

(4) The ornamentation, with cherubim on the walls and with curtains, is similar.

(5) As M. Haran in particular has pointed out, both accounts describe a similarly elaborate architecture, which reflects a gradation of sanctity through the subdivision of the sanctuary area and through the attribution of different building materials to the three areas (gold and precious wood for the furniture of the holy of holies and of the outer sanctum; bronze for the articles of the court).[248]

However, the tabernacle account also mentions certain features that do not appear in the construction report in 1 Kgs 6–8, such as the various elements of the Priestly

---

NIHAN, *From Priestly Torah*, 43; C. D. CRAWFORD, "Between Shadow and Substance: The Historical Relationship of Tabernacle and Temple in Light of Architecture and Iconography," in *Levites and Priests in Biblical History and Tradition*, ed. M. Leuchter and J. M. Hutton, Ancient Israel and Its Literature 9 (Atlanta: SBL Press, 2011), 117–33; BOORER, *Vision of the Priestly Narrative*, 306–10.

[244] UTZSCHNEIDER, *Das Heiligtum und das Gesetz*, 270–74.

[245] The east-west orientation is expressed in Exod 27:12–16: the court with its door (v.16) faces the east. For the east-west orientation of the Solomonic temple, see 1 Kgs 7:39; Ezek 8:16; 43:4; 47:1.

[246] The Septuagint (GBL) has 40 cubits for the length. 2 Chr 3:3 (MT and LXX) and Ezek 41:2, 4 (MT) agree with MT. According to M. NOTH, *Könige*, BKAT 11 (Neukirchen-Vluyn: Neukirchener Verlag, 1968), 97, 100, the LXX corrected the text in view of the indication of the length of the great hall in v. 17.

[247] The measurements of the tabernacle can be deduced from Exod 26:15–30. The height ratio is 1:3 (tabernacle: 10 cubits; temple: 30 cubits). The calculation of the width is not without problems: "Exod 26:22–23 refers to six קרשים, that is, 9 cubits, since each is 1.5 cubits wide, plus two corner frames for which no measurements are given. Some scholars assume that the corner frames round out the width to 10 cubits, thus making the width, like the length, half of that of the Solomonic temple" (BOORER, *Vision of the Priestly Narrative*, 306–7). Scholars who believe that the ground plan of the Priestly tabernacle is half that of the Solomonic temple include HARAN, *Temples*, 151, n. 4; NIHAN, *From Priestly Torah*, 43, n. 121; KEEL, *Die Geschichte Jerusalems*, 2:927; BOORER, *Vision of the Priestly Narrative*, 310. The halving of the size in the tabernacle account presumably aims to accommodate the particular circumstances of the wilderness (see KEEL, *Die Geschichte Jerusalems*, 2:927).

[248] HARAN, *Temples*, 189–94.

garments. The mention of the ephod and the Urim and Thummim, articles typically associated with traditions of the historical books, in particular the books of Samuel, is worth noting.[249] Furthermore, one should note that other objects (utensils) that have a prominent place in the tabernacle account are probably not in the primary report of the First Temple's construction (1 Kgs 6–7*), namely the lampstands and the table for the "bread of the face," and also the golden altar (see 1 Kgs 7:48–49).

To be sure, ten lampstands and the table for the "bread of the face" are mentioned together with the golden altar in a short passage at the end of the report in 1 Kgs 6–7 (7:48–50). However, some commentaries offer good arguments for ascribing the whole passage, or specifically the golden altar, the table for the "bread of the face," the ten lampstands, the flower, the lamps, and the tongs (cf. 1 Kgs 7:48–49) to a secondary layer.[250] It is indeed striking that *all* items appended in 7:48–49 are found in the tabernacle account at the same location (Exod 25:23–39) and made or overlaid with gold. Significantly, neither table nor lampstands are mentioned among the objects carried away by the Babylonians according to 2 Kgs 25:13–17 (cf., however, Jer 52:19, where luminaries are mentioned).[251] The lampstands are also absent from Ezekiel's temple vision (Ezek 40–43). Possibly all the objects mentioned in 1 Kgs 7:48–49 were added later under the influence of the tabernacle account, where they are mentioned prominently.

Accordingly, given their absence from the primary temple construction account in 1 Kgs 6–8*, these cultic objects – lampstand, table for "the bread of the face," Urim and Thummim, ephod – should be considered a "proprium" of the tabernacle account. Interestingly, all these items play an important role in texts of 1–2 Samuel dealing with specific cult regulations of the sanctuaries in Shiloh and Nob.[252] The ark, another utensil occupying a central place in the tabernacle account, probably has its literary origin in 1–2 Samuel too.[253] These points of contact with the narrative tradition of 1–2 Samuel can be explained in two different ways: (1) This feature may point to the author's intention to express Israel's cultic diversity. In the time of Israel's first kings, Israel venerated YHWH at various cult sites. The author aimed to anchor the cultic variety in the pivotal Sinai revelation, thus establishing an etiology for it. (2) Alternatively, the author may have seen the cultic motifs taken up by 1–2 Samuel in close relation to the temple in Jerusalem. Even though the items in question may not have been mentioned in 1 Kgs 6–8*, in a synchronic reading of Samuel–Kings the author of the tabernacle account may have thought them to be present in the sanctuary and in the cult established by Solomon. The priests engaged by David, Abiathar,

---

[249] For the ephod as garment, see 1 Sam 2:18; 22:18; 2 Sam 6:14. For the ephod as oracular instrument, see 1 Sam 2:28; 14:3; 21:10; 22:18; 23:6, 9; 30:7. For the Urim and Thummim, see 1 Sam 14:41–42 LXX; 28:6.

[250] See Noth, *Könige*, 166; Würthwein, *Die Bücher der Könige*; 84; V. Fritz, *Das erste Buch der Könige*, ZBK 10.1 (Zurich: TVZ, 1996), 84–85.

[251] See Würthwein, *Die Bücher der Könige*, 84.

[252] For the lampstand, see 1 Sam 3:3; for the "bread of the face," see 1 Sam 21:7; for the ephod and the Urim and Thummim, see above, n. 249.

[253] See 1 Sam 3:3; 4:1–7:1; 2 Sam 6; 7:2; 11:11; 15:24–29.

and Zadok[254] are assumed to be familiar with and responsible for the use of certain of these cultic objects (the ephod and the Urim and Thummim).[255] For the author, the Solomonic temple was also influenced by traditions from the north. The strong affinities between the tabernacle and the Solomonic temple concerning plan, orientation, measurements, and materials make the second interpretation more likely.

Notwithstanding the aforementioned commonalities and parallels with the temple of Jerusalem, the tabernacle account seems to distinguish itself purposefully from the latter in certain respects. As mentioned above, the beginning of the account in Exod 25:1–7* emphasizes the voluntary donations of the Israelites, creating a contrast with Solomon's exacted labor and taxation to build the sanctuary (see 1 Kgs 5:27–30, and further 10:14).[256] However, this funding model based on voluntary contributions was perhaps the only way to fund the rebuilding of the temple, given the absence of a powerful native authority.[257] In addition, the motif of the cherubim appears transformed in comparison to the temple construction report. Whereas in 1 Kgs 6:23–28 the tremendous cherubim, standing side by side, either carry or represent the deity, the cherubim of the tabernacle account function to protect the ark (by spreading their wings upon it; see Exod 25:18–20).[258] Furthermore, in P's reinterpretation of the motif, the cherubim are also considerably smaller (cf. the size of the ark in Exod 25:10 with the size of the cherubim in 1 Kgs 6:23–24). These deviations are certainly theologically meaningful; they will be dealt with further below. Likewise, the cultic traditions taken up from 1–2 Samuel are reinterpreted as well. The literary traditions of the ephod on the one hand and the Urim and Thummim on the other have been combined and integrated into one and the same vestment. As for the Urim and Thummim, it is possible, as a few scholars assume, that the author's idea was not that they would be taken from their pocket but that they would just be worn.[259] Their presence over the high priest's heart is probably meant to give his judgment the status of divine oracle. The designation "breastpiece of justice" gives further support to this interpretation.[260]

---

[254] Zadok is linked to the Elide (and Aaronide) priesthood in 2 Sam 8:17.

[255] For the ephod, see 1 Sam 14:3 (used as oracular instrument by Ahijah, uncle of Abiathar); 23:6, 9; 30:7 (used as oracular instrument by Abiathar). For the Urim and Thummim, see 1 Sam 14:41–42 LXX.

[256] See PROPP, *Exodus 19–40*, 372.

[257] See above, II.10.6.3.

[258] On the function of the cherubim in 1 Kgs 6, see WÜRTHWEIN, *Die Bücher der Könige*, 67. The statement mentioning the ark in this chapter, 6:19, which is often considered a secondary addition, does not mention the placement of the ark under the wings of the cherubim. Similarly, YHWH's epithet in the ark narrative ("YHWH of hosts who sits *above* the cherubim"; see 1 Sam 4:4; 2 Sam 6:2) reflects a concept that is different from the Priestly notion of the ark placed *under* the wings of the cherubim.

[259] See KEEL, *Die Geschichte Jerusalems*, 2:934. According to Propp's assumption, "the Priestly Writer coopted an ancient divinatory symbol about which he felt considerable ambivalence." See PROPP, *Exodus 19–40*, 443 with reference to HOUTMAN, *Exodus*, 2:456.

[260] The concept as such may, as indicated above (II.10.7.1), be influenced by Egyptian legal custom.

Nevertheless, it cannot be excluded that the Urim and Thummim were used by the high priest in difficult legal disputes (see Neh 7:65 // Ezra 2:63). An important innovation in comparison with the Jerusalem temple and its cult is furthermore the extraordinary weight that is given to the high priest, which is especially evident in the royal features of his vestments and consecration (Exod 28; see 10.5 above).

One should further note that certain elements of Solomon's temple, such as the molten sea and the two pillars, Jachin and Boaz, have not been included in the tabernacle account. Such "omission" probably is due to the adaptation to a mobile wilderness sanctuary.

Summing up this section, we note that there is no conclusive evidence to demonstrate the dependence of the tabernacle account on premonarchic or early monarchic tent traditions from Israel or beyond. There are, however, clues for Egyptian influence on certain elements of the tabernacle and Aaron's vestment (breastpiece of "judgment").

Important for the interpretation of the tabernacle is the fact that Exod 25–29 shares striking parallels and commonalities with the temple construction report in 1 Kgs 6–8; the numerous common points and the few meaningful differences make it likely that the Priestly author(s) composed this core unit as a response to the conception and theology of the Solomonic temple. Moreover – and this point seems to be overlooked in scholarship – this author integrated several elements from cult traditions present in 1–2 Samuel too. The author of the Tabernacle account, living in a time remote from the period when Solomon's temple existed, based his account on information given by the books of Samuel–Kings, with whose contents he was obviously acquainted.

10.8 Aim of the Tabernacle Account

Scholars view the aim of the tabernacle account in different ways. Many see this foundation myth as an etiology for the temple of Jerusalem. For others, P's tabernacle was conceived as a sanctuary prototype not only for the Jerusalem shrine but also for several Judean and Israelite sanctuaries. A third group of scholars emphasizes the utopian and allegedly temple-critical traits of the composition.

10.8.1 Etiology for the Jerusalem Temple?

According to a pointed remark by Wellhausen, the tabernacle in reality was not the prototype but rather a copy of the Jerusalem temple.[261] In Wellhausen's view, "Q"'s (=P's) focus on the temple in Jerusalem was exclusive, reaffirming the principle of Deuteronomistic cult centralization, although this exigence is never found *expressis*

---

[261] Cf. WELLHAUSEN, *Prolegomena zur Geschichte*, 37: "Denn diese (*scil.* die Stiftshütte) ist in Wahrheit nicht das Urbild, sondern die Kopie des jerusalemischen Tempels."

verbis in Priestly texts, as Wellhausen himself recognized.[262] Given the aforementioned similarities between P's ideal sanctuary and the Solomonic temple, a majority of scholars share Wellhausen's view that the tabernacle account is primarily centered on Jerusalem and its sanctuary. To this, we may add the observation that the system of coordinated chronological information in the Priestly texts aims toward the construction of the sanctuary by Solomon; this is a further clue that P[C] had the Jerusalem temple in view.[263]

However, current scholarship sees the reference more specifically to the second (planned or already rebuilt) sanctuary in Persian-era Jerusalem, rather than the first, Solomonic temple.[264] The tabernacle would thus function as a model for the planned temple or as an etiology for the rebuilt Second Temple and its cult. This idea is bound up with indications of a postexilic setting for P[G]/P[C] and the tabernacle account. In favor of this theory, we may note that some important elements – the seven-branched lampstand, the table, the office and vestments of the high priest – did indeed find their way into the Second Temple, suggesting some affinity between the tabernacle and the Second Temple.[265] At first sight, however, the fact that a few important pieces of furniture – namely the ark and the "cover" (with the cherubim) – apparently were not integrated into the Second Temple might argue against this thesis (although there were probably efforts to reproduce at least the ark; see Jer 3:16).[266] Perhaps one should consider the possibility that the author wanted to integrate the ark, together with the cherubim, into his tabernacle plan merely for "historical" reasons. Since the ark and the cherubim play an important role in certain texts related to the temple of Jerusalem (2 Sam 6; 7; 1 Kgs 6–8), we might argue that the author's aim was to legitimize these central elements of the First Temple rather than to let them be reproduced in the planned (or rebuilt) Second Temple.

Furthermore, a few scholars, including Wellhausen and Otto, view the priesthood promoted by the tabernacle account, the Aaronides, as descendants of the preexilic Jerusalem clergy (the "Zadokites").[267] By depicting Aaron as the first high priest, the Priestly author anchored the Jerusalemite priesthood in the exodus, Israel's founding myth. According to Wellhausen, this became necessary because "Zadok was of no use for the Mosaic period since he first lived under Solomon."[268] Situated in the

---

[262] Cf. Wellhausen, *Prolegomena zur Geschichte*, 34–38.

[263] See below, III.1.2.2 (b) (3).

[264] See, among others, L. Schmidt, *Studien zur Priesterschrift*, 259; Nihan, *From Priestly Torah*, 383–94; Albertz, *Exodus 19–40*, 379–80. Concerning this question of P's focus, Wellhausen does not seem to distinguish between First and Second Temple (see Wellhausen, *Prolegomena zur Geschichte*, 34–38). Noth left open the question of which of the two temples the author was focused on (see Noth, *Das zweite Buch Mose*, 163).

[265] See also Blum, *Studien*, 305.

[266] See also Blum, *Studien*, 305.

[267] Cf. Wellhausen, *Prolegomena zur Geschichte*, 122–24; Otto, *Das Gesetz*, 180–82.

[268] Wellhausen, *Prolegomena zur Geschichte*, 122: "(....) dass Sadok für die mosaische Zeit nicht zu gebrauchen war, weil er erst unter Salomo lebte."

postmonarchic era, the seemingly archaic tabernacle account provides a better legitimation for the Jerusalem temple than do the texts in Samuel–Kings that record the foundation and building of the temple in the time of David and Solomon. The Priestly narrative about the wilderness sanctuary establishes the long continuity of cultic affairs, from the time of the exodus, through the time of the Judean monarchy, to Persian-era Yehud. Another goal of this reconstitution, as scholars also point out, was for the priesthood, and especially the high priest, to fill as much as possible the power-political vacuum created by the long absence of Davidic kingship.[269] Other scholars, however, conjecture that Aaron was the eponym of the priesthood of Bethel and that the Aaronides originally belonged or were connected to the latter. This argument is based on the (allegedly) central role that Bethel plays in the Priestly passages dealing with Jacob[270] and the connection of the non-Priestly story about Israel's (and Aaron's) apostasy in Exod 32 with the apostasy of Jeroboam I (see further below).[271] Because of the striking parallels and commonalities with the Jerusalem temple described in the construction report in 1 Kings 6–8, this second option seems less likely.

10.8.2 Prototype for Several YHWH Sanctuaries in the Persian Era?

Some scholars question the unilateral focus on the Jerusalem temple, assuming instead that the tabernacle account was conceived as a model for several Judean and Israelite sanctuaries in the Persian era. Their main argument is the tabernacle's location in the wilderness of Sinai, which is interpreted as marking neutrality toward competing sanctuaries.[272] At first sight, certain observations seem to give further support to this second view. The tabernacle account takes up not only elements from the Jerusalem cult tradition but also important motifs from northern traditions (as reflected in 1–2 Samuel), such as the ark, the "bread of the face," the ephod, and the Urim and Thummim. Furthermore, it addresses itself to the Israel of the twelve tribes (see Exod 28:9–12, 17–21, 29) and thus stresses Israel's ethnic diversity in a symbolic and artificial way. However, the inclusion of the cultic items mentioned in 1–2 Samuel does not attenuate the strong focus on Jerusalem (see above),[273] and the pan-Israelite view is not incompatible with the interests of the Jerusalem priesthood or lay circles (as the later example of 1–2 Chronicles shows). With Blum, one should address a fundamental objection to the interpretation of the tabernacle account as a model for multiple sanctuaries: According to P^C's compositional logic, legitimate worship takes place

---

[269] See below, II.10.9.

[270] See above, II.6.5 (a).

[271] See below, II.10.10.2.

[272] Cf. B. J. DIEBNER, "Gottes Welt, Moses Zelt und das salomonische Heiligtum," in *Lectio difficilior probabilior? Festschrift Fr. Smyth-Florentin*, ed. T. Römer, *DBAT* 12 (Heidelberg: Wiss.-theol. Seminar, 1991), 127–54; RÖMER, "Der Pentateuch," 92. See also ALBERTZ, *Exodus 19–40*, 193–94, and KNAUF, *Josua*, 19.

[273] See the previous section, II.10.7.

only at one place, the tabernacle founded on Mount Sinai, the unique sanctuary established on the basis of YHWH's instructions to Moses.[274] J. W. Watts, however, has argued that the Priestly author was less concerned with spatial centralization than with the monopoly of the Aaronide priesthood over the cultic service. According to him, the logic of centralization would allow the uniform cult to be held at multiple shrines.[275] Concretely, the tabernacle account would have laid the ideological basis for the coexistence of the two sanctuaries in Jerusalem and Garizim (or reflected and legitimized the two interconnected shrines).[276] Nevertheless, the spatial dimension plays an important role in the tabernacle account; for example, the importance of the place of YHWH's encounter with Moses or the Israelites is underlined by the local adverbs שָׁם and שָׁמָּה ("there," see Exod 25:21 and 29:42).[277] Admittedly, the location of the tabernacle in the wilderness, far from Jerusalem, and its mobility may have facilitated the decentralization of the cult in the Persian era. Moreover, epigraphical finds at Mount Gerizim make it likely that the Priestly biblical traditions – at least in Hellenistic times – held important status for the Samaritan community frequenting this sanctuary.[278]

---

[274] See BLUM, "Issues and Problems," 32.

[275] See J. W. WATTS, *Ritual and Rhetoric in Leviticus: From Sacrifice to Scripture* (Cambridge: Cambridge University Press, 2007); IDEM, "The Torah as the Rhetoric of Priesthood," in *The Pentateuch as Torah: New Models for Understanding Its Promulgation and Acceptance*, ed. G. N. Knoppers and B. M. Levinson (Winona Lake, IN: Eisenbrauns, 2007), 319–32; IDEM, *Leviticus 1–10*, 104–7.

[276] See WATTS, *Ritual and Rhetoric in Leviticus*, 149–50; IDEM, "The Torah as the Rhetoric of Priesthood," 320; WATTS, *Leviticus 1–10*, 104.

[277] See also RHYDER, *Centralizing the Cult*, 99, who underlines the "interdependence of the Aaronide priests and YHWH's sanctuary."

[278] Material culture and numerous Aramaic and Hebrew inscriptions found on Mount Gerizim reveal striking commonalities and analogies with both the Priestly core texts (P^c) and the presumably later Priestly texts (P^s). Numerous inscriptions on ashlars (probably stemming from the Hellenistic era) document dedications to YHWH by members of the Yahwistic community (for the *editio princeps* see Y. MAGEN, H. MISGAV, and L. TSFANIA, eds., *Mount Gerizim Excavations, I: The Aramaic, Hebrew and Samaritan Inscriptions*, JSP 2 [Jerusalem: Staff Officer of Archaeology, 2004]). Concerning the dating of the inscriptions see also: J. DUŠEK, *Aramaic and Hebrew Inscriptions from Mt. Gerizim and Samaria between Antiochus III and Antiochus IV Epiphanes*, CHANE 54 (Leiden: Brill, 2012), 6–62; K. DE HEMMER GUDME, *Before the God in This Place for Good Remembrance: A Comparative Analysis of the Aramaic Votive Inscriptions from Mount Gerizim*, BZAW 441 (Berlin: de Gruyter, 2013), 78–84; R. PUMMER, "Samaritan Studies – Recent Research Results," *The Bible, Qumran, and the Samaritans*, ed. M. Kartveit, G.N. Knoppers, StSam 10; SJ 104 (Berlin: de Gruyter, 2016), 66–7. The ashlars apparently formed part of the inner wall of the temple on Mount Gerizim. The dedications "could be seen as being in line with the mythological foundation for the practice of giving gifts to Yahweh's sanctuary, described in Exodus 25:1-9" (DE HEMMER GUDME, *Before the God in This Place for Good Remembrance*, 149). The votive inscriptions contain the recurrent phrase "for the good remembrance before Yahweh," which resembles the motif of the "remembrance before YHWH" in the Priestly tabernacle account (cf. Exod 28:12, 29; 30:16; 39:7) and in late Priestly texts (cf. Num 5:15, 18; 10:10; 31:54). The names Phinehas and Eleazar are attested in a number of inscriptions (five and three, respectively); in some, the names are associated with priests. A small bell with a silver clapper, found in the area of the sacred precinct, resembles the small bells hanging from

Nevertheless, the question arises as to whether the author of the tabernacle account intended his sanctuary model to apply to more than one sanctuary. The clear allusions to the Jerusalem temple make this rather unlikely. Furthermore, as will be shown below (10.9), the strong focus on Aaron the high priest fits well with the situation in Jerusalem in the 5th century BCE (the possible time when the tabernacle account was written), but probably not with that of Garizim at the same time. As for the motif of the tabernacle's location in the wilderness and its mobility, it is understandable within the geographical situation of the narrative. Since the Priestly author wanted to base the Aaronides' legitimation on the Sinai revelation, he located the initial sanctuary on Sinai; and to ensure the tradition's contiunuity, he conceived it as a movable shrine. The absence of any allusions to the legitimacy of multiple cult sites (which contrasts with the clear hint in the non-Priestly verse Exod 20:24) also speaks against the interpretation of the Tabernacle as a model for several YHWH sanctuaries.

10.8.3 Utopian Literature and Temple Critique?

Some scholars see the tabernacle account as utopian literature, recognizing undertones critical of the preexilic Jerusalem temple. They emphasize both the aforementioned differences between the tabernacle and the Jerusalem temple according to the construction account in 1 Kgs 6–8 and the central motif of the tent. The most extreme position, as expressed by T. Fretheim, argues that the Priestly authors were entirely opposed to rebuilding the temple in Jerusalem after the end of the exile.[279] Others, noting the emphasis on the tent motif in the tabernacle account, see in P a corrective to the theology of YHWH's presence and "dwelling" in the Jerusalemite temple traditions.[280] They emphasize the fact that P's sanctuary is movable and the motif of YHWH's encounters (יעד niphal) with Moses (Exod 25:22) and with Israel (29:43). P's alleged opposition to YHWH's dwelling in the sanctuary is also underlined by Weimar, who on the basis of literary-critical considerations argues that the Priestly author conceived of an "empty" sanctuary lacking the typical characteristics of a temple (in his analysis, all prescriptions concerning the tent's furniture are "eliminated").[281]

---

the fringes of the robe of the high priest as described in Exod 28:33–35. These examples of parallels and correspondences with the prescriptions of the tabernacle account might indicate the high esteem in which the YHWH community held the Priestly legislative texts in the Hellenistic period and perhaps also before.

[279] T. E. FRETHEIM, "The Priestly Document: Anti-Temple?," VT 18 (1968): 313–29.

[280] NOTH, Überlieferungsgeschichtliche Studien, 266–67; VON RAD, Theologie des Alten Testaments I, 247; B. JANOWSKI, "Die Einwohnung Gottes in Israel. Eine religions- und theologiegeschichtliche Skizze zur biblischen Schekina-Theologie, 3–40," in Das Geheimnis der Gegenwart Gottes: Zur Schechina-Vorstellung in Judentum und Christentum, ed. B. Janowski and E. E. Popkes, WUNT 318 (Tübingen: Mohr Siebeck, 2014), 19–25; M. EMMENDÖRFFER, Gottesnähe: Die Rede von der Präsenz JHWHS in der Priesterschrift und verwandten Texten, Göttingen: Vandenhoeck & Ruprecht, 2019.

[281] See WEIMAR, "Sinai und Schöpfung," 349, 383–84.

What is the weight of these diverse arguments? First, we should ask whether P conceived YHWH's "wandering" through the wilderness within the tabernacle as an ideal. This question should be answered in the negative. First, as shown above, the tabernacle mobility is explicable within the geographical situation of the narrative. This motif enabled the author to demonstrate the continuity over time of the tradition founded on Sinai. One particular argument against interpreting the tabernacle as an ideal is that, as shown above, the tent terminology derives in part precisely from Jerusalem temple theology.[282] There, the lexemes משכן and שכן refer to YHWH's permanent dwelling rather than to a temporary residence. Moreover, the motif of YHWH's encounter with Israel in Exod 25–29 does not contradict the idea that YHWH "dwells" in the temple; rather, the deity's ongoing presence in the shrine consists of regular encounters with Israel on the occasion of the sacrificial cult.[283]

What speaks against the "utopia" explanation in general is the fact that most parts of the tabernacle account and the related sacrificial legislation constitute concrete laws and decrees that were feasibly practicable. In fact, several elements from the material concerning furniture, priestly attire, and cult procedures were realized in the Second Temple (see above). Significantly, there are, as shown above, no compelling literary-critical arguments for the exclusion of the instructions concerning the tabernacle furniture in Exod 25:10–40 from the tabernacle account.[284]

In summary, we state that the tabernacle has a strong affinity with the temple of Jerusalem and in particular with related literary traditions in the books of Samuel and Kings. With regard to the subtle critique a few of these references express, it is likely that the tabernacle account was composed in critical support of the rebuilding of the temple of Jerusalem (or the latter's achievement).

10.9 Setting of the Tabernacle Account

The dates proposed by European and North American scholars for the composition of P^G/P^C are rather vague, spanning the late Neo-Babylonian (second third of the sixth century BCE) to the early Persian period (last third of the sixth and beginning of the fifth century BCE).[285] Scholars who dare to be more precise are rare.[286] Does the tabernacle account provide data that confirm at least the above general estimation, or does it bear clues to a more precise historical location?

---

[282] See above, II.10.7.

[283] See also BOORER, *Vision of the Priestly Narrative*, 370.

[284] See the argument above in II.10.4.1 (b).

[285] Cf. RÖMER, "Der Pentateuch," 93.

[286] According to de Pury, P^G was written between 535 and 530, in the last years of Kyros's reign. The author dreamed of the rebuilding of the temple, but concrete measurements were not yet initiated ("Vom Neubau des Tempels in Jerusalem wird bereits geträumt, noch ist aber nichts in die Wege geleitet worden"). See DE PURY, "Der priesterschriftliche Umgang mit der Jakobgeschichte," in *Die Patriarchen und die Priesterschrift*, 49.

The extent of the tabernacle account (including some parts of the Sinaitic sacrificial legislation) and the great concentration of prescriptions in it makes a compositional setting in relation to a great temple building (or rebuilding) project, most likely that of the Second Temple in Jerusalem, a tempting suggestion. Information about the foundation and reconstruction of the Jerusalem temple comes from the biblical books Haggai, Zechariah, and Ezra. Whereas the relevant texts in Haggai and Zechariah stem from a time close to the event in question, the relevant passages in Ezra were probably written much later. Haggai 1–2 and Zech 4:4–8 and 8:9–13 bear witness to concerted efforts by certain Judean groups in the time of Darius I to rebuild the sanctuary in Jerusalem. Interestingly, these texts refer to the foundation of the "house of yhwh" and the beginning of the temple building but never to the latter's achievement.[287] Precise information about the temple's achievement and dedication, however, is found in Ezra 6:15–18. How to deal with this discrepancy between Haggai and Zechariah on the one hand and Ezra on the other? For several reasons, the credibility of the information in Ezra 6:15–18 about the circumstances and the precise date of the temple's achievement (3 Adar, in the sixth year of Darius I [515 BCE]) should be doubted: (1) The assertion in Ezra 6:14 that the building activity of the Judean elders was based on decrees not only of Cyrus and Darius but also of Artaxerxes does not fit the following report. (2) Both the absence of Zerubbabel and Jeshua and the presence of Levites – who are not mentioned elsewhere in Ezra 4–6 – at the event are awkward. (3) In Ezra 6:15–18, unlike the preceding and subsequent contexts, the author does not refer to any official documents. (4) With regard to the difficulties the building project has met (see Hag 1), a period of only four or five years for the building and completion of the sanctuary seems short; in particular, one must wonder why the books of Haggai and Zechariah know nothing about it.[288] As for the striking absence of any information about the building's achievement in Haggai and Zechariah, with Grabbe one may see in it a hint of a (considerable) delay in the temple's completion.[289] This silence about the temple's achievement in Haggai and Zechariah is all the more remarkable as both books underwent a redactional development (in the case of Zechariah possibly up to Hellenistic times) as most recent commentators agree. Perhaps there was a long building process, in stages, with no official finishing and dedication, which would not be without analogy.[290] This prolongation might have been caused by reluctance of (a

---

[287] See Hag 2:18; Zech 8:9.

[288] The last two points are referred to by GRABBE, *History of the Jews*, 284.

[289] GRABBE, *History of the Jews*, 282–85.

[290] GRABBE, *History of the Jews*, 285, mentions as an analogy the medieval cathedrals that often took decades or even centuries to be built. Parallels closer in time are the long building periods for the sanctuary of Edfu in Egypt in the ptolemaic era between 237 and 57 BCE (see C. DE WIT, "Inscriptions dédicatoires du temple d'Edfou. I. E. IV, 1–16," *CdE* 36/71 [1961]: 56–97; IDEM, "Inscriptions dédicatoires du temple d'Edfou. II. E. VII, 1–20," *CdE* 36/72 [1961]: 277–320), and for the Temple of Herod (see John 2:20; Josephus, De Bello Judaico I,401; V,36f; V,184–237; V,238–45; Antiquitates Judaicae XV,380–425; XX,219; Mishna-Tractate Middot). In both cases, the cult was apparently maintained over long phases of the construction. I thank Axel Bühler,

part of) the Judean population concerning this project or/and the dearth of available resources for building the temple.

If this was the case, then the tabernacle account as a programmatic text need not predate the new sanctuary's foundation and first phase of construction but may presuppose an early form of the rebuilt temple (but not the final product). Thus, it is imaginable that the tabernacle account was conceived both as confirmation (for certain items of the sanctuary that had already been realized) and as program (for certain elements yet to be integrated into the temple).[291]

The extensive description of Aaron's vestments in Exod 28 provides a further clue. His majestic and kinglike depiction may betray the ambitions of priestly circles to take, in a certain sense, the place of the king. As Nihan has argued, such attempts are conceivable in a time when the weakening or disappearance of Zerubbabel, governor of Judah and Davidic heir, had attenuated the hopes for restoring national independence and the Davidic monarchy.[292] The sudden weakening of Zerubbabel can be cautiously inferred from the fact that in the books of Haggai and Zechariah great hopes are placed on him regarding the building of the temple and its completion; but that in the end the completion of the temple building is never mentioned. Also, through editorial insertions, Joshua the high priest seems to have been put at the side of Zerubbabel[293] or even to have replaced him.[294] An element of Aaron's vestments points to the Persian era as well. According to the instruction of Exod 28:9–29, the two shoulder pieces of the high priest's ephod should hold two carnelian stones with seal engravings of the names of Israel's twelve sons, and, similarly, the pectoral should contain twelve gemstones with seal engravings of the same twelve names, corresponding to the twelve tribes of Israel. As shown above, the rationale is that Aaron, whenever he

---

Geneva, for pointing to the parallel of the temple of Edfu and both Jan Rückl, Prague, and Yuval Gadot, Tel Aviv, for that of the temple of Herod.

[291] See also KRATZ, *Composition*, 245.

[292] See NIHAN, *From Priestly Torah*, 394.

[293] In Haggai, Josua's mentions apparantly all belong to the redactional framework of the book. See J. WÖHRLE, *Die frühen Sammlungen des Zwölfprophetenbuches: Entstehung und Komposition*, BZAW 360 (Berlin: de Gruyter, 2006), 288–94.319; J. RÜCKL, "The Leadership of the Judean Community according to the Book of Haggai," in *Transforming Authority: Concepts of Leadership in Prophetic and Chronistic Literature*, ed. by K. Pyschny and S. Schulz (Berlin: De Gruyter, 2021), 77–81.

[294] The oracle in Zech 6:9–15, which in its present form refers to Joshua the high priest, seems to have been originally intended for both Zerubbabel (as the main character) and Joshua. The idea that Joshua would have been the original recipient of the first crown seems unlikely in light of the mention of the "priest" sitting on the other throne in v. 13b (see WÖHRLE, *Die frühen Sammlungen des Zwölfprophetenbuches*, 341–47; NIHAN, *From Priestly Torah*, 394, n. 514). In the context of this question, one should also consider the passage Zech 3:1–7, which focuses on Joshua the high priest alone and ascribes to him a strong position of power. This text is viewed by scholars to be a later addition to the book because it contrasts with the dyarchic concept (the governor and the high priest officiating in comparable positions of power alongside each other) found in other parts of the book (see Zech 4 and 6:9–15*). See WÖHRLE, *Die frühen Sammlungen des Zwölfprophetenbuches*, 332–36.

enters the sanctuary, carries the twelve names on his shoulders and over his heart in order to evoke YHWH's remembrance of Israel (literally: "as a reminder before YHWH at all times" [v. 29: לזכרן לפני יהוה תמיד]). As a few scholars have suggested, this prescription was probably influenced by the frequent ancient Near Eastern use of seals and other objects as votives to a deity for the sake of the latter's attention and favor (זכרון).[295] What is uncommon in ANE votive practice, however, is the dedication of an object in favor of a tribe or a territory. Nevertheless, as Nihan points out, this element has a strong parallel in the frequently attested administrative Yehud seal impressions from the Persian era.[296] Most of these contain the toponym Yehud (*yhwd*) as an element; many seal inscriptions consist uniquely of this toponym.[297] The motif of the engraved gemstonses in Exod 28 may indeed have been inspired by the use of the Yehud seals by Judean governors and officials. The high priest who represents Israel before YHWH competes with Yehud's officials. Yet, the choice of the names of the twelve tribes of Israel instead of Judah or Israel deserves attention. The concept of a twelve-tribe Israel is relatively late. In a developed form, it seems to appear for the first time in the narrative of the birth of Jacob's sons in Gen 29:31–30:24.[298]

The extraordinary weight given to the high priest – as expressed in different "royal" elements of his outfitting – suggests a setting for the tabernacle account in the early – but not too early – Achaemenid period (first half of the fifth century BCE). For the author of the tabernacle account, the high priest, along with the secular governor, must already have become an actor of some weight in the postexilic community. In this respect, it is important to note that there is abundant evidence for the application of the concept of the high priest to the *Jerusalemite* priesthood in the Persian era, which contrasts with the lack of evidence for such an institution in other Yahwistic sanctuaries in the same period. According to the books of Haggai and Zechariah, Joshua son of Jehozadak occupied the office of the high priest in Jerusalem during

---

[295] See W. ZWICKEL, "Die Edelsteine im Brustschild des Hohenpriesters und beim himmlischen Jerusalem," in *Edelsteine in der Bibel*, ed. W. Zwickel (Mainz: von Zabern, 2002), 50–70; J. TIGAY, "The Priestly Reminder Stones and Ancient Near Eastern Votive Practices," in *Shay: Studies in the Bible, Its Exegesis and Language Presented to Sara Japhet*, ed. M. Bar Asher, D. Rom-Shiloni, E. Tov, and N. Wazana (Jerusalem: Bialik, 2007), 119–38; C. NIHAN, "Le pectoral d'Aaron et la figure du grand prêtre dans les traditions sacerdotales du Pentateuque," in *Congress Volume Stellenbosch 2016*, ed. L. C. Jonker, G. R. Kotzé, and C. M. Maier, VTSup 177 (Leiden: Brill, 2017), 23–55.

[296] See C. NIHAN, "Le pectoral d'Aaron," 23–55.

[297] Following the edition and classification by O. LIPSCHITS, D. VANDERHOOFT, *The Yehud Stamp Impressions. A Corpus of Inscribed Impressions from the Persian and Hellenistic Periods in Judah* (Winona Lake, IN: Eisenbrauns, 2011), 79 (73%) out of 108 seals stemming of the early period (late 6th–5th century BCE) contain the element Yehud. 44 (types 5 and 6) (39%) consist of only the toponym (Yehud).

[298] See J.-D. MACCHI, *Israël et ses tribus selon Genèse 49*, OBO 145 (Fribourg: Presses Universitaires; Göttingen: Vandenhoeck & Ruprecht, 1999), 272; NIHAN, *From Priestly Torah*, 394, here n. 517. According to Macchi's analysis, there is no literary echo in early Deuteronomistic texts (see MACCHI, *Israël et ses tribus*, 272).

the rule of Darius the Great.[299] The book of Nehemiah mentions the high priests Eliashib and Joiada being in office in the fifth century BCE.[300] There is also an extra-biblical attestation in the Elephantine correspondence from the end of the fifth century BCE.[301] The author of the petition letter TAD A 4.7 (// 4.8) (= Cowley 30 [// 31]), Yedanyah, a priest and apparently the leader of the Judean community of Yeb, uses the expression "high priest" (כהנא רבא) for Yehohanan, the high priest of Jerusalem (see l. 18) but never for himself or another YHWH priest in Elephantine. He is, like his priestly colleagues, simply called "priest" (כהנא, see l. 1). Significantly, among the Samarian addressees of the petition neither a high priest nor other priests are mentioned (see TAD A 4.7, l. 29; cf. TAD A 4.9, l. 1).[302] The earliest evidence for the use of the expression *high priest* by the Samarians comes from a much later period. One of the numerous votive inscriptions found on Mount Gerizim (possibly stemming from the early second century BCE) probably associated the name of a donor with a (the) high priest.[303] This correspondence between the high priest's position in the tabernacle account and historical evidence in the Jerusalem clergy of the fifth century BCE era may be taken as a further indication that the tabernacle account focuses on the temple of Jerusalem and the organization of its cult rather than any other sanctuary.

---

[299] See Hag 1:1, 12, 14; 2:2, 4; Zech 3:1, 3, 6, 8–9; 6:11. In most of these texts Joshua bears the title "high priest"; only in the passage Zech 3:1–9 the title is partly omitted (probably because of repetition).

[300] See Neh 3:1, 20–21; 12:10, 22–23; 13:28.

[301] The petition TAD A 4.7, l. 30 // TAD A 4.8, contains a precise date (see l. 30, and l. 29 respective): "The twentieth of Marheshwan, seventeenth year of King Darius" (=407 BCE). The memorandum TAD A 4.9, which bears no date, must have been written shortly after the petition of TAD A 4.7 // TAD A 4.8.

[302] According to TAD A 4.7 // 4.8, the Judeans in Yeb had sent a first petition to Bagavahyah the governor of Jerusalem, to "Yehohanan the High Priest and his colleagues the priests who are in Jerusalem, Avastana the brother of Anani and the nobles of Judah" (l. 17–18) and furthermore to "Delayah and Shelemyah sons of Sanballat governor of Samaria" (l. 29). The memorandum in reply to TAD A 4.7 // 4.8 was commissioned by Bagavahyah and Delaiah (cf. TAD A 4.9, l.1). In light of his juxtaposition with Bagavahyah in TAD A 4.9, it seems probable that Delaiah succeeded his father Sanballat as governor of Samaria or at least held a high a position in the Persian administration of Samaria. See J. Dušek, *Les manuscrits araméens du Wadi Daliyeh et la Samarie vers 450–332 av. J.-C.* (Leiden: Brill, 2007), 528; Pummer, "Samaritan Studies – Recent Research Results," 63.

[303] See inscription 384 according to the *editio princeps*: Magen, Misgav, and Tsfania, eds., *Mount Gerizim Excavations*, I 255. Concerning the dating of the inscriptions: Dušek, *Aramaic and Hebrew Inscriptions from Mt. Gerizim and Samaria between Antiochus III and Antiochus IV Epiphanes*, 6–62; de Hemmer Gudme, *Before the God in This Place for Good Remembrance*, 78–84; Pummer, "Samaritan Studies – Recent Research Results," 66–7.

10.10 The Literary Relationship to Neighboring Non-Priestly Units and the Literary Profile of the Tabernacle Account

10.10.1 Relationship to Non-Priestly Texts in Exodus 19–24

Since the non-Priestly texts in this section are numerous and often not related to each other, a thorough treatment of all of these texts and their relationship to the Priestly tabernacle account is not possible. Instead, our point of departure will be important intertextual contacts between the tabernacle account and some non-Priestly units.

As shown above, the pre-Priestly itinerary notice in Exod 19:2 mentions Israel's stay in the desert of Sinai[304] Most recent analyses agree that the pre-Priestly stratum in Exod 19–24* reported Moses's ascension to the mountain of God (Mt. Sinai) and the promulgation of one law (either the Decalogue or the Covenant Code) in Exod 19–24*.[305] There are indications that the tabernacle account is dependent on certain non-Priestly texts in the first part of the Sinai pericope (Exod 19–24). Important motifs from the introduction of the tabernacle account (Exod 24:15b–18a*) – Mount Sinai, the cloud – appear in determined grammatical form (i.e., with the article) despite the fact that they are being used for the first time in the Priestly strand.[306] The probable conclusion from this is that Exod 24:15b–18a* presupposes the preceding non-Priestly texts, in which these motifs play an important role (Mount Sinai in Exod 19:18–20; the cloud in Exod 19:16). Since Exod 24:15b–18a* is an integral part of the tabernacle account, we should deduce that the latter, in its entirety, depends on non-Priestly Sinai texts. Moreover, even if we exclude Exod 24:15b–18a* from the base layer of P, we are nevertheless confronted with the problem that the expression "the cloud" (הענן, determined form) is used in Exod 40:34(–35) without having been previously introduced. Thus, it is difficult to escape the conclusion that the tabernacle account was composed for and positioned within the pre-Priestly Sinai narrative. An alternative but more speculative explanation of this difficulty, which followers of the source theory prefer, is that similar text sequences were lost from P during the process of combining P and non-P.

In the tabernacle instructions, another motif betrays P's dependence on the Pre-Priestly Sinai narrative: the עדת ("testimony"). It is striking to see that among the sacred articles belonging to the tabernacle, the עדת is one of the rare items for whom an instruction to manufacture is lacking.[307] Moreover, in the preceding Priestly texts, the עדת is not introduced either, so that within the context of P it is not clear to whom the term refers. Since in both, P and non-P, it is a matter of laws, which YHWH

---

[304] See above, II.9.3.3.

[305] LEVIN, *Der Jahwist*, 364–65; OSWALD, *Israel am Gottesberg*, 123; RÖMER, "Der Penta-teuch," 92; ALBERTZ, *Exodus 19–40*, 10–12.

[306] See above, II.10.3.2.

[307] Another example are the Urim and Thummim; see Exod 28:30 (MT, LXX); for the variant of SP, see above, II.10.2.2 (c).

proclaimed on Sinai, the expression probably has as reference laws on a written document.[308] This is also suggested by the fact that the term recalls Akkadian *adû / adê* and Aramaic עדין, which both mean a covenant contract or a contractual obligation. Concretely, the reference could be to "the book of the covenant" (ספר הברית) mentioned in Exod 24:7, to the two tablets referred to in 24:12, or to the "words" of the Decalogue (see 20:1). It seems most likely that the reference is to the two tablets and (or) the Decalogue: the compound term ארון העדת corresponds to the Deuteronomistic expressions ארון הברית, "ark of covenant," and ארון ברית יהוה, "ark of the covenant of YHWH," and probably depends on it.[309] ארון העדת occurs frequently in the tabernacle account (see Exod 25:22; 26:33, 34; 30:6, 26; 31:7; 39:35; 40:3, 5, 21), and it probably belongs to the primary stratum.[310]

Furthermore, it is imaginable that the Priestly author (redactor) presupposed the motif of Moses's stay on the mountain for forty days and forty nights (in Exod 24:18b), which gave him the occasion to insert the long instruction section of the tabernacle account.[311]

10.10.2 Relationship to Non-Priestly Texts in Exodus 32–34

What is the literary-historical relationship to the non-Priestly texts in Exod 32–34 which interrupt the tabernacle account? Traditionally, most parts in Exod 32–34, such as the story of Israel's apostasy with the golden bull in Exod 32*[312] and the legislative text 34:10–27[313], are considered old and (much) predating the Priestly tabernacle

---

[308] UTZSCHNEIDER, "Tabernacle," 283.

[309] Thus ALBERTZ, *Exodus 19–40*, 158.

[310] See also Num 4:5; 7:89; Josh 4:16. – According to S. Boorer, the expression עדת ("testimony") would refer to the specific instructions for the tabernacle as outlined in Exod 25–29*. See BOORER, *Vision of the Priestly Narrative*, 313, n. 260: "These verses do not ... refer to the stone tablets referred to in 31:18, but in some way to the instructions for the tabernacle as outlined in Exod 25–29*." However, those instructions are never called עדות (the "model" shown to Moses is called תבנית).

[311] See LEVIN, *Der Jahwist*, 365; H. SAMUEL, *Von Priestern zum Patriarchen: Redaktions- und traditionsgeschichtliche Studien zu Levi und den Leviten in der Literatur des Zweiten Tempels*, BZAW 448 (Berlin: de Gruyter, 2014), 289. An indication that it is a relatively old motif within the Sinai tradition is its reuse in the Elijah cycle (see 1 Kgs 19:8); see also LEVIN, *Der Jahwist*, 365, n. 9.

[312] See NOTH, *Das zweite Buch Mose*, 200–203; E. AURELIUS, *Der Fürbitter Israels: Eine Studie zum Mosebild im Alten Testament*, ConBOT 27 (Stockholm: Almqvist & Wiksell, 1988), 204; J. SCHARBERT, *Exodus*, NEchtB 24 (Würzburg: Echter Verlag, 1989), 120–21; CRÜSEMANN, *Die Tora*, 66–71; OSWALD, *Israel am Gottesberg*, 123; J. C. GERTZ, "Beobachtungen zu Komposition und Redaktion in Exodus 32–34," in *Gottes Volk am Sinai: Untersuchungen zu Ex 32–34 und Dtn 9–10*, ed. M. Köckert and E. Blum (Gütersloh: C. Kaiser, Gütersloher Verlagshaus, 2001), 88–106.

[313] See NOTH, *Das zweite Buch Mose*, 213–16; J. HALBE, *Das Privilegrecht Jahwes: Ex 34, 10–26; Gestalt und Wesen, Herkunft und Wirken in vordeuteronomischer Zeit*, FRLANT 114 (Göttingen: Vandenhoeck & Ruprecht, 1975), 510–22; SCHARBERT, *Exodus*, 128–29; CRÜSEMANN, *Die Tora*, 148–51.

account. A few recent treatments of these chapters, however, see most of Exod 32–34 as secondary additions to the earlier non-P Sinai pericope (in Exod 19–24) and the Priestly tabernacle account.[314] Especially interesting and important is this question in the case of the golden bull story (Exod 32*) because Aaron as artisan of the idol plays a central role in the latter, contrasting drastically Aaron the majestic and positive high priest of P. There are linguistic common points as well: the story about the golden bull[315] opens with assertions that are reminiscent of formulations in the tabernacle account and other Priestly texts (see Exod 32:1–5).[316]

According to most literary-critical analyses, Exod 32:1–5 is part of the reconstructed original kernel of the story.[317] It is important to note that Exod 32 also has several intertextual contacts with non-Priestly texts in the Sinai pericope.[318] The unit presup-

---

[314] See Otto, "Die nachpriesterliche Pentateuchredaktion," 83–101; Kratz, *Composition*, 134–36; A. Berlejung, *Die Theologie der Bilder: Herstellung und Einweihung von Kultbildern in Mesopotamien und die alttestamentliche Bilderpolemik*, OBO 162 (Fribourg: Presses Universitaires; Göttingen: Vandenhoeck & Ruprecht, 1998), 355–56; M. Konkel, "Exodus 32–34 and the Quest for an Enneateuch," in *Pentateuch, Hexateuch, or Enneateuch? Identifying Literary Works in Genesis through Kings*, ed. T. B. Dozeman, T. Römer, and K. Schmid (Atlanta: Society of Biblical Literature, 2009), 169–84.

[315] The translation "bull" for עֵגֶל is more appropriate than the common rendering "calf," which seems to suggest a pejorative meaning (in the context of Exod 32 and 1 Kgs 12:26–33, see Noth, *Die Israelitischen Personennamen*, 151). The traditional understanding of "calf" is obviously influenced by the deprecation of the idolatrous act by the authors of both stories. However, a disapproving meaning is contradicted by other occurrences of the term; cf. in particular the onomastically attested עֶגְלִיו ("a bull is yhwh"). See *HALOT* 784 and J. Pakkala, "Jeroboam without Bulls," *ZAW* 120 (2008): 501, n. 1.

[316] See V. A. Hurowitz, "The Golden Calf and the Tabernacle," *Shnaton* 7 (1983–84): 51–59 (Hebrew), 9–10 (English); H. Utzschneider, *Das Heiligtum und das Gesetz: Studien zur Bedeutung der Sinaitischen Heiligtumstexte (Ex 25–40, Lev 8–9)*, OBO 77 (Fribourg: Presses Universitaires; Göttingen: Vandenhoeck & Ruprecht, 1988), 85–87; Gertz, "Beobachtungen zu Komposition und Redaktion in Exodus 32–34," 89–91. For the parallel with Lev 9:2, 3, 8, see Frevel, *Mit Blick*, 178–79; K. Schmid, "Israel am Sinai: Etappen der Forschungsgeschichte zu Ex 32–34 in seinen Kontexten," in *Gottes Volk am Sinai: Untersuchungen zu Ex 32–34 und Dtn 9–10*, ed. M. Köckert and E. Blum (Gütersloh: C. Kaiser, Gütersloher Verlagshaus, 2001), 32.

[317] See, among others, Wellhausen, *Die Composition*, 91–92; Aurelius, *Der Fürbitter Israels*, 60–68; H.-C. Schmitt, "Die Erzählung vom Goldenen Kalb Ex. 32* und das Deuteronomistische Geschichtswerk," in *Rethinking the Foundations: Historiography in the Ancient World and in the Bible; Essays in Honour of John Van Seters*, ed. S. L. McKenzie and T. Römer, BZAW 294 (Berlin: de Gruyter, 2000), 237–38; Kratz, *Composition*, 135; Gertz, "Beobachtungen zu Komposition und Redaktion in Exodus 32–34," 95–97; Samuel, *Von Priestern zum Patriarchen*, 272. Differently, Noth, *Das zweite Buch Mose*, 200–202, and Otto, *Deuteronomium 1–11*, 955–57, exclude Aaron from the primary account. Their arguments are not compelling. Although it is probable that Aaron was added secondarily in certain texts (Exod 32:25, 35; Deut 9:20), one should not conclude that the original tradition focused exclusively on the people as the guilty party. There is no literary-critical signal in Exod 32:1–6 that argues for separating Aaron from the intrigue.

[318] Aurelius, *Der Fürbitter Israels*, 68–70; Blum, *Studien*, 54–56; Gertz, "Beobachtungen zu Komposition und Redaktion in Exodus 32–34," 88–89.

Table 3.   Parallels between Exodus 32:1–5 and Priestly texts

Golden bull story	Parallels in the tabernacle account and other Priestly texts
[1] Now when the people saw that Moses delayed to come down from the mountain, the people assembled before [against] [ויקהל על] Aaron, and said to him "Up, make [עשה] us gods who will go before us; as for this Moses, the man who brought us up from the land of Egypt, we do not know what has become of him."	Cf. Exod 35:1: And Moses assembled [ויקהל] all the congregation of the Israelites together. Cf. Exod 25:8: "they should make [ועשו] a sanctuary for me."
[2] And Aaron said to them, "Break off the gold rings [נזמי הזהב] which are in the ears of your wives, your sons, and your daughters, and bring them to me."	Cf. Exod 35:22: Then all whose hearts moved them, both men and women, came and brought brooches and earrings [נזם] and signet rings and bracelets, all articles of gold [זהב].
[3] Then all the people broke off the gold rings [נזמי הזהב] which were in their ears, and brought them to Aaron.	Cf. Exod 35:22.
[4] And he took this from their hand, and fashioned it with a graving tool, and made it into a molten bull [עגל]; and they said, "This are your gods, O Israel, who brought you up from the land of Egypt."	Cf. Lev 9:2: And he [Moses] said to Aaron, "Take for yourself a young bull [עגל] for a sin offering and a ram for a burnt offering, both without defect, and offer them before YHWH." Cf. also 9:3, 8.
[5] Now when Aaron saw this, he built an altar before it; and Aaron announced and said, "Tomorrow shall be a feast to YHWH [חג ליהוה]!"	Cf. Exod 12:14, and also Lev 23:41 and Num 29:12: "you shall celebrate it as a feast to YHWH [חג ליהוה]."

poses the image interdiction of the Covenant Code in Exod 20:23 (see especially 32:8: "They have quickly turned aside from the way which I commanded them"), Israel's first divine service in 24:4–5, which it spoofs,[319] and probably also the cultic meal in 24:11 (ויאכלו וישתו, "and they ate and drank," cf. 32:6). Furthermore, Gertz points out that certain commonalities that Exodus 32 shares with the tabernacle account it shares equally with non-Priestly texts outside the Sinai pericope.[320] For example, the motif of the golden earrings appears in the Gideon narrative (Gideon uses them for fabricating the ephod; see Judg 8:24–26). Here the linguistic commonality is even stronger (Judg 8:24–26 uses the same expression, נזמי הזהב). The syntagma חג ליהוה is also found or has a parallel in non-Priestly texts (see Exod 13:6 and Deut 16:1 [פסח ליהוה]). As

---

[319] Cf. the common expressions ויבן מזבח, "and he built an altar," 24:4 // 32:5; ויעלו עלת, "and they offered burnt offerings," 24:5 // 32:6; שכם *hiphil*, "to rise early," 24:4 // 32:6; cf. also תחת ההר, "at the foot of the mountain," 24:4 // 32:19.

[320] GERTZ, "Beobachtungen zu Komposition und Redaktion in Exodus 32–34," 91–93.

will be shown below, there are also strong similarities with the narrative of Jeroboam's golden bulls (עֶגְלֵי זָהָב) in 1 Kgs 12:26–33.

How, then, to position Exod 32 in the literary history of the Sinai pericope and, in particular, how to define its relationship to the tabernacle account? I share Kratz's general impression that after Exod 19–24, Israel's apostasy comes about so suddenly that I am inclined to regard the story as a secondary addition.[321] Similarly, Noth considered Exod 32 to be a (relatively) late and "alien" addition to the pentateuchal narrative.[322] A further indication that this unit is of rather late origin is the numerous shared motifs and expressions with other texts in different parts of the Hebrew Bible and the obvious or probable dependence on some of them (e.g., the image interdiction in the Covenant Code [and Decalogue?]; Exod 24:4–5, 11; the narrative of Jeroboam's golden bulls).

The story of Jeroboam's bulls in 1 Kgs 12:26–33, deserves particular attention because it shares a key motif, the golden bull (bulls), with Exod 32. Almost all scholars assume that Exod 32 depends on 1 Kgs 12. The main argument is the apparent quotation of 1 Kgs 12:28 in Exod 32:4, as evidenced by the striking plural ("These are your gods, O Israel, who brought you up out of the land of Egypt"), which in the context of Exod 32 is not fitting (because Aaron makes only *one* molten bull).[323] The basic idea of making a bull, the idolatrous act, is therefore borrowed from the passage in 1 Kgs 12:26–33.[324]

Given these clues pointing to the late origin of Exod 32, we can now address the question of the literary-historical relationship between the latter unit and the tabernacle account. The parallels and common points make it likely that one text is dependent on the other. Exodus 32 can be read as a composition that purposefully contrasts with the tabernacle account; the reverse is less likely. The most compelling piece of evidence that Exod 32* presupposes the tabernacle account is the choice of Aaron as the artisan who made the idol and the figure responsible for "the feast for YHWH." Aaron does not have a cultic function in the non-Priestly Sinai pericope. Thus, if the story of the golden bull was indeed reacting to an existing Sinai narrative, the latter most probably included the Priestly tabernacle narrative (instruction account and short conclusion). The contrasting elements in Exod 32 are the depiction of Aaron as an "apostate" (cf.

---

[321] KRATZ, *Composition*, 134.

[322] NOTH, *Überlieferungsgeschichte*, 13: Exod 32 is "nicht nur ... ein Spätling, sondern auch ... ein Fremdling innerhalb der Pentateucherzählung."

[323] See, among others, NOTH, *Das zweite Buch Mose*, 204; LEVIN, *Der Jahwist*, 367; KRATZ, *Composition*, 165; SCHMID, *Literaturgeschichte*, 120.

[324] The age of the bull motif in the literary history of the narrative of Jeroboam's apostasy is a matter of debate. Some scholars consider it the oldest element in the passage of Jeroboam's apostasy; see, for example, R. KITTEL, *Die Bücher der Könige*, HKAT I/5 (Göttingen: Vandenhoeck & Ruprecht, 1900), 107–11; NOTH, *Überlieferungsgeschichtliche Studien*, 282–83; G. HENTSCHEL, *1. Könige*, NEchtB 10 (Würzburg: Echter, 1984), 86–87; KRATZ, *Composition*, 165; 211, with n. 18. Recently, Juha Pakkala has expressed the opposite view, arguing that the bulls are generally ignored by the authors of 1–2 Kings, who constantly refer to "Jeroboam's sin" and declare it to be the main reason for the destruction of Israel. Instead of the bulls, the high places are the central target of their criticism (see PAKKALA, "Jeroboam without Bulls").

Aaron's position as majestic high priest in Exod 28), and the violent breaking-off of the earrings (cf. the voluntary nature of the people's donation in the tabernacle account [25:2–7]). However, since the conclusion of the previous sections is that we should distinguish between different strata within the tabernacle account, we should consider the possibility that the story of the golden bull does not necessarily presuppose the secondary parts of Exod 30–31, 35–40 and Lev 4–10. As indicated above, there are certain indications favoring this idea. Frevel offers a possible contrasting element in a Priestly text in comparison with the story of the golden bull: according to Frevel, the young bull (עגל) in Lev 9:2, 3, 8 alludes to the molten bull (עגל מסכה) in Exod 32. Frevel's interpretation is plausible; in this case, it is a Priestly text that seems to be reacting to Exod 32. However, there are, as shown in the previous section, strong indications that Lev 9 does not belong to the most original layer of the Priestly Sinai pericope.[325] Similarly, Moses's regular gathering of the Israelites in Exod 35:1 may purposefully contrast the "rebellious" gathering of the people around Aaron, and the donation of the golden earrings in 35:22 perhaps constitutes a back reaction related to the violent breaking-off of the earrings of the Israelites in Exod 32. The latter may be indicated by the fact that the instruction for the donation in 25:2–7 mentions only gold as raw material (among others) but no specific piece of jewelry.

For what reason does the author of Exod 32 blame the "Priestly" Aaron for an idolatrous act typically known from the former kingdom of the north? With regard to the close parallel with 1 Kgs 12:26–33, scholars believe that Aaron, the protagonist of the story, and the Aaronides stood in a close relationship to the sanctuary of Bethel.[326] This cannot be excluded but remains rather speculative. Aaron's depiction as an idolatrous priest might have other causes. The association with Bethel's famous iconic cult might simply have aimed to harm the Aaronides' reputation.

The motif of the *idolatry* may be explained as follows: The author invented Aaron's idolatrous act because of the rich imagery present throughout the tabernacle account (see in particular the cherubim, the seven-branched lampstand with its "flowers," and Aaron's precious vestments, which in fact are reminiscent of the vestments of divine statues). The great importance given to the ark in Exod 25–29 may also have caused criticism (see Jer 3:16). For the author of Exod 32, the description of the tabernacle in 25–29 may have come close to an "idolatrous" theology (cf.

---

[325] See above, II.10.6.2 (b).

[326] See, among others, ALBERTZ, *Exodus 19–40*, 193–94. Albertz (194, n. 10) also points to a few texts associating Eleazar and Phinehas with the hill country of Ephraim and Bethel (see Josh 24:33 and Judg 20:26–28). K. KOENEN, "Aaron/Aaroniden," WIBILEX, https://www.bibelwis-senschaft.de/stichwort/11012/, further refers to the names of the two first sons of Aaron (Nadab and Abihu, mentioned in Exod 6:23; 24:1, 9; 28:1; Lev 10:1; Num 3:2, 4; 26:60–61), which are very similar to those of the sons of Jeroboam I (Abijah and Nadab), the founder of the sanctuaries of Bethel and Dan. However, one should not draw historical conclusions from Aaron's first two sons, who are obviously literary "creations" (the conformity of their names to those of the two sons of Jeroboam I – the only two members of Jeroboam's family whose names are known! – is too blatant). For a possible motive for the "invention," see above, II.10.6.2 (b).

the same terminology [use of עָשָׂה] related to the fabrication of the tabernacle on the one hand and the bull idol on the other).[327]

A further unit within Exod 32–34 that has an interesting intertextual point of contact with the tabernacle account is the enigmatic pericope about a tent that Moses should erect outside the camp and call "tent of meeting" (Exod 33:7–11). What is the literary relationship between the two dissimilar "tent accounts"? According to the classical Documentary Hypothesis, the short Ohel Moed text is considered an old piece of tradition stemming from the Elohist source. Scholars also surmised that this unit would have influenced the Priestly tabernacle account. Today, an increasing number of scholars consider the text part of a relatively late Deuteronomistic or Pentateuch redaction covering several texts in Exodus–Deuteronomy.[328] Some among these scholars classify Exod 33:7–11 as post-Priestly.[329] Although we cannot enter fully into the discussion here, some arguments adduced for the latter view seem valuable. A closer look at the passage reveals subtle connection with its immediate and more distant preceding context: The fact that Moses erects the "tent of meeting" outside the camp should be understood as a consequence of the refusal of YHWH to go up "in the midst" of the people (see Exod 33:3). At the same time, 33:7–11 reacts to the Priestly tabernacle account. Since the tent, designated with the definite article, is not properly introduced at the beginning (in v. 7), it is tempting to identify it with the Priestly tabernacle mentioned in Exod 25–31. In contrast to Priestly theology, which assumes that YHWH dwells (שָׁכַן) permanently in the sanctuary, 33:7–11 emphasizes that the pillar of cloud descends *at times*. The placement of the tent outside of the camp opposes the Priestly statement that YHWH will reside "among" (בְּתוֹךְ) the Israelites (see Exod 25:8, cf. 29:46). An indication that this passage is of late origin are important thematic and linguistic commonalities that 33:7–11 shares with several presumably late Non-Priestly texts in Numbers and Deuteronomy (Num 11:14–17, 24–30; 12:1–10; Deut 31:14–15, 23).

Another crucial question pertains to the classification of the two statements relating to Moses's descent from Mount Sinai (Exod 32:15 and 34:29), which contain the

---

[327] Perhaps the author of Ps 106:19–20 understood Exod 32 in this sense and took the same line: the designation *tabnît* ("model, image, idol") for the molten image of the bull might be a polemic against the positive use of this expression in the tabernacle account.

[328] See A. H. J. GUNNEWEG, "Das Gesetz und die Propheten. Eine Auslegung von Ex 33,7–11; Num 11,4–12,8; Dtn 31,14f.; 34,10," *ZAW* 102 (1990): 169–80, in particular 172–75; BLUM, *Studien*, 61–62, 76–77; OTTO, "Die nachpriesterliche Pentateuchredaktion," 91–92; R. ACHENBACH, *Die Vollendung*, 178–80, 293–94; IDEM, "The Story of the Revelation at the Mountain of God and the Redactional Editions of the Hexateuch and the Pentateuch," in *A Critical Study of the Pentateuch: An Encounter between Europe and Africa*, ed. E. Otto and J. H. Le Roux (Münster: Lit Verlag, 2005); R. ALBERTZ, "Ex 33,7–11, ein Schlüsseltext für die Rekonstruktion der Redaktionsgeschichte des Pentateuch," *Biblische Notizen* 149 (2011): 13–43; J. JEON, "The Non-Priestly Ohel Moed," The Torah.com, accessed 17.08.2021 (https://www.thetorah.com/article/the-non-priestly-ohel-moed).

[329] See the critics mentioned in the preceding footnote, except BLUM, *Studien*, 61–62, 76–77, who assigns the unit to his (pre-Priestly) KD.

Priestly expression עֵדֻת, "testimony" (as element of the expression "tablets of the testimony"), though typical Priestly vocabulary is otherwise absent. Current scholars tend to attribute these statements to a post-Priestly Pentateuch redactor who took up the Priestly term עֵדֻת.[330] Others assign the texts (or parts of them) to P.[331] Given the emphasis on the tablets (לֻחֹת, which are written recto verso by the finger of God), which do not play a role in P^C, the former attribution seems more likely. Since no other statement reports Moses's descent from the mountain, perhaps the primitive form of Exod 34:29* was part of the pre-Priestly strand (Moses descended from Mount Sinai with a shining face).[332] Exodus 34:28a may have been intended as a *Wiederaufnahme* of 24:18b.

Summing up this section, we note that the tabernacle account as a comprehensive, carefully elaborated composition can be read as an independent, self-contained unit; it was, in a first stage, perhaps composed as such (cf. in particular Exod 25–29*). The sudden and unprepared appearance of a certain motifs, however, reveals that the tabernacle account depends on preceding non-Priestly texts, suggesting that it was the author's (authors') intention to integrate the tabernacle account into the existing non-P Sinai narrative.[333] The relationship between the P and non-P strata in the Sinai pericope (Exod 19–40) cannot be defined in a general way. On the one hand, it was shown that the Priestly tabernacle account depends on certain passages in the preceding section Exod 19–24; on the other hand, it seems that most parts of Exod 32–34 were inserted by a post-Priestly redactor (or post-Priestly redactors).

---

[330] SCHARBERT, *Exodus*, 120; C. DOHMEN, "Was stand auf den Tafeln vom Sinai und was auf denen vom Horeb? Geschichte und Theologie eines Offenbarungsrequisits," in *Vom Sinai zum Horeb: Stationen alttestamentlicher Glaubensgeschichte*, ed. F.-L. Hossfeld (Würzburg: Echter, 1989), 19–23, 43; OSWALD, *Israel am Gottesberg*, 209–10; FREVEL, *Mit Blick*, 143–44; OWCZAREK, *Die Vorstellung vom Wohnen Gottes*, 42, 215–16; NIHAN, *From Priestly Torah*, 49.

[331] ALBERTZ, *Exodus 19–40*, 261–62, 266, 276; B. J. SCHWARTZ, "The Priestly Account of the Theophany," 114, 126–27.

[332] ALBERTZ, *Exodus 19–40*, 306–7, 321–23.

[333] See also ALBERTZ, *Exodus 19–40*, 147.

III. Synthesis

As stated in the introduction, an important methodological principle of this study is its focus on each individual Priestly section or unit. The crucial questions concerning identification, inner stratification, literary profile, and relationship to the non-P "environment" have been discussed separately for each unit. This methodological decision was based on preliminary observations favoring the idea that the Priestly texts form a stratum that is more composite and less homogeneous than was previously thought.

In what follows, the results reached for each unit or section will be synthesized. This final part is structured according to the main topics related to the Priestly texts, that is, (1) the question of the inner differentiation of the Priestly texts, (2) their literary profile, and (3) their relationship to the non-Priestly texts. The question of the historical location(s) will be addressed in the first paragraph dealing with the different strata of P.

1. Stratigraphy of P: Sources and Redactions in the Priestly Texts of Genesis 1–Exodus 40

The present analysis shares many results with other investigations on P. The firm starting points for the identification of the Priestly texts are the generally shared observations regarding their language (distinct vocabulary), style (repetition, concentric structure), and theological convictions (theonym theology). Current scholarship agrees on the general attribution of texts to P or to non-P; only a few verses are disputed.[1]

There is less agreement among scholars about the inner differentiation (stratification) of the Priestly texts. As for the question concerning the existence of older sources of the Priestly composition, several scholars advocate a "book" or "record" of tôlĕdōt, which would be the ostensible source of Gen 5 and other P genealogical texts as well.[2] Scholars also allow for the possibility of sources in the case of Gen 1, the miracle account in Exod 7–11, and the tabernacle account (and, outside of Gen 1–Exod 40, in Lev 1–3).[3] The present study agrees, in principle, with the latter four assumptions. Nevertheless, concerning these four cases, we must distinguish between *Vorlagen* that were composed by Priestly authors in order to be integrated into P^C on the one hand (i.e., Exod 7–11 and the tabernacle account) and sources that were written independently of P^C and that should be considered proto-Priestly units on the other (i.e., Gen 1* and Lev 1–3*). Concerning the supposed "book of genealogies," however, this study maintains that the title "This is the record of the tôlĕdōt" in Gen 5:1 is misleading and that the author is only pretending to rely on an ancient and reliable tradition. The title's usage should be seen in the light of competition with the genealogy in

---

[1] See above, I.2.1.

[2] See above, n. 1 in section I.2.

[3] See, for instance, Blum, *Studien*, 250–52; Römer, "From the Call of Moses," 121–50.

Gen 4 (visibly, the author of Gen 5 depends on Gen 2–4, which uses אדם as a proper name). There are strong indications that Gen 5 is a redactional composition that aims to link the proto-Priestly creation story with the proto-Priestly flood story.[4]

The present work distinguishes itself from most other studies in that it also points out the contours of older sources with distinct stylistic and ideological features for other Priestly texts, such as the flood narrative and the Priestly Abraham narrative.

Generally, the differentiation between P[c] and secondary Priestly texts suggested here agrees with the view of many scholars. Some of these secondarily inserted texts seem to be influenced by the so-called Holiness Code, both its vocabulary and its theological agenda. Others share common points with Priestly (Priestly-like) texts in Numbers. Precise conclusions concerning the relationship between these texts and H and other secondary Priestly texts in Leviticus, Numbers, and other books, however, go beyond the framework of the present investigation, which focuses on the Priestly texts in Gen 1–Exod 40.

An important result of the above analyses is the observation that the texts assigned to P[c] sometimes deviate from one another linguistically. I agree with those scholars who reckon with several Priestly authors, a sort of "school," rather than with only one.[5]

1.1 Origins of P: Four Proto-P Compositions in Genesis 1–25

1.1.1 The Linguistic and Theological Distinctiveness of the Proto-Priestly Units

There are indications favoring the idea that several Priestly texts in the primeval history and the Abraham narrative rely on sources that distinguish themselves linguistically and ideologically from P[c]. Since these units were reworked by the Priestly redactors before their integration into the comprehensive Priestly composition, one must distinguish between a proto-Priestly ground layer and one or several secondary Priestly redactional layers. In what follows, the most important redaction-critical conclusions of the relevant analyses above are summarized and distinctive linguistic and thematic features of these proto-Priestly units are outlined.

(a) Genesis 1:1–2:1*

Many scholars assume that the present version of the creation story in Gen 1:1–2:4a is a reworking of an older source, which is identified either with the word account statements or the deed account assertions. The analysis of the unit presented here confirmed this literary-critical distinction, concluding that the word account statement was the basic framework of the primary story. Arguments were made on three

---

[4] On this question, see above, II.2.5.

[5] See, in particular, BLUM, "Noch einmal"; and see below, III.1.2.1.

different levels, related to differences between the two accounts in spelling, vocabulary, and theology:

Table 4.   Differences between the primary composition and
           the Priestly redaction in Genesis 1

Primary layer (word account)	Redaction (deed account)
1. Spelling – למינו, "after its (their) kind" in 1:11 – חיתו ארץ "the wild animals of the earth" in 1:24	– למינהו, "after its (their) kind" in 1:12 [2×], 21, 25 – חית הארץ, "the wild animals of the earth" in 1:25
2. Literary structure, vocabulary – ברא and ברך *piel* are absent. – Structuring sequence of eight works.	– Structuring sequence of עשׂה, "to make" as verb for "ordinary" creation acts on the one hand and ברא, "to create" + ברך *piel*, "to bless" for the creation of humanity, sea animals, and birds on the other. – Structuring sequence of six working days (cf. מלאכה, "work", עשׂה, "to make") on the one hand and one day of rest (שׁבת) on the other.
3. Theology The respective living spaces of the sea animals and of the land animals participate in the creation: 1:20 And God said, "Let the waters bring forth [ישׁרצו המים] swarms of living creatures, and let birds fly above the earth across the dome of the sky." (And it was so.)[6] 1:24 And God said, "Let the earth bring forth [תוצא הארץ] living creatures of every kind: cattle and creeping things and wild animals of the earth [וחיתו ארץ] of every kind." And it was so.	Elohim is the lone creator: 1:21 So God created [ויברא אלהים] the great sea monsters and every living creature that moves, of every kind, with which the waters swarm, and every winged bird of every kind. And God saw that it was good. 1:25 God made [ויעשׂ אלהים] the wild animals of the earth [חית הארץ] of every kind, and the cattle of every kind, and everything that creeps upon the ground of every kind. And God saw that it was good.
Announcement sentence in 1:26 expresses the idea of the "plurality" of Elohim (the first-person plural is used three times). 1:26 And God said, "Let us make [נעשׂה] humankind [אדם] in our image [בצלמנו], according to our likeness [בצלמנו] …"	In the execution sentence in 1:27, Elohim appears as a lone actor. 1:27 And God created man [האדם] in his own image, in the image of God he created him; male and female he created them.

---

[6] The correspondence formula occurs only in the LXX. See above, II.1.2.2 (a).

Even though it seems impossible to identify the full extent of the base layer (word account), the analysis nevertheless has shown that the redactor preserved his source text to a great extent (each section of the eight creative works contains a word account statement). Given certain linguistic (vocabulary) and theological (monotheistic) features, the deed account as secondary redaction should be assigned to the Priestly composition. In contrast, the presumed ground layer, which contains elements that are alien to the theology of P, probably constitutes a proto-Priestly composition. Motifs in the word account that are difficult to combine with the theology of P include the "birth" of certain beings by the earth and the sea and the internal "plurality" of Elohim as it is expressed in 1:26. Moreover, God, as presented in Gen 1, does not dwell in heaven (as hinted at in the Priestly texts Gen 17:22 and 35:13), but is beyond all spaces (including that of heaven) that he has created (see Gen 1:6–8).[7] The expression צבא is used differently in the proto-Priestly creation account on the one hand and in the later Priestly texts on the other: in Gen 2:1, the term צבא refers to the "host" of all beings populating the living spaces of the created world (וכל צבאם, "and all their host"). In the Priestly texts of Exodus and Numbers, the same expression designates Israel as an organized army or, when used in the plural (as always in Exodus), as "regiments" of an army.[8]

In view of its formal, conceptual, and theological coherence, the creation account may have been conceived as an independent and self-contained unit, not necessarily as a component of a more extensive and continuous work comprising several parts. With regard to its marked positive ontology and theology, Gen 1:1–2:1* matches well with certain creation psalms (Pss 8; 19; 104) but may also be compared with myths of "beginning" in antiquity alluding to a utopian "golden age."

(b) Genesis 6–9 P

The Priestly Flood narrative shows clear signs of redactional growth although the reconstruction of the precise contours of the presumed ground layer in Gen 6–9 P seems difficult.

Given the lack of coherence with the story's plot, some or all of the time indications and calendrical systems reflected in the text should be assigned to secondary Priestly layers.

There is an intriguing linguistic difference between the passage of YHWH's instruction to Noah and two statements related to the fulfillment of that instruction: in the former the distributive notion has to be deduced from the context (see Gen 6:19, 20: שנים, "two [of every kind]"), while in the latter the idea is expressed by repetition (7:9 and 7:15: שנים שנים, "two of every kind") which is in agreement with the conventions

---

[7] See SCHÜLE, *Der Prolog*, 102; SCHMID, *Schöpfung*, 88–89.
[8] See Exod 6:26; 7:4; 12:17, 41, 51 and the frequent use of the noun in Num 1–10 and 31.

of Late Biblical Hebrew and which is often found in Priestly texts in Exodus, Leviticus and Numbers.[9] This difference points to redactional development too.

Furthermore, there are strong indications that 9:1–7, a passage with its own particular structure, is not an integral part of the primary story. The language of holy war in 9:2 with expressions that are predominantly used in late Dtr texts may point to a later author in 9:1–7 (or 9:2–7), as compared with the concluding unit narrating God's covenant with all creatures and his solemn abdication of violence (9:8–17).

The remaining primary kernel of the Priestly flood story forms a well-marked unit with a coherent plot and a particular theological main theme, namely the "conversion" of God as revealed at the end of the story (9:8–17). In an innovative manner, the author adapts the conflicting positions of the gods toward humans in the Mesopotamian flood tradition to the monotheistic conception. Within an innerbiblical discourse, the purpose of this adaptation is to respond to the presentation of YHWH as a god of irrevocable judgment in prophetic and Deuteronomistic texts. Because of its particular theology, the Priestly flood story does not match certain central Priestly texts in Exodus, namely the Priestly plague narrative and the Priestly story of the parting of the sea. God's striking and solemn renunciation of violence as presented in Gen 6–9* P stands in tension with YHWH's bellicose acts against Pharaoh and the Egyptians. This discrepancy is all the more blatant as in Exod 14 P the Egyptian army's devastation by YHWH is accomplished by the same element water as in Gen 6–9* P.

(c) Genesis 10 P

The Priestly stratum of the genealogy in Gen 10, constituting a unified and coherent unit, forms the "natural" continuation of the proto-Priestly flood story. The composition is tightly connected to the flood narrative through the names of the three main ancestors (and world regions), which are identical with those of Noah's three sons (Shem, Ham, and Japheth). The fact that the tripartite table opens with Japheth fits with the geographical location of the ark's landing (at Mount Ararat).

Although the Table of Nations (P) is often considered a key text of P^G/P^C (as representing the Persian *oikumene*), a closer look reveals that it would be better assigned to a proto-Priestly level and understood in a Neo-Babylonian or Neo-Assyrian context. In contrast to the Persian monumental inscriptions, which consistently have Persia, Media, and Elam at their beginning, there is no visible hierarchy in the tripartite composition of Gen 10 P; remarkably, Persia is not mentioned, and Media and Elam are assigned to two different "world regions" (Japhet and Shem, respectively). Cush's prominent position within Ham and Canaan's association with the latter are better understood in an earlier (Neo-Assyrian or Neo-Babylonian) period than in the Persian era. The composition with its universal perspective matches well with the

---

[9] See POLZIN, *Late Biblical Hebrew*, 47–51; *GKC* §123c, d, with n. 2, §134q. See furthermore above II.3.2 (a).

similarly universal and (or) multiethnic scope of other proto-Priestly units (Gen 1, flood narrative, Abraham narrative).

(d) Priestly Abraham Narrative

Through its literary profile and its theology, the Priestly Abraham narrative clearly distinguishes itself from the Priestly texts dealing with Isaac, Jacob, Esau and Joseph. In contrast to the latter, the Abraham story of P is self-contained and independent of the non-Priestly strand.[10] It has striking singularities in comparison with P[C]: two pivotal texts use the Tetragram, which stands in tension with the theonym theology of the Priestly composition. The allusions to the moon cult in the toponyms Ur-Chasdim and Harran and certain personal names are peculiar features.[11] The subtle point of the story, that it is the local deity El Shaddai/YHWH rather than Sîn, the moon god, who brings fecundity and progeny to Sarah and Abraham, makes better sense in the context of a proto-Priestly Abraham narrative than in the comprehensive Priestly composition. The same holds true for the insistence on Abraham being the father of a multitude of nations and the multiethnic scope of the story, which contrasts with the strong focus on Israel in Priestly texts in the subsequent sections.

(e) Other "Vorlagen" of the Priesty Compositon

There are other Priestly texts within Gen 1–Exod 40 that have a regular and sophisticated structure, such as the Priestly miracle story in Exod 7–11, the Priestly story of the parting of the sea in Exod 14, and the tabernacle account. They give the impression that they were, in an initial stage, composed as single units and might therefore be considered *Vorlagen* of P[C] too. Nevertheless, since the style and theology of these texts are typically Priestly, they are well integrated into the overall Priestly composition. Furthermore, in contrast to the proto-Priestly texts in Genesis, they do not appear as well-marked units having a clear beginning and end. Moreover, they bear signs of dependence on the non-Priestly strand. Probably these "sources" were composed by the authors of the Priestly composition themselves.[12]

1.1.2 General Commonalities between the Proto-Priestly Compositions in Genesis 1–25

The four presupposed literary *Vorlagen* in Gen 1–25 (creation account, flood narrative, Table of Nations, Abraham narrative) have several commonalities and are connected to one another through certain common expressions and motifs and also have

---

[10] Only a few of its texts, such as the indications of the patriarchs' ages, are not anchored in the narrative's plot and depend on the non-P context; they should be ascribed to a secondary redactional layer.

[11] See II.6.5.2.

[12] See above, II.7.4, II.8.5, and II.10.10, and below, III.2.3 (2).

theological ideas in common.[13] They are each self-contained and independent from the non-Priestly strand. All four compositions share the formula "these are the *tôlĕdōt* of …" The phrase in 2:4a was perhaps the title of the creation story in Gen 1:1–2:1* originally, having the same function as the formula in the other three units.[14] Other striking parallels and commonalities between the proto-Priestly units are the enumeration and categorization of animals in Gen 1:1–2:1* and Gen 6–9 P, the approbation formulae of Gen 1 and the "non-approbation" statement in 6:12a ("God looked at the earth, and behold: it was corrupt"), and geographical correspondences between the flood story (which ends in the north at Ararat), the Table of Nations (which begins in the north with Japheth and ends in the east with Arpachshad), and the Terah narrative (which begins in the east at "Ur of the Chaldeans").

The four units share a common multiethnic (Abraham narrative) and universal (creation story, flood narrative, Table of Nations) scope and theology. The use of the theonym אלהים in the context of the "universalistic" proto-Priestly history of origins seems deliberate and meaningful. First, the deity's name is not the specific designation of Israel's national god (יהוה); אלהים as a general, unspecific term seems an appropriate designation for the creator of the universe. Second, as shown above in the analysis of Gen 1, the author of this story probably chose the term אלהים because of its morphological specificity (though a plural in form, the noun is consistently used as a singular). Regarding the plurality of God in 1:26, the designation אלהים might express the idea that the deity is simultaneously one and multiple.[15] Regarding the subtlety of the אלהים terminology in Gen 1:1–2:1*, it is questionable that the author of the latter text, as commonly assumed, conceived it to aim at the hierarchic concept of a three-stage revelation of God in Pᶜ (God's manifestations as Elohim and El Shaddai represent preliminary stages in comparison with his revelation as YHWH, which is, according to Pᶜ, his only valid name; see Exod 6:3).

1.1.3 The Noah and Abraham Narratives

Particularly strong similarities are observable between the Noah and the Abraham stories: Noah and Terah have both three sons. After the statement about their births (procreations), each story's focus immediately moves to the youngest son (Japhet, Haran) and the descendant(s) of the latter (10:1–2; 11:27–28).

A shared central motif of both narratives is that of the covenant (ברית). The covenant concept found in the two proto-Priestly accounts should probably be understood as a response to the Deuteronomic/Deuteronomistic covenant idea (see further below). The Priestly (proto-Priestly) covenant tradition differs in two ways from the latter. First, Deuteronomic/Deuteronomistic ideology emphasizes fulfillment of

---

[13] See also above, II.1.5, II.3.7.2.
[14] See above, II.1.3.6 (b) and II.1.3.7.
[15] See above, II.1.3.9.

the covenant and obedience to the law, whereas in Gen 6–9* P and the proto-Priestly Abraham narrative the covenant is not conditional. The *běrît* given to Noah and Abraham is irrevocable.[16] Second, according to both the proto-Priestly flood account and the proto-Priestly Abraham narrative, the covenant is not addressed to Israel alone but is directed to a multiethnic or even universal beneficiary (the covenant with Noah in Gen 6–9 includes all humans and all animals).

Another shared element of the proto-Priestly flood story and the Abraham narrative, is the honor associated with Noah and Abraham: they were "blameless" (תמים) and "walked with/before God" (6:9; 17:1). Together with the absence of animal sacrifices, these motifs may point to an alternative model of allegiance to YHWH that was opposed to the traditional cult with animal sacrifice. Noah and Abraham do not venerate YHWH at a particular sanctuary but rather live, wherever they go, in the presence of the deity.

1.1.4 Redaction-Critical Conclusion

Prima facie, the common assumption that the flood and the Abraham narratives (primary P stratum) on the one hand and the Priestly Sinai pericope, the center of the Priestly composition, on the other stem from the same author is problematic. In fact, this theory cannot explain the presence of two completely different models of allegiance to God/YHWH. For what reason would the author of P^C – who according to common scholarly interpretation is primarily interested in the authorization of Israel's theocratic institutions and sacrificial cultus – have prefaced his work with accounts about two honored non-Israelite figures who received the deity's covenant by virtue of their blameless but cultless conduct?

Generally, the dichotomy in the Priestly composition is explained by the idea that the Priestly author wanted to anchor the Sinai cult legislation in the covenant given to Abraham. According to a few Priestly texts (Gen 17:17–22; 28:1–5; Exod 6:2–9), God's covenant with Abraham is in fact directed to Isaac and Jacob (Israel) and finds its fulfillment at Sinai. Therefore, it seems as a consequence that in P no particular covenant is concluded at Sinai. Influenced by Zimmerli's seminal study, many scholars explain this arrangement as a result of the Priestly author's opposition to the pre-Priestly (Deuteronomistic) covenant:[17] whereas the pre-Priestly covenant concluded at Sinai/Horeb, with its pattern of edited laws on the one hand and blessings and curses on the other, is conditional, the covenant of P constitutes an unconditional

---

[16] The order of circumcision (17:9–14) and the report of its fulfillment by Abraham should be ascribed to a secondary layer. Regarding the Priestly flood account, the dietary laws (Gen 9:1–7), which are not directly related to the establishment of the covenant (9:8–17) anyway, probably belong to a secondary stratum as well (cf. above, II.3.4 [e]).

[17] See ZIMMERLI, "Abrahambund und Sinaibund." Scholars following Zimmerli are, among others, VON RAD, *Die Priesterschrift*, 175–76; BLUM, *Studien*, 294–95; NIHAN, "Priestly Covenant," 91–103.

gift and is independent of the people's obedience to the decrees proclaimed by God at Sinai. However, even though one may interpret P^C in this sense, namely, that the Sinai legislation of P is based on the "covenant of grace" concluded with Abraham, it is striking that this idea, which would connect the two parts – the "Priestly ancestor narrative" and the "tabernacle account" – is not developed. In no part of this section is the reader reminded that Abraham's covenant is now finding its fulfillment. This disjointedness, in addition to the aforementioned tension between conflicting statements about the covenant in Gen 17, speaks against the idea that the covenant originally concluded with Abraham in P (proto-P) was meant to extend (to be directed) to the Sinai event.

Another theory aiming to prove the coherence of P^C as a unified document concerns the striking absence of altar building and animal sacrifice in both the Priestly flood narrative and the ancestral narrative. This feature is explained by the principle of the Priestly author to restrict legitimate sacrifices to the comprehensive YHWH worship constituted at Sinai.[18] Indubitably, this explanation applies nicely on the level of the Priestly document. However, as shown above, in the context of the individual units (flood story, Abraham narrative), there is another interpretation for the absence of cultic actions (sacrifices) by the main protagonists (Noah, Abraham): their author(s) promoted a model of allegiance to YHWH that was opposed to the traditional cult with animal sacrifice. Such promotion of "cultless" allegiance to God (YHWH) would fit nicely with a setting for these stories among Judeans after the destruction of the temple in the Neo-Babylonian era (see below). Operation of the regular cult at the sanctuary in Jerusalem was no longer possible; a large part of the Judean population lived in exile, without access to a Yahwistic sanctuary.

A further indication of the original independence of the proto-Priestly Noah and Abraham accounts is that they differ from the Priestly texts in Exodus in their literary design. Both protagonists are introduced and endowed with honorable qualities (Gen 6:9; 17:1), unlike Moses and Aaron, the pivotal figures in the Priestly texts of Exodus, who are not introduced at all. More generally, all Priestly units in question (Gen 1*, Gen 6–10 P, and the Priestly Abraham narrative) distinguish themselves from P^C through their particular theological profile. Distinct motifs include the inner pluralism of אלהים, the concept of a peaceful deity, universalism, and a marked multiethnic scope. These elements remain without resonance in the Priestly composition and stand in tension with Priestly texts in the subsequent sections (i.e. Exod 7–11 P and 14 P). Taken together, these aspects of disparateness and incoherence on the level of the comprehensive Priestly composition point to the texts' formation at different stages. The (proto-)Priestly creation account and the Noah and Abraham narratives were composed independently of P's Sinai account and predate the latter. Only later did Priestly authors (redactors) take up the former texts, integrating them into their

---

[18] Cf. WELLHAUSEN, *Prolegomena zur Geschichte*, 38; GILDERS, "Sacrifice before Sinai and the Priestly Narratives," 57–72; LEVIN, "Die Priesterschrift als Quelle," 29.

overall work and transforming their theology by directing Abraham's covenant with
yhwh/El Shaddai to Israel.

How tightly are the four proto-Priestly units connected with each other? Is it imaginable that they were edited or even composed simultaneously? The comparison of
the four texts reveals shared motifs and commonalities as well as differences.[19] As
shown above, the connectedness of the proto-Priestly compositions (Gen 1*; Gen
6–9*; Gen 10*; proto-Priestly Abraham narrative) is subtle but particular. The fact
that all four share the title "these are the procreations/history of …" (אלה תולדת) may
point to common or successive editions of the four compositions (each one written
on its own small scroll or sheet?).[20]

The term תולדת seems polysemous; the first sense is "descendants," literally, "procreations," but
most instances can also be understood as "history."[21] Originally, this proto-Priestly composition
might have contained as many as eight *tôlĕdōt* series, including the aforementioned four plus
those of Ishmael, Isaac, Esau, and Jacob, which are included in the *tôlĕdōt* of Terah and which
each introduce a genealogy.

The formal and theological commonalities shared by these four units point to their
mutual adjustment and a common edition. However, these shared elements should
not detract from the fact that each text has its own linguistic and stylistic characteristics and self-contained structure. This is in particular the case for the proto-Priestly
creation account: given its regular structure with climactic development, and its
marked theology (positive ontology), the proto-Priestly creation account may have
been composed as an independent unit. The particular structure and style of individual passages may also be due to the tradition from which a unit was borrowed. The
proto-Priestly Table of Nations seems to have been built on an elaborate, tripartite list
of nations stemming from Phoenician traders.

---

[19] Note that there are differences in vocabulary between Gen 1* and the proto-Priestly flood
narrative and between the latter and the proto-Priestly Abraham narrative (see II.3.7.2 and
II.6.7 [b]).

[20] Evidence for short texts, written on short scrolls or single sheets, is found in Elephantine
and also in Qumran (see Tov, Scribal Practices, ch. 2, p. 74), for an example of a short literary
text see the combination A of Deir 'Alla, which seems to be a copy from a papyrus sheet (cf. the
reconstruction in Blum, Die altaramäischen Wandinschriften vom Tell Deir 'Alla und ihr insti-
tutioneller Kontext, 26 with n. 23; 29).

[21] See J. Scharbert, "Der Sinn der Toledot-Formel in der Priesterschrift," in *Wort – Gebot
– Glaube: Beiträge zur Theologie des Alten Testaments; Festschrift für W. Eichrodt*, ed. H. J.
Stoebe, J. J. Stamm, and E. Jenni, ATANT 59 (Zurich: Zwingli-Verlag, 1970), 52; Weimar, "Die
Toledot-Formel," 84; Lohfink, "Die Priesterschrift," 204, with n. 38. Concerning the function
of the *tôlĕdōt* formulae in P^G/P^C, see Scharbert, "Der Sinn"; Weimar, "Die Toledot-Formel";
Blum, *Die Komposition*, 432–46.

1.1.5 The Setting of the Proto-P Units

A setting in the late monarchic or Neo-Babylonian era seems plausible for all four units and for the common edition.[22] As for the primary composition in Gen 1, certain affinities to Egyptian cosmology and to an architectural element of the pre-exilic temple may favor a setting in the monarchic era. For the other three units, the Neo-Babylonian period seems probable. These settings are especially likely given that the covenant concept found in the proto-Priestly Noah and Abraham narratives should probably be understood as a response to the Deuteronomic/Deuteronomistic covenant idea.

The question concerning the origin of the "theological" covenant concept in the Hebrew Bible is a subject of much debate. Studies by H. U. Steymans and Otto note strong indications that the covenant notion in the book of Deuteronomy was influenced by the Neo-Assyrian oath of allegiance (*adê*).[23] In particular, the series of curses in Deut 28 has significant parallels in the *adê*. Deuteronomy adapts this concept and binds Israel to YHWH and to certain principles and prescriptions associated with YHWH.[24] The term ברית also plays an important role in 2 Kgs 22–23, according to which King Josiah carried out a reform based on a "forgotten" book found in the temple. The discovered book is called the "book of the covenant" (2 Kgs 23:2, 21). Furthermore, it is said that Josiah made a covenant, a "loyalty oath," before YHWH, binding himself and his people to the principles and prescripts of the recovered book (2 Kgs 23:3).[25] The unity and dating of the report in 2 Kgs 22–23 are much debated, as are the question of the historicity of the account (legend?) of the book's discovery and the elements of Josiah's reform.[26] Nevertheless, most scholars agree in dating a primary version of 2 Kgs 22–23 to the late monarchic period and in considering some of the reforms plausible.[27]

---

[22] See the treatment of this question in the relevant sections of the analyses.

[23] Cf. H. U. STEYMANS, *Deuteronomium 28 und die adê zur Thronfolgeregelung Asarhaddons: Segen und Fluch im Alten Orient und in Israel*, OBO 145 (Fribourg: Presses Universitaires; Göttingen: Vandenhoeck & Ruprecht, 1995); IDEM, "Deuteronomy 28 and Tell Tayinat," *Verbum et Ecclesia* 34, art. 870 (2013), http://dx.doi.org/10.4102/ve.v34i2.870; E. OTTO, *Das Deuteronomium: Politische Theologie und Rechtsreform in Juda und Assyrien*, BZAW 284 (Berlin: de Gruyter, 1999), 64–69; IDEM, "Die Ursprünge der Bundestheologie im Alten Testament und im Alten Orient," *ZAR*, 4 (1998), 41–42.

[24] However, in Deuteronomy, the term ברית is rare (see Deut 5:3; 7:9, 11; 28:69), and it is not certain that it belongs to part of the book stemming from the Neo-Assyrian period, see OTTO, *Deuteronomium 1–11*, 1:678–80. Nevertheless, the idea of a covenant as a mutual commitment between YHWH and Israel is clearly expressed, especially in Deut 13 and 28.

[25] Since W. M. L. de Wette, scholars have generally associated the scroll discovered in the temple with the book of Deuteronomy or a primary form of it. More recently, however, several scholars have voiced skepticism about the value of the biblical account.

[26] Cf., among many others, RÖMER, *So-Called Deuteronomistic History*, 49–55; J. BEN-DOV, "Writing as Oracle and as Law: New Contexts for the Book-Find of King Josiah," *JBL* 127 (2008): 222–39.

[27] See, for instance, RÖMER, *So-Called Deuteronomistic History*, 53–54, 104; C. UEHLINGER, "Was There a Cult Reform under King Josiah? The Case for a Well-Grounded Minimum," in *Good Kings and Bad Kings*, ed. L. L. Grabbe, JSOTSup 393 (London: T&T Clark, 2005), 279–316.

Regarding the emphasis on the unconditional nature of the covenant and on its multiethnic and universal beneficiaries, it is probable that the proto-Priestly Noah and
Abraham narratives were reacting to the nationalist and demanding Deuteronomic/
Deuteronomistic covenant concepts of the periods of the late Judean monarchy and
the early exile. Their particular targets were the theology of judgment (via the flood
narrative) and that of the loss of the land (via the Abraham narrative). The emphasis on the permanence of right of usufruct of the land (cf. עוֹלָם) in Gen 17 insinuates
that Jerusalem's fall and the temple's pillaging by the Neo-Babylonians could not affect
the validity of the land promise addressed to Abraham. Given these clues, both the
flood and the Abraham narrative should be dated after the conquest of Jerusalem by
Nebuchadnezzar II. The striking allusions to the religion of the moon god Sîn, who
was favored by the Neo-Babylonian king Nabonidus, provide further evidence for the
Abraham narrative's setting in the Neo-Babylonian period.

Likewise, a setting for the Table of Nations no later than the Neo-Babylonian era
seems confirmed, as evidenced by its selection of toponyms.[28]

1.2 The Priestly Composition (P^c)

1.2.1 General Characterization

In general, a relatively coherent Priestly strand with linguistic, conceptual, and ideological commonalities is identifiable in Genesis and Exodus. However, with the exception of the first half of the book of Genesis (Gen 1–25), this strand lacks continuity.
Several gaps in the Priestly narrative thread require complementary material from the
surrounding units of the non-P strand, and in several cases a Priestly text has been
influenced by neighboring non-P texts. Therefore, this composition should be considered a redaction, namely, a series of smaller or larger textual units inserted in or
combined with non-Priestly texts, rather than an independent source.[29] Moreover, the
Priestly units sometimes deviate from one another linguistically.[30]

– For instance, certain elements of the burial notices in the Priestly ancestral narrative
  contradict one another.
– As shown above, in the Priestly texts of Genesis and Exodus 1–15 the expression
  עֵדָה, "congregation," appears only in Exod 12.[31] One might be inclined to correlate
  the use of this term with the enactment of the first cultic law for Israel (i.e., the
  Passover prescription in Exod 12:1–8). Yet if this were the intention of the author,

---

[28] See above, II.4.8.
[29] On this question, see below, III.2.
[30] See the assembled observations above, II.6.8 and II.7.4 (b).
[31] Cf. Exod 12:3, 6, 19, 47.

one should expect the use of the expression עֵדָה in the main parts of the tabernacle account, in Exod 25–29 and 40, too.

– The situation is similar to that of the term קָהָל, "assembly." It plays a central role in three Priestly texts in Genesis (Gen 28:3; 35:11; 48:4) but occurs only once in Exodus (Exod 12:6); see further below.

– Likewise, the term צָבָא, "host," frequently referring to Israel as an organized "army" in the book of Numbers, also appears sporadically in a few Priestly texts in Exodus (always in the plural, in the sense of "regiments": in the introduction to the miracle narrative [6:26; 7:4] and in the notice concerning Israel's exodus [12:41, 51]; among these texts 7:4 and 12:41 are commonly assigned to P^G/P^C). It is absent from the Priestly texts in Genesis (except Gen 1 where it appears with a different meaning [host of the beings in the different living spaces]) and from central Priestly texts in Exodus too (the story of the miracle at the sea and the tabernacle account).

– Strikingly, one pericope, Exod 6:2–9, shares a significant number of linguistic commonalities with the book of Ezekiel; much more than any other Priestly unit, it is strongly influenced by this book.[32]

– It is also astonishing that toponyms are used in a sporadic and very uneven manner. In Exod 1–15, only one Priestly text mentions toponyms. The statement in question, the detailed itinerary notice in Exod 14:2, fulfills a central function in the plot (through the mention of Baal Zaphon). However, it does not match the end of the Priestly Passover account (Exod 12:41, 51), which recounts Israel's exodus without mentioning any toponym.

Nevertheless, most of the units are interrelated by shared themes and motifs. This conflicting evidence – namely, formal disparateness and differences of vocabulary and style on one hand and thematic and conceptional coherence on the other – point to different authors who shared the task of composing this work. They were working on it together, at the same time, each author on his own part or assignment. Recently, Blum maintained that P^C/P^s was a work by several authors, perhaps members of a sort of temple school.[33]

Most of the shared motifs and topics can be subsumed under *two central themes*. First, the Priestly authors "nationalize" the proto-Priestly units. Divine promises made to humans in general or to specific nations are redirected to Israel. These promises concern the gift of God's covenant, which includes God's assistance, fruitfulness and multiplication, and the possession of the land. The revelation of YHWH's name is

---

[32] See above, II.7.3 (b).

[33] See BLUM, "Noch einmal," 53, n. 67. Blum reckons with a formation in multiple stages through generations. In general, he abstains from differentiation between Priestly strata: "man wird ernsthaft ... mit der Möglichkeit rechnen müssen, dass ein Werk wie KP – selbst mit der Beschränkung auf eine wie immer geartete Erstedition ('KP^s') – nicht auf einen individuellen Tradenten, sondern auf eine Gruppe (innerhalb einer mit dem Tempel verbundenen 'Schule'?) zurückgeht, vermutlich am Ende des (mehr als zweistufigen) Redaktionsprozesses über mehrere Schreibergenerationen."

restricted to Israel alone. Relatedly, the Priestly author glosses over Jacob's problematic behavior described in the non-Priestly stratum. Second, a real *proprium* of the Priestly composition, in contrast to the non-Priestly strand, is the constitution of the sacrificial cult at Mount Sinai and of a particular priesthood, namely, the Aaronides. This theme is already alluded to in the book of Genesis, by means of correspondences between the end of the creation account in Gen 1 and the end of the tabernacle account and by the promise that Israel will be a "*(cultic) assembly* (קהל) of peoples" (Gen 28:3; 35:11; 48:4). Yet this theme is only fully developed in the book of Exodus, where it is closely connected with the figure of Aaron. It is concretized in detail in the tabernacle account. Many scholars believe that the tabernacle account aims to give a theological-historical foundation for the temple of Jerusalem by anchoring it in the normative Sinai event.[34] Certain observations related to the tabernacle account and, additionally, the striking system of coordinated chronological information indeed show that P^C has a particular interest in the temple of Jerusalem.[35]

In what follows, some important subtopics and thematic motifs that can be associated to one or both of these two central themes are briefly outlined.

1.2.2 Dominant Themes and Motifs

(a) Redirecting the Covenant and Certain Promises to Israel Alone

(1) The Motif of Blessing and Fruitfulness and Multiplication Applied to Israel

The blessing motif, denoted by the double expression פרה, "to be fruitful" /רבה, "to multiply," and the lexeme ברא, "to create," are characteristic elements of the Priestly redaction in Gen 1. Divine blessing and the order to procreate and multiply are addressed only to sea animals, birds (in Gen 1:22), and humans (in 1:28), not to land animals. The redactor alludes to a relationship of competition between humans and land animals, who have to share the same living space.

The blessing motif and the double term רבה/פרה reappear in other Priestly texts, first in Gen 9:1–7, at the end of the flood story (see 9:1, 7, in the *qal* imperative). However, in contrast to Gen 1, the blessing and order to be fruitful and multiply in Gen 9:1, 7 are addressed neither to women nor to animals but only to men. Perhaps this shift should be interpreted to indicate that the restriction and hierarchalization visible in Gen 1 (the land animals are deprived of the blessing) become more pronounced after the flood.

The motif of fruitfulness and multiplication reappears in the ancestral narrative. Since Abraham and Sarah are not able to respond to God's order to reproduce, the deity has to intervene to "provide" multiplication and fruitfulness himself (17:2, 6, רבה

---

[34] See above, II.10.8–9.
[35] See below, III.1.2.2 (b) (3).

and פרה in the *hiphil*, with God/YHWH as subject; note also the inverse order of the two verbs). Other Priestly texts (Gen 28:3; 35:11; 48:4; Exod 1:7) show marks of this redaction layer as well (use of רבה/פרה in *qal* or *hiphil*). Additionally, the expressions שרץ, "to increase greatly," and עצם, "to become mighty," both lacking in Gen 1, and מלא את, "to fill" (cf. 1:22, 28), occur in Exod 1:7. According to Exod 1:7, the Israelites "were fruitful and increased greatly, and multiplied, and became exceedingly mighty, so that the land [of Egypt] was filled with them." This text, containing five different terms expressing the Israelites' growth, marks an obvious climax. According to the author of Exod 1:7, in a certain sense, the Israelites have fulfilled God's order to fill the earth in Gen 1:28. Following this climax, these characteristic expressions and motifs do not appear again in Priestly texts. The word pair רבה/פרה occurs only one other time, in Lev 26:9 (H). On close examination, Exod 1:7 does not fit the global scope of the blessing motif and the orders of Gen 1:28, in that it states that Israel filled a particular land (ארץ) – the land of Egypt – and not the earth (ארץ), as was demanded of humankind in Gen 1:28. Apparently, it was more important to the redactor(s) to exploit an important theme conceived for the creation account in Gen 1 by applying it to Israel than it was to maintain conceptual coherence. Considered as a whole, the network of intertextual connections based on the blessing motif and the lexemes פרה and רבה does not seem very coherent; the use of the motifs does not always fit the function the terms have in Gen 1, nor are they always well anchored in their immediate context. For instance, the back reference in the Abraham narrative to Gen 1 by means of רבה *hiphil* and פרה *hiphil* seems somewhat forced. It is bizarre that Abraham and Sarah, the heroes of the narrative, are unable to fulfill God's commandment to procreate (expressed in Gen 1:28; 9:1, 7) – a fact that could be interpreted as a deficiency in God's creation. This latter incoherence is certainly due to the presence of the sterility motif in the proto-Priestly Abraham account.

(2) Redirection of Abraham's Covenant to Israel

The Priestly texts in Genesis and Exod 1–6 contain several articulations of the covenant. A fundamental idea of the proto-Priestly narratives is that God (YHWH) concluded covenants with both Noah and Abraham. Later Priestly authors took up the covenant idea and reformulated it. The covenant addressed to Abraham, which was originally unconditional and centered on the promise of a rich, multiethnic offspring and the land of Canaan (see Gen 17:1–8*), was later supplemented with the order of circumcision and was additionally addressed to only one of Abraham's sons, Isaac. These later elements in Gen 17 (see 17:9–14, 16–22) prepare for the limitation of the covenant to Israel, which is apparent in a few Priestly texts in the Jacob-Esau and Joseph narratives (Gen 28:3–4; 35:11–12) and more explicitly in the Priestly texts at the beginning of the book of Exodus (2:24; 6:3–4), according to which God (YHWH) concluded a covenant not only with Abraham but also with Isaac and Jacob.

Exodus 2:24

²⁴ So God heard their [the Israelites'] groaning; and God remembered his covenant with Abraham, Isaac, and Jacob.

Exodus 6:3–4

³ And I appeared to Abraham, Isaac, and Jacob, as El Shaddai, but by my name, YHWH, I did not make myself known to them. ⁴ And I also established my covenant with them, to give them the land of Canaan, the land in which they sojourned.

(3) The Theonym Concept

It is generally acknowledged that P implements a stringent theonym ideology. The story of origins (Gen 1–11 P) uses the name Elohim. El Shaddai is the name of the deity who appears to Abraham and Jacob. The deity's genuine name, YHWH, is first revealed to Moses, from which point the deity uses this name in his interactions with the people of Israel. This theonymic concept seems consistent throughout P – regardless of its disputed extent – with the exception of two central texts in the proto-Priestly Abraham narrative, however, which contain the Tetragram (Gen 17:1b and 21:1b).³⁶ At these two points, the Priestly authors left the proto-Priestly narrative unchanged, leaving the conceptual difference between the source text and the Priestly redaction visible. Whereas the proto-Priestly Abraham narrative equated El Shaddai with YHWH, the Priestly composition maintains that God's true name is reserved to Israel alone.

(4) The Shift from a "Multitude of Nations" (Abraham's Descendance) to "Company of Nations" (Israel)

The Priestly texts of the Jacob-Esau narratives twice formulate the statement (or wish) that Jacob will become "an assembly of peoples (nations)," once in the form of a wish, once as a divine promise:

Genesis 28:3–4

³ And may El Shaddai bless you and make you fruitful and multiply you, that you may become an assembly of peoples [קהל עמים]. ⁴ May he also give you the blessing of Abraham, to you and to your descendants with you; that you may possess the land of your sojournings, which God gave to Abraham.

Genesis 35:11

¹¹ God also said to him, "I am El Shaddai; be fruitful and multiply; a nation [גוי] and an assembly of nations [וקהל גוים] shall come from you, and kings shall come forth from you."

How should the expression "a (cultic) assembly of peoples (nations)" be understood? The term קהל is rare in the supposed Pᶜ but occurs often in the late Priestly passages

---

³⁶ See above, II.6.6.4.

of the book of Numbers.[37] It has clearly a religious (cultic) connotation and probably foreshadows Israel's constitution as a religious congregation at Sinai. It is striking,
however, that the term is absent from the tabernacle account.

Since the promise (or wish) is addressed to Jacob the reference of the terms "peoples" and "nations" are Israel and Judah. The kings mentioned in Gen 35:11 are the
later Israelite and Judean kings.[38] The peculiar sequence in 35:11 – "a nation [גוי] and
an assembly of nations [וקהל גוים] shall come from you" – probably reflects different
eras in Israel's history (as recorded in the historical books of the Bible). First, Jacob-
Israel constituted one nation (גוי); then, in the period of the two monarchies, Israel
was split into two separate entities (גוים), the Southern and the Northern Kingdoms.

The term גוים indeed is used as a designation for the two parts of Israel in Ezekiel
37:22:

Ezekiel 37:22
[22] and I will make them one nation [לגוי אחד] in the land, on the mountains of
Israel; and one king will be king for all of them; and they will no longer be two
nations [לשני גוים], and they will no longer be divided into two kingdoms [לשתי
ממלכות].

Obviously, the author of the Priestly texts in the Jacob-Esau section on the one hand
and in Ezekiel on the other do not share the same conception of Israel's inner organization. According to the astonishing statement of the Priestly author, Israel constitutes
a union of different "nations" or *ethnē*.

The choice of the term *nations* by the Priestly author is significant. The statements
that Jacob (Israel) will be a cultic assembly of nations (גוים/עמים) parallel Abraham's
promising designation as "father of multiple nations [גוים]" in the proto-Priestly Abraham narrative (Gen 17:4–5), a further example of the creative transformation of a
proto-Priestly motif by the Priestly redactor of the ancestral narrative. As in other
examples, a nationalizing tendency is clear: whereas the promise concerns both Israel
and ethnically related nations in the Abraham narrative, the wish in Gen 28:3–4 and
the promise in 35:11 include only Israelite "nations."

Although the designation "congregation of (distinct) nations" certainly arose from
historiographical interest (the promise envisages the kingdoms of Israel and Judah),

---

[37] Cf. all occurrences in Priestly texts: Gen 28:3; 35:11; 48:4; Exod 12:6; 16:3; Lev 4:13, 14, 21;
16:17, 33; Num 10:7; 14:5; 15:15; 16:3, 33; 17:12; 19:20; 20:4, 6, 10, 12. Since the expression קהל,
"cultic assembly," for Israel is frequent in Deuteronomy and Deuteronomistic texts in Josh and
1 Kings (see the designations "assembly of yhwh" [Deut 23:2, 3 (2×), 4 (2×), 9] and "assembly
of Israel" [Deut 31:30; Josh 8:35; 1 Kgs 8:14 (2×), 22, 55; 12:3; cf. also Deut 5:22; 1 Kgs 8:65]), it
is probable that the author of the Priestly texts in Genesis borrowed it from Deuteronomy and
Deuteronomistic texts.

[38] So Blum, *Die Komposition*, 457.

it probably hints at the coexistence of distinct communities in Yehud, Samaria, and Elephantine in the Persian period as well.[39]

(5) Possession of the Land

Several Priestly texts in the ancestral narrative and in Exod 1–6 evoke the theme of the possession of the land of Canaan, which is promised to Abraham and then to the line Isaac-Jacob (Israel) (see Gen 17:8; 28:4; 35:12; Exod 6:2–9). This limitation of the promise to Israel alone matches the redirection of YHWH's covenant with Abraham to Israel (see above). Consequently, in P^C the promised land of Canaan includes the northern and southern parts of Palestine but neither Edom and adjacent Arab territories nor the Transjordan areas. The land promise is already fulfilled during the patriarchs' lifetime.[40] The latter do not own the land but instead have the right to sojourn in it. Consequently, אחזה should be understood as "right of usufruct." Nevertheless, in the context of the promise of the land of Canaan, P also uses the lexemes ירש, "to take possession; become heir, owner" (Gen 28:4), and מורשה, "acquisition, property" (Exod 6:8). In Gen 28:4, Jacob, by the extension, may represent Israel. If so, Gen 28:4 and Exod 6:8 probably allude to the non-Priestly account of Israel's conquest of the land in which the verb ירש, "to take possession (of the promised land)," is an important key word. Thus apparently two concepts of land possession stand side by side in P^C. Probably the Priestly author distinguishes between the land possession of the ancestors (which consists in the usufruct of the land) on the one hand and the more secure, long-term land ownership of the Israelites on the other.[41]

Related to this second notion is the achievement of control over the land (כבש, "to subdue") by Joshua in Josh 18:1. The same expression appears in Num 32:22, 29. The question is whether Josh 18:1 and Num 32 should both be assigned to the initial Priestly composition. Since the lexeme כבש appears only once in P^C and is used differently there (in Gen 1:28 the expression refers to the subjection of the earth rather than of the land), these texts probably belong to a later redaction layer. Nevertheless, the latter argument looses its force in light of the Priestly Exod 1:7 which similarly applies a global assertion in Gen 1 (about the growth of the humans) to the Israelites (Exod 1:7 is commonly assigned to P^G/P^C).

(6) The *tôlĕdōt* Formulae (אלה תולדות)

There are a total of thirteen *tôlĕdōt* formulae (אלה תולדות, "these are the *tôlĕdōt* of," once זה ספר תולדת, "this is the book of the *tôlĕdōt* of") in the Hebrew Bible, of which

---

[39] BLUM, *Die Komposition*, 456–58. See also E. A. Knauf, who, however, has different interpretations for Gen 17:4, 5 on the one hand and Gen 35:11 on the other. According to Knauf, the former text would target Judah (the Persian province of Yehud) and the latter passages Israel (the Persian province of Samaria); see KNAUF, *Josua*, 154 (Knauf does not offer any argument for his interpretation).

[40] See above, II.6.6.6.

[41] Similarly ALBERTZ, *Exodus 19–40*, 126.

eleven are found in Genesis, one in Numbers, and one in the book of Ruth.[42] The instances in Genesis are generally all assigned to the Priestly strand. Certain anomalies in Num 3:1–4 (mention of Moses and Aaron at the beginning of the genealogy, the circumstantial phrase in 3:1b, and the passage's remoteness from the *tôlĕdōt* in Genesis) lead most scholars to rightly consider the text a late, post-Priestly addition. The passage presupposes the episode about the offering of the "strange fire" in Lev 10, which recent commentaries have considered a late Priestly or post-Priestly insertion.[43] As noted above, the term's first sense is "descendants, procreations," but in several instances the translation "history" seems more appropriate (i.e., the *tôlĕdōt* of Noah, of the sons of Noah, of Terah, and of Jacob). In the Priestly composition, the last entry is the *tôlĕdōt* of Jacob, which includes a more comprehensive history than do the *tôlĕdōt* of Ishmael, Isaac, and Esau. In fact, the *tôlĕdōt* of Jacob encompasses all the history of Israel, which begins with the Joseph story but covers the following books.[44] The focus on Israel is visible again.

As often observed the heading "*tôlĕdōt* of Jacob" in Gen 37:2 does not fit well as a heading for the Joseph story. Since in P^c the latter unit functions as a transition bringing Jacob-Israel to Egypt, where the people increase greatly and become a great nation (Exod 1:7), the *tôlĕdōt* formula nevertheless matches the overall agenda of the Priestly composition.[45]

(b) Constitution of the Sacrificial Cult

Diverse topics are related to the constitution of the sacrificial cult at Sinai and at the later temple in Jerusalem, although this is not apparent at first sight for all of them. There is also a religious activity (Passover feast) that is supposed to happen outside of the central sanctuary, on a family basis.

(1) Paralleling Israel's Liberation and Its Constitution as Cultic Assembly with the Cosmic Order

Scholars emphasize the presence of intertextual correspondences between the creation narrative in Gen 1:1–2:4a and the end of the tabernacle account (Exod 39–40).

---

[42] Gen 2:4; 5:1; 6:9; 10:1; 11:10, 27; 25:12, 19; 36:1, 9; 37:2; Num 3:1; Ruth 4:18.

[43] See above, II.10.6.2 (c).

[44] See LOHFINK, "Die Priesterschrift," 204, n. 38. According to BLUM, *Die Komposition*, 432–37, the *tôlĕdōt* of Jacob would end with Jacob's burial. Speaking against Blum's understanding is the fact that other *tôlĕdōt* sections do not end with the death (and the burial) of the relevant ancestor mentioned in the *tôlĕdōt* formula (i.e., *tôlĕdōt* of Adam, *tôlĕdōt* of Noah's sons, *tôlĕdōt* of Shem, *tôlĕdōt* of Terah). Furthermore, the ensemble of *tôlĕdōt* sections in P, which according to Blum's understanding would limit themselves to the book of Genesis, would not match the comprehensive outline of P^c.

[45] Perhaps in the course of the formation of P^c the heading "*tôlĕdōt* of Jacob" was displaced from its original location at the beginning of the genealogy of Jacob in Gen 35:22b–26 (proto-P) to the beginning of the Joseph story (37:2).

The parallel between the accomplishment of God's creation and the tabernacle's construction at Sinai creates an *inclusio*,[46] with the shared motifs of achievement of the work, final approbation, and God's and Moses's blessing, using the common expressions מלאכה, "work," כלה *piel*, "to complete," ראה, "to see," עשׂה, "to make," הנה, "behold," and ברך *piel*, "to bless": The author(s) state(s) that God/Moses achieved his work (common terms, כלה *piel* and מלאכה, cf. Gen 2:2a with Exod 40:33b). Also relevant are Gen 1:31a/Exod 39:43a (final approbation by God/Moses; common terms, מלאכה, ראה, עשׂה, and הנה); Gen 2:1a/Exod 39:32a (statement of the work's achievement; common term, כלה *pual* and *qal*); and Gen 2:3a (1:27)/Exod 39:43b (God's/ Moses's blessing; common term, ברך *piel*). Yet, one should take into account that most of the shared motifs in Gen 1:1–2:4a belong to the final section Gen 2:2–3 which shows signs of later origin.[47] Furthermore, also the texts on the other side of the narrative bridge, in Exod 39–40, are perhaps (all) late supplements (since they belong to the secondary fulfillment section of the tabernacle account).[48] For instance, the term מלאכה, "work" occurs three times in Gen 2:2–3, but never in the preceding section, Gen 1:1–2:1; the same expression is very frequently used in the secondary parts of the tabernacle account, while it is completly absent from the older instruction section (Exod 25–29).[49]

As is often noted, the story of the parting of the sea (Exod 14 P) evokes the Priestly creation too, through the shared motifs of the splitting of the sea and the revealing of the dry land. Whereas the verb for splitting is different (compare בקע *qal*, "to split," and *niphal*, "to be split," in Exod 14:16, 21, with בדל *hiphil*, "to separate," in Gen 1), the designation of the dry land is the same (יבשה, Exod 14:16, 22, 29; Gen 1:9, 10).

What is the theological significance of these intertextual links between Gen 1 and Exod 14; 39–40? Both rabbinical tradition and modern scholars have suggested, that creation is finally achieved by YHWH's dwelling in the midst of his people.[50] In particular, it is said that the Priestly composition reflects a structure present in Enuma Elish in which creation and the construction of a sanctuary for the deity are closely linked, the latter constituting a microcosm of the former. After the victory over the chaotic powers (Tiamat), Marduk is enthroned in the earthly abode (Esagila in Babylon).[51] Considered in isolation, however, the creation account in Gen 1 (the proto-Priestly account) does not reflect this idea: creation is fully achieved with the formation of

---

[46] Cf., among others, POLA, *Die ursprüngliche Priesterschrift*, 227–29, 361; JANOWSKI, "Tempel und Schöpfung," 46; BLUM, *Studien*, 301–12.

[47] See above, II.1.3.6 (c).

[48] See above, II.10.4.2.

[49] מלאכה appears 5 times in Exod 31 and 24 times in Exod 35–40.

[50] Cf. *Pesiqta de Rab Kahana* 8–9 (see P. SCHÄFER, "Tempel und Schöpfung: Zur Interpretation einiger Heiligtumstraditionen in der rabbinischen Literatur," in *Studien zur Geschichte und Theologie des Rabbinischen Judentums*, ed. P. Schäfer, Kairós 16 [Leiden: Brill, 1978], 131–32); VON RAD, *Theologie des Alten Testaments I*, 247; JANOWSKI, *Sühne als Heilsgeschehen*, 311–12; ZENGER, *Gottes Bogen*, 171–72; NIHAN, *From Priestly Torah*, 54–55.

[51] See Enuma Elish VI 60–61.

humans, and the whole is deemed "very good" (Gen 1:31; 2:1). Blum and Janowski see the difficulty of the aforementioned interpretation – its conflict with Gen 1:31; 2:1 – and adjust it as follows: YHWH's taking up residence among Israel is not the achievement of the creation but rather constitutes the reestablishment of the creation (after its corruption and the flood event).[52] Even though on the level of the endtext such an interpretation is possible it is not the only one. Alternatively, one might see in these intertextual contacts simply an attempt by the authors of Exod 14 P and the tabernacle account to create parallels between the reported events (miracle at the sea, construction of the tabernacle) on the one hand and God's creation on the other. Moreover, there is a difference between the Priestly composition and Enuma Elish that seems to be overlooked in scholarship but nevertheless might be significant. While it is true that both the Esagil and the Priestly tabernacle are built at the beginning of the second year according to the respective calendars,[53] the point of reference is different: in Enuma Elish it is the creation; in Pᶜ, it is Israel's exodus from Egypt (see Exod 40:17). Given that Pᶜ depends on Enuma Elish, one should interpret this difference in the sense that the Priestly author highlights the exodus event at the expense of the creation. This may be further confirmed by the fact that whereas none of the Priestly chronological and calendarial notices refer to the creation, the exodus event, in contrast, appears as a reference point in those notices several times (see Exod 12:2, 40–41; 19:1; 40:17; and 1 Kgs 6:1).

(2) Introducing Aaron as first high priest and eponym of the priesthood

Aaron is pivotal in Pᶜ because of his role as high priest in the tabernacle account and in the sacrificial legislation. At the same time, he is an enigmatic figure. During his introduction in Exod 7:1, almost no information is given about him. All that the reader is told is that he is Moses's brother. What is the purpose of this detail (which is repeated many times in Priestly texts [Pᶜ and Pˢ]; see Exod 7:1; 28:1, 2, 4, 41; Lev 16:2; Num 20:8; 27:13; Deut 32:50)? It probably aims to hint at – or to postulate – Aaron's Levitical descent. As Moses's brother, Aaron is a Levite too. Furthermore: as a redaction layer, Pᶜ presupposes the pre-Priestly story in Exod 2:1–10, which emphasizes Moses' Levitical origin (see 2:1). Possibly Pᶜ presupposes and accepts the requirements of Deut 18:1–5. Only as a Levite is Aaron authorized to fulfill the tasks of the high priest. At the same time, it seems that Pᶜ subverts Levitical priestly traditions that trace their lineage to Moses as common ancestor (see Exod 2:1; Deut 33:8–10; Judg 18:30; cf. also 1 Sam 2:27–28). Possibly Aaron should replace Moses as the ancestor of the Israelite priesthood founded at Mount Sinai.

One important goal of the Priestly miracle story, as a complementary layer to the non-P plague story, is to introduce Aaron into the plot and to give him – the future high priest – an important role, namely, that of a charismatic prophet. Endowed with

---

[52] See BLUM, *Studien*, 245, and JANOWSKI, "Tempel und Schöpfung," 62.
[53] This correspondence is emphasized by NIHAN, *From Priestly Torah*, 55.

magical forces, he participates in YHWH's demonstration of power. He competes with and defeats the Egyptian magicians and thus takes over the role occupied by Moses in the non-P story (while the latter occasionally still exercising this role too). Aaron's role is probably parallel to that of his Egyptian competitors, the חרטמים, "soothsayer priests, magicians."[54] Like them, Aaron is a priest with magic abilities, although there are certain differences in their actions. The Egyptian magicians perform the miracles בלהטיהם, "with their enchantments" (7:11, 22; 8:3, 14), whereas Aaron acts on instruction received by Moses, who received it from YHWH.

As shown above, the motif of Aaron's assistance to Moses in Exod 1–12 was probably introduced by the author of the Priestly miracle account in Exod 7–11.[55] It was only later that the motif was taken up by non-Priestly authors and inserted in both the non-Priestly plague story in Exod 7–11 and the non-Priestly stratum of Exod 4–5. In the following parts of the book of Exodus as well, Aaron is mentioned in both Priestly and non-Priestly texts. This raises the question whether Aaron was first introduced into the book of Exodus by the Priestly author(s) or whether P took up an existing non-P tradition about Aaron. Scholars often consider the brief mentions of Aaron in Exod 15:20; 17:8–13, 18 and 24:14 to stem from old pre-Priestly traditions.[56] The mention of Nadab and Abihu, Aaron's two firstborn sons, in Exod 24:1, 9 would also reflect an ancient tradition (preserved in E or JE).[57] Similarly, the story of Israel's apostasy with the golden bull in Exod 32, in which Aaron plays a central role, has traditionally been considered pre-Priestly. Several recent treatments, however, offer good arguments for classifying at least some of these texts as post-Priestly.

In Exod 15:20 Miriam is, surprisingly, introduced as sister of Aaron alone, whereas one would expect the specification "sister of Moses and Aaron." Therefore Noth and Kratz consider here an "ancient" place of Aaron before his depiction as priest in P.[58] Yet, as argued above, there are indications that the song of Miriam is a post-Priestly composition; therefore, one might see in this specification a polemical hint in favor of Aaron and against Moses.[59]

The short story on Israel's victory against the Amalekites in Exod 17:8–13 presents some puzzling features, as has been shown in recent publications by C. Berner and J. Jeon.[60] Joshua appears out of the blue as military leader just as in the book of Joshua and organizes an ad-hoc army of the people which is capable to withstand the warlike tribe of the Amalekites. This picture contrasts with the reminiscence of the conflict found in Deut 25:17–18 that reports Amalek's

---

[54] See above, II.7.4 (a).

[55] See above, II.7.5 (c).

[56] NOTH, *Überlieferungsgeschichte*, 196; A. CODY, *A History of Old Testament Priesthood*, AnBib 35 (Rome: Pontifical Biblical Institute, 1969), 146–56; VALENTIN, *Aaron: Eine Studie zur vorpriesterschriftlichen Aaron-Überlieferung*, OBO 18 (Fribourg: Presses Universitaires; Göttingen: Vandenhoeck & Ruprecht, 1978), 198–203; BLUM, *Studien*, 362.

[57] See for instance PROPP, *Exodus 19–40*, 292–93.

[58] NOTH, *Überlieferungsgeschichte*, 197–98, with n. 506; KRATZ, *Composition*, 288, n. 55.

[59] See above, II.8.6.

[60] See BERNER, "Das Wasserwunder von Rephidim," 208–9; J. JEON, "Egyptian Iconography and the Battle with Amalek (Exodus 17:8–16) Revisited," *Sem* 61 (2019): 89–115.

villain attack but ignores Israel's victory. It is striking that the story assembles the leading figures of the Hexateuch – Moses, Aaron, Joshua (and adds furthermore Hur who may be the ancestor of Bezalel mentioned in the Priestly stratum; cf. Exod 31:2; 35:30; 38:22). These observations favor the idea that the story is an artificial and theological construction, which was composed late.

In Exod 18 Aaron is only briefly mentioned (18:12). Because of its particular style (many speeches; protagonists [YHWH/God, Moses, Jitro] and key words occur in a certain frequency [20 times and 10 times, respectively]) and its theology (Moses' Midianite family should be declared as YHWH-worshippers), this chapter is considered late (post-Priestly) in some recent studies.[61] The motif that Aaron, the later high priest, is invited to Jethro's feast of Sacrifice probably should enhance the legitimacy of this somewhat unorthodox cultic event.

Aaron appears again in Exod 24 in two different literary contexts. In the passage Exod 24:1, 9–11, Aaron, along with his two sons Nadab and Abihu and the seventy elders, has the privilege of ascending the mountain of God, seeing the deity, and eating before it. Given the language and motifs close to P, Ezekiel and late prophetic texts, recent scholarship assigns the texts to a late, harmonizing Pentateuch redaction that encompasses large portions of the Pentateuch.[62] It is indeed striking that the text simultaneously glorifies the elders and the Aaronide priests. Since the names Nadab and Abihu allude to the unlucky (Abijah) and negatively connoted (Nadab) sons of Jeroboam I, the texts in Exodus evoking them (Exod 6:23; 24:1, 9; 28:1b) most probably presuppose the anti-Jeroboam polemic in Exod 32. The aforementioned texts counter the apostasy story of Exod 32 by putting Aaron, Nadab, and Abihu in a positive light by assigning important roles to them at crucial moments in the wilderness episode. In Exod 24:13–14 Aaron offices together with Hur as judge during Moses' absence. Probably this motif is influenced by both Aaron and Hur's simultaneous mention in Exod 17:8–13 and by Jethro's suggestion that Moses delegate juridical tasks to selected men in Exod 18.

As for the story of Israel's apostasy in Exod 32, there are reasons to consider it a polemical reaction to the Priestly tabernacle account (see above II.10.10.2.).

Was Aaron invented by the Priestly author(s)? Aaron as a fictional figure would match the imaginary tabernacle.[63] If correct, it would be worth considering Hanna Liss's idea that Aaron is an artificial name, built on the Hebrew designation of the ark, אָרוֹן, by insertion of a ה (on analogy to Abraham's name).[64] The choice of this particular artificial name for the priesthood's eponym would make sense given the importance of the ark in the tabernacle account. The ark, together with the "cover" and the cherubim, is the first piece of furniture to be fabricated and the place where YHWH meets with Moses (see Exod 25:10–22).

---

[61] See KRATZ, *Composition*, 281.289; ALBERTZ, *Exodus 1–18*, 299–301.

[62] See J. L. SKA, "Le repas d'Ex 24,11," *Bib* 74 (1993), 305–27; OTTO, "Die nachpriesterliche Pentateuchredaktion," 80.

[63] Also OTTO, *Deuteronomium 1–11*, 1:992 assumes the fictional character of the Aaron figure in P.

[64] See MATHYS, "Künstliche Personennamen im Alten Testament," 221: "Mündliche Mitteilung von Hanna Liss, Heidelberg: אַהֲרֹן ist um ה erweitertes אָרוֹן ('Lade'); sie verweist auf die Parallele von Abram und Abraham hin."

(3) Chronological Information

The Priestly strand contains considerable chronological information, in particular statements about the ages of the ancestors. As shown in detail above, this material appears predominantly in the book of Genesis and in Exod 1–12 and is part of a comprehensive chronological framework that covers Gen 1–1 Kgs 6. The period from Abraham's birth to the construction of the temple of Solomon lasts precisely 1,200 years. Israel departs from Egypt exactly 720 years after Abraham's birth. Israel's stay in Egypt lasts 430 years, and the length of the ancestor's sojourn in land of Canaan amounts precisely a half of it (215 years).[65]

It is significant that the first (inserted) part of the chronological designation in 1 Kgs 6:1aα has the same shape as the chronological statements in Genesis and Exodus.

1 Kings 6:1aα

ויהי בשמונים שנה וארבע מאות שנה לצאת בני ישראל מארץ מצרים[1aα]

[1aα] In the four hundred and eightieth year [lit., in the eightieth year and in the four hundredth year] after the Israelites left the land of Egypt,

A striking shared characteristic is the repetition of the noun *year* (שנה), which is almost consistently used for multiunit numbers in the relevant Priestly texts.[66] Significantly, this particular spelling does not occur again in 1–2 Kings or elsewhere in the Former Prophets.[67] It is also absent from Priestly texts, which are generally attributed to a secondary Priestly stratum (Gen 47:9; Exod 6:16, 18, 20). *Prima vista*, one should conclude from this observation that the chronological designation in 1 Kgs 6:1aα (up to מצרים) stems from the same author as the other chronological notices and not from the so-called Deuteronomist, as Noth and many commentators have suggested.[68] But more important than this question is the observation that this chronologi-

---

[65] See I.2.5.

[66] Chronological statements with multiunit numbers appear in the following Priestly texts: Gen 5:3, 5, 6, 7, 8, 10, 11, 13, 14, 16, 17, 18, 20, 21, 23, 25, 26, 27, 28, 30, 31; 9:28, 29; 11:13, 12, 15, 16, 17, 19, 20, 21, 24, 25, 32; 12:4; 16:16; 17:1; 23:1; 25:7, 17; 35:28; 37:2; 47:28 (2×); Exod 12:40, 41. In most instances, the term שנה, "year" / שנים, "years," appears twice or three times (after each digit). There are only few exceptions: in Gen 5:3, 21; 11:12, 16, 20, 24 the term שנה "year" is used only once. As for the statements in 37:2; 47:28, which both contain the number seventeen (שבע עשרה), the deviation is to be explained by the genitive construction: the two digits are closely connected. – The particular spelling with the repetition of the noun *year* is shared by SP but is lacking consistently in LXX. The deviation in LXX should most probably be attributed to the translators, who in this case resisted a literal translation.

[67] Chronological statements are numerous in the books Judges, 1–2 Samuel, and in particular in 1–2 Kings (cf. the chronological information in the regnal formulae). Multiunit numbers appear in Joshua 14:10 (2×); 24:29; Judg 2:8; 3:14; 10:2, 3, 8; 2 Sam 5:5; 1 Kgs 2:11; 6:38; 7:1; 14:20, 21 (2×); 15:1, 10, 33; 16:8, 10, 15, 23 (2×), 29 (2×) *et passim*. In each of these texts the term שנה / שנים appears only once.

[68] See Noth, *Überlieferungsgeschichtliche Studien*, 18–27; idem, *Könige*, BKAT 11 (Neukirchen-Vluyn: Neukirchener Verlag, 1968), 110; Würthwein, *Die Bücher der Könige*, 62; Fritz, *Das erste Buch der Könige*, ZBK 10.1 (Zurich: TVZ, 1996), 68–69; Koenen, "1200 Jahre," 504.

cal system is based on chronological indications in Genesis and Exodus, *all* of which
are assigned to the Priestly composition (or Priestly *Grundschrift*), as it is delimited
by most scholars.[69] The notice in 1 Kings 6:1aα is a part of this system, or, to put it
more accurately, it is its *aim* (as indicated by the round period of 1,200 years between
Abraham's birth and Solomon's construction of the temple). Further support for the
idea that P[C]'s chronological system is related to 1–2 Kings comes from the choice of
430 years in Exod 12:40, 41 MT for the period of Israel's stay in Egypt.[70] This number
of years is surprising first because of the extraordinary length of the period (which
cannot be deduced form the plot[71]) and second because it is not a round and theologically meaningful number. The only possible reference point within the Hebrew Bible
is the calculation from the regnal formulae in the books of Kings, according to which
the period from Solomon's building of the temple to the capture of Jerusalem and end
of the Judean monarchy lasted 430 years. The correspondence between the two periods probably is not accidental.[72]

One might object that the information in Exod 12:40–41 is not shared by SP and LXX, that LXX
deviates from MT in 1 Kgs 6:1aα, and furthermore that the calculation of the period between
the construction of the temple and Jerusalem's capture is based uniquely on MT. Nevertheless, it
seems that MT has preserved the original indications of a chronological system, most elements
of which also appear in the other main textual witnesses. With the exception of the indications
in Exod 12:40–41 and 1 Kgs 6:1aα, LXX and SP share all relevant numbers with MT.[73] In the
case of Exod 12:40–41 the alternative reading of SP and LXX (the 430 years encompass the Israel's sojourning in both Canaan and Egypt) can easily be explained as a harmonization with the
information in Exod 6:16–25 (P[S]).[74] As for the notice in 1 Kgs 6:1aα, the alternative reading of
LXX may be explained by the intention of the translator (the scribe of LXX *Vorlage*) to move the
aim of the referential system from the reign of the flawed Solomon to the brave Asa (according
to LXX, Asa's instauration took place precisely five hundred years after Israel's exodus).[75] Furthermore, several among the mentioned numbers are not round and theologically meaningful,
namely, 75, 60, 17, 147, and 430.[76] They seem to make sense only as elements of a chronological
system aimed toward a specific key event like the one mentioned in 1 Kgs 6:1a.

---

[69] See I.2 (5) and II.6.4 (a).

[70] Concerning the textual problem, see above, II.7.2 (e), (f).

[71] Perhaps the indication even contradicts the latter: according to Exod 2:1 (presupposed by
P[C]), whose meaning is highly disputed however, the mother of Moses seems to be a daughter of
Levi; if so, only three generations lie between Jacob and Moses (see SCHMID, *Genesis and the
Moses Story*, 5 [here "grandchild of Levi" should be replaced by "child of Levi" or "daughter of
Levi"], 141).

[72] KOENEN, "1200 Jahre," 198–99. A connection between the indication in Exod 12:40–41 and
the period between the construction of Solomon's temple and its destruction is also assumed in
J. BARR, "Why the World Was Created in 4004 BC: Archbishop Ussher and Biblical Chronology," *BJRL* 67 (1984): 589, and SCHMID, *Genesis and the Moses Story*, 18, 130.

[73] Gen 12:4; 16:16; 17:1; 21:5; 25:26; 47:28.

[74] See, above, II.7.2 (e), (f).

[75] See, above, I.2.5.

[76] See Gen 25:26; 47:28; Exod 12:40–41 (the number 430 is shared by all three main textual
witness).

But what is the reason for the parallel between Israel's stay in Egypt and the duration of the First Temple (denoted by the identical length of the two periods)? In both cases, the 430 years mark a period of *monarchic rule*. Since Israel's stay in Egypt – after Joseph's death – is marked by the people's bondage in service to Pharaoh, the Egyptian king, might it be that the Priestly author depicted Israel and Judah's monarchies negatively? Gen 17:6, 16; 35:11; 36:31, predict or state the emergence of the kingdoms of Israel, Judah, and Edom. One may detect a historiographic interest in these statements and perhaps also a positive estimation of the two kingdoms. It is, however, important to note that since, according to our analysis, three of these statements belong to the proto-Priestly Abraham narrative, they are not necessarily significant for the theology of P^C. More relevant in this respect are other motifs found in its "core text," the tabernacle account, which may indeed indicate a critical distance toward the monarchy as an institution. First, the donation offering in Exod 25:1–7*, which is a voluntary endowment, probably intentionally contrasts with Solomon's enforced labor and taxation to build his temple (1 Kgs 5:27–30; 10:14).[77] Likewise, Aaron's majestic attire, described at length in Exodus 28 and reminiscent of the vestments of the Judean king in several respects, might reflect an antimonarchical stance on the part of P^C.[78] The Priestly authors were opposed to the idea that a Judean king would exercise authority over temple and cultic affairs, as it was practiced in the monarchic era. Paralleled are the temple being under the jurisdiction of the king on the one hand and Israel being under the dominion of the Pharaoh on the other. This astonishing juxtaposition may have been influenced by the blanket negative assessment of the Israelite and Judean kingships at the end of the book of Kings (see 2 Kgs 23:32, 37). Looking at it that way, the parallel between Israel's stay in Egypt on the one hand and Israel's and Judah's monarchies on the other seems deliberate and meaningful.

(4) The Passover Festival

By letting the Israelites celebrate Passover just before leaving Egypt (see Exod 12:1–13), the Priestly author (P^C) takes up the historical setting given to the Passover festival by Deuteronomy (see Deut 16:1–8). In response to the latter text, which has transferred the celebration of Passover to the central sanctuary, P^C passes it back into the domain of the family, in agreement with the presumably common ancient custom.[79] In so doing, P^C was certainly considering the situation of the Judeans living in exile, either in Babylonia or Egypt, far away from Jerusalem. Another difference from Deut 16:1–8 is the specification of the day of celebration (fourteenth day of the first month). This date probably refers to the full moon. However, the day is rather casually mentioned (in the context of preparation of the lamb) and with no specific designation referring

---

[77] See above, II.10.7.2.
[78] See above, II.10.9.
[79] Cf. ALBERTZ, *Exodus 1–18*, 212–13.

to the full moon. This fits the absence of a specific designation for the month (in Deut 16, the traditional name חדש האביב, "month of the ears," is used).

1.2.3 The Extent of the Priestly Composition

Because the analysis herein has been limited to the Priestly texts in Gen 1–Exod 40, the questions concerning aim, extent, and setting can only be answered preliminarily. The preceding section showed that the Priestly composition evokes several themes, including the growth of the people, the gift of the land, the promise of kingdoms, and the revelation of God's true name to Israel. The main theme, however, at least regarding the length of the corresponding texts, is the constitution of Israel's cult and its priesthood at Sinai. Even if one were open to the view that the primary Priestly stratum (P^c) has additional narrative goals, such as the death of Moses (cf. Deut 34:7) and the subduing of the land of Canaan (Josh 18:1), one would still have to acknowledge that these are not pursued with the same focus and urgency as is the Priestly Sinai legislation. Furthermore, whereas the aforementioned narrative aims (the death of Moses, the control and possession of the land) are also present in non-P texts, the Priestly core – the tabernacle account and the sacrificial legislation – is P^c's *proprium*. Moreover, as L. Perlitt has shown, the few P-like elements in Deut 34, which reports Moses's view of the land and his death, should be classified post-Priestly.[80] As for the notice in Josh 18:1, it contains terms that are predominantly used in late Priestly texts (as קהל *niphal* and עדה).

With regard to the major focus on the Sinai revelation, one should ask whether this specific theme is taken up beyond the description of the sacrificial cult at Mount Sinai in Exod 25–Lev 3*. This question relates first to certain texts in the book of Numbers, in which the tent of meeting appears frequently and plays an important role, in particular in Num 1–4. However, several motifs and linguistic features of these Priestly texts are reminiscent of the language of the books of Ezra, Nehemiah, and Chronicles. Generally, the P-like texts in Numbers are interested in the relationship between Aaronides, Levites, and elders, whereas the Priestly texts of Genesis and Exodus ignore Levites and elders.[81] For these reasons, a recent tendency among scholars is to assign them to late Priestly or post-Priestly strata.[82]

Texts in the Former Prophets may also be relevant. This possibility is further suggested by P^c's literary profile as a redaction. As redactors, the Priestly authors were also able to compose texts for books that were "distant" from the core of P^c in the

---

[80] See PERLITT, "Priesterschrift im Deuteronomium?," 65–87, in particular the meticulous examination of Deut 34:7–8 (containing the indication of the years of Moses life and the days of his lamentation by the Israelites), which is traditionnally assigned to P, in 77–80.

[81] See ACHENBACH, *Die Vollendung*, esp. 141–72.

[82] See, among others, POLA, *Die ursprüngliche Priesterschrift*, 51–99; BAUKS, "Genesis 1," 345; ACHENBACH, *Die Vollendung*; NIHAN, *From Priestly Torah*, 20–30; RÖMER, "Der Pentateuch," 141, 144–45.

Sinai pericope; in such cases, the narrative connection was assured by the non-Priestly strand. For example, the Priestly chronological designation in 1 Kgs 6:1aα is located at a considerable remove from P^C's center, raising the question whether other texts in the Former Prophets that share certain linguistic and ideological characteristics with Priestly texts might also belong to the first Priestly redaction. Such texts marked by Priestly language (sometimes late Priestly language) include those referring to the presence of the tent of meeting at Shiloh or Jerusalem (Josh 18:1; 19:51; 1 Sam 2:22 MT; 1 Kgs 8:4); the connectedness of the ark with YHWH's glory in 1 Sam 4:21–22; YHWH's statement that he has not dwelt in a house but has moved about "in tent and tabernacle" (2 Sam 7:6–7); and the ark's move to the temple (1 Kgs 8:1–11, esp. 8:4, 6–8, 10–11). Thematically, these texts are linked to the tabernacle account as the "core text" of the P^C in that they demonstrate the continuity of legitimate Yahwistic worship established at Sinai into the period of the Israelite and Judean monarchies and beyond. In particular, the passage in 1 Kgs 8:1–11, which appears in close proximity to 1 Kgs 6:1, deserves attention. It contains several typical Priestly motifs, expressions, and even entire sentences. Most commentators generally qualify them as "Priestly-like," "im Sinn der Priesterschrift," or "Priestly revision."[83]

Most scholars, however, fail to specify the literary classification of 1 Kgs 8:1–11 further, in particular to define their relationship to the Priestly texts in the Pentateuch.[84] Remarkable parallels with the tabernacle account are as follows:[85]

The motif of cherubim spreading their wings upon the ark and protecting it appears only here and in the tabernacle account (cf. 8:6–7 with Exod 25:18–20). In contrast to the arrangement of the Solomonic temple according to 8:6–7, where the griffins and the ark are clearly separated one from the other, in the tabernacle account the cherubim protrude from the *kappōret* and are perhaps formed from a single ingot. How are the two texts related to one another? 1 Kings 8:6(–7) is often considered to belong to the ancient kernel of the report of the ark's move to the temple. The connection between cherubim and ark is probably already pre-Priestly, as it also appears in the ark account.[86] Possibly the author of the tabernacle account was influenced by the conception of 1 Kgs 8:6–7, although he "simplified" the imagery and reduced the size of the cherubim. The particular interest given to the poles of the ark in 1 Kgs 8:8 has struck commentators.[87]

---

[83] See NOTH, *Könige*, 178–81; WÜRTHWEIN, *Die Bücher der Könige*, 84–88; FRITZ, *Das erste Buch der Könige*, 87; M. COGAN, *I Kings: A New Translation with Introduction and Commentary*, AB 10 (New York: Doubleday, 2001), 278–81; M. A. SWEENEY, *I and II Kings: A Commentary*, OTL (Louisville: Westminster John Knox, 2007), 131.

[84] An exception is Achenbach, who assigns most of the mentioned texts to his "theocratic redaction" ("theokratische Bearbeitung"); see R. ACHENBACH, "Der Pentateuch, seine theokratischen Bearbeitungen und Josua–2 Könige," in *Les Dernières Rédactions du Pentateuque, de l'Hexateuque et de l'Ennéateuque*, ed. T. Römer and K. Schmid, BETL 203 (Leuven: Peeters, 2007), 225–34.

[85] See J. HUTZLI, "Priestly(-like) Texts in Samuel and Kings."

[86] See in particular 2 Sam 6:2, where the reference to "YHWH of hosts who is enthroned above the cherubim" seems well anchored in the story.

[87] See NOTH, *Könige*, 179–80; WÜRTHWEIN, *Die Bücher der Könige*, 87; FRITZ, *Das erste Buch der Könige*, 87; COGAN, *1 Kings*, 250.

Again, this interest also appears in Exod 25:11–15. The statement that they "are there until this day" in 1 Kgs 8:8 (MT) and the instruction in Exod 25:15 (MT, SP) that the poles should never be removed from the rings of the ark are probably related to each other.[88] 1 Kings 8:8 is often considered a secondary insertion into its context. The expression קדש, "sanctuary," which also appears in 8:10 and in several Priestly texts, may favor assignment to a Priestly or post-Priestly stratum.[89]

The short, climactic report in 1 Kgs 8:10–11, which describes the filling of the temple by the cloud and the glory of YHWH, relies on expressions and motifs found in the Priestly text Exod 40:34–35 (namely, מלא, "to fill"; יכל, "to be able"; כבוד יהוה, "the glory of YHWH"). Probably it was influenced by the latter text, as is commonly assumed.[90] The question arises, however, in which time interval to the "source" text the passage in Kgs 8:10–11 was written. Could it have been written by the same circle of authors?

To my knowledge, short Priestly passages like those in 1 Kgs 6:1aα or 1 Kgs 8:10–11 are never assigned to P^G/P^C (nor to P^S). However, P^C's obvious (but not uncritical) focus on the temple of Jerusalem raises the question whether Priestly authors would not have taken a natural interest in intervening in the historic books of the Hebrew Bible and in particular in the report of the construction of Solomon's temple in 1 Kgs 6–8. Scholars working on Priestly texts and defending the source model will have difficult time accepting the idea that the Priestly composition reached 1–2 Samuel and 1 Kings because, in these books, texts with Priestly characteristics are rare and, of course, do not form a continuous strand. But scholars who consider P a redaction layer may be more open to such a conclusion.[91]

1.2.4 Purpose (Aim) of P^C

What is the purpose of the Priestly narrative and its center, the establishment of the cult and the Aaronide priesthood? Generally, as shown above, European and American scholars see in P^G/P^C an attempt to legitimize the Aaronide priesthood and to provide the cultic constitution of the Second Temple in Jerusalem. The composition

---

[88] Interestingly, the statement in 1 Kgs 8:8 is absent from LXX. Was it left out because a scribe of LXX *Vorlage* or the translator was aware that the ark was no longer present in the temple? On account of this blatant contradiction, it seems unlikely that a scribe of MT would have added the plus.

[89] See HUTZLI, "Priestly(-like) Texts in Samuel and Kings," 229. קדש meaning "sanctuary" is predominantly used in Priestly texts and Ezekiel (cf. Exod 26:33; 28:29, 35, 43; 29:30; 31:11; 35:19; 39:1, 41; Lev 4:6; 6:23; 10:4, 18; 16:2, 3, 16, 17, 20, 23, 27; Num 4:12; 8:19; 28:7; Ezek 41:21, 23; 42:13, 14; 44:19, 27; 45:2; 46:19; Ps 60:8; 68:18, 25; 74:3; 134:2; 2 Chr 5:11; 29:5, 7; 35:5).

[90] See NOTH, *Könige*, 180–81; WÜRTHWEIN, *Die Bücher der Könige*, 88; FRITZ, *Das erste Buch der Könige*, 87; COGAN, *I Kings*, 278–81; SWEENEY, *I and II Kings*, 131.

[91] Both the "classical" delimitation (Gen 1–Deut 34) and the more restricted demarcation proposed by recent European treatments (Gen 1–Exod 40/Lev 16) seem to be established according to criteria that fit the source model. One such important criterion was (is) the quantitative presence of Priestly texts and their mutual connectedness in a certain section. When following the redaction model, however, this criterion is less important.

of P^C should be understood against the background of the struggle between different priesthoods in the exilic and postexilic periods. An important aspect of this question pertains to the provenance of the Aaronides. Certain indications raise doubts about the antiquity of the so-called Aaronide priesthood. It is indeed difficult to find traces of a preexilic or exilic Aaronide priesthood in the Hebrew Bible.[92] There are certain indications favoring the idea that Aaron was unknown in the pre-Priestly exodus-Sinai texts (see above).[93] Polemical texts in the Hebrew Bible dealing with or alluding to struggles in which Aaron as high priest is involved all seem to presuppose P^C's introduction of Aaron as priest in Exod 28.

As shown above, one such text is Exod 32, which depicts Aaron as an apostate priest.[94] It is a polemical reaction to the Priestly tabernacle account, which assigns Aaron and his family the central role in the Sinai cult legislation. In 32:26–29, Aaron is superseded and replaced by the Levites. If this latter passage belongs to the primary story, then this anti-Aaronide tendency goes along with a marked pro-Levite bias.[95] As for the association with Bethel and the kingship of Jeroboam I in Exod 32, these do not necessarily hint at the existence of a time-honored Aaron tradition at Bethel but likely, as has been shown above, have other causes.[96]

In the book of Numbers, the hierarchical relationship between Aaron and the Levites is a major theme. A majority of European scholars agree in classifying the relevant texts as post-Priestly too.[97]

Strikingly, outside of the Pentateuch, Aaron and his sons appear only in late postexilic writings (Chronicles, Ezra, Nehemiah, a few psalms) and in a few presumably late assertions (insertions) in other books (Josh 21:19; 24:5, 33; Judg 20:28; 1 Sam 12:6, 8; Mic 6:4).[98] Accord-

---

[92] See J. BLENKINSOPP, "The Judean Priesthood," *CBQ* 60 (1998): 37; E. OTTO, "Priestertum II, Religionsgeschichtlich 1., Alter Orient und Altes Testament," *RGG* 6:1648; and see further below, and further below.

[93] See above, II.7.5 (c) and III.1.2.2 (b) (2).

[94] See above, II.10.10.2.

[95] See SAMUEL, *Von Priestern zum Patriarchen*, 278–80.

[96] See above, II.10.10.2.

[97] See above, III.1.2.3, n. 82.

[98] A detailed discussion of these texts, which are generally considered late, cannot be provided within the scope of this paragraph. For Josh 21:19; 24:5, 33 see ACHENBACH, "Der Pentateuch, seine theokratischen Bearbeitungen," 235–37; for Judg 20:28 see IDEM, "Der Pentateuch, seine theokratischen Bearbeitungen," 241; U. BECKER, *Richterzeit und Königtum: Redaktionsgeschichtliche Studien zum Richterbuch*, BZAW 192 (Berlin: de Gruyter, 1990), 276–77. Josh 24:33 and Judg 20:28 are probably conceptually related to the late Phinehas texts in Exod 6:14–27 and Num 25 (see above II.7.3 [c]). 1 Sam 12:6, 8 should be seen in connection with the similar statement in Joshua 24:5. Both texts obviously depend on the Priestly texts in the Pentateuch, see E. AURELIUS, *Zukunft jenseits des Gerichts: Eine redaktionsgeschichtliche Studie zum Enneateuch*, BZAW 319 (Berlin: de Gruyter, 2003), 180–82. The same holds true for YHWH's sending of Moses, Aaron and Miriam in Mic 6:4, which is worded the same as the commission given to Moses and Aaron in Josh 24:5 and 1Sam 12:8 (identical formulation with שלח). The inclusion of Miriam (cf. 1Chr 5:29) may indicate that Mic 6:4 is still later than the two former texts. Significantly, the pericope Micah 6:3–5 follows the pattern of enumerating a selection of YHWH's salvation acts apparent in both Josh 24:2–13 and 1Sam 12:6–13, see H. UTZSCHNEIDER, *Micha*, ZBK 24.1 (Zurich: TVZ, 2005), 43. As for the larger section Mic 6:1–8, scholars consider

ing to a few critics, the oracle of the anonymous "man of God" in 1 Sam 2:27–36 would have a pro-Zadokite and anti-Aaronite tendency.[99] However, a close reading of this pericope reveals that whereas a pro-Zadokite bias in this text is obvious (see 2:35–36), the Aaronides are absent from it.[100] In Chronicles, Ezra, and Nehemiah, the Aaronides are connected with the Zadokite genealogy.

This silence on Aaron and the Aaronides in preexilic texts gives the impression that the Aaronides appear out of the blue. Their sudden emergence may favor the idea that Aaron was an imaginary figure invented in order to provide better legitimation for a certain priesthood, most probably, as hinted at in particular by the tabernacle account, that of the second Jerusalem temple.

According to a widespread view, P[G]/P[C] focuses on the temple of Jerusalem and the organization of its cult in the late Neo-Babylonian or early Persian era. The aim of the Priestly composition was to offer the constitution of the sacrificial cult in the planned or previously built Second Temple of Jerusalem. There are, as shown above, indeed remarkable parallels between the Priestly wilderness sanctuary and the report of the building of the temple in 1 Kgs 6–7, revealing an implicit focus of the tabernacle account on the Jerusalem temple.[101] Furthermore, the coordinated chronological information scattered throughout the Priestly texts in Genesis–Exodus and including that in 1 Kgs 6:1aα points to the construction of the Jerusalem temple "480 years after the exodus" and 1,200 years after Abraham's birth. It does not seem possible to dissociate the relevant chronological texts from the Priestly stratum.

---

it a late "Deuteronomistic" redaction because of several linguistic and thematic communalities with texts in the Former Prophets, see H. W. WOLFF, *Dodekapropheton 4: Micha*, BK 14.4 (Neukirchen-Vluyn: Neukirchener Verlag, 1985), 142–45; J. WÖHRLE, *Die frühen Sammlungen des Zwölfprophetenbuches: Entstehung und Komposition*, BZAW 360 (Berlin: de Gruyter, 2006).

[99] R. ACHENBACH, "Levitische Priester und Leviten im Deuteronomium: Überlegungen zur sog. 'Levitisierung' des Priestertums," *ZABR* 5 (1999): 302, with n. 59; R. P. GORDON, *1 & 2 Samuel: A Commentary* (Grand Rapids: Zondervan, 1999), 85.

[100] The oracle is directed against the "house of Levi" rather than against Aaron. The statement in 2:28 identifies the condemned "house of Eli" with the tribe of Levi. This becomes evident from its clear intertextual reference to the statement in Deut 18:5 about the election of the Levites (cf. 1 Sam 2:28aα: "And I chose [בחר] him out of all the tribes of Israel [מכל שבטי ישראל]" with Deut 18:5a: "For YHWH your God has chosen [בחר] him out of all your tribes [מכל שבטיך]"). The father of the "house of Eli" is Levi. Moreover, the expression of YHWH's "revelation to the house of Eli's father" (2:27) probably alludes to the story of YHWH's revelation to Moses in Exod 2–4*; Moses is designated as a "man of the house of Levi" in Exod 2:1. Note furthermore that the circumstantial phrase "when they were (slaves) in Egypt" in 1 Sam 2:27 precludes a reference to Aaron, who was, according to P's presentation, elected as high priest *after* Israel left Egypt. The following scholars recognize in this section an anti-Levitical tendency: P. MOMMER, *Samuel: Geschichte und Überlieferung*, WMANT 63 (Neukirchen-Vluyn: Neukirchener Verlag, 1991), 9; HUTZLI, *Die Erzählung von Hanna und Samuel*, 167–82; RÜCKL, *Sure House*, 192–231; N. MACDONALD, "David's Two Priests," in *Writing, Rewriting, and Overwriting in the Books of Deuteronomy and the Former Prophets. Essays in Honour of Cynthia Edenburg*, ed. I. Koch, T. Römer, and O. Sergi, BETL 304 (Leuven: Peeters, 2019), 243–47.

[101] See above, II.10.7.2, II.10.8.1.

Recently, however, a few scholars have argued that P^C's founding myth of the sanctuary aimed to apply not only to Jerusalem but also to other Yahwistic sanctuaries, for example at Gerizim or Bethel. However, as shown above, the arguments put forward by these scholars do not necessarily favor such a conclusion.[102] The location of the tabernacle, Israel's first sanctuary, in the wilderness of Sinai need not be interpreted as taking a neutral stance toward competing sanctuaries but rather can be explained by the need to better legitimate the Jerusalem priesthood by anchoring it in the exodus tradition. P^C's focus on Israel as a whole, with its emphasis on Israel's diversity (cf. the recurrent motif of the twelve tribes) and its two main components (Israel and Judah; cf. Gen 28:3; 35:11), does not stand in contradiction to the concept of a centralized cult in Jerusalem (a similar theology is found in 1–2 Chronicles).[103]

With regard to the seemingly central role given to Bethel in Gen 35:9–15, scholars see the Aaronides in close relation to the priesthood of Bethel. It is indeed the only place where concrete cultic activity before the Sinai pericope happens in P (see Gen 35:14–15).[104] Yet Blum's careful analysis of 35:11–15 makes it likely that the latter is reacting instead to the Bethel etiology in Gen 28 and reformulating Bethel's status as place of revelation. Bethel is not the place of YHWH's dwelling but just a place where the deity "spoke" to Jacob and afterward departed from it.[105]

In conclusion, one can state that P^C's intention is to offer a historical foundation and constitution for the Second Temple of Jerusalem and its cult. This sanctuary, however, was intended to serve as the unique sanctuary of the inhabitants of both Judah and Israel (Samaria), who together formed one unique קהל ("cultic assembly").

1.2.5 Possible Historical Location

Most European and American scholars agree on the approximate setting of P^G/P^C in the late Babylonian or early Persian era. The vagueness in dating is bound up with the fact that the central contents of the Priestly composition lack clear historical references. Nevertheless, certain motifs hint at a setting in the Persian era. As shown in detail above in the analysis of the tabernacle account, the importance given to the high priest and the absence of a royal figure in P's constitution of Israel's cult matches well with the time of damped or lost hope for a restoration of the Judean monarchy after the disappearance (deposition?) of Zerubbabel, governor and Davidic heir (end of sixth or beginning of fifth century BCE).[106] In this situation, the Jerusalemite priesthood and in particular the high priest may have aimed to gain influence and power. Earlier texts envisage inner-Judean power relations differently. Significantly, in the

---

[102] See above, II.10.8.2.

[103] Likewise, 1–2 Chronicles focuses on the twelve-tribe Israel, which is centered on the Jerusalem sanctuary.

[104] A. ROFÉ, Introduction, 228–29; GUILLAUME, Land, 183–87.

[105] Cf. BLUM, Die Komposition, 265–70; IDEM, "Noch einmal," 47–50.

[106] See above, II.10.9.

books of Haggai* and Zechariah 1–8* (first redactions), which can be dated to the two
last decades of the sixth century BCE, hopes and expectations are projected on both
the Davidic governor and the high priest (Joshua) or only on the former.[107] The temple
plan in Ezek 40–48, whose primary form may predate P^C, also gives some importance
to the secular, Davidic ruler (נשׂיא, "prince";[108] see also 37:25–38).[109] In this respect one
should furthermore take into account certain particularities of the Priestly texts (P^C),
such as the motif of the twelve tribes of Israel and the presupposition of the larger historical work in Genesis–2 Kings, and its connectedness with certain texts and contents of the latter (conquest of the land; history of the Israelite and Judean kingdoms)
possibly hint at a later period (fifth century BCE). Nevertheless, as for the comparison with Ezek 40–48, one should also consider the possibility that P^C developed its
distinct concept contemporaneously with the former. Such competition between the
two concepts is all the more conceivable since, as stated above, it should be assumed
that the rebuilding of the temple in Jerusalem in reality took longer than most scholars believe on the basis of the indication of Ezra 6:15–18. This would have left enough
time for a debate on different concepts.[110] Note, furthermore, that the two plans agree
on important details, such as orientation and length/width ratio of the temple building (that could have actually corresponded to the plan of the Second Temple).

Furthermore, it is noteworthy that in P^C, the miracle at the sea plays out "in front
of Baal Zaphon" (Exod 14:2), which probably denotes the sanctuary of Zeus Casios
mentioned by Herodotus.[111] The sanctuary of Baal Zaphon/Zeus Casios usually is
identified with Ras Qasrun on the northern coast of Sinai. Apparently, relevant

---

[107] According to recent treatments, the literary history of the relevant textual units shows a
shift from exclusive support for the governor (Zerubbabel) to balanced promoting of both the
governor and the high priest (Joshua). Initially, the oracles of Haggai (primary form of the book)
aimed to legitimize Zerubbabel as ruler in Judea by hinting at his leading role in the foundation and reconstruction of the Second Temple in Jerusalem. The mentions of Joshua the high
priest as an addressee of Haggai's oracles together with Zerubbabel (Hag 1:1, 12, 14; 2:2, 4) most
likely did not belong to the original stratum of the book but instead stem from a later redactor.
See J. Wöhrle, *Die frühen Sammlungen des Zwölfprophetenbuches*, 288–94.319; J. Rückl, "The
Leadership of the Judean Community according to the Book of Haggai," 77–81. In the book of
Zechariah, too, some texts that focus on Joshua's role as high priest seem to stem from later authors or editors, see above II.10.9.

[108] For the understanding of the "prince" in Ezekiel as Davidic ruler, see Zimmerli, *Ezechiel
25–48*, 915–18; Rudnig, *Heilig und profan*, 137–64, in particular 154–64.

[109] The historical setting of Ezekiel's temple constitution is disputed. According to
T. A. Rudnig, *Heilig und profan: Redaktionskritische Studien zu Ez 40–48*, BZAW 287 (Berlin:
de Gruyter, 2000), 194–97, large parts of Ezek 40–48 and 37:25–38 belong to the relatively early
"Gola redaction." In terms of dating, he is very cautious and vague (approximately between 550
and 450 BCE), except for the the temple plan (before 520). For K. Schmid the massive conceptual divergences from the theology of the tabernacle account point to pre-Priestly origins of Ezek
40–48. Opting for a much later date: N. MacDonald, *Priestly Rule: Polemic and Biblical Interpretation in Ezekiel 44*, BZAW 476 (Berlin: de Gruyter, 2015).

[110] See above, II.10.9.

[111] See Herodotus, *Persian Wars* 2:6, 158; 3:5. The historian names a mountain facing Lake

material remains from the Persian era but none from previous periods, have been found at Ras Qasrun.[112]

The question of the geographical setting of P is difficult to answer.[113] According to the above analysis, P^C has a clear, implicit focus on Jerusalem and the rebuilding of its temple in the Persian era. Therefore, it would seem reasonable to assume that it stems from Priestly circles living in Persian-era Jerusalem. But recent archaeological perspectives cast doubt on the notion that Jerusalem was a center of scribal activity and production of biblical writings in the beginning of the Persian period. First, there is almost no evidence of Hebrew inscriptions in Yehud around 586–350 BCE, and, secondly, the province Yehud appears to have been only sparsely populated at this time.[114] Therefore, one might be tempted to assume the Golah in Babylon as the place of origin for the bulk of biblical writings stemming from this period.[115] However, if we assume a later date for P than usually assumed, in the middle of the 5th century BCE, Jerusalem seems more feasible as a place of composition, since political conditions had consolidated, and the return of exiles had led to a modest increase in population in that time. Certain *aegyptiaca* in Priestly texts in Exodus are intriguing; they may be explained by the fact that the circle of authors included returnees from Egypt too.

1.3 Secondary Priestly Redactions (H and P^s)

Regarding linguistic and ideological particularities, several Priestly passages in Gen 1– Exod 40 should not probably be assigned to the Priestly composition outlined above. As for the redaction-historical classification of these texts, it remains partly speculative, given that the latter are mainly linked to texts units outside the books of Genesis– Exodus that could not be investigated in the framework of this study.

The majority of these presumably secondarily inserted texts seem to have been

---

Serbonis in Egypt the "Casian mountain" (Κάσιον ὄρος), pointing to a high sanctuary dedicated to Baal Zaphon, who was called Zeus Casios in Greek.

[112] See G. I. DAVIES, "The Wilderness Itineraries and Recent Archaeological Research," in *Studies in the Pentateuch*, ed. J. A. Emerton, VTSup 41 (Leiden: Brill, 1990), 163–64. Davies quotes (in translation) E. OREN, preliminary report, in *Qadmaniot Sinai (Sinai in Antiquity)*, ed. Z. Meshel and I. Finkelstein (Tel Aviv: Tel Aviv University Press, 1980), 101–58.

[113] Remarkably, among recent studies on P only few address this question. Jerusalem seems often tacitly assumed to be the place of origin. According to de Pury, P was composed in Jerusalem during the last years of Cyrus' reign (see DE PURY, "Der priesterschriftliche Umgang mit der Jakobgeschichte," 49). Wöhrle identifies the Priestly authors with returnees from the Babylonian Golah (see WÖHRLE, *Fremdlinge*, 188–89).

[114] See O. LIPSCHITS, "Persian Period Finds from Jerusalem: Facts and Interpretations," *JHS* 9, art. 20 (2009), doi:10.5508/jhs.2009v9.a20; I. FINKELSTEIN, Jerusalem and Judah 600–200 BCE: Implications for Understanding Pentateuchal Texts, in *The Fall of Jerusalem and the Rise of the Torah*, ed. P. Dubovský, D. Markl and J.-P. Sonnet (eds.), FAT 107 (Tübingen: Mohr Siebeck, 2016), 3–18.

[115] FINKELSTEIN, Jerusalem and Judah 600–200 BCE, 14–5.

influenced by the so-called Holiness Code, both its vocabulary and its theological agenda. These texts include passages validating Abraham's ownership of the burial site at Machpelah (Gen 23 and back references to this text in Gen 25:9–10; 49:29–30, 32; 50:13b), the sequence in Gen 17 dealing with circumcision (vv. 9–14, 23–27), further legislative texts concerning Mazzoth (Exod 12:14–20), and the participation of foreigners in the Passover festival (Exod 12:43–50), and finally the Sabbath theme developed in Exod 16:22–26. Mazzoth together with Passover is declared to be a pilgrimage festival (חג). Certain texts specify the Sabbath as a "strict Sabbath" (שבת שבתון; see Exod 16:23; 31:15; 35:2; Lev 23:3). Specific arguments for the attribution of each of these texts to a second Priestly layer close to H were given in the relevant paragraphs. Precise conclusions concerning the relationship between these texts and H, however, go beyond the framework of the present investigation, which focuses on the Priestly texts in section Gen 1–Exod 40.

There are also some texts that do not have typical features of H but have other characteristics that point to their secondary nature. Because of the absence of striking commonalities which they would share among themselves they are difficult to classify; they are assigned to Pˢ, which however should not be considered a unified stratum within P. Rather it should be used as provisional designation of different sorts of later additions written in the style of Pᶜ.[116] Such a text is the manna story in Exod 16, which is traditionally ascribed to Pᴳ/Pᶜ. Exod 1:1–5, a text with characteristics of P, seems also to have been written at a later time, after the separation of Genesis from Exodus, in order to render the transition smoother.

The Priestly flood story alludes to distinct calendars (a schematic moon calendar and an exact moon calendar combined with a solar calendar). The proto-Priestly flood narrative probably did not contain any chronological designations but was reworked by different redactors. Yet, as most commentators note, the precise and certain differentiation of literary strata on the basis of inconsistencies between the various chronological designations is not possible. The 365-day solar calendar, on which Gen 8:14 is probably based, is also referenced in Gen 5 both through the total of the years of Enoch's life (5:23) and the parallelization with the Mesopotamian ancestor Enmeduranki, who is associated with Sippar, the center of the sun god.

One important question is whether the few statements that cast Moses in a rather negative light (see the motif of Moses's inept speech in Exod 6:12bγ, 30; cf. 14:15) should be ascribed to a secondary Priestly layer (Pˢ). In fact, apart from these statements, Moses is consistently depicted positively in the Priestly composition, in particular in its core parts (the tabernacle account and the sacrificial legislation). Are these passages connected with Priestly texts in the books of Numbers and Deuteronomy dealing with Moses and Aaron's enigmatic offense at Kadesh (see Num 20:1–13) and its consequence (Moses and Aaron are prevented from entering the promised land; they are "replaced" by Joshua on the one hand and Eleazar and Phinehas on the

---

[116] See NIHAN, "Priestly Covenant," 88–89.

other)? The transgression at Kadesh probably lay in Moses's inappropriate question addressed to the assembled Israelites (see Num 20:10) and his twofold striking of the rock (see v. 11). At any rate, Moses's action demonstrated doubt and unbelief to the deity (cf. v. 12). A thorough redaction-critical analysis of this and related texts – Num 20:1–13, 22–29; 27:12–14; Deut 32:50–52; 34:1, 7–9 – is needed in order to answer this question.[117]

A further secondary Priestly stratum is present in Exod 6:14–25; 28:1b; Lev 9; 10; Num 3:2–4; 25; 26:60–61. They throw the particular Aaronide line that leads to Eleazar and to Phinehas into relief. The narrative in Lev 9–10 presupposes the "anti"-Priestly text in Exod 32. These units take up Aaron's association with Bethel present in the latter text. Leviticus 9 subtly rehabilitates Aaron by letting him offer a young bull (עגל) as a sin offering (חטאת) for himself (cf. Lev 9:2, 3, 8). Moreover, Nadab and Abihu, whose names are strikingly reminiscent of the sons of Jeroboam I, Abijah, and Nadab, are probably introduced as an allusion to the apostasy of Exod 32 too. The "creation" and removal of these two figures in Lev 10 give the authors the opportunity to reconceptualize the Aaronide priesthood by putting forward an entirely positive lineage comprising the high priests of the second and third generation, Eleazar and Phinehas. The author(s) of these texts apparently cannot help but "accept" the accusation of apostasy and the Aaronides' association with Jeroboam I in Exod 32. Accordingly, they try to integrate this background into the Priestly plot and to transform it.[118] In some of these texts, Moses seems to be overshadowed or overtaken by the Aaronides (see in particular Exod 6:14–27; Num 25; Lev 10). With regard to their tendency, these units are perhaps correlated with the aforementioned statements that put Moses in an unfavorable light (Exod 6:12bγ, 30; 14:15).

---

[117] In current scholarship they often are ascribed to a late post-Priestly redaction; see KRATZ, *Composition*, 108–12, 207; ACHENBACH, *Die Vollendung*, 302–34 ("Pentateuch redaction"); C. NIHAN, "La mort de Moïse (Nb 20,1–13; 20,22–29; 27,12–23) et l'édition finale du livre des Nombres," in *Les dernières rédactions du Pentateuque, de l'Hexateuque et de l'Ennéateuque*, ed. T. Römer and K. Schmid, BETL 203 (Leuven: Peeters, 2007), 145–82 ("theocratic redaction"). Other scholars consider only single statements about Moses's and Aaron's offense secondary additions (in particular Num 20:12 and 20:24); see FREVEL, *Mit Blick*, 237–44, 306–36; D. FRANKEL, The Murmuring Stories of the *Priestly School: A Retrieval of Ancient Sacerdotal Lore*, VTSup 89 (Leiden: Brill, 2002), 263–312.

[118] A similar strategy can be observed in the fulfillment report of the tabernacle account: by alluding to the Korahites' rebellion (see Num 16–17) in Exod 38:22 (LXX, Monacensis) and (possibly also) to the temple-women episode (see 1 Sam 2:22 MT) in Exod 38:8, the author "acknowledges" these scandalous events. This raises the question whether these allusions are, as often surmised, late insertions into Exod 35–40 or whether they should be ascribed to the base layer of this section. The lack of literary-critical signals and several indications of a late date for the entire section of the fulfillment account make the second possibility more likely. Lev 9–10 and Exod 35–40 presuppose (late) post-Priestly texts and should therefore be assigned to a second Priestly redaction.

2. The Literary Profile of the Priestly Texts in Genesis 1–Exodus 40

The question of literary profile is one of the most hotly debated in current research on the Priestly pentateuchal texts. One should distinguish roughly between three scholarly positions, which are reflected in three distinct models: the source model, the redaction model, and the model reckoning with both source and redactional material. In the following, arguments put forward for each of these models, their merits, and their deficiencies will be discussed in relation to the results of the present investigation.

2.1 Arguments for the Source Model

Important arguments supporting the source theory are as follows:[1] the Priestly texts have a distinct ideological tendency with marked aspects such as strict monotheism, the theology of YHWH's name (YHWH reveals his name only at Sinai), and strict cult centralization (cult and sacrifice begin only in the Sinai wilderness, after the consecration of the tabernacle). Because of P's distinct theological profile, many scholars reject the idea that P was written as a redaction layer built on already-existing non-P compositions that stand in tension with or contradict the Priestly ideological outline. Despite a few incoherences, these distinct *theologoumena* are clearly visible in the Priestly texts of Genesis and Exodus. In addition to a few ideological incongruities, one should note that the Priestly units sometimes deviate from one another linguistically.[2] Nevertheless, the Priestly texts in Genesis and Exodus form a relatively coherent strand with identifiable linguistic, conceptual, and ideological commonalities. Undoubtedly, the distinctiveness of both the linguistic and the ideological outlines of the Priestly composition would fit well with a composition conceived as a *source*. However, certain contradictory evidence favoring the redaction model (see the following paragraph) raises the question whether the authors might nevertheless have conceived their texts as a supplementary layer reacting to theologically distinct texts and aiming to correct them within one and the same work. There is an argument for answering this question affirmatively. One should take into consideration the possibility that the Priestly authors, for certain reasons, wished to contribute to a large "Israelite" account that was destined to be representative of different ideological movements rather than to relegate their writings to a separate document. Even though an independent document would accentuate the Priestly ideological outline, the Priestly authors may have

---

[1] See in the introduction 1.1. (2). Scholars who consider P a source are listed in n. 9.
[2] See the assembled observations above, II.7.4 (b) and III.1.2.1.

preferred to present their composition in the framework of a common already existing normative account and foundation myth in order to give it greater visibility.

A second important argument advanced in favor of the source theory is the fact that in certain sections P and non-P share the same content, creating doublets. Scholars explain this particular element of the textual profile as a result of the combination of the P source with the non-P source by a redactor. Prime examples are the flood narrative in Exod 6–9 and the story of the parting of the sea in Exod 14. In both units, specific content is told twice, by P and by non-P. However, the analyses of these units have shown that alternative explanations are possible and even more appropriate than the model reckoning with the fusion of two sources. For both stories, the present study proposes a model that assumes one source text which was supplemented by redactional additions. In Gen 6–9, the Priestly narrative constitutes the independent base layer, on which the non-Priestly elements were later built. In Exod 14 the situation is different, insofar as neither the Priestly story nor the non-P layer is independent from texts in their environements. There is an indication that the Priestly narrative depends on the larger non-Priestly context: its beginning (Exod 14:1–3) looks back on the non-P itinerary notice in 13:20. At the same time, the non-P passages show signs of depending on the Priestly story. In both cases, Gen 6–9 and Exod 14, the doublets can be explained by the redactor's intention to renarrate certain content found in the base layer in order to correct it ideologically. For instance, by repeating the announcement of the flood, the non-Priestly redactor of Gen 6–8 aimed to specify the cause for the flood (i.e., humanity's evil). The reformulation of God's order to enter the ark gave the redactor occasion to introduce the distinction between clean and unclean animals into the plot. For a similar reason, the sending-out of the raven, an unclean bird, has been "corrected." In non-P the dove, which is considered a clean animal, is sent out. In the story of the parting of the sea, the non-Priestly redactor(s) renarrated the miracle in order to adjust it to the specific YHWH-war theology and to make sure that YHWH rather than Moses is the author of the salvation act.

What supports the source model prima facie is that large sections within the Priestly strand are composed of self-contained units that do not show any significant dependence on the non-Priestly strand. The Priestly primeval narrative is largely independent of the non-Priestly strand. The only exception is Gen 5, which presupposes the non-Priestly story in Gen 4 but was nevertheless conceived for an independent Priestly primeval history. As for the Priestly creation story, Gen 6–9 P, and the Priestly Table of Nations, they all constitute autonomous and self-contained units and do not bear any clear signs of dependence on non-P.

Some scholars nevertheless detect a gap between Gen 1:1–2:4a; 5 on the one hand and the Priestly flood story on the other, because P does not explain the sudden emergence of evil. They argue that the Priestly composition would depend on the non-Priestly story of the fall of mankind in Gen 2–3 non-P.[3] However, in my view, this "gap" is theologically meaningful and

---

[3] See among others Cross, *Canaanite Myth*, 302; Blum, *Studien*, 280.

intended by the author of the proto-Priestly flood narrative: the author used the interaction of the statement "God looked at the earth, and behold: it was corrupt" (6:12a) with the repeated approbation formula of Gen 1 to juxtapose the "bad" condition of the world with the good creation at the beginning, without explaining the massive decline. The author intended to leave the question of how evil entered the world open. This should not be understood as an expression of theological incapacity but may be interpreted as theologically wise restraint and consciousness of the limits of human knowledge.[4]

Similarly, the self-contained Priestly Abraham narrative, its primary stratum, should be considered an autonomous composition, independent from the non-Priestly strand.

Given their elaborate internal structure, the following units in Exodus might be considered "source texts" or *Vorlagen* as well: the story of the five miracles, the story of the parting of the sea, and the tabernacle account. Nevertheless, analysis of these texts has shown that they were probably never connected with one another within an independent and separate Priestly document. There are indications that they were conceived for the larger non-Priestly context (see no. 13 and no. 14 in the table below).

In contrast to these source, or source-like texts, however, there are other sections where the Priestly thread is interrupted here and there and bears clear signs of dependence on non-Priestly texts. This will be demonstrated in the following section.

To sum up this section, although certain aspects of the Priestly texts seem favorable to the source model and there are indications that Priestly units were conceived as autonomous compositions (e.g., Gen 6–9 P), there is no compelling evidence for the model's global validity.

2.2 Arguments for the Redaction Model

Scholars supporting the redaction model point to certain sections of P that show significant dependence on non-P texts. In the sections in question the Priestly texts are sparse, and often they are tightly linked with non-Priestly texts; in a few cases the connection is syntactic in nature. Moreover, the Priestly thread, considered in isolation, is interrupted here and there, presupposing the contents of neighboring non-Priestly texts. These features are visible in particular in the Jacob-Esau and Joseph narratives but also in Exod 1–14. In these sections, P is incomprehensible in several instances without the neighboring non-P texts.

The following table lists the most important Priestly texts that bear signs of strong dependence on non-P texts. All texts in question are assigned to P[G] in Elliger's and Lohfink's compilations, although there is some question about the classification of

---

[4] See OTTO, *Das Gesetz*, 190 and the quotation in n. 446. CARR, *Reading*, 77, and WÖHRLE, *Fremdlinge*, 151, n. 12 do not detect a gap either.

Gen 25:26b by Elliger.[5] For a few among the listed texts scholars have offered alternative classifications (non-P, P^s). They are referred to in table 5.

One can distinguish three levels of dependence:

A: Assertion of P depends syntactically and/or conceptually on the non-P strand; it depends on *specific* information given by the immediate non-Priestly context (e.g., Abraham's departure from Harran in Gen 12:1–4a [cf. no. 1]; the non-P itinerary in Exod 13:20 [cf. no. 13]).

B: Assertion or motif in P depends on commonly known data in non-P (e.g., upheaval of Sodom and Gomorrah [no. 2]; Moses's stay in Egypt [no. 10]).

C: The syntax and contents of the Priestly narrative are coherent, but P "borrows" typical non-P vocabulary, which does not appear elsewhere in Priestly texts (P^c), from neighboring non-P texts (e.g., no. 9, no. 11).

In some of the fourteen cases in table 5, not only are the two texts in question listed (dependent Priestly text, non-Priestly reference text), but also the preceding Priestly text. This way it can be made visible that the P passage in question does not depend on the latter, but only on the non-Priestly text.

---

[5] The lack of any mention of this text in Elliger's compilation is probably due to a typing error: the indication "15b" after "19f" does not make sense (see ELLIGER, "Sinn," 121) and should be replaced by "26b." In Gen 25, verse 26b is the only (possible) Priestly text following vv. 19–20 (P).

Table 5.   Priestly texts depending on non-P: Three levels of dependence

Number of case and Scripture reference	Level of dependence
No. 1: Genesis 12:4b	**= A**
Gen 11:31–32 (P): [31] And Terah took Abram his son, and Lot the son of Haran, his grandson, and Sarai his daughter-in-law, his son Abram's wife; and they went out together from Ur of the Chaldeans in order to enter the land of Canaan; and they went as far as Harran, and settled there. [32] And the days of Terah were two hundred and five years; and Terah died in Harran.	Gen 12:4b (P) depends syntactically on the statement about Abraham's departure in 12:4a (non-P). P has not reported Abraham's departure from Harran.
Gen 12:1–4a (non-P): [1] *YHWH said to Abram, "Go forth from your country, from your relatives, and from your father's house to the land that I will show you. (...)"* [4a] *So Abram went forth as YHWH had spoken to him; and Lot went with him.*	
Gen 12:4b–5 (P): [4b] Abram was seventy-five years old when he departed from Harran. [5] And Abram took Sarai his wife and Lot his nephew, and all their possessions which they had accumulated, and the persons which they had acquired in Harran, and they set out for the land of Canaan; thus they came to the land of Canaan.	
No. 2: Genesis 19:29	**= B**
Gen 17 (P, YHWH's revelation to Abraham): "(...) [21] But my covenant I will establish with Isaac, whom Sarah will bear to you at this set time next year." [22] And when he finished talking with him, God went up from Abraham.	Gen 19:29 (P) presupposes the preceding non-P story about YHWH's destruction of Sodom and Gomorrah and about Lot and his family's rescue in Gen 19.
(Gen 18–19 [non-P], Story of Abraham's hospitality to the three men and YHWH's destruction of Sodom and Gomorrah)	
Gen 19:29 (P): [29] Thus it came about, when God destroyed the cities of the valley, that God remembered Abraham, and sent Lot out of the midst of the overthrow, when he overthrew the cities in which Lot lived.	

Number of case and Scripture reference	Level of dependence

No. 3: Genesis 25:26b

$= A$

Gen 25:20 (P): [20] and Isaac was forty years old when he took Rebekah, the daughter of Bethuel the Aramean of Paddan-aram, the sister of Laban the Aramean, to be his wife.

Gen 25:21–26a (non-P): [21] Isaac pleaded with YHWH on behalf of his wife, because she was barren; and YHWH responded to his plea, and his wife Rebekah conceived. (…) [24] When her days to be delivered were fulfilled, behold, there were twins in her womb. [25] Now the first came forth red, all over like a hairy garment; and they named him Esau. [26a] And afterward his brother came forth with his hand holding on to Esau's heel, so his name was called Jacob,

Gen 25:26b (P): [26b] and Isaac was sixty years old when she gave birth to them.

Gen 25:26b (P) continues the non-P birth story of Jacob and Esau (Gen 25:21–26a), syntactically depending on it.

No. 4: Genesis 31:18

$= A$

Gen 28:8–9 (P): [8] So Esau saw that the daughters of Canaan displeased his father Isaac; [9] and Esau went to Ishmael, and married, besides the wives that he had, Mahalath the daughter of Ishmael, Abraham's son, the sister of Nebaioth.

Gen 28–31 (non-P, Jacob-Laban story): (…) 31:17: [17] Then Jacob arose and put his children and his wives upon camels

Gen 31:18 (P): [18] and he drove away all his livestock and all his possessions which he had accumulated, his acquired livestock which he had accumulated in Paddan-aram, to go to the land of Canaan to his father Isaac.

Since P is silent about Jacob's prosperous sojourn in Paddan-aram, Gen 31:18 (P) presupposes the non-P stories about Jacob's accumulation of livestock in the homeland of Rebecca's family. Moreover, the statement in 31:18 lacks an explicit subject (Jacob); it continues the preceding non-P phrase (Gen 31:17), syntactically depending on it. It is impossible to read 31:18 (P) as the immediate continuation of 28:9 (P).

No. 5: Genesis 41:46a[6]

$= B$

Gen 37:2 (P): [2] Joseph, when seventeen years of age, was pasturing the flock with his brothers while he was still a youth, along with the sons of Bilhah and the sons of Zilpah, his father's wives. And Joseph brought back a bad report about them to their father.

(Gen 37–41 [non-P Joseph story])

Gen 41:46a (P): [46a] Now Joseph was thirty years old when he stood before Pharaoh, king of Egypt.

Since P does not contain a report about Joseph's stay and high position in Egypt, Gen 41:46a (P) is not comprehensible without the information of the non-P Joseph story. Thus, P complements the non-P Joseph story.

---

[6] K. Schmid and T. Römer exclude Gen 41:46a from P[G]. See SCHMID, "So-Called Yahwist," 46–47; RÖMER, "Joseph Story," 198. See the discussion above, II.6.4 (h) (1).

Number of case and Scripture reference	Level of dependence
No. 6: Genesis 46:6	= A

Gen 41:46a (P): [46a] Now Joseph was thirty years old when he stood before Pharaoh, king of Egypt.

Gen 41–46 (non-P, Joseph story): (…) 46:5: [5] And Jacob arose from Beersheba; and the sons of Israel carried their father Jacob and their little ones and their wives, in the wagons which Pharaoh had sent to carry him.

Gen 46:6 (P): [6] And they took their livestock and their possessions which they had accumulated in the land of Canaan, and came to Egypt, Jacob and all his descendants with him.

Since the statement reporting Jacob and his sons' move to Egypt in Gen 46:6 (P) has the unspecified subject "they", it depends syntactically on the preceding non-Priestly context (46:5). The unspecified subject shows furthermore that 46:6 does not fit as the immediate continuation of the previous Priestly text 41:46a.

No. 7: Genesis 49:31	= B

Gen 49:31 (P): [31] "There they buried Abraham and his wife Sarah, there they buried Isaac and his wife Rebekah, and there I buried Leah."

The absence of Rachel's interment in the cave of Machpelah in 49:31 (P) is due to the non-P statement in Gen 35:19 about Rachel's burial "on the way to Ephrat." Obviously, P presupposes this statement.

No. 8: Genesis 49:33	= A

Gen 49:33 (P): [33] When Jacob finished charging his sons, he gathered up his feet into the bed and breathed his last, and was gathered to his people.

Depends on the mention of the bed in non-P (Gen 47:31; 48:2).

No. 9: Exodus 1:7[7]	= C

Exod 1:7 (P): [7] But the Israelites were fruitful and increased greatly, and multiplied, and became mighty (ויעצמו) exceedingly, so that the land was filled with them.

Is influenced by the close non-Priestly context, where the root עצם appears twice (עצום, "mighty" in 1:9; עצם, "become mighty" in 1:20). Note that the root is absent elsewhere in P.

No. 10: Exodus 6:2–3	= B

Exod 6:2–3 (P): [2] God spoke further to Moses and said to him, I am YHWH; [3] and I appeared to Abraham, Isaac, and Jacob, as El Shaddai, but by my name, YHWH, I did not make myself known to them.

Presupposes Moses's introduction in Exod 2:1–10 (non-P).

---

[7] Römer, *Moïse*, 44–45, considers ויצמו a harmonizing addition. See the discussion above, II.7.5 (a).

Number of case and Scripture reference	Level of dependence

No. 11: Exodus 6:6[8]

Exod 6:6 (P): [6] "Say, therefore, to the Israelites, 'I am YHWH, and I will bring you out from under the burdens (סבלת) of the Egyptians, and I will deliver (והצלתי) you from their bondage. I will also redeem you with an outstretched arm and with great judgments.'"

= C

Takes up vocabulary from non-Priestly texts in Exod 1–5 (נצל hiphil, סבלות).

No. 12: Exodus 12:40–41

Exod 12:1–13, 28 (P, Passover instruction): (…) [11] Now you shall eat it in this manner: with your loins girded, your sandals on your feet, and your staff in your hand; and you shall eat it in haste – it is YHWH's Passover. [12] For I will go through the land of Egypt on that night, and will strike down all the first-born in the land of Egypt, both man and beast; and against all the gods of Egypt I will execute judgments – I am YHWH. [13] And the blood shall be a sign for you on the houses where you live; and when I see the blood I will pass over you, and no plague will befall you to destroy you when I strike the land of Egypt." [28] And the Israelites went and did so; just as YHWH had commanded Moses and Aaron, so they did.

(Exod 12:29–33*, 37a [non-P, report of the killing of the firstborn and notice on Israel's departure])

Exod 12:40–41 (P): [40] Now the time that the Israelites lived in Egypt was four hundred and thirty years. [41] And it came about at the end of four hundred and thirty years, to the very day, that all the hosts of the YHWH went out from the land of Egypt.

= B

Exod 12:40–41 (P) depends on the non-P report of the killing of the firstborn and Israel's permission from Pharaoh to leave his country (Exod 12:29–33).

---

[8] OTTO, "Forschungen zur Priesterschrift," 10, n. 45, considers vv. 6–8 a secondary insertion stemming from his *Pentateuchredaktion*. KUENEN, *Historisch-kritische Einleitung*, 1.1:315–16, and BAENTSCH, *Exodus–Leviticus–Numeri*, assigned vv. 6–8 to a secondary Priestly tradtition or to R^P. See the discussion above, II.7.3 (b).

Number of case and Scripture reference	Level of dependence
No. 13: Exodus 14:1–3	**= A**

Exod 12:41 (P): [41] And it came about at the end of four hundred and thirty years, to the very day, that all the hosts of the YHWH went out from the land of Egypt.

Exod 13:20 (non-P): [20] *Then they set out from Succoth and camped in Etham on the edge of the wilderness.*

Exod 14:1–3 (P): [1] Now YHWH spoke to Moses, saying, [2] "Tell the Israelites to turn back and camp before Pi-hahiroth, between Migdol and the sea; you shall camp in front of Baal Zaphon, opposite it, by the sea. [3] For Pharaoh will say of the Israelites, 'They are wandering aimlessly in the land; the wilderness has closed against (before) them.'"[9]

The detailed itinerary notice in Exod 14:2 (P) does not match the end of the Priestly Passover account (Exod 12:40–41), which recounts Israel's exodus without mentioning any toponyms. Exod 14:3 (P) is dependent on the non-P itinerary in 13:20, according to which the Israelites "camped in Etham on the edge of the wilderness."

| **No. 14: Exodus 24:15b–16aα, 18a**[10] | **= A** |

Exod 19:1 (P): [1] In the third month after the Israelites had gone out of the land of Egypt, on that very day they came into the wilderness of Sinai.

(Exod 19 [non-P, beginning of the Sinai pericope: Israel camps in front of the mountain; theophany])

Exod 24:15b–16aα, 18α (P): [15b] And the cloud (הֶעָנָן) covered the mountain (הָהָר). [16aα] And the glory of YHWH settled upon Mount Sinai. [18a] And Moses entered the midst of the cloud as he went up to the mountain.

Two central motifs in Exod 24:15b–16aα, 18α (P), the mountain and the cloud, are not introduced in the preceding Priestly texts but are mentioned in the beginning of the non-Priestly Sinai pericope (Exod 19). When the Priestly stratum is read as a continuous source, the definite forms (הָהָר and הֶעָנָן) come as a surprise, unless one assigns a cataphoric function to the article (which seems unlikely).

From the examples shown in the table above one may draw the following conclusions: Texts labeled A manifestly depend on non-P texts, and it is difficult to escape the conclusion that they are redactional in nature. Texts labeled B and C, considered on their own, are not necessarily redactional. For instance, the incompleteness of certain "fragmentary" B texts may be explained by the prominence of the presupposed non-P motif (this explanation would apply in the case of the absence of an appropriate introduction for Moses in Exod 6) or by the loss of a Priestly text during the process of combining P and non-P (this might explain the lack of a report of the killing of Egypt's firstborn). However, when found in close proximity to A texts, a B or C text may give further support to the idea that the relevant Priestly passage or section constitutes a redaction.

---

[9] For the translation and meaning of Exod 14:3 see II.8.5.

[10] Schmid, "Der Sinai," 116–17, 126–27 ascribes Exod 24:15b–18 to a secondary Priestly (P^s) or post-Priestly (Pentateuch redactor) stratum. See above, II.10.3.2.

Most of the quoted texts belong to the Jacob-Esau and Joseph narratives and to the exodus section; examples from the Priestly primeval section are absent. Thus a first cautious conclusion should be that at least some of the Priestly texts in Gen 25–Exod 40 were written as redactional supplements to the non-Priestly texts.

With regard to this evidence, scholars defending the source model argue that where Priestly passages appear "incomplete," certain P elements must have been lost during the process of joining together the non-P and P texts. Another explanation is that P was written in constant but implicit relation to non-P material that would have been known to the reader. However, neither explanation takes into account the fact that there are entire sections in P where no gaps are visible and where P constitutes an uninterrupted thread, as for instance in the primeval history and in the Terah-Abraham narrative. Is it conceivable that the redactors would have completely preserved the Priestly thread in some sections but not in others? Can one imagine that one and the same Priestly author composed his text in constant relation to non-P in one section and in another not at all? As for the second explanation, it can apply to cases where P relies on well-known non-Priestly data, as for instance Moses's stay in Egypt, which would be presupposed in Exod 6:2 (read in the context of an independent P document). However, it cannot apply either to the few cases where a Priestly assertion depends syntactically on non-P or to those where a P statement relies on specific information given only in the non-Priestly stratum.

It is remarkable that entire Priestly sections and large textual units do not contain any of the mentioned features of dependence on non-P. This speaks against the global validity of the redaction model. As shown above, the Priestly primeval narrative and the Priestly Abraham narrative, its primary stratum, should be considered autonomous compositions, independent from the non-Priestly strand. The two above-cited texts from the Abraham narrative (no. 1, no. 2) do not belong to the story's base stratum (proto-Priestly narrative) and are not significant for the classification of the latter.

Summing up, we state that the redaction model is adequate for some but not all textual evidence.

2.3 Source *and* Redaction

The conclusion of the two previous sections is that we should roughly distinguish between two distinct literary profiles within the Priestly texts in Genesis and Exodus: The Priestly texts in the Jacob-Esau and Joseph section and in Exod 1–40 were written as a redaction complementing the non-Priestly (and pre-Priestly) Jacob and Joseph narratives and pre-Priestly Exodus story. In contrast, the Priestly texts in the primeval narrative and the proto-Priestly Abraham narrative were conceived as self-contained and independent units. The present investigation is in agreement with a few other studies that argue that the question of the profile of P in Gen 1–Exod 40 should be

answered individually for the different sections.[11] R. H. Pfeiffer was the first to express
the idea that some P texts, such as the Priestly primeval narrative, were composed as
autonomous narratives whereas others were written as revisions of non-Priestly texts
(i.e., the Priestly Abraham, Jacob-Esau and Joseph narratives).[12] Whereas Pfeiffer's
analysis was limited to the book of Genesis, more recently Blum, Gertz, and Wöhrle
have proposed similar models, distinguishing between two literary profiles within the
Priestly strand of Genesis–Exodus and beyond. Blum detects the two "source" and
"redaction" profiles in diverse sections in Genesis–Exodus. According to his theory,
both Priestly "source" texts and complementary Priestly passages were composed as
"preliminary works" (*Vorarbeiten*), which were then combined with the pre-Priestly
texts.[13] As for Gertz and Wöhrle, they tentatively distinguish between the literary profile of entire sections within the Priestly strand, identifying two large parts as source
texts (P texts in Gen 1–11 and Exod 1–40 [Gertz] or Gen 1–11 and Exod 6–40 [Wöhrle])
and a third part as a redaction building on non-Priestly texts (P texts in the ancestral narrative in Gen 12–50 [Gertz] or Gen 12–Exod 4 [Wöhrle]).[14] Their conclusions
are based on observations concerning the continuity and coherence of the narrative
in the different parts of the Priestly strand. According to Gertz and Wöhrle, Gen 1–11
P and Exod 1–40 P (Wöhrle: Gen 1–11 P and Exod 6–40 P) constitute fairly uninterrupted and coherent narrative threads. Both Gertz and Wöhrle seem to assign all
three parts to *the same compositional level* (they were written at the same time by the
same author[s]).

The present study shares the methodological concern that the visibly different outlines of Priestly texts may indicate distinct modes of literary composition. As for the
analysis of the different sections, however, my observations and conclusions differ
from those of Gertz, Wöhrle and partly Blum in three important points. First, the
above investigation provided evidence for an independent Priestly Abraham narrative (constituting a source text). Second, the study argues that the Priestly texts in the
exodus section are redactional in nature. Finally, I will argue that the differences in
the literary profile have implications for the redaction history of the Priestly writings.

(1) Gertz and Wöhrle (the latter within the framework of meticulous investigation)
classify all Priestly texts of the ancestral narrative as redactional and dependent
on the non-Priestly thread. However, as shown above, the Priestly Abraham
narrative (base stratum) contrasts with the Priestly texts in the Jacob, Esau,
and Joseph sections insofar as it is self-contained and has its own theological
profile distinct from that of the Priestly composition. It should be considered
a proto-Priestly unit that predates the latter. A few other scholars, like Römer

---

[11] See above I.1.1, with n. 13.
[12] R. Pfeiffer, "Non-Israelite Source," 67. His proposal, expressed in a short 1930 article
about the literary history of the book of Genesis, did not find much resonance in scholarship.
[13] Blum, *Studien*, 229–85; idem, "Noch einmal," 32–64.
[14] Gertz, *Tradition*, 390–91; idem, "Genesis 5," 90–91; Wöhrle, *Fremdlinge*, 147–60.

and Blum, have also observed that in the Abraham section P forms a continuous and self-contained strand, though none have arrived at the above literary-historical conclusion.[15]

(2) Gertz and Wöhrle, in agreement with scholars defending the source model, maintain that large parts or even all Priestly portions of Exod 1–40 (Wöhrle Exod 6–40) can be read as a continuous and self-contained narrative. Nevertheless, there are a few gaps and incoherences in this section. First, Moses is not introduced; the transition from Exod 2:25 to 6:2 does not seem smooth (see the previous section). Second, there are no reports of YHWH's striking the Egyptian firstborn and of the celebration of Israel's first Passover, despite the fact that both events are announced (in Exod 12:1–13). After the instruction for the Passover and the announcement of the killing of the Egyptian firstborn, P only briefly mentions Israel's exodus from Egypt. Third, after this episode P can only be identified again beginning in Exod 14, where the Priestly layer relates Israel's (YHWH's) ultimate victory over the Egyptians at the Sea of Reeds. But it is striking that the detailed itinerary notice (14:2) does not hark back to P's statement of Israel's leaving Egypt but rather relies on an itinerary notice from the non-P strand (13:20; cf. 14:3). Finally, the motifs of the "mountain" (ההר) and "cloud" (ענן) in the tabernacle account are not properly introduced and depend on the preceding non-Priestly texts. In other passages in Exodus, P also seems to be connected to preceding (or subsequent) non-Priestly texts by taking up certain motifs and specific expressions (עצם, "to become mighty"[16]; סבלות, "burden bearing, compulsory labor";[17] נצל hiphil, "to pull out, deliver"[18]) that do not appear elsewhere in the Priestly strand.[19] In this respect, the Priestly texts in Exod 1–40 resemble the more fragmentary Priestly strand in the Jacob-Esau and Joseph sections. Scholars rightly point out the regular and sophisticated composition of some units in the exodus section (i.e., the Priestly miracle narrative, the story of the parting of the sea, the tabernacle account). However, because there are certain gaps between them in the Priestly strand, we can conclude that they were probably never connected to one another within an independent and separate Priestly document. Rather, the texts in question should be interpreted as a first step in the composition of independent units, before they were integrated into a combined P–non-P strand (see Blum's theory).

(3) The present study, in contrast to those of Pfeiffer, Blum, Gertz, and Wöhrle, associates the two dissimilar literary profiles with distinct literary strata: the source texts (primeval history, Abraham narrative) predate the redactional texts (complementary passages in the Jacob-Esau and Joseph narratives); the former

---

[15] RÖMER, "Der Pentateuch," 105; BLUM, "Noch einmal," 53.
[16] Cf. Exod 1:9, 20.
[17] Cf. Exod 1:11; 2:11; 5:4, 5 (all texts belong to non-P strands).
[18] Cf. Exod 2:19; 3:8; 5:23 (2×); 12:27; 18:4, 8, 9, 10 (2×) (all texts belong to non-P strands).
[19] Cf. BLUM, Studien, 234–35; RÖMER, Moïse, 151.

are classified as "proto-Priestly"; the latter are assigned to P[C] or P[S] (see above, III.1). The aforementioned scholars, though they stress the differences in the literary profile of P, do not consider the possibility that their observations might be evaluated diachronically to indicate the inner differentiation of the Priestly strand. In their analyses, the observed differences in the literary profile do not serve as indicators of distinct Priestly layers. They attribute source and redactional texts in P to the same literary layer (P[G]/P[C]).[20]

The redaction-critical differentiation between proto-P and P[C] suggested in the present study may render the "source and redaction" model more plausible. Read through the lens of the latter model (as conceived by Blum, Gertz, and Wöhrle) only, without a diachronic perspective, the Priestly literary work may appear rather disparate, something of miscellany, raising the question why one and the same Priestly author (or group of authors) would have composed only source texts in large sections (the primeval history and Abraham narrative) and in other, similarly extensive divisions (the Jacob-Esau, Joseph, and exodus sections) only redactional texts.[21] Assigning the "source texts" to proto-Priestly authors and the "redactional texts" to later Priestly redactors allows us to overcome this difficulty.

---

[20] See already in "Methodological Considerations," I.2.3 (c).

[21] This disparateness is also conceded by WÖHRLE, *Fremdlinge*, 158, n. 31: "Nun könnte gegen das hier vorgetragene Modell eingewandt werden, dass ein so umrissenes priesterliches Werk, bei dem die Urgeschichte und ab Exod 6 auch die Exoduserzählungen von den priesterlichen Autoren eigenständig formuliert, die Vätergeschichte und der Beginn der Exoduserzählung aber unter Aufnahme vorgegebener Überlieferungen gestaltet wurden, ein recht disparates Werk wäre."

3. The Literary-Historical Relationship between the Priestly and Non-Priestly Strata in Genesis 1–Exodus 40

The present study agrees with the majority view among European scholars that the relationship between the P and non-P strata in Gen 1–Exod 40 cannot be defined in global terms. The question required individual treatment for each section and each unit. The differentiation between proto-P, P^C, and P^S (H) on the one hand and among different non-P layers on the other renders the question more complex but leads to more nuanced answers. It may explain evidence that appears contradictory according to more simplistic models (which still hold to the classical Documentary Hypothesis and its fixed relationship between non-Priestly sources and P and [or] which do not reckon with inner stratification of P). In some cases, conclusions remain preliminary in nature. This caution is a result of the main focus of this study, namely, the question of inner differentiation within the Priestly stratum and that of its profile. It is not possible herein to subject the non-Priestly units to the same thorough assessment that we did the Priestly texts.

An important result of the investigation is that the proposed proto-Priestly accounts in the book of Genesis constitute self-contained units which are independent from neighboring and more remote non-Priestly texts. The four proto-Priestly compositions, each of which deals with a specific topic (creation, flood, primary geography, and Abraham narrative), probably provided the impulse for the composition of distinct parallel non-Priestly versions or of complementary non-P insertions into the proto-Priestly texts (*Fortschreibungen*): the narrative of the fall of mankind in Gen 2–3; the story of Cain and Abel in Gen 4*; the non-Priestly additions to Flood narrative; the story of the tower of Babel; and the non-Priestly stories about Abraham. In three of four cases (creation, flood, primeval geography), this result agrees with several recently published studies (with the difference that the latter do not distinguish between a proto-Priestly and a Priestly stage).[1]

The tentative reconstruction of the formation of the primeval narrative is as follows

---

[1] Arguing for the dependence of Gen 2–3 on Gen 1 is OTTO, "Die Paradieserzählung"; BLENKINSOPP, "Post-Exilic Lay Source," 54–55; DE PURY, "P^G as the Absolute Beginning," 28–30 (see above, II.1.6). Arguing for the dependence of Gen 6–8 (non-P) on Gen 6–9 (P) are BLENKINSOPP, *Pentateuch*; SKA, "Story of the Flood" = IDEM, "relato del diluvio"; BOSSHARD-NEPUSTIL, *Vor uns die Sintflut*; ARNETH, *Durch Adams Fall*; SCHMID, *Literaturgeschichte*, 154–55 (see above, II.3.6). Arguing for the dependence of Gen 11 on Gen 10 P: WITTE, *Die biblische Urgeschichte*, 90; BOSSHARD-NEPUSTIL, *Vor uns die Sintflut*, 210–12; SCHÜLE, *Der Prolog*, 402–3; DE PURY, "P^G as the Absolute Beginning," 30–32. Arguing for the dependence of Gen 10 (non-P) on Gen 10 (P): WENHAM, *Genesis 1–15*, 215; KNOHL, "Nimrod," 1:45–52; WITTE, *Die biblische Urgeschichte*, 110–16; NIHAN, "L'écrit sacerdotal," 180–82.

Figure 1.   Formation of the primeval narrative

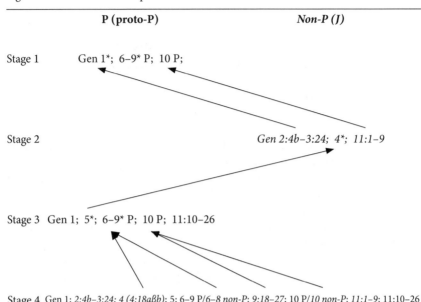

P (proto-P)	**Non-P (J)**
Stage 1 Gen 1*; 6–9* P; 10 P;	
Stage 2	*Gen 2:4b–3:24; 4*; 11:1–9*
Stage 3 Gen 1; 5*; 6–9* P; 10 P; 11:10–26	

Stage 4 Gen 1; *2:4b–3:24; 4 (4:18aβb)*; 5; 6–9 P/*6–8 non-P*; *9:18–27*; 10 P/*10 non-P*; *11:1–9*; 11:10–26
(Combined P–non-P stratum)

Non-italics: text belongs to P
Italics: text belongs to non-P
→:   reacts to

(see fig. 1): At its beginning stand the three proto-Priestly units, namely, creation account, flood story, and Table of Nations. This provoked the composition of a parallel non-Priestly primeval narrative (Gen 2:4–3:24; 4*; 11:1–9). The author of the latter, traditionally designated as "J" (the Yahwist), aimed to correct the optimistic theology of the proto-Priestly units (in particular Gen 1* and Gen 10 P) and cast the nature of the humans and the development of humanity in a negative light. A further concern of this author, apparently, was to identify YHWH as the creator god, in opposition to the universalistic designation Elohim chosen by the authors of Gen 1* and Gen 6–10*. Later, the proto-Priestly accounts were supplemented with two "bridging" units – the unilinear genealogies in Gen 5 and Gen 11:10–26 – which reinforced the cohesion between them. In a fourth stage, the proto-Priestly and the non-Priestly primeval narratives were combined and complemented with non-Priestly insertions (*Fortschreibungen*: non-Priestly flood story, story of Canaan's curse, non-P additions in the Table of Nations).

Concerning the relationship between P and non-P in the Abraham narrative, scholarship has moved in a new direction in the last decades. Though scholars traditionally considered the P strand to depend in general on most non-P entities in this

Figure 2.   Formation of the Abraham narrative

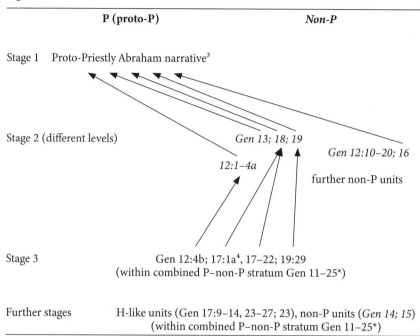

| P (proto-P) | *Non-P* |

Stage 1   Proto-Priestly Abraham narrative[3]

Stage 2 (different levels)   *Gen 13; 18; 19*

12:1–4a   *Gen 12:10–20; 16*

further non-P units

Stage 3   Gen 12:4b; 17:1a[4], 17–22; 19:29
(within combined P–non-P stratum Gen 11–25*)

Further stages   H-like units (Gen 17:9–14, 23–27; 23), non-P units (*Gen 14; 15*)
(within combined P–non-P stratum Gen 11–25*)

Non-italics: text belongs to P
Italics: text belongs to non-P
→:   reacts to

section, some critics have more recently offered good arguments for classifying several non-P units – Gen 15; 20; 21:8–21; 22 – as post-Priestly. One among these scholars, A. de Pury, went much further, arguing that most non-P texts in Gen 12–25 depend on P.[4] The present investigation drew on de Pury's observations and considerations concerning this question, confronting them with the traditional view and focusing in particular on the relationship between the (proto-)Priestly Abraham narrative and the non-Priestly stories in Gen 12 non-P; 13 non-P; 16 non-P; 18; and 19 non-P, which are commonly considered pre-Priestly. The distinction between a proto-Priestly stratum and later redactional, Priestly additions, as is suggested in the present study, may provide a new impulse to this discussion and help to overcome the impasse. The tentative conclusion is to classify the mentioned non-P units as post-proto-Priestly. Their

---

[2] Gen 11:27–25:9 P; 25:13–16; 25:19; 35:22b–27; 36*.

[3] Consistent with the age indication in Gen 17:1a are the statements in 16:16; 17:17b and 21:5; they all depend on the non-Priestly statement of Abraham's old age in 18:11 (see above, II.6.4 [a3]).

[4] See above, II.6.10.

authors reacted to the proto-Priestly narrative in various ways: While the latter depicts Abraham as the "father of multiple nations" and illustrates the origins of Ishmael, Israel, and Edom, the combined Gen 13; 18–19 complements this narrative by creating stories about the origins of Israel, Moab, and Ammon. The non-P story in Gen 16, with its striking concentration of conflict motifs, contrasts the pacifist proto-Priestly standpoint and might be motivated to correct the latter. The next step was the merging of the proto-Priestly and non-Priestly strands. During this process, or shortly thereafter, some Priestly texts were added. These Priestly additions responded to the non-Priestly texts in question and aligned the proto-Priestly stratum with them, while preparing the limitation of the Abrahamic covenant to Israel alone within the concept of the comprehensive Priestly composition (P^C). In a still later phase, other non-P texts were written, presupposing the unified P-non-P stratum (Gen 15; 22). On the other side, a few distinct units with H-like traits (Gen 17:9–14, 23–27; 23) were inserted as well (see fig. 2).

In the Jacob-Esau and Joseph narratives, the Priestly texts are extremely sparse; they do not form a self-contained strand and obviously complement the non-Priestly plot. Probably, the non-Priestly strand also contains some post-Priestly texts. However, since the non-Priestly texts are much more numerous and more extensive than the sporadic Priestly passages and furthermore often not related to each other, the relationship between P and non-P could not have been dealt with comprehensively. For example, the question of which of the two passages dealing with Jacob's name change, Gen 32:28–29 (non-P) or 35:10 (P^C), predates the other remains open.

In Exodus the situation is similar to that in the Jacob-Esau and Joseph narratives: the Priestly texts supplemented a preexisting non-Priestly strand. In contrast to the Jacob-Esau and Joseph narratives, however, the complementary P elements are more comprehensive, also constituting a few well-elaborated compositions. The non-Priestly strand in this section contains some post-Priestly texts. Yet the relationship between Priestly and non-Priestly material could not be examined in each case. Nevertheless, the investigation aimed to contribute to the vivid scholarly discussion about the literary origins of certain key motifs found in both the Priestly and non-Priestly strands, specifically Israel's move from Canaan to Egypt, YHWH's revelation (or self-presentation) to Moses, and Aaron's assistance to Moses during the latter's negotiation with Pharaoh. The first theme, which concerns the transition between the books of Genesis and Exodus, was probably part of the pre-Priestly stratum (including the Joseph story and the beginning of the non-Priestly exodus narrative [Exod 1:8–15*]). YHWH's self-presentation in Exod 6:2–9 (P^C) likely predated the revelation account in Exod 3 (non-Priestly stratum). And finally, certain indications favor the idea that Aaron's accompaniment of Moses was invented by P^C and only later taken up by non-Priestly authors, who further modified Aaron's function (in non-P, he becomes Moses's mouthpiece, whereas in P^C he acts as a magician). Similarly, the Priestly tabernacle account (primary form: Exod 25–29*, 39–40*, Lev 1–3) and Aaron's role as high priest probably antedated the story of Israel and Aaron's apostasy with the golden bull in Exod 32*, which seems to have been a polemical reaction to it.

Afterward, later Priestly and non-Priestly authors added further texts. Within the Priestly stratum, the Priestly Sinai legislation in particular was augmented (additions in Exod 35–40 and in Lev 1–16). One of the motives of the intervening later Priestly authors was to react on their turn to the (diachronically) "intermediate" non-Priestly texts.

In sum, contrary to what scholars often argue, the Priestly strand, traditionally considered the latest pentateuchal "source," was responsible for several important elements of "tradition" that were only later taken up and reworked by non-Priestly authors. However, certain of these genuinely Priestly motifs and themes go back to the stage of the proto-Priestly accounts, which originally had nothing to do with the comprehensive Priestly composition.

Abbreviations

ÄAT	Ägypten und Altes Testament
AB	Anchor Bible
ABD	*Anchor Bible Dictionary*. Edited by David Noel Freedman. 6 vols. New York: Doubleday, 1992
ABRL	Anchor Bible Reference Library
ABS	Archaeology and Biblical Studies
ADPV	Abhandlungen des Deutschen Palästina-Vereins
AIL	Ancient Israel and Its Literature
AJSL	*American Journal of Semitic Languages and Literatures*
ANET	*Ancient Near Eastern Texts Relating to the Old Testament*. Edited by James B. Pritchard. 3rd ed. Princeton: Princeton University Press, 1969
AOAT	Alter Orient und Altes Testament
AR	*Archiv für Religionswissenschaft*
ArchB	Archaeology and Bible
AS	Assyriological Studies
ATANT	Abhandlungen zur Theologie des Alten und Neuen Testaments
ATD	Das Alte Testament Deutsch
ATSAT	Arbeiten zu Text und Sprache im Alten Testament
AYBRL	Anchor Yale Bible Reference Library
BBB	Bonner biblische Beiträge
BEATAJ	Beiträge zur Erforschung des Alten Testaments und des antiken Judentums
BeO	*Bibbia e oriente*
BETL	Bibliotheca Ephemeridum Theologicarum Lovaniensium
Bib	*Biblica*
BibLeb	*Bibel und Leben*
BJRL	*Bulletin of the John Rylands University Library of Manchester*
BK	*Bibel und Kirche*
BKAT	Biblischer Kommentar, Altes Testament
BNP	*Brill's New Pauly: Encyclopaedia of the Ancient World*. Edited by Hubert Cancik. 22 vols. Leiden: Brill, 2002–2011
BThSt	Biblisch-theologische Studien
BWANT	Beiträge zur Wissenschaft vom Alten und Neuen Testament
BZ	*Biblische Zeitschrift*
BZABR	Beihefte zur Zeitschrift für altorientalische und biblische Rechtsgeschichte
BZAW	Beihefte zur Zeitschrift für die alttestamentliche Wissenschaft
CAT	Commentaire de l'Ancien Testament
CBQ	*Catholic Biblical Quarterly*
CdE	*Chronique d'Égypte*
CHANE	Culture and History of the Ancient Near East
CM	Cuneiform Monographs
ConBOT	Coniectanea Biblica: Old Testament Series
COS	*The Context of Scripture*. Edited by William W. Hallo. 3 vols. Leiden: Brill, 1997–2002
DBAT	*Dielheimer Blätter zum Alten Testament und seiner Rezeption in der Alten Kirche*

DDD	*Dictionary of Deities and Demons in the Bible.* Edited by Karel van der Toorn, Bob Becking, and Pieter W. van der Horst. Leiden: Brill, 1995. 2nd rev. ed. Grand Rapids: Eerdmans, 1999
DJD	Discoveries in the Judaean Desert
EBR	*Encyclopedia of the Bible and Its Reception.* Edited by Hans-Josef Klauck et al. Berlin: de Gruyter, 2009–
ErIsr	*Eretz-Israel*
EstBib	*Estudios bíblicos*
ETS	Erfurter theologische Studien
FAT	Forschungen zum Alten Testament
FB	Forschung zur Bibel
FRLANT	Forschungen zur Religion und Literatur des Alten und Neuen Testaments
GAT	Grundrisse zum Alten Testament
HAT	Handbuch zum Alten Testament
HBAI	*Hebrew Bible and Ancient Israel*
HBM	Hebrew Bible Monographs
HCOT	Historical Commentary on the Old Testament
HKAT	Handkommentar zum Alten Testament
HS	*Hebrew Studies*
HSS	Harvard Semitic Studies
HThKAT	Herders Theologischer Kommentar zum Alten Testament
HTR	*Harvard Theological Review*
HUCA	*Hebrew Union College Annual*
ICC	International Critical Commentary
IECOT	International Exegetical Commentary on the Old Testament
IEKAT	Internationaler exegetischer Kommentar zum Alten Testament
ITS	*Indian Theological Studies*
JA	*Journal Asiatique*
JANESCU	*Journal of the Ancient Near Eastern Society of Columbia University*
JAOS	*Journal of the American Oriental Society*
JBL	*Journal of Biblical Literature*
JBTh	*Jahrbuch für Biblische Theologie*
JCS	*Journal of Cuneiform Studies*
JHS	*Journal of Hellenic Studies*
JQR	*Jewish Quarterly Review*
JRAS	*Journal of the Royal Asiatic Society*
JSOT	*Journal for the Study of the Old Testament*
JSOTSup	Journal for the Study of the Old Testament Supplement Series
JSP	*Journal for the Study of the Pseudepigrapha*
JSS	*Journal of Semitic Studies*
JTS	*Journal of Theological Studies*
KAT	Kommentar zum Alten Testament
KEH	Kurzgefasstes exegetisches Handbuch zum Alten Testament
KHC	Kurzer Hand-Commentar zum Alten Testament
LÄ	*Lexikon der Ägyptologie.* Edited by Wolfgang Helck, Eberhard Otto, and Wolfhart Westendorf. Wiesbaden: Harrassowitz, 1972
LAPO	Littératures anciennes du Proche-Orient
LASBF	*Liber Annuus Studii Biblici Franciscani*
LD	Lectio Divina
MThSt	Marburger theologische Studien
NAWG	*Nachrichten (von) der Akademie der Wissenschaften in Göttingen*

NBL	*Neues Bibel-Lexikon.* Edited by Manfred Görg and Bernhard Lang. 3 vols. Zurich: Benziger, 1991–2001
NCBiC	New Cambridge Bible Commentary
NEA	*Near Eastern Archaeology*
NEchtB	Neue Echter Bibel
NICOT	New International Commentary on the Old Testament
NSKAT	Neuer Stuttgarter Kommentar, Altes Testament
OBO	Orbis Biblicus et Orientalis
OTE	*Old Testament Essays*
OTL	Old Testament Library
OTS	Old Testament Studies
OtSt	*Oudtestamentische Studiën*
PTMS	Princeton Theological Monograph Series
RB	*Revue biblique*
RGG	*Religion in Geschichte und Gegenwart.* Edited by Hans Dieter Betz. 4th ed. Tübingen: Mohr Siebeck, 1998–2007
RHR	*Revue de l'histoire des religions*
RlA	*Reallexikon der Assyriologie.* Edited by Erich Ebeling et al. Berlin: de Gruyter, 1928–
RSR	*Recherches de science religieuse*
SAACT	State Archives of Assyria Cuneiform Texts
SANE	Sources of the Ancient Near East
SBAB	Stuttgarter biblische Aufsatzbände
SBS	Stuttgarter Bibelstudien
SCS	Septuagint and Cognate Studies
Sem	*Semitica*
SJ	Studia Judaica
SJLA	Studies in Judaism in Late Antiquity
SJOT	*Scandinavian Journal of the Old Testament*
StSam	Studia Samaritana
TB	Theologische Bücherei: Neudrucke und Berichte aus dem 20. Jahrhundert
TDOT	*Theological Dictionary of the Old Testament.* Edited by G. Johannes Botterweck and Helmer Ringgren. Translated by John T. Willis et al. 8 vols. Grand Rapids: Eerdmans, 1974–2006
Transeu	*Transeuphratène*
TRE	*Theologische Realenzyklopädie.* Edited by Gerhard Krause and Gerhard Müller. Berlin: de Gruyter, 1977–
TRu	*Theologische Rundschau*
TTZ	*Trierer theologische Zeitschrift*
TWAT	*Theologisches Wörterbuch zum Alten Testament.* Edited by G. Johannes Botterweck and Helmer Ringgren. Stuttgart: Kohlhammer, 1970–
TZ	*Theologische Zeitschrift*
UF	*Ugarit-Forschungen*
VeEc	*Verbum et Ecclesia*
VT	*Vetus Testamentum*
VTSup	Supplements to Vetus Testamentum
VWGTh	Veröffentlichungen der Wissenschaftlichen Gesellschaft für Theologie
WAW	Writings from the Ancient World
WBC	Word Biblical Commentary
WMANT	Wissenschaftliche Monographien zum Alten und Neuen Testament
WO	*Die Welt des Orients*

WUNT	Wissenschaftliche Untersuchungen zum Neuen Testament
YNER	Yale Near Eastern Researches
ZABR	*Zeitschrift für altorientalische und biblische Rechtsgeschichte*
ZAH	*Zeitschrift für Althebraistik*
ZAW	*Zeitschrift für die alttestamentliche Wissenschaft*
ZBK	Zürcher Bibelkommentare
ZKT	*Zeitschrift für katholische Theologie*
ZTK	*Zeitschrift für Theologie und Kirche*

Bibliography

ACHENBACH, REINHARD. "Das Kyros-Orakel in Jesaja 44,24–45,7 im Lichte altorientalischer Parallelen." *ZABR* 11 (2005): 155–94.

ACHENBACH, REINHARD. "Das Versagen der Aaroniden: Erwägungen zum literarhistorischen Ort von Leviticus 10." Pages 55–70 in *"Basel und Bibel": Collected Communications to the XVIIth Congress of the International Organization for the Study of the Old Testament, Basel 2001*. Edited by Matthias Augustin and Hermann Michael Niemann. BEATAJ 51. Frankfurt: Lang, 2004.

ACHENBACH, REINHARD. "Der Pentateuch, seine theokratischen Bearbeitungen und Josua–2 Könige." Pages 225–53 in *Les dernières rédactions du Pentateuque, de l'Hexateuque et de l'Ennéateuque*. Edited by Thomas Römer and Konrad Schmid. BETL 203. Leuven: Peeters, 2007.

ACHENBACH, REINHARD. *Die Vollendung der Tora: Studien zur Redaktionsgeschichte des Numeribuches im Kontext von Hexateuch und Pentateuch*. BZABR 3. Wiesbaden: Harrassowitz, 2003.

ACHENBACH, REINHARD. "Levitische Priester und Leviten im Deuteronomium: Überlegungen zur sog. 'Levitisierung' des Priestertums." *ZABR* 5 (1999): 301–4.

ACHENBACH, REINHARD. "Theocratic Reworking in the Pentateuch." Pages 53–78 in *Chronicles and the Priestly Literature of the Hebrew Bible*. Edited by Jaeyoung Jeon and Louis C. Jonker. BZAW 528. Berlin: de Gruyter, 2021.

AEJMELAEUS, ANNELI. "Septuagintal Translation Techniques: A Solution to the Problem of the Tabernacle Account." Pages 116–30 in *Collected Essays: On the Trail of Septuagint Translators*. Kampen: Kok Pharos, 1993.

AHN, GREGOR. *Religiöse Herrscherlegitimation im Achämenidischen Iran: Die Voraussetzungen und die Struktur ihrer Argumentation*. Acta Iranica 31. Leiden: Brill; Leuven: Peeters, 1992.

ALBERTZ, RAINER. *Exodus 1–18*. ZBK 2.1. Zurich: TVZ, 2012.

ALBERTZ, RAINER. *Exodus 19–40*. ZBK 2.2. Zurich: TVZ, 2015.

ALBERTZ, RAINER. *Religionsgeschichte Israels in alttestamentlicher Zeit: Vom Exil bis zu den Makkabäern*. 2nd ed. GAT 8.2. Göttingen: Vandenhoeck & Ruprecht, 1997.

ALBERTZ, RAINER. "Wilderness Material in Exodus (Exodus 15–18)." Pages 151–68 in *The Book of Exodus: Composition, Reception, and Interpretation*. Edited by Thomas B. Dozeman, Craig A. Evans, and Joel N. Lohr. VTSup 164. Leiden: Brill, 2014.

ALBRIGHT, WILLIAM F. "The Babylonian Matter in the Predeuteronomic Primeval History (JE) in Gen 1–11." *JBL* 58 (1939): 91–103.

ALFRINK, BERNARDUS. "L'expression נֶאֱסַף אֶל עַמָּיו." *OtSt* 5 (1948): 118–31.

ALLEN, JAMES P. "From the Memphite Theology." *COS* 1:21–23.

ALLEN, JAMES P. "The Cosmology of the Pyramid Texts." Pages 1–28 in *Religion and Philosophy in Ancient Egypt*. Edited by William Kelly Simpson. New Haven: Yale University Press, 1989.

ALTMANN, PETER. *Banned Birds. The Birds of Leviticus 11 and Deuteronomy 14*. Archaeology and Bible 1. Tübingen: Mohr Siebeck, 2019.

AMIT, YAIRAH. *Hidden Polemics in Biblical Narrative*. Translated by Jonathan Chipman. BibInt 25. Leiden: Brill, 2000.

AMIT, YAIRAH. "הבריאה ולוח הקדושה." Pages 13*–29* in *Tehillah le-Moshe: Biblical and Judaic Studies in Honor of Moshe Greenberg*. Edited by Mordechai Cogan, Barry L. Eichler, and Jeffrey H. Tigay. Winona Lake, IN: Eisenbrauns, 1997.

ARNETH, MARTIN. *Durch Adams Fall ist gänzlich verderbt …: Studien zur Entstehung der alttestamentlichen Urgeschichte*. FRLANT 217. Göttingen: Vandenhoeck & Ruprecht, 2007.

ARNOLD, BILL T. *Genesis*. NCBiC. Cambridge: Cambridge University Press, 2009.

ARTEMOV, NIKITA. "Belief in Family Reunion in the Afterlife in the Ancient Near East and Mediterranean." Pages 27–41 in *La famille dans le Proche-Orient ancien: Réalités, symbolismes, et images; Proceedings of the 55th Rencontre Assyriologique Internationale at Paris, 6–9 July 2009*. Edited by Lionel Marti. Winona Lake, IN: Eisenbrauns, 2014.

AURELIUS, ERIK. *Der Fürbitter Israels: Eine Studie zum Mosebild im Alten Testament*. ConBOT 27. Stockholm: Almqvist & Wiksell, 1988.

AURELIUS, ERIK. *Zukunft Jenseits des Gerichts: Eine redaktionsgeschichtliche Studie zum Enneateuch*. BZAW 319. Berlin: de Gruyter, 2003.

AVIGAD, NAHMAN, and BENJAMIN SASS. *Corpus of West Semitic Stamp Seals*. Jerusalem: Israel Academy of Sciences and Humanities, 1997.

BADEN, JOEL S. *The Composition of the Pentateuch: Renewing the Documentary Hypothesis*. AYBRL. New Haven: Yale University Press, 2012.

BADEN, JOEL S. "The Original Place of the Priestly Manna Story in Exodus 16." *ZAW* 122 (2010): 491–504.

BADEN, JOEL S., and JEFFREY STACKERT. "Convergences and Divergences in Contemporary Pentateuchal Research." Pages 17–37 in *The Oxford Handbook of the Pentateuch*. Edited by Joel S. Baden and Jeffrey Stackert. Oxford: Oxford University Press, 2021.

BAENTSCH, BRUNO. *Exodus–Leviticus–Numeri*. HKAT I/2. Göttingen: Vandenhoeck & Ruprecht, 1903.

BARNOUIN, MICHEL. "Recherches numériques sur la généalogie de Gen. V." *RB* 77 (1970): 347–65.

BARR, JAMES. "Why the World Was Created in 4004 BC: Archbishop Ussher and Biblical Chronology." *BJRL* 67 (1984): 575–608.

BARTLETT, JOHN R. *Edom and the Edomites*. JSOTSup 77. Sheffield: Sheffield Academic, 1989.

BAUKS, MICHAELA. "Die Begriffe מורשה und אחזה in P᷍ᵍ: Überlegungen zur Landkonzeption der Priestergrundschrift." *ZAW* 116 (2004): 171–88.

BAUKS, MICHAELA. *Die Welt am Anfang: Zum Verhältnis von Vorwelt und Weltentstehung in Gen 1 und in der altorientalischen Literatur*. WMANT 74. Neukirchen-Vluyn: Neukirchener Verlag, 1997.

BAUKS, MICHAELA. "Genesis 1 als Programmschrift der Priesterschrift (P᷍ᵍ)." Pages 333–45 in *Studies in the Book of Genesis: Literature, Redaction and History*. Edited by André Wénin. BETL 155. Leuven: Peeters, 2001.

BAUMGART, NORBERT CLEMENS. *Die Umkehr des Schöpfergottes: Zu Komposition und religionsgeschichtlichem Hintergrund von Gen 5–9*. Herders biblische Studien 22. Freiburg im Breisgau: Herder, 1999.

BEAULIEU, PAUL-ALAIN. *The Reign of Nabonidus, King of Babylon, 556–539 B.C.* YNER 10. New Haven: Yale University Press, 1989.

BECKER, UWE. *Richterzeit und Königtum: Redaktionsgeschichtliche Studien zum Richterbuch*. BZAW 192. Berlin: de Gruyter, 1990.

BEDFORD, PETER R. "Temple Funding and Priestly Authority in Achaemenid Judah." Pages 336–51 in *Exile and Return: The Babylonian Context*. Edited by Jonathan Stökl and Caroline Waerzeggers. BZAW 478. Berlin: de Gruyter, 2015.

BEN-DOV, JONATHAN. "Writing as Oracle and as Law: New Contexts for the Book-Find of King Josiah." *JBL* 127 (2008): 222–39.

BENZ, FRANK L. *Personal Names in Phoenician and Punic Inscriptions.* Rome: Biblical Institute Press, 1972.

BERGER, PAUL-RICHARD. "Ellasar, Tarschisch und Jawan, Gn 14 und 10." *WO* 13 (1982): 50–78.

BERLEJUNG, ANGELIKA. *Die Theologie der Bilder: Herstellung und Einweihung von Kultbildern in Mesopotamien und die alttestamentliche Bilderpolemik.* OBO 162. Fribourg: Presses Universitaires; Göttingen: Vandenhoeck & Ruprecht, 1998.

BERNAT, DAVID A. *Sign of the Covenant: Circumcision in the Priestly Tradition.* AIL 3. Atlanta: SBL Press, 2009.

BERNER, CHRISTOPH. "Das Wasserwunder von Rephidim (Ex 17,1–7) als Schlüsseltext eines nachpriesterschriftlichen Mosebildes." *VT* 63 (2013): 193–209.

BERNER, CHRISTOPH. "Der literarische Charakter der Priesterschrift in der Exoduserzählung: Dargestellt an Exodus 1 bis 14." Pages 94–133 in *Abschied von der Priesterschrift? Zum Stand der Pentateuchdebatte.* Edited by Friedhelm Hartenstein and Konrad Schmid. VWGTh 40. Leipzig: Evangelische Verlagsanstalt, 2015.

BERNER, CHRISTOPH. *Die Exoduserzählung: Das literarische Werden einer Ursprungslegende Israels.* FAT 73. Tübingen: Mohr Siebeck, 2010.

BERNER, CHRISTOPH. "Gab es einen vorpriesterlichen Meerwunderbericht?" *Bib* 95 (2014): 1–25.

BERNHARDT, KARL-HEINZ. "ברא II 2." *TDOT* 2:245.

BIENKOWSKI, PIOTR. "Sippar." Page 274 in *Dictionary of the Ancient Near East.* Edited by Piotr Bienkowski and A. R. (Alan Ralph) Millard. Philadelphia: University of Pennsylvania Press, 2010.

BLENKINSOPP, JOSEPH. "Abraham as Paradigm in the Priestly History in Genesis," *JBL* 128 (2009): 225–41.

BLENKINSOPP, JOSEPH. "The Judean Priesthood during the Neo-Babylonian and Achaemenid Periods: A Hypothetical Reconstruction." *CBQ* 60 (1998): 25–43.

BLENKINSOPP, JOSEPH. *The Pentateuch: An Introduction to the First Five Books of the Bible.* ABRL. New York: Doubleday, 1992.

BLENKINSOPP, JOSEPH. "A Post-Exilic Lay Source in Genesis 1–11." Pages 113–26 in *Abschied vom Jahwisten: Die Komposition des Hexateuch in der jüngsten Diskussion.* Edited by Jan Christian Gertz, Konrad Schmid, and Markus Witte. BZAW 315. Berlin: de Gruyter, 2002.

BLOCH, RENÉ. "Baucis." BNP. 2006. https://doi.org/10.1163/1574-9347_bnp_e214090.

BLOCH-SMITH, ELIZABETH. *Judahite Burial Practices and Beliefs about the Dead.* JSOTSup 123. Sheffield: Sheffield Academic, 1992.

BLUM, ERHARD. "Der vermeintliche Gottesname 'Elohim.'" Pages 97–119 in *Gott nennen: Gottes Namen und Gott als Name.* Edited by Ingolf U. Dalferth and Philipp Stoellger. Religion in Philosophy and Theology 35. Tübingen: Mohr Siebeck, 2008.

BLUM, ERHARD. *Die Komposition der Vätergeschichte.* WMANT 57. Neukirchen-Vluyn: Neukirchener Verlag, 1982.

BLUM, ERHARD. "Die literarische Verbindung von Erzvätern und Exodus: Ein Gespräch mit neueren Forschungshypothesen." Pages 119–56 in *Abschied vom Jahwisten: Die Komposition des Hexateuch in der jüngsten Diskussion.* Edited by Jan Christian Gertz, Konrad Schmid, and Markus Witte. BZAW 315. Berlin: de Gruyter, 2002.

BLUM, ERHARD. "Issues and Problems in the Contemporary Debate Regarding the Priestly Writings." Pages 31–44 in *The Strata of the Priestly Writings: Contemporary Debate and Future Directions.* Edited by Sarah Shectman and Joel S. Baden. AThANT 95. Zurich: TVZ, 2009.

BLUM, ERHARD. "The Linguistic Dating of Biblical Texts – An Approach with Methodological Limitations." Pages 303–26 in *The Formation of the Pentateuch: Bridging the Academic Cultures of Europe, Israel, and North America*. Edited by Jan Christian Gertz et al. FAT 111. Tübingen: Mohr Siebeck, 2016.

BLUM, ERHARD. "Noch einmal: Das literargeschichtliche Profil der P-Überlieferung." Pages 32–64 in *Abschied von der Priesterschrift? Zum Stand der Pentateuchdebatte*. Edited by Friedhelm Hartenstein and Konrad Schmid. VWGTh 40. Leipzig: Evangelische Verlagsanstalt, 2015.

BLUM, ERHARD. *Studien zur Komposition des Pentateuch*. BZAW 189. Berlin: de Gruyter, 1990.

BOGAERT, PIERRE-MAURICE. "L'importance de la Septante et du 'Monacensis' de la Vetus Latina pour l'exégèse du livre de l'Exode (chap. 35–40)." Pages 399–428 in *Studies in the Book of Exodus: Redaction – Reception – Interpretation*. Edited by Marc Vervenne. BETL 126. Leuven: Leuven University Press, 1996.

BOGAERT, PIERRE-MAURICE. "L'Orientation du parvis du sanctuaire dans la version grecque de l'Exode (Ex., 27, 9–13 LXX)." *L'Antiquité classique* 50 (1981): 79–85.

BOGAERT, PIERRE-MAURICE. "La construction de la Tente (Ex 36–40) dans le Monacensis de la plus ancienne version latine: L'autel d'or et Hébreux 9,4." Pages 62–76 in *L'enfance de la Bible hébraïque: Histoire du texte de l'Ancien Testament*. Edited by A. Schenker and P. Hugo. MdB 52. Geneva: Labor et Fides, 2005.

BOORER, SUZANNE. *The Vision of the Priestly Narrative: Its Genre and Hermeneutics of Time*. AIL 27. Atlanta: SBL Press, 2016.

BOSSHARD-NEPUSTIL, ERICH. *Vor uns die Sintflut: Studien zu Text, Kontexten und Rezeption der Fluterzählung Genesis 6–9*. BWANT 165. Stuttgart: Kohlhammer, 2005.

BOTTÉRO, JEAN. *L'Épopée de Gilgamesh: Le grand homme qui ne voulait pas mourir*. Paris: Gallimard, 1992.

BOTTÉRO, JEAN. *Mythes et rites de Babylone*. Paris: H. Champion, 1985.

BRINKMAN, J. A. (JOHN ANTHONY). "Ur. A. III. Philologisch. Mitte 2.–1. Jahrtausend." *RlA* 14:364–67.

BUDDE, KARL. *Die biblische Urgeschichte (Gen 1–12, 5)*. Giessen: Ricker, 1883.

BUDDE, KARL. "Wortlaut und Werden der ersten Schöpfungsgeschichte." *ZAW* 35 (1915): 65–97.

BÜHLER, AXEL. "The Demotic Literature and the Priestly Exodus: The *Legend of Sesostris*, the *Inaros Cycle*, and the Battles of Magicians compared to the Priestly Exodus." In *The Historical Location of P*. Edited by Jürg Hutzli and Jordan Davis. ArchB. Tübingen: Mohr Siebeck, forthcoming.

BÜHRER, WALTER. *Am Anfang …: Untersuchungen zur Textgenese und zur relativ-chronologischen Einordnung von Gen 1–3*. Göttingen: Vandenhoeck & Ruprecht, 2014.

BURROWS, ERIC. "Notes on Harrian." *JRAS* 2 (1925): 277–84.

BURSTEIN, STANLEY M. *The Babyloniaca of Berossus*. SANE 1.5. Malibu, CA: Undena, 1978.

CALMEYER, PETER. "Hose." *RlA* 4:472.

CARR, DAVID M. *Genesis 1–11*. IECOT. Stuttgart: Kohlhammer, 2021.

CARR, DAVID M. *Reading the Fractures of Genesis: Historical and Literary Approaches*. Louisville: Westminster John Knox, 1996.

CASSUTO, UMBERTO. *A Commentary on the Book of Exodus*. Jerusalem: Magnes, 1967.

CASSUTO, UMBERTO. *A Commentary on the Book of Genesis, Part I*. Jerusalem: Magnes, 1972.

CHAINE, JOSEPH. *Le livre de la Genèse*. LD 3. Paris: Cerf, 1947.

CHILDS, BREVARD S. *The Book of Exodus*. OTL. Louisville: Westminster John Knox, 1974.

COATS, GEORGE W. *Rebellion in the Wilderness: The Murmuring Motif in the Wilderness Traditions of the Old Testament*. Nashville: Abingdon, 1968.

COATS, GEORGE W. "The Wilderness Itinerary." *CBQ* 34 (1972): 135–52.

CODY, AELRED. *A History of Old Testament Priesthood.* AnBib 35. Rome: Pontifical Biblical Institute, 1969.

COGAN, MORDECHAI. *I Kings: A New Translation with Introduction and Commentary.* AB 10. New York: Doubleday, 2001.

CONRAD, JOACHIM. *Karl Heinrich Grafs Arbeit am Alten Testament: Studien zu einer wissenschaftlichen Biographie.* Edited by Uwe Becker. BZAW 425. Berlin: de Gruyter, 2011.

CORTESE, ENZO. "The Priestly Tent (Ex 25–31.35–40): Literary Criticism and Theology of P." *LASBF* 48 (1998): 9–30.

CRAWFORD, CORY D. "Between Shadow and Substance: The Historical Relationship of Tabernacle and Temple in Light of Architecture and Iconography." Pages 117–33 in *Levites and Priests in Biblical History and Tradition.* Edited by Mark Leuchter and Jeremy M. Hutton. AIL 9. Atlanta: SBL Press, 2011.

CROSS, FRANK MOORE. *Canaanite Myth and Hebrew Epic: Essays in the History of Religion in Israel.* Cambridge: Harvard University Press, 1973.

CROSS, FRANK MOORE. "4QExod–Lev^f." Pages 133–44 in *Qumran Cave 4. VII.* Edited by Eugene Ulrich et al. DJD 12. Oxford: Clarendon, 1994.

CRÜSEMANN, FRANK. "Die Eigenständigkeit der Urgeschichte. Ein Beitrag zur Diskussion um den 'Jahwisten.'" Pages 11–29 in *Die Botschaft und die Boten: Festschrift für Hans Walter Wolff zum 70. Geburtstag.* Edited by Jörg Jeremias and Lothar Perlitt. Neukirchen-Vluyn: Neukirchener Verlag, 1981.

CRÜSEMANN, FRANK. *Die Tora: Theologie und Sozialgeschichte des alttestamentlichen Gesetzes.* 2nd ed. Munich: Kaiser, 1997.

DAVIES, GRAHAM I. "The Wilderness Itineraries and Recent Archaeological Research." Pages 161–75 in *Studies in the Pentateuch.* Edited by J. A. Emerton. VTSup 41. Leiden: Brill, 1990.

DAVIES, PHILIP R. "Biblical Hebrew and the History of Ancient Judah: Typology, Chronology and Common Sense." Pages 150–63 in *Biblical Hebrew: Studies in Chronology and Typology.* Edited by Ian Young. JSOTSup 369. London: T&T Clark, 2003.

DAVILA, JAMES R. "New Qumran Readings for Genesis One." Pages 3–11 in *Of Scribes and Scrolls: Studies on the Hebrew Bible, Intertestamental Judaism and Christian Origins presented to John Strugnell on the Occasion of His Sixtieth Birthday.* Edited by Harold W. Attridge, John J. Collins, and Thomas H. Tobin. Lanham, MD: University Press of America, 1990.

DAY, JOHN. "The Flood and the Ten Antediluvian Figures." Pages 211–23 in *On Stone and Scroll: Essays in Honour of Graham Ivor Davies.* Edited by James K. Aitken, Katharine J. Dell, and Brian A. Mastin. BZAW 420. Berlin: de Gruyter, 2011.

DE BREUCKER, GEERT. "Berossos: His Life and His Work." Pages 15–28 in *The World of Berossos: Proceedings of the 4th International Colloquium on "The Ancient Near East between Classical and Ancient Oriental Traditions," Hatfield College, Durham, 7th–9th July 2010.* Edited by Johannes Haubold et al. Classica et Orientalia 5. Wiesbaden: Harrassowitz, 2013.

DE WIT, CONSTANT. "Inscriptions dédicatoires du temple d'Edfou. I. E. IV, 1–16." *CdE* 36/71 (1961): 56–97.

DE WIT, CONSTANT. "Inscriptions dédicatoires du temple d'Edfou. II. E. VII, 1–20." *CdE* 36/72 (1961): 277–320.

DELITZSCH, FRANZ. *A New Commentary on Genesis.* Edinburgh: T&T Clark, 1888.

DHORME, PAUL. "Abraham dans le cadre d'histoire." *RB* 37 (1928): 367–85, 481–511.

DIEBNER, BERND JÖRG. "Gottes Welt, Moses Zelt und das salomonische Heiligtum." Pages 127–54 in *Lectio difficilior probabilior? L'exégèse comme expérience de décloisonnement; Mélanges offerts à Françoise Smyth-Florentin*. Edited by Thomas Römer. DBAT 12. Heidelberg: Wiss.-theol. Seminar, 1991.

DIEBNER, BERND JÖRG, and HERMANN SCHULT. "Alter und geschichtlicher Hintergrund von Genesis 24." *DBAT* 10 (1975): 10–17.

DIETRICH, WALTER, HANS-PETER MATHYS, THOMAS RÖMER, and RUDOLF SMEND. *Die Entstehung des Alten Testaments: Neuausgabe*. Theologische Wissenschaft 1. Stuttgart: Kohlhammer, 2014.

DILLMANN, AUGUST. *Die Genesis*. 3rd ed. KEH 11. Leipzig: Hirzel, 1875.

DILLMANN, AUGUST, and AUGUST WILHELM KNOBEL. *Die Bücher Exodus und Leviticus*. Leipzig: Hirzel, 1880.

DOHMEN, CHRISTOPH. "Was stand auf den Tafeln vom Sinai und was auf denen vom Horeb? Geschichte und Theologie eines Offenbarungsrequisits." Pages 9–50 in *Vom Sinai zum Horeb: Stationen alttestamentlicher Glaubensgeschichte*. Edited by Frank-Lothar Hossfeld. Würzburg: Echter, 1989.

DOLD, ALBAN. "Versuchte Neu- und Erstergänzungen zu den altlateinischen Texten im Cod. Clm 6225 der Bayer. Staatsbibliothek." *Bib* 37 (1956): 39–58.

DOZEMAN, THOMAS B. *Commentary on Exodus*. Grand Rapids: Eerdmans, 2009.

DOZEMAN, THOMAS B. "The Priestly Wilderness Itineraries and the Composition of the Pentateuch." Pages 257–88 in *The Pentateuch: International Perspectives on Current Research*. Edited by Thomas B. Dozeman, Konrad Schmid, and Baruch J. Schwartz. FAT 78. Tübingen: Mohr Siebeck, 2011.

DRIVER, G. R. (GODFREY ROLLES). "Resurrection of Marine and Terrestrial Creatures." *JSS* 7 (1962): 12–22.

DRIVER, S. R. (SAMUEL ROLLES). *Notes on the Hebrew Text of the Books of Samuel*. Oxford: Clarendon, 1890.

DRIVER, S. R. (SAMUEL ROLLES). *A Treatise on the Use of the Tenses in Hebrew and Some Other Syntactical Questions*. Grand Rapids: Eerdmans, 1998.

DUHM, BERNHARD. *Das Buch Jesaja*. 2nd ed. HKAT III/1. Göttingen: Vandenhoeck & Ruprecht, 1902.

DURAND, JEAN-MARIE, and MICHAËL GUICHARD. "Les rituels de Mari." *Florilegium Marianum* 3 (1997): 19–78.

DUŠEK, JAN. *Aramaic and Hebrew Inscriptions from Mt. Gerizim and Samaria between Antiochus III and Antiochus IV Epiphanes*. CHANE 54. Leiden: Brill, 2012.

DUŠEK, JAN. *Les manuscrits araméens du Wadi Daliyeh et la Samarie vers 450–332 av. J.-C.* Leiden: Brill, 2007.

DUSSAUD, RENÉ. "Les Phéniciens au Négeb et en Arabie d'après un texte de Ras Shamra." *RHR* 108 (1933): 5–46.

EBELING, ERICH. "Androgyn." *RlA* 1:106–7.

EERDMANS, B. D. (BERNARDUS DIRK). *Alttestamentliche Studien I: Die Komposition der Genesis*. Giessen: Töpelmann, 1908.

EHRLICH, ARNOLD B. *Randglossen zur hebräischen Bibel 1*. Leipzig: Hinrichs, 1908.

EISSFELDT, OTTO. *Hexateuch-Synopse*. Leipzig: Hinrichs, 1922.

EITAN, ISRAEL. "Two Onomatological Studies." *JAOS* 49 (1929): 30–33.

ELLIGER, KARL. *Kleine Schriften zum Alten Testament*. Edited by Hartmut Gese and Otto Kaiser. TB 32. Munich: Kaiser, 1966.

ELLIGER, KARL. *Leviticus*. HAT I/4. Tübingen: Mohr Siebeck, 1966.

ELLIGER, KARL. "Sinn und Ursprung der priesterlichen Geschichtserzählung." *ZTK* 49 (1952): 121–43.

FINKELSTEIN, ISRAEL. "Jerusalem and Judah 600–200 BCE: Implications for Understanding Pentateuchal Texts." Pages 3–18 in *The Fall of Jerusalem and the Rise of the Torah*. Edited by Peter Dubovský, Dominik Markl and Jean-Pierre Sonnet. FAT 107. Tübingen: Mohr Siebeck, 2016.

FINKELSTEIN, ISRAEL, and THOMAS RÖMER. "Comments on the Historical Background of the Abraham Narrative: Between 'Realia' and 'Exegetica.'" *HeBAI* 3 (2014): 3–23.

FINKELSTEIN, ISRAEL, and NEIL ASHER SILBERMAN. *David and Solomon: In Search of the Bible's Sacred Kings and the Roots of Western Civilization*. New York: Free Press, 2006.

FINKELSTEIN, JACOB JOEL. "The Antediluvian Kings: A University of California Tablet." *JCS* 17 (1963): 39–51.

FINN, ARTHUR HENRY. "The Tabernacle Chapters." *JTS* 16 (1914–15): 449–82.

FISCHER, GEORG. "Keine Priesterschrift in Ex 1–15?" *ZKT* 117 (1995): 203–11.

FISCHER, GEORG, and DOMINIK MARKL. *Das Buch Exodus*. NSKAT 2. Stuttgart: Katholisches Bibelwerk, 2009.

FISCHER, IRMTRAUD. *Die Erzeltern Israels: Feministisch-theologische Studien zu Genesis 12–36*. BZAW 222. Berlin: de Gruyter, 1994.

FISHBANE, MICHAEL. *Biblical Interpretation in Ancient Israel*. Oxford: Oxford University Press, 1985.

FLEMING, DANIEL E. "Mari's Large Public Tent and the Priestly Tent Sanctuary." *VT* 50 (2000): 489–90.

FOHRER, GEORG. *Ezechiel, mit einem Beitrag von K. Galling*. HAT I/13. Tübingen: Mohr Siebeck, 1955.

FOSTER, BENJAMIN R. "Epic of Creation." *COS* 1:390–402.

FRANKEL, DAVID. *The Murmuring Stories of the Priestly School: A Retrieval of Ancient Sacerdotal Lore*. VTSup 89. Leiden: Brill, 2002.

FRETHEIM, TERENCE E. "The Priestly Document: Anti-Temple?" *VT* 18 (1968): 313–29.

FREVEL, CHRISTIAN. *Mit Blick auf das Land die Schöpfung erinnern: Zum Ende der Priestergrundschrift*. Herders biblische Studien 23. Freiburg im Breisgau: Herder, 2000.

FRITZ, VOLKMAR. *Das erste Buch der Könige*. ZBK 10.1. Zurich: TVZ, 1996.

FRITZ, VOLKMAR. *Israel in der Wüste: Traditionsgeschichtliche Untersuchung der Wüstenüberlieferung des Jahwisten*. MThSt 7. Marburg: Elwert, 1970.

GANZEL, TOVA. *Ezekiel's Visionary Temple in Babylonian Context*. BZAW 539. Berlin: de Gruyter, 2021.

GARDINER, ALAN H. *The Admonitions of an Egyptian Sage*. Leipzig: J. C. Hinrichs, 1909.

GARR, W. RANDALL. "The Grammar and Interpretation of Exodus 6:3." *JBL* 111 (1992): 403–4.

GASTER, THEODOR HERZL. "Heaven 1." *ABD* 3:551–52.

GEORGE, ANDREW R. *The Babylonian Gilgamesh Epic*. 2 volumes. Oxford: Oxford University Press, 2003.

GEORGE, ANDREW R. *Gilgamesh: The Babylonian Epic Poem and Other Texts in Akkadian and Sumerian*. London: Penguin Books, 2003.

GERTZ, JAN CHRISTIAN. "Antibabylonische Polemik im priesterlichen Schöpfungsbericht?" *ZTK* 106 (2009): 137–55.

GERTZ, JAN CHRISTIAN. "Beobachtungen zu Komposition und Redaktion in Exodus 32–34." Pages 88–106 in *Gottes Volk am Sinai: Untersuchungen zu Ex 32–34 und Dtn 9–10*. Edited by Matthias Köckert and Erhard Blum. Gütersloh: Gütersloher Verlagshaus, 2001.

GERTZ, JAN CHRISTIAN. *Das erste Buch Mose (Genesis): Die Urgeschichte Gen 1–11*. ATD 1. Göttingen: Vandenhoeck & Ruprecht, 2021.

GERTZ, JAN CHRISTIAN. "Genesis 5: Priesterliche Redaktion, Komposition oder Quellenschrift?" Pages 65–93 in *Abschied von der Priesterschrift? Zum Stand der Pentateuchdebatte*. Edited by Friedhelm Hartenstein and Konrad Schmid. VWGTh 40. Leipzig: Evangelische Verlagsanstalt, 2015.

GERTZ, JAN CHRISTIAN. "The Miracle at the Sea: Remarks on the Recent Discussion about Origin and Composition of the Exodus Narrative." Pages 91–120 in *The Book of Exodus: Composition, Reception, and Interpretation*. Edited by Thomas B. Dozeman, Craig A. Evans, and Joel N. Lohr. VTSup 164. Leiden: Brill, 2014.

GERTZ, JAN CHRISTIAN. *Tradition und Redaktion in der Exoduserzählung: Untersuchungen zur Endredaktion des Pentateuch*. FRLANT 186. Göttingen: Vandenhoeck & Ruprecht, 2000.

GERTZ, JAN CHRISTIAN. "Von Adam zu Enosch: Überlegungen zur Entstehungsgeschichte von Gen 2–4." Pages 215–36 in *Gott und Mensch im Dialog: Festschrift für Otto Kaiser zum 80. Geburtstag*. Edited by Markus Witte. BZAW 345. Berlin: de Gruyter, 2004.

GESE, HARTMUT. "Der bewachte Lebensbaum und die Heroen: Zwei mythologische Ergänzungen zur Urgeschichte der Quelle J." Pages 78–85 in *Wort und Geschichte: Festschrift für Karl Elliger zum 70. Geburtstag*. Edited by Hartmut Gese and Hans Peter Rüger. AOAT 18. Kevelaer: Butzon & Bercker; Neukirchen-Vluyn: Neukirchener Verlag, 1973.

GESUNDHEIT, SHIMON. "Introduction: The Strengths and Weaknesses of Linguistic Dating." Pages 295–302 in *The Formation of the Pentateuch: Bridging the Academic Cultures of Europe, Israel, and North America*. Edited by Jan Christian Gertz, Bernard M. Levinson, Dalit Rom-Shiloni, and Konrad Schmid. FAT 111. Tübingen: Mohr Siebeck, 2016.

GILDERS, WILLIAM K. "Sacrifice before Sinai and the Priestly Narratives." Pages 57–72 in *The Strata of the Priestly Writings: Contemporary Debate and Future Directions*. Edited by Sarah Shectman and Joel S. Baden. AThANT 95. Zurich: TVZ, 2009.

GLASSNER, JEAN-JACQUES. *Mesopotamian Chronicles*. WAW 19. Atlanta: SBL Press, 2004.

GONZALEZ, HERVÉ. "Jawan, 1: Hebrew Bible/Old Testament." *EBR* 13:1–2.

GORDON, ROBERT P. *1 & 2 Samuel: A Commentary*. Grand Rapids: Zondervan, 1999.

GÖRG, MANFRED. "עַ רָקִיע *rāqîaʿ*." *TDOT* 13:646–53.

GRABBE, LESTER L. *A History of the Jews and Judaism in the Second Temple Period, Volume 1: Yehud; A History of the Persian Province of Judah*. London: T&T Clark, 2007.

GRAEFE, ERHART. *Untersuchungen zur Wortfamilie bjɜ*. Cologne: University of Cologne, 1971.

GRAF, FRITZ. "Hyrieus." BNP. 2006. https://doi.org/10.1163/1574-9347_bnp_e520260.

GREENBERG, MOSHE. *Ezekiel 1–20: A New Translation with Introduction and Commentary*. AB 22A. New York: Doubleday, 1983.

GREENBERG, MOSHE. *Ezekiel 21–37: A New Translation with Introduction and Commentary*. AB 22A. New York: Doubleday, 1997.

GROSS, MELANIE. "Ḥarrān als kulturelles Zentrum in der altorientalischen Geschichte und sein Weiterleben." Pages 139–54 in *Kulturelle Schnittstelle: Mesopotamien, Anatolien, Kurdistan; Geschichte, Sprachen, Gegenwart*. Edited by Lea Müller-Funk, Stephan Procházka, Gebhard J. Selz, and Anna Telič. Vienna: Institut für Orientalistik der Universität Wien, 2014.

GROSS, WALTER. "Bundeszeichen und Bundesschluss in der Priesterschrift." *TTZ* 87 (1978): 78–115.

GROSS, WALTER. *Die Pendenskonstruktion im biblischen Hebräisch*. ATSAT 27. St. Ottilien: EOS Verlag, 1987.

GROSS, WALTER. "Gen 1,26.27; 9,6: Statue oder Ebenbild Gottes? Aufgabe und Würde des Menschen nach dem hebräischen und dem griechischen Wortlaut." *JBTh* 15 (2001): 11–38.

GRÜNWALDT, KLAUS. *Exil und Identität: Beschneidung, Passa und Sabbat in der Priester-schrift.* BBB 85. Frankfurt: Hain, 1992.

GUDME, ANNE KATRINE DE HEMMER. *Before the God in This Place for Good Remembrance: A Comparative Analysis of the Aramaic Votive Inscriptions from Mount Gerizim.* BZAW 441. Berlin: de Gruyter, 2013.

GUILLAUME, PHILIPPE. *Land and Calendar: The Priestly Document from Genesis 1 to Joshua 18.* New York: T&T Clark, 2009.

GUNKEL, HERMANN. *Genesis.* 3rd ed. HKAT I/1. Göttingen: Vandenhoeck & Ruprecht, 1922.

HA, JOHN. *Genesis 15: A Theological Compendium of Pentateuchal History.* BZAW 181. Berlin: de Gruyter, 1989.

HAAS, VOLKERT, and DORIS PRECHEL. "Mondgott A. II Bei den Hethitern." *RlA* 8:370–71.

HALBE, JÖRN. *Das Privilegrecht Jahwes: Ex 34, 10–26; Gestalt und Wesen, Herkunft und Wirken in vordeuteronomischer Zeit.* FRLANT 114. Göttingen: Vandenhoeck & Ruprecht, 1975.

HAMILTON, VICTOR P. *The Book of Genesis, Chapters 1–17.* NICOT. Grand Rapids: Eerd-mans, 1990.

HANHART, ROBERT. "The Translation of the Septuagint in Light of Earlier Tradition and Subsequent Influences." Pages 339–79 in *Septuagint, Scrolls and Cognate Writings.* Edited by George J. Brooke and Barnabas Lindars. SCS 33. Atlanta: Scholars Press, 1992.

HARAN, MENAHEM. "Shiloh and Jerusalem." *JBL* 81 (1962): 14–24.

HARAN, MENAHEM. *Temples and Temple Service in Ancient Israel.* Oxford: Oxford Univer-sity Press, 1978.

HARL, MARGUERITE. *La Bible d'Alexandrie, I: La Genèse; Traduction du texte grec de la Septante; Introduction et Notes.* Paris: Cerf, 1986.

HARTENSTEIN, FRIEDHELM, and KONRAD SCHMID, eds. *Abschied von der Priesterschrift? Zum Stand der Pentateuchdebatte.* VWGTh 40. Leipzig: Evangelische Verlagsanstalt, 2015.

HARTLEY, JOHN E. *Leviticus.* WBC. Waco, TX: Word, 1992.

HECKL, RAIK. "Die Exposition des Pentateuchs: Überlegungen zum literarischen und theo-logischen Konzept von Genesis 1–3*." Pages 3–37 in *Ex oriente Lux: Studien zur Theo-logie des Alten Testaments; Festschrift für Rüdiger Lux zum 65. Geburtstag.* Edited by Angelika Berlejung and Raik Heckl. Leipzig: Evangelische Verlagsanstalt, 2011.

HENDEL, RONALD S. "'Begetting' and 'Being Born' in the Pentateuch: Notes on Historical Linguistics and Source Criticism." *VT* 50 (2000): 38–46.

HENDEL, RONALD S. "A Hasmonean Edition of MT Genesis? The Implications of the Edi-tions of the Chronology in Genesis 5." *HeBAI* 1 (2012): 1–17.

HENDEL, RONALD S. "How Old Is the Hebrew Bible? A Response to Konrad Schmid." *ZAW* 133 (2021): 361–70.

HENDEL, RONALD S. *The Text of Genesis 1–11: Textual Studies and Critical Edition.* New York: Oxford University Press, 1998.

HENDEL, RONALD S., and JAN JOOSTEN. *How Old Is the Hebrew Bible? A Linguistic, Textual, and Historical Study.* AYBRL. New Haven: Yale University Press, 2018.

HENTSCHEL, GEORG. *1. Könige.* NEchtB 10. Würzburg: Echter, 1984.

HERMANT, DOMINIQUE. "Analyse littéraire du premier récit de la création." *VT* 15 (1965): 437–51.

HESS, RICHARD S. *Studies in the Personal Names of Genesis 1–11.* AOAT 234. Kevelaer: Butzon & Bercker; Neukirchen-Vluyn: Neukirchener Verlag, 1993.

HIEKE, THOMAS. *Die Genealogien der Genesis.* Freiburg im Breisgau: Herder, 2003.

HIEKE, THOMAS. *Levitikus 1–15.* HThKAT. Freiburg im Breisgau: Herder, 2008.

Hölscher, Gustav. *Drei Erdkarten: Ein Beitrag zur Erderkenntnis des hebräischen Altertums*. Sitzungsberichte der Heidelberger Akademie der Wissenschaften 3. Heidelberg: Winter, 1948.

Holzinger, Heinrich. *Exodus*. KHC 2. Freiburg im Breisgau: Mohr, 1900.

Holzinger, Heinrich. *Genesis*. KHC 1. Freiburg im Breisgau: Mohr, 1898.

Homan, Michael M. *To Your Tents, O Israel! The Terminology, Function, Form, and Symbolism of Tents in the Hebrew Bible and the Ancient Near East*. CHANE 12. Leiden: Brill, 2002.

Hornung, Erik. *Der Eine und die Vielen: Ägyptische Gottesvorstellungen*. Darmstadt: Wissenschaftliche Buchgesellschaft, 1973.

Horowitz, Wayne. "The Isles of the Nations: Genesis X and Babylonian Geography," Pages 35–43 in *Studies in the Pentateuch*. Edited by J. A. Emerton. VTSup 41. Leiden: Brill, 1990.

Hossfeld, Frank-Lothar, and Erich Zenger. *Psalmen: 101–150*. HThKAT. Freiburg im Breisgau: Herder, 2008.

Houtman, Cornelis. *Exodus*. 4 volumes. HCOT. Kampen: Kok, 1993–2002.

Hughes, Jeremy. *Secrets of the Times: Myth and History in Biblical Chronology*. JSOTSup 66. Sheffield: Sheffield Academic, 1990.

Humbert, Paul. "Die literarische Zweiheit des Priester-Codex in der Genesis (Kritische Untersuchung der These von von Rad)." *ZAW* 58 (1940–41): 30–57.

Hurowitz, Victor Avigdor. "The Golden Calf and the Tabernacle." *Shnaton* 7 (1983–84): 51–59 (Hebrew), 9–10 (English).

Hurowitz, Victor Avigdor. *I Have Built You an Exalted House: Temple Building in the Bible in Light of Mesopotamian and Northwest Semitic Writings*. JSOTSup 115. Sheffield: Sheffield Academic, 1992.

Hurowitz, Victor Avigdor. "The Priestly Account of Building the Tabernacle." *JAOS* 105 (1985): 21–30.

Hurvitz, Avi. "Dating the Priestly Source in Light of the Historical Study of Biblical Hebrew a Century after Wellhausen." *ZAW* 100 (1988): 88–100.

Hurvitz, Avi. *A Linguistic Study of the Relationship between the Priestly Source and the Book of Ezekiel: A New Approach to an Old Problem*. Cahiers de la Revue biblique 20. Paris: Gabalda, 1982.

Hurvitz, Avi, in Collaboration with Leeor Gottlieb, Aaron Hornkohl, Emmanuel Mastéy. *A Concise Lexicon of Late Biblical Hebrew. Linguistic Innovations in the Writings of the Second Temple Period*. VTSup 160. Leiden: Brill, 2014.

Hutzli, Jürg. *Die Erzählung von Hanna und Samuel: Textkritische und literarische Analyse von 1. Samuel 1–2 unter Berücksichtigung des Kontextes*. AThANT 89. Zurich: TVZ, 2007.

Hutzli, Jürg. "Interventions présumées des scribes concernant le motif de l'arbre sacré dans le Pentateuque." *Sem* 56 (2014): 313–31.

Hutzli, Jürg. "J's Problem with the East: Observations on the So-Called Yahwist Texts in Genesis 1–25, Followed by Literary Historical Conclusions." Pages 99–120 in *The Social Groups behind the Pentateuch*. Edited by Jaeyoung Jeon. AIL 44. Atlanta: SBL Press, 2021.

Hutzli, Jürg. "La conception du ciel dans la tradition sacerdotale de la Bible hébraïque." *JA* 300 (2012): 595–607.

Hutzli, Jürg. "La fureur divine et son détournement en Nb 25." Pages 177–99 in *Colères et repentirs divins: Actes du colloque organisé par le Collège de France, Paris, les 24 et 25 avril 2013*. Edited by Jean-Marie Durand, Lionel Marti, and Thomas Römer. OBO 274. Fribourg: Presses Universitaires; Göttingen: Vandenhoeck & Ruprecht, 2015.

HUTZLI, JÜRG. "Priestly(-like) Texts in Samuel and Kings," Pages 223–42 in *Writing, Rewriting, and Overwriting in the Books of Deuteronomy and the Former Prophets; Essays in Honour of Cynthia Edenburg*. Edited by Ido Koch, Thomas Römer, and Omer Sergi. BETL 304. Leuven: Peeters, 2019.

HUTZLI, JÜRG. "The Procreation of Seth by Adam in Gen 5:3 and the Composition of Gen 5." *Sem* 54 (2012): 147–62.

HUTZLI, JÜRG. "Tradition and Interpretation in Gen 1:1–2:4a." *JHS* 10, art. 12 (2010). https://doi.org/10.5508/jhs.2010.v10.a12.

HUTZLI, JÜRG. "Transgression et initiation: Tendances idéologiques et développement littéraire du récit de Genèse 2–3." Pages 113–33 in *Tabou et Transgressions: Actes du colloque organisé par le Collège de France, Paris, les 11 et 12 avril 2012*. Edited by Jean-Marie Durand, Michaël Guichard, and Thomas Römer. Fribourg: Presses Universitaires; Göttingen: Vandenhoeck & Ruprecht, 2015.

HUTZLI, JÜRG. "Überlegungen zum Motiv der Ansammlung der Wasser unterhalb des Himmels an einem Ort (Gen 1,9)." *TZ* 62 (2006): 10–16.

JACOB, BENNO. *Das Buch Genesis*. Repr. ed. Stuttgart: Calwer, 2000.

JACOBSEN, THORKILD. "The Eridu Genesis." *JBL* 100 (1981): 513–29.

JACOBSEN, THORKILD. *The Sumerian King List*. AS 11. Chicago: University of Chicago Press, 1939.

JANOWSKI, BERND. "Die Einwohnung Gottes in Israel: Eine religions- und theologiegeschichtliche Skizze zur biblischen Schekina-Theologie, 3–40." Pages 19–25 in *Das Geheimnis der Gegenwart Gottes: Zur Schechina-Vorstellung in Judentum und Christentum*. Edited by Bernd Janowski and Enno Edzard Popkes. WUNT 318. Tübingen: Mohr Siebeck, 2014.

JANOWSKI, BERND. *Sühne als Heilsgeschehen: Traditions- und religionsgeschichtliche Studien zur priesterschriftlichen Sühnetheologie*. WMANT 55. Neukirchen-Vluyn: Neukirchener Verlag, 1982.

JANOWSKI, BERND. "Tempel und Schöpfung: Schöpfungstheologische Aspekte der priesterschriftlichen Heiligtumskonzeption." *JBTh* 5 (1990): 37–69.

JAPHET, SARA. *I and II Chronicles: A Commentary*. OTL. Louisville: Westminster John Knox, 1993.

JEON, JAEYOUNG. *The Call of Moses and the Exodus Story: A Redactional-Critical Study in Exodus 3–4 and 5–13*. FAT II/60. Tübingen: Mohr Siebeck, 2013.

JEON, JAEYOUNG. "Egyptian Iconography and the Battle with Amalek (Exodus 17:8–16) Revisited." *Sem* 61 (2019): 89–115.

JEON, JAEYOUNG. "The Elders Redaction (ER) in the Pentateuch: Scribal Contributions of an Elders Group in the Formation of the Pentateuch." Pages 73–98 in *The Social Groups behind the Pentateuch*. Edited by Jaeyoung Jeon. AIL 44. Atlanta: SBL Press, 2021.

JEON, JAEYOUNG. "A Source of P? The Priestly Exodus Account and the Book of Ezekiel." *Sem* 58 (2016): 77–92.

JEPSEN, ALFRED. "Zur Chronologie des Priesterkodex." *ZAW* 47 (1929): 251–55.

JERICKE, DETLEF. *Die Ortsangaben im Buch Genesis: Ein historisch-topographischer und literarisch-topographischer Kommentar*. FRLANT 248. Göttingen: Vandenhoeck & Ruprecht, 2013.

JOOSTEN, JAN. "The Distinction between Classical and Late Biblical Hebrew as Reflected in Syntax." *HS* 46 (2005): 330–34.

JOOSTEN, JAN. *People and Land in the Holiness Code: An Exegetical Study of the Ideational Framework of the Law in Leviticus 17–26*. VTSup 67. Leiden: Brill, 1996.

JÜNGLING, HANS-WINFRIED. *Richter 19: Ein Plädoyer für das Königtum; Stilistische Analyse der Tendenzerzählung Ri 19,1–30a; 21,25*. AnBib 84. Rome: Pontifical Biblical Institute, 1981.

KAUFMANN, YEHEZKEL. *The Religion of Israel from Its Beginnings to the Babylonian Exile.* Translated by Moshe Greenberg. Chicago: University of Chicago Press, 1960.

KEEL, OTHMAR. "Die Brusttasche des Hohenpriesters als Element priesterschriftlicher Theologie." Pages 379–91 in *Das Manna fällt auch heute noch: Beiträge zur Geschichte und Theologie des Alten, Ersten Testaments; Festschrift für Erich Zenger.* Edited by Frank-Lothar Hossfeld and Ludger Schwienhorst-Schönberger. Herders biblische Studien 44. Freiburg im Breisgau: Herder, 2004.

KEEL, OTHMAR. *Die Geschichte Jerusalems und die Entstehung des Monotheismus.* 2 volumes. Orte und Landschaften der Bibel 4.1–2. Göttingen: Vandenhoeck & Ruprecht, 2007.

KEEL, OTHMAR, and SILVIA SCHROER. *Schöpfung: Biblische Theologien im Kontext altorientalischer Religiosität.* Göttingen: Vandenhoeck & Ruprecht, 2002.

KEEL, OTHMAR, and CHRISTOPH UEHLINGER. *Göttinnen, Götter und Göttersymbole: Neue Erkenntnisse zur Religionsgeschichte Kanaans und Israels aufgrund bislang unerschlossener ikonographischer Quellen.* 5th ed. Freiburg im Breisgau: Herder, 2001.

KELLERMANN, DIETHER. "מִשְׁכָּן *miškān.*" *ThWAT* 5:62–69.

KEPPER, MARTINA. "Genesis, Das erste Buch Mose." Pages 107–19 in *Einleitung in die Septuaginta.* Edited by Siegfried Kreuzer. Vol. 1 of *Handbuch zur Septuaginta (LXX.H).* Edited by Martin Karrer, Wolfgang Kraus, and Siegfried Kreuzer. Gütersloh: Gütersloher Verlagshaus, 2016.

KILIAN, RUDOLF. *Die vorpriesterlichen Abrahamüberlieferungen.* Bonn: Hanstein, 1966.

KING, THOMAS J. *The Realignment of the Priestly Literature: The Priestly Narrative in Genesis and Its Relation to Priestly Legislation and the Holiness School.* PTMS 102. Eugene, OR: Pickwick, 2009.

KITCHEN, KENNETH A. "The Tabernacle—A Bronze Age Artefact." *ErIsr* 24 (1993): 119–29.

KITTEL, RUDOLF. *Die Bücher der Könige.* HKAT I/5. Göttingen: Vandenhoeck & Ruprecht, 1900.

KITTEL, RUDOLF. *Geschichte des Volkes Israel, Erster Band: Palästina in der Urzeit, das Werden des Volkes, Geschichte der Zeit bis zum Tode Josuas.* 7th ed. Stuttgart: Kohlhammer, 1932.

KLEIN, RALPH W. "Archaic Chronologies and the Textual History of the OT." *HTR* 67 (1974): 255–63.

KNAUF, ERNST AXEL. "Die Priesterschrift und die Geschichten der Deuteronomisten." Pages 101–18 in *The Future of Deuteronomistic History.* Edited by Thomas Römer. BETL 147. Leuven: Peeters, 2000.

KNAUF, ERNST AXEL. "Genesis 36,1–43." Pages 291–300 in *Jacob: Commentaire à plusieurs voix de Gen. 25–36; Mélanges offerts à Albert de Pury.* Edited by Jean-Daniel Macchi and Thomas Römer. Geneva: Labor et Fides, 2001.

KNAUF, ERNST AXEL. "Ishmael (Son of Abraham and Hagar)." *EBR* 13:352–55.

KNAUF, ERNST AXEL. *Ismael: Untersuchungen zur Geschichte Palästinas und Nordarabiens im 1. Jahrtausend v. Chr.* 2nd ed. ADPV. Wiesbaden: Harrassowitz, 1989.

KNAUF, ERNST AXEL. *Josua.* ZBK 6. Zurich: TVZ, 2008.

KNAUF, ERNST AXEL. *Richter.* ZBK 7. Zurich: TVZ, 2016.

KNOHL, ISRAEL. "Nimrod and the Dates of P and J." Pages 45–52 in volume 1 of *Birkat Shalom: Studies in the Bible, Ancient Near Eastern Literature, and Postbiblical Judaism Presented to Shalom M. Paul on the Occasion of His Seventieth Birthday.* Edited by Chaim Cohen et al. 2 volumes. Winona Lake, IN: Eisenbrauns, 2008.

KNOHL, ISRAEL. *The Sancuary of Silence: The Priestly Torah and the Holiness School.* Minneapolis: Augsburg Fortress, 1995.

KOCH, KLAUS. *Die Priesterschrift von Exodus 25 bis Leviticus 16: Eine überlieferungsgeschichtliche und literarkritische Untersuchung.* FRLANT 71. Göttingen: Vandenhoeck & Ruprecht, 1959.

KOCH, KLAUS. "P—kein Redaktor! Erinnerung an zwei Eckdaten der Quellenscheidung." *VT* 37 (1987): 446–67.

KÖCKERT, MATTHIAS. *Abraham: Ahnvater – Vorbild – Kultstifter.* Biblische Gestalten 31. Leipzig: Evangelische Verlagsanstalt, 2017.

KÖCKERT, MATTHIAS. "Das Land in der priesterlichen Komposition des Pentateuch." Pages 147–62 in *Von Gott reden: Beiträge zur Theologie und Exegese des Alten Testaments; Festschrift für Siegfried Wagner zum 65. Geburtstag.* Edited by Dieter Vieweger and Ernst-Joachim Waschke. Neukirchen-Vluyn: Neukirchener Verlag, 1995.

KÖCKERT, MATTHIAS. "Die Geschichte der Abrahamüberlieferung." Pages 103–28 in *Congress Volume: Leiden, 2004.* Edited by André Lemaire. VTSup 109. Leiden: Brill, 2006.

KÖCKERT, MATTHIAS. "Gen 20–22 als nachpriesterliche Erweiterung der Vätergeschichte." Pages 157–76 in *The Post-Priestly Pentateuch: New Perspectives on Its Redactional Development and Theological Profiles.* Edited by Federico Giuntoli and Konrad Schmid. FAT 101. Tübingen: Mohr Siebeck, 2015.

KÖCKERT, MATTHIAS. "Wie wurden Abraham- und Jakobüberlieferung zu einer 'Vätergeschichte' verbunden?" *HeBAI* 3 (2014): 43–66.

KOENEN, KLAUS. "Aaron/Aaroniden." *WiBiLex.* https://www.bibelwissenschaft.de/stichwort/11012/.

KOENEN, KLAUS. "1200 Jahre von Abrahams Geburt bis zum Tempelbau." *ZAW* 126 (2014): 494–505.

KOHATA, FUJIKO. *Jahwist und Priesterschrift in Exodus 3–14.* BZAW 166. Berlin: de Gruyter, 1986.

KONKEL, MICHAEL. "Exodus 32–34 and the Quest for an Enneateuch." Pages 169–84 in *Pentateuch, Hexateuch, or Enneateuch? Identifying Literary Works in Genesis through Kings.* Edited by Thomas B. Dozeman, Thomas Römer, and Konrad Schmid. Atlanta: SBL Press, 2009.

KRAELING, EMIL G. "Geographical Notes." *AJSL* 41 (1925): 193–94.

KRAELING, EMIL G. "Terach." *ZAW* 40 (1922–23): 153–54.

KRATZ, REINHARD G. *The Composition of the Narrative Books of the Old Testament.* Translated by John Bowden. London: T&T Clark, 2005.

KRATZ, REINHARD G., and HERMANN SPIECKERMANN. "Schöpfer/Schöpfung II." *TRE* 30:258–83.

KRÜGER, THOMAS. "Das menschliche Herz und die Weisung Gottes." Pages 65–92 in *Rezeption und Auslegung im Alten Testament und in seinem Umfeld: Ein Symposion aus Anlass des 60. Geburtstags von Odil Hannes Steck.* Edited by Reinhard G. Kratz and Thomas Krüger. OBO 153. Fribourg: Presses Universitaires; Göttingen: Vandenhoeck & Ruprecht, 1997.

KRÜGER, THOMAS. "Erwägungen zur Redaktion der Meerwundererzählung (Exodus 13:17–14:31)." *ZAW* 108 (1996): 519–33.

KRÜGER, THOMAS. "Genesis 1:1–2:3 and the Development of the Pentateuch." Pages 125–38 in *The Pentateuch: International Perspectives on Current Research.* Edited by Thomas B. Dozeman, Konrad Schmid, and Baruch J. Schwartz. FAT 78. Tübingen: Mohr Siebeck, 2011.

KRÜGER, THOMAS. "Schöpfung und Sabbat in Genesis 2,1–3." Pages 155–69 in *Sprachen – Bilder – Klänge: Dimensionen der Theologie im Alten Testament und in seinem Umfeld; Festschrift für Rüdiger Bartelmus zu seinem 65. Geburtstag.* Edited by Christiane Karrer-Grube and Jutta Krispenz. AOAT 359. Münster: Ugarit-Verlag, 2009.

KUENEN, ABRAHAM. "Beiträge zur Hexateuchkritik, VII: Manna und Wachteln (Ex. 16.)." Pages 276–94 in *Gesammelte Abhandlungen zur biblischen Wissenschaft: Aus dem Holländischen übersetzt von K. Budde*. Freiburg im Breisgau: Herder, 1894.

KUENEN, ABRAHAM. *An Historico-Critical Inquiry into the Origin and Composition of the Hexateuch (Pentateuch and Book of Joshua)*. Translated by Philip Henry Wicksteed. London: Macmillan, 1886.

KUENEN, ABRAHAM. *Historisch-critisch onderzoek naar het ontstaan en de verzameling van de boeken des Ouden Verbonds I*. Leiden: Engels, 1861.

KUENEN, ABRAHAM. *Historisch-kritische Einleitung in die Bücher des alten Testaments hinsichtlich ihrer Entstehung und Sammlung*. 3 volumes. Leipzig: Schulze, 1885–94.

KVANVIG, HELGE S. *Primeval History: Babylonian, Biblical, and Enochic; An Intertextual Reading*. Leiden: Brill, 2011.

LAMBERT, MAYER. "A Study of the First Chapter of Genesis." *HUCA* 1 (1924): 3–12.

LAMBERT, WILFRED GEORGE. "The Qualifications of Babylonian Diviners." Pages 141–58 in *Festschrift für Rykle Borger zu seinem 65. Geburtstag am 24. Mai 1994*. Edited by Stefan M. Maul. CM 10. Groningen: Styx, 1998.

LAMBERT, WILFRED GEORGE, and A. R. (ALAN RALPH) MILLARD. *Atra-Ḥasis: The Babylonian Story of the Flood*. Repr. ed. Winona Lake, IN: Eisenbrauns, 1999.

LE BOULLUEC, ALAIN, and PIERRE SANDEVOIR. *La Bible d'Alexandrie, I: L'Exode; Traduction du texte grec de la Septante; Introduction et Notes*. Paris: Cerf, 1986.

LECOQ, PIERRE. *Les inscriptions de la Perse achemenide: Traduit du vieux perse, de l'élamite, du babylonien et de l'araméen*. Paris: Gallimard, 1997.

LEMAIRE, ANDRÉ. "Le sabbat à l'époque royale israélite." *RB* 80 (1973): 161–85.

LEMAIRE, ANDRÉ. "Sabbat." *NBL* 3:388–91.

LEMMELIJN, BÉNÉDICTE. *A Plague of Texts? A Text-Critical Study of the So-Called "Plagues Narrative" in Exodus 7:14–11:10*. OTS 56. Leiden: Brill, 2015.

LEVIN, CHRISTOPH. *Der Jahwist*. FRLANT 157. Göttingen: Vandenhoeck & Ruprecht, 1993.

LEVIN, CHRISTOPH. "Die Priesterschrift als Quelle: Eine Erinnerung." Pages 9–31 in *Abschied von der Priesterschrift? Zum Stand der Pentateuchdebatte*. Edited by Friedhelm Hartenstein and Konrad Schmid. VWGTh 40. Leipzig: Evangelische Verlagsanstalt, 2015.

LEVIN, CHRISTOPH. "Tatbericht in der priesterschriftlichen Schöpfungserzählung." *ZTK* 91 (1994): 115–33.

LEVINE, BARUCH A. "Late Language in the Priestly Source: Some Literary and Historical Observations." *WJCS* 8 (1983): 69–82.

LICHTHEIM, MIRIAM. "I. Instructions. Merikare (1.35)." *COS* 1:65.

LINAFELT, TOD. Review of *A Prophet Reads Scripture: Allusion in Isaiah 40–66*, by Benjamin D. Sommer. *JQR* 90 (2000): 501–4.

LIPIŃSKI, EDWARD. "Les Chamites selon Gen 10, 6–10 et 1 Chr 1, 8–16." *ZAH* 5 (1992): 135–52.

LIPIŃSKI, EDWARD. "Les Sémites selon Gen 10,21–30 et 1 Chr 1,17–23." *ZAH* 6 (1993): 193–215.

LIPIŃSKI, EDWARD. "צָפוֹן." *TDOT* 12:435–42.

LIPSCHITS, ODED. "Abraham zwischen Mamre und Jerusalem." Pages 187–209 in *The Politics of the Ancestors: Exegetical and Historical Perspectives on Genesis 12–36*. Edited by Mark G. Brett and Jakob Wöhrle. FAT 124. Tübingen: Mohr Siebeck, 2018.

LIPSCHITS, ODED. "Persian Period Finds from Jerusalem: Facts and Interpretations." *JHS* 9, art. 20 (2009). https://doi.org/10.5508/jhs.2009.v9.a20.

LIPSCHITS, ODED, THOMAS RÖMER, and HERVÉ GONZALEZ. "The Pre-Priestly Abraham Narratives from Monarchic to Persian Times." *Sem* 59 (2017): 261–96.

LIPSCHITS, ODED and DAVID S. VANDERHOOFT. *The Yehud Stamp Impressions: A Corpus of Inscribed Impressions from the Persian and Hellenistic Periods in Judah.* Winona Lake, IN: Eisenbrauns, 2011.

LO SARDO, DOMENICO. *Post-Priestly Additions and Rewritings in Exodus 35–40: An Analysis of MT, LXX, and Vetus Latina.* FAT II/119. Tübingen: Mohr Siebeck, 2020.

LOHFINK, NORBERT. "Die Priesterschrift und die Geschichte." Pages 183–225 in *Congress Volume: Göttingen, 1977.* Edited by J. A. Emerton. VTSup 29. Leiden: Brill, 1978.

LOHFINK, NORBERT. "Die Schichten des Pentateuch und der Krieg," Pages 255–315 in *Studien zum Pentateuch.* SBAB 4. Stuttgart: Katholisches Bibelwerk, 1988.

LOHFINK, NORBERT. *Studien zum Pentateuch.* SBAB 4. Stuttgart: Katholisches Bibelwerk, 1988.

LÖHR, MAX. *Untersuchungen zum Hexateuchproblem, I: Der Priestercodex in der Genesis.* BZAW 38. Giessen: Töpelmann, 1924.

LUBSCZYK, HANS. "Wortschöpfung und Tatschöpfung: Zur Entwicklung der priesterlichen Schöpfungslehre in Gen 1,1–2,4a." *BibLeb* 6 (1965): 191–208.

MACCHI, JEAN-DANIEL. *Israël et ses tribus selon Genèse 49.* OBO 145. Fribourg: Presses Universitaires; Göttingen: Vandenhoeck & Ruprecht, 1999.

MACCHI, JEAN-DANIEL. "'Ne ressassez plus les choses d'autrefois': Esaïe 43,16–21, un surprenant regard deutéro-ésaïen sur le passé." *ZAW* 121 (2009): 225–41.

MACDONALD, NATHAN. "David's Two Priests." Pages 243–62 in *Writing, Rewriting, and Overwriting in the Books of Deuteronomy and the Former Prophets; Essays in Honour of Cynthia Edenburg.* Edited by Ido Koch, Thomas Römer, and Omer Sergi. BETL 304. Leuven: Peeters, 2019.

MACDONALD, NATHAN. *Priestly Rule: Polemic and Biblical Interpretation in Ezekiel 44.* BZAW 476. Berlin: de Gruyter, 2015.

MAGEN, YITZHAK. "The Dating of the First Phase of the Samaritan Temple on Mount Gerizim in Light of the Archaeological Evidence." Pages 157–211 in *Judah and the Judeans in the Fourth Century B.C.E.* Edited by Oded Lipschits, Gary N. Knoppers, and Rainer Albertz. Winona Lake, IN: Eisenbrauns, 2007.

MAGEN, YITZHAK. *Mount Gerizim Excavations, II: A Temple City.* JSP 8. Jerusalem: Staff Officer of Archaeology, 2008.

MAGEN, YITZHAK, HAGGAI MISGAV, and LEVANA TSFANIA, eds. *Mount Gerizim Excavations, I: The Aramaic, Hebrew and Samaritan Inscriptions.* JSP 2. Jerusalem: Staff Officer of Archaeology, 2004.

MAIBERGER, PAUL. *Das Manna. Eine literarische, etymologische und naturkundliche Untersuchung.* ÄAT 6. Wiesbaden: Harrassowitz, 1983.

MARTI, LIONEL. "From Ur to Harran: History of Origins or Late Rewriting." In *The Historical Location of P.* Edited by Jürg Hutzli and Jordan Davis. ArchB. Tübingen: Mohr Siebeck, forthcoming.

MATHYS, HANS-PETER. "Die Ketubim." Pages 591–92 in *Die Entstehung des Alten Testaments.* Edited by Walter Dietrich et al. Theologische Wissenschaft 1. Stuttgart: Kohlhammer, 2014.

MATHYS, HANS-PETER. "Künstliche Personennamen im Alten Testament." Pages 218–49 in *"… der seine Lust hat am Wort des Herrn!": Festschrift für Ernst Jenni zum 80. Geburtstag.* Edited by Jürg Luchsinger, Hans-Peter Mathys, and Markus Saur. AOAT 336. Münster: Ugarit-Verlag, 2007.

MATHYS, HANS-PETER. "Numbers and Chronicles: Close Relatives 2." Pages 79–107 in *Chronicles and the Priestly Literature of the Hebrew Bible.* Edited by Jaeyoung Jeon and Louis C. Jonker. BZAW 528. Berlin: de Gruyter, 2021.

MATHYS, HANS-PETER. "Numeri und Chronik: Nahe Verwandte." Pages 555–78 in *The Books of Leviticus and Numbers.* Edited by Thomas Römer. BETL 215. Leuven: Peeters, 2008.

MAUL, STEFAN M. *Das Gilgamesch-Epos: Neu übersetzt und kommentiert.* Munich: Beck, 2005.

MAZAR, AMIHAI. "The Search for David and Solomon: An Archaeological Perspective." Pages 117–40 in *The Quest for the Historical Israel: Debating Archaeology and the History of Early Israel.* Edited by Israel Finkelstein, Amihai Mazar, and Brian B. Schmidt. ABS 17. Atlanta: SBL Press, 2007.

McEVENUE, SEAN E. *The Narrative Style of the Priestly Writer.* AnBib 50. Rome: Pontifical Biblical Institute, 1971.

METTINGER, TRYGGVE N. D. *The* Dethronement of Sabaoth: *Studies in the Shem and Kabod Theologies.* ConBOT 18. Lund: Gleerup, 1982.

MEYERS, CAROL. "Realms of Sanctity: The Case of the 'Misplaced' Incense Altar in the Tabernacle Texts of Exodus." Pages 33–46 in *Texts, Temples, and Traditions: A Tribute to Menahem Haran.* Edited by Michael V. Fox et al. Winona Lake, IN: Eisenbrauns, 1996.

MILGROM, JACOB. "H$_R$ in Leviticus and Elsewhere in the Torah." Pages 24–40 in *The Book of Leviticus: Composition and Reception.* Edited by Rolf Rendtorff, Robert A. Kugler, with the Assistance of Sarah Smith Bartlet. VTSup 93. Leiden: Brill, 2003.

MILGROM, JACOB. *Leviticus 1–16: A New Translation with Introduction and Commentary.* AB 3. New York: Doubleday, 1991.

MILGROM, JACOB. *Leviticus 17–22: A New Translation with Introduction and Commentary.* AB 3A. New York: Doubleday, 2000.

MILGROM, JACOB. *Leviticus 23–27: A New Translation with Introduction and Commentary.* AB 3B. New York: Doubleday, 2001.

MILGROM, JACOB. "Priestly ('P') Source." *ABD* 5:460.

MILGROM, JACOB. *Studies in Cultic Theology and Terminology.* SJLA 36. Leiden: Brill, 1983.

MOMMER, PETER. *Samuel: Geschichte und Uberlieferung.* WMANT 63. Neukirchen-Vluyn: Neukirchener Verlag, 1991.

MORGENSTERN, JULIAN. "The Sources of the Creation Story: Gen 1:1–2:4." *AJSL* 36 (1919–20): 169–212.

NA'AMAN, NADAV. "The Pre-Priestly Abraham Story as a Unified Exilic Work." *SJOT* 29 (2015): 157–81.

NELSON, RICHARD D. "The Role of the Priesthood in Deuteronomistic History." Pages 132–47 in *Congress Volume: Leuven, 1989.* Edited by J. A. Emerton. VTSup 43. Leiden: Brill, 1991.

NELSON, RICHARD D. "Studies in the Development of the Tabernacle Account." Ph.D. diss., Harvard University, 1987.

NEUMANN-GORSOLKE, UTE. *Herrschen in den Grenzen der Schöpfung: Ein Beitrag zur alttestamentlichen Anthropologie am Beispiel von Psalm 8, Genesis 1 und verwandten Texten.* Neukirchen-Vluyn: Neukirchener Verlag, 2004.

NIHAN, CHRISTOPHE. *From Priestly Torah to Pentateuch: A Study in the Composition of the Book of Leviticus.* FAT II/25. Tübingen: Mohr Siebeck, 2007.

NIHAN, CHRISTOPHE. "L'écrit sacerdotal entre mythe et histoire." Pages 151–91 in *Ancient and Modern Scriptural Historiography / L'historiographie biblique, ancienne et moderne.* Edited by George J. Brooke and Thomas Römer. Leuven: Peeters, 2007.

NIHAN, CHRISTOPHE. "La mort de Moïse (Nb 20,1–13; 20,22–29; 27,12–23) et l'édition finale du livre des Nombres." Pages 145–82 in *Les dernières rédactions du Pentateuque, de l'Hexateuque et de l'Ennéateuque.* Edited by Thomas Römer and Konrad Schmid. BETL 203. Leuven: Peeters, 2007.

NIHAN, CHRISTOPHE. "Le pectoral d'Aaron et la figure du grand prêtre dans les traditions sacerdotales du Pentateuque." Pages 23–55 in *Congress Volume: Stellenbosch, 2016*. Edited by Louis C. Jonker, Gideon R. Kotzé, and Christl M. Maier. VTSup 177. Leiden: Brill, 2017.

NIHAN, CHRISTOPHE. "The Priestly Covenant: Its Reinterpretation, and the Composition of 'P.'" Pages 87–128 in *The Strata of the Priestly Writings: Contemporary Debate and Future Directions*. Edited by Sarah Shectman and Joel S. Baden. AThANT 95. Zurich: TVZ, 2009.

NÖLDEKE, THEODOR. *Untersuchungen zur Kritik des Alten Testaments*. Kiel: Schwers, 1869.

NOTH, MARTIN. *Das dritte Buch Mose: Leviticus*. ATD 6. Göttingen: Vandenhoeck & Ruprecht, 1962.

NOTH, MARTIN. *Das zweite Buch Mose: Exodus*. ATD 5. Göttingen: Vandenhoeck & Ruprecht, 1958.

NOTH, MARTIN. *Die Israelitischen Personennamen im Rahmen der gemeinsemitischen Namengebung*. BWANT 3. Stuttgart: Kohlhammer, 1928.

NOTH, MARTIN. *A History of Pentateuchal Traditions*. Translated by Bernhard W. Anderson. Englewood Cliffs, NJ: Prentice Hall, 1972.

NOTH, MARTIN. *Könige*. BKAT 11. Neukirchen-Vluyn: Neukirchener Verlag, 1968.

NOTH, MARTIN. *Überlieferungsgeschichte des Pentateuchs*. 2nd ed. Darmstadt: Wissenschaftliche Buchgesellschaft, 1960.

NOTH, MARTIN. *Überlieferungsgeschichtliche Studien*. Halle: Niemeyer, 1943.

NOTTER, VIKTOR. *Biblischer Schöpfungsbericht und ägyptische Schöpfungsmythen*. SBS 68. Stuttgart: Katholisches Bibelwerk, 1974.

OEMING, MANFRED. *Das Buch der Psalmen: Psalm 1–41*. NSKAT 13.1. Stuttgart: Katholisches Bibelwerk, 2000.

OLYAN, SAUL M. "Exodus 31:12–17: The Sabbath according to H, or the Sabbath according to P and H?" *JBL* 124 (2005): 201–9.

OREN, ELIEZER D. "Preliminary report." Pages 101–58 in *Qadmaniot Sinai (Sinai in Antiquity)*. Edited by Ze'ev Meshel and Israel Finkelstein. Tel Aviv: Tel Aviv University Press, 1980.

OSBORNE, WILLIAM R. "Anteriority and Justification." *OTE* 25/2 (2012): 369–82.

OSWALD, WOLFGANG. *Israel am Gottesberg: Eine Untersuchung zur Literaturgeschichte der vorderen Sinaiperikope Ex 19–24 und deren historischem Hintergrund*. OBO 159. Fribourg: Presses Universitaires; Göttingen: Vandenhoeck & Ruprecht, 1998.

OTTO, ECKART. "Das Buch Levitikus zwischen Priesterschrift und Pentateuch." Review of *From Priestly Torah to Pentateuch*, by Christophe Nihan. *TRu* 74 (2009): 470–79.

OTTO, ECKART. *Das Deuteronomium: Politische Theologie und Rechtsreform in Juda und Assyrien*. BZAW 284. Berlin: de Gruyter, 1999.

OTTO, ECKART. *Das Deuteronomium im Pentateuch und Hexateuch: Studien zur Literaturgeschichte von Pentateuch und Hexateuch im Lichte des Deuteronomiumrahmens*. FAT 30. Tübingen: Mohr Siebeck, 2000.

OTTO, ECKART. *Das Gesetz des Mose: Eine Literatur- und Rechtsgeschichte der Mosebücher*. Darmstadt: Wissenschaftliche Buchgesellschaft, 2007.

OTTO, ECKART. *Deuteronomium 1–11*. 2 volumes. HThKAT. Freiburg im Breisgau: Herder, 2011–12.

OTTO, ECKART. "Die nachpriesterliche Pentateuchredaktion im Buch Exodus." Pages 61–111 in *Studies in the Book of Exodus: Redaction – Reception – Interpretation*. Edited by Marc Vervenne. BETL 126. Leuven: Leuven University Press, 1996.

OTTO, ECKART. "Die Paradieserzählung Genesis 2–3: Eine nachpriesterschriftliche Lehrerzählung in ihrem religionsgeschichtlichen Kontext." Pages 167–92 in *"Jedes Ding hat seine Zeit …": Studien zur israelitischen und altorientalischen Weisheit; Diethelm Michel zum 65. Geburtstag.* Edited by Anja Angela Diesel et al. BZAW 241. Berlin: de Gruyter, 1996.

OTTO, ECKART. "Die Priesterschrift und das Deuteronomium im Buch Levitikus: Zur Integration des Deuteronomiums in den Pentateuch." Pages 161–85 in *Abschied von der Priesterschrift? Zum Stand der Pentateuchdebatte.* Edited by Friedhelm Hartenstein and Konrad Schmid. VWGTh 40. Leipzig: Evangelische Verlagsanstalt, 2015.

OTTO, ECKART. "Die Ursprünge der Bundestheologie im Alten Testament und im Alten Orient." *ZAR* 4 (1998): 1–84.

OTTO, ECKART. "Forschungen zur Priesterschrift." *TRu* 62 (1997): 1–50.

OTTO, ECKART. "Gab es 'historische' und 'fiktive' Aaroniden im Alten Testament." *ZABR* 7 (2001): 403–14.

OTTO, ECKART. "Priestertum II, Religionsgeschichtlich 1., Alter Orient und Altes Testament." *RGG* 6:1646–49.

OTTO, ECKART. "Sabbat." *RGG* 7:712–13.

OWCZAREK, SUSANNE. *Die Vorstellung vom Wohnen Gottes inmitten seines Volkes in der Priesterschrift.* Europäische Hochschulschriften 23. Bern: Lang, 1998.

PAKKALA, JUHA. "Jeroboam without Bulls." *ZAW* 120 (2008): 501–25.

PERLITT, LOTHAR. "Priesterschrift im Deuteronomium?" Pages 65–87 in *Lebendige Forschung im Alten Testament.* Edited by Otto Kaiser. BZAW 100. Berlin: de Gruyter, 1988.

PÉTER-CONTESSE, RENÉ. *Lévitique 1–16.* CAT IIIa. Geneva: Labor et Fides, 1993.

PFEIFFER, HENRIK. "Gottesbezeichnungen/Gottesnamen (AT), 3: El Schaddaj/Schaddaj ("Allmächtiger"?)." *WiBiLex.* https://www.bibelwissenschaft.de/stichwort/19928/.

PFEIFFER, ROBERT H. (ROBERT HENRY). "A Non-Israelite Source of the Book of Genesis." *ZAW* 48 (1930): 66–73.

PIROT, LOUIS, and ALBERT CLAMER. *La Sainte Bible, I: Genèse.* Paris: Letouzey et Ané, 1953.

POHLMANN, KARL-FRIEDRICH. *Das Buch des Propheten Hesekiel (Ezechiel) Kapitel 20–48.* ATD 22.2. Göttingen: Vandenhoeck & Ruprecht, 2001.

POLA, THOMAS. "Back to the Future: The Twofold Priestly Concept of History." Pages 39–65 in *Torah and the Book of Numbers.* Edited by Christian Frevel, Thomas Pola, and Aaron Schart. FAT II/62. Tübingen: Mohr Siebeck, 2013.

POLA, THOMAS. *Die ursprüngliche Priesterschrift: Beobachtungen zur Literarkritik und Traditionsgeschichte von P^g.* WMANT 70. Neukirchen-Vluyn: Neukirchener Verlag, 1995.

POLZIN, ROBERT. *Late Biblical Hebrew: Toward an Historical Typology of Biblical Hebrew Prose.* Harvard Semitic Monographs 12. Missoula, MT: Scholars Press, 1976.

POPPER, JULIUS. *Der biblische Bericht über die Stiftshütte: Ein Beitrag zur Geschichte der Composition und Diaskeue des Pentateuch.* Leipzig: Hunger, 1862.

POSENER, GEORGES. "Sur l'orientation et l'ordre des points cardinaux chez les Egyptiens." *NAWG* 1 (1965): 69–78.

PRESTEL, PETER, and STEFAN SCHORCH. "Genesis/Das erste Buch Mose." Pages 145–51 in *Septuaginta Deutsch, Erläuterungen und Kommentare (I).* Edited by Martin Karrer and Wolfgang Kraus. Stuttgart: Deutsche Bibelgesellschaft, 2011.

PROCKSCH, OTTO. *Die Genesis.* 2nd ed. KAT 1. Leipzig: Deichert, 1924.

PROPP, WILLIAM HENRY. *Exodus 1–18: A New Translation with Introduction and Commentary.* AB 2. New York: Doubleday, 1999.

PROPP, WILLIAM HENRY. *Exodus 19–40: A New Translation with Introduction and Commentary.* AB 2A. New York: Doubleday, 2006.

PUMMER, REINHARD. "Samaritan Studies – Recent Research Results." Pages 57–77 in *The Bible, Qumran, and the Samaritans*. Edited by Magnar Kartveit and Gary N. Knoppers. StSam 10; SJ 104. Berlin: de Gruyter, 2018.

PURY, ALBERT DE. "Abraham: The Priestly Writer's 'Ecumenical' Ancestor." Pages 163–81 in *Rethinking the Foundations: Historiography in the Ancient World and in the Bible; Essays in Honor of John Van Seters*. Edited by Steven L. McKenzie, Thomas Römer, and Hans Heinrich Schmid. BZAW 294. Berlin: de Gruyter, 2000.

PURY, ALBERT DE. *Die Patriarchen und die Priesterschrift / Les Patriarches et le document sacerdotal: Gesammelte Studien zu seinem 70. Geburtstag / Recueil d'articles, à l'occasion de son 70e anniversaire*. Edited by Jean-Daniel Macchi, Thomas Römer, and Konrad Schmid. AThANT 99. Zurich: TVZ, 2010.

PURY, ALBERT DE. "Genèse 12–36." Pages 217–38 in *Introduction à l'Ancien Testament*. Edited by Thomas Römer et al. 2nd ed. Geneva: Labor et Fides, 2009.

PURY, ALBERT DE. "Gottesname, Gottesbezeichnung und Gottesbegriff: 'Elohim als Indiz zur Entstehungsgeschichte des Pentateuch." Pages 25–47 in *Abschied vom Jahwisten: Die Komposition des Hexateuch in der jüngsten Diskussion*. Edited by Jan Christian Gertz, Konrad Schmid, and Markus Witte. BZAW 315. Berlin: de Gruyter, 2002.

PURY, ALBERT DE. "Pg as the Absolute Beginning." Pages 13–42 in *Die Patriarchen und die Priesterschrift / Les Patriarches et le document sacerdotal: Gesammelte Studien zu seinem 70. Geburtstag / Recueil d'articles, à l'occasion de son 70e anniversaire*. Edited by Jean-Daniel Macchi, Thomas Römer, and Konrad Schmid. AThANT 99. Zurich: TVZ, 2010.

PURY, ALBERT DE, THOMAS RÖMER, and KONRAD SCHMID. *L'Ancien Testament commenté: La Genèse*. Paris: Bayard; Geneva: Labor et Fides, 2016.

QIMRON, ELISHA. *The Hebrew of the Dead Sea Scrolls*. HSS 29. Atlanta: Scholars Press, 1986.

RAD, GERHARD VON. *Das Erste Buch Mose: Genesis*. 11th ed. ATD 2–4. Göttingen: Vandenhoeck & Ruprecht, 1981.

RAD, GERHARD VON. *Die Priesterschrift im Hexateuch literarisch untersucht und theologisch gewertet*. BWANT 65. Stuttgart: Kohlhammer, 1934.

RAD, GERHARD VON. *Theologie des Alten Testaments, Band I: Die Theologie der geschichtlichen Überlieferung Israels*. 10th ed. Munich: Kaiser, 1992.

REDFORD, DONALD B. *A Study of the Biblical Story of Joseph (Genesis 37–50)*. VTSup 20. Leiden: Brill, 1970.

REINDL, JOSEPH. "Der Finger Gottes und die Macht der Götter: Ein Problem des ägyptischen Diasporajudentums und sein literarischer Niederschlag." Pages 49–60 in *Dienst der Vermittlung: Festschrift zum 25-jährigen Bestehen des Philosophisch-Theologischen Studiums im Priesterseminar Erfurt*. Edited by Wilhelm Ernst et al. ETS 37. Leipzig: St. Benno, 1977.

RENDSBURG, GARY A. "Late Biblical Hebrew and the Date of 'P.'" *JANESCU* 12 (1980): 65–80.

RENDTORFF, ROLF. "L'histoire biblique des origines (Gen 1–11) dans le contexte de la rédaction 'sacerdotale' du Pentateuque." Pages 83–94 in *Le Pentateuque en question: Les origines et la composition des cinq premiers livres de la Bible à la lumière des recherches récentes*. Edited by Albert de Pury. Geneva: Labor et Fides, 1989.

RENDTORFF, ROLF. *Leviticus*. BKAT 3.1. Neukirchen-Vluyn: Neukirchener Verlag, 1985.

RENDTORFF, ROLF. *The Problem of the Process of Transmission in the Pentateuch*. Translated by John J. Scullion. JSOTSup 89. Sheffield: JSOT Press, 1990.

RENDTORFF, ROLF. "Two Kinds of P? Some Reflections on the Occasion of the Publishing of Jacob Milgrom's Commentary on Leviticus 1–16." *JSOT* 60 (1993): 75–81.

RHYDER, JULIA. *Centralizing the Cult: The Holiness Legislation in Leviticus 17–26*. FAT 134. Tübingen: Mohr Siebeck, 2019.

Rofé, Alexander. "An Enquiry into the Betrothal of Rebekah." Pages 27–39 in *Die Hebräische Bibel und ihre zweifache Nachgeschichte: Festschrift für Rolf Rendtorff zum 65. Geburtstag*. Edited by Erhard Blum. Neukirchen-Vluyn: Neukirchener Verlag, 1990.

Rofé, Alexander. *Introduction to the Literature of the Hebrew Bible*. Biblical Studies 9. Jerusalem: Simor, 2009.

Rofé, Alexander. "La composizione de Gen 24." *BeO* 129 (1981): 161–65.

Röhrig, Meike J. *Innerbiblische Auslegung und priesterliche Fortschreibungen in Lev 8–10*. FAT II/128. Tübingen: Mohr Siebeck, 2021.

Römer, Thomas. "Abraham Traditions in the Hebrew Bible outside the Book of Genesis." Pages 159–80 in *The Book of Genesis: Composition, Reception, and Interpretation*. Edited by Craig A. Evans, Joel N. Lohr, and David L. Petersen. VTSup 152. Leiden: Brill, 2012.

Römer, Thomas. "The Creation of Humans and Their Multiplication: A Comparative Reading of Athra-Hasis, Gilgamesh XI and Genesis 1; 6–9." *ITS* 50 (2013): 123–31.

Römer, Thomas. "Der Pentateuch." Pages 53–166 in *Die Entstehung des Alten Testaments*. Edited by Walter Dietrich et al. Theologische Wissenschaft 1. Stuttgart: Kohlhammer, 2014.

Römer, Thomas. "The Exodus Narrative according to the Priestly Document." Pages 157–74 in *The Strata of the Priestly Writings: Contemporary Debate and Future Directions*. Edited by Sarah Shectman and Joel S. Baden. AThANT 95. Zurich: TVZ, 2009.

Römer, Thomas. "From the Call of Moses to the Parting of the Sea: Reflections on the Priestly Version of the Exodus Narrative." Pages 121–50 in *The Book of Exodus: Composition, Reception, and Interpretation*. Edited by Thomas B. Dozeman, Craig A. Evans, and Joel N. Lohr. VTSup 164. Leiden: Brill, 2014.

Römer, Thomas. "Gen 15 und Gen 17: Beobachtungen und Anfragen zu einem Dogma der 'neueren' und 'neuesten' Pentateuch-kritik." *DBAT* 26 (1989–90): 32–47.

Römer, Thomas. "Genèse 15 et les tensions de la communauté juive postexilique dans le cycle d'Abraham." *Transeu* 7 (1994): 107–21.

Römer, Thomas. "The Hebrew Bible and Greek Philosophy and Mythology: Some Case Studies." *Sem* 57 (2015): 185–203.

Römer, Thomas. "Israel's Sojourn in the Wilderness and the Construction of the Book of Numbers." Pages 419–45 in *Reflection and Refraction: Studies in Biblical Historiography in Honour of A. Graeme Auld*. Edited by Robert Rezetko et al. VTSup 113. Leiden: Brill, 2007.

Römer, Thomas. "The Joseph Story in the Book of Genesis: Pre-P or Post-P?" Pages 185–201 in *The Post-Priestly Pentateuch: New Perspectives on Its Redactional Development and Theological Profiles*. Edited by Federico Giuntoli and Konrad Schmid. FAT 101. Tübingen: Mohr Siebeck, 2015.

Römer, Thomas. *L'Ancien Testament commenté: L'Exode*. Paris: Bayard; Geneva: Labor et Fides, 2017.

Römer, Thomas. "La construction d'Abraham comme ancêtre œcuménique." *RSR* 26 (2014): 7–23.

Römer, Thomas. *Moïse en version originale*. Paris: Bayard; Geneva: Labor et Fides, 2015.

Römer, Thomas. *The So-Called Deuteronomistic History: A Sociological, Historical and Literary Introduction*. London: T&T Clark, 2007.

Rösel, Martin. "Die Chronologie der Flut in Gen 7–8: Keine neuen textkritischen Lösungen." *ZAW* 110 (1998): 590–93.

Rösel, Martin. *Übersetzung als Vollendung der Auslegung: Studien zur Genesis-Septuaginta*. BZAW 223. Berlin: de Gruyter, 1994.

Roskop, Angela R. *The Wilderness Itineraries: Genre, Geography, and the Growth of Torah*. History, Archaeology, and Culture of the Levant 3. Winona Lake, IN: Eisenbrauns, 2011.

RÜCKL, JAN. "The Leadership of the Judean Community according to the Book of Haggai." Pages 59–84 in *Transforming Authority: Concepts of Leadership in Prophetic and Chronistic Literature*. Edited by Katharina Pyschny and Sarah Schulz. BZAW 518. Berlin: de Gruyter, 2021.

RÜCKL, JAN. *A Sure House: Studies on the Dynastic Promise to David in the Books of Samuel and Kings*. Fribourg: Presses Universitaires; Göttingen: Vandenhoeck & Ruprecht, 2016.

RUDNIG, THILO ALEXANDER. *Heilig und profan: Redaktionskritische Studien zu Ez 40–48*. BZAW 287. Berlin: de Gruyter, 2000.

RUDNIG, THILO ALEXANDER. "König ohne Tempel: 2 Samuel 7 in Tradition und Redaktion." *VT* 61 (2011): 426–46.

RUDOLPH, WILHELM. *Der "Elohist" von Exodus bis Joshua*. BZAW 68. Berlin: Töpelmann, 1938.

RUPPERT, LOTHAR. *Genesis: Ein kritischer und theologischer Kommentar*. 4 volumes. FB 70. Würzburg: Echter, 1992–2008.

RUPRECHT, EBERHARD. "Stellung und Bedeutung der Erzählung vom Mannawunder." *ZAW* 86 (1974): 269–307.

RÜTERSWÖRDEN, UDO. "Der Bogen in Genesis 9: Militärhistorische und traditionsgeschichtliche Erwägungen zu einem biblischen Symbol." *UF* 20 (1988): 248–63.

RÜTERSWÖRDEN, UDO. *Dominium terrae: Studien zur Genese einer alttestamentlichen Vorstellung*. BZAW 215. Berlin: de Gruyter, 1993.

RUWE, ANDREAS. *'Heiligkeitsgesetz' und 'Priesterschrift': Literaturgeschichtliche und rechtssystematische Untersuchungen zu Leviticus 17,1–26,2*. FAT 26. Tübingen: Mohr Siebeck, 1999.

SÁENZ-BADILLOS, ANGEL. *A History of the Hebrew Language*. Translated by John Elwolde. Cambridge: Cambridge University Press, 1993.

SAMUEL, HARALD. *Von Priestern zum Patriarchen: Redaktions- und traditionsgeschichtliche Studien zu Levi und den Leviten in der Literatur des Zweiten Tempels*. BZAW 448. Berlin: de Gruyter, 2014.

SANDERSON, JUDITH E. *An Exodus Scroll from Qumran: 4QpaleoExodᵐ and the Samaritan Tradition*. HSS 30. Atlanta: Scholars Press, 1986.

SARNA, NAHUM M. *The JPS Torah Commentary: Genesis*. Philadelphia: Jewish Publication Society of America, 1989.

SAUNERON, SERGE. "Le créateur androgyne." *Mélanges Mariottes* 32 (1961): 242–44.

SAUNERON, SERGE, and JEAN YOYOTTE. "La naissance du monde selon l'Égypte ancienne: La naissance du monde." Pages 17–91 in *Sources Orientales I: La naissance du monde*. Paris: Éditions du Seuil, 1959.

SAUR, MARKUS. *Der Tyroszyklus des Ezechielbuches*. BZAW 386. Berlin: de Gruyter, 2008.

SCHÄFER, PETER. "Tempel und Schöpfung: Zur Interpretation einiger Heiligtumstraditionen in der rabbinischen Literatur." Pages 122–33 in *Studien zur Geschichte und Theologie des Rabbinischen Judentums*. Edited by Peter Schäfer. Kairós 16. Leiden: Brill, 1978.

SCHAPER, JOACHIM. *Priester und Leviten im achämenidischen Juda: Studien zur Kult- und Sozialgeschichte Israels in persischer Zeit*. FAT 31. Tübingen: Mohr Siebeck, 2000.

SCHARBERT, JOSEF. "Der Sinn der Toledot-Formel in der Priesterschrift." Pages 45–56 in *Wort – Gebot – Glaube: Beiträge zur Theologie des Alten Testaments; Walther Eichrodt zum 80. Geburtstag*. Edited by Hans Joachim Stoebe, Johann Jakob Stamm, and Ernst Jenni. AThANT 59. Zurich: Zwingli-Verlag, 1970.

SCHARBERT, JOSEF. *Exodus*. NEchtB 24. Würzburg: Echter, 1989.

SCHAUDIG, HANSPETER. *Die Inschriften Nabonids von Babylon und Kyros' des Grossen*. AOAT 256. Münster: Ugarit-Verlag, 2001.

SCHELLENBERG, ANNETTE. *Der Mensch, das Bild Gottes? Zum Gedanken einer Sonderstellung des Menschen im Alten Testament und in weiteren altorientalischen Quellen.* AThANT 101. Zurich: TVZ, 2011.

SCHMID, KONRAD. "Der Sinai und die Priesterschrift." Pages 114–27 in *"Gerechtigkeit und Recht zu üben" (Gen 18,19): Studien zur altorientalischen und biblischen Rechtsgeschichte, zur Religionsgeschichte Israels und zur Religionssoziologie; Festschrift für Eckart Otto zum 65. Geburtstag.* Edited by Reinhard Achenbach and Martin Arneth. BZABR 13. Wiesbaden: Harrassowitz, 2010.

SCHMID, KONRAD. "Die Unteilbarkeit der Weisheit: Überlegungen zur sogenannten Paradieserzählung und ihrer theologischen Tendenz." *ZAW* 114 (2002): 21–39.

SCHMID, KONRAD. "Differenzierungen und Konzeptualisierungen der Einheit Gottes in der Religions- und Literaturgeschichte Israels." Pages 11–38 in *Der eine Gott und die Götter: Polytheismus und Monotheismus im antiken Israel.* Edited by Manfred Oeming and Konrad Schmid. AThANT 82. Zurich: TVZ, 2003.

SCHMID, KONRAD. *Genesis and the Moses Story: Israel's Dual Origin in the Hebrew Bible.* Siphrut 3. Winona Lake, IN: Eisenbrauns, 2010.

SCHMID, KONRAD. "Gibt es eine 'abrahamitische Ökumene' im Alten Testament? Überlegungen zur religionspolitischen Theologie der Priesterschrift in Genesis 17." Pages 67–92 in *Die Erzväter in der biblischen Tradition: Festschrift für Matthias Köckert.* Edited by Anselm C. Hagedorn and Henrik Pfeiffer. BZAW 400. Berlin: de Gruyter, 2009.

SCHMID, KONRAD. "How Old Is the Hebrew Bible? A Response to Ronald Hendel and Jan Joosten." *ZAW* 132 (2020): 622–31.

SCHMID, KONRAD. "Israel am Sinai: Etappen der Forschungsgeschichte zu Ex 32–34 in seinen Kontexten." Pages 9–40 in *Gottes Volk am Sinai: Untersuchungen zu Ex 32–34 und Dtn 9–10.* Edited by Matthias Köckert and Erhard Blum. Gütersloh: Gütersloher Verlagshaus, 2001.

SCHMID, KONRAD. *Literaturgeschichte des Alten Testaments: Eine Einführung.* Darmstadt: Wissenschaftliche Buchgesellschaft, 2008.

SCHMID, KONRAD. "Loss of Immortality? Hermeneutical Aspects of Genesis 2–3 and Its Early Receptions." Pages 58–78 in *Beyond Eden: The Biblical Story of Paradise and Its Reception History.* Edited by Konrad Schmid and Christoph Riedweg. FAT II/34. Tübingen: Mohr Siebeck, 2008.

SCHMID, KONRAD. "The Neo-Documentarian Manifesto: A Critical Reading." *JBL* 140/3 (2021): 461–79.

SCHMID, KONRAD. *Schöpfung.* TdT 4. Tübingen: Mohr Siebeck, 2012.

SCHMID, KONRAD. "The So-Called Yahwist and the Literary Gap between Genesis and Exodus." Pages 29–50 in *A Farewell to the Yahwist? The Composition of the Pentateuch in Recent European Interpretation.* Edited by Thomas B. Dozeman and Konrad Schmid. Atlanta: SBL Press, 2006.

SCHMIDT, BRIAN B. "Moon." *DDD* 585–93.

SCHMIDT, LUDWIG. "Die Priesterschrift in Exodus 16." *ZAW* 119 (2007): 483–98.

SCHMIDT, LUDWIG. *Literarische Studien zur Josephsgeschichte.* BZAW 167. Berlin: de Gruyter, 1986.

SCHMIDT, LUDWIG. *Studien zur Priesterschrift.* BZAW 214. Berlin: de Gruyter, 1993.

SCHMIDT, WERNER H. *Die Schöpfungsgeschichte der Priesterschrift: Zur Überlieferungsgeschichte von Genesis 1,1–2,4a und 2,4b–3,24.* 3rd ed. WMANT 17. Neukirchen-Vluyn: Neukirchener Verlag, 1973.

SCHMIDT, WERNER H. *Exodus.* BKAT 2.1. Neukirchen-Vluyn: Neukirchener Verlag, 1988.

SCHMITT, HANS-CHRISTOPH. "Die Erzählung vom Goldenen Kalb Ex. 32* und das Deuteronomistische Geschichtswerk." Pages 235–50 in *Rethinking the Foundations: Historiography in the Ancient World and in the Bible; Essays in Honour of John Van Seters*. Edited by Steven L. McKenzie and Thomas Römer. BZAW 294. Berlin: de Gruyter, 2000.

SCHMITT, HANS-CHRISTOPH. "'Priesterliches' und 'prophetisches' Geschichtsverständnis in der Meerwundererzählung Ex 13,17–14,31." Pages 139–55 in *Textgemäß: Aufsätze und Beiträge zur Hermeneutik des Alten Testaments; Festschrift für Ernst Würthwein zum 70. Geburtstag*. Edited by Antonius H. J. Gunneweg and Otto Kaiser. Göttingen: Vandenhoeck & Ruprecht, 1979.

SCHNABEL, PAUL. *Berossos und die babylonisch-hellenistische Literatur*. Leipzig: Teubner, 1923.

SCHRADER, LUTZ. "Kommentierende Redaktion im Noah-Sintflut-Komplex der Genesis." *ZAW* 110 (1998): 489–502.

SCHÜLE, ANDREAS. *Der Prolog der hebräischen Bibel: Der literar- und theologiegeschichtliche Diskurs der Urgeschichte (Gen 1–11)*. AThANT 86. Zurich: TVZ, 2006.

SCHÜLE, ANDREAS. *Die Urgeschichte (Genesis 1–11)*. ZBK 1.1. Zurich: TVZ, 2009.

SCHWAGMEIER, PETER. "Exodos, Exodus, Das zweite Buch Mose." Pages 120–35 in *Einleitung in die Septuaginta*. Edited by Siegfried Kreuzer. Vol. 1 of *Handbuch zur Septuaginta (LXX.H)*. Edited by Martin Karrer, Wolfgang Kraus, and Siegfried Kreuzer. Gütersloh: Gütersloher Verlagshaus, 2016.

SCHWALLY, FRIEDRICH. "Die biblischen Schöpfungsberichte." *AR* 9 (1906): 159–75.

SCHWARTZ, BARUCH J. "The Documentary Hypothesis." Pages 165–87 in *The Oxford Handbook of the Pentateuch*. Edited by Joel S. Baden and Jeffrey Stackert. Oxford: Oxford University Press, 2021.

SCHWARTZ, BARUCH J. "The Priestly Account of the Theophany and Lawgiving at Sinai." Pages 103–34 in *Texts, Temples, and Traditions: A Tribute to Menahem Haran*. Edited by Michael V. Fox et al. Winona Lake, IN: Eisenbrauns, 1996.

SEEBASS, HORST. *Genesis I: Urgeschichte*. Neukirchen-Vluyn: Neukirchener Verlag, 1996.

SEEBASS, HORST. *Genesis II/1: Vätergeschichte (11,27–22,24)*. Neukirchen-Vluyn: Neukirchener Verlag, 1999.

SEEBASS, HORST. *Genesis III: Josephsgeschichte (37,1–50,26)*. Neukirchen-Vluyn: Neukirchener Verlag, 2000.

SEIDL, THEODOR. "Levitikus 16—'Schlussstein' des priesterlichen Systems der Sündenvergebung." Pages 219–48 in *Levitikus als Buch*. Edited by Heinz-Josef Fabry and Hans-Winfried Jüngling. BBB 119. Berlin: Philo, 1999.

SELMS, ADRIANUS VAN. "A Forgotten God: LAḤ." Pages 318–26 in *Studia Biblica et Semitica Theodoro Christiano Vriezen*. Edited by Willem Cornelis van Unnik and A. S. van der Woude. Wageningen: Veenman, 1966.

SERGI, OMER. "The Composition of Nathan's Oracle to David (2 Samuel 7:1–17) as a Reflection of Royal Judahite Ideology." *JBL* 129 (2010): 261–79.

SHECTMAN, SARAH. "Rachel, Leah and the Composition of Genesis." Pages 207–22 in *The Pentateuch: International Perspectives on Current Research*. Edited by Thomas B. Dozeman, Konrad Schmid, and Baruch J. Schwartz. FAT 78. Tübingen: Mohr Siebeck, 2011.

SHECTMAN, SARAH. *Women in the Pentateuch: A Feminist and Source-Critical Analysis*. HBM 23. Sheffield: Sheffield Phoenix, 2009.

SHECTMAN, SARAH. "Women in the Priestly Narrative." Pages 175–86 in *The Strata of the Priestly Writings: Contemporary Debate and Future Directions*. Edited by Sarah Shectman and Joel S. Baden. AThANT 95. Zurich: TVZ, 2009.

SHUPAK, NILI. "The Admonitions of an Egyptian Sage: The Admonitions of Ipuwer (1.42)." *COS* 1:94.

SIMONS, JAN. *Geographical and Topographical Texts of the Old Testament.* Leiden: Brill, 1959.

SKA, JEAN LOUIS. "The Call of Abraham and Israel's Birth-Certificate (Gen 12:1–4a)." Pages 46–66 in *The Exegesis of the Pentateuch: Exegetical Studies and Basic Questions.* FAT 66. Tübingen: Mohr Siebeck, 2009.

SKA, JEAN LOUIS. "El relato del diluvio: Un relato sacerdotal y algunos fragmentos redaccionales posteriores." *EstBib* 52 (1994): 37–62.

SKA, JEAN LOUIS. "Le repas d'Ex 24,11." *Bib* 74 (1993): 305–27.

SKA, JEAN LOUIS. "Les plaies d'Égypte dans le récit sacerdotal (Pᵍ)." *Bib* 60 (1979): 23–35.

SKA, JEAN LOUIS. "Quelques exemples de sommaires proleptiques dans les récits bibliques." Pages 315–26 in *Congress Volume: Paris, 1992.* Edited by J. A. Emerton. VTSup 61. Leiden: Brill, 1995.

SKA, JEAN LOUIS. "Sommaires proleptiques en Gn 27 et dans l'histoire de Joseph." *Bib* 73 (1992): 518–27.

SKA, JEAN LOUIS. "The Story of the Flood: A Priestly Writer and Some Later Editorial Fragments." Pages 1–22 in *The Exegesis of the Pentateuch: Exegetical Studies and Basic Questions.* FAT 66. Tübingen: Mohr Siebeck, 2009.

SKEHAN, PATRICK W., EUGENE ULRICH, and JUDITH E. SANDERSON. *Palaeo-Hebrew and Greek Biblical Manuscripts with a Contribution by P. J. Parsons.* DJD 9. Oxford: Clarendon, 1992.

SKINNER, JOHN. *A Critical and Exegetical Commentary on Genesis.* ICC. Edinburgh: T&T Clark, 1910.

SMEND, RUDOLF. *Die Erzählung des Hexateuch: Auf ihre Quellen untersucht.* Berlin: Reimer, 1912.

SMITH, MARK S. *The Priestly Vision of Genesis 1.* Minneapolis: Augsburg Fortress, 2010.

SODEN, WOLFRAM VON. "Der altbabylonische Atramḫasis-Mythos." Pages 612–45 in *Texte aus der Umwelt des Alten Testaments, III: Weisheitstexte, Mythen, Epen, 3.1, Weisheitstexte.* Edited by Otto Kaiser. Gütersloh: Mohn, 1990.

SOGGIN, JAN ALBERTO. *Das Buch Genesis.* Darmstadt: Wissenschaftliche Buchgesellschaft, 1997.

SOMMER, BENJAMIN D. *A Prophet Reads Scripture: Allusion in Isaiah 40–66.* Contraversions: Jews and Other Differences. Stanford, CA: Stanford University Press, 1998.

SPEISER, EPHRAIM AVIGDOR. "Akkadian Myths and Epics: The Creation Epic." *ANET* 60–72.

SPEISER, EPHRAIM AVIGDOR. *Genesis: A New Translation with Introduction and Commentary.* AB 1. New York: Doubleday, 1964.

SPERLING, S. DAVID. "Pants, Persians and the Priestly Source." Pages 373–85 in *Ki Baruch Hu: Ancient Near Eastern, Biblical, and Judaic Studies in Honor of Baruch A. Levine.* Edited by Robert Chazan, William Wolfgang Hallo, and Lawrence H. Schiffman. Winona Lake, IN: Eisenbrauns, 2003.

SPIEGELBERG, WILHELM. *Ägyptische Randglossen zum Alten Testament.* Strasbourg: Schlesier & Schweikhardt, 1904.

STACKERT, JEFFREY. "Compositional Strata in the Priestly Sabbath: Exodus 31:12–17 and 35:1–3." *JHS* 11, art. 15 (2012). https://doi.org/10.5508/jhs.2011.v11.a15.

STADE, BERNHARD. *Biblische Theologie des Alten Testaments I.* Tübingen: Mohr Siebeck, 1905.

STAMM, JOHANN JAKOB. "Hebräische Frauennamen." Pages 301–39 in *Hebräische Wortforschung: Festschrift zum 80. Geburtstag von Walter Baumgartner.* Edited by Benedikt Hartmann et al. VTSup 16. Leiden: Brill, 1967.

STAUBLI, THOMAS. "Verortungen im Weltganzen: Die Geschlechterfolgen der Urgeschichte mit einem ikonographischen Exkurs zur Völkertafel." *BK* 58 (2003): 20–29.

Steck, Odil Hannes. "Der Mensch und die Todesstrafe." *TZ* 53 (1997): 118–30.

Steck, Odil Hannes. *Der Schöpfungsbericht der Priesterschrift: Studien zur literarkritischen und überlieferungsgeschichtlichen Problematik von Genesis 1,1–2,4a.* FRLANT 115. Göttingen: Vandenhoeck & Ruprecht, 1975.

Steins, Georg. "'Sie sollen mir ein Heiligtum machen': Zur Struktur und Entstehung von Ex 24,12–31,18." Pages 159–67 in *Vom Sinai zum Horeb: Stationen alttestamentlicher Glaubensgeschichte.* Edited by Frank-Lothar Hossfeld. Würzburg: Echter, 1989.

Steuernagel, Carl. "Bemerkungen zu Genesis 17." Pages 172–79 in *Beiträge zur alttestamentlichen Wissenschaft: Karl Budde zum siebzigsten Geburtstag am 13. April 1920.* Edited by Karl Marti. BZAW 34. Giessen: Töpelmann, 1920.

Steymans, Hans Ulrich. *Deuteronomium 28 und die adê zur Thronfolgeregelung Asarhaddons: Segen und Fluch im Alten Orient und in Israel.* OBO 145. Fribourg: Presses Universitaires; Göttingen: Vandenhoeck & Ruprecht, 1995.

Steymans, Hans Ulrich. "Deuteronomy 28 and Tell Tayinat." *VeEc* 34, art. 870 (2013). https://doi.org/10.4102/ve.v34i2.870.

Streck, Michael P. "Ur." *NBL* 3:975.

Streibert, Christian. *Schöpfung bei Deuterojesaja und in der Priesterschrift: Eine vergleichende Untersuchung zu Inhalt und Funktion schöpfungstheologischer Aussagen in exilisch-nachexilischer Zeit.* Frankfurt: Lang, 1993.

Sweeney, Marvin A. *I and II Kings: A Commentary.* OTL. Louisville: Westminster John Knox, 2007.

Tal, Abraham. *Biblia Hebraica Quinta: Genesis.* Stuttgart: Deutsche Bibelgesellschaft, 2016.

Talon, Philippe. *The Standard Babylonian Creation Myth Enūma Eliš.* SAACT 4. Helsinki: Neo-Assyrian Text Corpus Project, 2005.

Tengström, Sven. *Die Toledot-Formel und die literarische Struktur der priesterlichen Erweiterungsschicht im Pentateuch.* ConBOT 1.7. Lund: Gleerup, 1982.

Theuer, Gabriele. *Der Mondgott in den Religionen Syrien-Palästinas: Unter besonderer Berücksichtigung von KTU 1.24.* Fribourg: Presses Universitaires; Göttingen: Vandenhoeck & Ruprecht, 2000.

Tiemeyer, Lena-Sofia. *For the Comfort of Zion: The Geographical and Theological Location of Isaiah 40–55.* VTSup 139. Leiden: Brill, 2011.

Tigay, Jeffrey H. "The Priestly Reminder Stones and Ancient Near Eastern Votive Practices." Pages 119–38 in *Shay: Studies in the Bible, Its Exegesis and Language Presented to Sara Japhet.* Edited by Moshe Bar Asher, Dalit Rom-Shiloni, Emanuel Tov, and Nili Wazana. Jerusalem: Bialik Institute, 2007.

Tournay, Raymond Jacques, and Aaron Shaffer. *L'Épopée de Gilgamesh.* LAPO 15. Paris: Cerf, 1998.

Tov, Emanuel. "Der Charakter der hebräischen Quellen der Septuaginta und ihr textkritisch-textgeschichtlicher Wert." Pages 78–102 in *Septuaginta Deutsch, Erläuterungen und Kommentare (I).* Edited by Martin Karrer and Wolfgang Kraus. Stuttgart: Deutsche Bibelgesellschaft, 2011.

Tov, Emanuel. "The Harmonizing Character of the Septuagint of Genesis 1–11." Pages 315–32 in *Die Septuaginta: Text, Wirkung, Rezeption, 4; Internationale Fachtagung veranstaltet von Septuaginta Deutsch (LXX.D), Wuppertal, 19.–22. Juli 2012.* Edited by Wolfgang Kraus and Siegfried Kreuzer. WUNT 325. Tübingen: Mohr Siebeck, 2014.

Tov, Emanuel. "The Nature and Background of Harmonizations in Biblical Manuscripts." *JSOT* 31 (1985): 3–29.

Tov, Emanuel. "Some Sequence Differences between the Masoretic Text and the Septuagint and Their Ramifications for Literary Criticism." Pages 411–18 in *The Greek and Hebrew Bible: Collected Essays on the Septuagint.* VTSup 72. Leiden: Brill, 1999.

Tov, Emanuel. *The Text-Critical Use of the Septuagint in Biblical Research.* 3rd ed. Winona Lake, IN: Eisenbrauns, 2015.

Tov, Emanuel. *Textual Criticism of the Hebrew Bible.* 3rd ed. Minneapolis: Augsburg Fortress, 2012.

Tov, Emanuel. "Textual Harmonization in the Stories of the Patriarchs." Pages 19–50 in *Rewriting and Interpreting the Hebrew Bible: The Biblical Patriarchs in the Light of the Dead Sea Scrolls.* Edited by Devorah Dimant and Reinhard G. Kratz. BZAW 439. Berlin: de Gruyter, 2013.

Tsevat, Matitiahu. "The Canaanite God Šalaḥ." *VT* 4 (1954): 41–49.

Uehlinger, Christoph. "Was There a Cult Reform under King Josiah? The Case for a Well-Grounded Minimum." Pages 279–316 in *Good Kings and Bad Kings.* Edited by Lester L. Grabbe. JSOTSup 393. London: T&T Clark, 2005.

Utzschneider, Helmut. *Das Heiligtum und das Gesetz: Studien zur Bedeutung der Sinaitischen Heiligtumstexte (Ex 25–40, Lev 8–9).* OBO 77. Fribourg: Presses Universitaires; Göttingen: Vandenhoeck & Ruprecht, 1988.

Utzschneider, Helmut. *Micha.* ZBK 24.1. Zurich: TVZ, 2005.

Utzschneider, Helmut. "Tabernacle." Pages 267–301 in *The Book of Exodus: Composition, Reception, and Interpretation.* Edited by Thomas B. Dozeman, Craig A. Evans, and Joel N. Lohr. VTSup 164. Leiden: Brill, 2014.

Utzschneider, Helmut, and Wolfgang Oswald. *Exodus 1–15.* IEKAT. Stuttgart: Kohlhammer, 2013.

Valentin, Heinrich. *Aaron: Eine Studie zur vor-priesterschriftlichen Aaron-Überlieferung.* OBO 18. Fribourg: Presses Universitaires; Göttingen: Vandenhoeck & Ruprecht, 1978.

Van Seters, John. *Abraham in History and Tradition.* New Haven: Yale University Press, 1975.

Van Seters, John. *The Life of Moses: The Yahwist as Historian in Exodus–Numbers.* Kampen: Kok Pharos, 1994.

Van Seters, John. *The Pentateuch: A Social-Science Commentary.* Trajectories 1. Sheffield: Sheffield Academic, 1999.

Van Seters, John. *Prologue to History: The Yahwist as Historian in Genesis.* Louisville: Westminster John Knox, 1992.

VanderKam, James C. *Calendars in the Dead Sea Scrolls: Measuring Time.* London: Routledge, 1998.

Verbrugghe, Gerald P., and John M. Wickersham. *Berossos and Manetho, Introduced and Translated: Native Traditions in Ancient Mesopotamia and Egypt.* Ann Arbor: University of Michigan Press, 1996.

Vermeylen, Jacques. "Tradition et rédaction en Genèse 1." *Transeu* 16 (1998): 127–47.

Vervenne, Marc. "The 'P' Tradition in the Pentateuch." Pages 67–90 in *Pentateuchal and Deuteronomistic Studies.* Edited by Christiaan H. W. Brekelmans and Johan Lust. BETL 94. Leuven: Peeters, 1990.

Vink, J. G. "The Date and the Origin of the Priestly Code in the Old Testament." Pages 1–144 in *The Priestly Code and Seven Other Studies.* Edited by J. G. Vink et al. OTS 15. Leiden: Brill, 1969.

Wade, Martha Lynn. *Consistency of Translation Techniques in the Tabernacle Accounts of Exodus in the Old Greek.* SCS 49. Leiden: Brill, 2003.

Wagenaar, Jan A. *Origin and Transformation of the Ancient Israelite Festival Calendar.* BZABR 6. Wiesbaden: Harrassowitz, 2005.

Watts, James W. *Leviticus 1–10.* HCOT. Leuven: Peeters, 2014.

Watts, James W. "The Torah as the Rhetoric of Priesthood." Pages 319–32 in *The Pentateuch as Torah: New Models for Understanding Its Promulgation and Acceptance.* Edited by Gary N. Knoppers and Bernard M. Levinson. Winona Lake, IN: Eisenbrauns, 2007.

WEIMAR, PETER. "Chaos und Kosmos: Gen 1,2 als Schlüssel einer älteren Fassung der priesterschriftlichen Schöpfungserzählung." Pages 196–211 in *Mythos im Alten Testament und seiner Umwelt: Festschrift für Hans-Peter Müller zum 65. Geburtstag*. Edited by Armin Lange, Hermann Lichtenberger, and Diethard Römheld. BZAW 278. Berlin: de Gruyter, 1999.

WEIMAR, PETER. "Die Toledot Formel in der priesterschriftlichen Geschichtsdarstellung." *BZ* 18 (1974): 65–93.

WEIMAR, PETER. "Gen 17 und die priesterliche Abrahamsgeschichte." *ZAW* 100 (1988): 22–60.

WEIMAR, PETER. "Sinai und Schöpfung: Komposition und Theologie der priesterschriftlichen Sinaigeschichte." *RB* 95 (1988): 337–85.

WEIMAR, PETER. *Studien zur Priesterschrift*. FAT 56. Tübingen: Mohr Siebeck, 2008.

WEINFELD, MOSHE. "God the Creator in Genesis 1 and in the Prophecy of Second Isaiah." *Tarbiz* 37 (1968): 105–32 (Hebrew).

WEIPPERT, MANFRED. "Edom: Studien und Materialien zur Geschichte der Edomiter auf Grund schriftlicher und archäologischer Quellen." Diss. theol., Tübingen, 1971.

WEIPPERT, MANFRED. "Schöpfung am Anfang oder Anfang der Schöpfung: Noch einmal zu Syntax und Semantik von Gen 1,1–3." *TZ* 60 (2004): 5–22.

WEIPPERT, MANFRED. "Tier und Mensch in einer menschenarmen Welt: Zum sogenannten *dominium terrae* in Genesis 1." Pages 35–55 in *Ebenbild Gottes – Herrscher über die Welt: Studien zu Würde und Auftrag des Menschen*. Edited by Hans-Peter Mathys. BThSt 33. Neukirchen-Vluyn: Neukirchener Verlag, 1998.

WELLHAUSEN, JULIUS. *Der Text der Bücher Samuelis untersucht*. Göttingen: Vandenhoeck & Ruprecht, 1871.

WELLHAUSEN, JULIUS. *Die Composition des Hexateuchs und der historischen Bücher des Alten Testaments*. Berlin: Reimer, 1899.

WELLHAUSEN, JULIUS. *Prolegomena to the History of Ancient Israel*. New York: Meridian Books, 1957. Reprint of *Prolegomena to the History of Israel*. Translated by J. (John) Sutherland Black and Allan Menzies, with preface by William Robertson Smith. Edinburgh: Black, 1885.

WELLHAUSEN, JULIUS. *Prolegomena zur Geschichte Israels*. Berlin: Reimer, 1895.

WENHAM, GORDON J. *Genesis 1–15*. WBC. Waco, TX: Word, 1987.

WENHAM, GORDON J. *Genesis 16–50*. WBC. Waco, TX: Word, 1994.

WEST, M. L. (MARTIN LITCHFIELD). *The East Face of Helicon: West Asiatic Elements in Greek Poetry and Myth*. Oxford: Clarendon, 1997.

WESTENDORF, WOLFHARDT. "Götter, androgyne." *LÄ* 2:633–35.

WESTERMANN, CLAUS. *Genesis 1–11*. BKAT 1.1. Neukirchen-Vluyn: Neukirchener Verlag, 1974.

WESTERMANN, CLAUS. *Genesis 12–36*. BKAT 1.2. Neukirchen-Vluyn: Neukirchener Verlag, 1981.

WESTERMANN, CLAUS. *Genesis 37–50*. BKAT 1.3. Neukirchen-Vluyn: Neukirchener Verlag, 1982.

WEVERS, JOHN WILLIAM. *Genesis*. Göttingen: Vandenhoeck & Ruprecht, 1974.

WEVERS, JOHN WILLIAM. *Notes on the Greek Text of Exodus*. SCS 30. Atlanta: SBL Press, 1990.

WEVERS, JOHN WILLIAM. *Text History of the Greek Exodus*. Göttingen: Vandenhoeck & Ruprecht, 1992.

WITTE, MARKUS. *Die biblische Urgeschichte: Redaktions- und theologiegeschichtliche Beobachtungen zu Genesis 1,1–11,26*. BZAW 265. Berlin: de Gruyter, 1998.

WÖHRLE, JAKOB. *Die frühen Sammlungen des Zwölfprophetenbuches: Entstehung und Komposition*. BZAW 360. Berlin: de Gruyter, 2006.

Wöhrle, Jakob. *Fremdlinge im eigenen Land: Zur Entstehung und Intention der priesterlichen Passagen der Vätergeschichte*. FRLANT 246. Göttingen: Vandenhoeck & Ruprecht, 2012.

Wöhrle, Jakob. "The Integrative Function of the Law of Circumcision." Pages 71–87 in *The Foreigner and the Law: Perspectives from the Hebrew Bible and the Ancient Near East*. Edited by Reinhard Achenbach, Rainer Albertz, and Jakob Wöhrle. BZABR 16. Wiesbaden: Harrassowitz, 2011.

Würthwein, Ernst. *Die Bücher der Könige: 1 Könige 1–16*. ATD 11.1. Göttingen: Vandenhoeck & Ruprecht, 1977.

Young, Ian, and Robert Rezetko, with the Assistance of Martin Ehrensvärd. *Linguistic Dating of Biblical Texts: An Introduction to Approaches and Problems*. 2 volumes. London: Equinox, 2009.

Zenger, Erich. *Gottes Bogen in den Wolken: Untersuchungen zu Komposition und Theologie der priesterschriftlichen Urgeschichte*. SBS 12. Stuttgart: Katholisches Bibelwerk, 1983.

Zenger, Erich. "Priesterschrift." TRE 27:435–46.

Ziegler, Leo. *Bruchstücke einer vorhieronymianischen Übersetzung des Pentateuch: Aus einem Palimpseste der k. Hof- und Staatsbibliothek zu München*. Munich, 1883.

Ziemer, Benjamin. *Abram–Abraham: Kompositionsgeschichtliche Untersuchungen zu Genesis 14, 15 und 17*. BZAW 350. Berlin: de Gruyter, 2005.

Ziemer, Benjamin. "Erklärung der Zahlen von Gen 5 aus ihrem kompositionellen Zusammenhang." *ZAW* 121 (2009): 1–18.

Zimmerli, Walther. "Abrahambund und Sinaibund: Ein Beitrag zum Verständnis der Priesterschrift." *TZ* 16 (1960): 268–80.

Zimmerli, Walther. *1. Mose 1–11*. 4th ed. ZBK 1.1. Zurich: TVZ, 1984.

Zimmerli, Walther. *1. Mose 12–25*. ZBK 1.1. Zurich: TVZ, 1976.

Zimmerli, Walther. *Ezechiel 25–48*. BKAT 12.2. Neukirchen-Vluyn: Neukirchener Verlag, 1969.

Zimmern, Heinrich. "Urkönige und Uroffenbarung." Pages 531–32 in volume 2 of *Die Keilinschriften und das Alte Testament*. Edited by Eberhard Schrader. 2 volumes. Berlin: Reuther & Reichard, 1902–3.

Zwickel, Wolfgang. "Die Edelsteine im Brustschild des Hohenpriesters und beim himmlischen Jerusalem." Pages 50–70 in *Edelsteine in der Bibel*. Edited by Wolfgang Zwickel. Mainz: von Zabern, 2002.

Index of Hebrew Bible, Deuterocanonical and Cognate Literature, New Testament

The letter "n" followed by a number refers to a footnote number.
The letter "t" followed by a number refers to a table number.

Index of Other Ancient Near Eastern and Greek Sources

The letter "n" followed by a number refers to a footnote number.

Index of Modern Authors

The letter "n" followed by a number refers to a footnote number.

Forschungen zum Alten Testament

Edited by

Corinna Körting (Hamburg) · Konrad Schmid (Zürich)
Mark S. Smith (Princeton) · Andrew Teeter (Harvard)

FAT I publishes works that give important momentum to Old Testament research all over the world. There are no religious or denominational preferences, and the series has no limits defined by certain positions. The sole determining factor for the acceptance of a manuscript is its high level of scholarship. Monographs, including habilitations, essay collections by established scholars and conference volumes on key subjects from the fields of theology and religious history define the profile of the series.

FAT II makes a point of publishing outstanding works of scholars at the beginning of their career and welcomes explorative research. As in *FAT I,* there are no religious or denominational preferences, and the series has no limits defined by certain positions. In addition to dissertations and monographs by recent doctorates and established scholars, *FAT II* publishes conference volumes on subjects from the fields of theology and religious history with an interdisciplinary focus.

FAT I:
ISSN: 0940-4155
Suggested citation: FAT I
All published volumes at
www.mohrsiebeck.com/fat1

FAT II:
ISSN: 1611-4914
Suggested citation: FAT II
All published volumes at
www.mohrsiebeck.com/fat2

Mohr Siebeck
www.mohrsiebeck.com